A literary & historical atlas of Europe

J G. 1860-1920 Bartholomew

EVERYMAN'S LIBRARY
EDITED BY ERNEST RHYS

REFERENCE

A LITERARY AND
HISTORICAL ATLAS OF
EUROPE

THIS IS NO. 496 OF *EVERYMAN'S LIBRARY*. THE PUBLISHERS WILL BE PLEASED TO SEND FREELY TO ALL APPLICANTS A LIST OF THE PUBLISHED AND PROJECTED VOLUMES ARRANGED UNDER THE FOLLOWING SECTIONS:

TRAVEL ❦ SCIENCE ❦ FICTION
THEOLOGY & PHILOSOPHY
HISTORY ❦ CLASSICAL
FOR YOUNG PEOPLE
ESSAYS ❦ ORATORY
POETRY & DRAMA
BIOGRAPHY
REFERENCE
ROMANCE

IN FOUR STYLES OF BINDING: CLOTH, FLAT BACK, COLOURED TOP; LEATHER, ROUND CORNERS, GILT TOP; LIBRARY BINDING IN CLOTH, & QUARTER PIGSKIN

LONDON: J. M. DENT & SONS, LTD.
NEW YORK: E. P. DUTTON & CO.

HISTORY

FIRST ISSUE OF THIS EDITION . 1910
REPRINTED 1912, 1914, 1915

INTRODUCTION

THIS is the second volume in a set of reference atlases which the publishers have in view for the readers of " Everyman's Library," their object being to provide the literary and historical student with all the necessary geographical data to illustrate the books which he is reading. It was found impossible to give sufficient detail of the whole World in one volume, and it was decided to give an Atlas to each Continent, whose special features could there be adequately treated. Extending the lines of the *Classical Atlas*, this book attempts to cover the geography of Europe, mapped out not only to define the frontiers and countries, but to illustrate history and literature —especially English literature. The changes in the face of Europe that have marked the growth of nations, that went on through the Middle Ages, and have continued to the times of Wellington and Napoleon, the Franco-Prussian War, and to the merging to-day of the military in the industrial struggle, may be followed in the 96 pages of coloured maps which come first in the volume. In addition, some 32 pages of maps in outline will be found covering—

(a) The great battles of the world. These are devised with an eye to Creasy's *Fifteen Decisive Battles*, and they go back to classic times; but it will be found that they help to illustrate many modern books too.

(b) Maps which relate to English literature. These do not exhaust the field, but they serve as examples of what the student, carrying on the process, may do for himself. By illustrating certain proverbial books and special authors, they show the reader how he may, with the coloured map for his guidance, go on to trace a map to illustrate his own favourite literary region or history-book.

(c) An Outline Map of England and Wales showing the situation of the greater monasteries and religious houses.

CONTENTS

COLOURED MAPS

	PAGE
THE WORLD ACCORDING TO ORTELIUS, 1570 . . .	1
THE WORLD, showing the Great Lines of International Commerce in connection with Europe	2, 3
OROGRAPHICAL CENTRAL EUROPE, showing the Height of each Country above Sea Level	4, 5
ETHNOGRAPHICAL CENTRAL EUROPE	6, 7
THE OLD WORLD, Early Explorers—World as known to Homer, B.C. 1000; Ptolemy, A.D. 150; and Martin Behaim, A.D. 1492	8, 9
BARBARIAN AND BYZANTINE EMPIRES, 525 A.D. . . .	10, 11
THE BARBARIAN MIGRATIONS—Huns, Angles, Saxons, Jutes, Goths, Vandals	12
BYZANTINE EMPIRE AT THE DEATH OF JUSTINIAN, 565 A.D.	13
EUROPE AT THE DEATH OF CHARLEMAGNE, 814 A.D. .	14, 15
EXPANSION OF CHRISTIANITY, from the Second to the Fourteenth Centuries	16, 17
SARACEN DOMINIONS	18
THE CRUSADES, 1096-1270.	19
EUROPE AT THE TIME OF THE CRUSADES, 1189 . .	20, 21
NORSE-VIKING INVASIONS—Kingdom of Canute . .	22
ANGLO-SAXON BRITAIN—" The Heptarchy " . .	23
NORMAN ENGLAND, showing Possessions of William I., and Dominions dependent on him	24, 25
ANGEVIN DOMINIONS IN THE TWELFTH CENTURY, showing Dominions of England and her Dependencies, and Dominions of France and her Dependencies . .	26, 27
OTTOMAN EMPIRE AT FALL OF CONSTANTINOPLE, 1453 .	28
SPANISH KINGDOMS AFTER 1513.	29
GERMANY AND N. ITALY, End of Fifteenth Century ..	30, 31
EUROPE AT THE BEGINNING OF THE REFORMATION, 1519	32, 33
FRANCE, 1618-1648	34, 35

Contents

	PAGE
GERMANY AND N. ITALY, from the Reformation to the Thirty Years' War, 1615-1648	36, 37
ITALY, from the Sixteenth to the Eighteenth Centuries .	38, 39
CENTRAL EUROPE, 1789	40, 41
CENTRAL EUROPE, 1810	42, 43
EUROPE, 1815	44, 45
MODERN EUROPE	46, 47
ECONOMIC MAP OF EUROPE, showing Chief Industrial Districts, Agricultural and Stock-rearing, and Fishing . . .	48, 49
PRINCIPAL RAILWAY AND STEAMBOAT ROUTES IN CENTRAL EUROPE AND THE MEDITERRANEAN . . .	50, 51
BRITISH ISLES, AGRICULTURAL DISTRICTS	52
BRITISH ISLES, LEADING INDUSTRIES	53
ENGLAND AND WALES, Northern Section . . .	54, 55
ENGLAND AND WALES, Southern Section . . .	56, 57
OROGRAPHICAL CENTRAL ENGLAND, showing the Height of each District above Sea Level	58, 59
OROGRAPHICAL SOUTH-EAST ENGLAND	60
OROGRAPHICAL CENTRAL SCOTLAND	61
SCOTLAND, Northern Section	62, 63
SCOTLAND, Southern Section	64, 65
IRELAND, Northern Section	66, 67
IRELAND, Southern Section	68, 69
HOLLAND AND BELGIUM	70, 71
FRANCE	72, 73
GERMANY	74, 75
CENTRAL GERMANY	76, 77
AUSTRIA-HUNGARY	78, 79
ITALY	80, 81
NORTHERN AND CENTRAL ITALY, with Environs of Rome .	82, 83
SPAIN AND PORTUGAL	84, 85
SWITZERLAND, showing Height of Mountains . .	86, 87
SCANDINAVIA—Sweden, Norway, and Denmark . .	88, 89
RUSSIA IN EUROPE	90, 91
KINGDOM OF POLAND—Before Union with Lithuania; at its Greatest Extent; in the Time of Napoleon I.—Present Limits of Russia, Prussia, and Austria . . .	92
CHANGES IN TURKEY IN EUROPE, 1856 to 1878 . .	93
BALKAN STATES	94, 95
DENSITY OF POPULATION, 1901	96

PAGE

A BRIEF SURVEY OF THE ENGLISH COINAGE FROM THE EARLIEST TIMES TO THE PRESENT DAY, BY BERNARD ROTH, F.S.A. 97

LINE MAPS

FIFTEEN DECISIVE BATTLES OF THE WORLD

BATTLE OF MARATHON, 29th September, 490 B.C. . . . 113

SYRACUSE AT THE TIME OF THE SIEGE, 415-413 B C. . . 114

BATTLE OF ARBELA 114

BATTLE OF METAURUS, 208 B.C. 115

BATTLEFIELD OF ARMINIUS AND VARUS, 9 A.D. . . . 115

BATTLE OF CHALONS, 451 A.D. 116

BATTLE OF TOURS OR POICTIERS, 732, showing Original Position of Charles Martel's Army 116

HASTINGS—BATTLE OF SENLAC, 14th October, 1066 . . 117

ORLEANS BEFORE JOAN OF ARC'S ENTRY 117

THE ARMADA, 1588 118

BATTLE OF BLENHEIM, 13th August, 1704 119

BATTLE OF PULTAWA, 28th June, 1709 119

VICTORY OF AMERICANS AT SARATOGA, 1777 . . . 120

BATTLE OF VALMY, 20th September, 1792 . . . 120

BATTLE OF WATERLOO, 18th June, 1815 121

FAMOUS BRITISH BATTLES

BATTLE OF BANNOCKBURN, 20th June, 1314 . . . 121

BATTLE OF CRECY, 25th August, 1346 122

BATTLE OF POICTIERS, 19th September, 1356 . . . 122

BATTLES AND SIEGES OF THE CIVIL WAR, 1642-1651 . 123

BATTLE OF AGINCOURT, 25th October, 1415 . . . 124

BATTLE OF EDGEHILL, 23rd October, 1642 . . . 124

BATTLE OF MARSTON MOOR, 2nd July, 1644 . . . 125

BATTLE OF NASEBY, 14th June, 1645 125

BATTLE OF DUNBAR, 3rd September, 1650 . . . 126

BATTLE OF THE NILE, 1st August, 1798 . . . 126

BATTLE OF COPENHAGEN, 2nd April, 1801 . . . 127

BATTLE OF TRAFALGAR, 21st October, 1805 . . . 127

MAPS ILLUSTRATING DISTRICTS CONNECTED WITH FAMOUS BOOKS AND THEIR AUTHORS

PAGE

ROUTE OF THE CANTERBURY PILGRIMS, from London to Canterbury 128

THE LAND OF BURNS 128

THE LAND OF SCOTT 129

"IVANHOE," showing the journeys of Cedric, Isaac, The Templar, etc. 129

MAP OF LONDON, illustrating "Pepys' Diary," "Evelyn's Diary," Dr. Johnson, etc. 130, 131

THE ARTHURIAN REGIONS 132

THE LAKE DISTRICT, associated with Wordsworth, Coleridge, Southey, De Quincey, Ruskin, etc. 133

DICKENS' WORKS, Places mentioned in 134

BALZAC'S "CATHERINE DE MEDICI" 135

GEORGE ELIOT'S COUNTRY 135

IRVING'S "CONQUEST OF GRANADA," Principal Towns mentioned in 136

DUMAS' NOVELS, Principal Places mentioned in . . 137

THE NETHERLANDS AND BELGIUM, illustrating Motley's "Rise of the Dutch Republic" 138

"THE CLOISTER AND THE HEARTH," Map to illustrate . 139

THE MONASTERIES OF ENGLAND AND WALES . . 140

BORROW'S "LAVENGRO," Places mentioned in . . 141

"WESTWARD HO!" Voyages of Amyas Leigh in the *Rose* and the *Vengeance* 142

PARIS AT THE TIME OF THE REVOLUTION . . . 143

MEDIÆVAL PARIS 144

A GAZETTEER OF TOWNS AND PLACES IN EUROPE HAVING A LITERARY OR HISTORIC INTEREST 145

INDEX 183

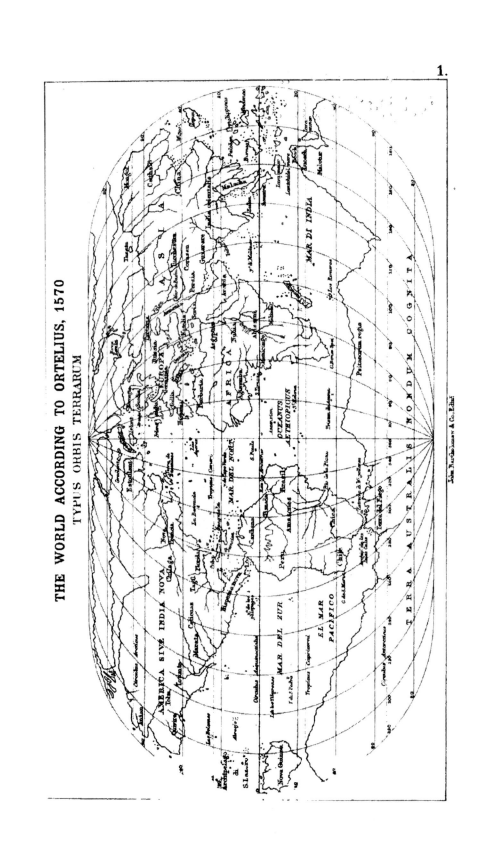

THE WORLD ACCORDING TO ORTELIUS, 1570

TYPUS ORBIS TERRARUM

AMERICA SIVE INDIA NOVA
EUROPA
A S I A
AFRICA
MAR DEL NORT
MAR DEL ZUR
EL MAR PACIFICO
OCEANUS AETHIOPICUS
MAR DI INDIA
TERRA AUSTRALIS NONDUM COGNITA
Nova Guinea
Archipelago di S. Lazaro
Peru
Amazones
Brasil
Chile
Chica
Terra del Fuego
Florida
Nova Francia
Chilaga
Estotilant
Tartaria
Russia
Germania
Gallia
Hispania
Barbaria
Aegyptus
Nubia
Arabia
Persia
Corasan
Tuchestan
Cathay
China
India orientalis
Mongol
Tangut
Circulus Arcticus
Circulus Aequinoctialis
Tropicus Capricorni
Tropicus Cancri
Circulus Antarcticus
Psittacorum regio

John Bartholomew & Co. Edin.

1.

2.

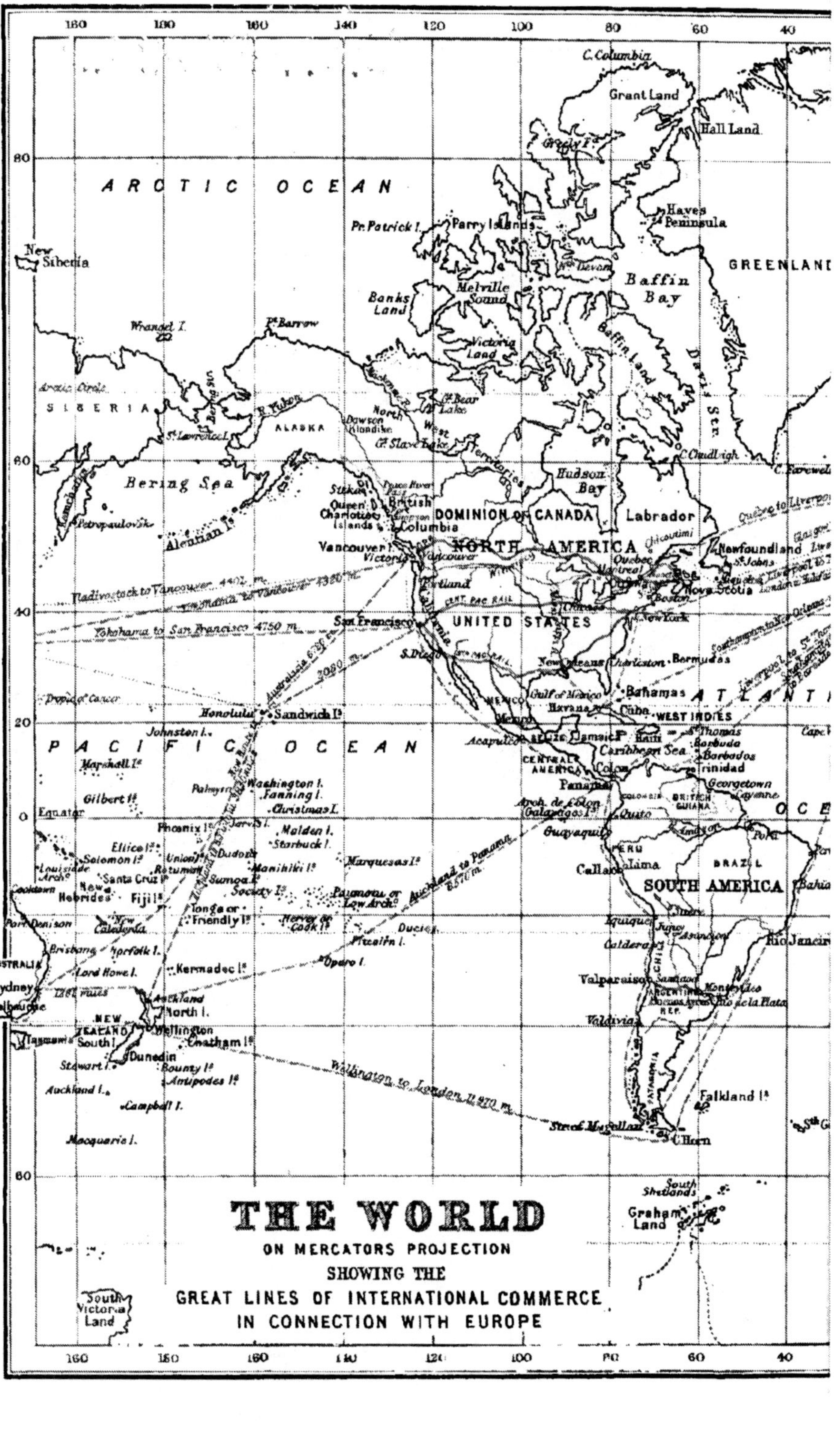
THE WORLD
ON MERCATORS PROJECTION
SHOWING THE
GREAT LINES OF INTERNATIONAL COMMERCE
IN CONNECTION WITH EUROPE
ARCTIC OCEAN
PACIFIC OCEAN
NORTH AMERICA
DOMINION OF CANADA
UNITED STATES
SOUTH AMERICA
GREENLAND
SIBERIA
ALASKA
Bering Sea
Baffin Bay
Hudson Bay
Labrador
Newfoundland
British Columbia
Vancouver
San Francisco
New Orleans
Charleston
Bermudas
Bahamas
Cuba
WEST INDIES
Caribbean Sea
Panama
Colon
Quito
Guayaquil
Callao
Lima
Valparaiso
Valdivia
Falkland Is
C. Horn
Honolulu
Sandwich Is
Fiji Is
AUSTRALIA
Sydney
Melbourne
NEW ZEALAND
Auckland
Wellington
Dunedin
Chatham Is
Yokohama to San Francisco 4750 m.
Wellington to London 11,970 m.
Auckland to Panama 6570 m.
Grant Land
Hall Land
Banks Land
Melville Sound
Victoria Land
Wrangel I.
New Siberia
Kermadec Is
Tonga or Friendly Is
Marquesas Is
Graham Land
South Shetlands
South Victoria Land

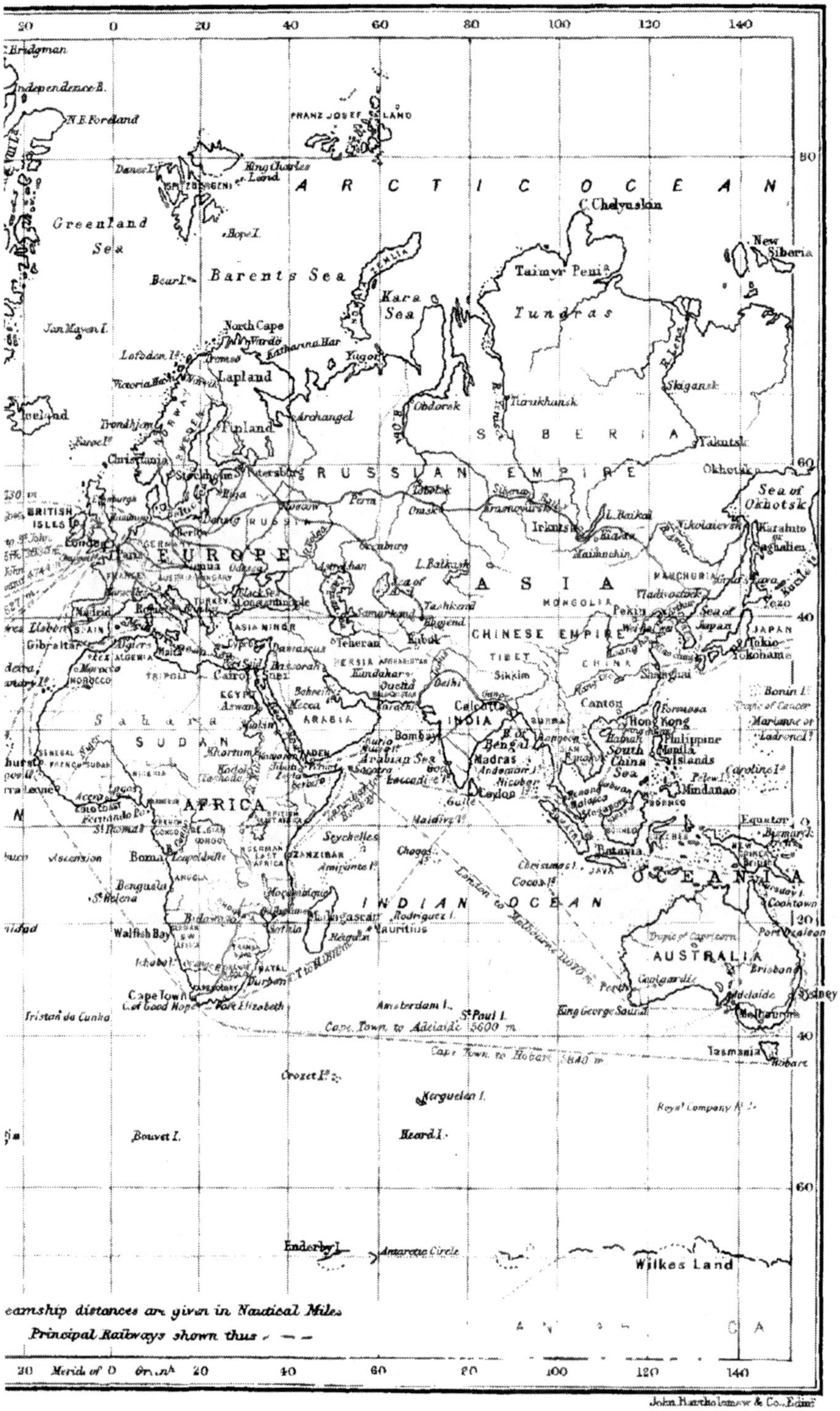
ARCTIC OCEAN
Greenland Sea
Barents Sea
Kara Sea
Franz Josef Land
King Charles Land
Spitzbergen
Hope I.
Bear I.
Jan Mayen I.
N.E. Foreland
Independence B.
Bridgman
Danes I.
C. Chelyuskin
Taimyr Peni.
Tundras
New Siberia
North Cape
Vardö
Lofoden Is.
Tromsö
Lapland
Yugor
Archangel
Finland
Iceland
Trondhjem
Faroe Is.
Christiania
Stockholm
Petersburg
Riga
Moscow
Perm
Tobolsk
Omsk
Obdorsk
Turukhansk
Yakutsk
Skigansk
SIBERIA
RUSSIAN EMPIRE
BRITISH ISLES
London
Paris
Berlin
Vienna
EUROPE
Odessa
Black Sea
Constantinople
Madrid
Lisbon
Gibraltar
Algiers
Malta
Tunis
Morocco
Tripoli
ALGERIA
SPAIN
FRANCE
GERMANY
AUSTRIA HUNGARY
TURKEY
RUSSIA
Orenburg
Astrakhan
Sea of Aral
L. Balkash
Tashkend
Samarkand
Khojend
Bokhara
Teheran
ASIA MINOR
Damascus
Cyprus
Port Said
Suez
Cairo
EGYPT
Aswan
Basra
Bahrein
Mecca
ARABIA
Kandahar
Quetta
Karachi
Delhi
Calcutta
INDIA
Bombay
Bengal
Madras
Goa
Laccadive Is.
Ceylon
Maldive Is.
Chagos
Andaman Is.
Nicobar
Sikkim
TIBET
ASIA
CHINESE EMPIRE
MONGOLIA
Irkutsk
L. Baikal
Kiakhta
Maimachin
Nikolaievsk
Sea of Okhotsk
Okhotsk
Karafuto or Saghalien
Yezo
MANCHURIA
Vladivostock
Pekin
Sea of Japan
JAPAN
Tokio
Yokohama
Shanghai
CHINA
Canton
Hong Kong
Formosa
Philippine Islands
Manila
South China Sea
Mindanao
Bonin I.
Tropic of Cancer
Marianne or Ladrone I.
Caroline Is.
Pelew I.
BURMA
Rangoon
Bangkok
Malacca
Singapore
Batavia
JAVA
Christmas I.
Cocos Is.
BORNEO
Equator
OCEANIA
NEW GUINEA
Cooktown
Port Darwin
AUSTRALIA
Tropic of Capricorn
Brisbane
Sydney
Adelaide
Melbourne
Perth
King George Sound
Coolgardie
Tasmania
Hobart
Sahara
SUDAN
SENEGAL
FRENCH SUDAN
NIGERIA
Accra
GOLD COAST
Lagos
Fernando Po
St. Thomas
Khartum
ADEN
Aden
Socotra
Arabian Sea
Kodok
Berbera
Jibuti
AFRICA
CONGO
Leopoldville
Boma
ANGOLA
Benguela
GERMAN EAST AFRICA
ZANZIBAR
Seychelles
Amirante Is.
Mozambique
Madagascar
Rodriguez I.
Mauritius
Reunion
Bulawayo
Walfish Bay
NATAL
Durban
Cape Town
C. of Good Hope
Port Elizabeth
Ascension
St. Helena
Tristan da Cunha
INDIAN OCEAN
London to Melbourne 11070 m
Amsterdam I.
St. Paul I.
Cape Town to Adelaide 5600 m
Cape Town to Hobart 5840 m
Crozet Is.
Kerguelen I.
Heard I.
Bouvet I.
Royal Company Is.
Enderby L.
Antarctic Circle
Wilkes Land
Steamship distances are given in Nautical Miles
Principal Railways shown thus
20 Merid. of Greenwich 20 40 60 80 100 120 140

John Bartholomew & Co., Edin.

4.

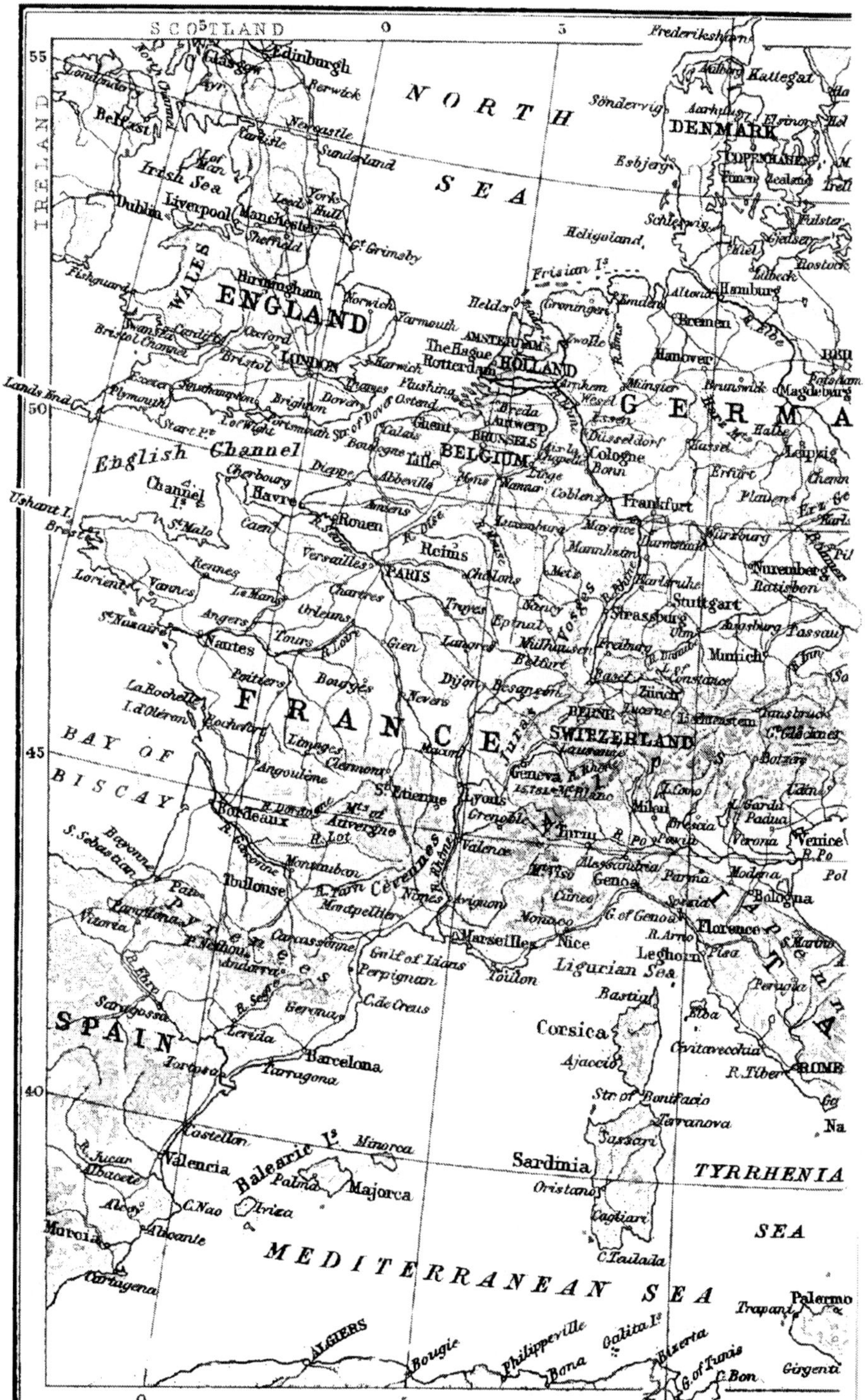
SCOTLAND
IRELAND
Edinburgh
Glasgow
Berwick
Belfast
Newcastle
Carlisle
Sunderland
Irish Sea
Dublin
Liverpool
Manchester
Leeds
York
Hull
Sheffield
Gt. Grimsby
WALES
Birmingham
ENGLAND
Norwich
Yarmouth
Bristol Channel
Oxford
Bristol
LONDON
Harwich
Lands End
Plymouth
Exeter
Southampton
Brighton
Dover
I. of Wight
Portsmouth
English Channel
Ushant I.
Brest
Cherbourg
Channel Is.
St. Malo
Havre
Caen
Rouen
Rennes
Lorient
Vannes
Le Mans
St. Nazaire
Nantes
Angers
Tours
Orleans
Chartres
Versailles
PARIS
Reims
Amiens
Dieppe
Boulogne
Calais
Abbeville
Lille
Ghent
Ostend
Flushing
Antwerp
Breda
BRUSSELS
BELGIUM
Liège
Namur
Mons
Rotterdam
The Hague
AMSTERDAM
HOLLAND
Helder
Groningen
Emden
Zwolle
Arnhem
Wesel
Essen
Düsseldorf
Cologne
Bonn
Aix la Chapelle
Coblenz
Frankfurt
Mayence
Mannheim
Darmstadt
Würzburg
Nuremberg
Ratisbon
Stuttgart
Karlsruhe
Strassburg
Ulm
Augsburg
Munich
Passau
Metz
Luxemburg
Nancy
Epinal
Vosges
Châlons
Troyes
Langres
Dijon
Gien
Bourges
Nevers
Mülhausen
Belfort
Freiburg
Basel
Constance
Zürich
Lucerne
BERNE
SWITZERLAND
Lausanne
Geneva
Mt. Blanc
Jura
Besançon
FRANCE
La Rochelle
I. d'Oléron
Rochefort
Poitiers
Limoges
Clermont
Angoulême
Bordeaux
R. Dordogne
Mts. of Auvergne
R. Lot
St. Etienne
Lyons
Grenoble
Valence
Macon
BAY OF BISCAY
Bayonne
S. Sebastian
Pau
Pamplona
Vitoria
Toulouse
Montauban
R. Tarn
Cevennes
Nimes
Avignon
R. Rhone
Montpellier
Carcassonne
Andorra
Perpignan
Gulf of Lions
C. de Creus
Marseilles
Toulon
Nice
Monaco
Cuneo
Turin
Alessandria
Genoa
G. of Genoa
Milan
Como
Brescia
Verona
Padua
Venice
R. Po
Parma
Modena
Bologna
Florence
R. Arno
Leghorn
Pisa
Perugia
Elba
Civitavecchia
R. Tiber
ROME
Ligurian Sea
Bastia
Corsica
Ajaccio
Str. of Bonifacio
Terranova
Sassari
Sardinia
Oristano
Cagliari
C. Teulada
TYRRHENIAN SEA
SPAIN
Saragossa
R. Ebro
Lerida
Gerona
Barcelona
Tarragona
Tortosa
Castellon
Valencia
R. Jucar
Albacete
Alcoy
Alicante
C. Nao
Murcia
Cartagena
Balearic Is.
Minorca
Majorca
Palma
Iviza
MEDITERRANEAN SEA
ALGIERS
Bougie
Philippeville
Bona
Galita I.
Bizerta
G. of Tunis
C. Bon
Tunis
Trapani
Palermo
Girgenti
NORTH SEA
Heligoland
Frisian Is.
Esbjerg
Sönderborg
Schleswig
Kiel
Lübeck
Altona
Hamburg
Bremen
R. Elbe
Hanover
Brunswick
Magdeburg
Potsdam
Halle
Leipzig
Cassel
Erfurt
Plauen
Münster
GERMANY
Frederikshavn
Aalborg
Kattegat
Aarhus
Elsinore
DENMARK
COPENHAGEN
Fünen
Zealand
Falster
Rostock
Innsbruck
Gr. Glockner
Bozen
Udine
Garda
Na
55
50
45
40
0
5

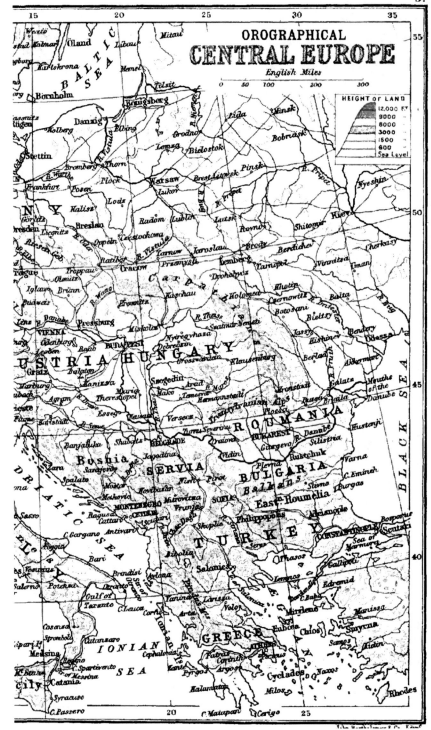

OROGRAPHICAL
CENTRAL EUROPE
English Miles
0 50 100 200 300
HEIGHT OF LAND
12,000 FT
9000
6000
3000
1500
600
Sea Level
BALTIC SEA
Öland
Bornholm
Königsberg
Danzig
Stettin
Warsaw
Brest Litovsk
Pinsk
Minsk
Kiev
Breslau
Cracow
Lemberg
Vienna
Pressburg
Buda Pest
AUSTRIA HUNGARY
Klausenburg
Szegedin
Odessa
Galatz
ROUMANIA
Bukarest
Belgrade
Bosnia
SERVIA
BULGARIA
Sofia
East Roumelia
Philippopolis
Adrianople
Constantinople
Sea of Marmora
TURKEY
Salonica
GREECE
Athens
Cyclades
Rhodes
Smyrna
Chios
IONIAN SEA
ADRIATIC SEA
BLACK SEA
Sicily
Messina
Catania
C. Matapan
Cerigo

6.

St Kilda
Hebrides
Scotland
Edinburgh
Dublin
Pwllheli
English
Welsh
ENGLISH
London
Amsterdam
Rhine
Christiania
Hamburg
Hanover
West
Franks
Cassel
Cologne
Flemings
Calais
Brussels
Aix la Chapelle
Wallons
Middle
Frankfurt
Channel Is
Brest
Rouen
Paris
North French
Orleans
Loire
Nantes
Luxemburg
Strassburg
High
Stuttgart
Alemanni
Basel
Lyons
Bordeaux
Milan
Genoa
Po
Bilbao
Tolosa
BASQUES
Toulouse
Provençals
Marseilles
Rhone
Florence
Corsica
Ajaccio
Madrid
Barcelona
Ebro
Valencia
Sardinia
SPANIARDS
Catalans
ROMANCE
FRENCH
10
0
50
40

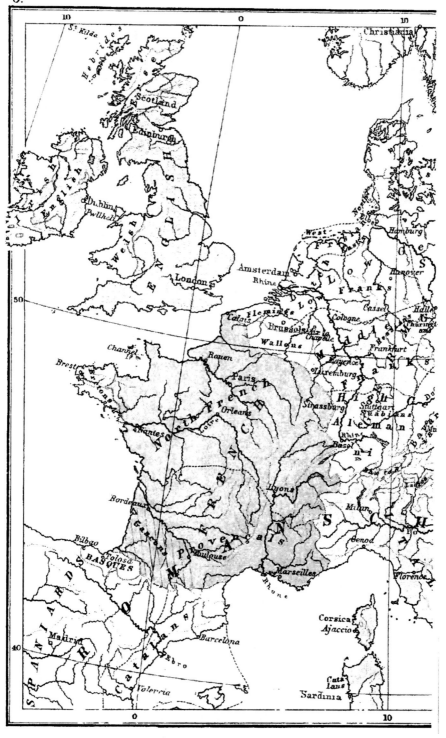

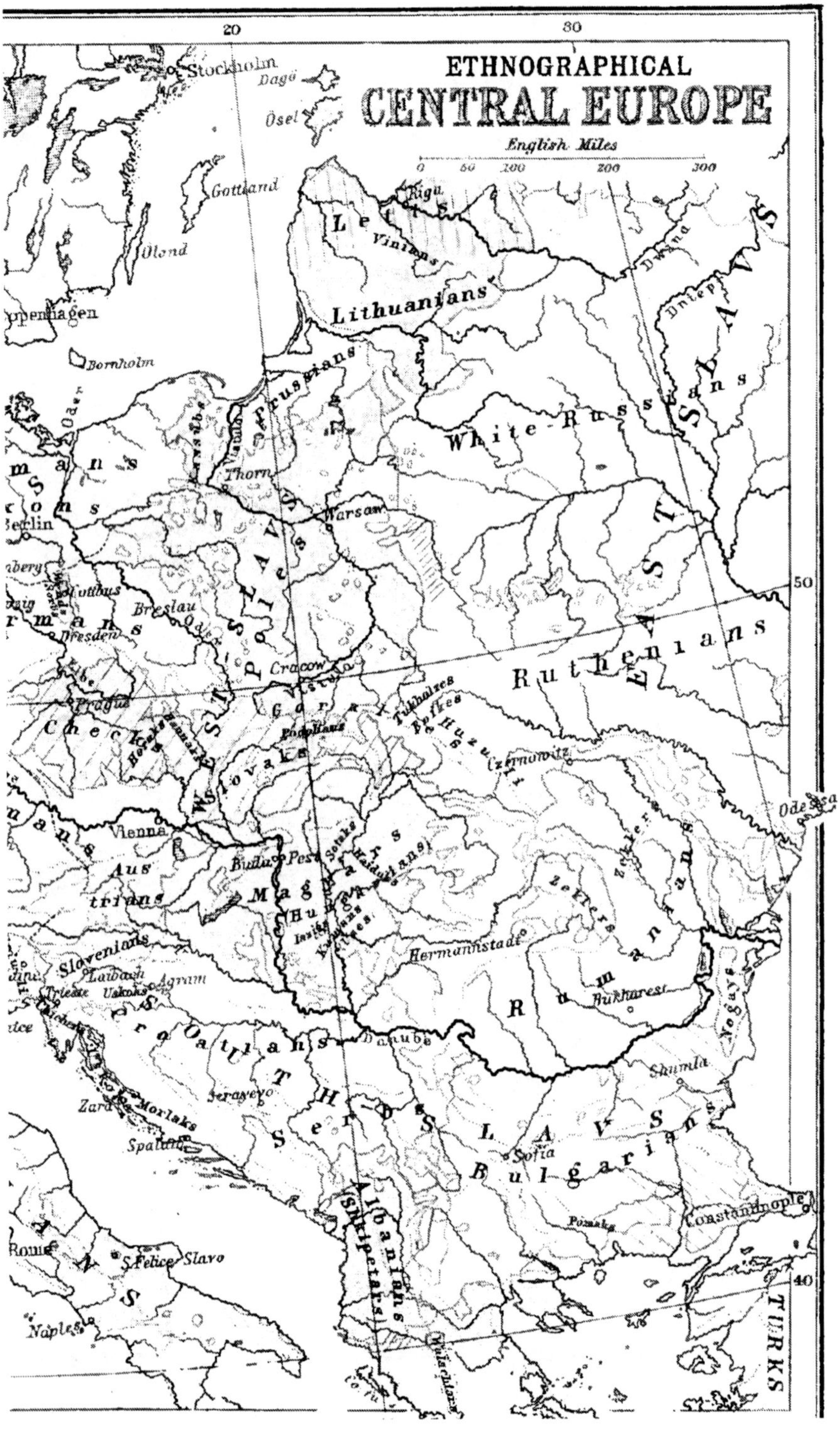
ETHNOGRAPHICAL
CENTRAL EUROPE
English Miles
0 50 100 200 300
20
30
50
40
Stockholm
Dagö
Ösel
Gottland
Öland
Copenhagen
Bornholm
Riga
Letts
Lithuanians
Prussians
White-Russians
Thorn
Warsaw
Berlin
Breslau
Dresden
Cracow
Prague
Czechs
Slovaks
Ruthenians
Czernowitz
Odessa
Vienna
Austrians
Buda
Pest
Magyars
Slovenians
Laibach
Agram
Trieste
Hermannstadt
Roumanians
Bukharest
Danube
Shumla
Serajevo
Zara
Morlaks
Spalato
Sofia
Bulgarians
Albanians
(Skipetars)
Constantinople
Pomaks
Rome
S.Felice Slavo
Naples
TURKS
EAST SLAVS
WEST SLAVS
Poles
Serbs
Croatians
Nogays

80 60 40 20 0 20 40 60 80 100 120

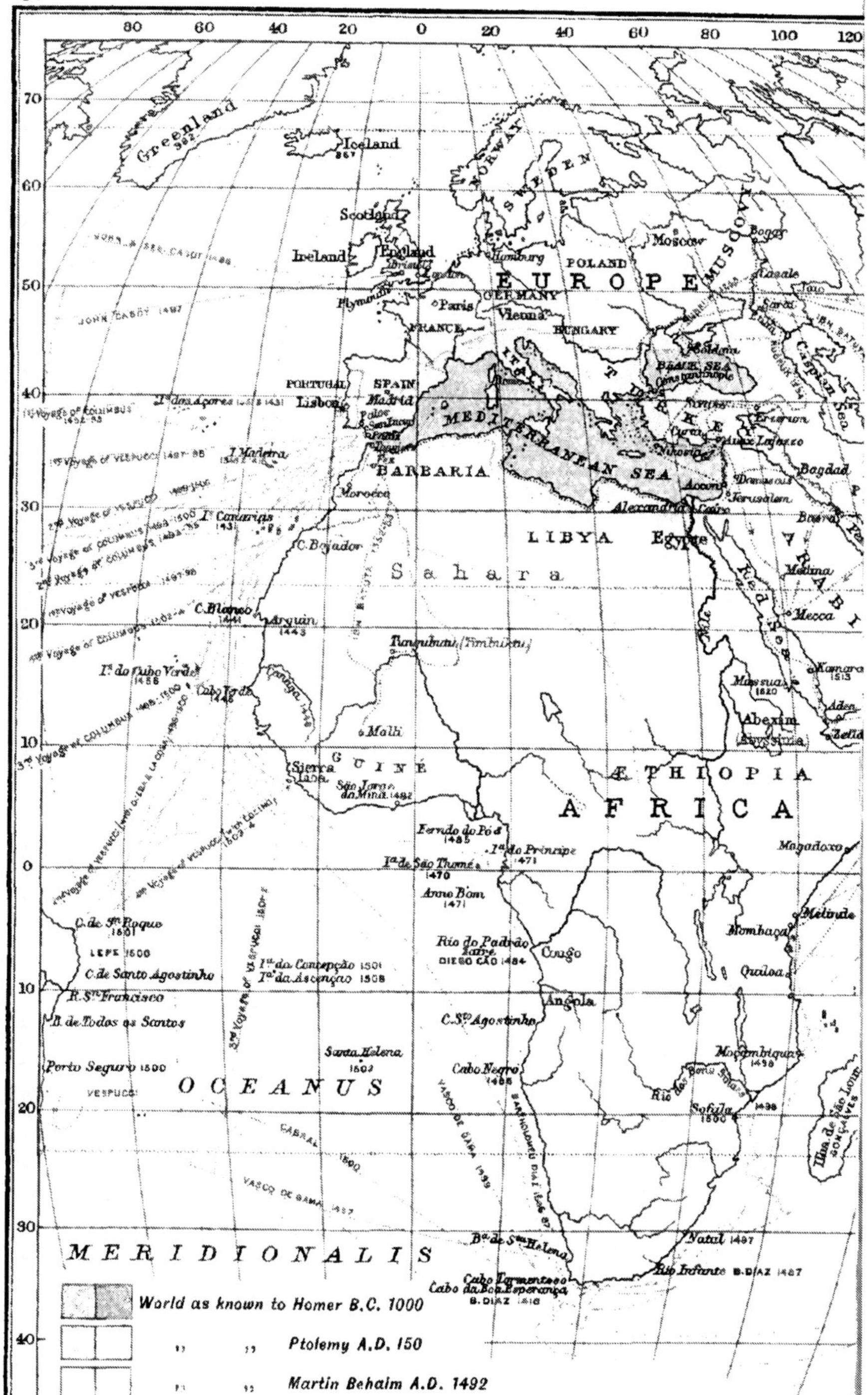

70

Greenland

Iceland

60

NORWAY SWEDEN

Scotland Moscow

50 Ireland England Hamburg POLAND
Plymouth Paris GERMANY Vienna
FRANCE HUNGARY E U R O P E

PORTUGAL SPAIN
Lisbon Madrid
40 I^as dos Açores

BARBARIA M E D I T E R R A N E A N   S E A

Morocco

Alexandria Cairo
Jerusalem

30 C. Bojador
L I B Y A   Egypt

S a h a r a

C. Blanco
Arguin

20 Bagdad

Ranpulnah (Timbuctu)

Medina

Mecca

I^as do Cabo Verde
Cabo Igde

10 Kanara

Malli Massuah
Abexim

GUINE

Sierra AFRICA
Leona ÆTHIOPIA
São Jorge A F R I C A
da Mina

0 Magadoxo
Ferndo do Pó
I^a do Principe
I^a de São Thomé
Anno Bom

C. de S^to Roque
LEPE
10 C. de Santo Agostinho Rio do Padrão Mombaça
R. S^to Francisco DIEGO CÃO Congo
B. de Todos os Santos Qualoa
Angola
C. S^to Agostinho
Porto Seguro Santa Helena Moçambique
20 Cabo Negro Sofala
O C E A N U S

CABRAL

VASCO DE GAMA

30
B^a de Sta Helena Natal
M E R I D I O N A L I S Rio Infante B. DIAZ
Cabo Tormentoso
Cabo da Boa Esperança
B. DIAZ

World as known to Homer B.C. 1000

40 ,,   ,,   Ptolemy A.D. 150

,,   ,,   Martin Behaim A.D. 1492

40 30 20 10 0 10 20 30 40 50

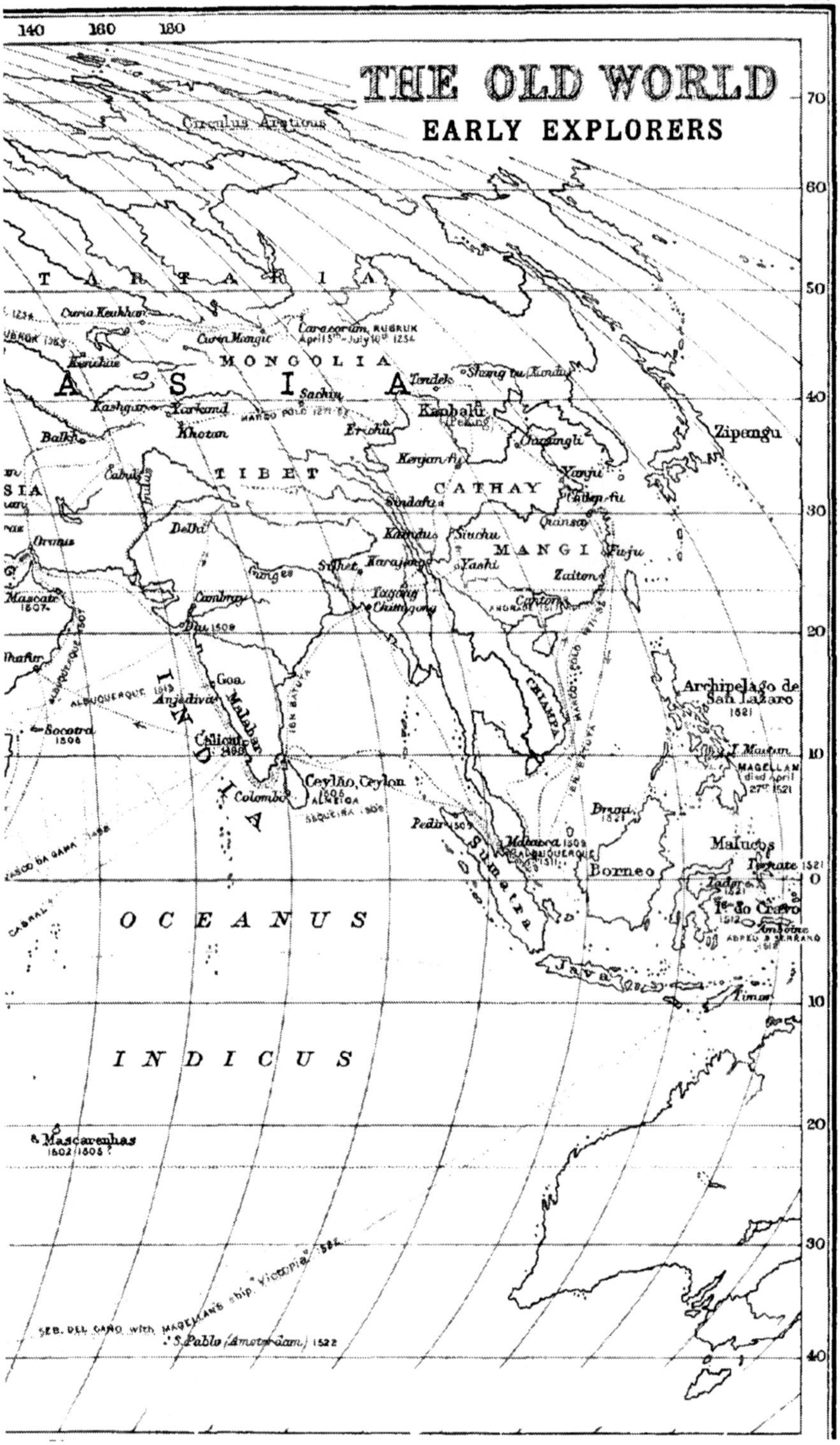
THE OLD WORLD
EARLY EXPLORERS
Circulus Arcticus
TARTARIA
MONGOLIA
ASIA
TIBET
CATHAY
MANGI
INDIA
OCEANUS
INDICUS
Caracorum
Kashgar
Yarkand
Khotan
Balkh
Cabul
Delhi
Ormus
Mascate 1507
Cambay
Diu 1509
Goa
Anjediva
Malabar
Calicut 1498
Socotra 1506
Ceylão, Ceylon
Colombo
Pedir
Malacca 1509
Sumatra
Borneo
Java
Timor
Ternate 1521
Amboina
Malucos
Archipelago de San Lazaro 1521
MAGELLAN
Zipangu
Kanbalu
Cauton
Zaiton
Fuju
Quinsay
Sachiu
CHAMPA
Mascarenhas
1502 1505
S. Pablo (Amsterdam) 1522
SEB. DEL CAÑO with MAGELLAN'S ship "Victoria"
ALBUQUERQUE
IBN BATUTA
MARCO POLO
VASCO DA GAMA 1498
CABRAL
140
160
180
70
60
50
40
30
20
10
0
10
20
30
40

CALEDONIA
Picts
Iona
Scots
HIBERNIA
Anglo Saxons
Eboracum
BRITAIN
Londinium
Jutes
JUTES
SAXONS
Frisians
Salians
Tornacum
Colonia
Liftinas
Rotomagus
Suessiones
Mogontia
THURINGIANS
Remi
Armorica
Syagrius
Parisii
Treves
Wormatia
EMPIRE OF THE FRANKS
Ripuarians
Alamanni
Regina
Andecavi
Aurelianum
Antheus
Metis
Stratisburg
Castra
Batava
Lauri
Juglada
Dario
Vindonissa
Novavium
Turones
Augustodunum
Tiburnia
Pictavium
Arpern
Burgundian
Genova
Modiolanum
Tridentum
Burdigala
Lugdunum
Vienne
KINGDOM
Flavia
Verona
Aquileia
Seg
Venetia
SUEVIAN
Lucus
Pompilona
Pollenia
Ravenna
Ravennia
KINGDOM
Palentia
Tolosa
Venausus
Avenio
Genua
Nasule
Ancon
Bracara
Alamasloca
Caesaraugusta
Narbena
Arelate
Pisae
Perusia
EMPIRE OF THE
Segovia
Ilerda
Massilia
Contin-rriga
Toletum
Gerunda
Corsica
Aleria
Conten
Roma
Hispolis
Dertosa
cellae
Ostia
Barcino
Turris
Tarraco
Beneventum
Neapolis
VISI-GOTHS
Segobriga
Oretian
Majorica
Minorica
Sardinia
Emerita
Valentia
Illiberis
Corduba
Evusus
EMPIRE
Carales
Co
Gades
Hispalis
Malaca
Carthage-
spartaria
Lilybaeum
Panorm
Tingis
OF THE
Hippo Zaritus
Sicilia
Ouida
Caesareu
Igilgilis
Agrigentum
Salda
Hippo Regius
Carthago
VANDALS
Hadrumentum
Thapsus
Leptis

English Miles
0 50 100 200 300 400 500

BARBARIAN
AND
BYZANTINE EMPIRES
525 A.D.
SLAVES
LONGOBARDS
HUNS
Heruli
GEPIDÆ
Sirmium
Singidunum
Naissus
Marcianopolis
Odessus
Sardica
Thracia
Sozopolis
Constantinople (Byzantium)
Heraclea
Sinope
Trapezus
Philippopolis
Hadrianopolis
Nicomedia
Pontus
Amasia
Scodra
Dyrrhachium
Thessalonice
Aulon
Abydus
Caesarea
BYZANTINE EMPIRE
Illyricum
Larissa
Synnada
Iconium
Asia
Nicopolis
Athenae
Smyrna
Ephesus
Laodicea
Tarsus
Antiochia
Patrae
Corinthus
Halicarnassus
Myra
Rhodus
Methone
Cyprus
Tripolis
Creta
Damascus
Tyrus
Jerusalem (Aelia)
Oriens
Cyrene
Berenice
Alexandria
Paraetonium
20
25
30
35
40
45
50
55

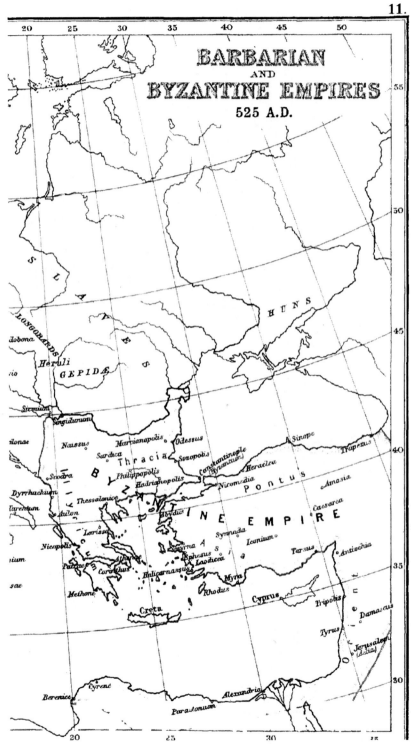

12.

THE BARBARIAN MIGRATIONS
English Miles
Huns
Angles, Saxons, Jutes
Goths
Vandals

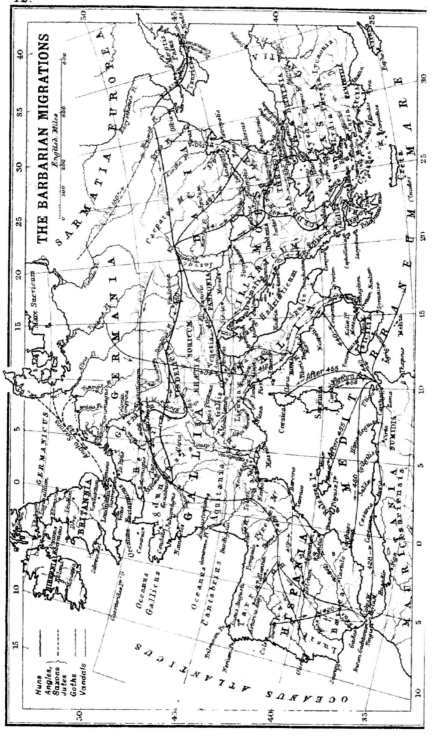

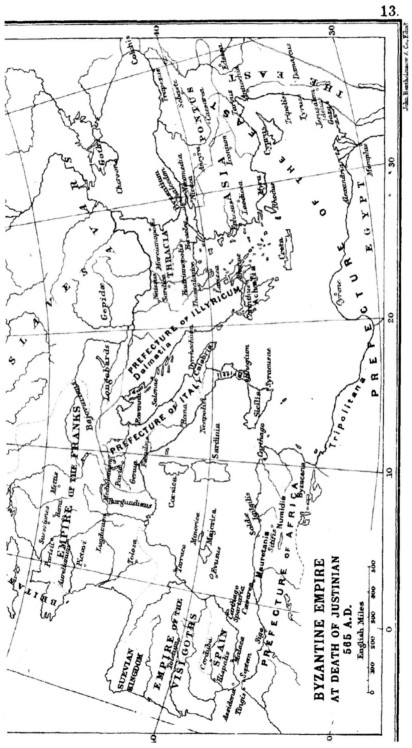

BYZANTINE EMPIRE
AT DEATH OF JUSTINIAN
565 A.D.
English Miles
0 100 200 300 400 500
EMPIRE OF THE FRANKS
SLAVES
AVARS
SUEVIAN KINGDOM
EMPIRE OF THE VISIGOTHS
SPAIN
PREFECTURE OF ITALY
PREFECTURE OF ILLYRICUM
PREFECTURE OF AFRICA
PREFECTURE OF THE EAST
EGYPT
THRACIA
ASIA
PONTUS
Dalmatia
Longobards
Gepidæ
Goths
Bajovarians
Burgundians
Suessiones
Parisii
Remi
Mettis
Aurelianum
Pictavi
Lugdunum
Mediolanum
Pavia
Genua
Tolosa
Toletum
Tarraco
Corduba
Hispalis
Malaca
Assidona
Tingis
Septem
Carthago Spartaria
Caesarea
Siga
Mauretania
Sitifis
Numidia
Saldae
Igilgilis
Carthago
Byzacena
Tripolitana
Corsica
Sardinia
Minorica
Majorica
Evusus
Ravenna
Roma
Neapolis
Salonae
Dyrrhachium
Calabria
Bruttii
Rhegium
Sicilia
Syracusae
Naissus
Sardica
Marcianopolis
Hadrianopolis
Heraclea
Thessalonica
Larissa
Corinthus
Athenae
Achaia
Creta
Byzantium
Chalcedon
Nicomedia
Nicaea
Ancyra
Ephesus
Laodicea
Myra
Rhodus
Iconium
Caesarea
Sebaste
Trapezus
Colchis
Chersona
Tarsus
Antiochia
Edessa
Cyprus
Tripolis
Tyrus
Damascus
Jerusalem
Gaza
Alexandria
Memphis
Cyrene
0
10
20
30
40

John Bartholomew & Co., Edinr.

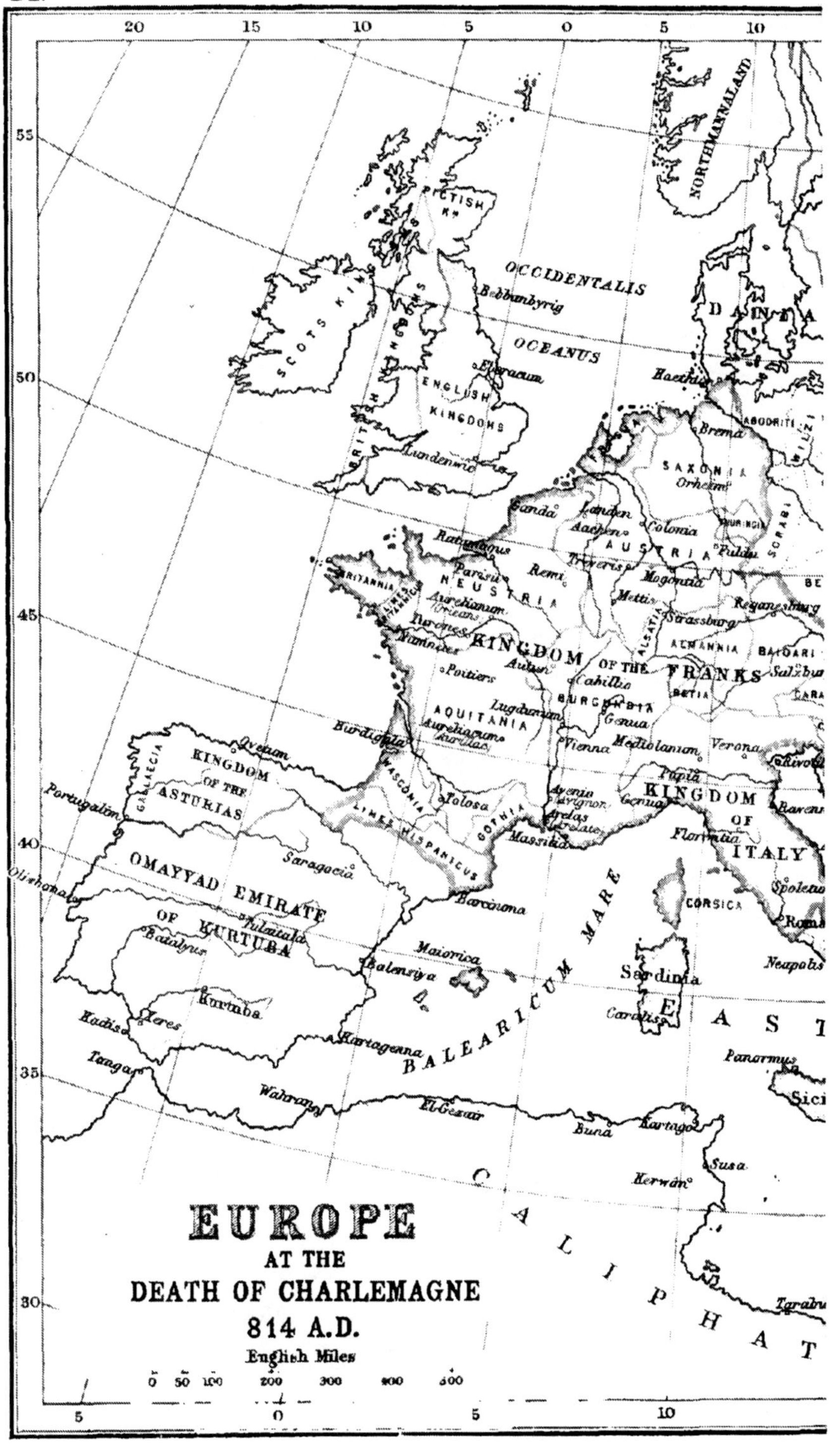
EUROPE
AT THE
DEATH OF CHARLEMAGNE
814 A.D.
English Miles
0 50 100 200 300 400 500
OCCIDENTALIS
OCEANUS
Bebbanbyrig
NORTHMANNALAND
PICTISH Kn
SCOTS Kn
ENGLISH
KINGDOMS
Eboracum
Lundenwic
DANIA
Haethby
Brema
ABODRITI
SAXONIA
Orheim
Ganda
Aachen
Colonia
AUSTRIA
Fulda
Treveris
Mogontia
Metti
Strassburg
Reganesburg
ALAMANNIA
BAIOARI
Salzburg
Parisii
NEUSTRIA
Remi
Aurelianum
Turones
Namnetes
KINGDOM
OF THE
FRANKS
Autun
Poitiers
Cabillo
BURGUNDIA
Lugdunum
AQUITANIA
Genua
Vienna
Mediolanum
Verona
Burdigala
Oviedo
KINGDOM
OF THE
ASTURIAS
GALLAECIA
Portugalom
WASCONIA
Tolosa
GOTHIA
LIMES HISPANICUS
Massilia
Arelas
KINGDOM
OF
ITALY
Florentia
Saragocia
OMAYYAD EMIRATE
OF KURTUBA
Tulaitala
Bataliyus
Barcinona
Maiorica
Balensiya
Kurtuba
Xeres
Kadis
Kartagenna
Tanga
BALEARICUM MARE
CORSICA
Sardinia
Caralis
Spoletum
Roma
Neapolis
Panormus
Sicilia
Wahran
El Gesair
Buna
Kartago
Susa
Kerwan
CALIPHATE
Tarabu
EAST

15.

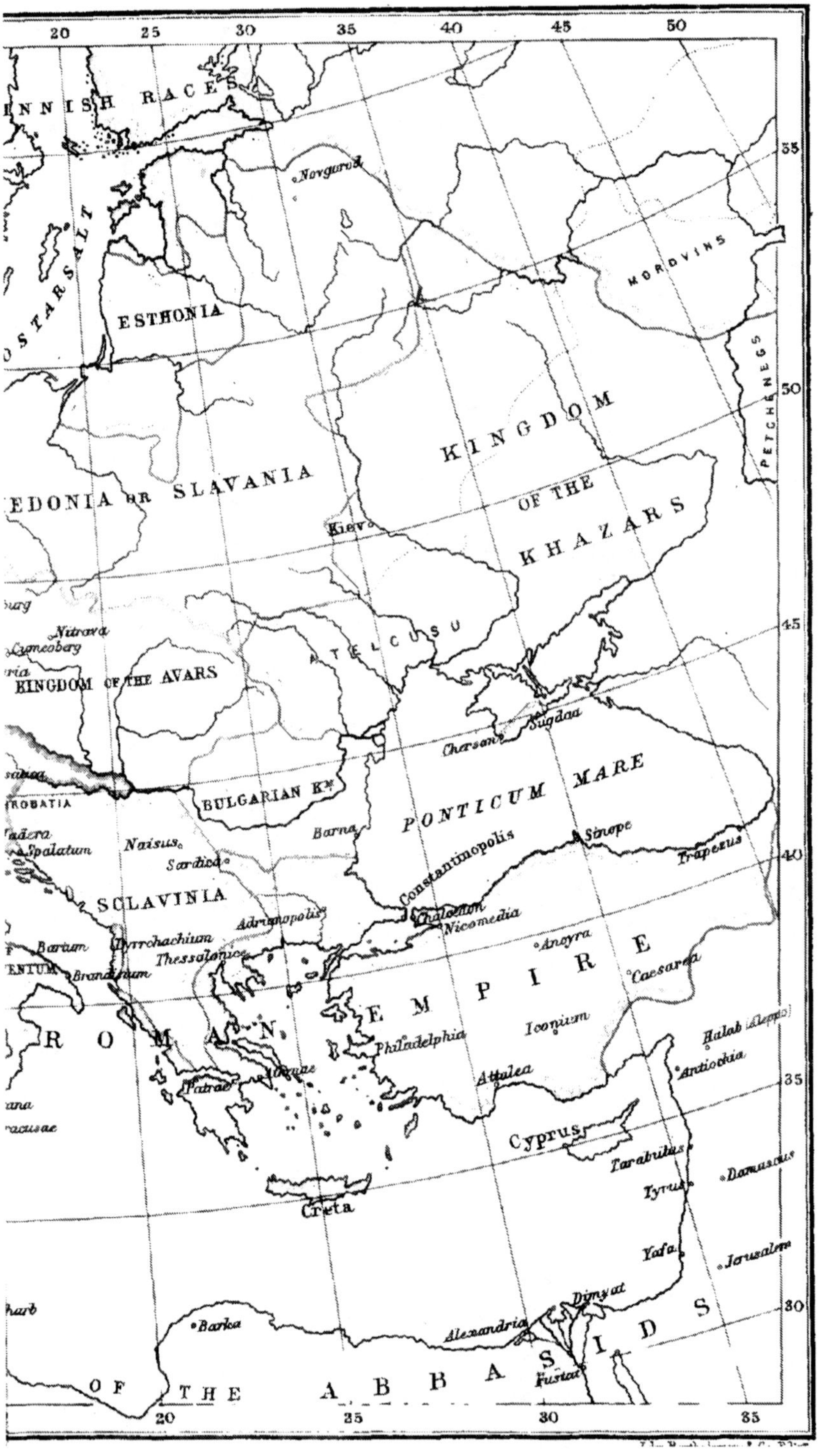
FINNISH RACES
OSTARSALT
ESTHONIA
Novgorod
MORDVINS
PETCHENEGS
KINGDOM OF THE KHAZARS
EDONIA OR SLAVANIA
Kiev
Nitrava
KINGDOM OF THE AVARS
ATELCUSU
Chersona
Sugdaa
BULGARIAN Kᵐ
PONTICUM MARE
CROBATIA
Jadera
Spalatum
Naisus
Sardica
Barna
Constantinopolis
Sinope
Trapezus
SCLAVINIA
Adrianopolis
Chalcedon
Nicomedia
Barium
Dyrrhachium
Thessalonica
Brundisium
Ancyra
Caesarea
ROMAN EMPIRE
Philadelphia
Iconium
Halab (Aleppo)
Antiochia
Athenae
Patrae
Attalea
Cyprus
Tarabulus
Damascus
Tyrus
Creta
Yafa
Jerusalem
Dimyat
Barka
Alexandria
Fustat
OF THE ABBASIDS

16.

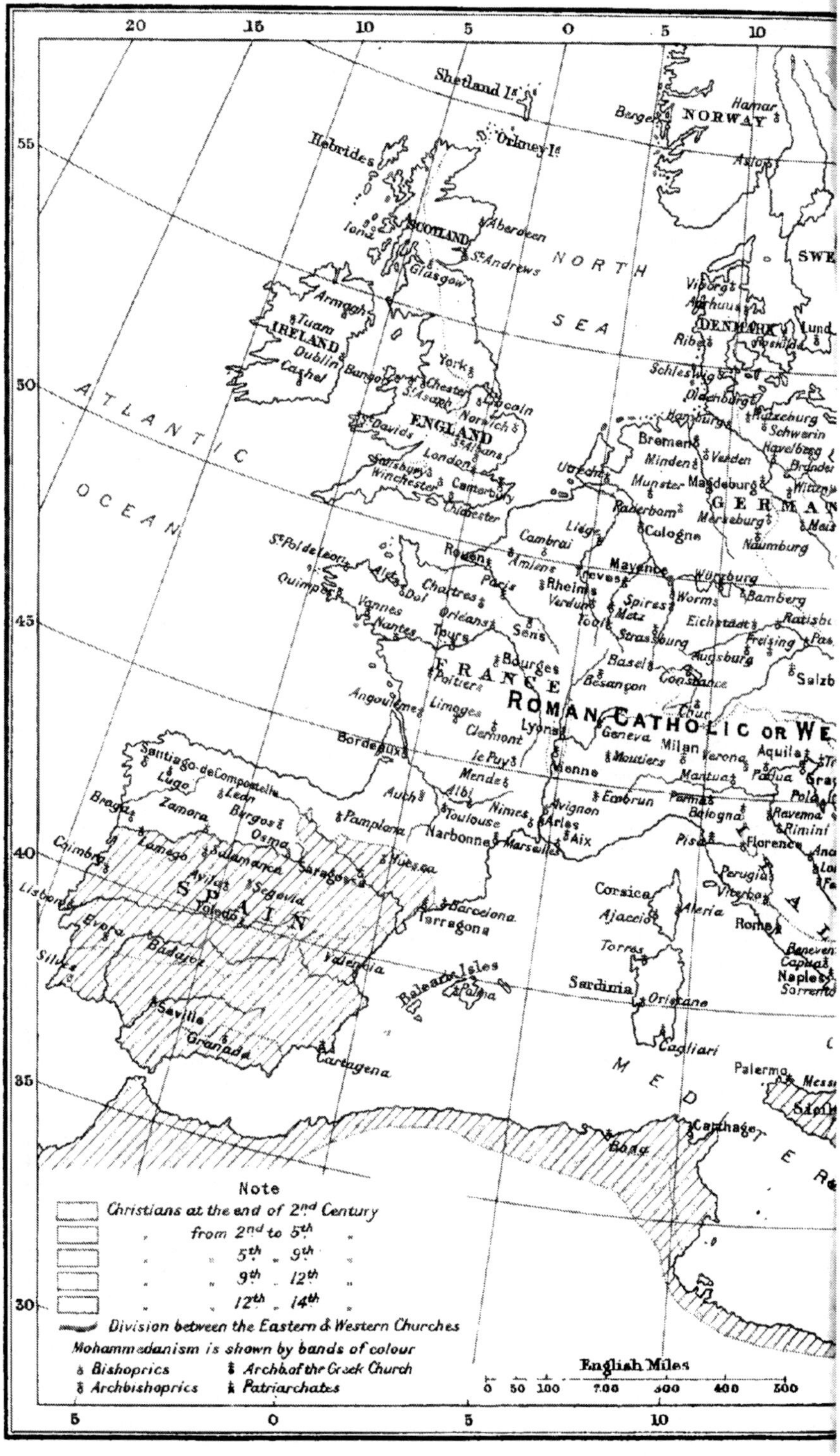

NORWAY
SCOTLAND
IRELAND
ENGLAND
DENMARK
FRANCE
SPAIN
ROMAN CATHOLIC OR WE
NORTH SEA
ATLANTIC OCEAN
Shetland Is.
Orkney Is.
Hebrides
Iona
Aberdeen
St Andrews
Glasgow
Armagh
Tuam
Dublin
Cashel
York
Chester
Lincoln
Norwich
St Davids
London
Salisbury
Winchester
Canterbury
Chichester
Bergen
Hamar
Viborg
Aarhuus
Ribe
Lund
Schleswig
Hamburg
Bremen
Minden
Verden
Munster
Magdeburg
Paderborn
Cologne
Merseburg
Naumburg
Schwerin
Havelberg
Utrecht
Liège
Cambrai
Mayence
Treves
Worms
Spires
Metz
Würzburg
Bamberg
Eichstadt
Ratisbon
Freising
Augsburg
Salzburg
Strassburg
Basel
Constance
Chur
Besançon
Rouen
Amiens
Paris
Rheims
Verdun
Toul
Chartres
Orleans
Sens
St Pol de Leon
Quimper
Vannes
Nantes
Tours
Dol
Bourges
Poitiers
Angoulême
Limoges
Clermont
Lyons
Geneva
Milan
Verona
Aquila
Mantua
Padua
Bordeaux
Le Puy
Vienne
Mende
Albi
Toulouse
Nimes
Avignon
Arles
Aix
Embrun
Parma
Bologna
Ravenna
Rimini
Pisa
Florence
Perugia
Viterbo
Rome
Benevento
Capua
Naples
Sorrento
Narbonne
Marseilles
Auch
Pamplona
Santiago de Compostella
Lugo
Leon
Braga
Zamora
Burgos
Osma
Lamego
Coimbra
Salamanca
Saragossa
Huesca
Avila
Segovia
Toledo
Lisbon
Evora
Badajoz
Silves
Valencia
Seville
Granada
Cartagena
Barcelona
Tarragona
Balearic Isles
Palma
Corsica
Ajaccio
Aleria
Torres
Sardinia
Oristano
Cagliari
Palermo
Carthage
Bona
MEDITERR
Note
Christians at the end of 2nd Century
from 2nd to 5th
5th 9th
9th 12th
12th 14th
Division between the Eastern & Western Churches
Mohammedanism is shown by bands of colour
Bishoprics
Archbishoprics
Archb. of the Greek Church
Patriarchates
English Miles
0 50 100 200 300 400 500

EXPANSION OF
CHRISTIANITY
RUSSIA
GREEK OR EASTERN CHURCH
HUNGARY
RN CHURCH
BLACK SEA
SEA
Novgorod
Dorpat
Osel
Arensburg
Gothland
Riga
Tver
Susdal
Polotsk
Smolensk
Vilna
Elbing
Marienburg
Kulm
Plock
Wloclawek
Breslau
Cracow
Kiev
Kamenetz
Gran
Varad
Alba
Csanad
Fünfkirchen
Rimnik
Tergovist
Caffa
Matriga
Cherson
Trebizond
Spalato
Ragusa
Antivari
Durazzo
Ochrida
Seres
Philippi
Salonica
Philippopolis
Adrianople
Eregli
Constantinople
Chalcedon
Nicomedia
Nicaea
Ancyra
Amasia
Kaisarieh
Broussa
Trani
Bari
Oria
Brindisi
Taranto
Otranto
Rossano
Severina
Corfu
Larissa
Leucas
Lepanto
Athens
Mitylene
Smyrna
Hierapolis
Laodicea
Ephesus
Stauropolis
Perga
Tarsus
Antioch
Laodicea
Rhodes
Constance
Famagusta
Nicosia
Emesa
Tripolis
Damascus
Tyre
Caesarea
Nazareth
Jerusalem
Gortyne
Damietta
Alexandria
20
25
30
35
40
45
50
55

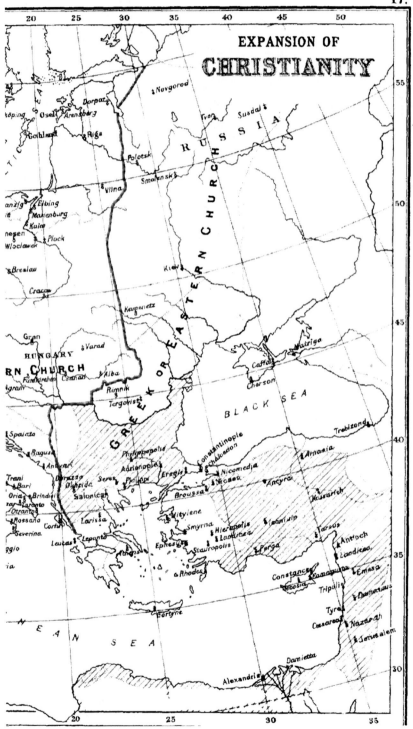

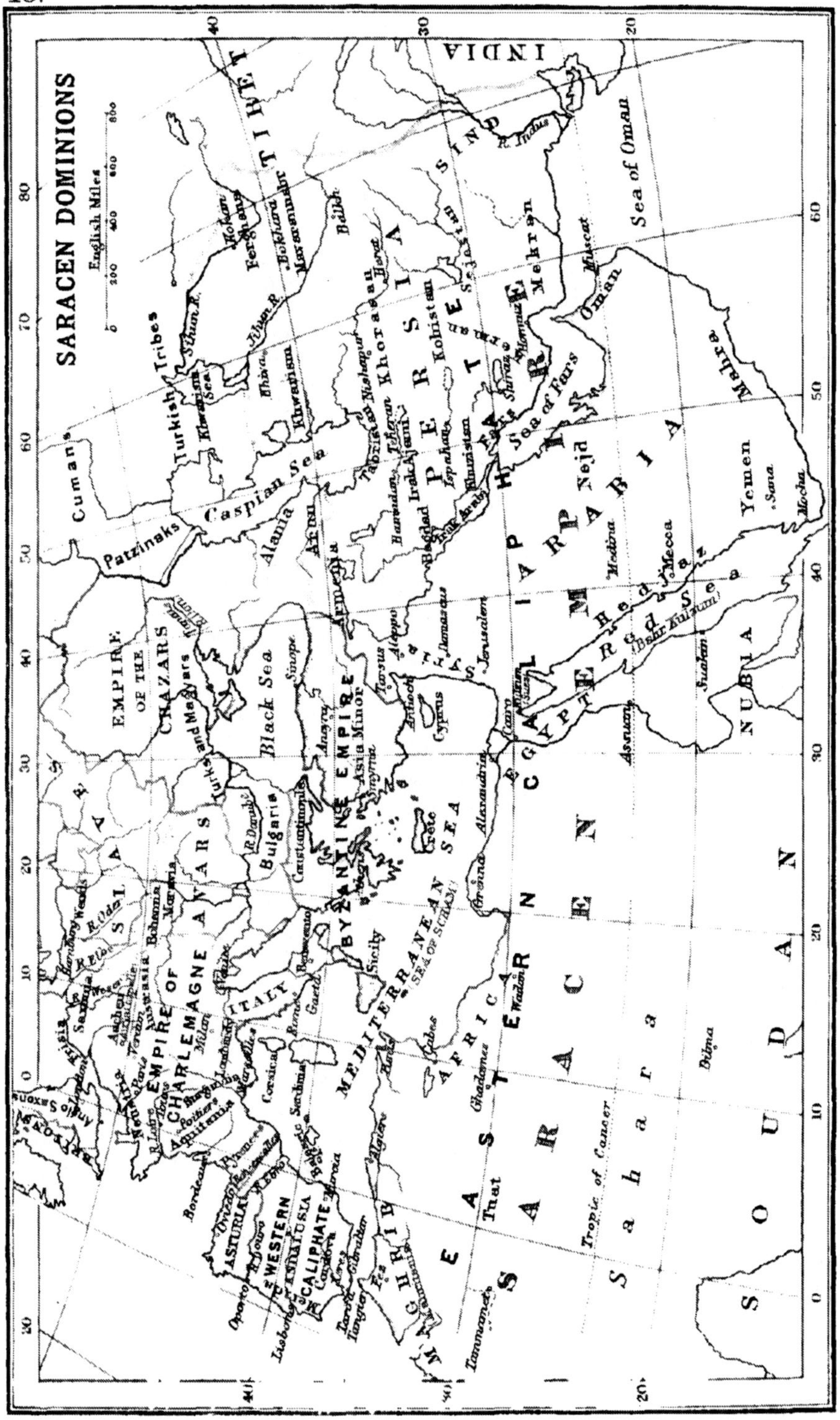
SARACEN DOMINIONS
English Miles
0 200 400 600 800
INDIA
TIBET
SIND
Sea of Oman
Oman
Muscat
Mekran
Sejestan
Kohistan
Khorasan
Herat
Balkh
Bokhara
Kokan
Ferghana
Maveraunnahr
Sihun R.
Jihun R.
Khiva
Khwarism
Khwarism Sea
Turkish Tribes
Cumans
Patzinaks
Caspian Sea
Alania
Armenia
Tabaristan
Nishapur
Tehran
Irak Ajami
Ispahan
Hamadan
Bagdad
Irak Arabi
Ahwaz
Farsistan
Shiraz
Sea of Fars
PERSIA
ARABIA
Nejd
Medina
Mecca
Yemen
Sana
Mocha
Mahra
Red Sea
Bahr Kulzum
Suakin
NUBIA
EGYPT
Assuan
Cairo
Alexandria
Damascus
Jerusalem
Aleppo
Syria
Tarsus
Antioch
Cyprus
EMPIRE OF THE CHAZARS
Turks and Magyars
Black Sea
Sinope
Angora
Asia Minor
Smyrna
BYZANTINE EMPIRE
Constantinople
Bulgaria
R. Danube
AVARS
SLAVS
R. Oder
R. Elbe
Bohemia
Moravia
EMPIRE OF CHARLEMAGNE
Saxons
Frisia
Aachen
Paris
Neustria
Austrasia
Aquitania
Burgundy
Poitiers
Marseilles
Milan
Lombards
ITALY
Rome
Gaeta
Benevento
Sicily
Crete
Corsica
Sardinia
MEDITERRANEAN SEA
(SEA OF SCHAM)
AFRICA
Tunis
Cabes
Ghadames
Barca
Waddan
Tripoli
Algiers
Fez
Tangier
MAGHRIB
EASTERN
WESTERN CALIPHATE
ANDALUSIA
ASTURIA
Leon
Cordova
Toledo
Lisbon
Oporto
Gibraltar
Bordeaux
Anglo Saxons
Britons
Sahara
Tropic of Cancer
Bilma
SOUDAN
SARACEN
Tuat

THE CRUSADES
1096-1270
English Miles
0 50 100 200 300 400
KINGDOM OF FRANCIA
KINGDOM OF ARAGON
KINGDOM OF HUNGARIA
KINGDOM OF SICILIA
BULGARIANS
SERVIA
EASTERN ROMAN EMPIRE
SELJUKS OF RUM
PONTUS
MEDITERRANEAN SEA
ALMOHADS
CORSICA
SARDINIA
Cyprus
Candia
EDESSA
BOHEMIA
STYRIA
CARINTHIA
TUSCIA
ROMANDIOLA
ALANS
CUMANS
Louis IX, 1270
Louis IX, 1248
Louis IX, 1249
Richard I, 1190
Richard I, 1191
Philip II, 1190
Philip II, 1191
Louis VII, 1147
Conrad III, 1147
Andrew of Hungary, 1217
John Bartholomew & Co., Edin

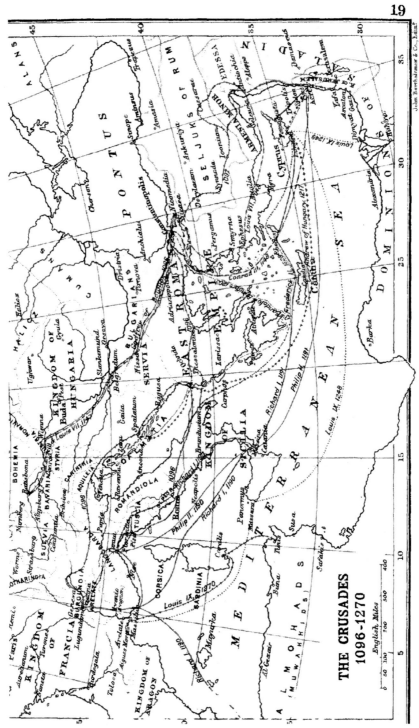

20.

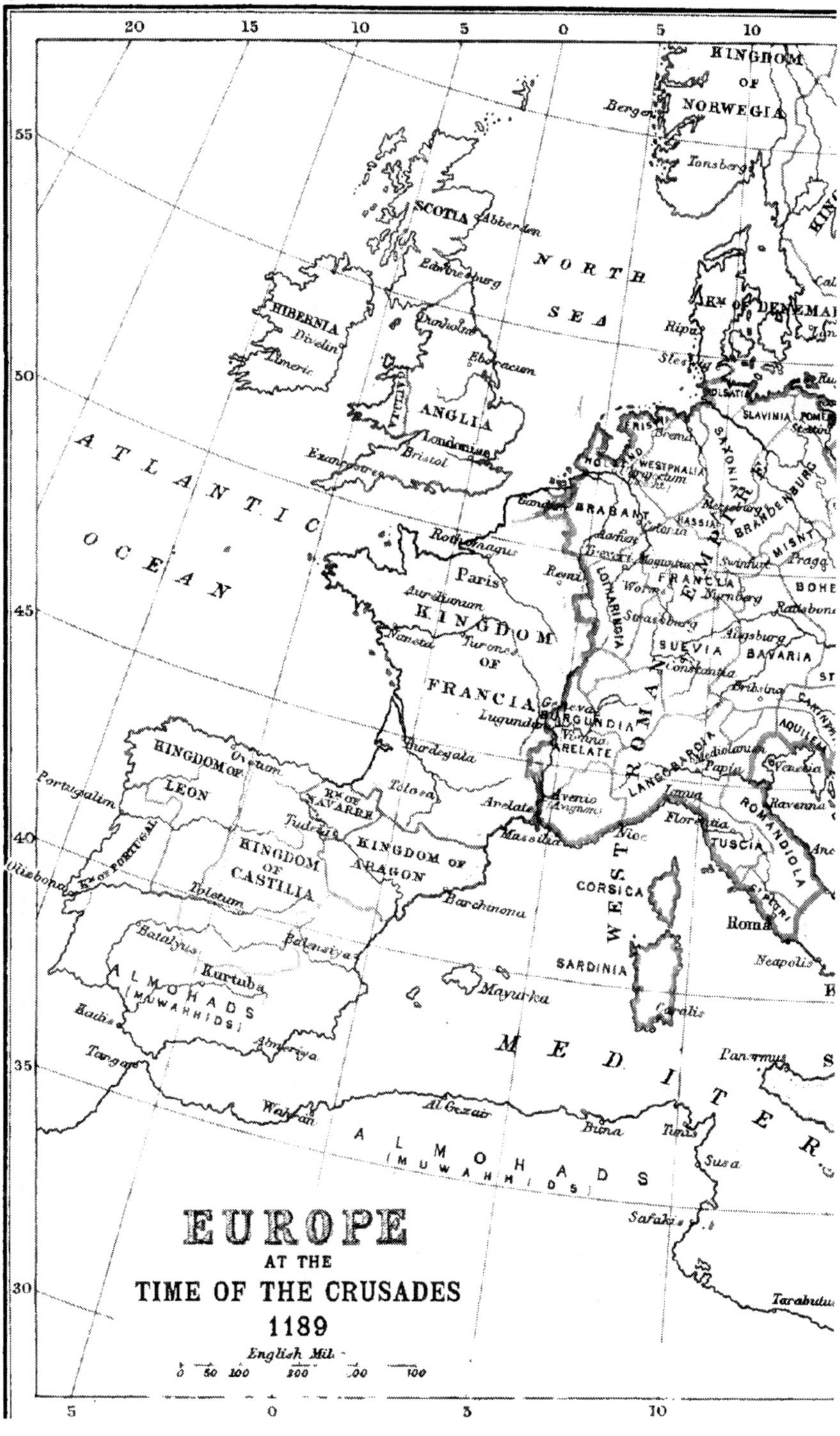
EUROPE
AT THE
TIME OF THE CRUSADES
1189
English Miles
KINGDOM OF NORWEGIA
Bergen
Tonsberg
SCOTIA
Abberdon
Edinburg
NORTH SEA
HIBERNIA
Divelin
Limeric
Eboracum
ANGLIA
London
Bristol
Exancester
ATLANTIC OCEAN
Rotomagus
Paris
Aurelianum
KINGDOM OF FRANCIA
Nameta
Turones
Burdegala
Tolosa
Lugundum
BRABANT
WESTPHALIA
SAXONIA
BRANDENBURG
HASSIA
Colonia
Treveri
Remi
Moguntiacum
LOTHARINGIA
FRANCIA
Worms
Nurnberg
Strassburg
Augsburg
SUEVIA
BAVARIA
Constantia
BURGUNDIA
ARELATE
Vienna
Arelate
Avenio
Massilia
LANGOBARDIA
Mediolanum
Papia
Venetia
Ravenna
Genua
Florentia
ROMANDIOLA
TUSCIA
SPOLETI
Roma
Neapolis
CORSICA
SARDINIA
Caralis
Mayurka
Barchinona
KINGDOM OF ARAGON
KINGDOM OF NAVARRE
Tudela
KINGDOM OF CASTILIA
Toletum
KINGDOM OF LEON
Ovetum
Portugalim
Olisbona
Batalyus
Kurtuba
ALMOHADS (MUWAHHIDS)
Kadis
Tanger
Almeriya
Balensiya
MEDITER
Al Gezair
Wahran
Buna
Tunis
Susa
Safakis
Palermus
Tarabulus
SLAVINIA
POMERANIA
Stettin
BOHEMIA
Prague
Ratisbona
Salzburg
AQUILEIA
MISNIA
Merseburg
HOLSATIA
FRISIA
Bremen
Ripa
Sleswig
Traiectum
WEST ROMAN EMPIRE

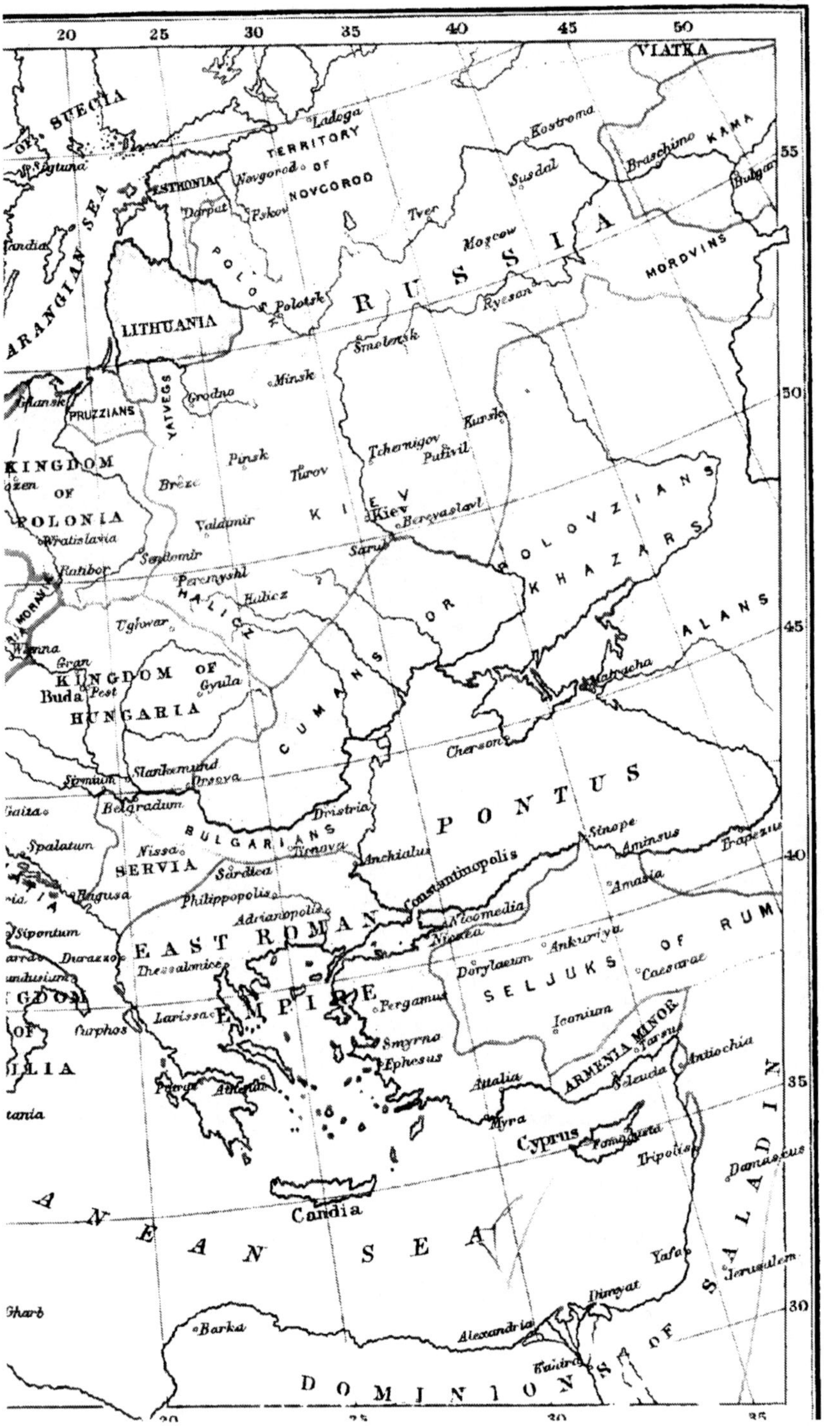
VIATKA
SUECIA
Ladoga
TERRITORY OF NOVGOROD
Novgorod
ESTHONIA
Darpat
Pskov
Tver
Kostroma
Susdal
KAMA
Braschimo
Bulgar
Moscow
R U S S I A
MORDVINS
POLO
Polotsk
Ryesan
LITHUANIA
Smolensk
Minsk
Grodno
PRUZZIANS
YATVEGS
Kursk
Tchernigov
Putivil
KINGDOM OF POLONIA
Pinsk
Turov
Valdimir
K I E V
Kiev
Pereyaslavl
Wratislavia
Sendomir
Ratibor
Peremyshl
HALICZ
Halicz
POLOVZIANS OR KHAZARS
ALANS
Ughwar
Wienna
Gran
KINGDOM OF HUNGARIA
Buda
Pest
Gyula
CUMANS
Matracha
Cherson
Slankamend
Orsova
PONTUS
Belgradum
Dristria
BULGARIANS
Tirnova
Sinope
Aminsus
Trapezus
Spalatum
Nissa
SERVIA
Sardica
Anchialus
Constantinopolis
Amasia
Ragusa
Philippopolis
Adrianopolis
EAST ROMAN EMPIRE
Nicomedia
Nicaea
RUM
Sipontum
Durazzo
Thessalonica
Dorylaeum
Ankuriya
SELJUKS OF RUM
Caesarae
Larissa
Pergamus
Iconium
Corphos
Smyrna
Ephesus
ARMENIA MINOR
Tarsus
Antiochia
Attalia
Seleucia
Myra
Cyprus
Famagusta
Tripolis
Damascus
Candia
A N E A N S E A
Yafa
Jerusalem
Dimyat
Barka
Alexandria
Kairo
DOMINIONS OF SALADIN
20
25
30
35
40
45
50
55

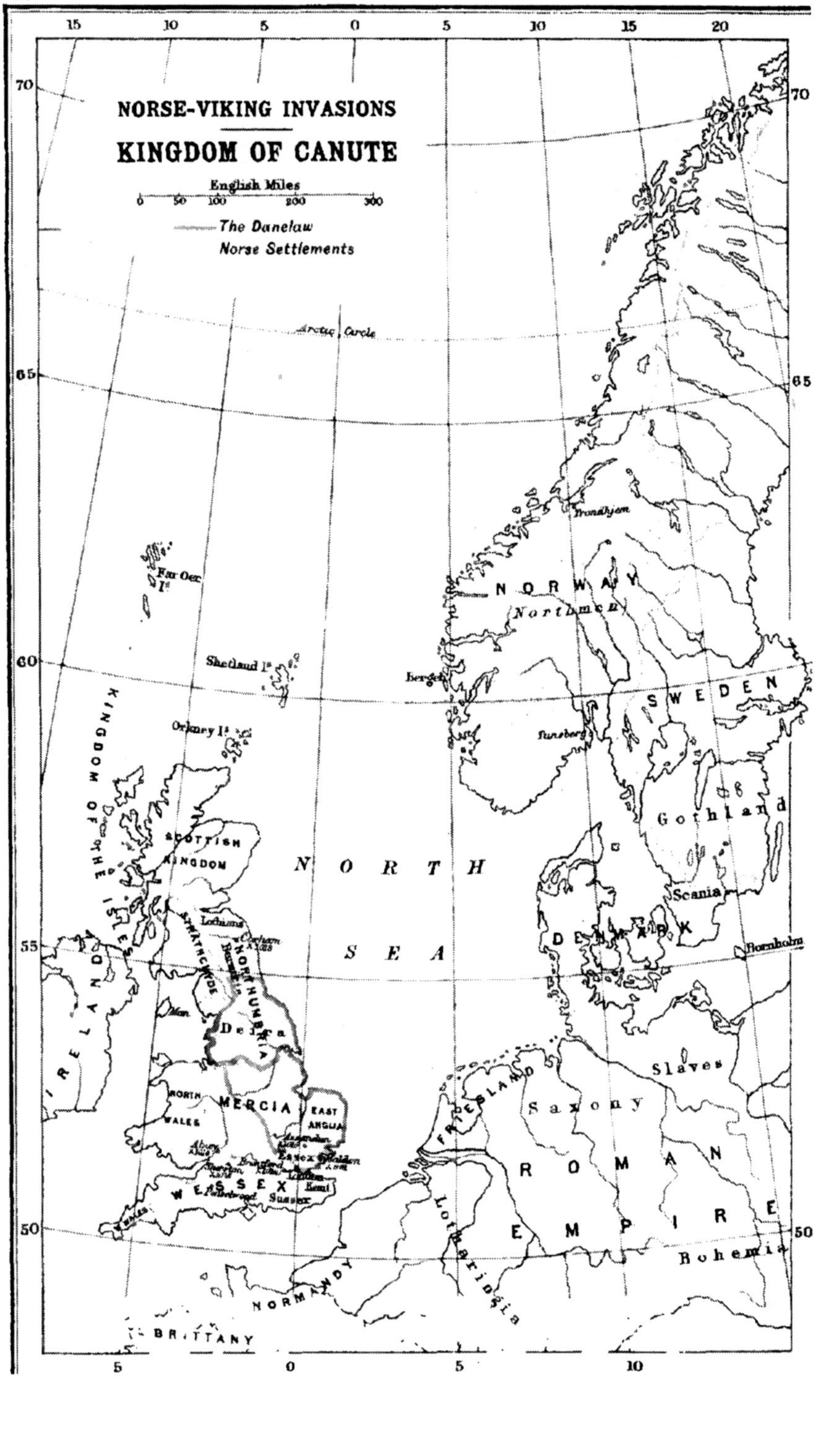

NORSE-VIKING INVASIONS

KINGDOM OF CANUTE

English Miles

| 0 | 50 | 100 | 200 | 300 |

The Danelaw
Norse Settlements

Arctic Circle

70

65

60

55

50

Far Oer Is.

Shetland Is.

Orkney Is.

KINGDOM OF THE ISLES

IRELAND

SCOTTISH KINGDOM

STRATHCLYDE

Lothians

Galloway

Man

NORTHUMBRIA

Deira

NORTH WALES

MERCIA

NORTH WALES

EAST ANGLIA

Essex

W E S S E X

Kent

Sussex

BRITTANY

NORMANDY

NORTH SEA

NORWAY
Northmen

Trondhjem

Bergen

Tunsberg

SWEDEN

Gothland

Scania

D E N M A R K

Bornholm

Slaves

FRIESLAND

Saxony

R O M A N

Lotharingia

E M P I R E

Bohemia

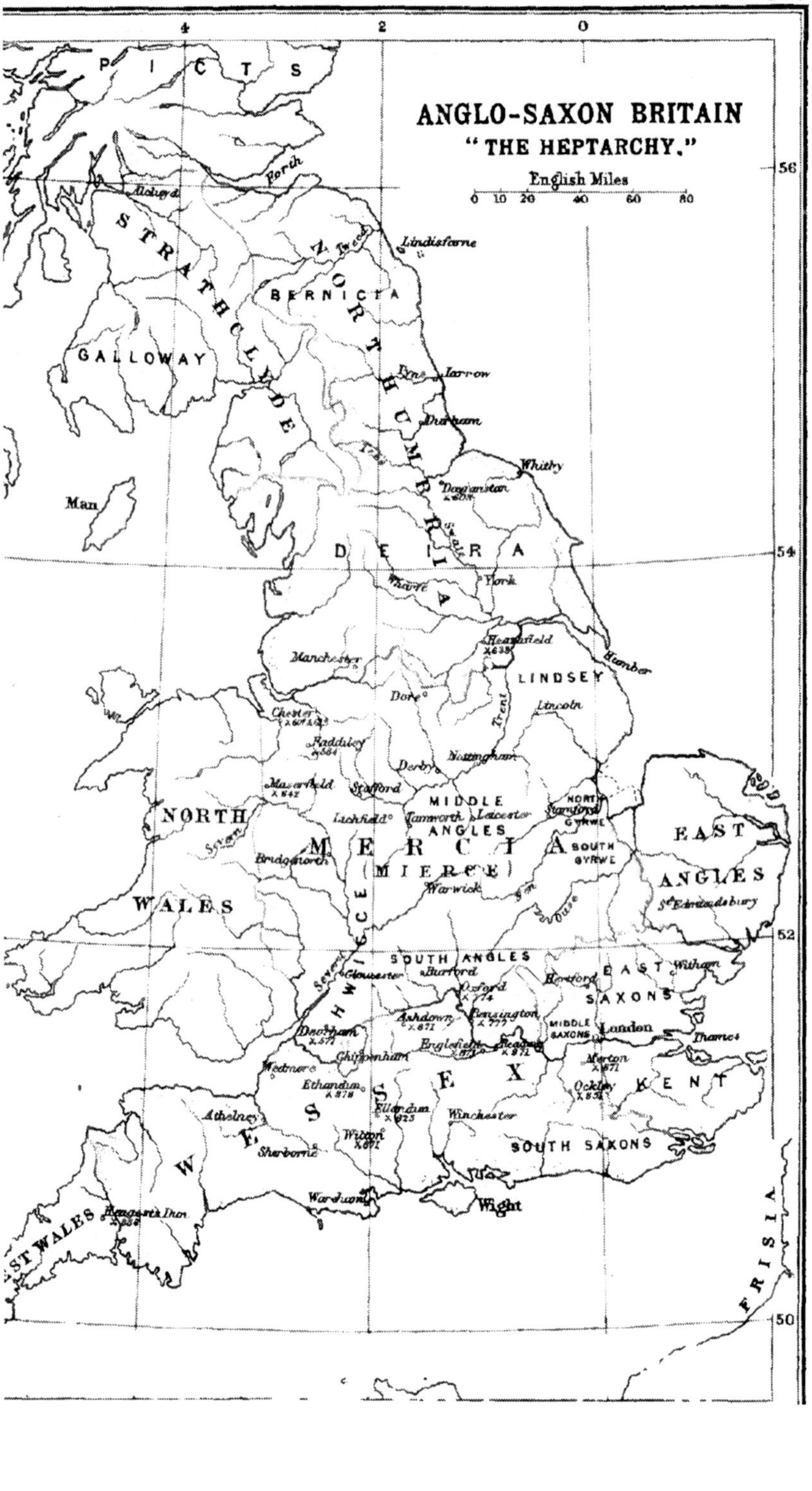
ANGLO-SAXON BRITAIN
"THE HEPTARCHY."
English Miles
0 10 20 40 60 80
4
2
0
56
54
52
50
PICTS
Forth
STRATHCLYDE
NORTHUMBRIA
BERNICIA
Lindisfarne
Tweed
GALLOWAY
Tyne
Jarrow
Durham
Whitby
Man
DEIRA
York
Swale
Wharfe
Heathfield
X 633
Humber
LINDSEY
Manchester
Dore
Lincoln
Trent
Chester
Derby
Nottingham
Stafford
MIDDLE ANGLES
Lichfield
Tamworth
Leicester
Maserfeld
X 642
NORTH WALES
Severn
Bridgnorth
MERCIA
(MIERCE)
Warwick
NORTH GYRWE
Stamford
SOUTH GYRWE
EAST ANGLES
St. Edmundsbury
HWICCE
SOUTH ANGLES
Gloucester
Burford
Oxford
X 774
Hertford
EAST SAXONS
Witham
Ashdown
X 871
Bensington
X 777
Deorham
X 577
MIDDLE SAXONS
London
Thames
Chippenham
Englefield
Reading
X 871
Wedmore
Merton
X 871
Ethandun
X 878
WESSEX
KENT
Ockley
X 851
Ellandun
X 823
Athelney
Winchester
Wilton
X 871
Sherborne
SOUTH SAXONS
Wareham
Wight
WEST WALES
Hengest's Dun
X 836
FRISIA

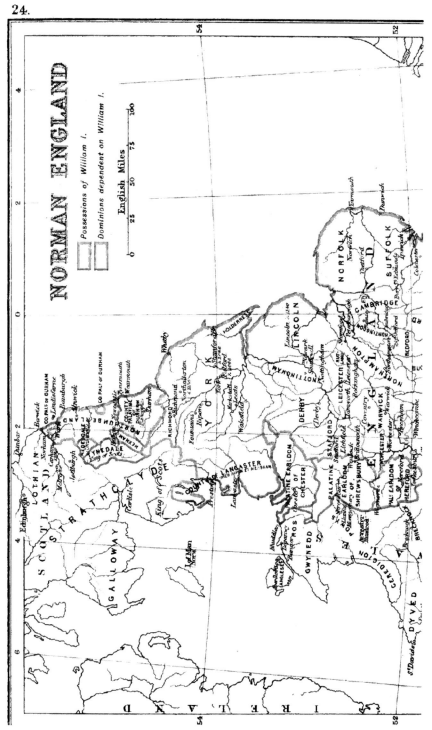

NORMAN ENGLAND

Possessions of William I.

Dominions dependent on William I.

English Miles

0   25   50   75   100

County of Flanders
Ponthieu
Vermandois
Beauvais
Champagne
Isle of France
NORMANDY
MAINE
Perche
BRITTANY
FRANCE
KENT
SUSSEX
SURREY
MIDDLESEX
HANTS
BERKS
WILTS
DORSET
SOMERSET
DEVON
CORNWALL
I. of Wight
Channel Islands
Jersey
Guernsey
Alderney
Sark
Ushant I.
Paris
Rouen
Calais
Boulogne
Amiens
Arras
Cherbourg
Caen
Bayeux
Lisieux
Falaise
Evreux
Rennes
Le Mans
Orleans
Compiegne
Winchester
Southampton
Salisbury
Exeter
Dover
Hastings
Sandwich
John Bartholomew & Co., Edin.

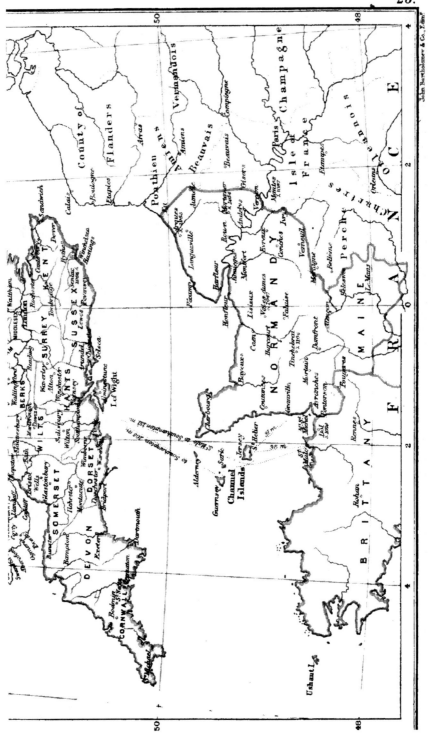

NORTH SEA
IRISH SEA
ENGLISH CHANNEL
ENGLAND
IRELAND
HOLLAND
BRABANT
LORRAINE
VERMANDOIS
AMIENS
VALOIS
VEXIN
LOTHIAN
STRATHCLYDE
GALLOWAY
WESTMORELAND
NORTHUMBERLAND
DURHAM
WELSH PRINCIPALITIES
MARCHER EARLDOMS
ULTONIA (ULSTER)
MIDIA (MEATH)
LAGENIA (LEINSTER)
CONNACTIA (CONNAUGHT)
MOMONIA (MUNSTER)
Berwick District
LONDON
York
Lincoln
Norwich
Colchester
Oxford
Winchester
Canterbury
Chester
Bristol
Dublin
Limerick
Cork
Dover
Calais
Boulogne
Bristol Chan.
North Chan.
I. of Wight
54
52
50

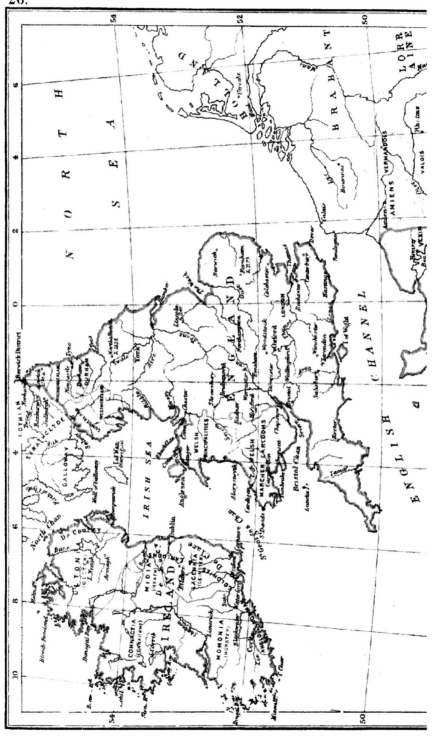

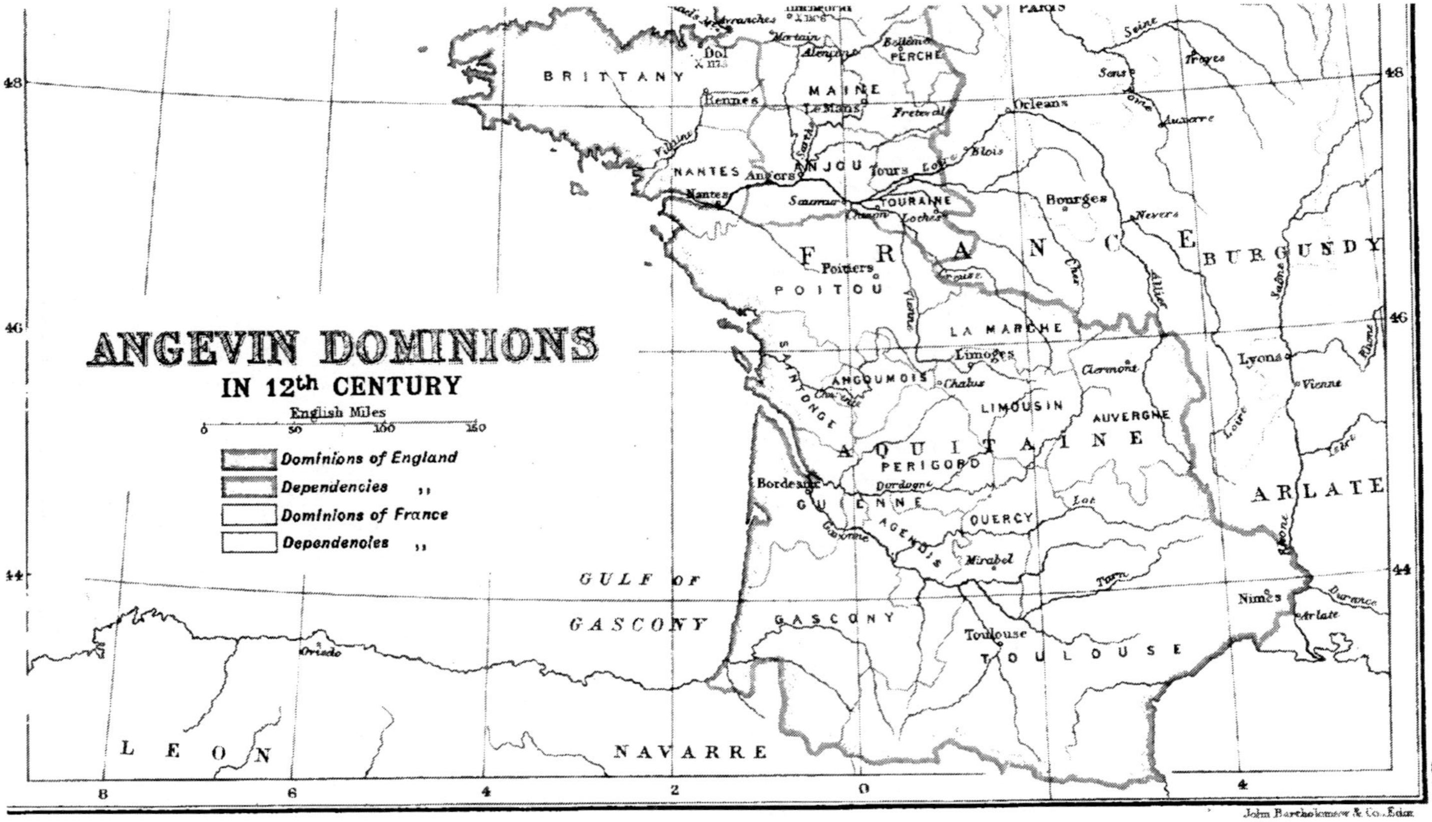
ANGEVIN DOMINIONS
IN 12th CENTURY
English Miles
0 50 100 150
Dominions of England
Dependencies ,,
Dominions of France
Dependencies ,,
BRITTANY
NANTES
Nantes
Rennes
Dol
Vilaine
MAINE
Le Mans
PERCHE
Alençon
Mortain
Fretevale
ANJOU
Angers
Tours
Saumur
Loire
Blois
TOURAINE
Loches
Orleans
PARIS
Seine
Sens
Troyes
Auxerre
Bourges
Nevers
Cher
Allier
F R A N C E
BURGUNDY
Poitiers
POITOU
Vienne
LA MARCHE
Limoges
Chalus
ANGOUMOIS
SAINTONGE
LIMOUSIN
Clermont
AUVERGNE
A Q U I T A I N E
PERIGORD
Dordogne
Bordeaux
GUIENNE
Garonne
AGENOIS
QUERCY
Lot
Mirabel
Tarn
Lyons
Vienne
Saône
Rhone
ARLATE
Isère
Durance
Nimes
Arlate
Toulouse
TOULOUSE
GASCONY
GULF OF
GASCONY
Oviedo
LEON
NAVARRE
48
46
44
8
6
4
2
0
4
John Bartholomew & Co. Edin.

OTTOMAN EMPIRE
AT FALL OF CONSTANTINOPLE
1453
English Miles
0 50 100 200 300 400
Ottoman Empire
Venetian Possessions
Genoese
Christian States of the East
HUNGARY
BOSNIA
SERVIA
WALLACHIA
MOLDAVIA
BULGARIA
KINGDOM OF THE TATARS
Cherkesses
BLACK SEA
GEORGIA
ARMENIA
AZERBIJAN
TREBIZOND
MESOPOTAMIA
EMPIRE OF THE MAMELUKES
SYRIA
OTTOMAN TURKS
KARAMAN
CYPRUS
MEDITERRANEAN SEA
ADRIATIC
VENICE
PAPAL STATES
NAPLES
Sicily
Barka
Constantinople
Rhodes

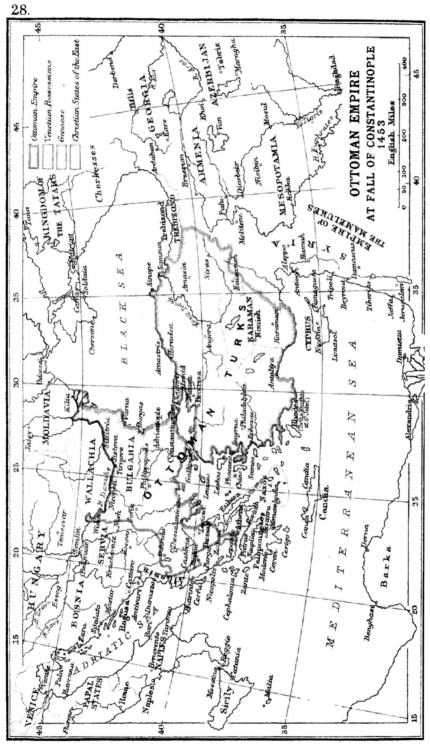

SPANISH KINGDOMS
AFTER 1513
English Miles
FRANCE
AFRICA
ATLANTIC OCEAN
MEDITERRANEAN SEA
Balearic Islands
Minorca
Majorca
Iviza
Formentera
Pyrenees
NAVARRE
ARAGON
Catalonia
Valencia
Murcia
Granada
Andalusia
CASTILE
Old Castile
New Castile
Leon
Asturias
Galicia
Estremadura
MADRID
LISBON
Oporto
Seville
Cordova
Cadiz
Malaga
Cartagena
Alicante
Barcelona
Zaragoza
Toledo
Valladolid
Burgos
Salamanca
Gibraltar
Strait of Gibraltar
Ceuta
Algiers
Marseilles
G. of Lions
John Bartholomew & Co. Edin.

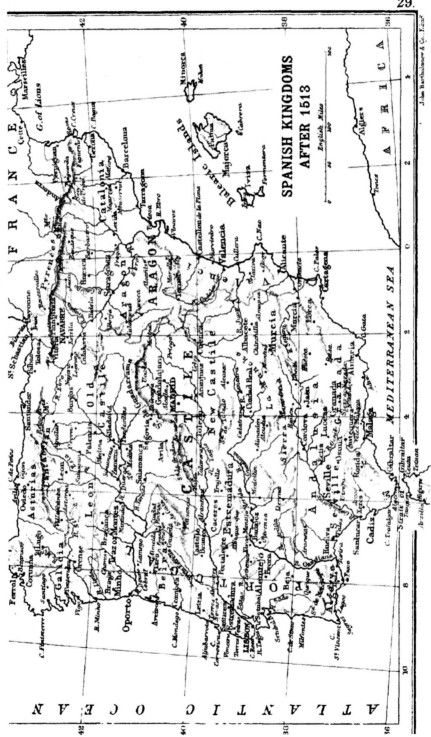

GERMANY & N. ITALY
END OF 15th CENTURY
POMERANIA
MECKLENBURG
BRANDENBURG
SILESIA
SAXONY
BOHEMIA
HOLSTEIN
SCHLESWIG
BREMEN
BRUNSWICK LÜNEBURG
MAGDEBURG
ANHALT
OLDENBURG
MÜNSTER
UTRECHT
FRIESLAND
GUELDERS
CLEVE
LIPPE
HESSE
WESTPHALIA
MARK
BERG
COLOGNE
JÜLICH
NASSAU
TRÈVES
MAYENCE
PALATINATE
UPPER PALATINATE
WÜRZBURG
NUREMBERG
LUXEMBURG
LIEGE
BRABANT
HAINAUT
FLANDERS
ZEELAND
VALOIS

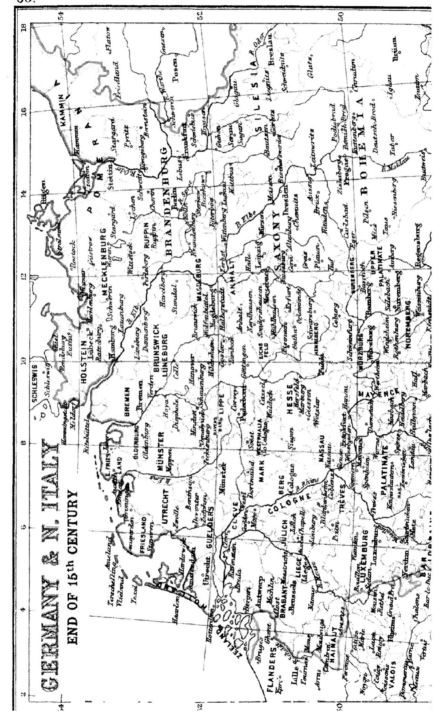

AUSTRIA
SALZBURG
STYRIA
CARINTHIA
CARNIOLA
CROATIA
TYROL
TRENT
VENICE
ISTRIA
FRANCHE COMTÉ
BURGUNDY
NEVERS
CHAROLAIS
FOREZ
VIVIERS
DAUPHINÉ
SAVOY
VALAIS
CONFEDERATION of SWITZERLAND
GRISONS
SUNDGAU
BREISGAU
MILAN
PIEDMONT
MONTFERRAT
SALUZZO
NICE
GENOA
PARMA
MODENA
FERRARA
LUCCA
FLORENCE
SIENA
PAPAL STATES
ADRIATIC SEA
Note to colours inside the Empire
Boundary of The Empire
Ecclesiastical Territories
Hapsburg Territories
Burgundian Territories
Wittelsbach, Wettin & Hohenzollern Terʳˢ
Other Lay Territories
Imperial Towns
English Miles
0 25 50 100

John Bartholomew & Co. Edinʳ

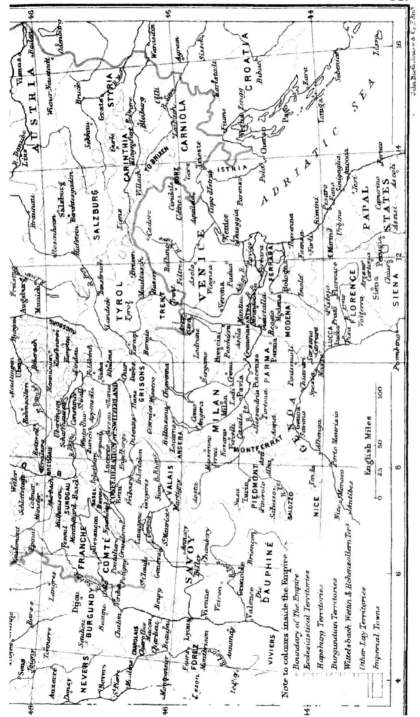

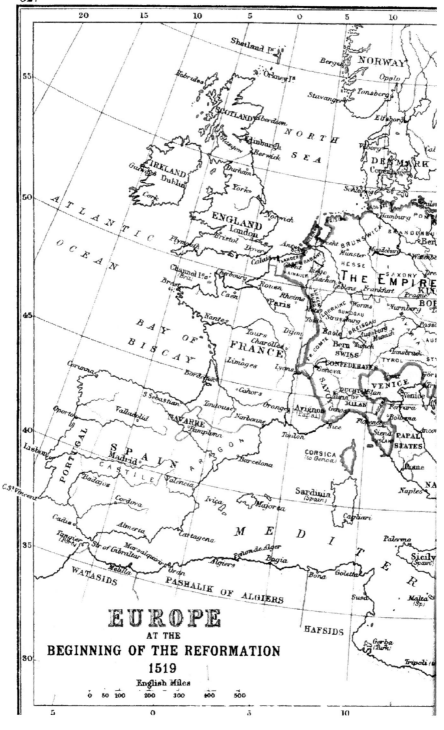

EUROPE
AT THE
BEGINNING OF THE REFORMATION
1519
English Miles
0 50 100 200 300 400 500
Shetland Is
Orkney Is
Hebrides
NORWAY
Bergen
Oslo
Tonsberg
Stavanger
Elfsborg
SCOTLAND
Aberdeen
Edinburgh
Glasgow
Berwick
NORTH SEA
IRELAND
Dublin
Galway
Cork
Durham
York
ENGLAND
London
Norwich
Bristol
Plymouth
Dover
Calais
DENMARK
Copenhagen
ATLANTIC OCEAN
Channel Is
Cherbourg
Brest
Caen
Rouen
Rheims
Paris
Antwerp
Utrecht
FLANDERS
BRABANT
HAINAULT
Ghent
Liege
Aachen
BRUNSWICK
Hamburg
Munster
HESSE
Magdeburg
BRANDENBURG
Berlin
Wittenberg
THE EMPIRE
SAXONY
Coblenz
Frankfurt
Prague
Worms
LORRAINE
SUNDGAU
Strasburg
Nurnberg
BREISGAU
Augsburg
Munich
Baale
Zurich
Bern
SWISS
CONFEDERATES
Geneva
TYROL
Innsbruck
Nantes
Tours
Dijon
BAY OF BISCAY
FRANCE
Charolles
Limoges
Lyons
Bordeaux
Cahors
Toulouse
Narbonne
Orange
Avignon
(Papal)
SAVOY
DUCHY OF MILAN
Milan
Genoa
VENICE
Venice
Ferrara
Bologna
Florence
Siena
TUSCANY
PAPAL STATES
Rome
Naples
Nice
Toulon
CORSICA
(to Genoa)
Sardinia
(Spain)
Cagliari
Corunna
S. Sebastian
Oporto
Valladolid
NAVARRE
Pamplona
ARAGON
Barcelona
PORTUGAL
SPAIN
Madrid
CASTILE
Lisbon
Badajos
Valencia
C. St. Vincent
Cordova
Iviça
Majorca
Cadiz
Almeria
Cartagena
MEDITER
Tangier
Str. of Gibraltar
Marsalquivir
Penon de Alger
Algiers
Bugia
Melilla
Oran
Bona
Goletta
WATASIDS
PASHALIK OF ALGIERS
HAFSIDS
Susa
Palermo
Sicily
(Spain)
Malta
Gerba
Tripoli

20
25
30
35
40
45
50
55
50
45
40
35
30
25
30
35
L. Ladoga
Viborg
Stolbovo
Vologda
Abo
Kevel
Narva
ESTHONIA
Novgorod
Uglitch
R U S S I A
Rostov
Nishni Novgorod
Kazan
KHANATE OF KAZAN
Stockholm
Gotland
Dorpat
Pskov
LIVONIA
Riga
Moscow
COURLAND
Dunaburg
Byeloi
Libau
Memel
Smolensk
Tula
RIAZAN
KHANATE OF ASTRAKHAN
Königsberg
Kovno
Vitepsk
LITHUANIA
Minsk
Mohilev
Yelets
Voronezh
Danzig
TEUTONIC ORDER
Grodno
Briansk
Thorn
Posen
Warsaw
Pinsk
PR. OF NOVGOROD SEVERSKI
Tchernigov
P O L A N D
Breslau
Lublin
VOLHYNIA
Kiev
KHANATE OF THE CRIMEA
Sandomir
Cracow
GALICIA
Lemberg
PODOLIA
Halicz
Trenczin
Tokay
Jassy
Vienna
KINGDOM OF HUNGARY
Pest
Buda
MOLDAVIA
YEDISAN
Klausenburg
Akerman
Kertch
Kaffa
Kronstadt
Mohacs
Tirgovishte
Baktchi Serai
GEORGIA
Semlin
Orsova
WALLACHIA
Sabac
Belgrade
Krajova
BLACK SEA
BOSNIA
Widdin
Nicopolis
Silistria
SERVIA
BULGARIA
Varna
Sinope
Samsun
Trebizond
Ragusa
OTTOMAN EMPIRE
Philippopolis
Kastamuni
Amasia
Scutari
Constantinople
Ismid
Barletta
Durazzo
Brusa
Angora
Brindisi
Salonika
Bergama
Kaisarieh
Larissa
Kutahiya
Corfu
Zeitun
Euboea I.
Konia
Adana
Lepanto
Chios I.
Smyrna
Karaman
Tarsus
Athens
Antioch
Zante
Duchy of Naxos
Adalia
Mistra
Rhodes
Cyprus (to Venice)
Nicosia
Tripoli
Damascus
Candia
Crete (to Venice)
SEA
Jaffa
Jerusalem
Damietta
Alexandria
BARKA
EGYPT
Suez
Cairo

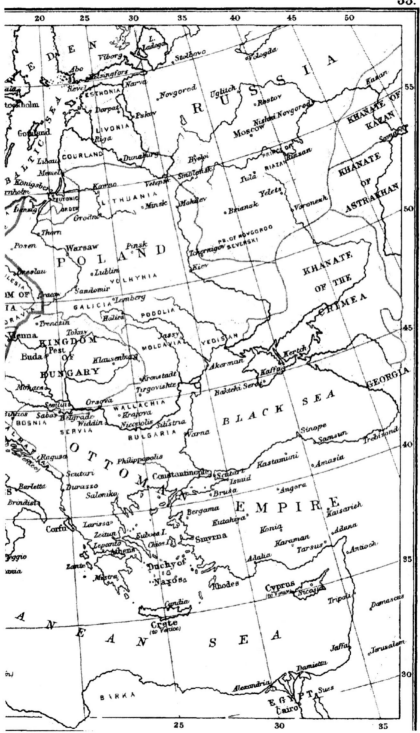

ENGLAND
WALES
ENGLISH CHANNEL
UNITED NETHERLANDS
SPANISH NETHERLANDS
LUXEMBURG
LIEGE
MÜNSTER
CLEVE
BERG
MARK
JULICH
TREVES
PALATINATE
LORRAINE
CHAMPAGNE
ILE DE FRANCE
NORMANDY
MAINE
BRITTANY
ANJOU
ORLEANS
SUNDGAU
FRANCHE
London
Paris

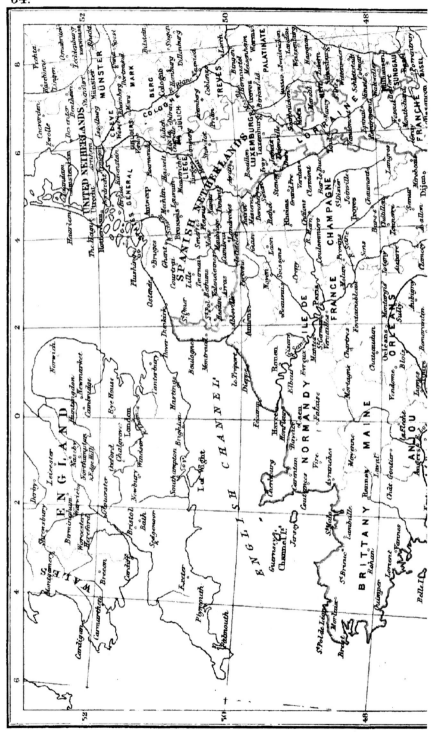

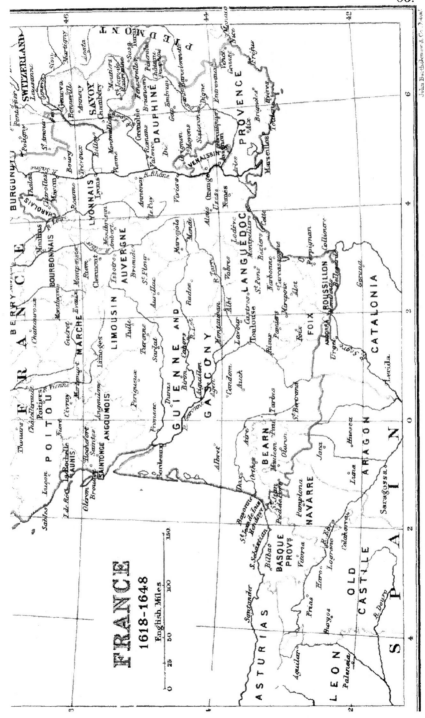

FRANCE
1618-1648
English Miles
0 25 50 100 150
F R A N C E
S P A I N
POITOU
BERRY
BURGUNDY
SWITZERLAND
BOURBONNAIS
MARCHE
LYONNAIS
SAVOY
LIMOUSIN
AUVERGNE
ANGOUMOIS
SAINTONGE
AUNIS
DAUPHINÉ
PIEDMONT
GUIENNE AND GASCONY
VENAISSIN
PROVENCE
LANGUEDOC
BEARN
FOIX
ROUSSILLON
NAVARRE
BASQUE PROVS
ASTURIAS
LEON
OLD CASTILE
ARAGON
CATALONIA
ANDORRA
Poitiers
Limoges
Lyons
Geneva
Chambéry
Grenoble
Bordeaux
Toulouse
Marseilles
Avignon
Nimes
Montpellier
Narbonne
Perpignan
Pamplona
Saragossa
Lerida
Bayonne
La Rochelle
Clermont
John Bartholomew & Co. Edin

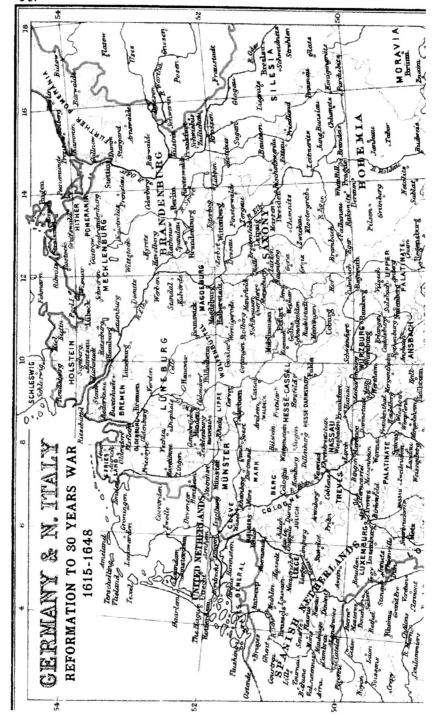

GERMANY & N. ITALY
REFORMATION TO 30 YEARS WAR
1615-1648
SCHLESWIG
HOLSTEIN
MECKLENBURG
HITHER POMERANIA
FURTHER POMERANIA
BRANDENBURG
SILESIA
SAXONY
BOHEMIA
MORAVIA
UPPER PALATINATE
ANSBACH
WÜRZBURG
MAGDEBURG
LÜNEBURG
BREMEN
OLDENBURG
E. FRIESLAND
MÜNSTER
CLEVE
MARK
BERG
COLOGNE
JULICH
TREVES
NASSAU
HESSE-CASSEL
HESSE DARMSTADT
PALATINATE
LUXEMBURG
LIEGE
UNITED NETHERLANDS
STATES GENERAL
SPANISH NETHERLANDS
WOLFENBÜTTEL
LIPPE
WALDECK

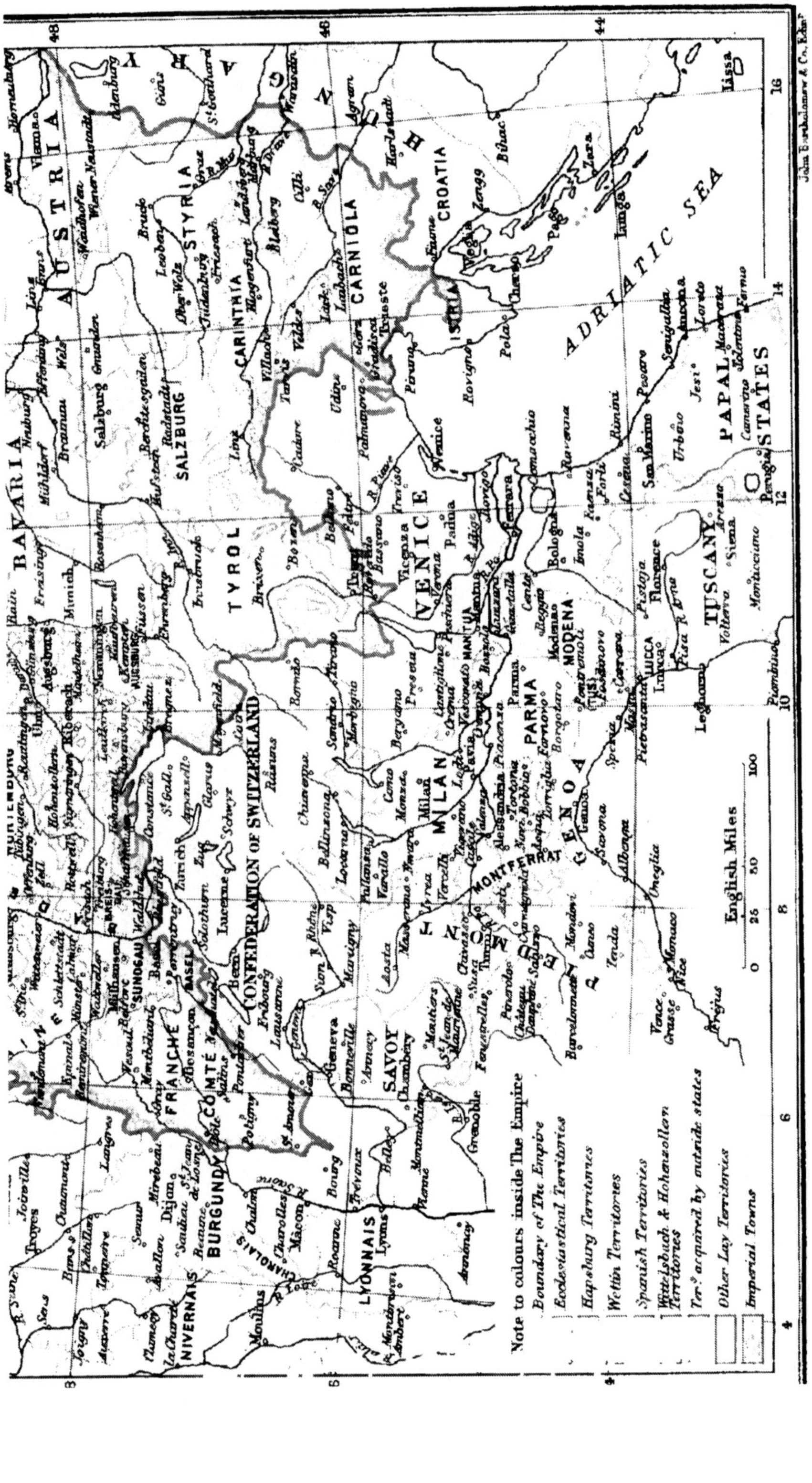
AUSTRIA
BAVARIA
SALZBURG
TYROL
STYRIA
CARINTHIA
CARNIOLA
CROATIA
ISTRIA
VENICE
MILAN
MANTUA
MODENA
PARMA
GENOA
MONTFERRAT
TUSCANY
LUCCA
PAPAL STATES
ADRIATIC SEA
CONFEDERATION OF SWITZERLAND
SAVOY
FRANCHE COMTÉ
BURGUNDY
NIVERNAIS
CHAROLAIS
LYONNAIS
SUNDGAU
English Miles
Note to colours inside The Empire
Boundary of The Empire
Ecclesiastical Territories
Hapsburg Territories
Wettin Territories
Spanish Territories
Wittelsbach & Hohenzollern Territories
Ter.s acquired by outside states
Other Lay Territories
Imperial Towns
John Bartholomew & Co. Edinr

SWITZERLAND
HUNGARY
OTTOMAN EMPIRE
Dalmatia
ADRIATIC SEA
Gulf of Venice
VENICE
MILAN
PIEDMONT
MONTFERRAT
GENOA
PARMA
MODENA
MANTUA
LUCCA
TUSCANY
PAPAL STATES
CORSICA
SAVOY
Istria
Trieste
Agram
Venice
Milan
Rome
Florence
Bologna
Ancona
Ravenna
Ragusa
Elba
Bastia
Ajaccio

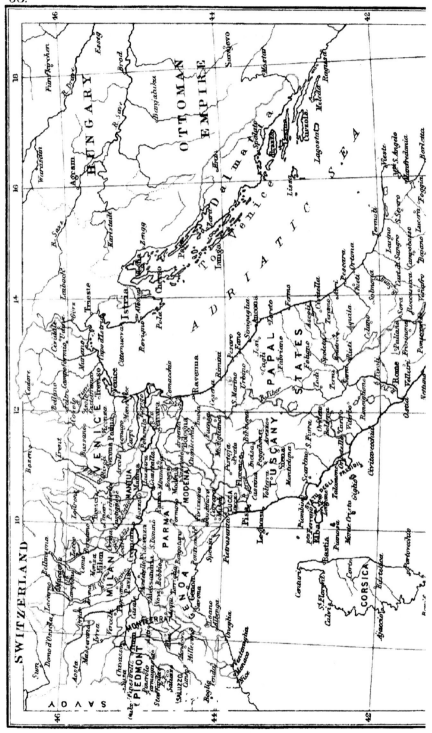

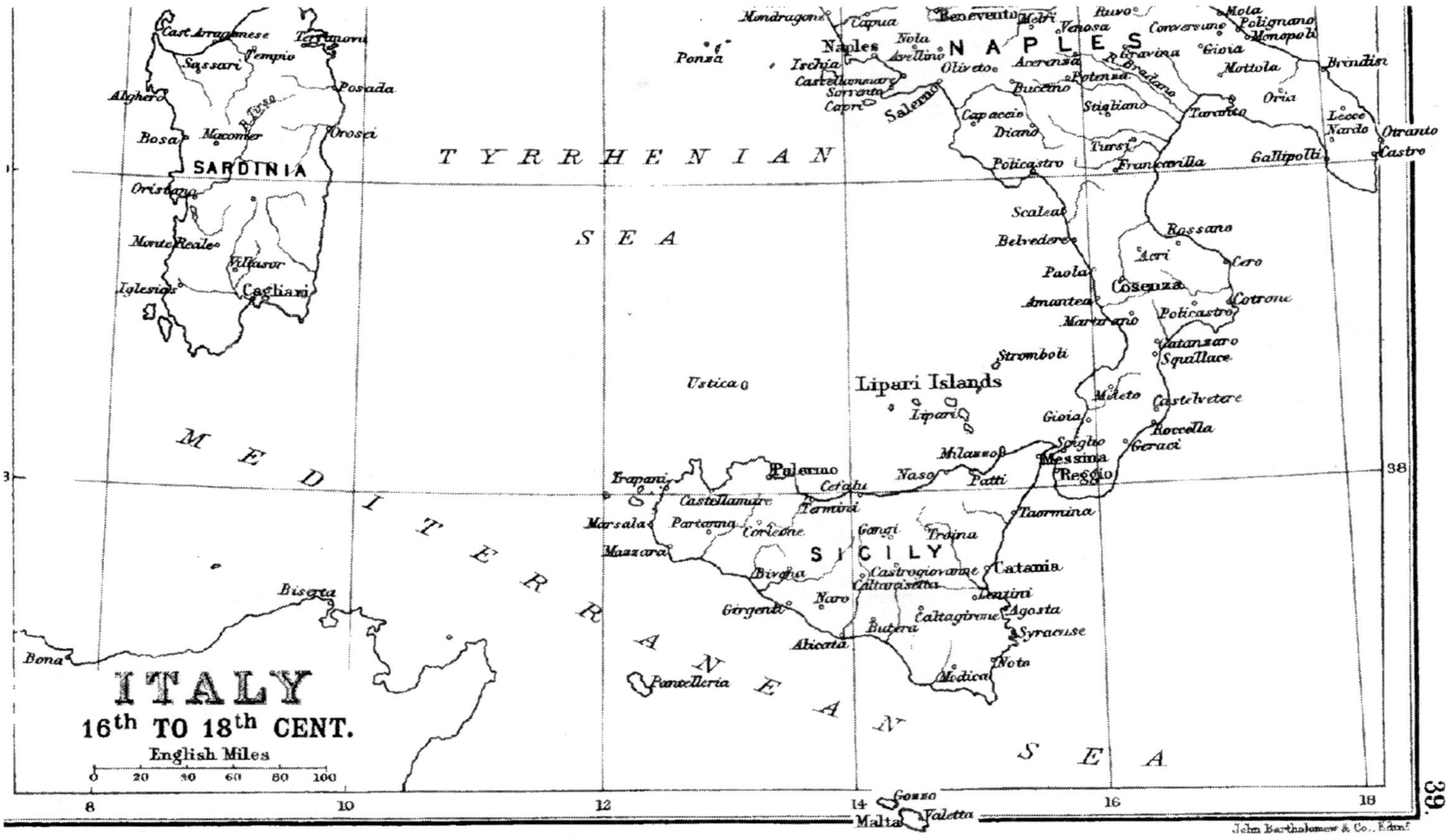
ITALY
16th TO 18th CENT.
English Miles
0 20 40 60 80 100
SARDINIA
NAPLES
SICILY
TYRRHENIAN SEA
MEDITERRANEAN SEA
Lipari Islands
Sassari
Tempio
Alghero
Bosa
Macomer
Posada
Orosei
Oristano
Monte Reale
Villasor
Iglesias
Cagliari
Ponza
Ischia
Naples
Capua
Nola
Avellino
Benevento
Salerno
Sorrento
Capri
Oliveto
Acerenza
Potenza
Venosa
Ruvo
Gravina
Conversano
Gioia
Mola
Polignano
Monopoli
Mottola
Oria
Brindisi
Taranto
Lecce
Nardo
Otranto
Castro
Gallipoli
Francavilla
Tursi
Stigliano
Buccino
Capaccio
Diano
Policastro
Scalea
Belvedere
Paola
Amantea
Martirano
Cosenza
Acri
Rossano
Cero
Cotrone
Catanzaro
Squillace
Castelvetere
Roccella
Geraci
Mileto
Gioia
Stromboli
Lipari
Ustica
Messina
Reggio
Milazzo
Patti
Naso
Cefalu
Termini
Palermo
Trapani
Castellamare
Marsala
Partanna
Corleone
Mazzara
Gangi
Troina
Taormina
Catania
Castrogiovanne
Caltanisetta
Naro
Girgenti
Alicata
Butera
Caltagirone
Lentini
Agosta
Syracuse
Noto
Modica
Pantelleria
Biserta
Bona
Gozzo
Malta
Valetta
8
10
12
14
16
18
38
John Bartholomew & Co., Edinr.

40.

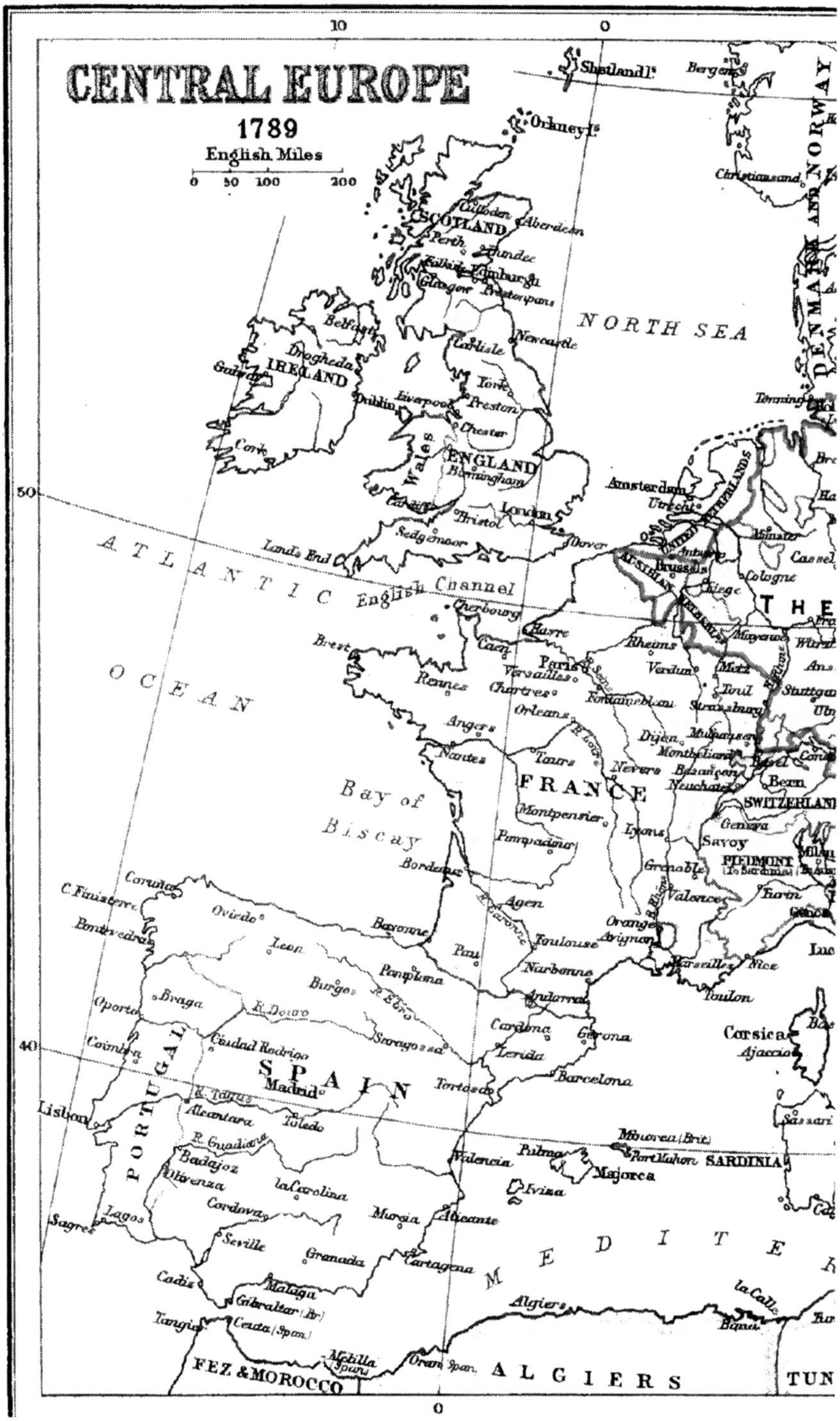
CENTRAL EUROPE
1789
English Miles
0 50 100 200
10
0
Shetland Is.
Bergen
Orkney Is.
NORWAY
DENMARK AND NORWAY
Christiansand
SCOTLAND
Culloden
Aberdeen
Perth
Dundee
Edinburgh
Glasgow
Prestonpans
NORTH SEA
Belfast
Drogheda
IRELAND
Galway
Dublin
Newcastle
Carlisle
York
Preston
Liverpool
Chester
Cork
Wales
ENGLAND
Birmingham
London
Bristol
Sedgemoor
Dover
Land's End
Amsterdam
Utrecht
UNITED NETHERLANDS
AUSTRIAN NETHERLANDS
Brussels
Antwerp
Liege
Cologne
Cassel
ATLANTIC
English Channel
OCEAN
Cherbourg
Havre
Caen
Brest
Rennes
Paris
Versailles
Chartres
Orleans
Rheims
Verdun
Metz
Toul
Strassburg
Fontainebleau
Stuttgart
Angers
Nantes
Tours
Nevers
Dijon
Mulhausen
Montbéliard
Basel
Besançon
Neuchatel
Bern
SWITZERLAND
FRANCE
Bay of
Biscay
Montpensier
Pompadour
Lyons
Geneva
Savoy
PIEDMONT
Bordeaux
Grenoble
Agen
Valence
Turin
Genoa
Orange
Avignon
Bayonne
Toulouse
Pau
Narbonne
Marseilles
Nice
Toulon
Andorra
Corunna
C. Finisterre
Oviedo
Pontevedra
Leon
Burgos
Pamplona
R. Ebro
Oporto
Braga
R. Douro
Saragossa
Cardona
Gerona
Lerida
Barcelona
Corsica
Ajaccio
Coimbra
Ciudad Rodrigo
PORTUGAL
SPAIN
Madrid
Tortosa
Lisbon
R. Tagus
Alcantara
Toledo
Minorca (Brit.)
Port Mahon
SARDINIA
Sassari
R. Guadiana
Badajoz
Olivenza
Valencia
Palma
Majorca
Iviza
la Carolina
Cordova
Murcia
Alicante
Lagos
Sagres
Seville
Granada
Cartagena
MEDITER
Cadiz
Malaga
Gibraltar (Br.)
Ceuta (Span.)
Tangier
Melilla (Span.)
Oran Span.
Algiers
la Calle
FEZ & MOROCCO
ALGIERS
TUN

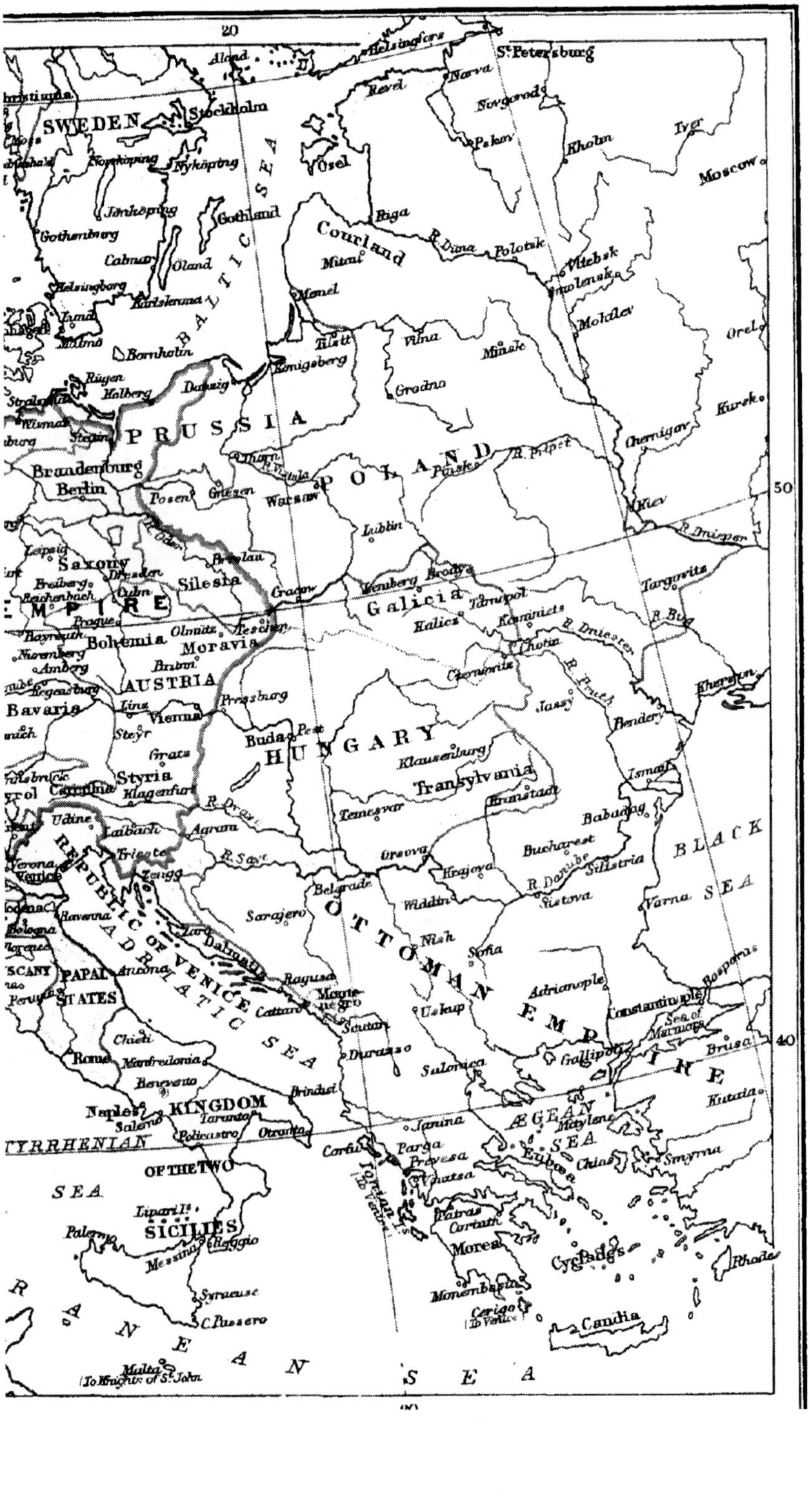
20
St Petersburg
Helsingfors
Aland
Stockholm
SWEDEN
Norrköping
Nyköping
Jönköping
Gothland
Gothenburg
Calmar
Öland
Helsingborg
Karlskrona
Malmö
Bornholm
BALTIC SEA
Ösel
Revel
Narva
Novgorod
Pskov
Kholm
Tver
Moscow
Riga
Courland
Mitau
R. Dina
Polotsk
Vitebsk
Smolensk
Mohilev
Orel
Memel
Tilsitt
Königsberg
Vilna
Minsk
Grodno
Kursk
Rügen
Kolberg
Danzig
Stralsund
Wismar
Stettin
PRUSSIA
POLAND
R. Pripet
Chernigov
Brandenburg
Berlin
Posen
Gnesen
Thorn
R. Vistula
Warsaw
Pinsk
Kiev
50
Lublin
R. Dnieper
Leipzig
Saxony
Dresden
Freiberg
Reichenbach
Culm
Silesia
Breslau
Cracow
Lemberg
Brody
Targowitz
EMPIRE
Galicia
Tarnopol
Prague
Olmütz
Teschen
Halicz
Kaminiets
R. Dniester
R. Bug
Bayreuth
Nuremberg
Amberg
Bohemia
Moravia
Brünn
Chotin
Czernowitz
R. Pruth
Regensburg
AUSTRIA
Pressburg
Jassy
Kherson
Bavaria
Linz
Vienna
Steyr
Buda
Pest
HUNGARY
Bender
Gratz
Klausenburg
Styria
Klagenfurt
Carinthia
Tyrol
Transylvania
Kronstadt
Ismail
R. Drave
Temesvar
Udine
Laibach
Agram
Babadag
Trieste
R. Save
Orsova
Bucharest
Verona
Venice
Zengg
Krajova
R. Danube
Silistria
BLACK SEA
REPUBLIC OF VENICE
Belgrade
Widdin
Sistova
Varna
Ravenna
Bologna
Sarajero
OTTOMAN EMPIRE
Zara
Dalmatia
Nish
Sofia
PAPAL STATES
Ancona
ADRIATIC SEA
Ragusa
Monte negro
Cattaro
Adrianople
Bosporus
Uskup
Constantinople
Sea of Marmora
Scutari
Rome
Chieti
Manfredonia
Durazzo
Salonica
Gallipoli
Brusa
40
Benevento
Brindisi
Kutaia
Naples
Salerno
KINGDOM
Taranto
Janina
ÆGEAN SEA
Policastro
Otranto
Corfu
Parga
Prevesa
Euboea
Chios
Smyrna
TYRRHENIAN
SEA
OF THE TWO
SICILIES
Lipari Is.
Palermo
Messina
Reggio
Patras
Corinth
Morea
Cyclades
Rhodes
Syracuse
C. Passero
Monembasia
Cerigo
(To Venice)
Candia
Malta
(To Knights of St. John)
MEDITERRANEAN SEA

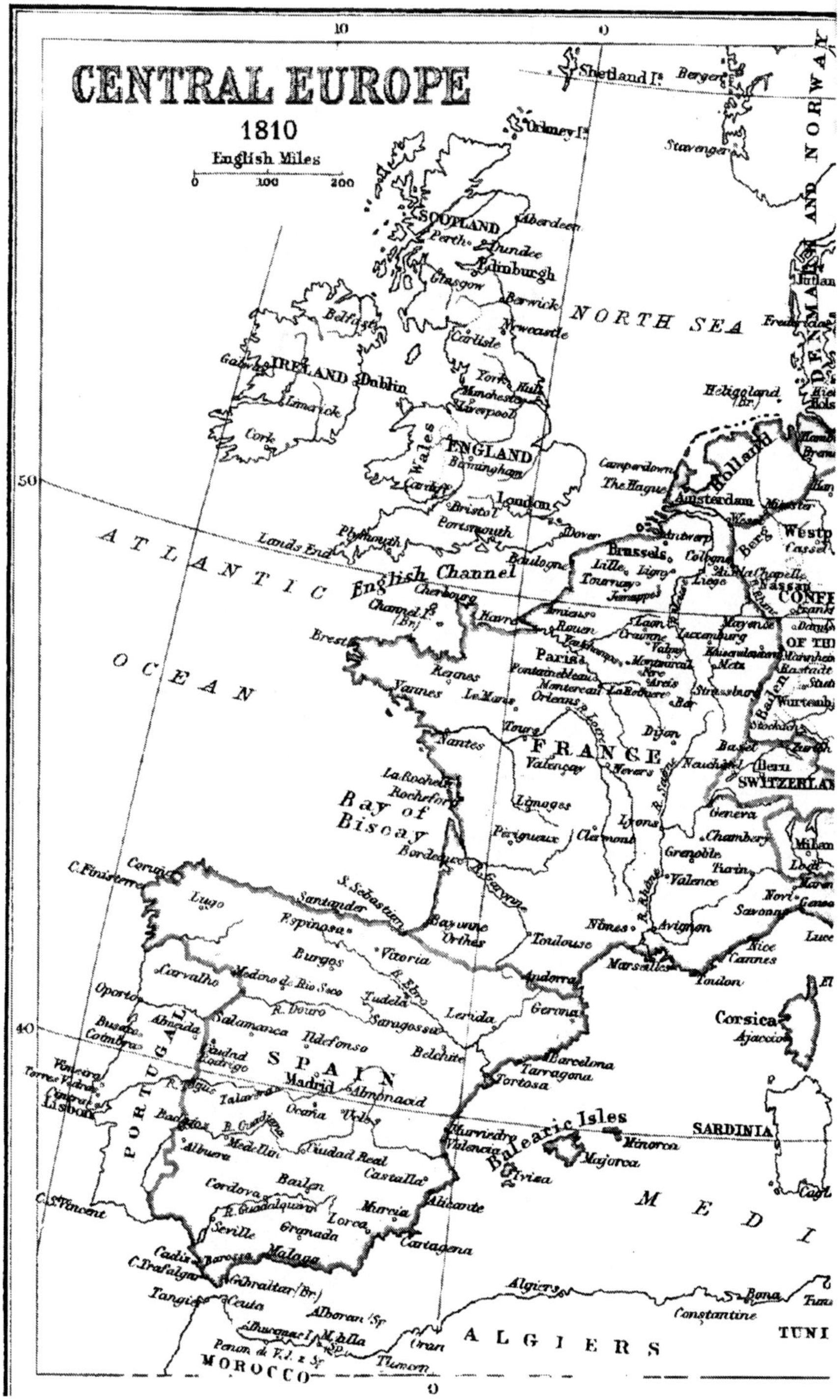
CENTRAL EUROPE
1810
English Miles
0 100 200
10
0
50
40
Shetland Is
Bergen
Orkney Is
Stavenger
NORWAY
SCOTLAND
Aberdeen
Perth
Dundee
Edinburgh
Glasgow
Berwick
NORTH SEA
Belfast
Newcastle
Carlisle
IRELAND
Dublin
Galway
Limerick
Cork
York
Hull
Manchester
Liverpool
Heligoland (Br.)
Wales
ENGLAND
Birmingham
Cardiff
Bristol
London
Portsmouth
Dover
Plymouth
Lands End
Camperdown
The Hague
Amsterdam
Holland
Brussels
Lille
Tournay
Jemappes
Ligny
Liege
Cologne
Aix la Chapelle
Berg
Nassau
Westp
Cassel
ATLANTIC
English Channel
Cherbourg
Channel Is (Br.)
Havre
Boulogne
Amiens
Rouen
Laon
Craonne
Luxemburg
Mayence
OF THE
Brest
OCEAN
Paris
Fontainebleau
Montereau
Arcis
La Rothiere
Bar
Metz
Strassburg
Baden
Rastadt
Wurtemb
Rennes
Vannes
Le Mans
Orleans
Tours
Dijon
FRANCE
Nantes
Valençay
Nevers
Basel
Neuchâtel
Bern
Zurich
SWITZERLAND
La Rochelle
Rochefort
Bay of Biscay
Limoges
Lyons
Geneva
Chambery
Milan
Perigueux
Clermont
Grenoble
Turin
Bordeaux
Valence
Lodi
Novi
Savona
Coruña
C. Finisterre
Lugo
Santander
S. Sebastian
Espinosa
Bayonne
Orthes
Toulouse
Nimes
Avignon
Nice
Cannes
Burgos
Vitoria
Marseilles
Toulon
Carvalho
Medina de Rio Seco
Tudela
R. Ebro
Andorra
Oporto
R. Douro
Saragossa
Lerida
Gerona
Corsica
Ajaccio
Busaco
Coimbra
Almeida
Salamanca
Ildefonso
Belchite
Barcelona
Tarragona
Tortosa
Vimeiro
Torres Vedras
Lisbon
PORTUGAL
SPAIN
Madrid
Almonacid
Talavera
Ocaña
Uclés
Badajoz
Albuera
Medellin
Ciudad Real
Murviedro
Valencia
Balearic Isles
Minorca
Majorca
Iviza
SARDINIA
Castalla
Cordova
Baylen
R. Guadalquivir
Murcia
Alicante
C. St Vincent
Seville
Granada
Lorca
Cartagena
MEDI
Cadiz
C. Trafalgar
Barossa
Malaga
Gibraltar (Br.)
Tangier
Ceuta
Alboran (Sp.)
Algiers
Bona
Constantine
Melilla
Oran
ALGIERS
TUNI
MOROCCO
Tlemcen
0

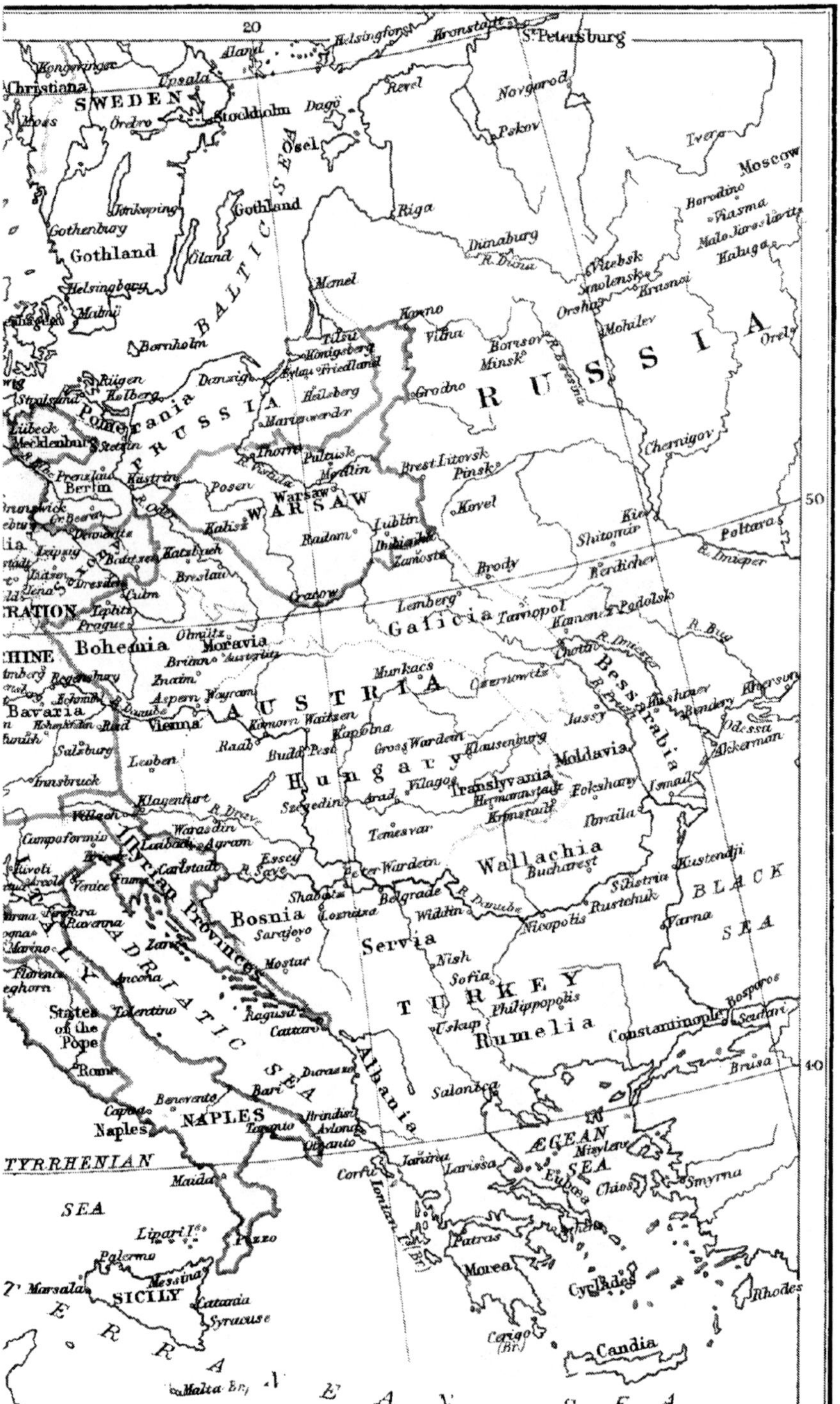

20
Helsingfors
Kronstadt
St Petersburg
Aland
Christiania
SWEDEN
Upsala
Stockholm
Dagö
Revel
Novgorod
Pskov
Tver
Moscow
Ösel
BALTIC SEA
Jönkoping
Gothland
Riga
Borodino
Viasma
Malo Jaroslavitz
Kaluga
Gothenburg
Gothland
Öland
Dünaburg
R. Düna
Vitebsk
Smolensk
Krasnoi
Helsingborg
Malmö
Memel
Orsha
Mohilev
Kovno
Vilna
Borisov
Minsk
Orel
Bornholm
Tilsit
Königsberg
Eylau
Friedland
Rügen
Kolberg
Danzig
Heilsberg
Grodno
RUSSIA
Stralsund
Pomerania
PRUSSIA
Marienwerder
Lübeck
Mecklenburg
Stettin
Thorn
Pultusk
Modlin
Brest Litovsk
Pinsk
Chernigov
Berlin
Küstrin
Posen
Warsaw
WARSAW
Kovel
50
Kalisz
Radom
Lublin
Zamość
Kiev
Zhitomir
Poltava
R. Dnieper
Leipzig
Bautzen
Katzbach
Dresden
Breslau
Brody
Berdichev
Jena
Culm
Cracow
Lemberg
Tarnopol
Kamenets Podolsk
Galicia
Prague
Bohemia
Olmütz
Moravia
Austerlitz
Brünn
R. Bug
Znaim
Munkacs
Czernowitz
Bessarabia
R. Dniester
Aspern
Wagram
AUSTRIA
Kishinev
Bender
Kherson
Bavaria
Vienna
Komorn
Waitzen
Kapolna
Jassy
Odessa
Akkerman
Salzburg
Leoben
Raab
Buda Pest
Gross Wardein
Klausenburg
Moldavia
Innsbruck
Hungary
Transylvania
Vilagos
Hermannstadt
Fokshany
Ismail
Klagenfurt
R. Drave
Arad
Szegedin
Kronstadt
Villach
Warasdin
Temesvar
Braila
Campoformio
Laibach
Agram
Illyrian Provinces
Essek
R. Save
Carlstadt
Peter Wardein
Wallachia
Bucharest
Kustendji
Venice
Fiume
Shabatz
Belgrade
R. Danube
Silistria
Rustchuk
BLACK SEA
Ferrara
Ravenna
Bosnia
Loznitza
Widdin
Nicopolis
Varna
Sarajevo
Zara
Servia
Marino
ADRIATIC SEA
Mostar
Nish
Sofia
Ancona
TURKEY
Philippopolis
Bosporus
Leghorn
States of the Pope
Tolentino
Ragusa
Cattaro
Uskup
Rumelia
Constantinople
Scutari
Rome
Albania
Durazzo
Brusa
40
Salonica
Benevento
Bari
Capua
Naples
NAPLES
Taranto
Brindisi
Avlona
Otranto
ÆGEAN SEA
Mitylene
TYRRHENIAN SEA
Corfu
Janina
Larissa
Euboea
Chios
Smyrna
Maida
Ionian Is.
Lipari Is.
Pizzo
Patras
Palermo
Messina
Morea
Cyclades
Rhodes
Marsala
SICILY
Catania
Syracuse
Cerigo (Br.)
Candia
MEDITERRANEAN SEA
Malta Br.
20

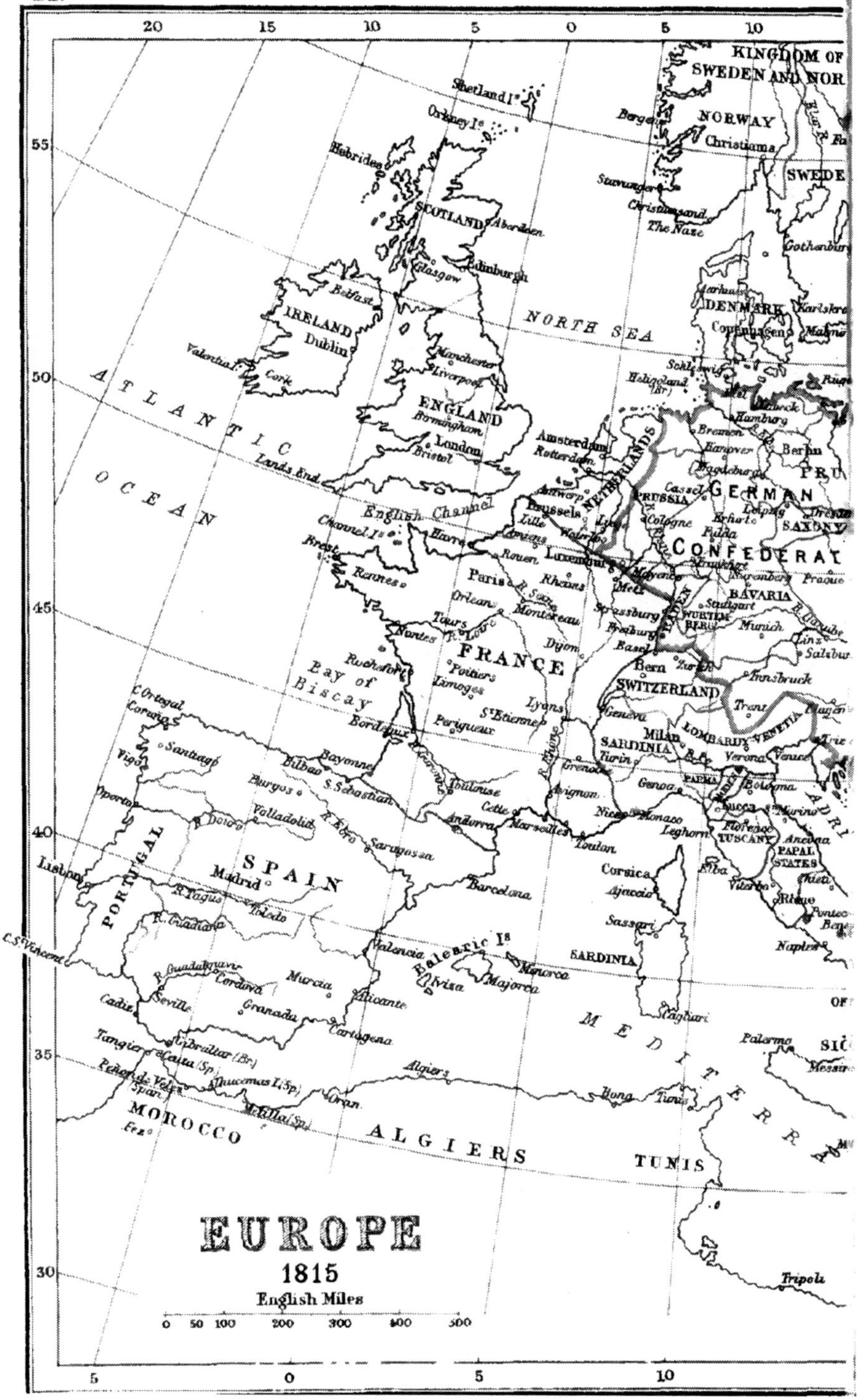
KINGDOM OF SWEDEN AND NOR
NORWAY
SWEDE
SCOTLAND
IRELAND
ENGLAND
NORTH SEA
ATLANTIC OCEAN
DENMARK
NETHERLANDS
PRUSSIA
GERMAN CONFEDERAT
SAXONY
BAVARIA
FRANCE
SWITZERLAND
SARDINIA
LOMBARDY VENETIA
TUSCANY
PAPAL STATES
SPAIN
PORTUGAL
Bay of Biscay
English Channel
MEDITERR
MOROCCO
ALGIERS
TUNIS
London
Paris
Madrid
Lisbon
Dublin
Edinburgh
Amsterdam
Brussels
Berlin
Munich
Milan
Turin
Florence
Naples
Marseilles
Algiers
Tripoli
EUROPE
1815
English Miles

20
25
30
35
40
45
50
Lake Ladoga
Onega
Viborg
Helsingfors
Kronstadt
St Petersburg
Vologda
Aland
G. of Finland
Reval
Stockholm
Yaroslav
Kazan
Nijni Novgorod
Pskov
Ösel
BALTIC SEA
Gothland
Tver
Moscow
Simbirsk
Riga
Syzran
Öland
R. Duna
Kaluga
Pensa
R. Volga
Memel
Vitebsk
Smolensk
RUSSIA
Saratov
Vilna
Minsk
Königsberg
Orel
Dantzig
W. Prussia
E. Prussia
Posen
Warsaw
Chernigov
R. Don
POLAND
Kalisz
Lublin
Kharkov
Kiev
Breslau
R. Dnieper
Cracow
Berdichev
Novocherkask
Lemberg
Taganrog
Rostov
R. Dniester
Pressburg
Czernowitz
R. Pruth
Odessa
Kherson
SEA OF AZOV
Kerch
Jassy
Buda Pest
Klausenburg
Moldavia
Crimea
R. Drave
Kronstadt
Galatz
Temesvar
R. Save
Wallachia
BLACK SEA
Poti
Bucharest
Belgrade
Servia
R. Danube
Rustchuk
Zara
Sarajevo
Varna
Sinope
Trebizond
Sofia
TURKEY
Philippopolis
Adrianople
Constantinople
Cettigne
Scutari
Angora
TURKEY IN ASIA
Bari
Brindisi
Salonica
Kaisarieh
Larissa
Corfu
ÆGEAN SEA
Eubœa
Smyrna
Konieh
Adana
Antioch
Athens
Patras
Rhodes
Cyclades
Cyprus
C. Matapan
Cerigo
Candia
Beyrout
Damascus
SEA
Jaffa
Jerusalem
Damietta
Alexandria
Barka
Cairo
EGYPT
55
50
45
40
35
30
25
30
35

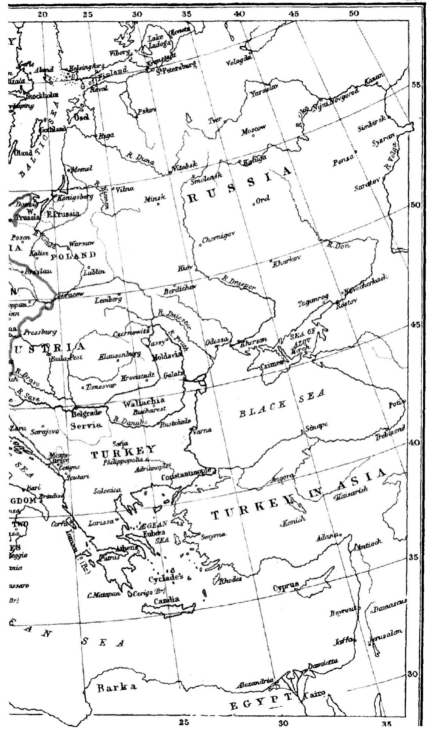

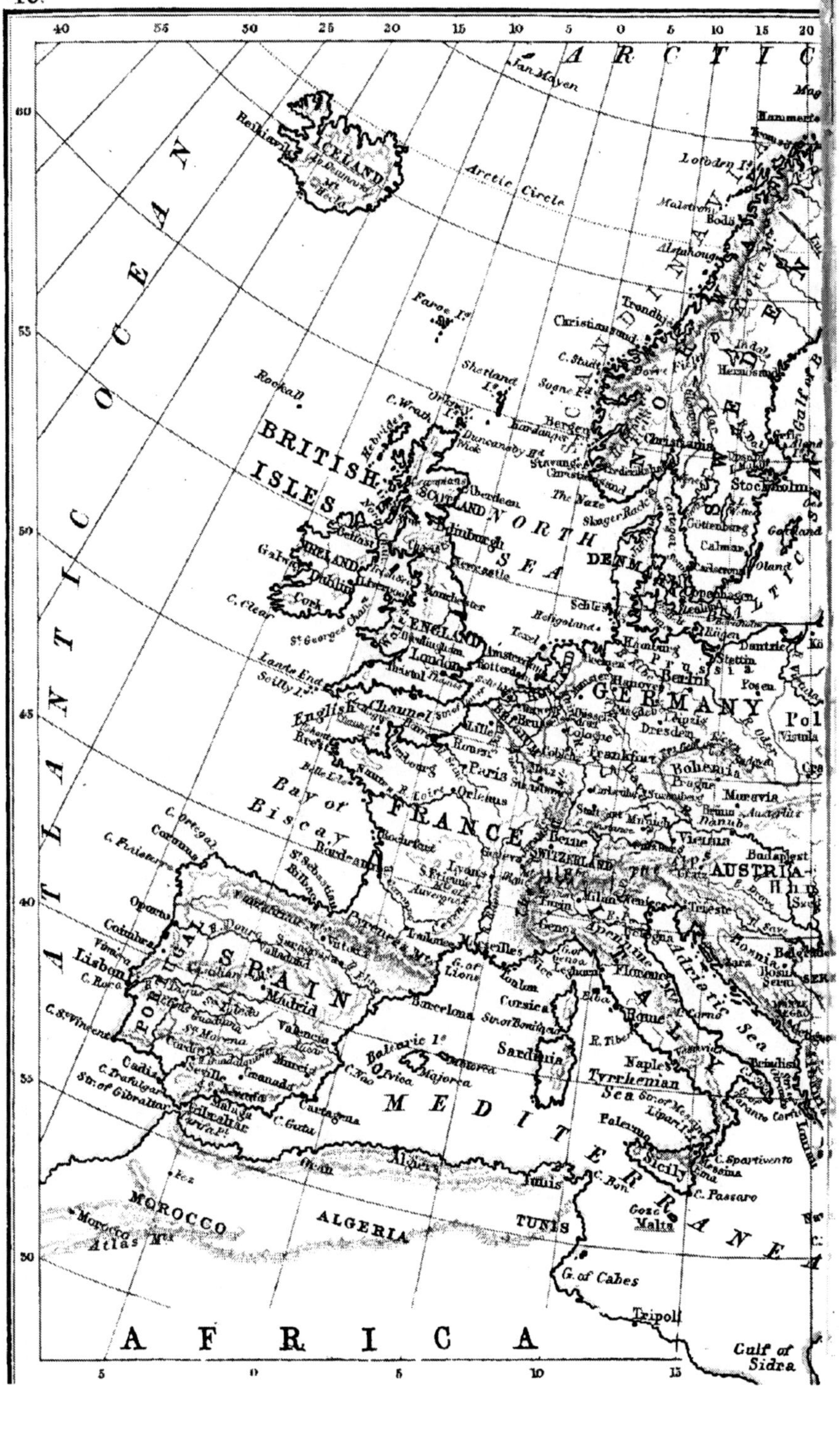
ARCTIC
Jan Mayen
ICELAND
Reikiavik
Mt. Hecla
Arctic Circle
Lofoden Is.
Malstrom
Faroe Is.
Christiansund
Trondhjem
Shetland Is.
Orkney Is.
Rockall
C. Wrath
Bergen
Stavanger
Christiania
Stockholm
The Naze
Skager Rack
Gottenburg
Calmar
Gottland
Oland
Carlscrona
Copenhagen
BRITISH
ISLES
SCOTLAND
Aberdeen
Edinburgh
Glasgow
Belfast
Newcastle
NORTH SEA
IRELAND
Dublin
Galway
Cork
C. Clear
St. Georges Chan.
Liverpool
Manchester
ENGLAND
Birmingham
London
Bristol
Lands End
Scilly Is.
Heligoland
Texel
Amsterdam
Rotterdam
Hamburg
Bremen
Hanover
Berlin
Stettin
Dantzic
Posen
Rügen
GERMANY
Leipzig
Dresden
Cologne
Frankfort
Bohemia
Prague
Moravia
Brünn
Vienna
Buda-pest
AUSTRIA
Pol
Vistula
English Channel
Brest
Nantes
Rouen
Paris
Orleans
Lille
Brussels
Belle Isle
R. Loire
Bay of Biscay
FRANCE
Bordeaux
Lyons
Geneva
Berne
Turin
Milan
Venice
Trieste
Genoa
Marseilles
Toulouse
G. of Lions
Nice
Leghorn
Florence
Corsica
Sardinia
Elba
Rome
R. Tiber
Naples
Tyrrhenian Sea
Adriatic Sea
Brindisi
Palermo
Sicily
Messina
C. Spartivento
C. Passaro
Malta
Gozo
C. Ortegal
Corunna
C. Finisterre
Oporto
Coimbra
Lisbon
C. Roca
C. St. Vincent
PORTUGAL
SPAIN
Madrid
Valladolid
Saragossa
Barcelona
Valencia
Murcia
Seville
Cadiz
C. Trafalgar
Str. of Gibraltar
Gibraltar
Malaga
Granada
Cartagena
C. Gata
C. Nao
Balearic Is.
Majorca
Minorca
MEDITERRANEAN
Algiers
Oran
Tunis
TUNIS
C. Bon
MOROCCO
Morocco
Atlas Mts.
Fez
ALGERIA
G. of Cabes
Tripoli
Gulf of Sidra
AFRICA
ATLANTIC OCEAN

MODERN
EUROPE
English Miles
0 100 200 300 400 500
OCEAN
White Sea
Kola Peninsula
Lapland
Finland
Great Russia
RUSSIA
West Russia
Little Russia
South Russia
Kirghiz Hordes
SIBERIA
ASIA
Ural Mountains
CASPIAN SEA
BLACK SEA
Sea of Azov
Crimea
Circassia
Caucasus Mount
ROUMANIA
BULGARIA
TURKEY
TURKEY IN ASIA
PERSIA
SYRIA
Cyprus
Candia
SEA
Moscow
St Petersburg
Archangel
Kazan
Astrakhan
Odessa
Kiev
Constantinople
Sebastopol
Tiflis
Smyrna
Alexandria
Port Said
Damascus
Teheran

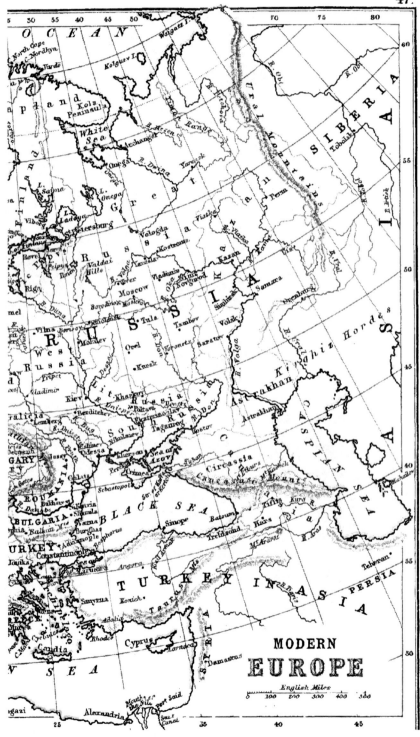

Chief Industrial Districts
Coalfields
Letters indicate the nature of the Chief Industries
C Cotton I Iron L Linen M Machinery S Silk W Wool
Agriculture and Stock-rearing
Fishing
Only Navigable Rivers are shown
Principal Railways
ECONOMIC MAP OF
EUROPE
English Miles
0 100 200 300 400 500
Trondhjem
Molde
Bergen
Stavanger
Christiansand
CHRISTIANIA
The Naze
The Skaw
Göteborg
DENMARK
COPENHAGEN
Malmö
Shetland Is
Orkney Is
Hebrides
Wick
SCOTLAND
Aberdeen
Perth
Dundee
Edinburgh
Glasgow
Londonderry
Belfast
IRELAND
Galway
Dublin
Limerick
Cork
Valencia I.
Manchester
Liverpool
Hull
ENGLAND
Birmingham
Bristol
LONDON
Plymouth
Southampton
Dover
Lands End
NORTH SEA
Heligoland
Kiel
Hamburg
Bremen
AMSTERDAM
Rotterdam
Antwerp
BRUSSELS
BELGIUM
Calais
Cologne
Cassel
GERMANY
Leipzig
Frankfurt
English Channel
Brest
Havre
Rouen
PARIS
Orleans
Tours
Nantes
Nevers
Dijon
Metz
Strassburg
Stuttgart
Nuremberg
Munich
Prague
Innsbruck
Basle
BERN
SWITZERLAND
Geneva
FRANCE
Bay of Biscay
Lyons
St Etienne
Bordeaux
Bayonne
Toulouse
Cette
Marseille
Toulon
Nice
Turin
Milan
Verona
Venice
Trieste
Genoa
Leghorn
Florence
Ancona
ITALY
ROME
Naples
Corsica
Ajaccio
Str. of Bonifacio
Sardinia
Sassari
Cagliari
Palermo
Sicily
Malta (British)
C. Ortegal
Coruña
C. Finisterre
Vigo
Oporto
Santander
Oviedo
Valladolid
S. Sebastian
PORTUGAL
SPAIN
MADRID
Saragossa
Barcelona
Toledo
Valencia
Cordova
Seville
Granada
Murcia
Cartagena
Cadiz
Malaga
Gibraltar (British)
Tarifa Pt.
Balearic Is
Majorca
Minorca
Iviza
Algiers
Tunis
TUNIS
MEDITERR

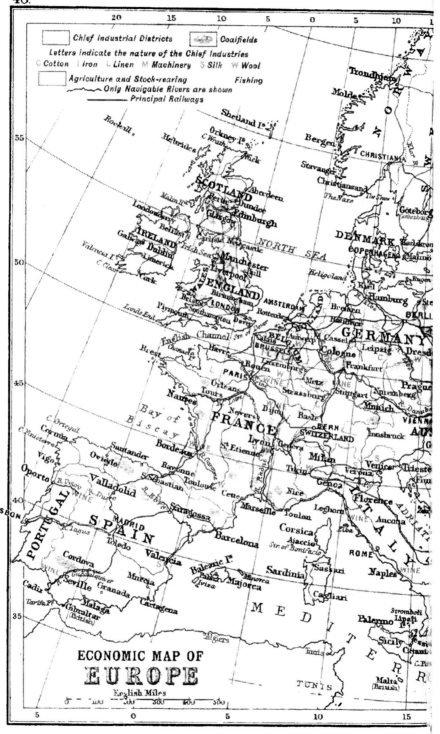

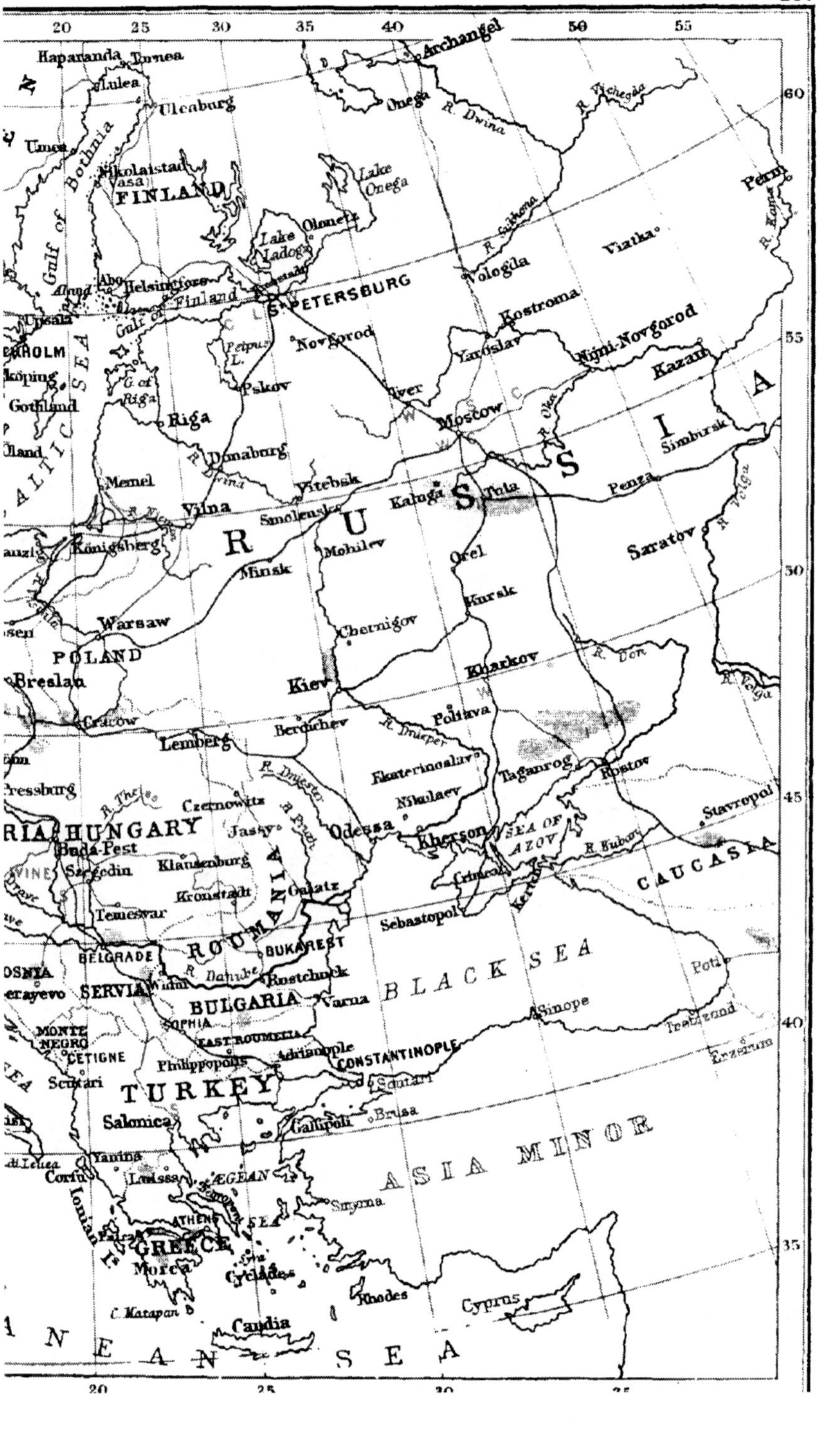

Haparanda
Tornea
Lulea
Uleaburg
Umea
Gulf of Bothnia
Nikolaistad
Vasa
FINLAND
Lake Onega
Lake Ladoga
Olonetz
Archangel
Onega
R. Dwina
R. Vichegda
Perm
Viatka
Vologda
R. Sukhona
Abo
Helsingfors
Aland
Gulf of Finland
Upsala
ST PETERSBURG
Kostroma
Yaroslav
Nijni-Novgorod
Kazan
Novgorod
Peipus L.
Pskov
G. of Riga
Riga
Gothland
Oland
Tver
Moscow
R. Oka
Simbirsk
Dunaburg
R. Dwina
Memel
Vitebsk
Vilna
Smolensk
Kaluga
Tula
Penza
R U S S I A
Königsberg
Minsk
Mohilev
Orel
Saratov
R. Volga
Kursk
Warsaw
Chernigov
POLAND
Breslau
Kiev
Kharkov
R. Don
Cracow
Poltava
Berdichev
R. Dnieper
Lemberg
R. Dniester
Ekaterinoslav
Taganrog
Rostov
Pressburg
R. Theiss
Czernowitz
R. Pruth
Nikolaev
Stavropol
HUNGARY
Jassy
Odessa
Kherson
SEA OF AZOV
R. Kuban
Buda-Pest
Szegedin
Klausenburg
Kronstadt
Galatz
Crimea
Kertch
CAUCASIA
Temesvar
Sebastopol
ROUMANIA
BELGRADE
BUKAREST
BLACK SEA
R. Danube
Rustchuck
Poti
SERVIA
Widin
BULGARIA
Varna
Sinope
SOPHIA
EAST ROUMELIA
Trebizond
MONTE NEGRO
CETIGNE
Philippopolis
Adrianople
CONSTANTINOPLE
Erzerum
Scutari
TURKEY
Salonica
Gallipoli
Brusa
Yanina
Corfu
Larissa
ÆGEAN SEA
ASIA MINOR
Smyrna
Ionian Is.
ATHENS
GREECE
Morea
Cyclades
Rhodes
Cyprus
C. Matapan
Candia
SEA

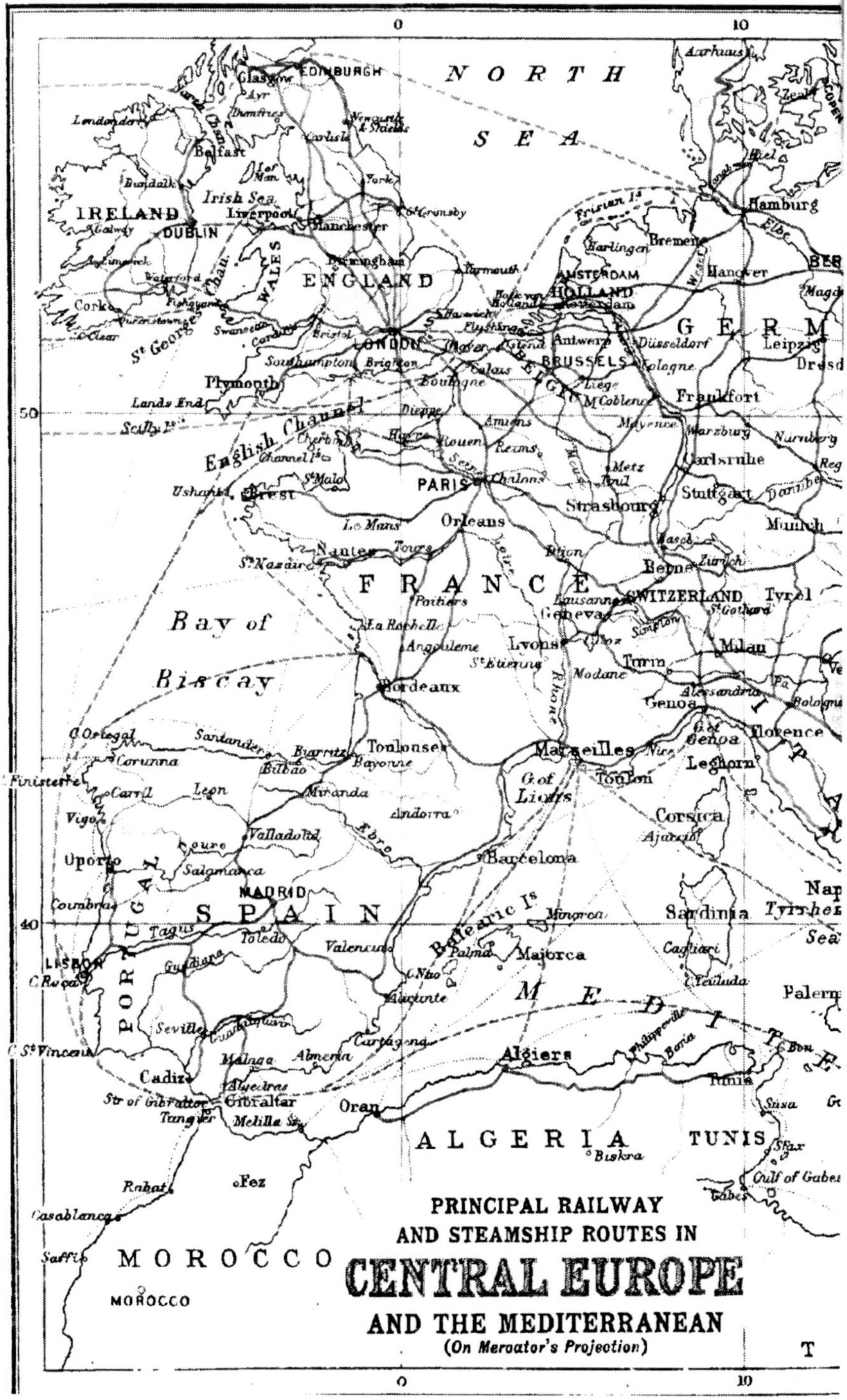
0
10
NORTH SEA
IRELAND
DUBLIN
Belfast
Irish Sea
Liverpool
Manchester
Birmingham
ENGLAND
WALES
LONDON
Plymouth
Southampton
Brighton
English Channel
Glasgow
EDINBURGH
Hamburg
Bremen
Hanover
AMSTERDAM
HOLLAND
Antwerp
BRUSSELS
Düsseldorf
Cologne
Frankfort
Leipzig
Strasbourg
Stuttgart
Munich
Berne
Zurich
SWITZERLAND
Tyrol
Geneva
Milan
Turin
Genoa
Florence
Leghorn
PARIS
Orleans
Nantes
FRANCE
Bay of Biscay
Bordeaux
Lyons
Marseilles
Toulon
Toulouse
Bayonne
Bilbao
Brest
Corsica
Sardinia
MADRID
SPAIN
PORTUGAL
LISBON
Oporto
Barcelona
Valencia
Balearic Is
Majorca
Cadiz
Seville
Gibraltar
Tangier
Oran
Algiers
ALGERIA
TUNIS
Tunis
MOROCCO
Fez
Rabat
Casablanca
50
40

PRINCIPAL RAILWAY AND STEAMSHIP ROUTES IN CENTRAL EUROPE AND THE MEDITERRANEAN (On Mercator's Projection)

20
30
50
40
Carlskrona
BALTIC SEA
Bornholm
Rugen
Memel
Tilsit
Konigsberg
Danzig
Schneidemuhl
Posen
Frankfort
Dunaburg
Vitebsk
Smolensk
Vilna
Minsk
Niemen
Dnieper
RUSSIA
Warsaw
Poland
Pripet
Breslau
Prague
Cracow
Vistula
Kiev
Lemberg
Berditchev
Dnieper
Brunn
Linz
Pressburg
VIENNA
BUDAPEST
AUSTRIA-HUNGARY
Dniester
Transylvania
Pruth
Odessa
Kherson
Trieste
Drave
Fiume
Galatz
Crimea
Save
Belgrade
Braila
RUMANIA
Bukharest
Sevastopol
Kustendje
Bosnia
Bosna Serai
SERVIA
R. Danube
BLACK SEA
BULGARIA
Varna
Monte negro
Mitrowica
Sophia
E. RUMELIA
Burgas
Adriatic Sea
Cetigne
Adrianople
Sinope
Foggia
TURKEY
Bosphorus
CONSTANTINOPLE
Brindisi
Salonica
Cavalla
Sea of Marmora
Dardanelles
Corfu
Asia Minor
Mitylene
Messina
GREECE
Smyrna
Ionian Sea
Corinth
Chios
Catania
Piraeus
ATHENS
Samos
Syra
Eregli
Mersina
C. Passero
Rhodes
Cerigo
Alexandretta
Malta
Canea
Cyprus
Crete
Limasol
Larnaca
Tripoli
Beirout
SEA
Tripoli
C. Misrata
Haifa
Gulf of Sidra
Jaffa
Alexandria
Port Said
TRIPOLI
EGYPT
CAIRO
Suez

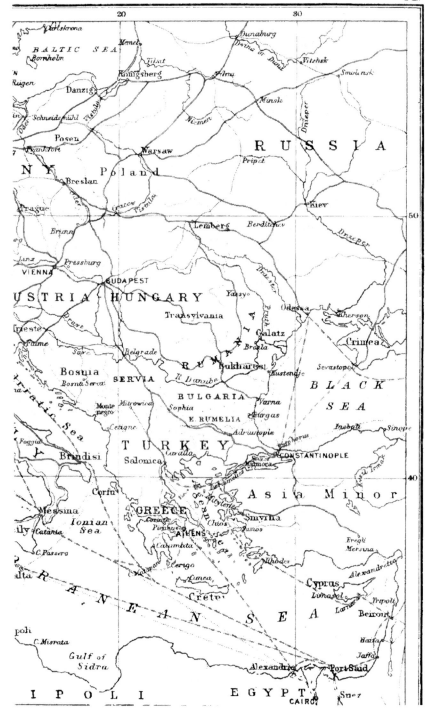

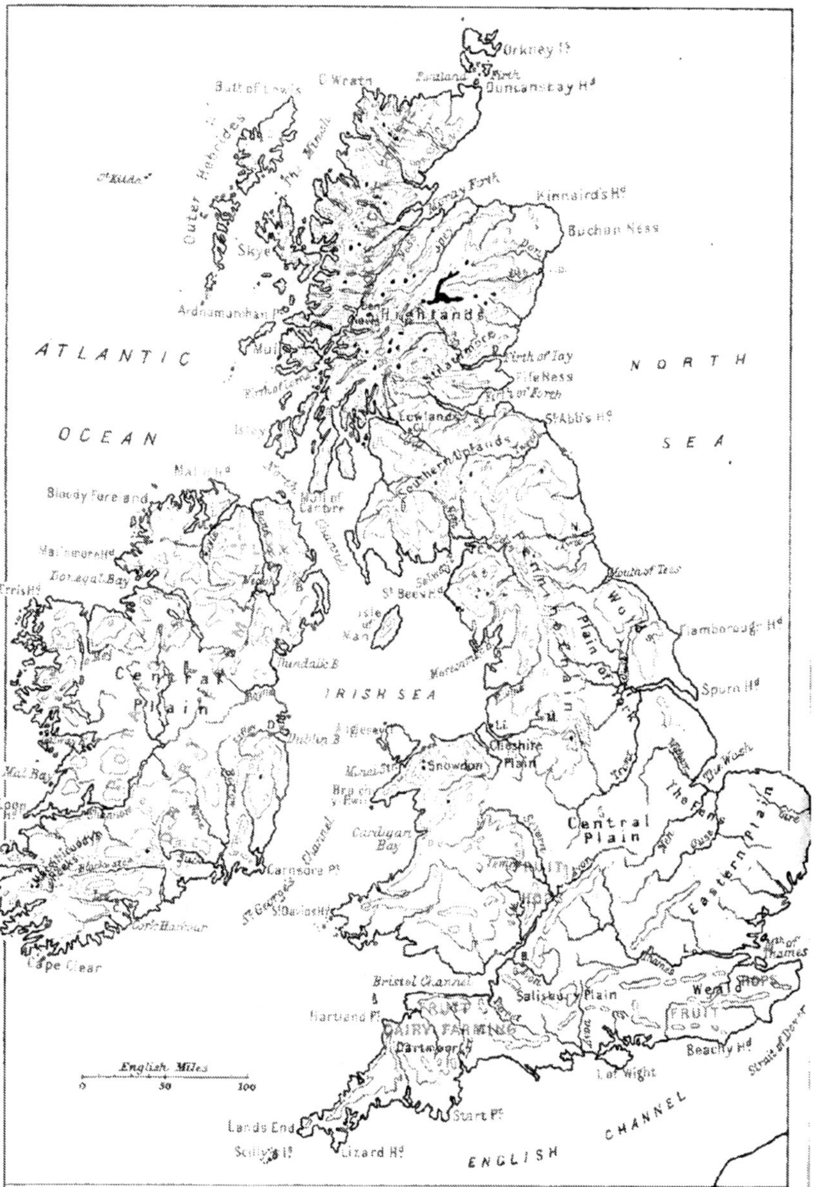
Orkney Is
C. Wrath
Duncansbay Hd
Butt of Lewis
Outer Hebrides
The Minch
Kinnairds Hd
Buchan Ness
Skye
Highlands
Ardnamurchan Pt
ATLANTIC
OCEAN
NORTH
SEA
Mull
Firth of Tay
Fife Ness
Firth of Forth
Islay
Lowlands
St Abb's Hd
Southern Uplands
Malin Hd
Bloody Foreland
Mull of Galloway
Donegal Bay
Erris Hd
Mouth of Tees
Isle of Man
St Bees Hd
Flamborough Hd
Central Plain
IRISH SEA
Dundalk B
Spurn Hd
Anglesey
Dublin B
Cheshire Plain
Snowdon
The Wash
Mal Bay
Central Plain
Eastern Plain
Cardigan Bay
Carnsore Pt
St Davids Hd
Cork Harbour
Cape Clear
Bristol Channel
Salisbury Plain
HOPS
FRUIT
DAIRY FARMING
Dartmoor
Hartland Pt
Beachy Hd
I. of Wight
Strait of Dover
English Miles
0
50
100
Lands End
Scilly Is
Lizard Hd
Start Pt
ENGLISH
CHANNEL

AGRICULTURAL DISTRICTS

HEIGHT OF LAND
Above 2500 Ft
1600 - 2500

Upland Pasture suitable for Sheep

Area suitable for Mixed Agriculture

Chief Wheat Districts

Districts where Cattle are most numerous

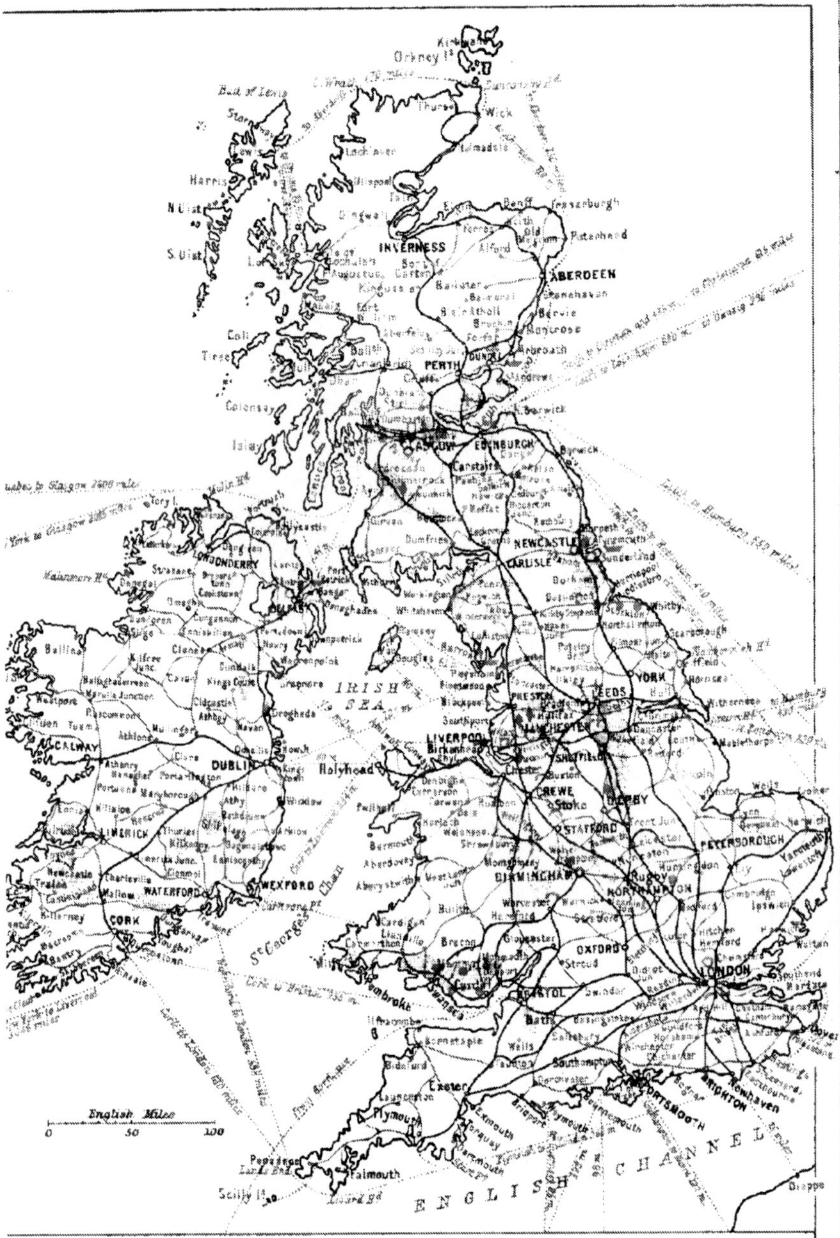
INVERNESS
ABERDEEN
PERTH
EDINBURGH
NEWCASTLE
CARLISLE
YORK
LEEDS
PRESTON
MANCHESTER
LIVERPOOL
CREWE
STAFFORD
DERBY
BIRMINGHAM
NORTHAMPTON
PETERBOROUGH
OXFORD
LONDON
BRISTOL
PORTSMOUTH
BRIGHTON
LONDONDERRY
BELFAST
DUBLIN
GALWAY
LIMERICK
WATERFORD
WEXFORD
CORK
IRISH SEA
ENGLISH CHANNEL
English Miles
0 50 100

LEADING INDUSTRIES

Industrial Regions
Coalfields

Cotton
Iron
Linen
Machinery
Pottery
Shipbuilding
Wool
Chemicals

54.

EDINBURGH
GLASGOW
SCOTLAND
Lanark
Berwick
Arran
FIRTH OF CLYDE
Ayr
Selkirk
Melrose
Hawick
Jedburgh
Cheviot Hills
Moffat
NORTHUMBERLAND
Dumfries
Stranraer
Port Patrick
Wigtown
Whithorn
Mull of Galloway
Burrow Hd.
SOLWAY FIRTH
Carlisle
Maryport
Cockermouth
Workington
CUMBERLAND
Whitehaven
St. Bees Hd.
Keswick
Appleby
WESTMORLAND
DURH
Ravenglass
Windermere
Kendal
Ayre Pt.
Ramsey
ISLE OF MAN
Snaefell
Laxey
Douglas
Port Erin
Calf of Man
Castletown
Barrow
Walney I.
Morecambe Bay
Lancaster
Fleetwood
Preston
IRISH SEA
Blackpool
LANCASHIRE
Lytham
Blackburn
Bradford
Halifax
Southport
Rochdale
Bolton
Bury
Wigan
Oldham
MANCHESTER
New Brighton
Bootle
Birkenhead
LIVERPOOL
Stockport
Holyhead
Holy I.
ANGLESEY
Beaumaris
Bangor
Carnarvon
Menai Strait
Snowdon
Conway
FLINT
Denbigh
CHESHIRE
Chester
Ruthin
Mold
Carnarvon Bay
CARNARVON
DENBIGH
Nantwich
Congleton
Hanley
Port Madoc
Pwllheli
Tremadoc Bay
Bala
Harlech
MERIONETH
STAFFORD
Stafford
Bardsey I.
Dolgelly
Barmouth
Shrewsbury
Lichfield
CARDIGAN
MONTGOMERY
SHROPSHIRE
Towyn
Aberdovey
R. Dovey
Montgomery
Wolverhampton
Bridgnorth
Dudley
BAY
Kidderminster

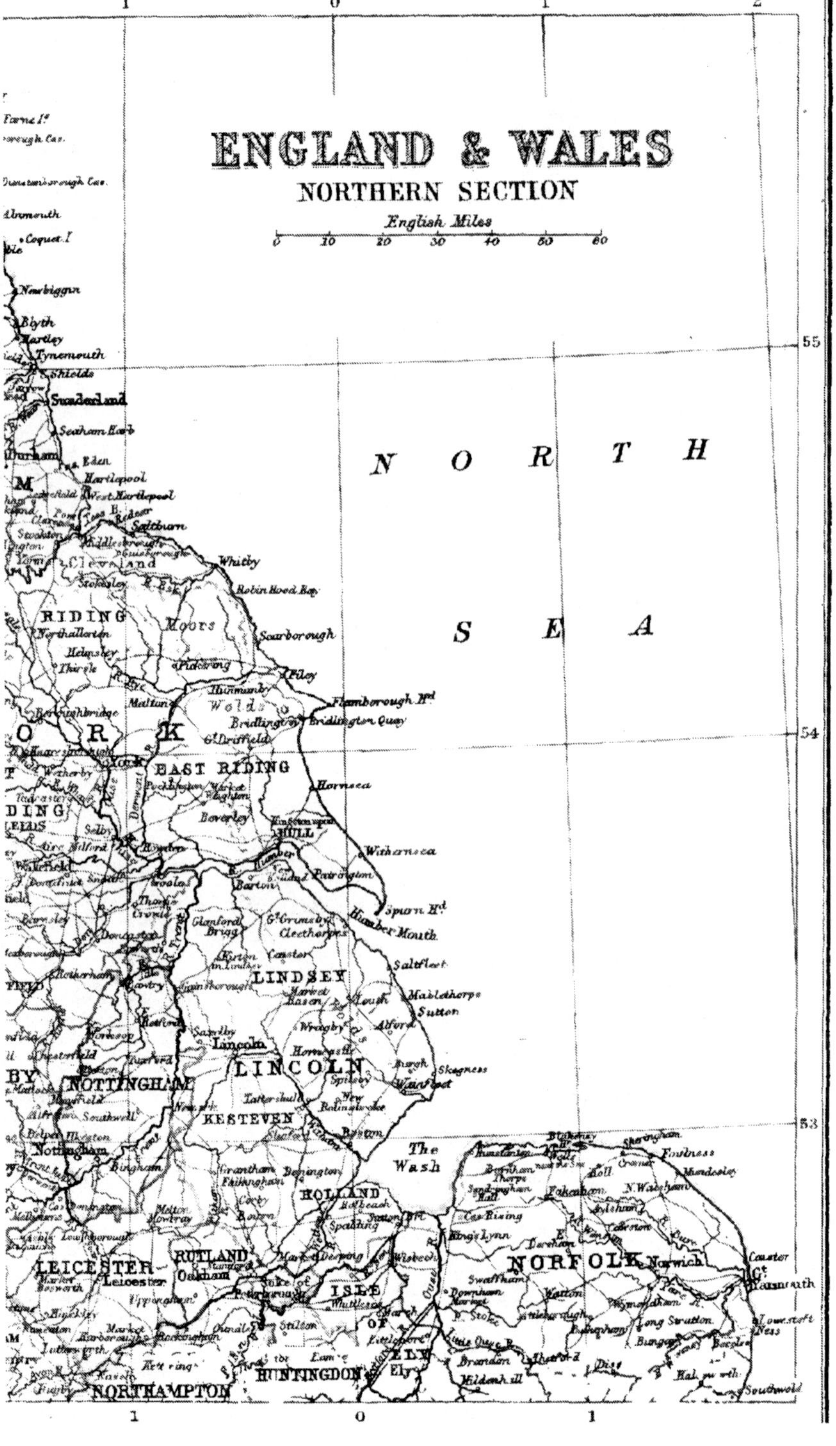
ENGLAND & WALES
NORTHERN SECTION
English Miles
0 10 20 30 40 50 60
NORTH SEA
Newbiggin
Blyth
Tynemouth
Shields
Sunderland
Seaham Harb
Hartlepool
West Hartlepool
Saltburn
Stockton
Cleveland
Whitby
Robin Hood Bay
RIDING
Northallerton
Moors
Scarborough
Helmsley
Thirsk
Pickering
Filey
Hunmanby
Malton
Wolds
Flamborough Hd
Bridlington Quay
Gt Driffield
EAST RIDING
Wetherby
Hornsea
Beverley
HULL
Selby
Withernsea
Wakefield
Patrington
Barton
Goole
Spurn Hd
Glanford Brigg
Gt Grimsby
Humber Mouth
Cleethorpes
Barnsley
Doncaster
Caistor
Saltfleet
LINDSEY
Rotherham
Gainsborough
Market Rasen
Louth
Mablethorpe
Sutton
Wragby
Alford
Retford
Lincoln
Horncastle
LINCOLN
Skegness
NOTTINGHAM
Spilsby
Wainfleet
Mansfield
Southwell
Tattershall
KESTEVEN
Boston
Nottingham
The Wash
Bingham
Grantham
Donington
Sheringham
Cromer
Fakenham
N. Walsham
HOLLAND
Holbeach
Spalding
Castle Rising
Kings Lynn
Melton Mowbray
Bourn
Loughborough
LEICESTER
Leicester
RUTLAND
Oakham
Market Deeping
Wisbech
NORFOLK
Norwich
Caister
Gt Yarmouth
Swaffham
Peterborough
ISLE OF ELY
Whittlesea
Wymondham
Lowestoft Ness
Stilton
Long Stratton
Thetford
Diss
Brandon
Bungay
Market Harborough
Kettering
HUNTINGDON
Ely
Mildenhall
Halesworth
Southwold
NORTHAMPTON
Rugby
1
0
1
2
55
54
53

CARDIGAN BAY
MONTGOMERY
SHROPSHIRE
RADNOR
CARDIGAN
HEREFORD
WORCESTER
PEMBROKE
CARMARTHEN
BRECKNOCK
GLOUCESTER
MONMOUTH
GLAMORGAN
BRISTOL CHANNEL
WILTSHIRE
SOMERSET
DEVON
DORSET
CORNWALL
Lyme Bay
Lundy I.
Bridgewater Bay
Barnstaple Bay
Bude Bay
Cardiff
Bristol
Bath
Exeter
Plymouth
Devonport
Dorchester
Portland I.
Bill of Portland
Start Pt
Continuation
On the same scale
Lands End
Falmouth B.
Lizard Hd
ENGLISH
CHANNEL
ISLANDS
Alderney
Guernsey
Herm
Sark
Jersey
St Helier
5
4
3
2
52
51
50

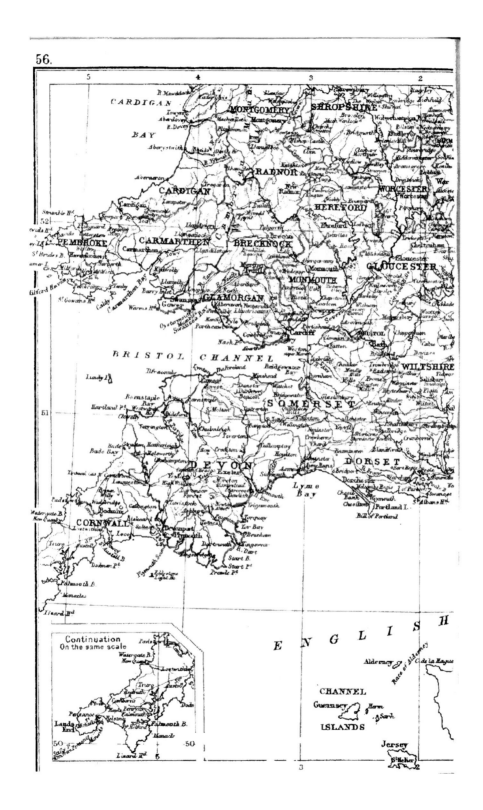

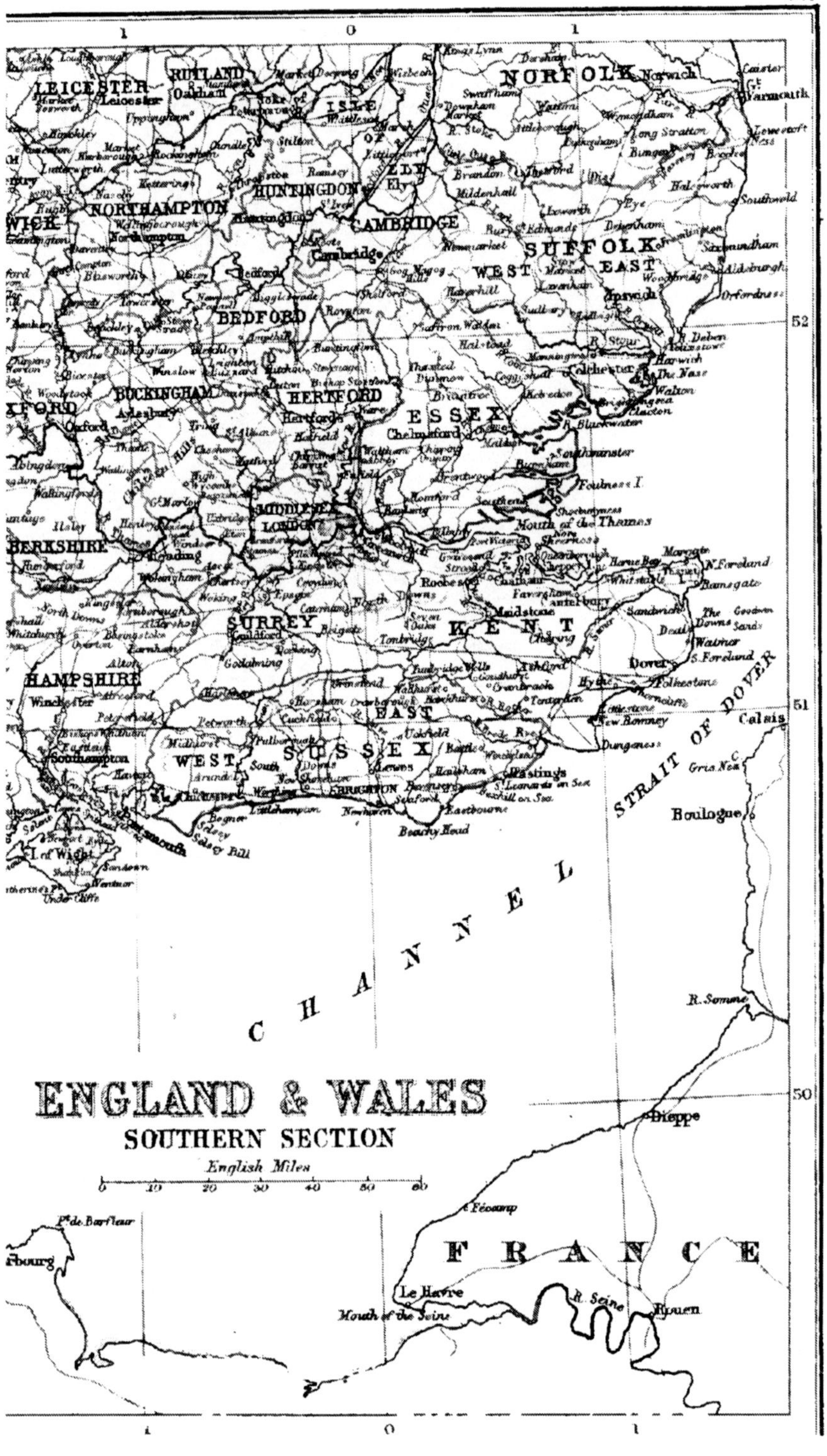
ENGLAND & WALES
SOUTHERN SECTION
English Miles
0 10 20 30 40 50 60
NORFOLK
SUFFOLK
EAST
WEST
CAMBRIDGE
ISLE OF ELY
HUNTINGDON
NORTHAMPTON
LEICESTER
RUTLAND
BEDFORD
BUCKINGHAM
HERTFORD
ESSEX
MIDDLESEX
LONDON
BERKSHIRE
SURREY
KENT
HAMPSHIRE
SUSSEX
I. of Wight
Mouth of the Thames
STRAIT OF DOVER
CHANNEL
FRANCE
Calais
Boulogne
R. Somme
Dieppe
Fécamp
Le Havre
Mouth of the Seine
R. Seine
Rouen
Pt. de Barfleur
Norwich
Gt. Yarmouth
Cambridge
Colchester
Harwich
Chelmsford
Maidstone
Canterbury
Dover
Folkestone
Hastings
Brighton
Eastbourne
Beachy Head
Portsmouth
Southampton
Winchester
Oxford
Reading
Leicester
Northampton
Bedford
Hertford
Aylesbury
Guildford
Dungeness
Ramsgate
Margate
N. Foreland
S. Foreland
Ipswich

Blackpool
Southshore
Lytham
R. Ribble
Southport
Birkdale
Ainsdale
Freshfield
Formby Pt
Hightown
Waterloo
New Brighton
Hoylake
Birkenhead
Parkgate
Flint
Mold
PRESTON
LANCASHIRE
Chorley
Bolton
Rochdale
Bury
Oldham
MANCHESTER
Ashton
Stalybridge
Glossop
STOCKPORT
BRADFORD
HALIFAX
Huddersfield
Ormskirk
Formby
Wigan
Leigh
St Helens
LIVERPOOL
Warrington
Runcorn
Helsby
CHESTER
CHESHIRE
Northwich
Macclesfield
Buxton
Chapel en le Frith
Bakewell
Congleton
Sandbach
Leek
CREWE
Nantwich
Wrexham
Ruabon
Whitchurch
Ellesmere
Oswestry
Wem
Market Drayton
Stone
STAFFORD
Stoke
Uttoxeter
Tutbury
Colwich
Rugeley
Newport
Penkridge
Cannock
Lichfield
Tamworth
SHROPSHIRE
SHREWSBURY
Minsterley
Montgomery
Church Stretton
Bishops Castle
Clun
Craven Arms
Ludlow
Knighton
Presteigne
Tenbury
Bridgnorth
Madeley
Coalport
Shifnal
WOLVERHAMPTON
Walsall
Wednesbury
Dudley
Stourbridge
Kidderminster
Bewdley
Bromsgrove
Droitwich
WORCESTER
BIRMINGHAM
Redditch
Kenilworth
Ashbourn
Matlock
Wirksworth

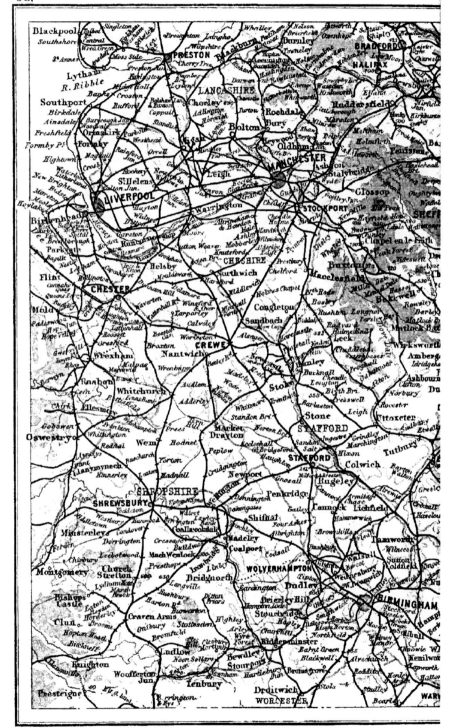

OROGRAPHICAL
CENTRAL ENGLAND
English Miles
0 5 10 15 20 25
HEIGHT OF LAND
2000 FT
1000
500
250
Sea Level
HULL
Withernsea
New Holland
Barton
Gt Grimsby
Spurn Hd
Selby
Howden
GOOLE
Pontefract
Doncaster
Brigg
Caistor
Rotherham
Bawtry
Gainsborough
Market Rasen
Louth
LINDSEY
Retford
Worksop
Tuxford
Lincoln
Wragby
LINCOLN
Horncastle
NOTTINGHAM
Mansfield
Southwell
Newark
Tattershall
Sleaford
Boston
NOTTINGHAM
Ilkeston
Bingham
Barkstone
Grantham
KESTEVEN
Swineshead
Trent Jun
Loughborough
Melton Mowbray
Spalding
Bourn
Deeping
LEICESTER
Leicester
Oakham
RUTLAND
Stamford
PETERBOROUGH
Whittlesea
Wigston
Hinckley
Uppingham
Wansford
Elton
Oundle
Holme
Market Harborough
Lutterworth
COVENTRY
RUGBY
Southam

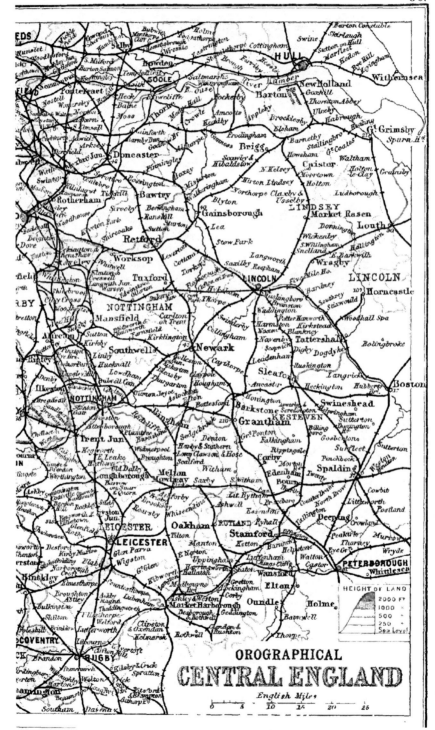

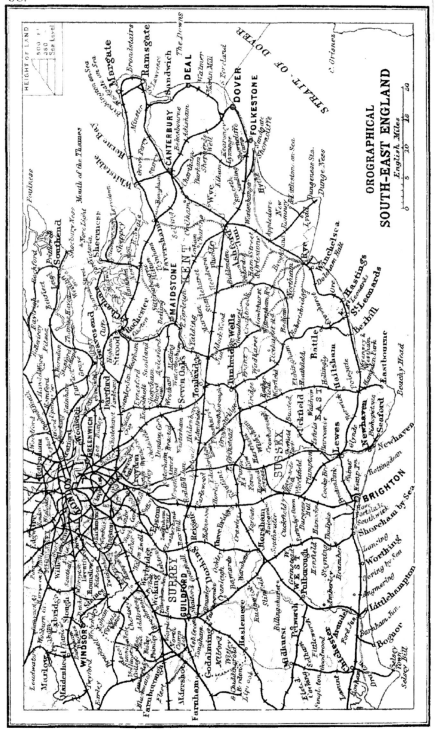

OROGRAPHICAL
SOUTH-EAST ENGLAND
English Miles
0 5 10 15 20
HEIGHT OF LAND
500 ft
250
Sea Level
STRAIT OF DOVER
The Downs
Mouth of the Thames
LONDON
GREENWICH
Woolwich
Southend
Sheerness
Margate
Ramsgate
Sandwich
DEAL
DOVER
FOLKESTONE
CANTERBURY
MAIDSTONE
KENT
Gravesend
Dartford
Rochester
Chatham
Faversham
Ashford
Tonbridge
Tunbridge Wells
Sevenoaks
Hastings
St Leonards
Bexhill
Eastbourne
Beachy Head
Battle
Hailsham
Rye
Winchelsea
Lewes
Newhaven
Seaford
SUSSEX
EAST
WEST
BRIGHTON
Shoreham by Sea
Worthing
Littlehampton
Bognor
Chichester
Arundel
Midhurst
Petworth
Pulborough
Horsham
Reigate
Dorking
Epsom
GUILDFORD
SURREY
Woking
Weybridge
Godalming
Haslemere
Farnham
Aldershot
Farnborough
WINDSOR
Slough
Uxbridge
Staines
Marlow
Maidenhead
Dungeness
Hythe
Herne Bay
Whitstable
Broadstairs
Selsey Bill

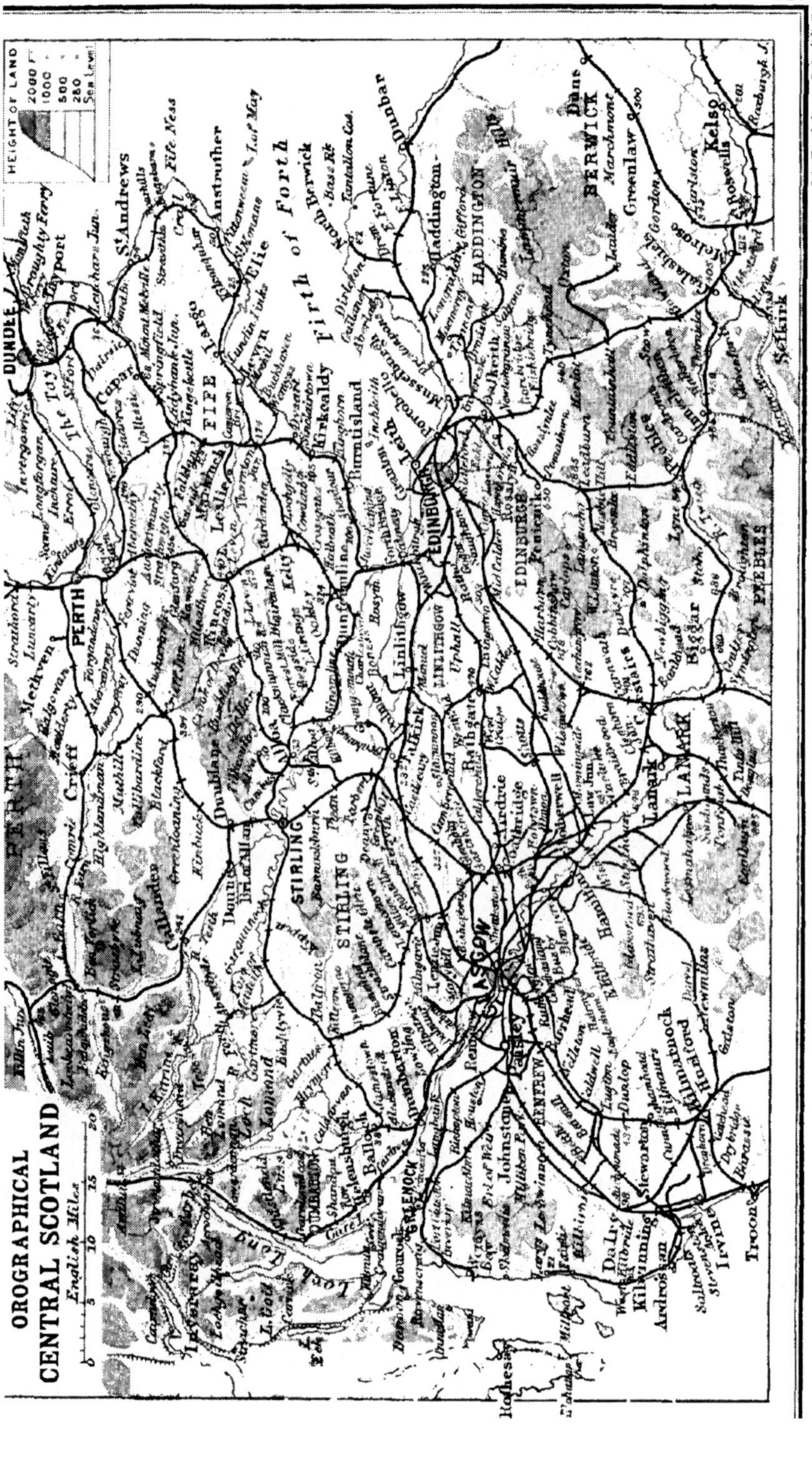
OROGRAPHICAL
CENTRAL SCOTLAND
English Miles
HEIGHT OF LAND
PERTH
DUNDEE
EDINBURGH
GLASGOW
STIRLING
FIFE
Firth of Forth
HADDINGTON
BERWICK
PEEBLES
LANARK
RENFREW
LINLITHGOW
John Bartholomew & Co. Edin'

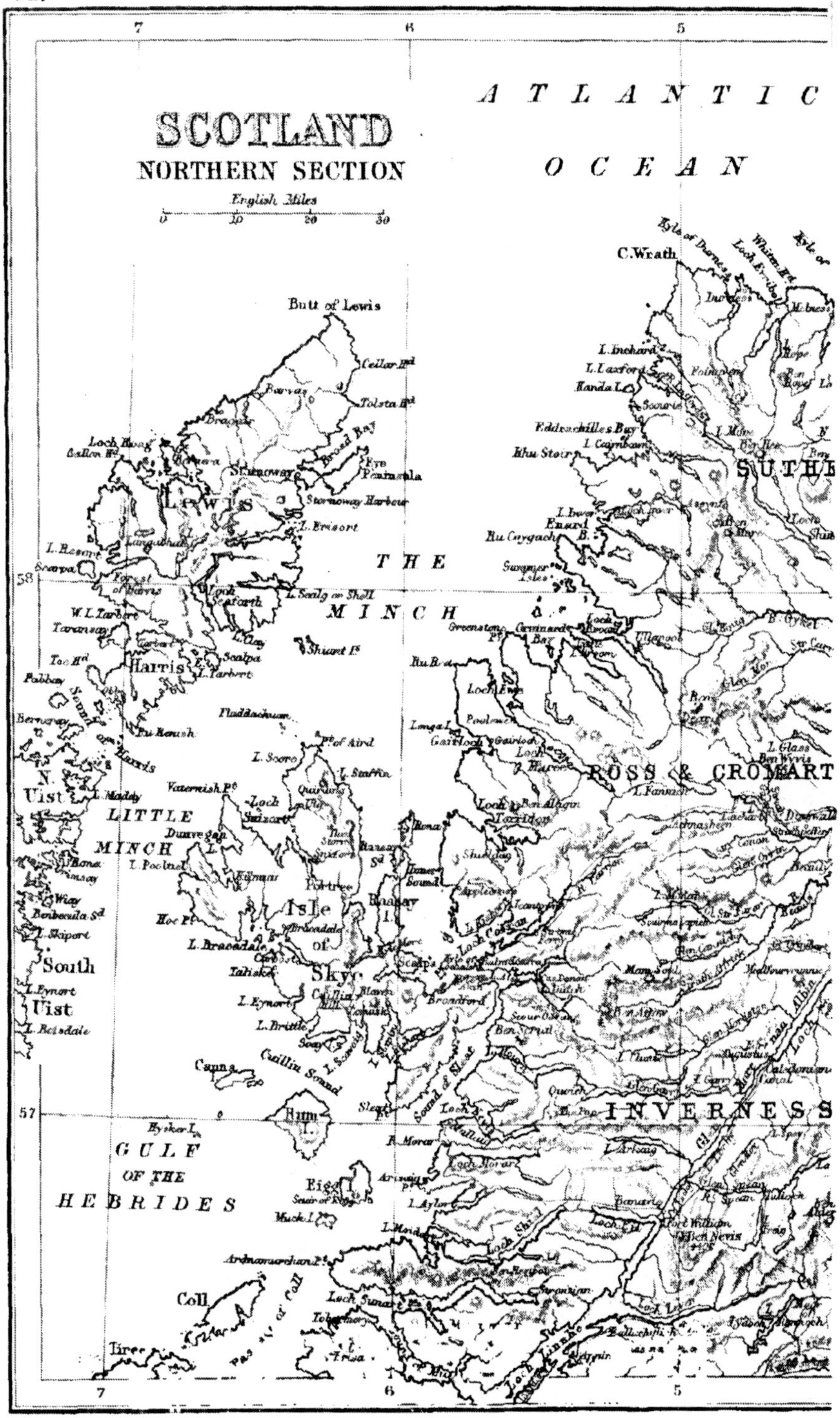
SCOTLAND
NORTHERN SECTION
English Miles
0 10 20 30
ATLANTIC
OCEAN
C.Wrath
Butt of Lewis
Lewis
Stornoway Harbour
THE
MINCH
Harris
N. Uist
LITTLE
MINCH
South
Uist
Isle
of
Skye
Canna
Rum I.
Eigg I.
Muck I.
Coll
Tiree
GULF
OF THE
HEBRIDES
SUTHE
ROSS & CROMART
INVERNESS
Fort William
Ben Nevis
7
6
5
58
57

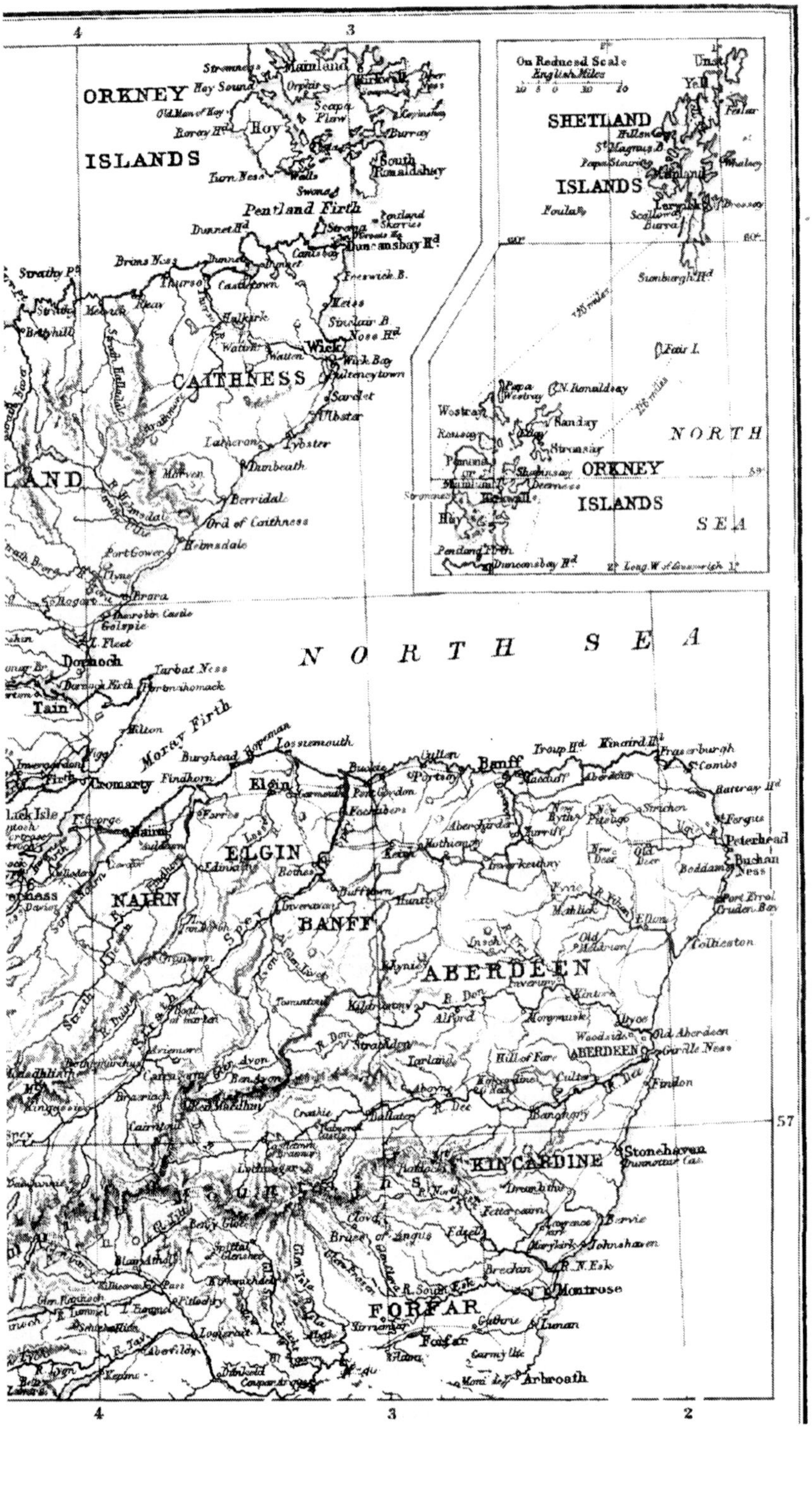
ORKNEY ISLANDS
Hoy
Pentland Firth
Mainland
Kirkwall
Scapa Flow
Burray
South Ronaldshay
Dunnet Hd
Duncansbay Hd
On Reduced Scale
English Miles
SHETLAND ISLANDS
Unst
Yell
Mainland
Lerwick
Foula
Sumburgh Hd
Fair I.
N. Ronaldsay
Westray
Sanday
Stronsay
Shapinsay
Rousay
Deerness
Stromness
NORTH SEA
ORKNEY ISLANDS
Thurso
Castletown
Halkirk
Watten
Wick
Wick Bay
CAITHNESS
Latheron
Lybster
Dunbeath
Berridale
Ord of Caithness
Helmsdale
Port Gower
Brora
Golspie
Dornoch
Dornoch Firth
Tarbat Ness
Tain
NORTH SEA
Moray Firth
Cromarty
Burghead
Lossiemouth
Findhorn
Elgin
Forres
Nairn
ELGIN
NAIRN
Banff
Portsoy
Cullen
Buckie
Keith
Huntly
BANFF
Fraserburgh
Kinnaird Hd
Troup Hd
Peterhead
Buchan Ness
Ellon
Collieston
ABERDEEN
Inverurie
Alford
Old Aberdeen
ABERDEEN
Girdle Ness
Findon
Banchory
Ballater
R. Dee
R. Don
Braemar
Stonehaven
KINCARDINE
Bervie
Johnshaven
Montrose
Brechin
FORFAR
Forfar
Arbroath
Lunan
Aberfeldy
Dunkeld
4
3
2
57

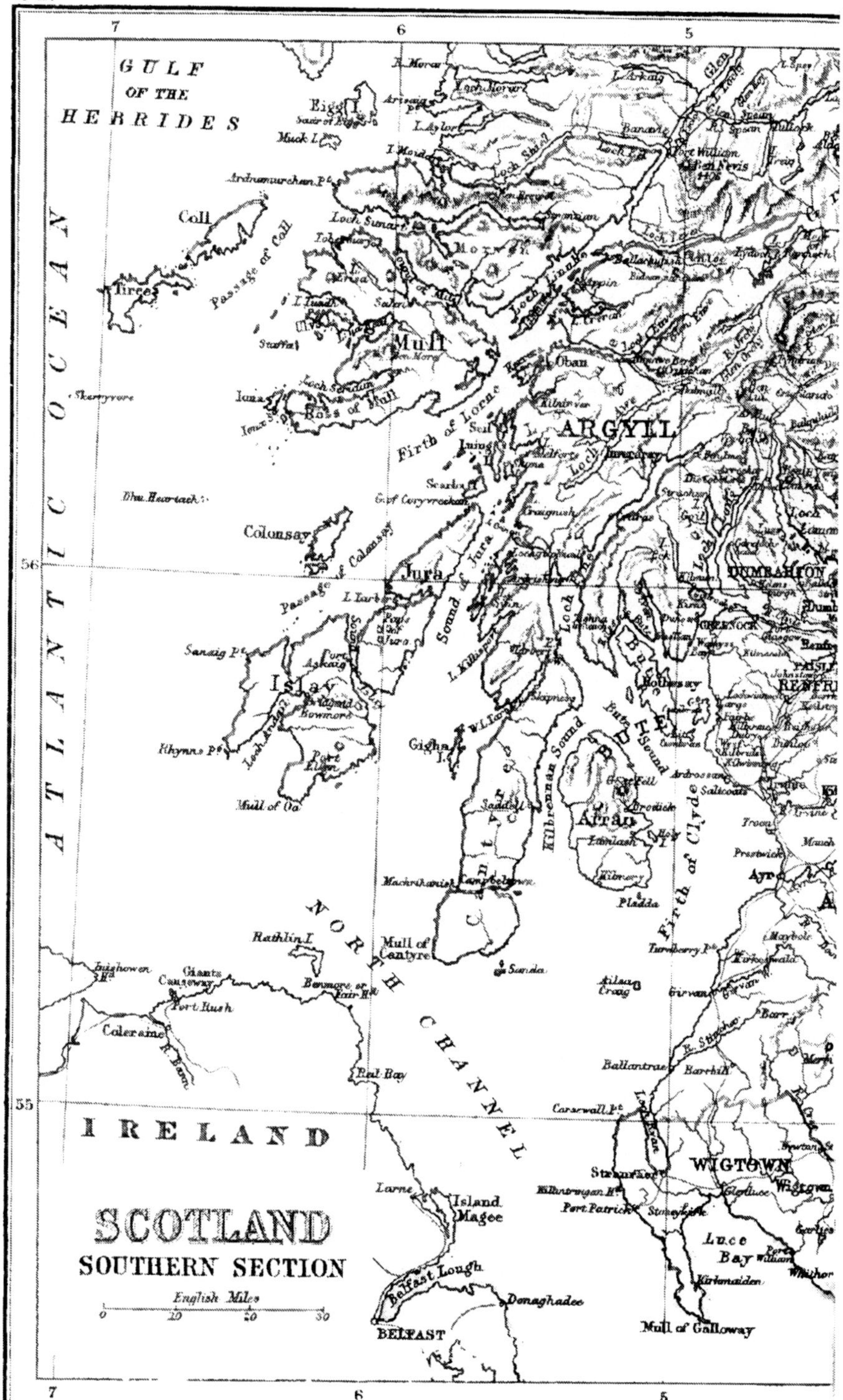
GULF OF THE HEBRIDES
ATLANTIC OCEAN
Eigg I.
Muck I.
Coll
Tiree
Passage of Coll
Mull
Iona
Ross of Mull
Firth of Lorne
Oban
ARGYLL
Colonsay
Passage of Colonsay
Jura
Sound of Jura
Islay
Port Askaig
Bowmore
Port Ellen
Mull of Oa
Sanaig Pt.
Rhynns Pt.
Gigha I.
Kilbrennan Sound
Campbeltown
Mull of Cantyre
Sanda
Rathlin I.
NORTH CHANNEL
Arran
Lamlash
Pladda
Firth of Clyde
Bute
Rothesay
Greenock
DUMBARTON
Ardrossan
Saltcoats
Troon
Prestwick
Ayr
Turnberry Pt.
Ailsa Craig
Girvan
Ballantrae
Carswall Pt.
Stranraer
WIGTOWN
Port Patrick
Luce Bay
Kirkmaiden
Mull of Galloway
Giants Causeway
Port Rush
Coleraine
Red Bay
IRELAND
Larne
Island Magee
Belfast Lough
Donaghadee
BELFAST
SCOTLAND
SOUTHERN SECTION
English Miles
0
10
20
30
7
6
5
56
55

4
3
2
KINCARDINE
Stonehaven
FORFAR
Forfar
Montrose
Arbroath
Brechin
PERTH
DUNDEE
Bell Rock L.Ho
St. Andrews Bay
St. Andrews
Cupar
FIFE
KINROSS
Firth of Forth
STIRLING
Stirling
NORTH SEA
56
Dunbar
Haddington
HADDINGTON
LINLITHGOW
EDINBURGH
St. Abbs Hd.
Eyemouth
Berwick
Duns
BERWICK
PEEBLES
Peebles
LANARK
Lanark
SELKIRK
Selkirk
Jedburgh
ROXBURGH
Hawick
Cheviot
DUMFRIES
Dumfries
Langholm
Lockerbie
Annan
55
Carlisle
SOLWAY FIRTH
Silloth
Maryport
Workington
Whitehaven
Keswick
Penrith
Appleby
ENGLAND
Bellingham
Haltwhistle
Hexham
Allendale
Kirkcudbright
RKCUDBRIGHT

John Bartholomew & Co. Edin.

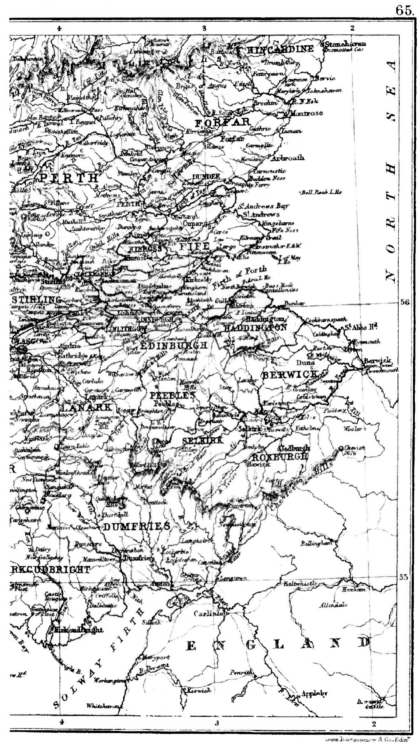

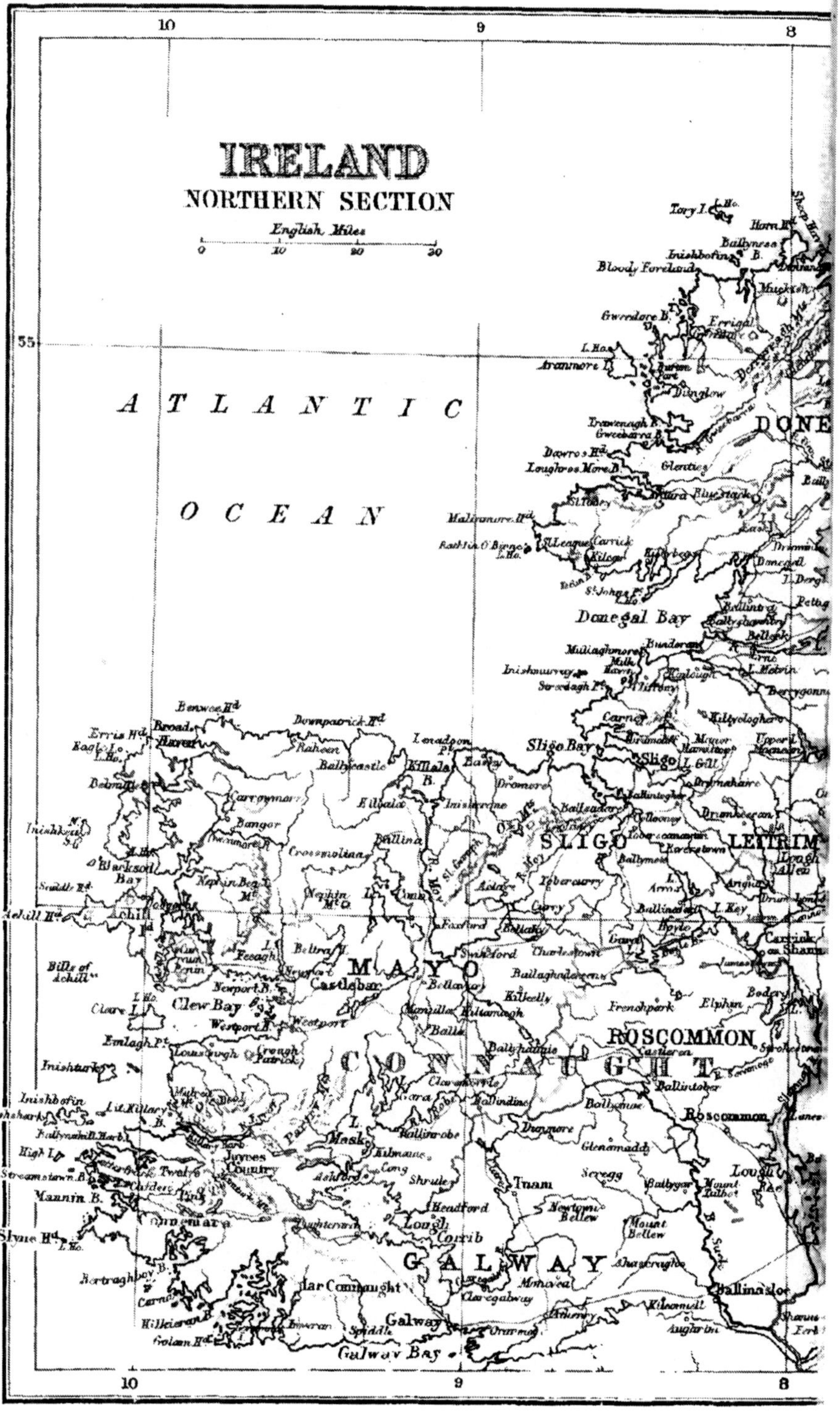
IRELAND
NORTHERN SECTION
English Miles
0
10
20
30
10
9
8
55
ATLANTIC
OCEAN
DONE
Donegal Bay
Sligo Bay
SLIGO
LEITRIM
MAYO
Castlebar
Clew Bay
Westport
CONNAUGHT
ROSCOMMON
Roscommon
GALWAY
Galway
Galway Bay
Tuam
Ballinasloe
Achill
Blacksod Bay
Killala B.
Ballina
Sligo
Lough Mask
Lough Corrib
Tory I.
Horn Hd.
Bloody Foreland
Gweedore B.
Aranmore I.
Dunglow
Killybegs
Donegal
Bundoran
Benwee Hd.
Broad Haven
Erris Hd.
Downpatrick Hd.
Ballycastle
Killala
Crossmolina
Newport
Swinford
Charlestown
Frenchpark
Elphin
Castlerea
Ballinrobe
Claremorris
Ballyhaunis
Headford
Mount Bellew
Clifden
Twelve Pins
Joyces Country
Killary B.
Inishbofin
Inishturk
Clare I.
Slyne Hd.
Mannin B.
Bertraghboy B.
Golam Hd.
Spiddle
Oranmore
Athenry
Loughrea
Lough Ree
Ballymote
Boyle
Carrick on Shannon
Lough Allen
Lough Gill
Tubbercurry
Foxford
Kiltimagh
Ballinlough
Dunmore
Glenamaddy
Ballygar
Mount Talbot
Kilconnell
Aughrim
Iar Connaught
Claregalway
Monivea
Cong
Shrule
Oughterard
Connemara
Mullaghmore
Inishmurray
Carney
Manor Hamilton
Drumshambo
Ballinamore
Keadue
L. Key
Easky
Dromore
Ballysadare
Collooney
Ballaghaderreen
Glenties
Ardara
Malinmore Hd.
Rathlin O'Birne I.
Loughros More B.
Dawros Hd.
Gweebarra B.
Mulrea
L. Conn
Nephin
Croagh Patrick
Louisburgh
Emlagh Pt.
Bills of Achill
Achill Hd.
Saddle Hd.
Inishkea
Belmullet
Bangor
Pontoon

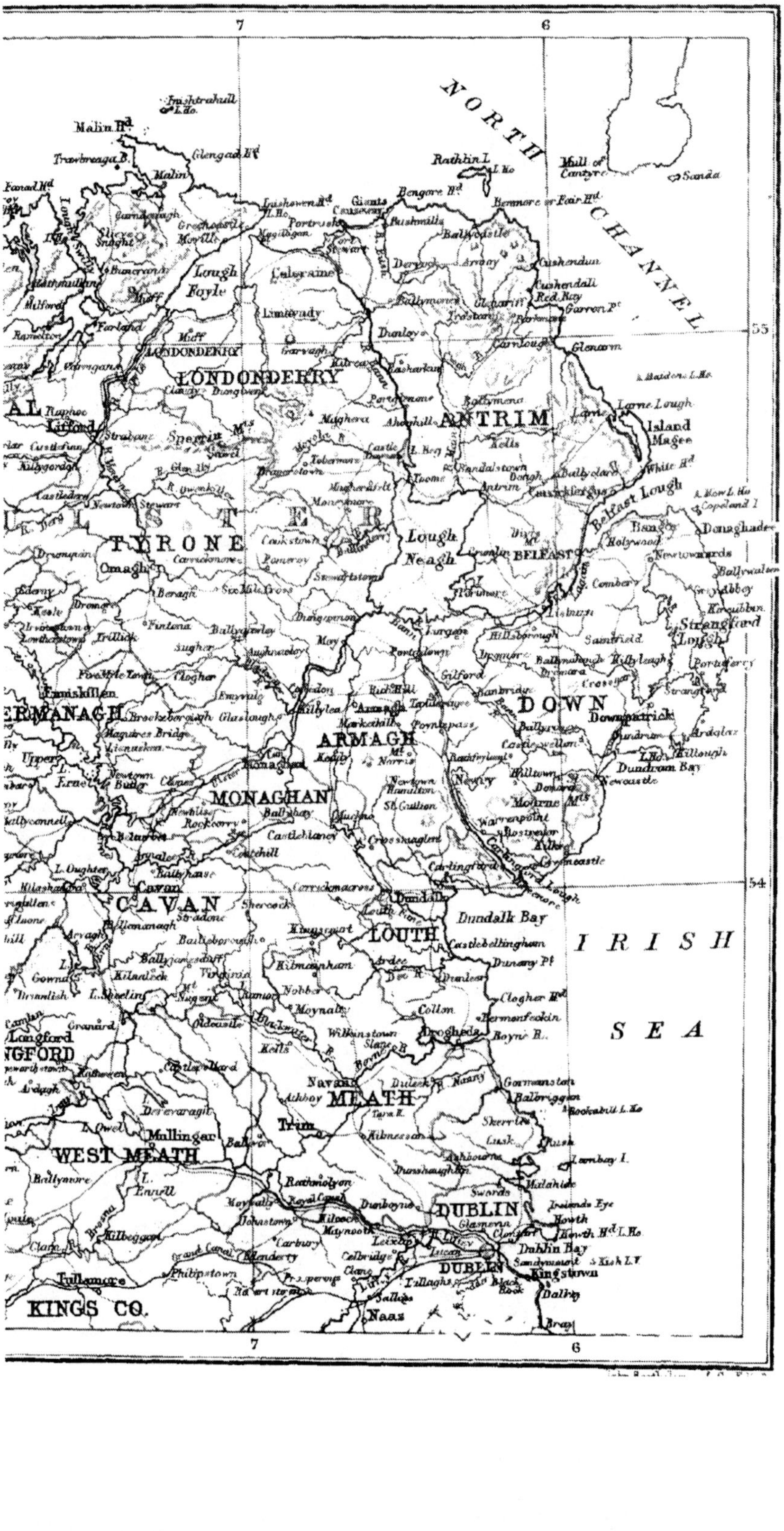
7
6
NORTH CHANNEL
IRISH SEA
Malin Hd
Rathlin I.
Mull of Cantyre
Sanda
Giants Causeway
Bushmills
Portrush
Coleraine
Lough Foyle
Limavady
Cushendun
Cushendall
Red Bay
Garron Pt
Glenarm
LONDONDERRY
ANTRIM
Larne Lough
Island Magee
White Hd
Ballymena
Kells
Antrim
Lifford
Strabane
Belfast Lough
Copeland I.
Bangor
Holywood
Donaghadee
Newtownards
BELFAST
Lough Neagh
TYRONE
Omagh
Cookstown
Pomeroy
Dungannon
Lurgan
Portadown
Strangford Lough
Saintfield
DOWN
Downpatrick
Dundrum Bay
Newcastle
Enniskillen
Maguires Bridge
ARMAGH
Armagh
Monaghan
MONAGHAN
Newry
Mourne Mts
Warrenpoint
Rostrevor
Kilkeel
Carlingford
Castleblaney
Carrickmacross
Cavan
CAVAN
Dundalk
Dundalk Bay
LOUTH
Castlebellingham
Ardee
Dunany Pt
Clogher Hd
Collon
Drogheda
Boyne R.
Longford
Granard
Kells
Navan
Slane
MEATH
Trim
Mullingar
WEST MEATH
Balbriggan
Skerries
Rush
Lambay I.
Malahide
Swords
Ireland's Eye
Howth
DUBLIN
Dublin Bay
Kingstown
Dalkey
Bray
Maynooth
Celbridge
Leixlip
Tallaght
Naas
Tullamore
KINGS CO.
55
54

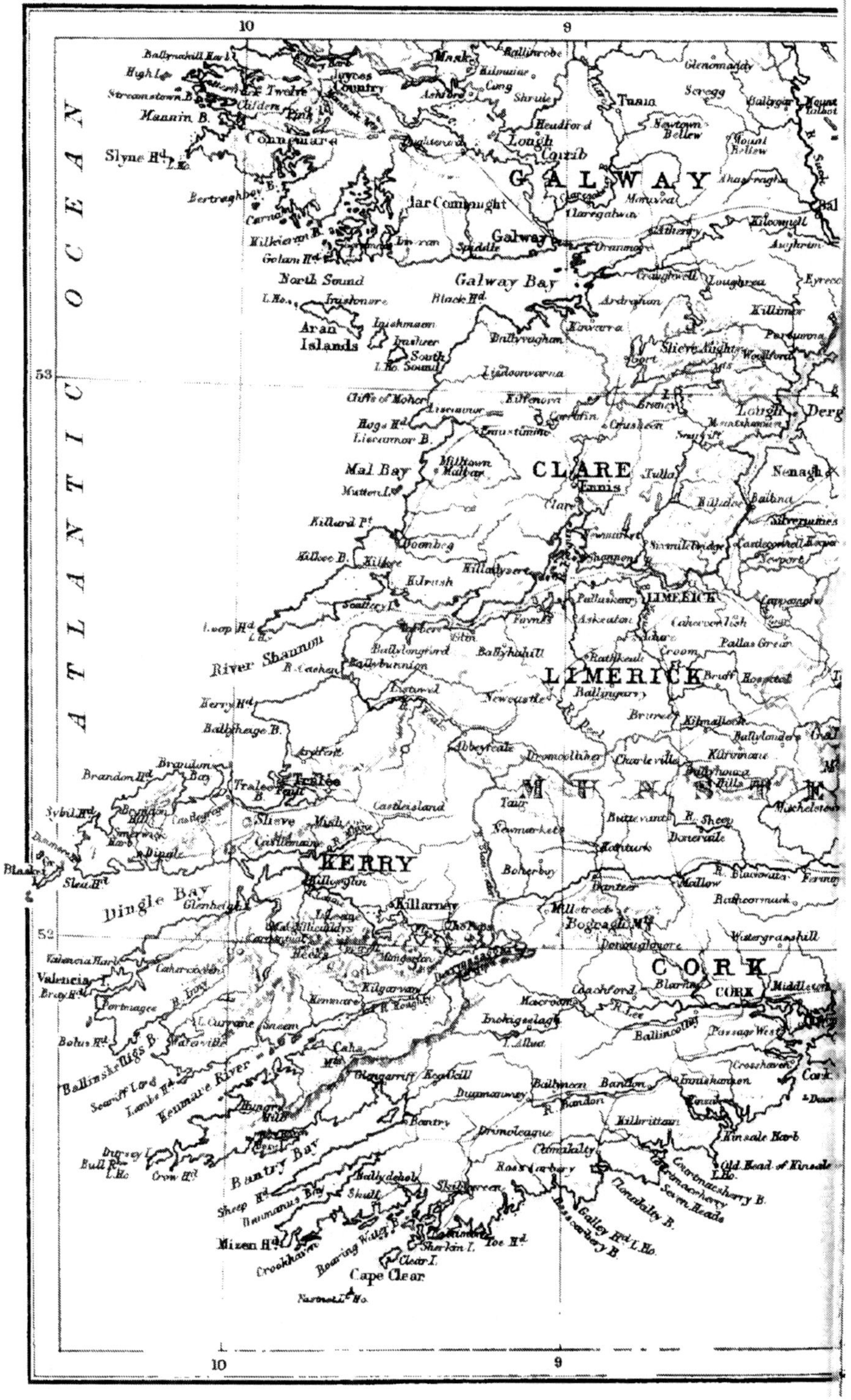
ATLANTIC OCEAN
GALWAY
CLARE
LIMERICK
KERRY
CORK
MUNSTER
Joyces Country
Twelve Pins
Connemara
Iar Connaught
Slyne Hd.
Galway
Galway Bay
North Sound
Aran Islands
Lough Corrib
Tuam
Headford
Loughrea
Ennis
Mal Bay
Loop Hd.
River Shannon
Tralee
Dingle Bay
Dingle
Killarney
Valencia I.
Kenmare River
Bantry Bay
Bantry
Mizen Hd.
Cape Clear
Skibbereen
Bandon
Kinsale Harb.
Old Head of Kinsale
Mallow
Fermoy
Lough Derg
Nenagh
Listowel
Castleisland
Newcastle
Kilmallock
Charleville
Macroom
Blarney
Middleton
10
9
53
52

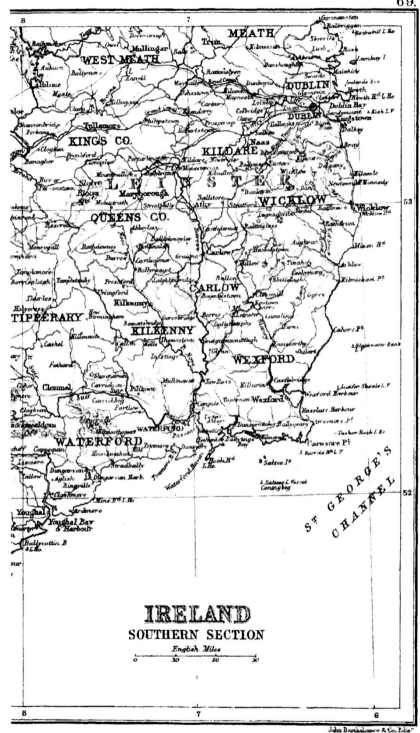

IRELAND
SOUTHERN SECTION
English Miles
0
10
20
30
MEATH
WEST MEATH
Mullingar
Trim
DUBLIN
Dublin Bay
Kingstown
Howth
KINGS CO.
Tullamore
KILDARE
Naas
LEINSTER
WICKLOW
Wicklow
QUEENS CO.
Maryborough
Athy
Carlow
CARLOW
TIPPERARY
KILKENNY
Kilkenny
WEXFORD
Wexford
Wexford Harbour
New Ross
Clonmel
WATERFORD
Waterford
Youghal
Youghal Bay & Harbour
Carnsore Pt.
ST GEORGE'S CHANNEL
53
52
8
7
6

John Bartholomew & Co. Edin.

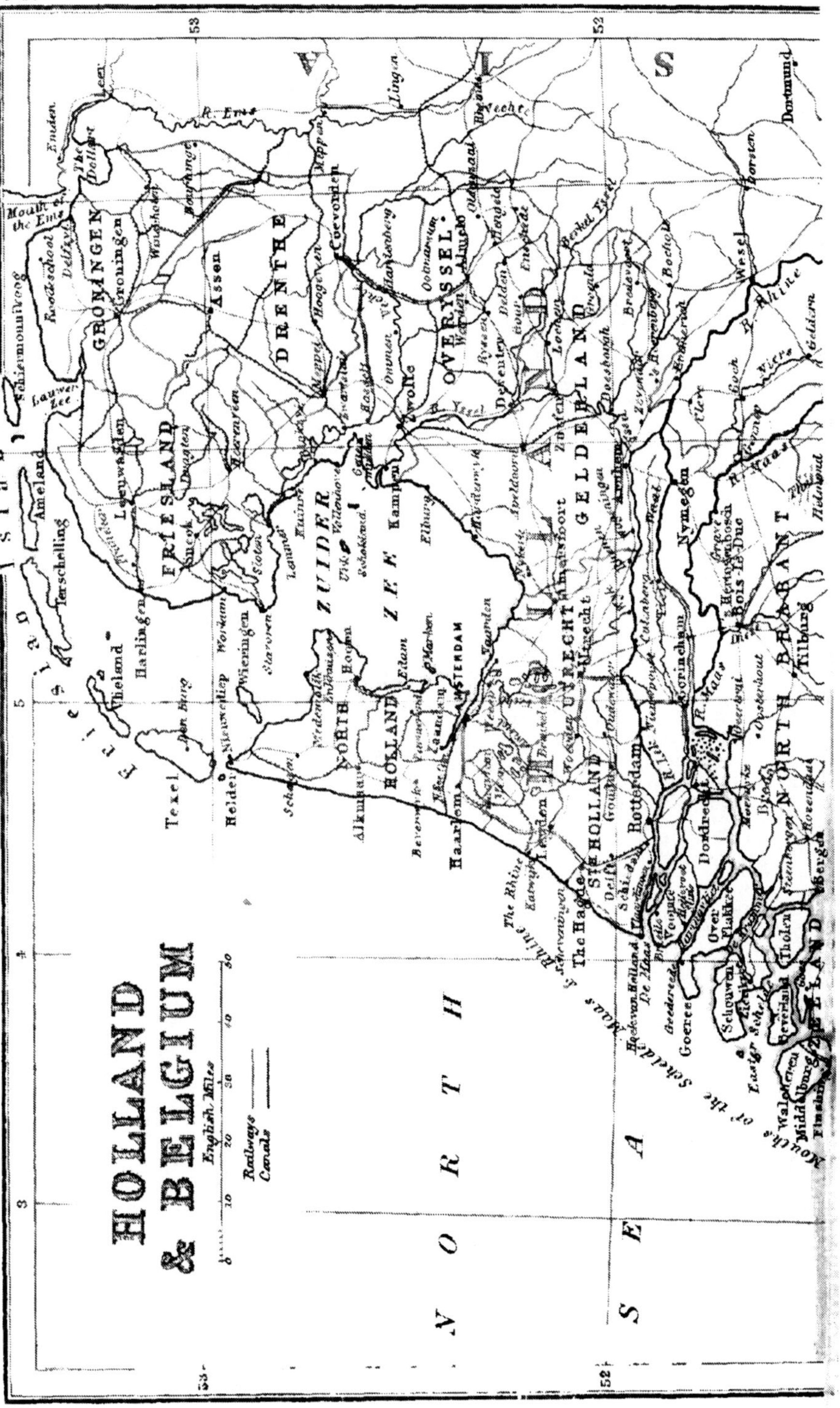
HOLLAND & BELGIUM
English Miles
Railways
Canals
NORTH SEA
ZUIDER ZEE
Friesland Islands
GRONINGEN
FRIESLAND
DRENTHE
OVERYSSEL
NORTH HOLLAND
SOUTH HOLLAND
UTRECHT
GELDERLAND
NORTH BRABANT
ZEELAND
Amsterdam
Haarlem
Rotterdam
The Hague
Leyden
Dordrecht
Groningen
Leeuwarden
Zwolle
Arnhem
Nymegen
Utrecht
Texel
Helder
Harlingen
Assen
Kampen
Gorinchem
Tilburg
Goeree
Schouwen
Middelburg
Wesel
Dortmund
Mouths of the Scheldt
Mouth of the Ems

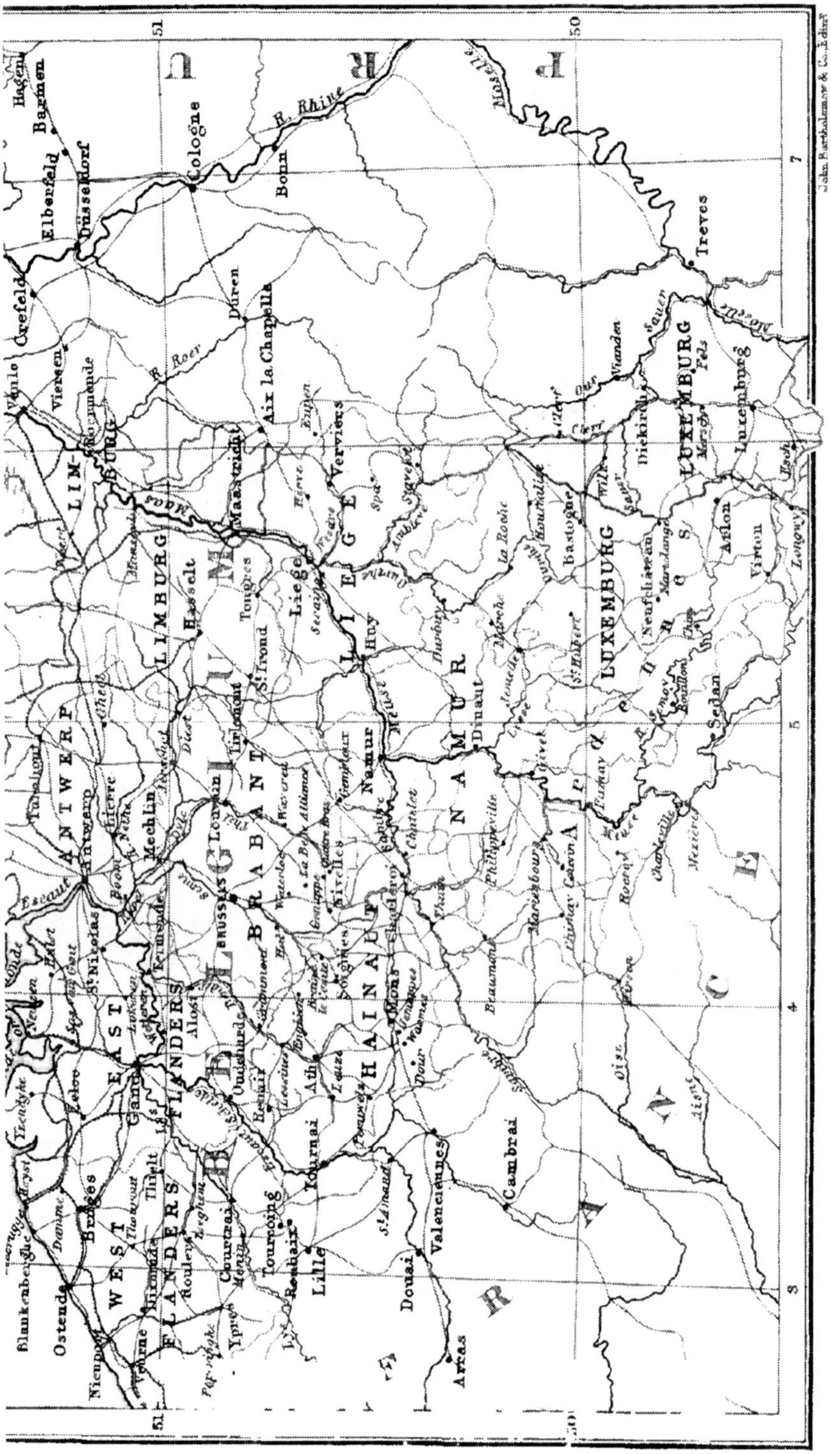

WEST FLANDERS
EAST FLANDERS
ANTWERP
LIMBURG
BRABANT
HAINAUT
NAMUR
LIEGE
LUXEMBURG
LUXEMBURG
Ostende
Blankenberghe
Nieuport
Bruges
Ypres
Courtrai
Gand
Alost
Antwerp
Mechlin
Louvain
Brussels
Namur
Liege
Hasselt
Maastricht
Verviers
Spa
Tongres
Huy
Dinant
Mons
Tournai
Lille
Roubaix
Tourcoing
Valenciennes
Cambrai
Douai
Arras
Sedan
Arlon
Bastogne
Aix la Chapelle
Cologne
Bonn
Düsseldorf
Elberfeld
Barmen
Crefeld
Düren
Venlo
Treves
Luxemburg
R. Rhine
R. Roer
Maas
Meuse
Escaut
Moselle
F R A N C E
P R U
51
50
3
4
5
7
John Bartholomew & Co. Edinr.

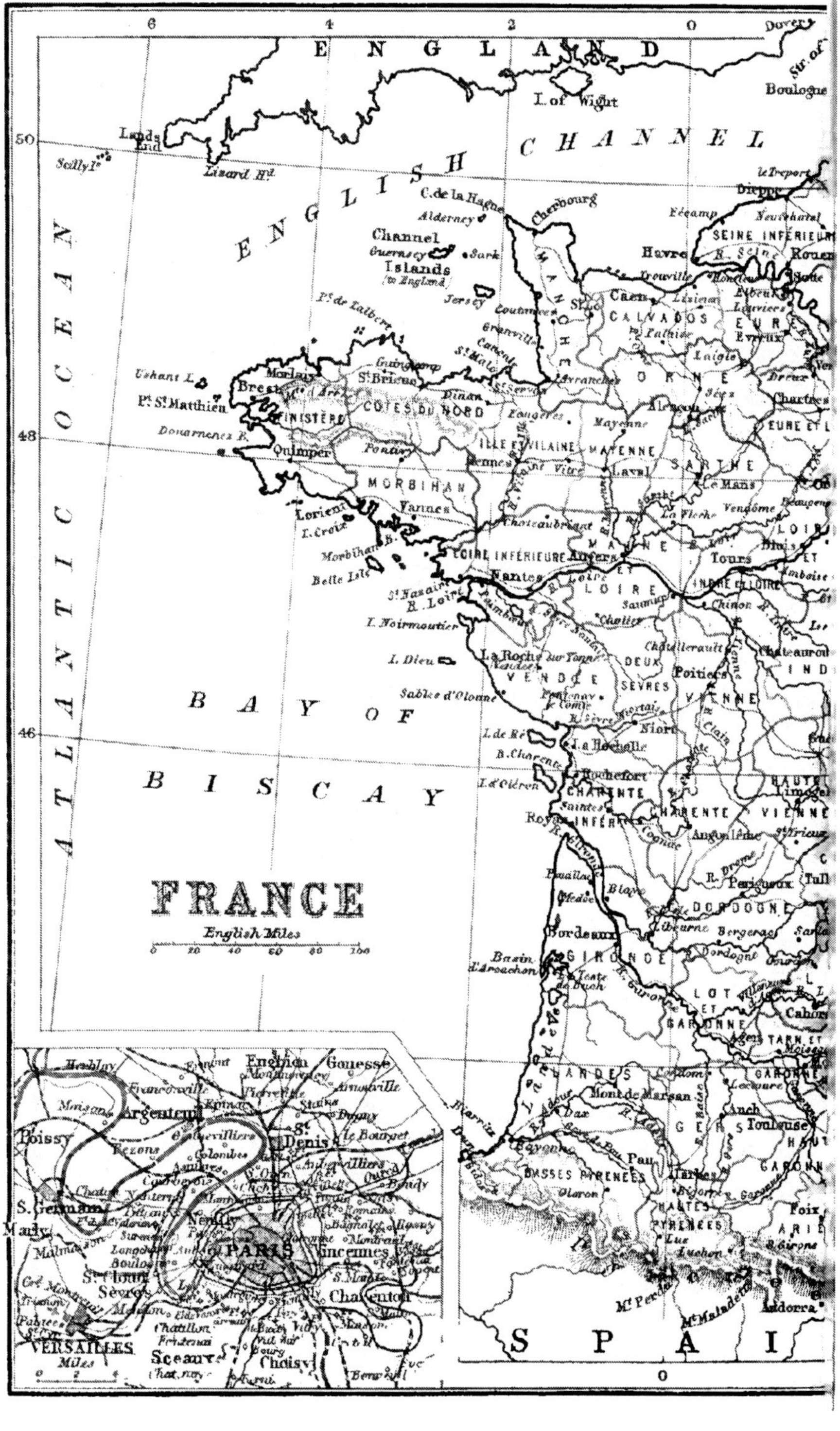
E N G L A N D
I. of Wight
Boulogne
Lands End
Scilly Is.
Lizard Hd.
E N G L I S H   C H A N N E L
C. de la Hague
Alderney
Cherbourg
Channel Islands (to England)
Guernsey
Sark
Jersey
Dieppe
Fécamp
Havre
Rouen
SEINE INFÉRIEURE
Caen
CALVADOS
EURE
Evreux
ORNE
Alençon
Chartres
Ushant I.
Brest
Pt. St. Matthieu
Morlaix
St. Brieuc
CÔTES DU NORD
FINISTÈRE
Douarnenez B.
Quimper
Dinan
Fougères
Mayenne
ILLE ET VILAINE
MAYENNE
Rennes
Vitré
Laval
SARTHE
Le Mans
MORBIHAN
Vannes
Lorient
Belle Isle
LOIRE INFÉRIEURE
Angers
Tours
Nantes
MAINE ET LOIRE
St. Nazaire
R. Loire
I. Noirmoutier
I. Dieu
La Roche sur Yon
VENDÉE
DEUX SÈVRES
Poitiers
VIENNE
Niort
La Rochelle
I. de Ré
Rochefort
CHARENTE
I. d'Oléron
Angoulême
Périgueux
DORDOGNE
Bordeaux
GIRONDE
Bassin d'Arcachon
LOT ET GARONNE
Agen
LANDES
Mont de Marsan
GERS
Auch
Toulouse
Bayonne
Pau
Tarbes
BASSES PYRÉNÉES
HAUTES PYRÉNÉES
Foix
Andorra
S P A I
A T L A N T I C   O C E A N
B A Y   O F   B I S C A Y
FRANCE
English Miles
0 20 40 60 80 100
Enghien
Gonesse
Argenteuil
Poissy
St. Denis
S. Germain
PARIS
Vincennes
St. Cloud
Sèvres
Charenton
VERSAILLES
Sceaux
Choisy
Miles
50
48
46
6
4
2
0

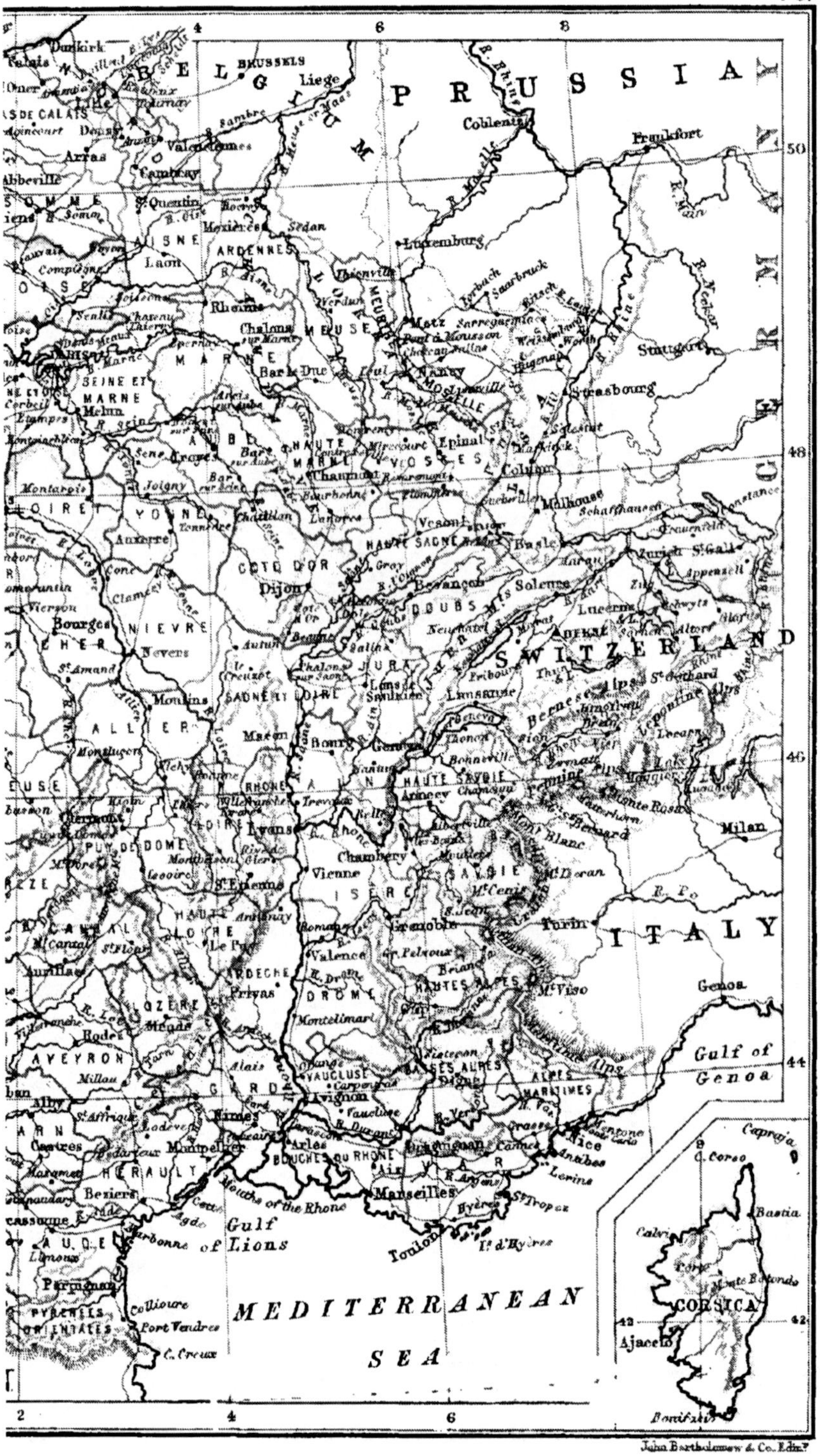
BELGIUM
BRUSSELS
Liege
PRUSSIA
Coblentz
Frankfort
Dunkirk
Arras
Cambray
Valenciennes
Abbeville
St. Quentin
Mezières
Sedan
Luxemburg
Thionville
Metz
Saarbruck
Nancy
Strasbourg
Stuttgart
Laon
Rheims
Chalons sur Marne
Bar le Duc
MARNE
MEUSE
AISNE
ARDENNES
SEINE ET MARNE
Melun
Etampes
Fontainebleau
Troyes
AUBE
HAUTE MARNE
Chaumont
Epinal
VOSGES
Colmar
Mulhouse
Basle
Zurich
St. Gall
Lucerne
Soleure
SWITZERLAND
Berne
Fribourg
Lausanne
Geneva
St. Gothard
Montargis
LOIRET
YONNE
Auxerre
Joigny
Chatillon
Langres
Vesoul
HAUTE SAONE
COTE D'OR
Dijon
Besançon
DOUBS
Gray
Beaune
Autun
NIEVRE
Nevers
Bourges
CHER
Vierzon
St. Amand
Moulins
ALLIER
Montluçon
SAONE ET LOIRE
Chalons sur Saone
Lons le Saulnier
JURA
Macon
Bourg
AIN
Annecy
HAUTE SAVOIE
Mont Blanc
Monte Rosa
Milan
RHONE
Lyons
LOIRE
St. Etienne
Clermont
PUY DE DOME
Chambery
SAVOIE
Mt. Cenis
Vienne
ISERE
Grenoble
Turin
ITALY
R. Po
HAUTE LOIRE
Le Puy
CANTAL
Aurillac
St. Flour
ARDECHE
Privas
Valence
DROME
Montelimart
HAUTES ALPES
Mt. Viso
Genoa
LOZERE
Mende
Rodez
AVEYRON
Millau
Alais
GARD
VAUCLUSE
Avignon
Nimes
BASSES ALPES
Digne
ALPES MARITIMES
Nice
Antibes
Gulf of Genoa
Alby
Castres
Lodeve
Montpellier
HERAULT
Beziers
Arles
BOUCHES DU RHONE
Aix
Marseilles
Draguignan
Toulon
Hyères
St. Tropez
Mouths of the Rhone
Gulf of Lions
Narbonne
AUDE
Limoux
Perpignan
PYRENEES ORIENTALES
Collioure
Port Vendres
C. Creux
MEDITERRANEAN SEA
Capraja
C. Corso
Bastia
Calvi
Corte
Monte Rotondo
CORSICA
Ajaccio
Bonifacio
50
48
46
44
42
2
4
6
8

John Bartholomew & Co. Edin.

DENMARK
SWED
Fredericia
Copenhagen
Malmö
Sound
Fünen
Zealand
Gr. Belt
Möen
Falster
Laaland
NORTH SEA
North Frisian Is.
Heligoland
SCHLESWIG-HOLSTEIN
Flensburg
Schleswig
Kiel Bay
Kiel
Fehmarn
Lübeck B.
Lübeck
Stralsund
Wismar
Rostock
Frisian Islands
Cuxhaven
Stade
Bremerhaven
Altona
HAMBURG
Schwerin
MECKLENBURG
Emden
Groningen
Leeuwarden
Harlingen
Assen
Oldenburg
OLDENBURG
Bremen
Vegesack
Harburg
Lüneburg
R. Elbe
Verden
Hoya
Zuyder Zee
Meppen
Zwolle
Deventer
HOLLAND
Arnhem
Hanover
Celle
Nienburg
Minden
Stendal
Uelzen
Brand
Spandau
Potsdam
Brandenburg
Brunswick
Magdeburg
Münster
Bielefeld
Lippe
Westphalia
Hamm
Soest
Paderborn
Dortmund
Crefeld
Duisburg
Düsseldorf
Barmen
Elberfeld
Cassel
Waldeck
Göttingen
Nordhausen
Halle
Leipzig
Dessau
Torgau
Wittenberg
Luckenwalde
Maastricht
COLOGNE
Aix-la-Chapelle
Liège
Bonn
Marburg
Nassau
Hersfeld
Mühlhausen
Erfurt
Weimar
Gotha
Jena
Thuringia
Altenburg
Zwickau
Chemnitz
KINGDOM OF SAXONY
BELGIUM
Coblenz
Wetzlar
Giessen
Fulda
Plauen
Annaberg
Wiesbaden
Frankfort
Hanau
Hof
Coburg
Eger
Bingen
Darmstadt
Aschaffenburg
Würzburg
Bamberg
Bayreuth
BO
Luxemburg
Treves
Kaiserslautern
Mannheim
Heidelberg
Worms
Thionville
Palatinate
Saarlouis
Saarbrück
Speyer
Landau
Metz
Forbach
Erlangen
Fürth
Nuremberg
Weiden
Amberg
Ansbach
Lorraine
Carlsruhe
Heilbronn
BAVARIA
Phalsburg
Strasburg
Nancy
Rastatt
Pforzheim
STUTTGART
Esslingen
Ludwigsburg
Nördlingen
Ratisbon or Regensburg
Straubing
Ingolstadt
R. Danube
WURTEMBERG
Tübingen
Reutlingen
Schlettstadt
Lahr
Ulm
Passau
Landshut
FRANCE
Colmar
Augsburg
Freiburg
Sigmaringen
Blenheim
MUNICH
Belfort
Mülhausen
Schaffhausen
Friedrichshafen
Memmingen
Kempten
Rosenheim
Salzburg
Basle
Constance
Lindau
R. Doubs
R. Rhine
SWITZERLAND
Tyrol
BADEN
ALSACE
Black Forest
Rhenish Prussia
HESSE
BAVARIA
PRUSSIA
HANOVER

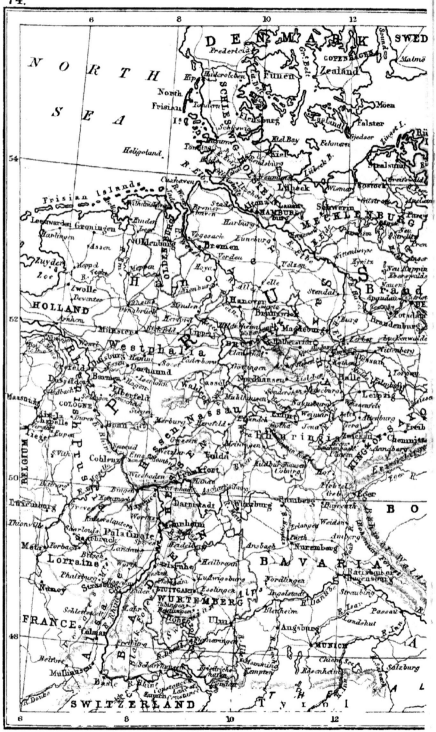

B A L T I C
S E A
RUSSIA
Memel
Bornholm
KÖNIGSBERG
Gulf of Danzig
Pillau
Danzig
Stolpmünde
Rügenwalde
Stolp
Lauenburg
Colberg
Cöslin
Belgard
Greifenberg
Stargard
Neu Stettin
Konitz
Dirschau
Elbing
Marienburg
Marienwerder
Graudenz
Strassburg
Thorn
Fordon
Bromberg
Alexandrovo
Insterburg
Gumbinnen
Tilsit
Labiau
Pillkallen
Angerburg
Lötzen
Lyck
Johannisburg
Neidenburg
Allenstein
Mlawa
R. Vistula
R. Bug
R. Netze
Wongrowitz
Gnesen
Inowrazlaw
Goplo See
Posen
Landsberg
Cüstrin
Frankfurt
Küstrin
R. Warthe
R. Oder
WARSAW
P O L A N D
R. Pilica
Kalisz
Kempen
Lissa
Rawicz
Glogau
Grünberg
Sagan
Sorau
Bunzlau
Görlitz
Liegnitz
Jauer
BRESLAU
Schweidnitz
Brieg
Waldenburg
Hirschberg
Glatz
Neisse
Neustadt
Oppeln
Rosenberg
Lublinitz
Beuthen
Königshutte
Gleiwitz
Kosel
Ratibor
Leobschütz
Oderburg
Cracow
R. Warta
R. Vistula
Galicia
Silesia
Moravia
A U S T R I A
H U N G A R Y
VIENNA
R. Elbe
Moldau R.
16
18
20
22
54
52
50
48
GERMANY
English Miles
0 20 40 60 80 100 150

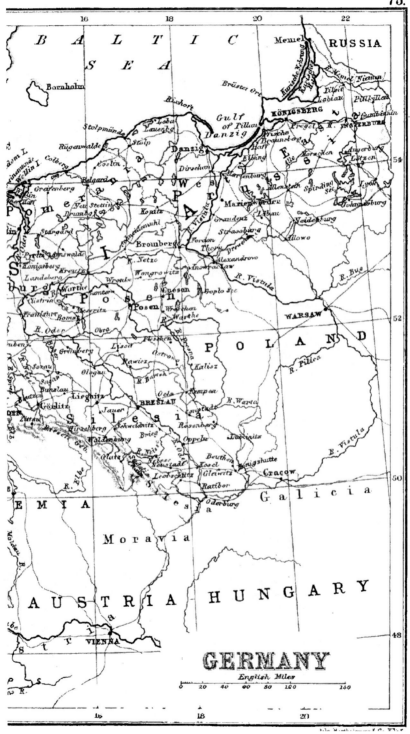

CENTRAL
GERMANY
English Miles
0 20 40 60 80
East Friesian Wangeroog
Nordeney
Borkum
SCHLESWIG
HOLSTEIN
Kiel Bay
Kiel
Fehmarn I.
Rügen I.
Pomeranian Bay
Stralsund
Rostock
Lübeck
Schwerin
MECKLENBURG
HAMBURG
Altona
Stettin
BERLIN
Potsdam
BRANDENBURG
Frankfurt
HANOVER
Lüneburg
Stade
BREMEN
OLDENBURG
Aurich
Osnabrück
Münster
WESTPHALIA
LIPPE
Bielefeld
Minden
Hildesheim
BRUNSWICK
Brunswick
Magdeburg
PROVINCE
MAGDEBURG
ANHALT
SAXONY
Halle
Merseburg
LEIPZIG
DRESDEN
SAXONY
Erfurt
Cassel
WALDECK
Arnsberg
Düsseldorf
COLOGNE
Crefeld
Dortmund
R. Elbe
R. Ems
Weser R.
Spree Wald
Guben
Cottbus
Cuxhaven
Göttingen
Celle
Gotha
Weimar
Eisenach
6
8
12
54
52

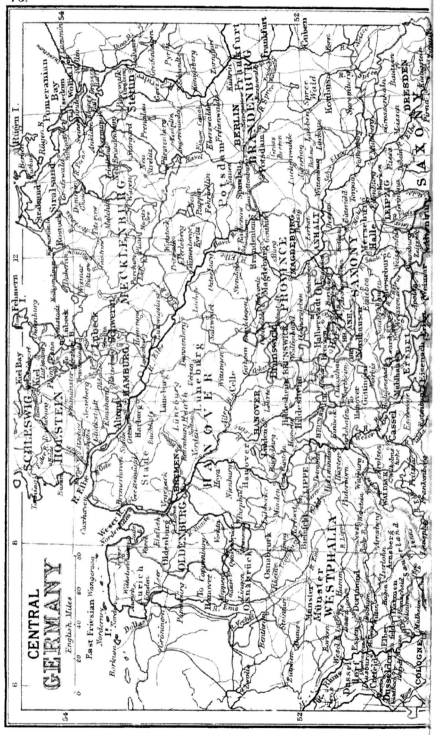

BAVARIA
WURTEMBERG
PRAGUE
MUNICH
FRANKFORT
STUTTGART
STRASSBURG
NASSAU
LORRAINE
Upper Bavaria
Lower Bavaria
Upper Palatinate
Palatinate
Swabia
Middle Franconia
Upper Franconia
Lower Franconia
Böhmer Wald
Ratisbon (Regensburg)
Nürnberg
Augsburg
Ingolstadt
Salzburg
Linz
Passau
Pilsen
Karlsbad
Mayence
Carlsruhe
Heidelberg
Würzburg
Bamberg
Baireuth
Coblenz
Treves
Metz
Nancy
Basle
Constance
Freiburg
Ulm
Darmstadt
Wiesbaden
Giessen
Hohenzollern
R. Moldau
R. Elbe
R. Eger
50
48
8
10
12
14
John Bartholomew & Co. Edinr

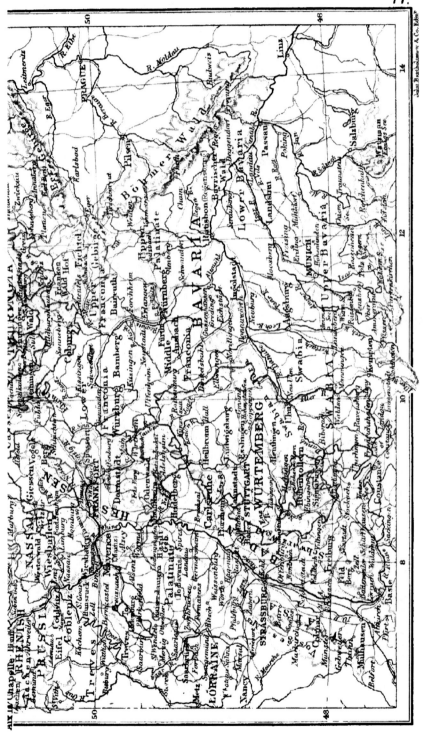

GERMANY

G E R M A N Y

SAXONY
Dresden • Breslau
Erz Gebirge • Reichenberg • Trautenau • Glatz • Neisse
Joachimsthal • Leitmeritz • Jung Bunzlau • Schnee Koppe
Karlsbad • Saaz • Theresienstadt • Sadowa • Königgratz
Eger • Prague • Kolin • Kuttenberg • Pardubitz • Sternberg
Bamberg • Mrienbad • BOHEMIA • Sazawa • Brittau • Olmutz
Nürnberg • Pilsen • Prabram • Polna • Prossnitz
B A V A R I A • Klattau • Sigmundsherberg • MORAVIA • Austerlitz • Ung. Hradisch
Regensburg • Budweis • Wittingau • Neuhaus • Brünn
R. Danube • Krumau • Gmünd • Znaim • Kalsburg
Passau • UPPER • Freystan • Horn • Tyrnau
Augsburg • MUNICH • Ried • Linz • Danube • VIENNA • Pressburg
AUSTRIA • Amstetten • St. Pölten • Neuhburg
Constance • Salzburg • Steyer • Scheibb • Neustadt • Raab
Dornbirn • Kufstein • Wels • Oedenburg
Feldkirch • Innsbruck • SALZBURG • Gnuern Chain • Bruck • Güns • Papa
Bludenz • Vorarlberg • Kitzbühel • Hoch Tauern • Mur • STYRIA • Veszprim
TYROL • High Tauern • Judenburg • Graz • Stermanager
Stelvio • Brixen • Villach • CARINTHIA • Leibnitz • Zala Egerszeg • Kanizaa
Ortler • Mt. Marmolata • Klagenfurt • Marburg • Gr. Kanizaa • Kaposvár
Bozen • Pontebba • Villach • Pettau
Bellano • Udine • Krainburg • Warasdin • Funfkirch
Trent • Laibach • CARNIOLA • Agram
L. di Garda • Görtz • GÖRITZ • Adelsberg • Gottschee • SLAVO
Verona • Treviso • Trieste • Piran • Karlstadt • Sisak • Nasic
Padua • Venice • ISTRIA • Fiume • CROATIA • Ogulin • Brod
Rovigno • Buccari • Zeng • Ottochatz • Dihac • Banialuka
Quarnero • Gospich • BOS
Bologna • ADRIATIC • Kliutch • Yattse
Pisa • Malada • Knin • Mt. Dinara • D'Valai
Lunga • Zara • Benkovas • DALMATIA • Kupres • Livno • Konietza
Incoronata • Sebenico • HERZE
Ancona • I T A L Y • Pta. della Planca • Spalato • Jduschi
Tiber • Lissa • Lesina • Metkov
S. Andrea • Curzola • S E A • Lagosta • Melada • Ragusa • Castel

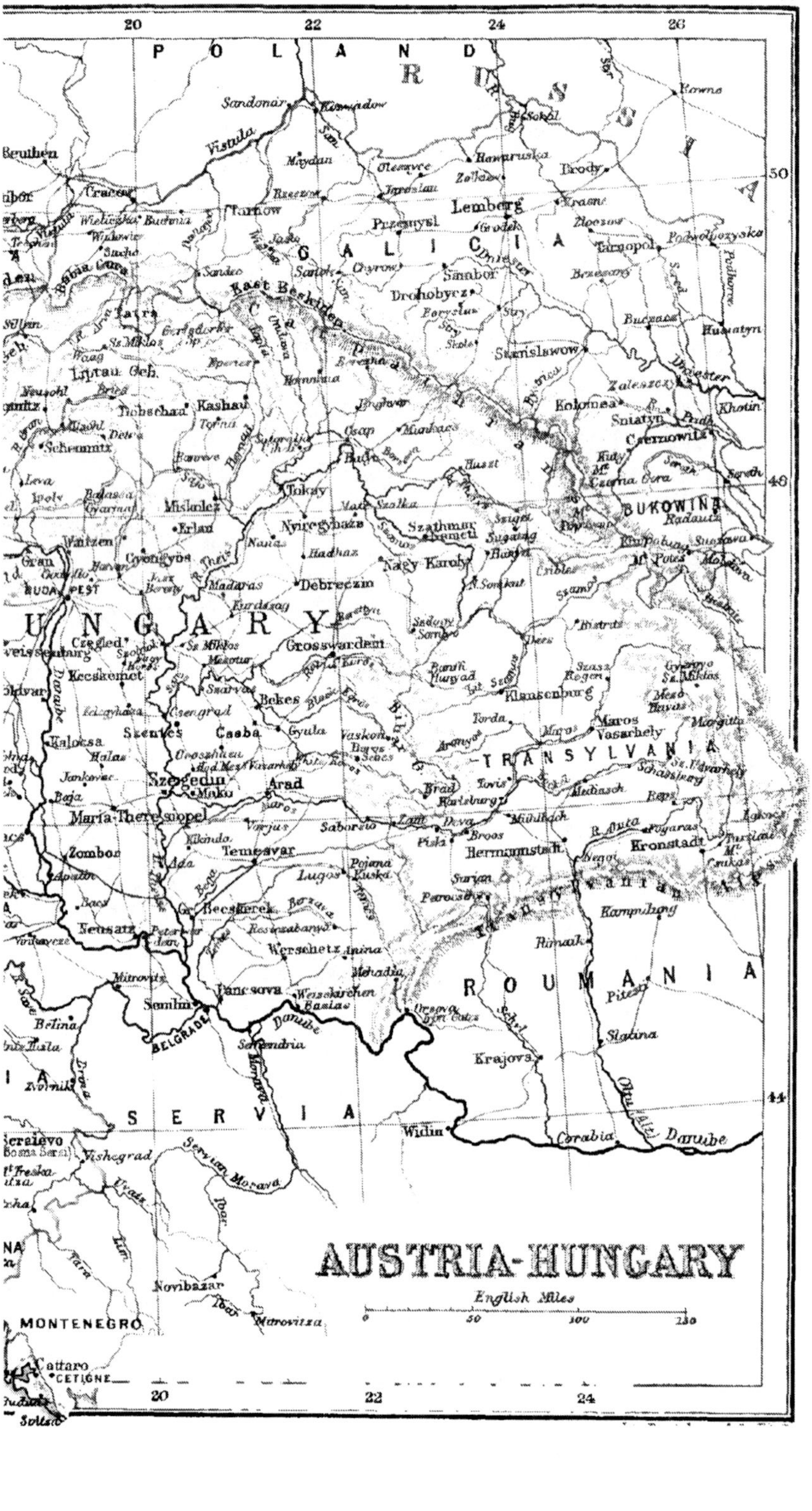

AUSTRIA-HUNGARY
English Miles
0 50 100 150
POLAND
RUSSIA
GALICIA
HUNGARY
TRANSYLVANIA
ROUMANIA
SERVIA
BUKOWINA
MONTENEGRO
Lemberg
Przemysl
Tarnow
Cracow
Brody
Tarnopol
Kolomea
Czernowitz
Stanislawow
Drohobycz
Sambor
Kashau
Tokay
Miskolcz
Erlau
Nyiregyhaza
Debreczin
Grosswardein
Szathmar
Nagy Karoly
Klausenburg
Maros Vasarhely
Hermannstadt
Kronstadt
Arad
Szegedin
Temesvar
Maria Theresiopel
Kecskemet
Czegled
Waitzen
Gran
Gyöngyös
Kalocsa
Zombor
Neusatz
Semlin
Belgrade
Pancsova
Werschetz
Mehadia
Krajova
Widin
Danube
Vistula
Cattaro
Cetigne
Seraievo
Novibazar
Mitrovitza
20
22
24
26
50
48
46
44

80.

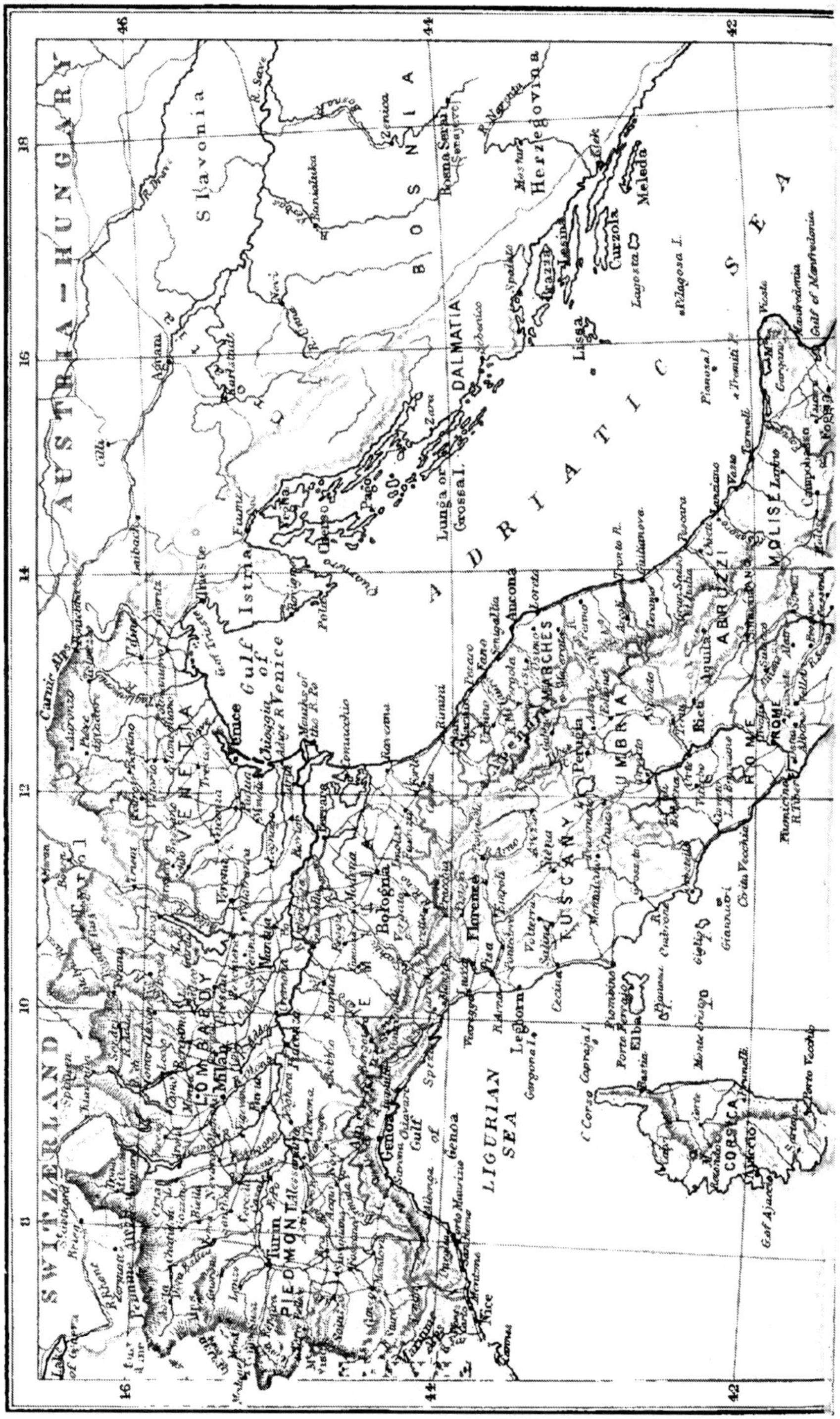

AUSTRIA – HUNGARY
SWITZERLAND
Slavonia
BOSNIA
Herzegovina
DALMATIA
ADRIATIC SEA
Gulf of Venice
Istria
LOMBARDY
VENETIA
PIEDMONT
TUSCANY
UMBRIA
MARCHES
ABRUZZI
MOLISE
ROME
CORSICA
LIGURIAN SEA
Gulf of Genoa
Milan
Turin
Genoa
Venice
Bologna
Florence
Leghorn
Perugia
Ancona
Trieste
Elba
Lissa
Curzola
Meleda

ITALY
English Miles
TYRHENIAN SEA
IONIAN SEA
MEDITERRANEAN SEA
GULF OF TARANTO
SARDINIA
SICILY
CAMPANIA
APULIA
BASILICATA
CALABRIA
Naples
Palermo
Cagliari
Tunis
Lipari Islands
Pontine Is
Ischia
Ventotene I.
Ustica I.
Pantellaria I.
Ægades
C. Bon
Galite I.
Bona
Reggio
Messina
Catania
Syracuse
Taranto
Brindisi
Cosenza
Catanzaro
Stromboli
Vulcano
Salerno
Sassari
Oristano
Nuoro
John Bartholomew & Co. Edinr.

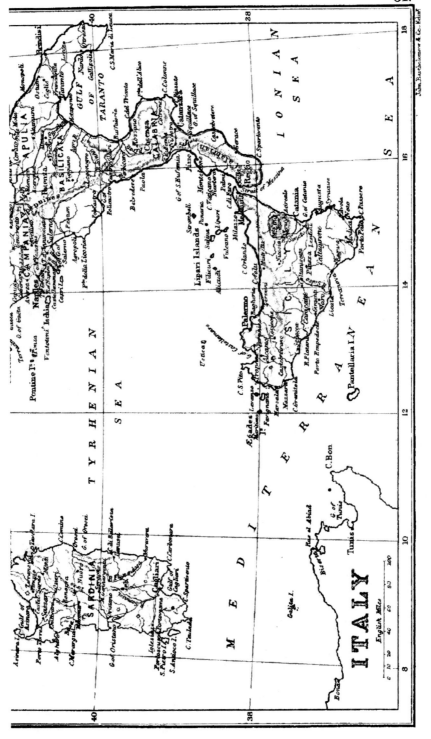

LOMBARDY
PIEDMONT
MILAN
TURIN
GENOA
Alessandria
Novara
Pavia
Cremona
Piacenza
Parma
Bergamo
Brescia
Como
Lecco
Cuneo
Savona
Albenga
Spezia
Sarzana
Carrara
Massa
Lucca
Pisa
Viareggio
Serravezza
Sondrio
GULF OF GENOA
Riviera di Ponente
Riviera di Levante
LIGURIAN SEA
FRANCE
Nice
Monaco
Mentone
S. Remo
Ventimiglia
Porto Maurizio
Antibes
Cannes
Grasse
LEGHORN (Livorno)
Gorgona I.
Piombino
Elba I.
Pianoso I.
Monte Cristo I.
Maritime Alps
Cottian Alps
Graian Alps
Pennine Alps
Mt. Blanc
Matterhorn
Aosta
Ivrea
Biella
Vercelli
Tortona
Voghera
Marengo
Novi
Acqui
Bobbio
Rapallo
Chiavari
Ventimiglia
Final Borgo
Alassio
Oneglia
English Miles
ROME
Albano
Frascati
Ostia
Porto
Ponte Galera
R. Tiber
Bosco di Muratella
Porcigliana
7
8
9
10
46
44

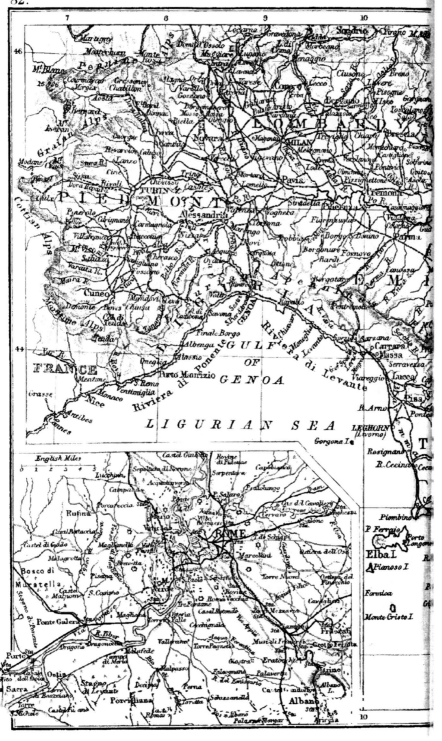

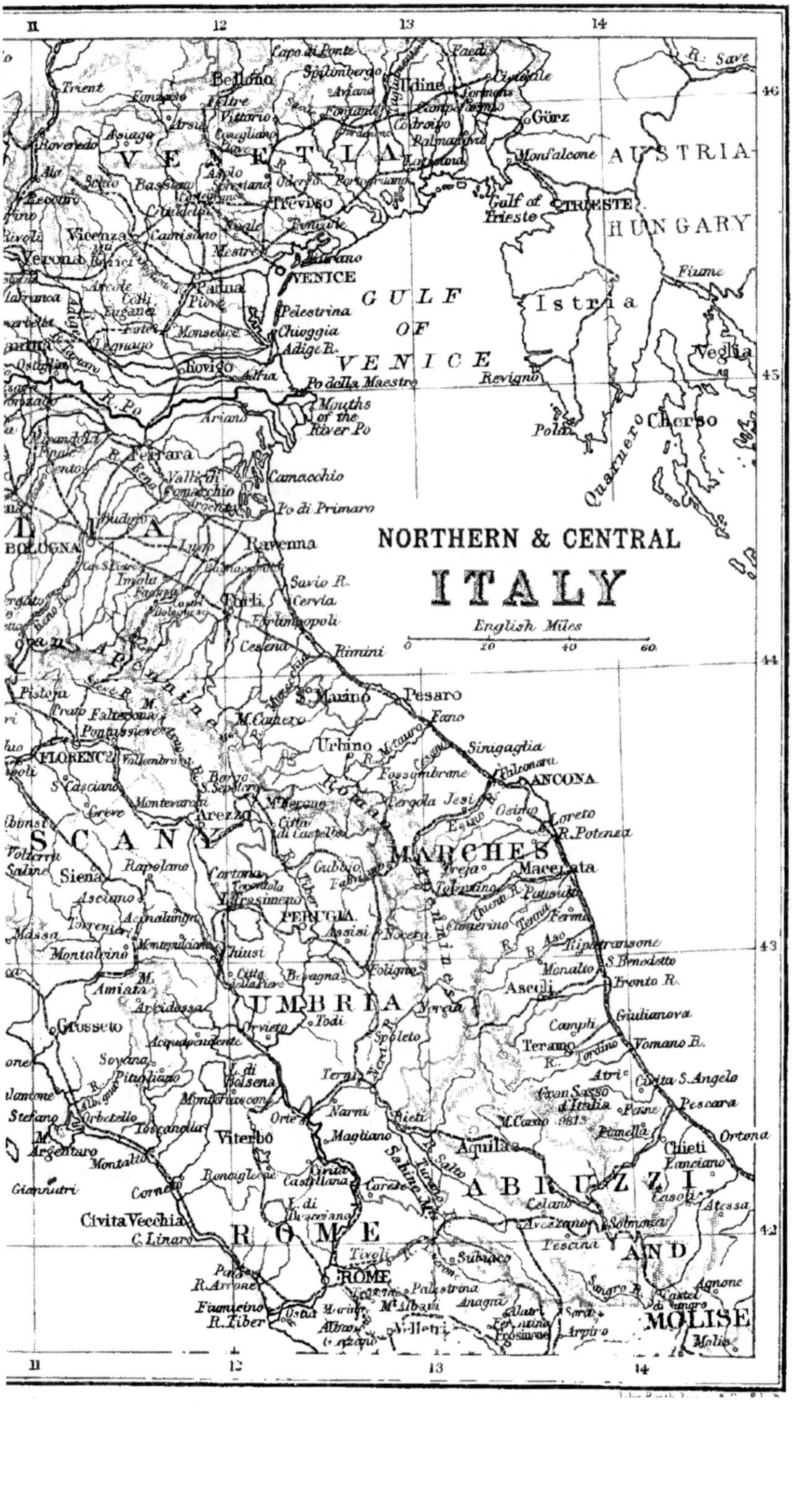
NORTHERN & CENTRAL
ITALY
English Miles
0 20 40 60
GULF OF VENICE
AUSTRIA HUNGARY
VENETIA
Istria
MARCHES
UMBRIA
ABRUZZI AND MOLISE
ROME
VENICE
BOLOGNA
FLORENCE
ANCONA
PERUGIA
ROME
Gulf of Trieste
TRIESTE
Mouths of the River Po
Belluno
Udine
Görz
Treviso
Vicenza
Verona
Padua
Rovigo
Ferrara
Ravenna
Forli
Rimini
Pesaro
Urbino
Siena
Arezzo
Grosseto
Viterbo
Orvieto
Spoleto
Terni
Aquila
Teramo
Ascoli
Macerata
Chieti
Civita Vecchia
Tivoli
Pola
Cherso
Veglia
Fiume

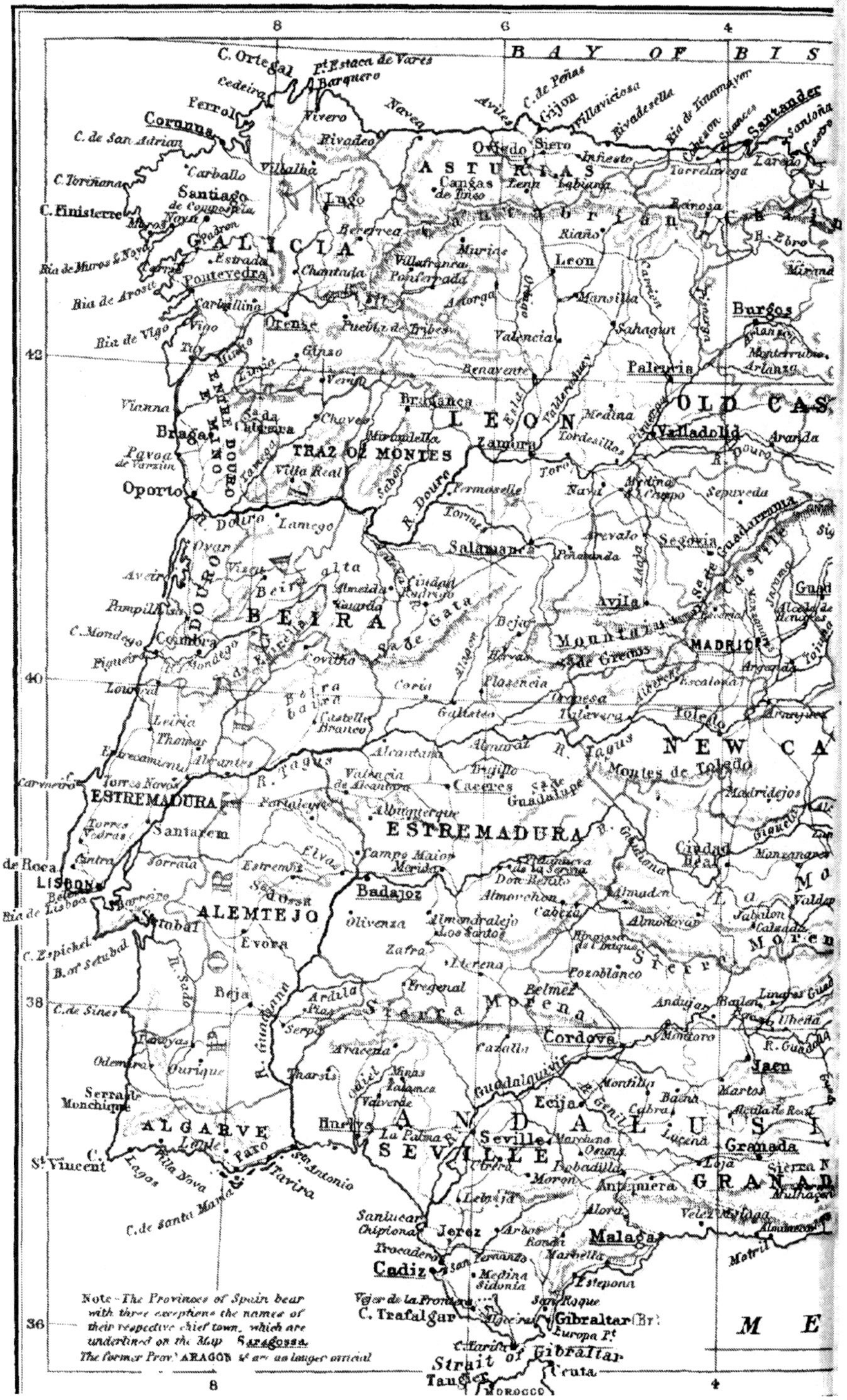
BAY OF BIS
C. Ortegal
Pt. Estaca de Vares
Barquero
Cedeira
Ferrol
Corunna
C. de San Adrian
Carballo
C. Toriñana
Santiago
de Compostela
C. Finisterre
GALICIA
Pontevedra
Ria de Arosa
Ria de Vigo
Vigo
Orense
Lugo
Rivadeo
Vivero
Villalba
Chantada
Villafranca
Ponferrada
Astorga
Oviedo
Siero
Gijon
Aviles
C. de Peñas
Villaviciosa
Rivadesella
ASTURIAS
Cangas de Onis
Leon
Riaño
Mansilla
Sahagun
Valencia
Benavente
Reinosa
Santander
Santoña
Castro
Laredo
Torrelavega
Burgos
R. Ebro
Miranda
Palencia
OLD CAS
Valladolid
Aranda
Tordesillas
Medina
Zamora
LEON
Toro
Nava
Medina del Campo
Sepulveda
Segovia
Arevalo
Peñaranda
Avila
Salamanca
Ciudad Rodrigo
Braganca
Mirandella
TRAZ OS MONTES
Villa Real
Chaves
Braga
Vianna
Pavoa de Varzim
Oporto
R. Douro
Lamego
Ovar
Aveiro
Vizeu
Beira alta
Almeida
Guarda
BEIRA
Pampilhosa
C. Mondego
Coimbra
Figueira
Covilha
Beira baixa
Castello Branco
Louzã
Leiria
Thomar
Entrocamento
Abrantes
Torres Novas
ESTREMADURA
Torres Vedras
Santarem
Cintra
LISBON
Belem
de Roca
Ria de Lisboa
Setubal
C. Espichel
B. of Setubal
ALEMTEJO
Evora
Beja
C. de Sines
Odemira
Ourique
Serra de Monchique
ALGARVE
Loulé
Faro
Lagos
Villa Nova
Tavira
St. Vincent
C. de Santa Maria
MADRID
Aranjuez
Toledo
Talavera
Oropesa
Plasencia
Coria
Galisteo
Alcantara
Almaraz
Trujillo
Caceres
Guadalupe
Valencia de Alcantara
Portalegre
Albuquerque
ESTREMADURA
Campo Maior
Merida
Badajoz
Olivenza
Almendralejo
Los Santos
Zafra
Llerena
Fregenal
Almaden
Almodovar
Pozoblanco
Belmez
Sierra Morena
Cordova
Montoro
Andujar
Baeza
Ubeda
Linares
Jaen
Martos
Montilla
Baena
Cabra
Lucena
Ecija
Guadalquivir
Seville
Carmona
Osuna
Moron
Lebrija
Jerez
Cadiz
Arcos
Ronda
Antequera
Loja
Granada
GRANADA
Malaga
Velez Malaga
Motril
Marbella
Estepona
San Roque
Gibraltar (Br.)
Europa Pt.
Strait of Gibraltar
Tangier
Ceuta
MOROCCO
C. Trafalgar
Vejer de la Frontera
Medina Sidonia
San Fernando
Sanlucar
Chipiona
Huelva
La Palma
ANDALUSIA
SEVILLE
Tharsis
Aracena
Cazalla
NEW CA
Montes de Toledo
Madridejos
Ciudad Real
Manzanares
Valdepeñas
Sierra de Gredos
Sa. de Gata
R. Tagus
R. Guadiana
Ayamonte
San Antonio
M E
Note - The Provinces of Spain bear with three exceptions the names of their respective chief town, which are underlined on the Map Saragossa.
The former Prov. ARAGON &c are no longer official
8
6
4
42
40
38
36

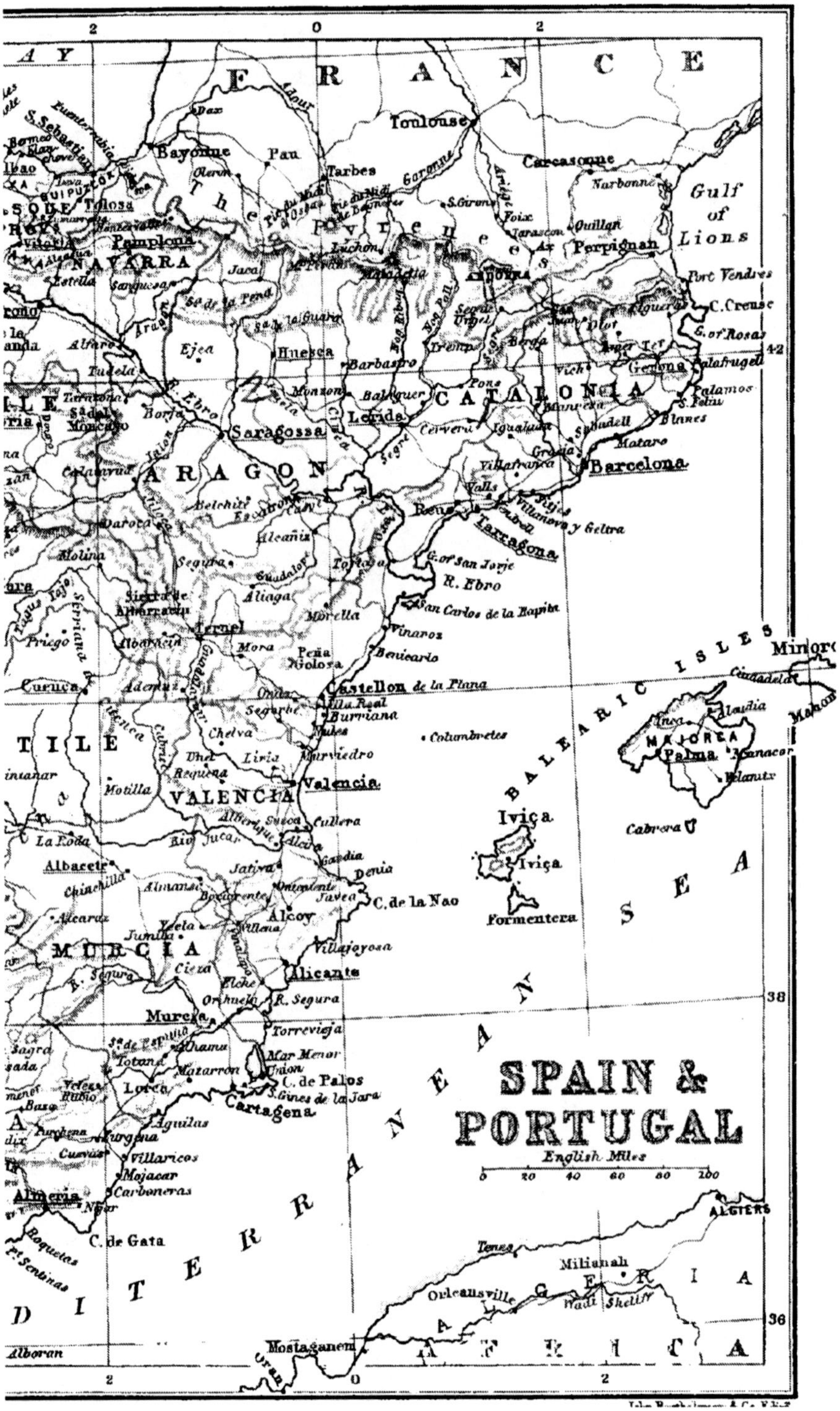

SPAIN & PORTUGAL
English Miles
0 20 40 60 80 100
F R A N C E
Toulouse
Carcasonne
Narbonne
Gulf of Lions
Perpignan
Port Vendres
C. Creuse
G. of Rosas
Bayonne
Pau
Tarbes
Dax
Foix
Tarascon
Quillan
Luchon
Andorra
NAVARRA
Pamplona
Tolosa
GUIPUZCOA
Estella
Sanguesa
Jaca
Huesca
Barbastro
Ejea
Alfaro
Tudela
Tarazona
Borja
Saragossa
Monzon
Balaguer
Lerida
CATALONIA
Tremp
Berga
Vich
Manresa
Gerona
Palafrugell
Palamos
S. Feliu
Blanes
Sabadell
Mataro
Barcelona
Igualada
Cervera
Villafranca
Valls
Reus
Sitjes
Villanova y Geltra
Tarragona
G. of San Jorje
R. Ebro
San Carlos de la Rapita
Vinaroz
Benicarlo
ARAGON
Belchite
Caspe
Alcañiz
Daroca
Calatayud
Molina
Segura
Guadalope
Tortosa
Aliaga
Morella
Teruel
Albarracin
Mora
Peña Golosa
Cuenca
Castellon de la Plana
Villa Real
Burriana
Onda
Segorbe
Nules
Columbretes
Chelva
Liria
Murviedro
Requena
Utiel
Motilla
VALENCIA
Valencia
Alberique
Sueca
Cullera
Alcira
Rio Jucar
Gandia
Denia
Jativa
Almansa
Onteniente
Javea
C. de la Nao
Alcoy
Villena
Yecla
Jumilla
Villajoyosa
La Roda
Albacete
Chinchilla
Alcaraz
MURCIA
R. Segura
Cieza
Alicante
Elche
Orihuela
R. Segura
Murcia
Torrevieja
Mar Menor
Alhama
Totana
Lorca
Mazarron
Union
C. de Palos
S. Gines de la Jara
Cartagena
Aguilas
Velez Rubio
Baza
Huercal Overa
Cuevas
Villaricos
Mojacar
Carboneras
Almeria
Nijar
C. de Gata
Roquetas
Alboran
BALEARIC ISLES
Minorca
Ciudadela
Mahon
Alcudia
Inca
MAJORCA
Palma
Manacor
Cabrera
Iviça
Formentera
MEDITERRANEAN SEA
Algiers
Tenez
Milianah
Orleansville
Wadi Shelif
ALGERIA
AFRICA
Mostaganem
Oran

SWITZERLAND
English Miles
0 10 20 30 40 50
Napoleon's March
The Affix "horn", i.e. peak, is contracted
as in Wildh. - Wildhorn
B. - Berg - Mountain
G. - Gebirge - Mountain Range
FRANCE
Lake of Geneva
BERNE
VAUD
FRIBOURG
NEUCHATEL
SOLOTHURN
VALLAIS
Besançon
Basel
Lausanne
Fribourg
Thun
Sion
Annecy
Albertville
Moutiers
Biella
Ivrea
Mont Blanc
Monte Rosa
Lorrach
Waldshut
Aarau
Bienne

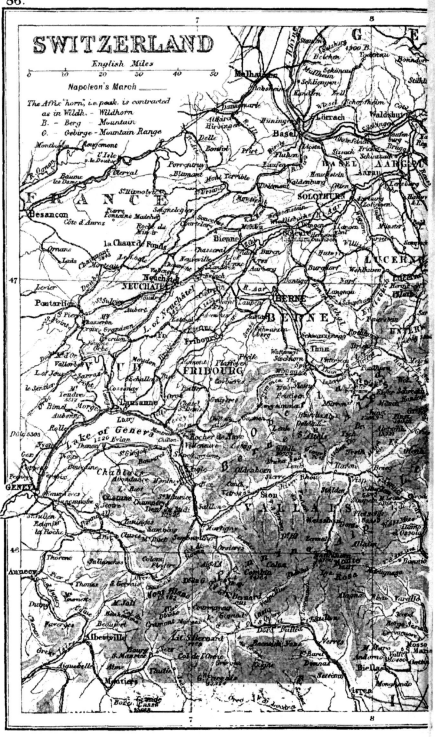

HEIGHT OF LAND
12,000 FT.
9000
6000
3000
1000
Sea Level
9
10
47
46
Constance
L. of Constance
THURGAU
Frauenfeld
Zurich
Ravensburg
Weingarten
Friedrichshafen
Lindau
Bregenz
Dornbirn
Feldkirch
Bludenz
Appenzell
APPENZELL
Herisau
St GALL
SCHWYZ
Schwyz
Glarus
GLARUS
Altdorf
URI
Chur
GRISONS
Thusis
Splügen
Vorder Rhein
Hinter Rhein
TICINO
Biasca
Bellinzona
Locarno
Maggia
Val Tellina
Bergamasque Alps
Dongo
Lecco
Como
Bergamo
Brescia
Monza
Gallarate
Busto Arsizio
Novara
Magenta
MILAN
Palazzolo
Treviglio
Edolo
Breno
Val Camonica
L. d'Iseo
Bormio

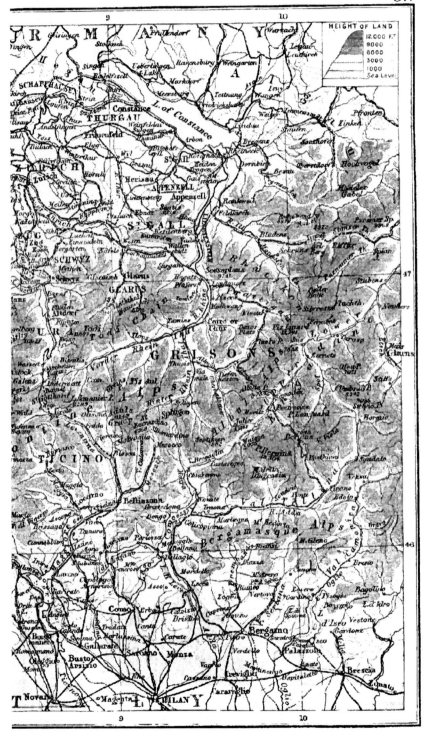

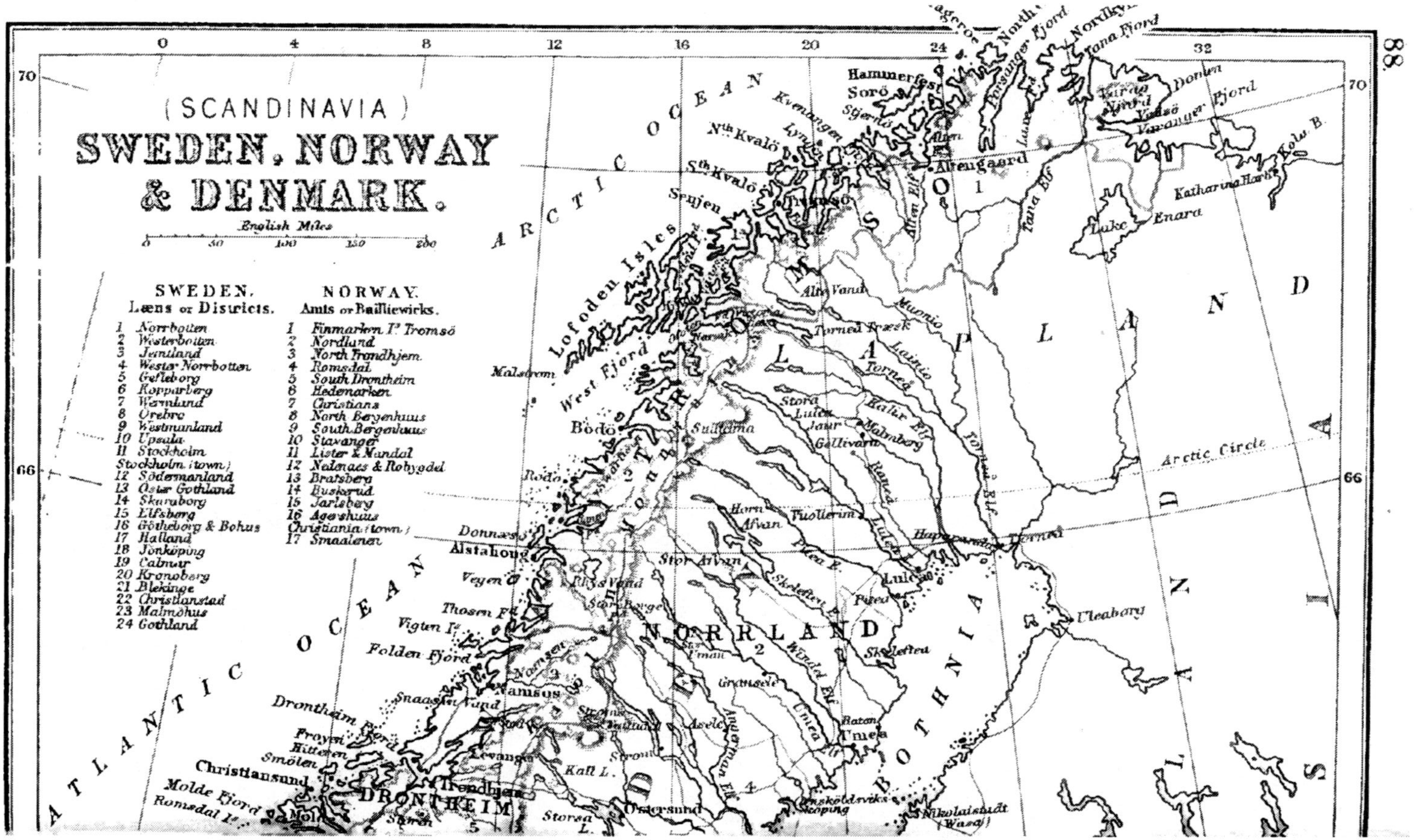
(SCANDINAVIA)
SWEDEN, NORWAY & DENMARK.
English Miles
0 50 100 150 200
SWEDEN. Læns or Districts.
1 Norrbotten
2 Westerbotten
3 Jemtland
4 Wester Norrbotten
5 Gefleborg
6 Kopparberg
7 Wermland
8 Örebro
9 Westmanland
10 Upsala
11 Stockholm
Stockholm (town)
12 Södermanland
13 Öster Gothland
14 Skaraborg
15 Elfsborg
16 Götheborg & Bohus
17 Halland
18 Jönköping
19 Calmar
20 Kronoberg
21 Blekinge
22 Christianstad
23 Malmöhus
24 Gothland
NORWAY. Amts or Bailliewicks.
1 Finmarken Iᵗ Tromsö
2 Nordland
3 North Trondhjem
4 Romsdal
5 South Drontheim
6 Hedemarken
7 Christians
8 North Bergenhuus
9 South Bergenhuus
10 Stavanger
11 Lister & Mandal
12 Nedenaes & Robygdel
13 Bratsberg
14 Buskerud
15 Jarlsberg
16 Agershuus
Christiania (town)
17 Smaalenen
ARCTIC OCEAN
ATLANTIC OCEAN
LAPLAND
FINLAND
NORRLAND
BOTHNIA
DRONTHEIM
Arctic Circle
Hammerfest
Sorö
Altengaard
Tromsö
Lofoden Isles
West Fjord
Malstrom
Bodö
Alstahoug
Donnæs
Namsos
Trondhjem
Christiansund
Molde Fjord
Romsdal
Dronthaim Fjord
Folden Fjord
Vigten Iˢ
Smölen
Hitteren
Froyen
Levanger
Östersund
Storsa L.
Kall L.
Umea
Luleå
Piteå
Skelleftea
Haparanda
Torneå
Uleaborg
Nikolaistadt (Wasa)
Ornsköldsvik
Tana Fjord
Porsanger Fjord
Varanger Fjord
Vadsö
Katharina Harb.
Lake Enara
Kola B.
Tana Elf
Alten Elf
Torneå Elf
Muonio
Lainio
Kalix Elf
Malmberg
Gellivara
Luleå
Stora Lulea Jaur
Ranea
Tuolterim
Hornafvan
Pitea E.
Stor Afvan
Skelleftea Elf
Windel Elf
Umea Elf
Angerman Elf
Snaasen Vand
Nth Kvalö
Sth Kvalö
Senjen
Lyngen
Kvenangen
Stjernö
Alten
Alten Vand
Torneå Træsk
Sulitelma
Nordkyn

GULF OF FINLAND
NORTH SEA
SKAGER RACK
CATTEGAT
SWEDEN
DENMARK
Stockholm
Christiania
Riga
Gothland
Bornholm
Oland
Dorpat
Revel
Helsingfors
Bergen
Stavanger
John Bartholomew & Co. Edin^r

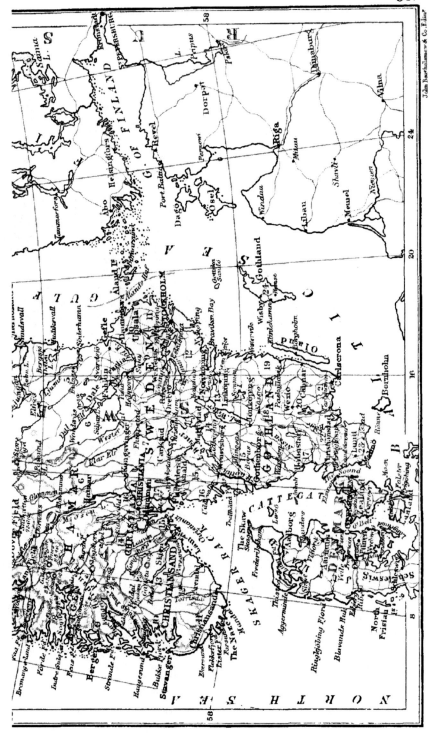

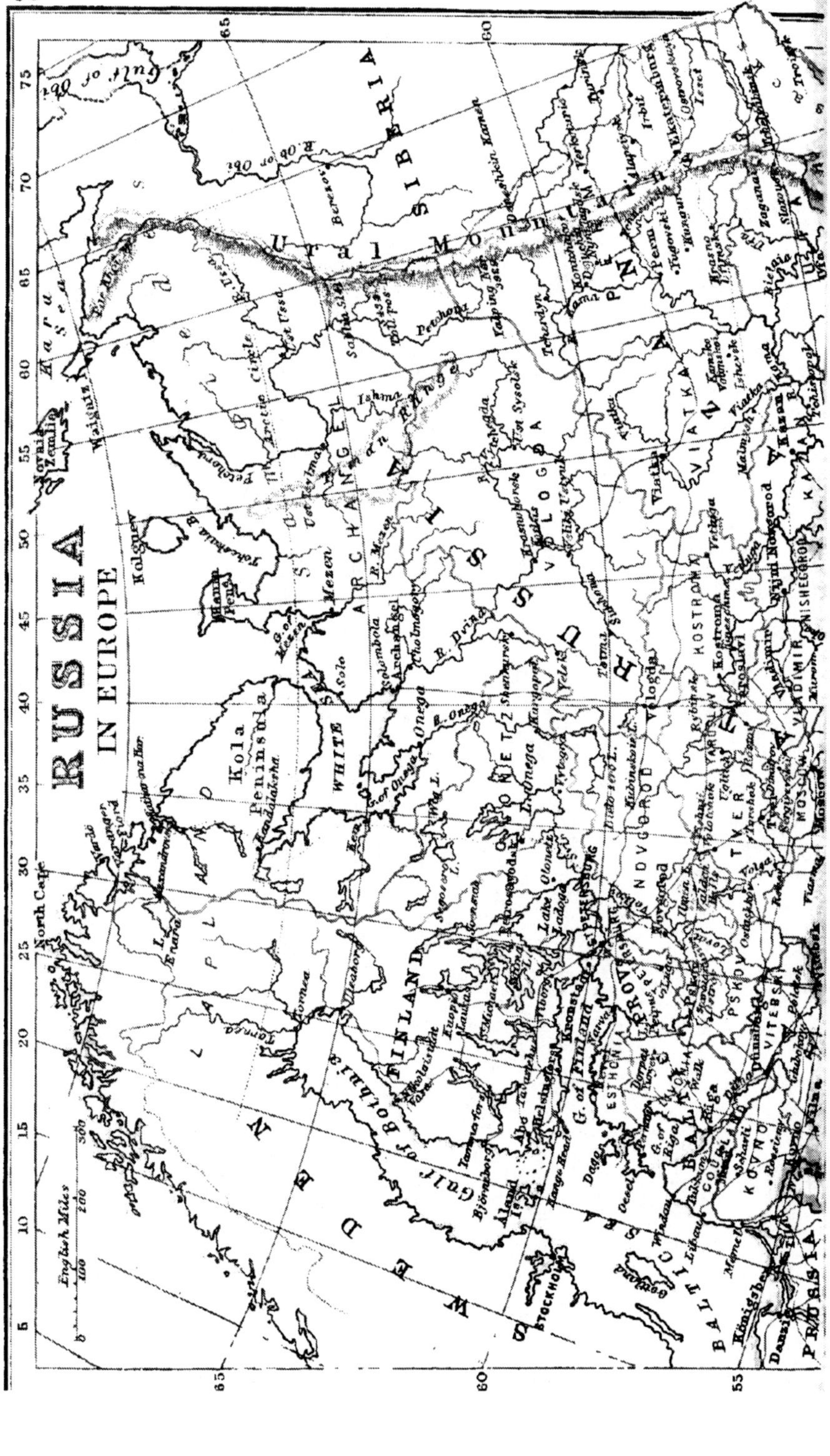
RUSSIA
IN EUROPE

BLACK SEA
CASPIAN SEA
Sea of Azov
SOUTH RUSSIA
CAUCASIA
ASIA MINOR
ROUMANIA
BULGARIA
TURKEY
AUSTRIA HUNGARY
POLAND
TRANSCASPIAN TERRITORY
Ust Urt plateau
URALSK
ASTRAKHAN
DON COSSACKS
KHERSON
Odessa
Kiev
Astrakhan
Constantinople
Trebizond
Baku

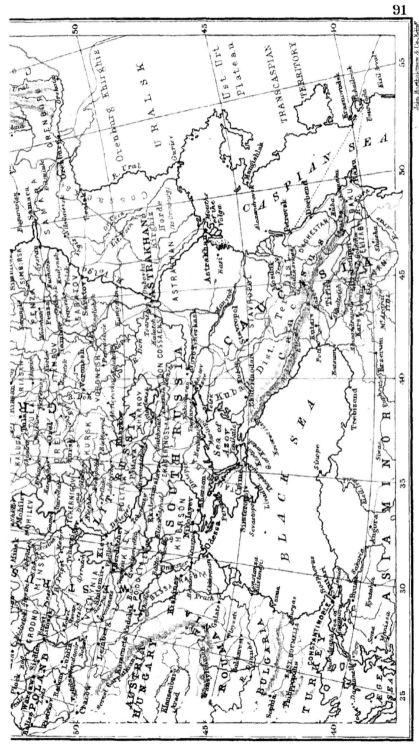

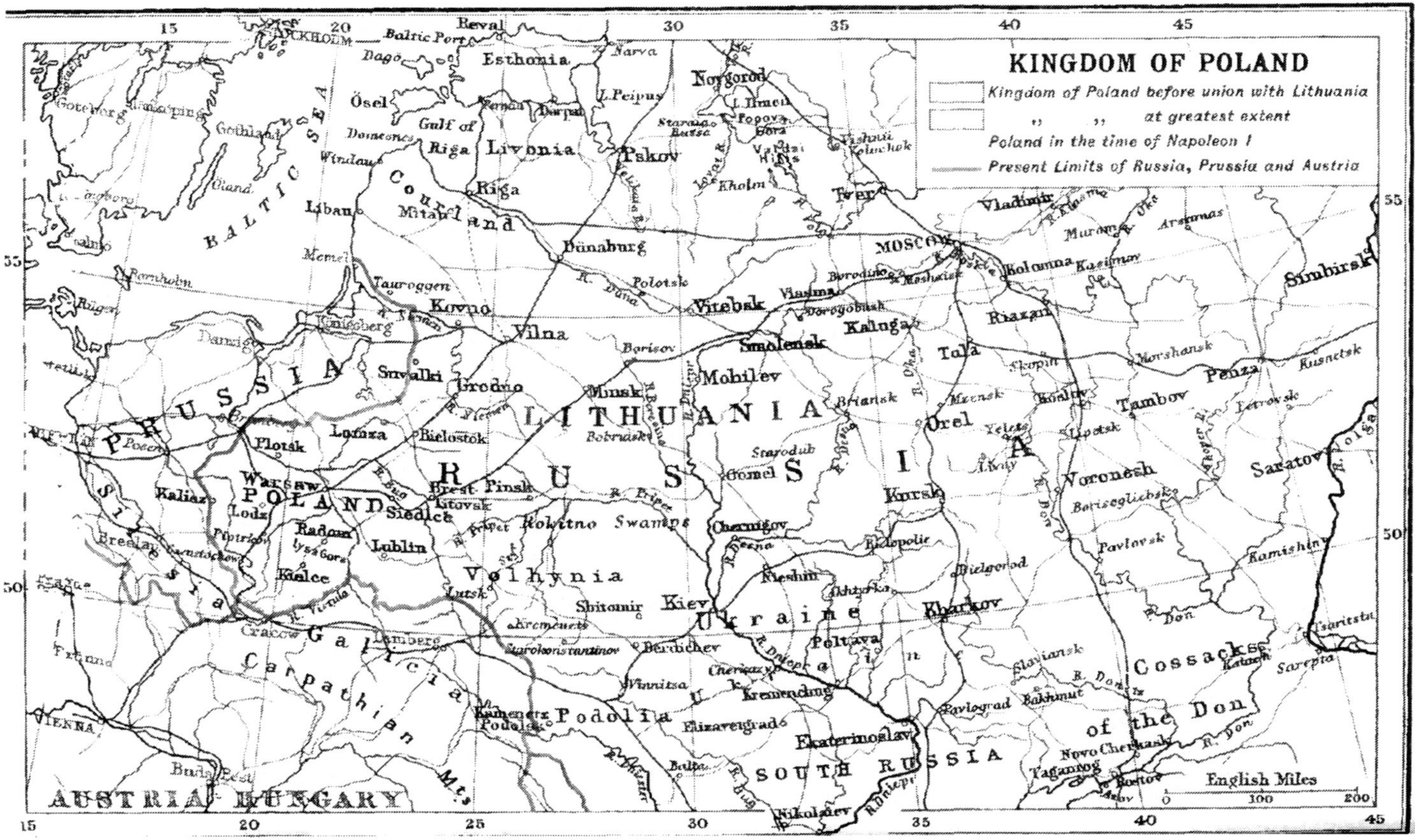
KINGDOM OF POLAND
Kingdom of Poland before union with Lithuania
" " at greatest extent
Poland in the time of Napoleon I
Present Limits of Russia, Prussia and Austria
English Miles
BALTIC SEA
Esthonia
Livonia
Courland
Ösel
Dagö
Gulf of Riga
Riga
Reval
Baltic Port
Narva
L. Peipus
Pskov
Novgorod
L. Ilmen
Tver
Vladimir
MOSCOW
Kolomna
Riazan
Tula
Kaluga
Smolensk
Vitebsk
Dünaburg
Polotsk
Libau
Memel
Tauroggen
Kovno
Vilna
Grodno
Suvalki
Königsberg
Danzig
Lomza
Bielostok
Plotsk
Warsaw
POLAND
Lodz
Kalisz
Radom
Lublin
Kielce
Siedlce
Brest Litovsk
Pinsk
Minsk
Borisov
Mobilev
Gomel
LITHUANIA
RUSSIA
PRUSSIA
Posen
Breslau
Cracow
Galicia
Carpathian Mts.
Lemberg
Volhynia
Lutsk
Shitomir
Kiev
Ukraine
Berdichev
Winnitsa
Podolia
Kamenetz Podolsk
Poltava
Kremenchug
Ekaterinoslav
Elizavetgrad
Nikolaiev
SOUTH RUSSIA
Kharkov
Kursk
Orel
Briansk
Chernigov
Voronesh
Tambov
Penza
Simbirsk
Saratov
Cossacks of the Don
Novo Cherkask
Taganrog
Rostov
Sarepta
Slaviansk
Bakhmut
Pavlograd
AUSTRIA HUNGARY
VIENNA
Buda Pest

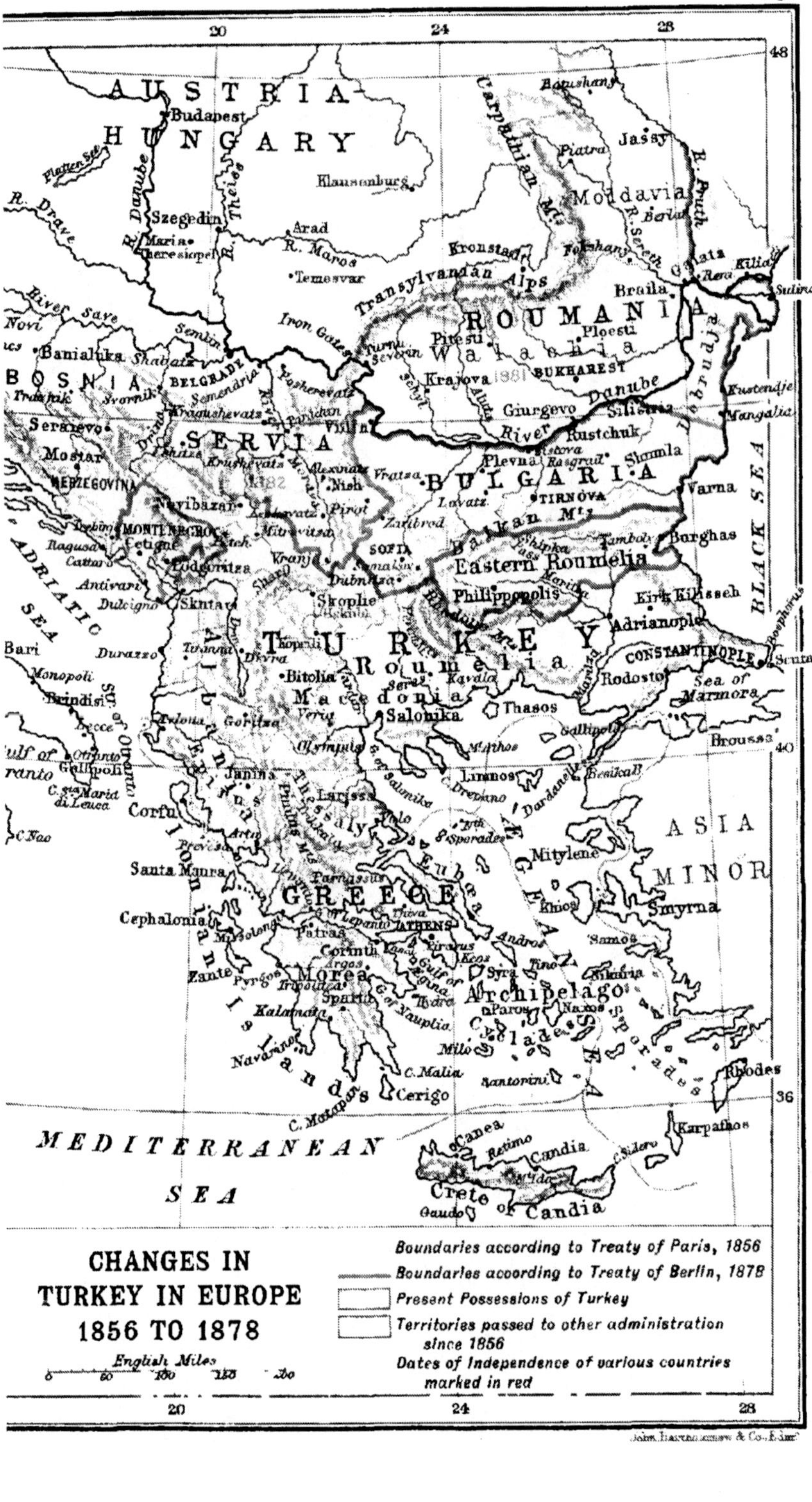
AUSTRIA
HUNGARY
Budapest
Szegedin
Arad
R. Maros
Temesvar
Klausenburg
Carpathian Mts
Jassy
Moldavia
R. Pruth
Kronstadt
Transylvanian Alps
Braila
Galatz
Sulina
ROUMANIA
Ploesti
Walachia
BUKHAREST
Giurgevo
Danube
Silistria
Rustchuk
Kustendje
Mangalia
Iron Gates
Semlin
Shabatz
BELGRADE
Semendria
Kragushevats
SERVIA
Nish
Pirot
Alexinatz
Vidin
BOSNIA
Banialuka
Seraievo
Mostar
HERZEGOVINA
Novibazar
MONTENEGRO
Cetigne
Ragusa
Cattaro
Podgoritza
Antivari
Dulcigno
Skutari
ADRIATIC SEA
Bari
Durazzo
Brindisi
Lecce
Otranto
Gallipoli
C. S. Maria di Leuca
Corfu
Santa Maura
Cephalonia
Zante
BULGARIA
Plevna
Lovatz
TIRNOVA
Shumla
Varna
Burghas
Balkan Mts
SOFIA
Eastern Roumelia
Philippopolis
Kirk Kilisseh
Adrianople
CONSTANTINOPLE
Bosphorus
Scutari
BLACK SEA
Skoplie
TURKEY
Roumelia
Bitolia
Macedonia
Salonika
Seres
Kavala
Thasos
Rodosto
Sea of Marmora
Brousa
Janina
Albania
Epirus
Larissa
Thessaly
Lemnos
Mitylene
Khios
Smyrna
ASIA MINOR
GREECE
Parnassus
ATHENS
Patras
Corinth
Argos
Tripolitza
Morea
Sparta
Kalamata
Navarino
Ionian Islands
Euboea
Andros
Syra
Tino
Naxos
Paros
Milo
Santorini
Archipelago
Cyclades
Sporades
Samos
Rhodes
Karpathos
Cerigo
C. Malia
C. Matapan
MEDITERRANEAN SEA
Canea
Retimo
Candia
Crete or Candia
Gaudo
C. Sidero
Boundaries according to Treaty of Paris, 1856
Boundaries according to Treaty of Berlin, 1878
Present Possessions of Turkey
Territories passed to other administration since 1856
Dates of Independence of various countries marked in red
English Miles
0 50 100 150 200
20
24
28
48
40
36
John Bartholomew & Co. Edin'

CHANGES IN TURKEY IN EUROPE 1856 TO 1878

AUSTRIA
HUNGARY
TRANSYLVANIA
MOLDAVIA
BESSARABIA
ROUMANIA
WALLACHIA
BULGARIA
EASTERN ROUMELIA
SERVIA
BOSNIA
HERZEGOVINA
MONTENEGRO
DALMATIA
SLAVONIA
BANAT
TURKEY
BLACK SEA
ADRIATIC SEA
Carpathian Mts
Dinaric Alps
BUDA PEST
River Danube
L. Balaton
Nagy Kanisza
Agram
Debreczin
Grosswardein
Szegedin
Temesvar
Maria Theresiopel
Zombor
Klausenburg
Hermanstadt
Kronstadt
Jassy
Kishenev
Galatz
Kilia
BUKHAREST
Ploesti
Krajova
BELGRADE
Semendria
Widin
Nish
SOFIA
Philippopolis
Adrianople
Kustendji
Varna
Shumla
Tirnova
Silistria
Rustchuk
Sistova
Nikopolis
Mostar
Serajevo
Cettinje
Cattaro
Ragusa
Skutari
Novibazar
Prisrend
Kostendil
Burgas
Midia
Temesvar
R. Pruth
R. Dniester
R. Drave or Drau
R. Save or Sau
R. Theiss
R. Szamos
R. Maros
R. Iskr
R. Timok
16
18
20
22
24
26
28
30
46
44
42

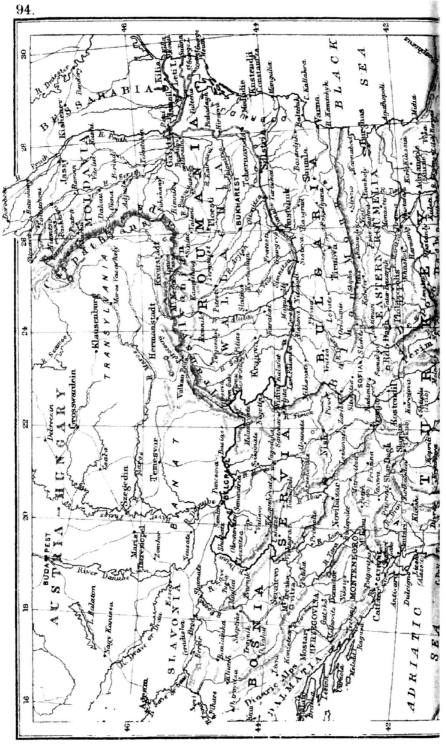

BALKAN STATES
English Miles
0 20 40 60 80 100 120 140 160
GREECE
THESSALY
EPIRUS
MOREA
ATHENS
Corinth
IONIAN SEA
MEDITERRANEAN SEA
ÆGEAN SEA
Grecian Archipelago
ASIA MINOR
SMYRNA
CRETE OR CANDIA
Cyclades
Southern Sporades
Northern Sporades
Strait of Otranto
Gulf of Taranto
SEA OF MARMORA
Brindisi
Taranto
Otranto
Corfu
Cephalonia
Zakynthos (Zante)
Santa Maura
Cerigo
Rhodes
Samos
Khios
Mitylene
Imbros
Limnos
Samothraki
Thasos
Andros
Milos
Thera (Santorin)
Euboea, Egripos or Negropont
Gallipoli
Salonica
Mt. Athos
Pindus
Broussa
John Bartholomew & Co., Edin.

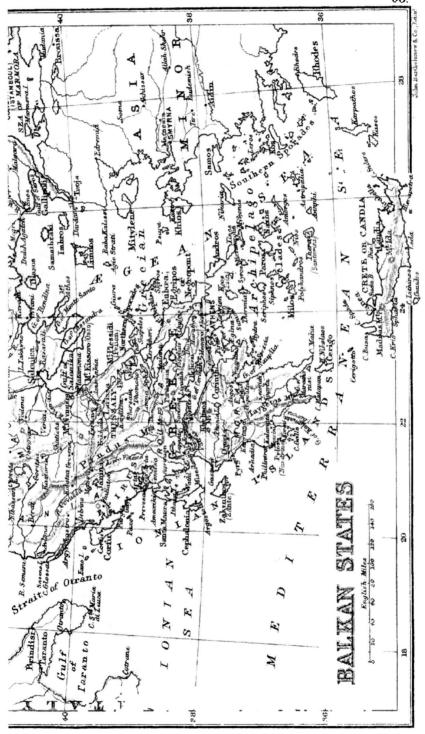

DENSITY OF POPULATION
Persons per square mile
Under 64
64 to 128
128 to 192
192 to 256
256 to 384
384 to 512
Above 512
Towns over 1,000,000 inhabitants
500,000
100,000
all smaller towns omitted
North Sea
Black Sea
Adriatic Sea
Bay of Biscay
English Channel

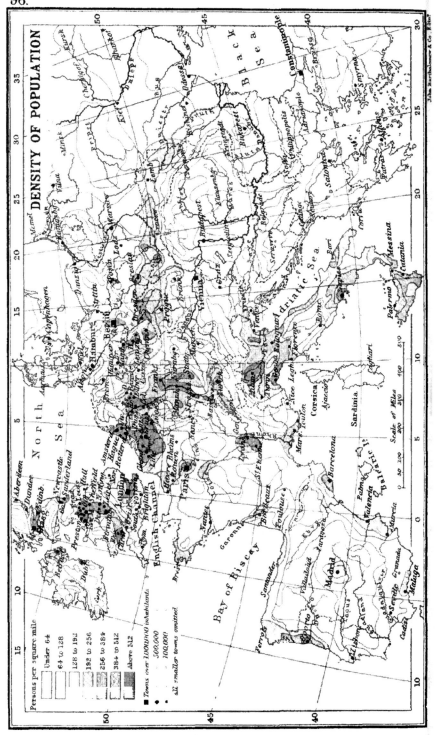

A

BRIEF SURVEY

OF THE

ENGLISH COINAGE

FROM THE

EARLIEST TIMES

TO THE

PRESENT DAY

PLATE I.

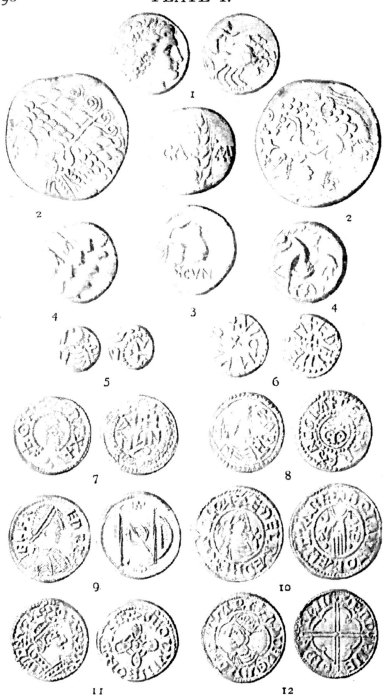

A BRIEF SURVEY

OF THE

ENGLISH COINAGE

FROM THE EARLIEST TIMES TO THE PRESENT DAY

By BERNARD ROTH, F.S.A.

*Vice-President of British Numismatic Society and Member of
Council of Royal Numismatic Society.*

THE ancient Britons were intimately related to their
neighbours the Gauls on the other side of the English
Channel, and through them early obtained a knowledge of
a well-designed coinage, chiefly of gold, which was minted
for nearly 250 years. According to Sir John Evans, the
gold uninscribed coins of the south coast were probably
first issued between 200 and 150 B.C. These gold coins
are usually described as staters, because they are degenerate
copies of the beautifully executed gold staters of Philip II.,
King of Macedon, father of Alexander the Great (B.C.
382-336).

Fig. I., Plate I., is a gold stater of that king; on the
obverse, i.e., the more important side, of the coin, which
usually carries the king's head or the chief symbol, is a
laureate head of Apollo or Hercules looking to the right;
on the other side (*reverse*) is a charioteer in a biga, or two-
horsed chariot, with two wheels.

Fig. II., Plate I., is an ancient British gold coin of about
B.C. 150, which is a barbarous copy of the perfect Greek art
seen in Fig. I. On the obverse is a large head to the left
with extremely ornate hair, etc., while on the reverse is a
very disjointed horse with the remnants of a winged
charioteer.

Fig. III., Plate I., is a fine specimen of a later ancient
British inscribed coin of Cunobelinus (Shakespeare's Cymbeline), a British king who flourished about A.D. 5: his

99

capital was Camulodonum, on the site of which is modern
Colchester. On the obverse is a horse with CVNO below,
and on the reverse is an ear of wheat with CA MV on either
side. The latest and most barbarously designed ancient
British coins were those of the Brigantes, a tribe who in-
habited Yorkshire, Lancashire, and other northern counties.
Some years before their conquest by the Romans in A D. 69,
their queen was Cartismandua, who is said to have treacher-
ously delivered up to the invaders Caractacus who had
taken refuge in her court.

Fig IV, Plate I, is a gold stater of the Brigantes, in
which it is still possible to find some distant resemblance to
the design on Philip's coin. On the obverse there are remains of the wreath with locks of hair, but it is difficult to
picture any likeness to a face. These ancient Britons were
far more civilised than many historians have described them
to be. I have several contemporary forgeries of ancient
British staters in my collection. They consist of copper
covered with a thin plating of gold: a high degree of
mechanical skill was required to produce such a forged coin.

For several centuries after the Roman invasion all traces
of a native coinage disappear till we come to the period of
the Sceats and Stycas The sceats were the earliest Saxon
coins struck in England, and were chiefly in silver, although
gold specimens are known.

Fig. V, Plate I., is a gold sceat which is supposed to have
been struck by Abbo, a Frankish moneyer who accompanied
St Augustine to England in A.D. 596: on the obverse is a
rude bust to the left with E behind, on the reverse traces
of letters around a dotted inner border enclosing a large
H-shaped ornament in centre, with letters above and
below. The stycas resemble the sceats, but are usually of
very base silver or copper

Fig. VI., Plate I., is a copper styca of Vigmund, Archbishop of York (A.D 837-854). The silver penny or, as it
was called in early days, the *novus denarius* was of Frankish
origin, and was first struck by Pepin the Short in 755. This
coin rapidly became popular all over Europe, and drove out,
not only the up to then current Roman coins, but also the
sceats and the stycas. Offa, King of Mercia (A.D. 757-796),
was the first English prince to strike silver pennies, and all
his coins are of beautiful types.

Fig. VII., Plate I., is a silver penny of King Offa, while Fig. VIII., Plate I., is one of his widowed queen, Cynethryth, who reigned for one year after his death   Contrary to the almost universal custom, the queen's name is on the reverse of the coin, while the name of the mint master, or moneyer, EOBA, is on the obverse, in front of the queen's bust.   For many centuries the silver penny was the only current English coin, and when smaller change was required it was cut into halves and quarters to form halfpennies and farthings, an operation which was often helped by the large cross on the reverse.

Fig. IX , Plate I., is a penny of Alfred the Great (871-901), with the monogram of London on the reverse: the portrait of the king on the obverse is fairly good, but the whole coin is far inferior in execution to those of King Offa and his queen.   Aethelred II. (979-1016) struck a large number of different types; one of the most interesting of his pennies is shown in Fig X., Plate I., with the king's head on the obverse and the so-called hand of Providence between Λ and ω descending from the clouds on the reverse.   Our Danish King Canute (1016-1035) issued a number of different pennies, of which Fig. XI., Plate I., is one which was minted at Dover.   Fig. XII., Plate I., is a penny of Harold I. (1035-1040), and Fig. XIII., Plate II , a penny of Harthacnut (1040-1042).   Silver pennies of Edward the Confessor (1042-1066) were struck in upwards of sixty different English towns, and are of various types.   Fig. XIV , Plate II., represents his " sovereign " type.   On the obverse the king is seen sitting on his throne, holding the sceptre in the right hand and the orb in the left; on the reverse we have what is termed a short cross voided with a martlet (bird) in each of the four quarters: this has usually been described as the Confessor's arms.   Harold II. (1066), although he reigned only a few months, struck some coins of which Fig. XV., Plate II., represents a penny, with the king's head to the left with the sceptre in front; on the reverse we find PAX (Peace) across the coin, which is rather incongruous, seeing he met his death so soon after at the Battle of Hastings.   William the Conqueror (1066-1087) struck pennies with a good portrait of himself, of which Fig. XVI., Plate II., is a fine specimen: it is usually termed the bonnet type, owing to the curious head dress or crown

PLATE II.

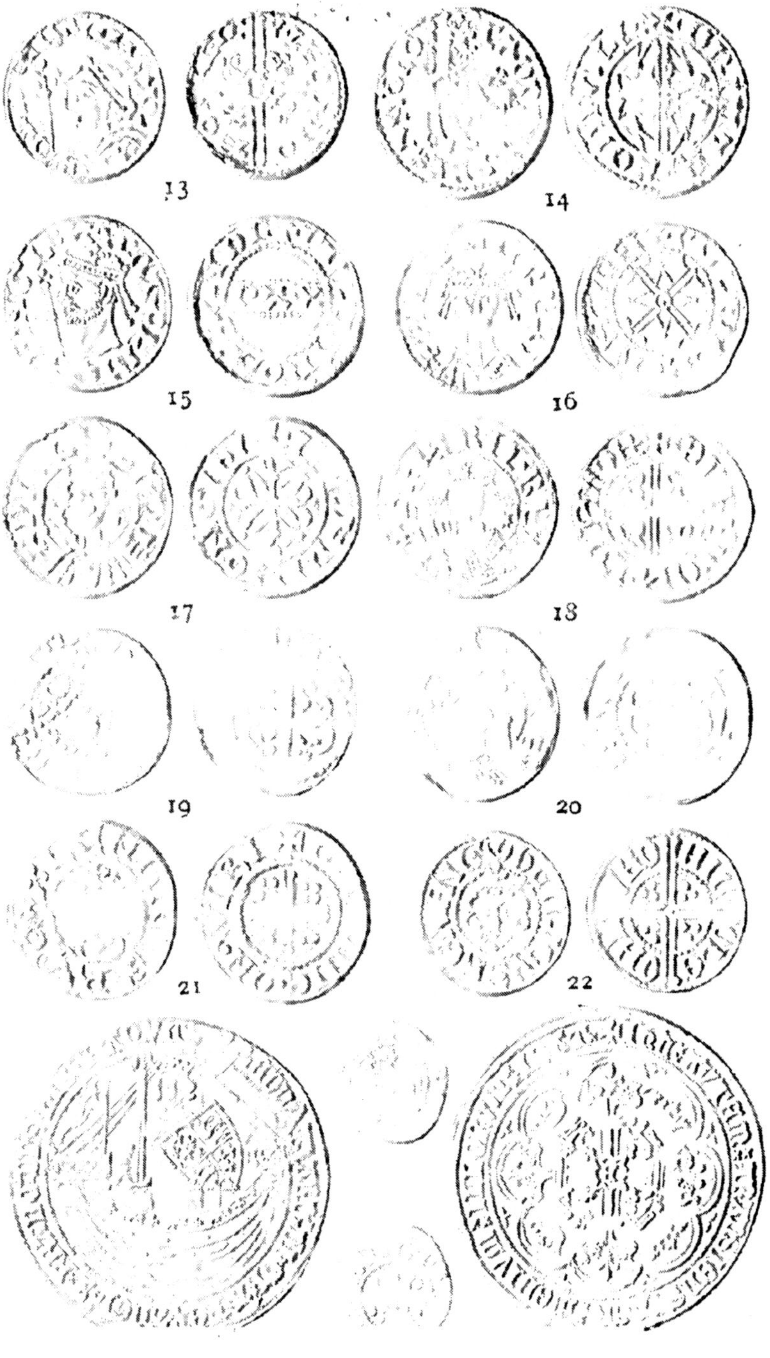

13
14
15
16
17
18
19
20
21
22
24
23
24

on the king's head   William Rufus (1087-1100) did not
vary much the coins of his father, and Fig. XVII., Plate II.,
represents a penny of his struck at Ipswich.

Henry I. (1100-1135) struck several types, of which
Fig. XVIII., Plate II., minted at London, is an interesting
specimen.   Stephen's troubled reign (1135-1154) is reflected
by the clumsy and badly struck pennies of his coinage.
One rarely ever meets with a well struck and round coin of
this king.   Fig. XIX , Plate II., is a Stephen penny struck
at Gloucester.   The Empress Matilda, daughter of Henry I.,
was Queen of England for a year during this reign, and
struck coins in several towns.

Fig. XX., Plate II., represents what is considered a fine
specimen of a Matilda penny.   In spite of the bad execution
of the coins of Stephen and Matilda, the silver employed
was not debased.   Henry II. (1154-1189), after his first
issue, struck the " short cross " penny, of which Fig. XXI.,
Plate II., is a specimen minted at Worcester.   This same
" short cross " penny was struck without alteration of type
and with the same name, Henricus, during the succeeding
reigns of Richard I. (1189-1199) and John (1199-1216), and
was continued unchanged during the greater portion of the
reign of Henry III. (1216-1272), till the year 1248, when
the " long cross " penny was struck: in this, the voided or
double-lined cross on the reverse extends to the margin of
the coin instead of only to the inner circle, as in the short
cross variety.   This king also added the numerals III. (or
the Latin equivalent) after his name, to distinguish himself
from his predecessors, the first time this device was employed in the English coinage (*see* Fig. XXII., Plate II.,
which is a long cross penny of Henry III.).

Edward I. (1272-1307) coined for the first time halfpennies
and farthings, instead of having pennies cut into halves
and quarters, as had been the custom till that time.   Fig.
XXIII., Plate II., is a farthing struck at York.   The coinage
of Edward II. (1307-1327) is so similar to that of Edward I.
that even experts differ amongst themselves as to whom they
should be assigned.   Edward III. (1327-1377) made several
important innovations: he not only issued a gold coinage,
but also larger silver coins, viz., groats (fourpence) and
half groats (twopence); his second gold coinage was the
Noble, shown in Fig. XXIV., Plate II.   This beautiful

PLATE III.

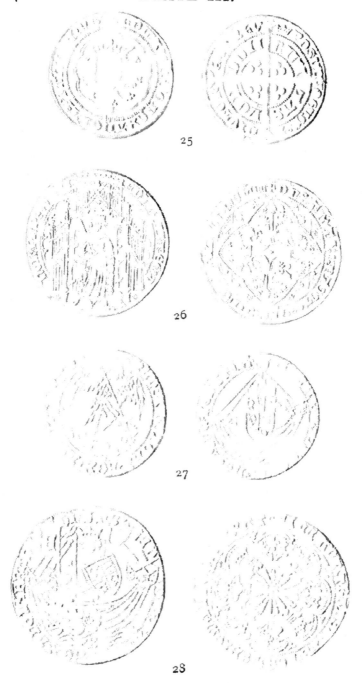

25

26

27

28

work of art was current for six shillings and eightpence
On the obverse the king standing in the ship, is supposed
to refer to the victory over the French fleet off Sluys in
1340. Fig. XXV., Plate III., is a groat of Edward III.
During this king's reign there was a great expansion of the
Norman possessions of the English crown, with a corre-
sponding increase in the output of Anglo-Gallic coins.
Fig. XXVI., Plate III., is a gold Pavillon or Royal d'Or of
his son, Edward the Black Prince. It is interesting to note
that there are four ostrich feathers on the obverse of the
coin, two on each side of the bust of that prince.

Richard II. (1377-1399) and Henry IV. (1399-1413),
Henry V. (1413-1422) and Henry VI. (1422-1461), made
little changes in the coinages, except that the last king
struck two new coins, the angel and half angel. Fig.
XXVII., Plate III., is the angel, which was current for six
shillings and eightpence. On the obverse is the Archangel
St. Michael piercing the dragon, and on the reverse a ship to
the right with the mast shaped like a cross, surmounted
by a top castle.

Edward IV (1461-1483) issued one new coin, the rose
noble, shown in Fig. XXVIII., Plate III., which differs from
the noble by having the rose on the side of the ship and in
the centre of the reverse. Rose nobles were not only struck
at the Tower, but also at Bristol, Coventry, York (Eboracum), and Norwich, and to distinguish these several mints
the initial letter of the town was placed on the waves below
the ship: thus in the rose noble figured there is a B for
Bristol. The coins of Edward V. (1483) were exactly like
his father's, and are only to be distinguished by their mint
marks. Richard III. (1483-1485) had no distinguishing
coins.

Henry VII. (1485-1509) struck a very fine new gold coin,
the sovereign, double the weight of the noble, viz, 240
grains, and was current for twenty shillings: it is shown in
Fig. XXIX., Plate IV. This same king also issued the
first shilling or testoon. Henry VIII. (1509-1547) struck
two new gold coins, the gold crown and the gold George
noble, which were current for five shillings, and six shillings
and eightpence respectively. Fig. XXX., Plate IV., is the
crown and Fig. XXXI., Plate IV., the George noble, which
has on the reverse St. George in armour on horseback and

PLATE IV.

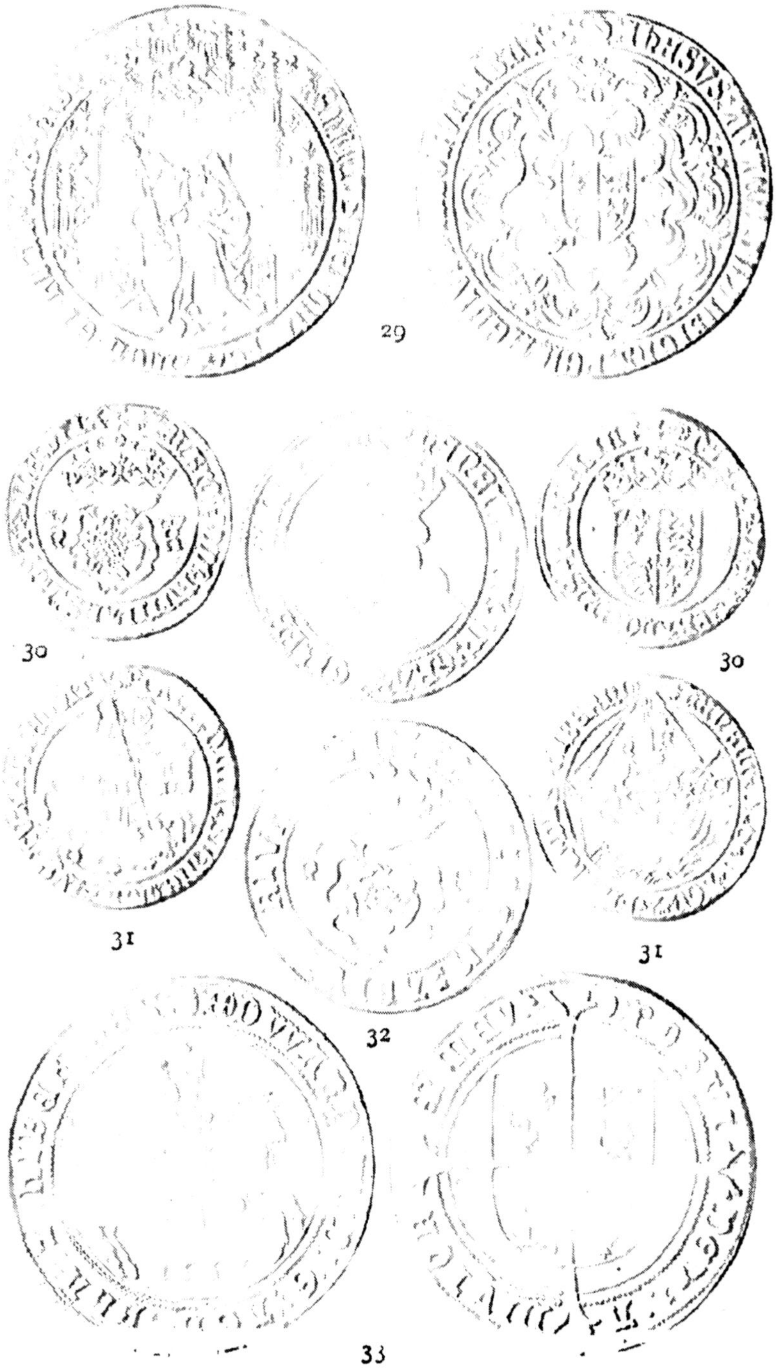

29

30 30

31 31

32

33

PLATE V. 107

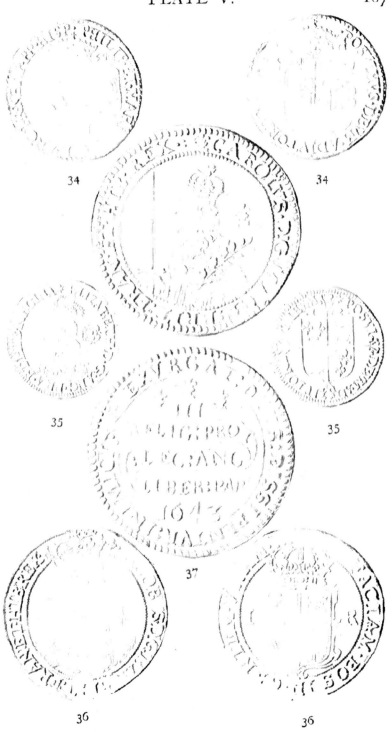

piercing the dragon. The shilling or testoon (Fig. XXXII., Plate IV.) gives a good portrait of the king.

Edward VI (1547-1553) struck the first silver crown, shown in Fig XXXIII., Plate IV. Mary (1553-1558), after her marriage with Philip II. of Spain, struck coins with the portrait of her husband as well as of herself, as seen in the shilling (Fig. XXXIV., Plate V.). The Spanish king's name is invariably placed first, before that of the English queen.

Elizabeth (1558-1603) issued a dated sixpence yearly for upwards of forty years, and Fig. XXXV., Plate V., is a milled sixpence of the year 1562: her dress is very ornate, as is the rule on all her coins.

When James VI. of Scotland became James I of England (1603-1625) he struck several coins to symbolise the union of the kingdoms. Fig XXXVI., Plate V , is the gold unite or sovereign. The reverse legend—" Faciam eos in gentem unam "—is from Ezekiel xxxvii. 22, " *I will make them one nation* in the land upon the mountains of Israel; and one king shall be king to them all: and they shall be no more two nations, neither shall they be divided into two kingdoms any more."

Charles I.'s troubled and tragic reign (1625-1649) produced innumerable new coins. While at Oxford, the gold three-pound piece (Fig. XXXVII., Plate V.) and the silver pound or twenty-shilling piece (Fig. XXXVIII., Plate VI.) were made out of the melted-down plate of the Oxford colleges. Amongst the many siege pieces of this reign, the shilling of Pontefract Castle (Fig. XXXIX., Plate VI) is very typical.

The Commonwealth coinage (1649-1660) is remarkable in having all the legends in good honest English instead of in Latin, and Fig XL., Plate VI., represents the gold broad or twenty-shilling piece. Oliver Cromwell (1653-1658) had some coins struck with his portrait, but it is doubtful whether they were ever in circulation. The crown, by Thomas Simon (Fig. XLI., Plate VII), is a fine work of art.

Charles II. (1660-1685) gave us the first five-guinea piece (Fig. XLII., Plate VII) His example was followed by James II. (1685-1688), William and Mary (1689-1694) (*see* Fig XLIII., Plate VII.), William (1694-1702), Anne (1702-1714), and the first two Georges (1714-1760).

George III. (1760-1820) was the last king to issue the

PLATE VI. 109

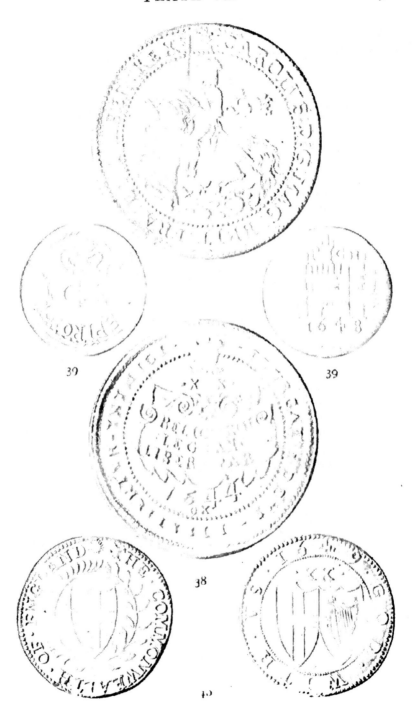

39   39

38

40

PLATE VII.

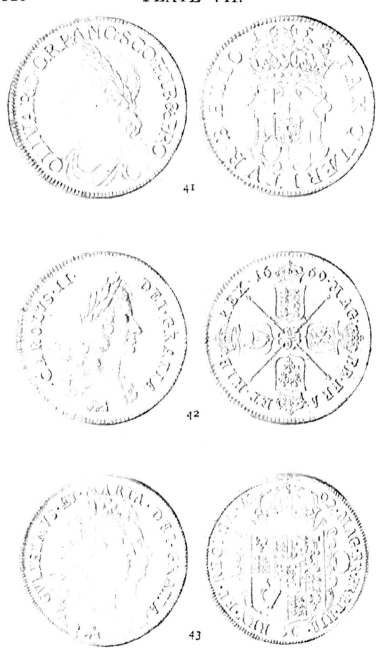

41

42

43

PLATE VIII.   III

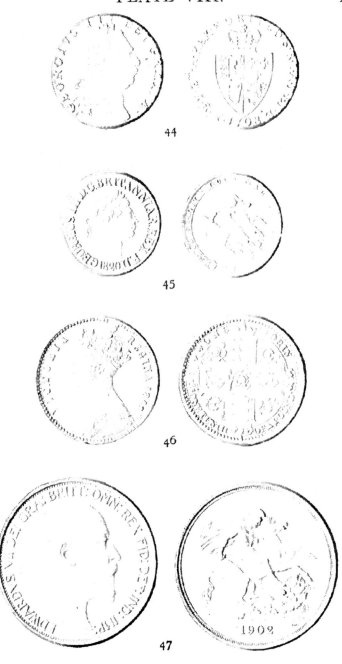

44

45

46

47

guinea, of which the spade variety (Fig. XLIV., Plate VIII)
is well known.   The modern sovereign of twenty shillings
was first struck by this king (Fig. XLV., Plate VIII.).

The coinages of George IV. (1820-1830) and William IV.
(1830-1837) have no new features.

Queen Victoria (1837-1901) issued two new silver coins,
the double florin of four shillings and the florin of two
shillings.   The first florin (Fig XLVI , Plate VIII.) was
issued in 1849, and as the words " Dei Gratia " were
omitted, it is known as the " godless or graceless florin."

Edward VII. (1901-1910) issued the same coins as his
mother, from the five-pound piece down to the farthing,
with the exception of the double florin. Fig. XLVII.,
Plate VIII., is his five-pound piece.

All the illustrations are from photographs of casts taken
from coins in the author's collection.

MAPS AND PLANS

OF

NOTABLE BATTLES AND DISTRICTS

CONNECTED WITH

FAMOUS AUTHORS AND THEIR BOOKS

PLANS OF CLASSICAL AND OTHER BATTLES DESCRIBED BY CREASY IN "FIFTEEN DECISIVE BATTLES OF THE WORLD"

ARMY UNDER GEN DATIS
100,000 Infantry
10,000 Cavalry
Trees felled by Greeks
Trees felled by Greeks
GREEK ATTACK
Athenians 9000 Men
Platœans 1000 Men
ARMY UNDER MILTIADES
First Position
BATTLE OF MARATHON
29th September 490 B.C.
Greeks
Persians

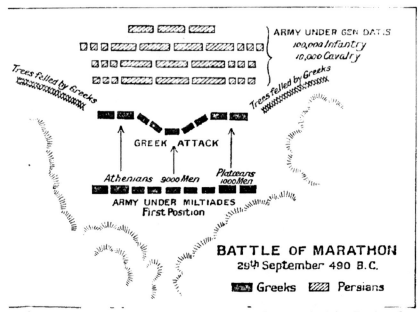

See Grote's " History of Greece." Creasy's " Fifteen Decisive Battles of the World." Rawlinson's " Herodotus," etc., etc.

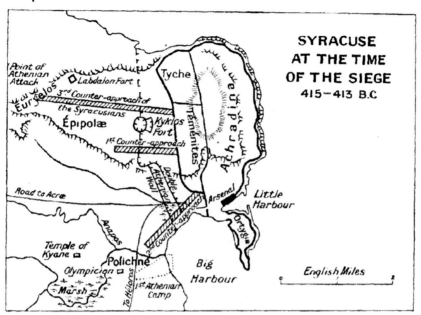

SYRACUSE
AT THE TIME
OF THE SIEGE
415–413 B.C
Point of Athenian Attach
Labdalon Fort
Euryelos
3rd Counter-approach of the Syracusians
Epipolæ
Kyklos Fort
1st Counter-approach
Tyche
Temenites
Achradina
Athenian Double Wall
Road to Acræ
Arsenal
Little Harbour
Ortygia
2nd Counter-approach
Anapos
Temple of Kyane
Polichne
Olympicion
Marsh
To Heloros
1st Athenian Camp
Big Harbour
English Miles

See Grote's "History of Greece." Creasy's "Fifteen Decisive Battles of the World," etc., etc.

Chariots
BATTLE OF
ARBELA
Alexander
Darius
Baggage
Brumeltus Fl
Hazir R

See Grote's "History of Greece." Creasy's "Fifteen Decisive Battles of the World," etc., etc.

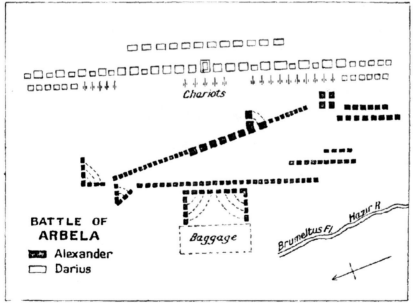

Retreat of Cavalry
CARTHAGINIAN ARMY UNDER ASDRUBAL
Infantry
Cavalry
Spaniards
Ligurians
Gauls
Elephants
River Metaurus
Cavalry
Lightly armed Troops
Infantry
Infantry
ROMAN ARMY UNDER M. LIVIUS & CL. NERO
BATTLE OF METAURUS
208 B.C.

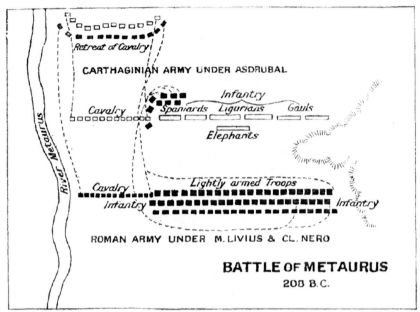

See Grote's "History of Greece." Creasy's "Fifteen Decisive Battles of the World," etc., etc.

BATTLEFIELD OF
ARMINIUS & VARUS
9 A.D.
Weser Fl.
Modern site of Detmold
Amisia Fl. (Ems)
Teutoburgiensis Saltus
Casia Sylva
Munitum
(Munster)
Lippia Fl. (Lippe)
Luppia (Lipstadt)
Aliso
(Elsen)
Germans
Romans
a Original Position of Combined Forces
b Varus advances & is attacked by Arminius

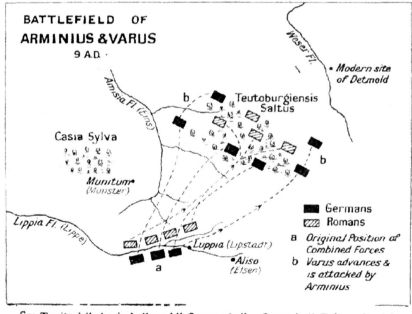

See Tacitus' "Agricola" and "Germania." Creasy's "Fifteen Decisive Battles of the World," etc., etc.

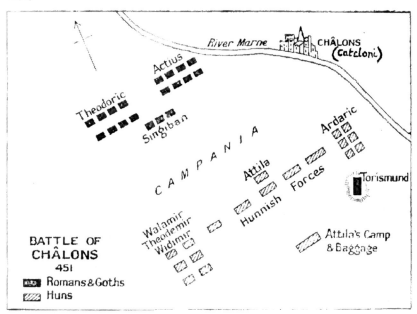

River Marne
CHÂLONS
(Catcloni)
Aetius
Theodoric
Singiban
CAMPANIA
Ardaric
Attila
Hunnish Forces
Torismund
Walamir
Theodemir
Widimir
Attila's Camp
& Baggage
BATTLE OF
CHÂLONS
451
Romans & Goths
Huns

See Gibbon's "Decline and Fall of the Roman Empire." Creasy's "Fifteen Decisive Battles of the World," etc., etc.

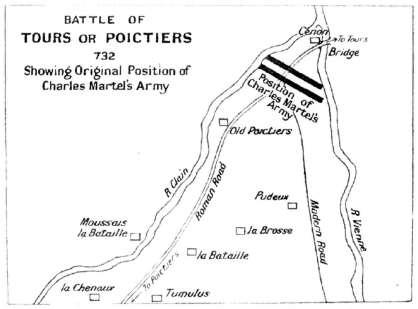

BATTLE OF
TOURS OR POICTIERS
732
Showing Original Position of
Charles Martel's Army
Cenon
To Tours
Bridge
Position of Charles Martel's Army
Old Poictiers
R. Clain
Roman Road
Pudeux
Modern Road
R. Vienne
Moussais la Bataille
la Brosse
la Bataille
To Poictiers
la Chenaux
Tumulus

See Gibbon's "Decline and Fall of the Roman Empire." Creasy's "Fifteen Decisive Battles of the World," etc., etc.

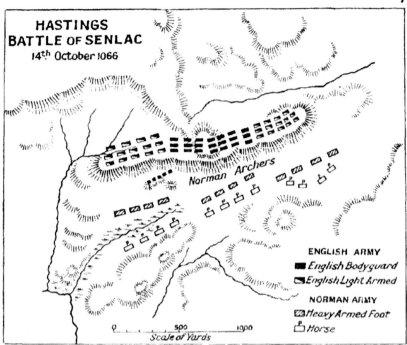

HASTINGS
BATTLE OF SENLAC
14th October 1066

Norman Archers

ENGLISH ARMY
█ English Bodyguard
▭ English Light Armed
NORMAN ARMY
▨ Heavy Armed Foot
♙ Horse

0   500   1000
Scale of Yards

See Thierry's " Norman Conquest."   Lytton's " Harold."   Creasy's " Fifteen Decisive Battles of the World," etc., etc.

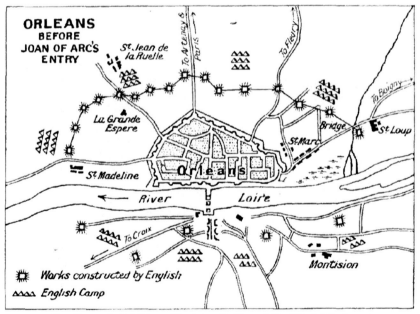

ORLEANS
BEFORE
JOAN OF ARC'S
ENTRY

St. Jean de
la Ruelle.

To Artenay &
Paris

To Fleury

To Bugny

La Grande
Espere

Bridge

St. Marc

St. Loup

St. Madeline

Orleans

River   Loire

To Croix

Montision

✦ Works constructed by English
▲▲▲▲ English Camp

See Creasy's " Fifteen Decisive Battles of the World," etc., etc.

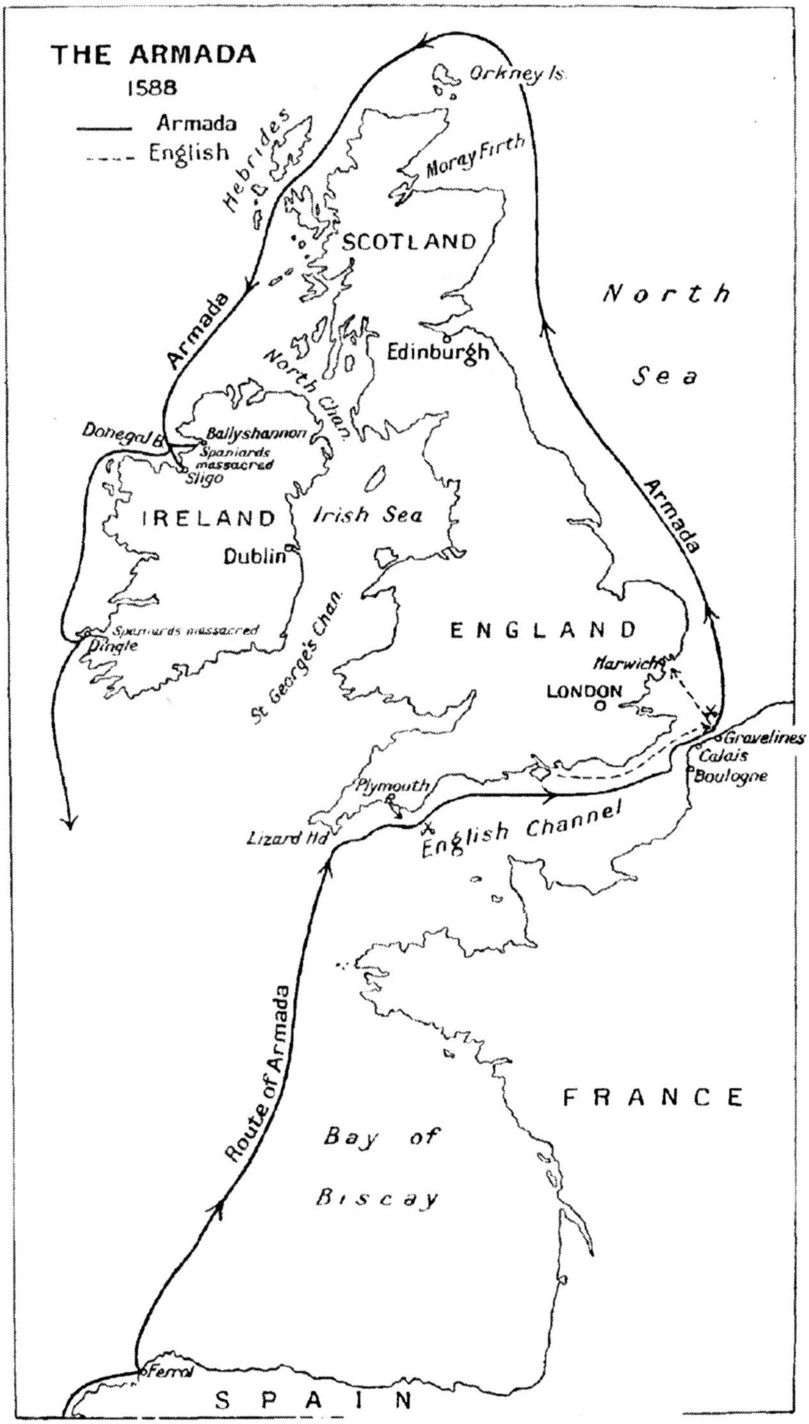
THE ARMADA
1588
Armada
English
Orkney Is.
Hebrides
Moray Firth
SCOTLAND
North
Sea
Armada
North Chan.
Edinburgh
Donegal B.
Ballyshannon
Spaniards massacred
Sligo
IRELAND
Irish Sea
Dublin
Armada
St George's Chan.
Spaniards massacred
Dingle
ENGLAND
Harwich
LONDON
Gravelines
Calais
Boulogne
Plymouth
Lizard Hd
English Channel
FRANCE
Route of Armada
Bay of
Biscay
Ferrol
SPAIN

See Strickland's "Life of Queen Elizabeth." Kingsley's "Westward Ho!"

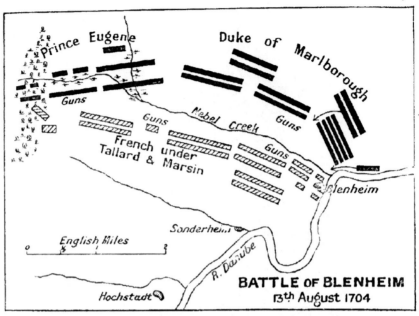

Prince Eugene
Duke of Marlborough
Guns
Guns
Nebel Creek
Guns
French under
Tallard & Marsin
Guns
Blenheim
Sonderheim
English Miles
R. Danube
Hochstadt
BATTLE OF BLENHEIM
13th August 1704

See Thackeray's "Henry Esmond." Creasy's "Fifteen Decisive Battles of the World," etc., etc.

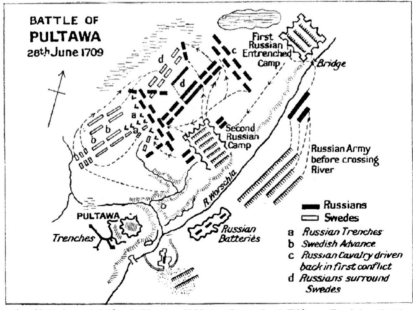

BATTLE OF
PULTAWA
28th June 1709
First
Russian
Entrenched
Camp
Bridge
Second
Russian
Camp
Russian Army
before crossing
River
R. Worschla
PULTAWA
Trenches
Russian
Batteries
Russians
Swedes
a Russian Trenches
b Swedish Advance
c Russian Cavalry driven back in first conflict
d Russians surround Swedes

See Voltaire's "Life of Charles XII." Creasy's "Fifteen Decisive Battles of the World," etc., etc.

VICTORY OF AMERICANS AT SARATOGA
1777
British
Americans
British Provision Boats
British Position
General Gates' Forces
Ford of the Fishkill
To Albany
Saratoga
Old Fort Hardy
Park Artillery
Landing Provisions
Hudson River
American Light Troops attacking British Provision Boats

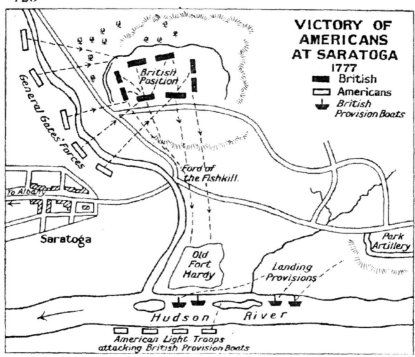

See Benjamin Franklin's "Autobiography." Creasy's "Fifteen Decisive Battles of the World," etc., etc.

BATTLE OF VALMY
20th September 1792
Maffrecourt
Hans
Somme Bionne
Valmy
Braux
To St Menehould
Donmartin
Dampierre
Gizacourt
To Châlons
R. Auve
Vailemont
Felcourt
R. Yevre
To Vitry
Prussians & Austrians
French

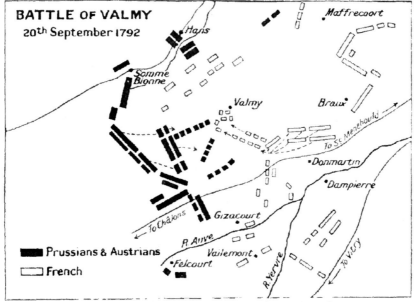

See Creasy's "Fifteen Decisive Battles of the World," etc., etc.

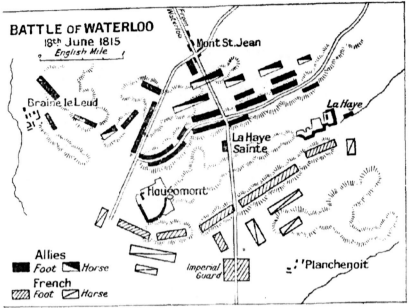

BATTLE OF WATERLOO
18th June 1815
English Mile
From Waterloo
Mont St. Jean
Braine le Leud
La Haye
La Haye Sainte
Hougomont
Allies
Foot
Horse
French
Foot
Horse
Imperial Guard
Planchenoit

See Gleig's "Life of Wellington." Creasy's "Fifteen Decisive Battles of the World," etc., etc.

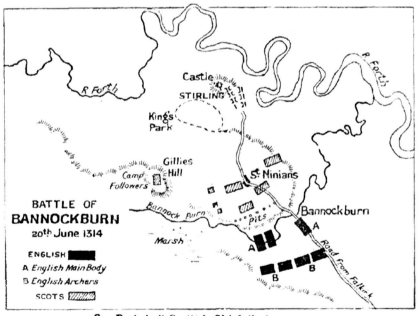

R Forth
R Forth
Castle
STIRLING
King's Park
Gillies Hill
Camp Followers
St Ninians
Bannock Burn
Pits
Bannockburn
Marsh
Road from Falkirk
A
A
B
B
BATTLE OF BANNOCKBURN
20th June 1314
ENGLISH
A English Main Body
B English Archers
SCOTS

See Porter's "Scottish Chiefs," etc., etc.

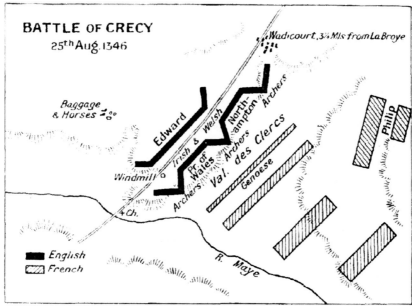

BATTLE OF CRECY
25th Aug. 1346
Wadicourt, 3½ Mls from La Broye
Baggage & Horses
Edward
Irish & Welsh
North-ampton
Archers
Pr. of Wales
Archers
Val. des Clercs
Genoese
Philip
Windmill
Archers
Ch.
R. Maye
English
French

See J. G. Edgar's "Cressy and Poictiers," etc., etc.

To Poictiers
King of France
Orleans
Dauphin
Cavalry
Hedge
Salisbury
Cavalry
Hedge
Warwick
Prince of Wales
Marshy Valley
Farm of Maupertuis
Beauvoir
BATTLE OF POICTIERS
19th Sept. 1356
½ Mile
English
French

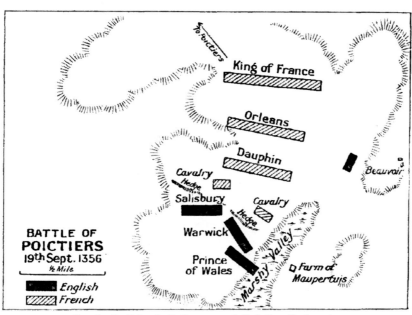

See J. G. Edgar's "Cressy and Poictiers," etc., etc.

BATTLES & SIEGES
OF THE
CIVIL WAR
1642 - 1651

Dunbar (Sept. 1650)

Philiphaugh
(Sept. 1645)

Marston Moor
(July 1644) •York *(Besieged June 1644)*

Bradford •

•*Preston* *Adwalton Moor*
(Sept. 1648) *(1643)* **Hull**

Gainsboro'
(July 1643)

Trent

•*Chester*
(Besieged 1645) •*Newark(Charles I surrenders to Scottish Army 1646)*
Nottingham
(Charles I sets up his Standard Aug 1642) •*Grantham*
(May 1643)

•*Shrewsbury*

•*Leicester*
(Seized by Charles 1645)

Severn •*Naseby (June 1645)*

•*Holmby Ho.(Charles I imprisoned 1648)*
•*Worcester* •*Northampton*
(Sept. 1651)
•*Ledbury* *Edgehill(1642)*
(April 1645)
Colchester
(Captured by Fairfax 1648)
Gloucester •*Woodstock*
(Besieged Aug to Sept 1643) *Oxford(Charles I Headquarters 1645)*
•*Chalgrove Field*
Thames *(June 1643)* *Brentford*
Uxbridge ●**LONDON**
Bristol (Besieged Sept 1645) •*Reading*
•*Roundway Down 1643*
•*Devizes* •*Newbury*
(Sept. 1643)
(Oct. 1644)
•*Bridgwater*
Langport
Parrett *(July 1645)*
• *Stratton*
(1643)
Carisbrooke Cas
(Charles I conveyed from Holmby House)

•*Plymouth*

See Carlyle's " Cromwell's Letters and Speeches." " Col. Hutchinson's
Memoirs." Scott's " Woodstock," etc., etc.

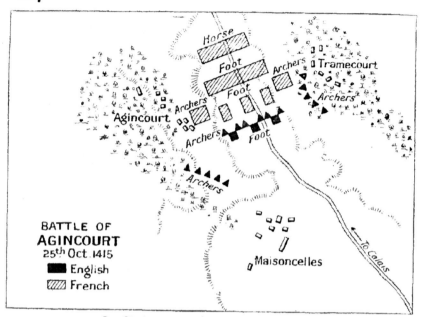

Horse
Foot
Foot
Archers
Tramecourt
Archers
Archers
Agincourt
Archers
Foot
Archers
BATTLE OF
AGINCOURT
25th Oct. 1415
English
French
Maisoncelles
To Calais

See Shakespeare's "Henry V.," etc., etc.

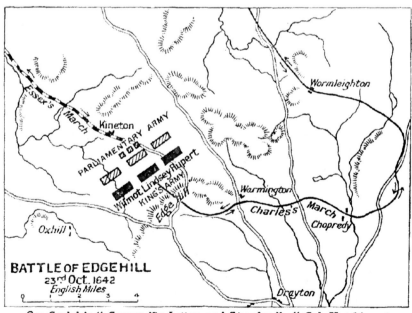

Wormleighton
Essex's March
Kineton
PARLIAMENTARY ARMY
Wilmot Lindsey Rupert
KING'S ARMY
Edge Hill
Warmington
Charles's March
Chopredy
Oxhill
BATTLE OF EDGEHILL
23rd Oct. 1642
English Miles
0 1 2 3 4
Drayton

See Carlyle's "Cromwell's Letters and Speeches." "Col. Hutchinson's Memoirs," etc., etc.

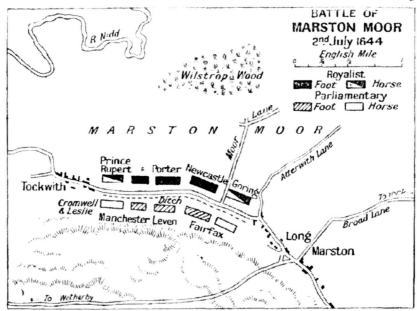

BATTLE OF
MARSTON MOOR
2nd July 1644
English Mile
Royalist
Foot
Horse
Parliamentary
Foot
Horse
R. Nidd
Wilstrop Wood
MARSTON MOOR
Lane
Moor
Atterwith Lane
Prince Rupert
Porter
Newcastle
Goring
Tockwith
Cromwell & Leslie
Ditch
Manchester
Leven
Fairfax
Long Marston
Broad Lane
To York
To Wetherby

See Carlyle's "Cromwell's Letters and Speeches." "Col. Hutchinson's Memoirs," etc., etc.

Reserve
Clipston
Rupert
Astley
Langdale
Broad Moor
Okey
Sulby Hedge
River Avon
Ireton
Skippon
Cromwell
Reserve
Mill Hill
BATTLE OF NASEBY
14th June 1645
English Mile
KING'S ARMY
Foot
Horse
PARLIAMENTARY ARMY
Foot
Horse
Baggage
Naseby

See Carlyle's "Cromwell's Letters and Speeches." "Col Hutchinson's Memoirs," etc., etc.

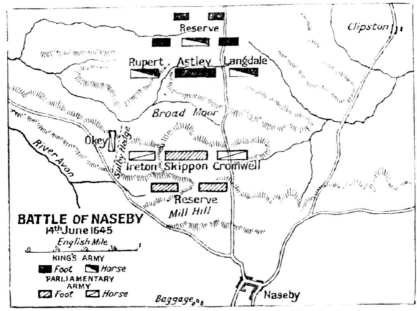

BATTLE OF DUNBAR
3rd Sept. 1650
English Mile
0
¼
½
¾
1
DUNBAR
Belhaven
Artillery
Spott Burn
ENGLISH
Foot
Horse
SCOTS
Foot
Horse

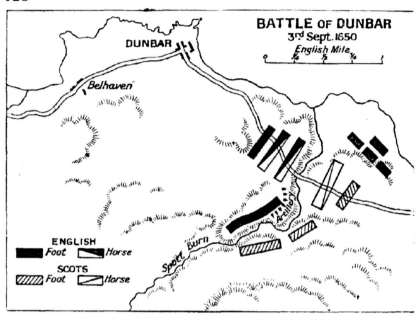

See Carlyle's "Cromwell's Letters and Speeches." "Col. Hutchinson's Memoirs," etc., etc.

Culloden aground
Nelson's Isle
Shoals
Wind
Shoals
Aboukir Castle
Village Cove
ABOUKIR BAY
BATTLE OF
THE NILE
1st August 1798
British Ships
French Ships
Fort

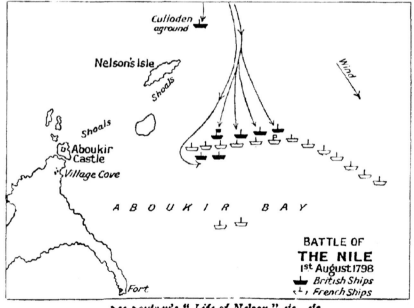

See Southey's "Life of Nelson," etc., etc.

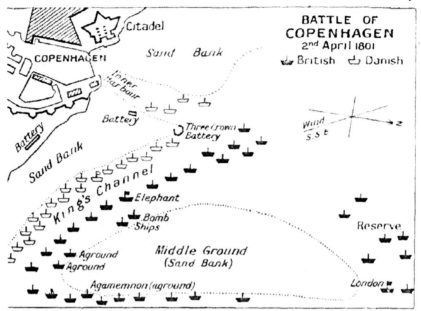

BATTLE OF
COPENHAGEN
2nd April 1801
British Danish
Citadel
COPENHAGEN
Sand Bank
Inner Harbour
Battery
Battery
Three Crown Battery
Wind S.S.E
Sand Bank
King's Channel
Elephant
Bomb Ships
Reserve
Middle Ground
(Sand Bank)
Aground
Aground
Agamemnon (aground)
London

See Southey's "Life of Nelson," etc., etc.

Téméraire
S Trinidad
Bucentaure
Victory
Redoutable
S. Anna
Royal Sovereign
Wind W.N.W
BATTLE OF
TRAFALGAR
21st October 1805
British Allies
Pr de Asturias

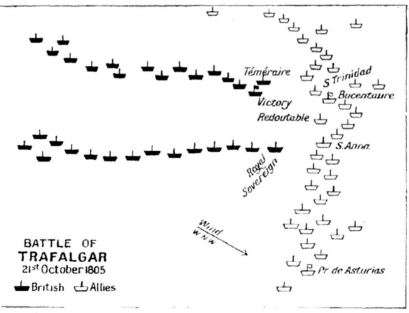

See Southey's "Life of Nelson," etc., etc.

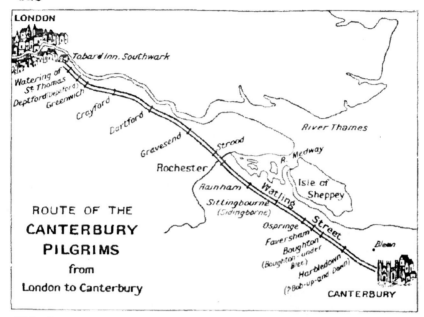

LONDON
Tabard Inn. Southwark
Watering of St Thomas
Deptford (Depeford)
Greenwich
Crayford
Dartford
Gravesend
Strood
Rochester
River Thames
R. Medway
Isle of Sheppey
Rainham
Watling Street
Sittingbourne (Sidingborne)
Ospringe
Faversham
Boughton (Boughton-under Blee)
Harbledown (? Bob-up-and-Down)
Blean
CANTERBURY
ROUTE OF THE
CANTERBURY
PILGRIMS
from
London to Canterbury

This shows only one of the pilgrims' routes to Canterbury, probably the one mentioned by Chaucer in his "Canterbury Tales." See also Stanley's "Memorials of Canterbury," etc., etc.

LAND OF BURNS
English Miles
0
2
4
6
8
Kilmarnock
Riccarton
R. Irvine
Cessnock W.
Lochlea
K Y L E
Mossgiel
Tarbolton
Mill
Mauchline
Muirkirk
Montgomerie
Ballochmyle
Catrine
AYR
R. Ayr (Sweet Afton)
Ochiltree
Lugar Water
Cumnock
Burns's Cottage
Alloway Kirk
Mount Oliphant
R. Nith
Afton Water
R. Doon
Dunaskin
Kirkoswald
Kilkerran

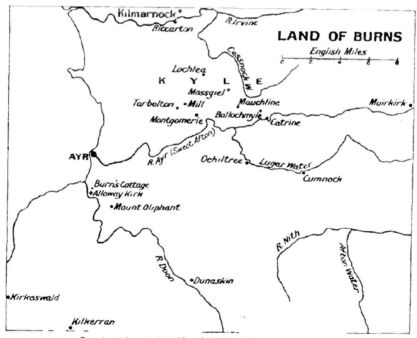

See Lockhart's "Life of Robert Burns," etc., etc.

LAND OF SCOTT
English Miles
0 2 4 6 8 10
Peebles
Cleikum Inn
Innerleithen (St Ronan's Well)
Black Dwarf's Cottage
Traquair Ho. (Tully Veolan)
Quair W
Elibank
Ashiestiel
Peel
Clovenfords
Galashiels
Abbotsford
Gala W.
Lauder
Leader W.
Allan W. (Glendearg)
Earlston
Smailholm
Darnick
Rhymer's Glen
Abbey
Melrose
(Kennquhair)
Dryburgh Abbey
Eildon Hills
Selkirk
Newark Cas.
Gordon Arms Inn
Yarrow W.
St Mary's Loch
Ettrick W
Ale W.
R Teviot
Jedburgh

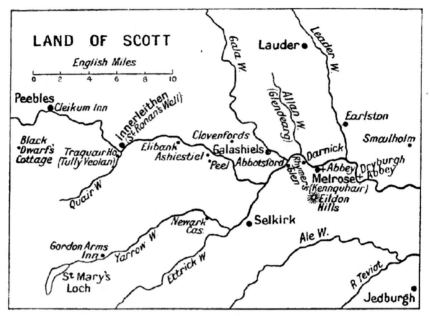

See Lockhart's "Life of Scott." The Waverley Novels. "Lady of the Lake," etc., etc.

"IVANHOE"
Cedric
Isaac
Brian de Bois-Guilbert
Jorvaulx Abbey
Ure
Fountains Abbey
York
Derwent
Ouse
Aire
Don
Rotherwood
Coningsburgh
Mersey
Sheffield
Torquilstone
Harthill Walk
Templestowe
Trent
Burton on Trent
Ashby de la Zouch

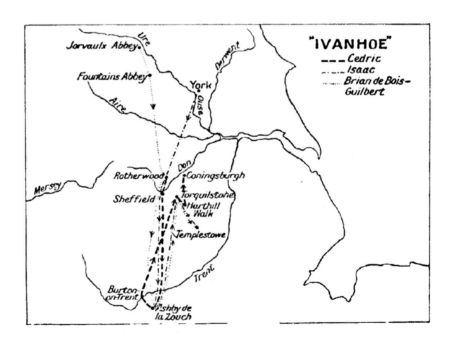

Stone Bldgs
LINCOLNS INN
NEW SQUARE
ROLLS
GARDEN
Cliffords Inn Gardens
FLEET STREET
BUTCHER ROW
STRAND
WYCH ST
Fountain Court
Pump Court
Temple
NORFOLK STREET
ARUNDEL

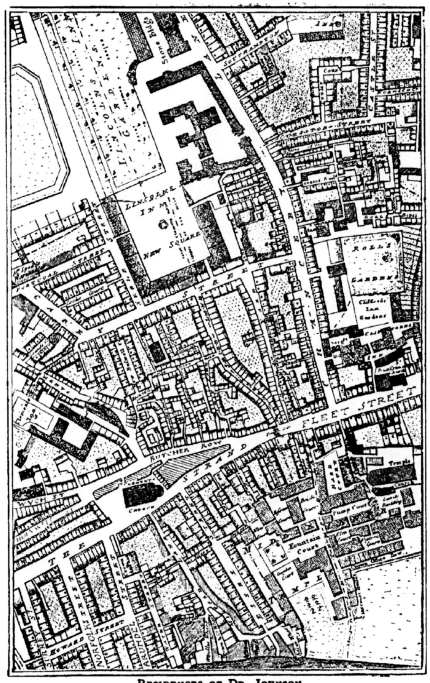

Residences of Dr. Johnson

Boswell Court, Gough Square, Johnson's Court, Fleet Street, Fetter Lane, Inner Temple Lane, 8 Bolt Court.

FLEET STREET
TEMPLE
TEMPLE GARDENS
SALISBURY SQUARE
CHURCH YARD
New Street
Temple
Grand Junction Wharf
Hawkes Wharf
Dorset Wharf
NEW RIVER OFFICE & YARD
TIMBER YARD
William Street
Tudor Street
Office

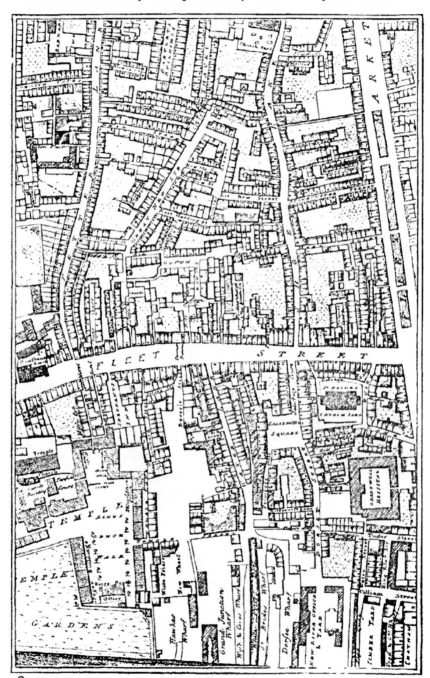

CHURCHES CONNECTED WITH THE JOHNSONIAN CIRCLE—OLIVER GOLDSMITH, JOSHUA REYNOLDS, ETC., ETC.

St. Clement's (Strand) · Temple Church . Other places

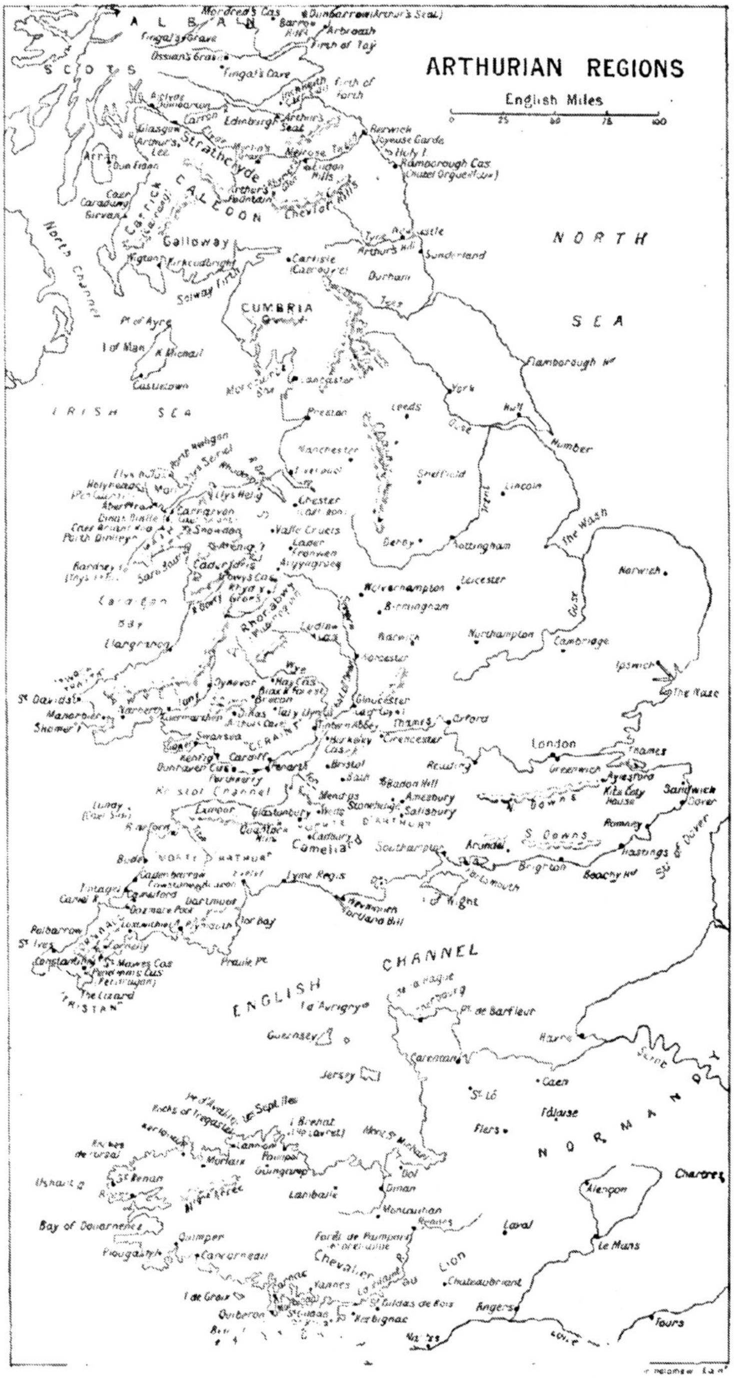

ARTHURIAN REGIONS
English Miles
0
25
50
75
100
NORTH
SEA
IRISH SEA
ENGLISH
CHANNEL
NORMANDY
SCOTS
Galloway
CUMBRIA
Strathclyde
Edinburgh
Arthur's Seat
Berwick
Joyeuse Garde
Carlisle
York
Lincoln
London
Thames
Glastonbury
Camelia
Tintagel
Amesbury
Salisbury
Winchester
Caerleon
Bristol
Norwich
Cambridge
Northampton
Birmingham
Nottingham
Sheffield
Leeds
Chester
Manchester
Preston
Lancaster
Durham
Sunderland
York
Hull
Humber
The Wash
Flamborough Hd
Southampton
Brighton
Hastings
Beachy Hd
Dover
Sandwich
Romney
Guernsey
Jersey
Caen
Falaise
Flers
Laval
Le Mans
Angers
Tours
Chartres
Alençon
Dinan
Vannes
Quimper
Morlaix
Chevalier au Lion
Lyme Regis
Dartmoor
Exmoor
The Lizard
I of Man
Castletown

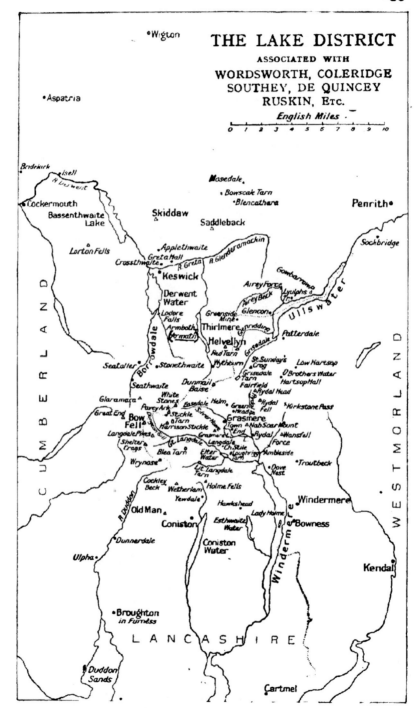

THE LAKE DISTRICT
ASSOCIATED WITH
WORDSWORTH, COLERIDGE
SOUTHEY, DE QUINCEY
RUSKIN, Etc.
English Miles
0 1 2 3 4 5 6 7 8 9 10
Wigton
Aspatria
Bridekirk
Isell
R. Derwent
Cockermouth
Bassenthwaite Lake
Skiddaw
Saddleback
Mosedale
Bowscale Tarn
Blencathara
Penrith
Sockbridge
Lorton Fells
Applethwaite
Greta Hall
Crossthwaite
R. Greta
R. Glenderamackin
Keswick
Derwent Water
Lodore Falls
Armboth
Thirlmere
Helvellyn
Red Tarn
Airey Force
Airey Beck
Lyulphs Tr.
Gowbarrow
Glencoyne
Greenside Mine
Ullswater
Patterdale
Grisedale
Borrowdale
Seatoller
Stonethwaite
Wythburn
St. Sunday's Crag
Grisedale Tarn
Low Hartsop
Brothers Water
Hartsop Hall
Seathwaite
Dunmail Raise
Fairfield
Rydal Head
Glaramara
White Stones
Easedale
Helm
Green Head
Rydal Fell
Kirkstone Pass
Great End
Pavey Ark
Stickle Tarn
Silver How
Grasmere
Bow Fell
Harrison Stickle
Town End
Nab Scar
Mount
Langdale Pikes
Gt. Langdale
Rydal
Wansfell Force
Shelter Crags
Blea Tarn
Langdale
Ch. Stile
Elter Water
Loughrigg Tarn
Ambleside
Wrynose
Lt. Langdale Tarn
Dove Nest
Troutbeck
Cockley Beck
Wetherlam
Holme Fells
Yewdale
Hawkshead
R. Duddon
Old Man
Coniston
Esthwaite Water
Lady Holme
Windermere
Bowness
Dunnerdale
Coniston Water
Ulpha
Kendal
Broughton in Furness
LANCASHIRE
Duddon Sands
Cartmel
CUMBERLAND
WESTMORLAND

See especially De Quincey's "Reminiscences of the Lake Poets."

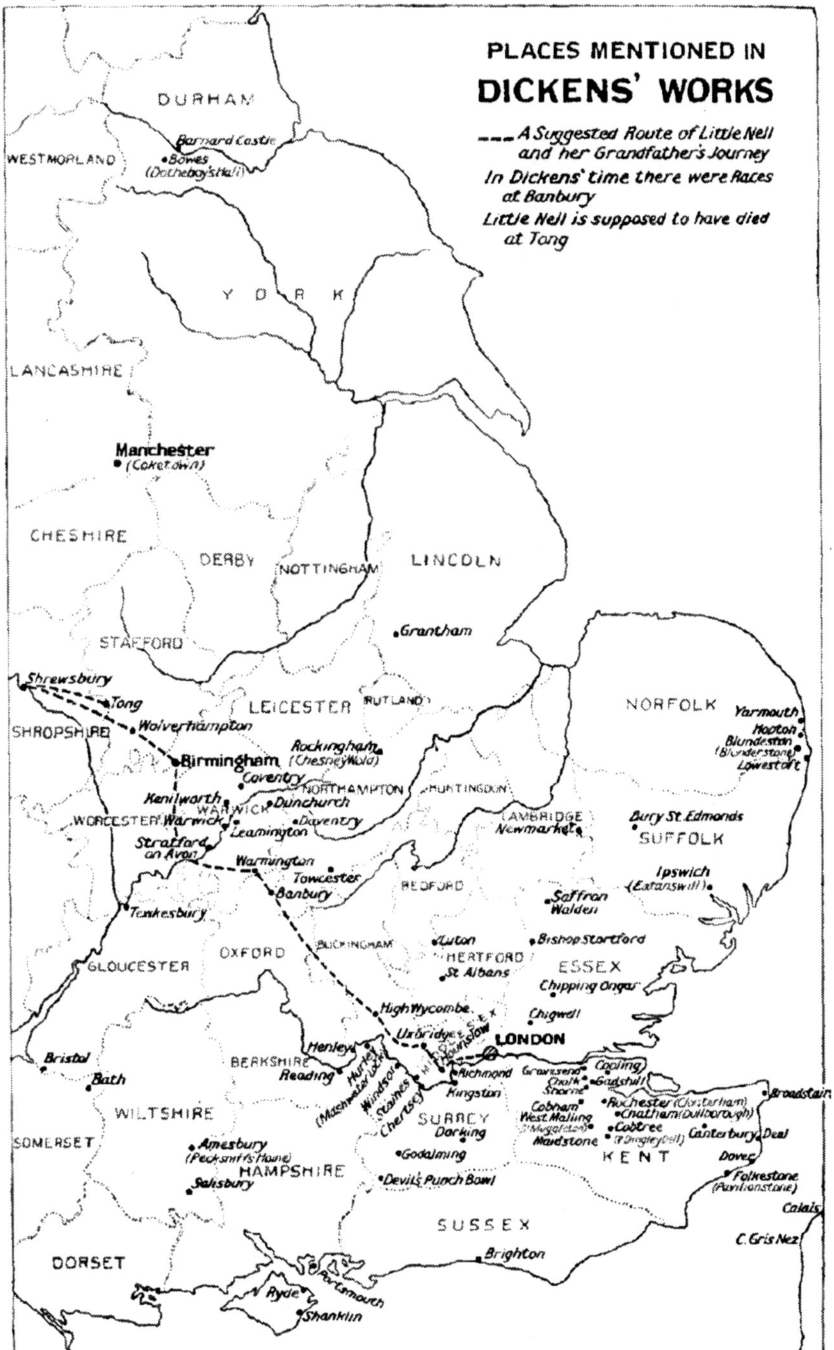

PLACES MENTIONED IN
DICKENS' WORKS
A Suggested Route of Little Nell and her Grandfather's Journey
In Dickens' time there were Races at Banbury
Little Nell is supposed to have died at Tong
DURHAM
Barnard Castle
Bowes
(Dotheboys Hall)
WESTMORLAND
YORK
LANCASHIRE
Manchester
(Coketown)
CHESHIRE
DERBY
NOTTINGHAM
LINCOLN
Grantham
STAFFORD
Shrewsbury
Tong
Wolverhampton
SHROPSHIRE
Birmingham
LEICESTER
RUTLAND
Rockingham
(Chesney Wold)
Coventry
NORTHAMPTON
HUNTINGDON
Kenilworth
Dunchurch
WARWICK
WORCESTER
Warwick
Leamington
Daventry
CAMBRIDGE
Newmarket
NORFOLK
Yarmouth
Hopton
Blundeston
(Blunderstone)
Lowestoft
Bury St. Edmonds
SUFFOLK
Stratford on Avon
Warmington
Towcester
Banbury
BEDFORD
Ipswich
(Eatanswill)
Saffron Walden
Tewkesbury
BUCKINGHAM
Luton
Bishop Stortford
HERTFORD
ESSEX
St. Albans
GLOUCESTER
OXFORD
Chipping Ongar
High Wycombe
Chigwell
Uxbridge
Hounslow
LONDON
Bristol
Henley
BERKSHIRE
Reading
Bath
Richmond
Kingston
Gravesend
Cooling
Gadshill
Rochester
Chatham
Cobham
West Malling
Maidstone
Cobtree
Canterbury
Deal
Dover
Broadstairs
WILTSHIRE
SURREY
Dorking
Godalming
SOMERSET
Amesbury
(Pecksniff's Home)
HAMPSHIRE
Salisbury
Devil's Punch Bowl
KENT
Folkestone
Calais
C. Gris Nez
SUSSEX
Brighton
DORSET
Ryde
Portsmouth
Shanklin

English Channel
PICARDY
Noyon
Compiègne
St. Denis
Rheims
Metz
Epernay
LORRAINE
Meaux
Châlons
St. Germain
Paris
ALENÇON
PERCHE
Corbeil
Etampes
Melun
ORLEANS
Joigny
Chaumont
Blois
Orleans
Tonnerre
Bourbon
Nantes
Tours
Chambord
Auxerre
Amboise
Veselay
Bourges
Nevers
Moncontour
Parthenay
Loches
BURGUNDY
FRANCHE COMTE
Poitiers
POITOU
BOURBON
Clermont
Bourg
Geneva
Limoges
Lyons
Venice
Bay of Biscay
PERIGORD
DAUPHINE
GUIENNE
ALBRET
ARMAGNAC
Nismes
Avignon
PROVENCE
Florence
Leghorn
Marseilles
Narbonne
Gulf of Lions
Rome

Gainsborough
(St. Oggs)
DERBY
(STONYSHIRE)
Lincoln (Lindum)
LINCOLN
North Sea
Matlock
Cromford
Wirksworth
(Snowfield)
Wooton Pk.
Ashbourne
(Oakbourne)
R. Derwent
R. Trent (Floss)
Ellastone
(Hayslope)
Norbury
(Norbourne)
R. Dove
STAFFORD
(LOAMSHIRE)
Stockingford
(Paddiford Common)
Nuneaton (Milby)
Arbury Pk.
(Cheverel Manor)
Chilvers Coton
(Shepperton)
Coventry
WARWICK

GEORGE ELIOT'S COUNTRY

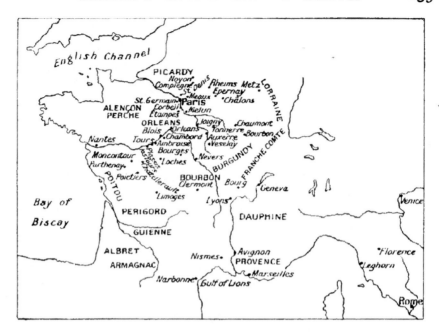

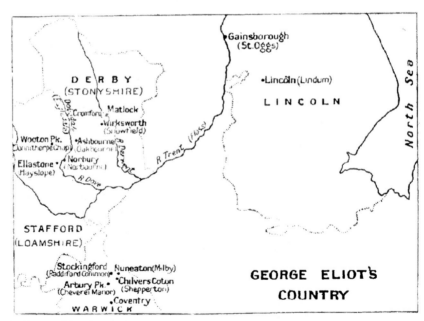

"George Eliot" was born at Arbury Park, and educated at Nuneaton and Coventry. Nearly all her works mention, or are closely associated with, the district marked on this map.

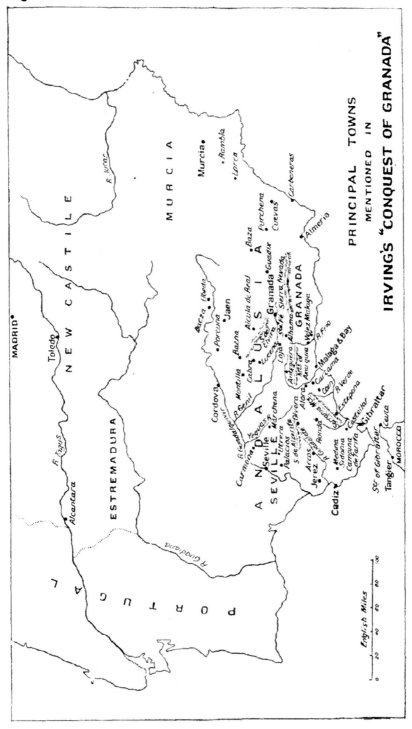

PRINCIPAL TOWNS
MENTIONED IN
IRVING'S "CONQUEST OF GRANADA"
MADRID
Toledo
NEW CASTILE
R. Tagus
Alcantara
ESTREMADURA
R. Guadiana
PORTUGAL
MURCIA
Murcia
Rambla
Lorca
Carboneras
Almeria
Purchena
Cuevas
Baza
Guadix
GRANADA
Granada
Sierra Nevada
Alcala de Real
Jaen
Ubeda
Baeza
Porcuna
Baena
Cordova
Montilla
Cabra
Lucena
Loja
Sta Fé
Alhama
Velez Malaga
R. Frio
Malaga & Bay
Cartama
Coin
Antequera
Alora
R. Verde
Estepona
Gibraltar
Ceuta
MOROCCO
Tangier
Str of Gibraltar
Medina Sidonia
Campana de Tarifa
Cadiz
Jerez
Arcos
Ronda
Olvera
Palacios
Utrera
Seville
SEVILLE
Carmona
Marchena
R. Guadalquivir
R. Genil
ANDALUSIA
English Miles

North Sea
ENGLAND
Hague
Utrecht
Zutphen
Leyden
NETHERLANDS
Antwerp
Bruges
Ghent
FLANDERS
Calais
Brussels
Malines
Vilvorde
Mons
BRABANT
Namur
Philipville
Charlemont
Valencie
Cateau Cambresis
English Channel
Dieppe
Montreuil
PICARDY
La Fère
CAUX
Harfleur
Caudebec
Rouen
Compiègne
Soissons
Rheims
NORMANDY
Mantes
St Germain
Paris
Meaux
Vincennes
St Maur
CHAMPAGNE
Chevreuse
Rambouillet
Chartres
Étampes
Fontainbleau
Melun
Montereau
LORRAINE
Nancy
BRETAGNE
Mayenne
Orleans
Pithiviers
Beaune
La Flèche
Durtal
ANJOU
Beaugency
Blois
Angers
Tours
Amboise
PLATEAU OF SOLOGNE
R. Loire
TOURAINE
La Charité
Arnay le Duc
BURGUNDY
Moncontour
1569
Charenton
Poitiers
La Châtre
POITOU
La Rochelle
Jarnac
Limoges
Angoulême
Lyon
St Andre de Cubsac
Bordeaux
R. Dordogne
GUYENNE
Catus
R. Lot
Montcuq
Cahors
Lauzerte
Nerac
Agen
Puymirol
Condom
Montauban
GASCONY
Auch
Toulouse
LANGUEDOC
Avignon
PROVENCE
Aix
NAVARRE
Pau
BEARN
Tarbes
Narbonne
ROUSILLON
SPAIN

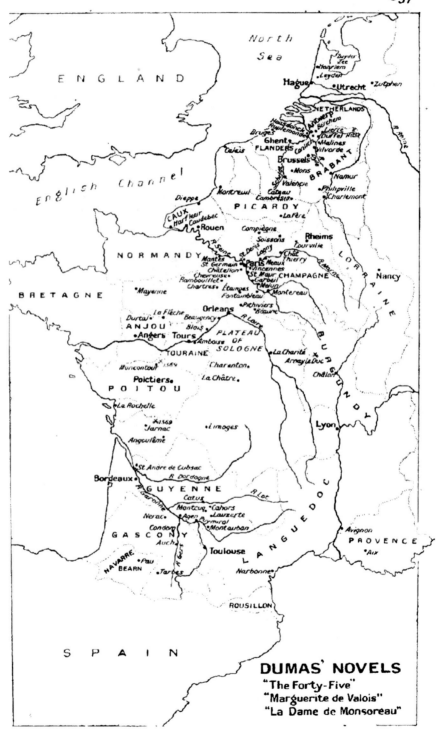

DUMAS' NOVELS
"The Forty-Five"
"Marguerite de Valois"
"La Dame de Monsoreau"

THE NETHERLANDS & BELGIUM
ILLUSTRATING
MOTLEY'S
"RISE OF THE DUTCH
REPUBLIC"
Groningen
FRIESLAND
Coerwoerden
Hardenberg
NORTH
SEA
ZUYDER
ZEE
Alkmaar
Haarlem
AMSTERDAM
Haarlem Meer
Naarden
Leyden (Siege 1583)
THE HAGUE
Zoeterwoude
Utrecht
Delft
Oudewater
Lochem
Zutfen
Rotterdam
R. Rhine
Schouwen
E. Schelde
Walchern
Middleburg
Flushing
W. Schelde
Tholen
Bergen-op-Zoom
Breda
Mook
Hertogenbosch
R. Maas
Antwerp
Bruges
Ghent
Mechlin
FLANDERS
Ingelmunster
Ypres
Courtray
Oudenarde
BRUSSELS
Aerschot
Louvain
Tirlemont
St Trond
Cologne
Maestricht
BRABANT
Jodoigne
Liege
Spa
Tournay
Soignies
Gemblours
Lens
HAINHAULT
Mons
Namur
Huy
Binche
Douay
Valenciennes
Arras
St Quentin
Luxembourg

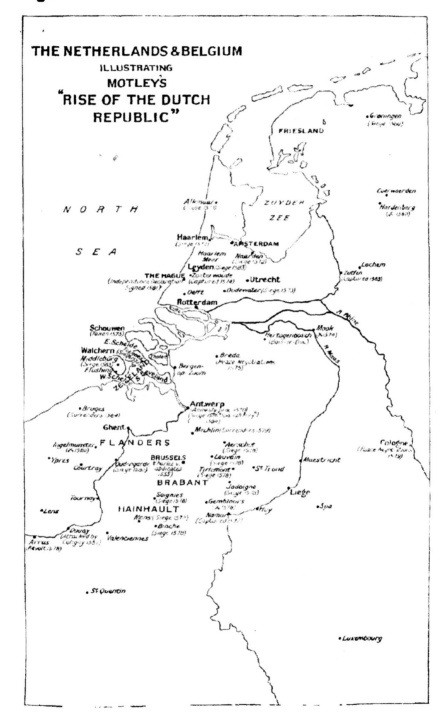

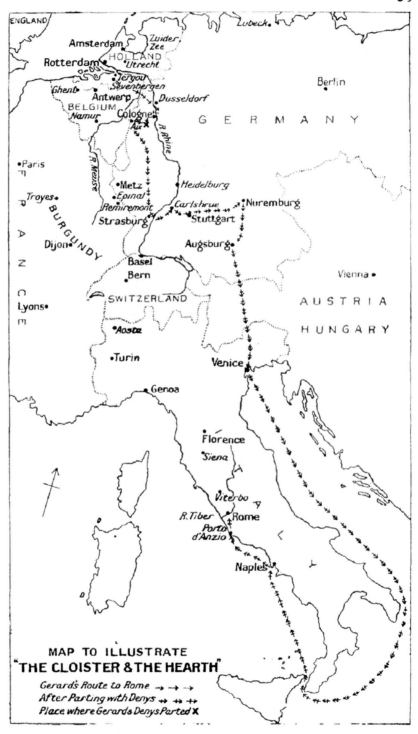

ENGLAND
Lubeck
Amsterdam
Zuider Zee
HOLLAND
Rotterdam
Utrecht
Tergou
Sevenbergen
Ghent
Antwerp
BELGIUM
Dusseldorf
Cologne
Namur
Aix
Berlin
GERMANY
R. Rhine
Paris
R. Meuse
Metz
Epinal
Remiremont
Heidelburg
Troyes
Carlshrue
Nuremburg
Stuttgart
Strasburg
BURGUNDY
FRANCE
Augsburg
Dijon
Basel
Bern
Vienna
SWITZERLAND
AUSTRIA HUNGARY
Lyons
Aosta
Turin
Venice
Genoa
Florence
Siena
Viterbo
R. Tiber
Rome
Porto d'Anzio
ITALY
Naples
MAP TO ILLUSTRATE
"THE CLOISTER & THE HEARTH"
Gerard's Route to Rome
After Parting with Denys
Place where Gerard & Denys Parted X

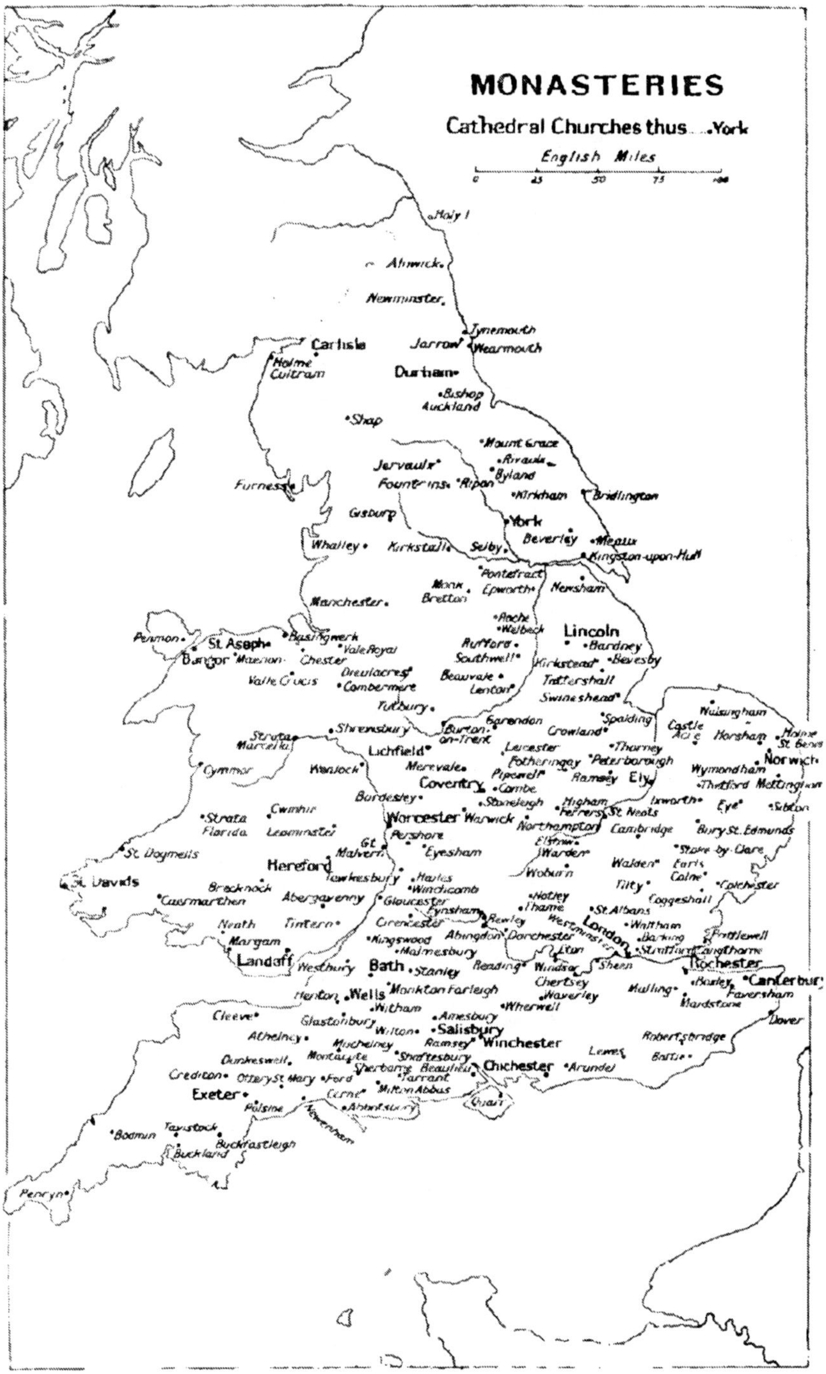
MONASTERIES
Cathedral Churches thus ... York
English Miles
0
25
50
75
100
Holy I
Alnwick
Newminster
Tynemouth
Carlisle
Jarrow
Wearmouth
Holme Cultram
Durham
Bishop Auckland
Shap
Mount Grace
Rivaulx
Byland
Jervaulx
Fountains
Ripon
Furness
Kirkham
Bridlington
Gisburn
York
Whalley
Kirkstall
Selby
Beverley
Meaux
Kingston-upon-Hull
Pontefract
Monk Bretton
Epworth
Newsham
Manchester
Roche
Welbeck
Lincoln
Penmon
St. Asaph
Basingwerk
Vale Royal
Chester
Bangor
Rufford
Bardney
Southwell
Kirkstead
Revesby
Valle Crucis
Dieulacres
Beauvale
Tattershall
Combermere
Lenton
Swineshead
Tutbury
Spalding
Strata Marcella
Shrewsbury
Burton-on-Trent
Garendon
Crowland
Castle Acre
Horsham
Walsingham
Lichfield
Leicester
Thorney
Norwich
Cymmer
Wenlock
Merevale
Fotheringay
Peterborough
Wymondham
Coventry
Pipewell
Ramsey
Ely
Thetford
Combe
Bordesley
Stoneleigh
Higham Ferrers
Ixworth
Eye
Strata Florida
Cwmhir
Leominster
Worcester
Warwick
Northampton
St. Neots
Cambridge
Bury St. Edmunds
St. Dogmells
Pershore
Gt. Malvern
Evesham
Warden
Stoke-by-Clare
Hereford
Walden
St. Davids
Tewkesbury
Hailes
Winchcomb
Woburn
Tilty
Colchester
Brecknock
Abergavenny
Gloucester
Notley
Thame
Caermarthen
Eynsham
Rewley
St. Albans
Coggeshall
Neath
Tintern
Cirencester
Abingdon
Dorchester
Westminster
London
Waltham
Barking
Prittlewell
Margam
Kingswood
Malmesbury
Landaff
Westbury
Bath
Stanley
Reading
Windsor
Eton
Sheen
Rochester
Canterbury
Chertsey
Waverley
Henton
Wells
Monkton Farleigh
Malling
Faversham
Witham
Wherwell
Maidstone
Cleeve
Glastonbury
Wilton
Amesbury
Salisbury
Dover
Athelney
Muchelney
Romsey
Winchester
Robertsbridge
Lewes
Dunkeswell
Montacute
Shaftesbury
Battle
Crediton
Ottery St. Mary
Ford
Sherborne
Beaulieu
Chichester
Arundel
Tarrant
Exeter
Cerne
Milton Abbas
Polsloe
Abbotsbury
Quarr
Tavistock
Bodmin
Buckfastleigh
Buckland
Penryn

See Froude's "Henry VIII.," also essay on "Dissolution of the Monasteries" in "Essays on Literature and History," etc., etc.

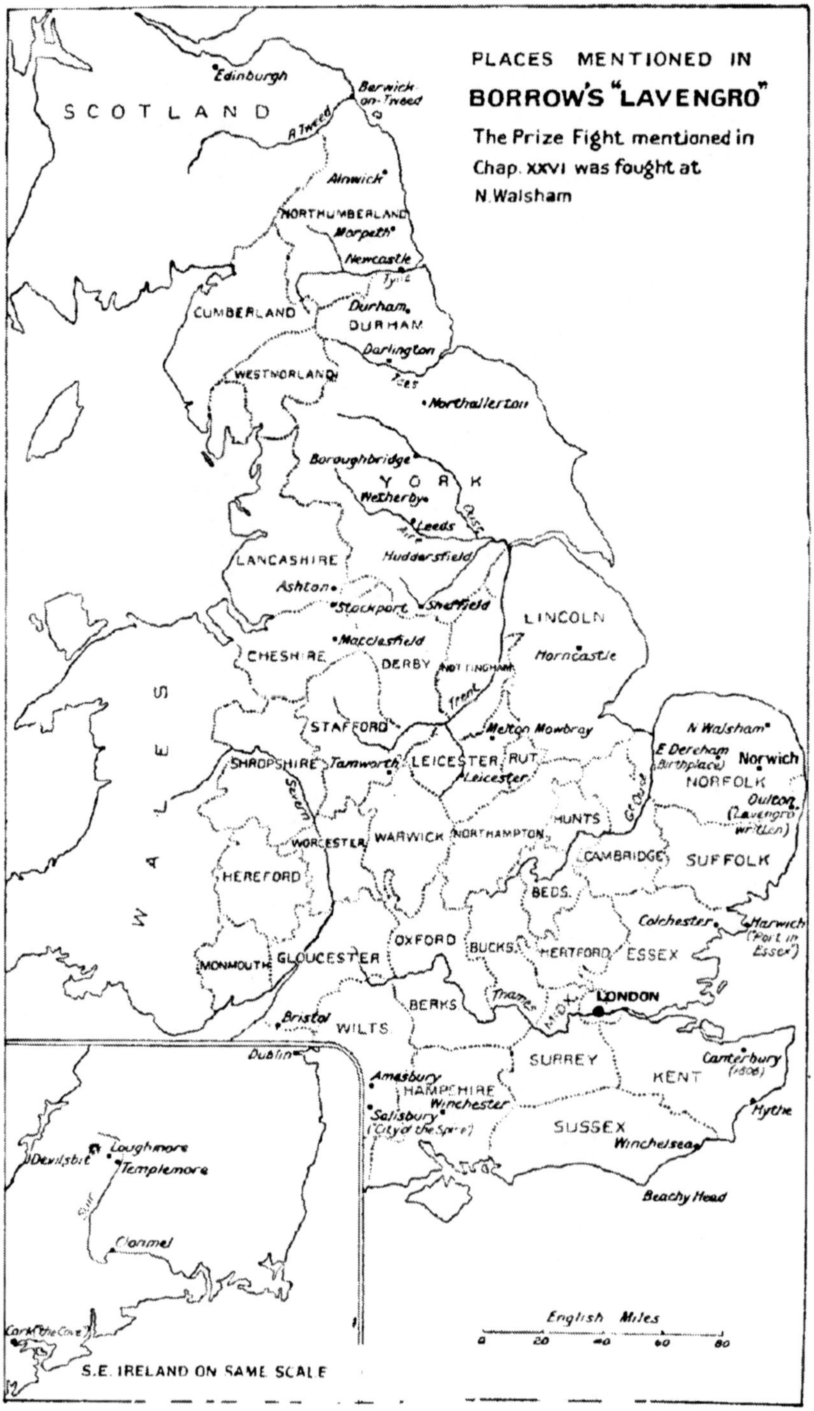
PLACES MENTIONED IN
BORROW'S "LAVENGRO"
The Prize Fight mentioned in Chap. XXVI was fought at N. Walsham
SCOTLAND
Edinburgh
Berwick on-Tweed
R. Tweed
Alnwick
NORTHUMBERLAND
Morpeth
Newcastle
Tyne
CUMBERLAND
Durham
DURHAM
Darlington
Tees
WESTMORLAND
Northallerton
Boroughbridge
YORK
Wetherby
Leeds
Aire
Ouse
LANCASHIRE
Huddersfield
Ashton
Stockport
Sheffield
LINCOLN
Macclesfield
CHESHIRE
DERBY
NOTTINGHAM
Horncastle
Trent
WALES
STAFFORD
Melton Mowbray
N. Walsham
SHROPSHIRE
Tamworth
LEICESTER
RUT
Leicester
E. Dereham (Birthplace)
Norwich
NORFOLK
Severn
Oulton (Lavengro written)
HUNTS
Gt. Ouse
WORCESTER
WARWICK
NORTHAMPTON
CAMBRIDGE
SUFFOLK
HEREFORD
BEDS.
Colchester
Harwich ("Port in Essex")
MONMOUTH
GLOUCESTER
OXFORD
BUCKS.
HERTFORD
ESSEX
BERKS
Thames
MDX.
LONDON
Bristol
WILTS.
Dublin
SURREY
KENT
Canterbury (1808)
Amesbury
HAMPSHIRE
Winchester
Salisbury ("City of the Spire")
SUSSEX
Hythe
Winchelsea
Loughmore
Devilsbit
Templemore
Suir
Clonmel
Beachy Head
English Miles
0
20
40
60
80
Cork (the Cove)
S.E. IRELAND ON SAME SCALE

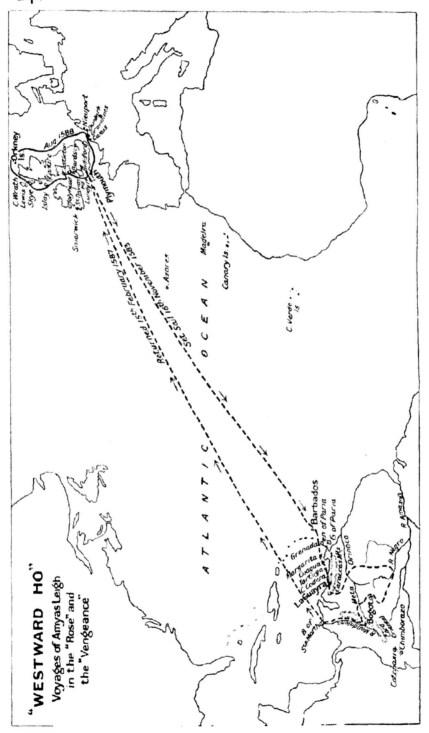

"WESTWARD HO"
Voyages of Amyas Leigh in the "Rose" and the "Vengeance"
ATLANTIC OCEAN
Returned 15th February 1587
Set Sail 16th November 1583
Azores
Madeira
Canary Is.
C. Verde Is
Orkney Is.
Aug 1588
C. Wrath
Lewis
Skye
Islay
Smerwick
Lundy
Plymouth
Nieuport
Calais
Barbados
Pen of Paria
G. of Paria
Grenada
Margarita
Cuagua
Tortuga
C. Codera
La Guayra
Orinoco
Meta
Bogota
R. Negro
R. Amazon
Chimborazo
Cotopaxi

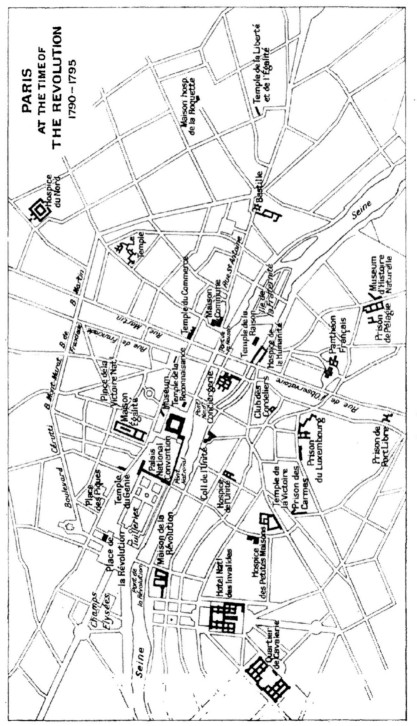

PARIS
AT THE TIME OF
THE REVOLUTION
1790 – 1795
Hospice du Nord
Maison hosp. de la Roquette
Temple de la Liberté et de l'Égalité
Bastille
Seine
Le Temple
Temple du Commerce
Maison Commune
Rue St Antoine
Ile de la Fraternité
Museum d'Histoire Naturelle
B. Martin
B. de
Franciade
Rue Martin
Rue de Franciade
Temple de la Raison
Hospice de la Humanité
Panthéon Français
Prison de Pélagie
Place de la Victoire Natl
Maison Égalité
Museum
Temple de la Reconnaissance
Pont Natl
Conciergerie
Club des Cordeliers
Rue de l'Observatoire
Prison du Luxembourg
Prison de Port Libre
B. Mont-Murat
Cérutti
Palais National Convention
Pont National
Coll de l'Unité
Hospice de l'Unité
Temple de la Victoire
Prison des Carmes
Boulevard
Place des Piques
Temple du Génie
Tuilleries
Maison de la Révolution
Hospice des Petites Maisons
Place de la Révolution
Hotel Natl des Invalides
Pont de la Révolution
Champs Elysées
Seine
Quartier de Cavalerie

See Carlyle, Burke, etc.

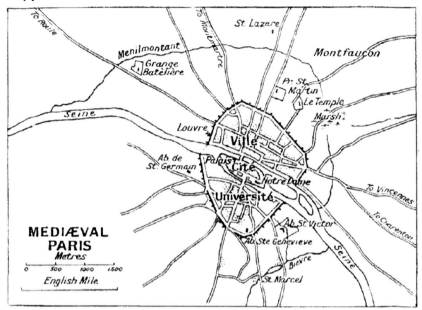

To Roule
To Montmartre
St. Lazare
Menilmontant
Montfauçon
Grange Batelière
Pr. St. Martin
Le Temple
Marsh
Seine
Louvre
Ville
Ab. de St. Germain
Palais
Cité
Notre Dame
To Vincennes
Université
To Charenton
MEDIÆVAL PARIS
Metres
0 500 1000 1500
English Mile
Ab. St. Victor
Ab. Ste Genevieve
Seine
Bievre
St. Marcel

See Balzac's "Catherine de Medici." Hugo's "Notre Dame." Dumas' Novels, etc., etc.

A GAZETTEER

OF

TOWNS AND PLACES IN EUROPE

HAVING A

LITERARY AND HISTORIC INTEREST

r.

A GAZETTEER
OF TOWNS AND PLACES IN EUROPE
HAVING A LITERARY & HISTORIC INTEREST[1]

ABBREVIATIONS

A. Author	f. Founded	W. War(s)	Scot. Scotland
Ass. Associations with	Res. Residence	En. England	Wa. Wales
Bp. Birthplace	Sc. Scene (of, in)	Ir. Ireland	

Aalesund, Norway. 62N. 6E. Bp. of Rollo, Norwegian chief, founder of the Duchy of Normandy.

Aarau, Switzerland. 47N. 8E. Assembly of the Diet of the Cantons, 1798, and proclamation of the Swiss Republic.

Abbots Langley, Herts, En. 51N. 0W. Bp. of Pope Adrian IV. (Nicholas Breakspear).

Abensberg, Bavaria. 48N. 11E. Defeat of Austrians by Napoleon, 1809.

Aberdeen, Scot. 57N. 2W. University: King's Coll., f. 1494; Marischal Coll., f. 1593. Names ass. with Barbour (tomb in cathedral), Hector Boece, Campbell, Byron, etc. Dr. Johnson at, 1773; 'Auld Brig o' Balgownie' near. (See Byron, 'Don Juan,' Cant. X.)

Aberdour, Fife, Scot., 56N. 3W. Richard Chancellour, navigator and discoverer of the Port Archangel, was lost in Aberdour Bay on his return home, 1556. (See Hakluyt, 'Voyages.')

Aberdour, Aberdeen, Scot. 57N. 2W. Ruins of castle where David Bruce was confined. (See old ballad of 'Sir Patrick Spens.')

Aberfoyle, Perth, Scot. 56N. 4W. (Sc. Scott, 'Rob Roy.')

Abergavenny, Monmouth, En. 51N. 3W. Old Roman settlement.

Abergele, Denbigh, Wa. 53N. 3W. Roman camp; victory of Gruffydd ap Llewelyn over Harold near; Dr. Johnson at 1774.

Abernethy, Perth, Scot. 56N. 3W. Ancient capital of the Picts.

Aberystwith, Cardigan, Wa. 52N. 4W. Castle built by Edward I., remains of Owen Glendower's dwelling; supposed grave of Taliesin, the poet.

Abingdon, Berks, En. 51N. 1W. Centre of struggle during Civil W.; 'Abingdon Law,' reference to summary execution of Royalist prisoners.

Abrantes, Portugal. 39N. 8W. Taken by Junot, 1807.

Acman, or Akeman Street, En. Old Roman road between Bath and Cirencester.

Acqui, Italy. 44N. 16E. Defeat of Austrians by Napoleon, 1796.

Addingham, Cumberland, En. 54N. 2W.

Circle of Druidic stones known as Long Meg and her daughters. (See Wordsworth's Sonnet.)

Agen, France. 44N. 0E. Bp. of the Gascon poet, Jasmin, d. 1864. (See Sainte-Beuve, 'Causeries du Lundi.')

Aghrim, Galway, Ir. 53N. 8W. Defeat of James II. by William of Orange, 1691.

Agincourt, France. 50N. 2E. Battle, Oct. 25, 1415.

Agosta (Augusta), Sicily. 37N. 15E. French victory over Admiral de Ruyter, 1676.

Aigues-Mortes, France. 43N. 4E. Tour Constance erected by S. Louis, S. Louis' port of embarkation for Crusades, 1248 and 1269.

Ailsa Craig, Firth of Clyde, Scot. 55N. 5W. (See Keats's Sonnet.)

Aird's Moss, near Sanquhar, Scot. 55N. 4W. Covenanters under the famous Cameron defeated and slain, 1680. (See 'Old Mortality.')

Airolo, Switzerland. 46N. 8E. The S. Gothard tunnel runs from here to Goeschenen; French driven back by Russians under Suvarov, 1799.

Aix-la-Chapelle (Aachen), Germany. 50N. 6E. Bp. and res. of Charlemagne; cathedral with his and Otho III.'s tomb; emperors crowned here till 16th century; treaty, Louis XIV. and Spain, 1668, terminating W. of Austrian Succession, 1748; Congress of Allies, 1818.

Ajaccio, Corsica. 41N. 8E. Bp. of Napoleon I.

Alarcos, Spain. 38N. 6W. Defeat of Alfonso IX. of Castile by the Moors, 1195.

Albi, France. 43N. 2E. Gave its name to the Albigenses, victims of the persecuting crusade of the Pope and Louis VIII., 13th century.

Albuera, Spain. 38N. 6W. Defeat of Soult by the English and Allies under Beresford, 1811.

Albufera, Spain. 39N. 0W. Defeat of English by Suchet near, 1812.

Alcala de Henares (Lat. Complutum), Spain. 40N. 3W. Complutensian (Polyglot) Bible printed, 1502-17; bp. of Cervantes, A. of 'Don Quixote.'

[1] *A large number of the places are not marked in the maps, but the latitude and longitude will enable the reader to locate their position. (See Introduction.)*

145

Alcala la Real, Spain. 37N. 4W. 'Royal' from its capture from Moors by Alfonso XI., 1340.

Alcantara, Spain. 39N. 6W. Famous order of knights f. after victory here over Moors by Alfonso IX., 1214.

Aldebury, or **Aldborough**, Norfolk, En. 52N. 1E. Bp. of Crabbe the poet (1754-1832).

Aldwinkle, Northants, En. 52N. 0W. Bp. of Dryden and Fuller.

Alencon, France. 48N. 0E. Bp. of Père Duchesne, leader of the Hébertistes, executed, 1794.

Alessandria, Italy. 44N. 8E. Post of defence of Lombard League against Frederick Barbarossa.

Alford, Aberdeen, Scot. 57N. 2W. Defeat of the Covenanters by Montrose, 1645.

Alfoxton Park, Somerset, En. 51N. 3W. Wordsworth's home, 1797-98.

Alfreton, Derby, En. 53N. 1W. King Alfred supposed founder.

Algarkirk, Lincoln, En. 52N. 0W. Grave of Algar, Earl of Mercia, killed fighting against the Danes.

Algeciras, Spain. 36N. 5W. Taken by Moors, 711; by Alfonso XI., 1344; naval engagement, English and French, 1801.

Alicante, Spain. 38N. 0W. Captured by English, 1706 (W. of Spanish Succession).

Alkmaar, Holland. 52N. 4E. Brave defence against Spaniards, who were forced to retreat by the opening of the dykes (see Motley, 'Dutch Republic'); convention for evacuation of Holland by English and Russians, 1799.

Allington, Kent, En. 51N. 0E. Bp. of Sir Thomas Wyatt, poet (1503-42).

Alloa, Clackmannan, Scot. 56N. 3W. Mary Stuart here as a child.

Alloway, Ayr, Scot. 55N. 4W. Bp. of Burns, and sc. 'Tam o' Shanter.'

Alma, river, Crimea. 44N. 33E. Battle, Sept. 20, 1854.

Almanza, Spain. 38N. 1W. Decisive victory of French over English and Portuguese (W. of Spanish Succession), 1707.

Almeria, Spain. 36N. 2W. Capital of province. A proverb commemorates the importance of this Moorish town:

'Cuando Almeria era Almeria,
Granada era su alquerie.'

Alney, island of, Severn, En. 51N. 2W. Single combat between Edmund Ironsides and Canute, 1015.

Alnwick, Northumberland, En. 55N. 1W. Seat of the Percies; sc. frequent warfare between English and Scots; Malcolm Canmore and his son slain, 1093.

Alost (Aalst), Belgium. 50N. 4E. First printing press in the Low Countries set up by Martens, a native (cir. 1475).

Alsace-Lorraine, 47-49N. 6-8E. Ceded to Germany by Treaty of Frankfort, 1871. (See Erckmann-Chatrian, 'Story of the Plébiscite,' 'Friend Fritz.')

Altdorf, Switzerland. 46N. 8E. Made famous by William Tell.

Altenkirchen, Rhen. Prussia. 50N. 7E. Austrians defeated by Kleber, 1796.

Althorp, Northants, En. 52N. 0W. Noted library, now at Manchester; masque by Ben Jonson, performed 1603.

Altrive, Selkirk, Scot. 55N. 3W. Home of Hogg, the Ettrick Shepherd (1772-1835).

Amalfi, Italy. 40N. 14E. Sacked by Robert Guiscard, 1075; discovery of famous MS. of the Pandects (Roman Laws), 1135; bp. of Masaniello (1623-47).

Ambleside, Westmoreland, En. 54N. 2W. Res. of Wordsworth (Rydal Mount), Miss Martineau, and Dr. Arnold.

Amboise, France. 47N. 0E. Noted castle, ancient res. of French kings, and bp. of Charles VIII.; meeting of Clovis and Alaric on island opposite, 506; death of L. da Vinci at Chateau de Clos-Lucé; Huguenot conspiracy, 1560; Edict of, 1563. (Sc. Dumas, 'The Two Dianas.')

Amesbury, Wilts, En. 51N. 1W. Vespasian's camp; nunnery f. by Queen Elfrida. (See Tennyson, 'Guinevere.')

Amiens, France. 49N. 2E. Magnificent early Gothic cathedral. Starting point of 12 Roman roads; Peace of (England, France, Holland, and Spain), 1802; battle, 1870 (Franco-Prussian W.); bp. of Peter the Hermit, preacher of First Crusade. (See Ruskin, 'Bible of Amiens.')

Ammergau, Ober and Unter, Bavaria. 47N. 11E. 'Passion Play' given at Ober-A. every 10 years since 1633.

Ampthill, Bedford, En. 52N. 0W. Where Catherine of Aragon awaited the issue of her trial; ruins of Houghton House, ass. Sir Philip Sidney.

Amsterdam, Holland. 52N. 4E. Bp. of Spinoza; home of Rembrandt.

Ancona, Italy. 43N. 13E. Trajan arch; surrender of Papal garrison to Piedmontese, 1860 (Unification of Italy).

Ancrum Moor, Roxburgh, Scot. 55N. 2W. English defeated by Scots, 1545.

Andelys, France. 49N. 1E. Ruins of Chateau Gaillard, built by King Richard I.; bp. of the Trouvères, Henri and Roger, and of the painter Poussin.

Andermatt, Switzerland. 46N. 8E. Famous Devil's Bridge over the Reuss; Suvarov and his Russians here, 1799.

Andernach (Antunnacum, Drusus' camp), Rhen. Prussia. 50N. 7E. Res. of Merovingian kings; tomb of Emperor Valentinian; defeat of Charles the Bald by sons of Louis the German, 876.

Angers, France. 47N. 0W. Castle built by S. Louis; Wellington military student at; bp. of good King René, father of Henry VI.'s queen.

Anglesey (Mona), Wa. 53N. 4W. Home of the Druids; conquered by Edward I.

Angouleme, France. 45N. 0E. Bp. of Marguerite, Queen of Navarre, A. of the 'Heptameron' (1492-1549).

Annan, Dumfries, Scot. 54N. 3W. Bp. of Edward Irving; Carlyle here at school, and

later mathematical tutor. (See Carlyle, 'Sartor Resartus,' Bk. 2, Chap. 3.)

Annonay, France. 45N. 4E. Bp. of brothers Montgolfier, discoverers of the balloon, and sc. their first ascent.

Antwerp, Holland (Hanse Town). 51N. 4E. Works by Rubens, and printing-press of Plantin, d. 1589; sack of the Spaniards, known as 'The Spanish Fury,' 1576, and in 1584; bp. of Van Dyke, Teniers, Rubens (?), etc.

Aosta (Augusta Prætoria), Italy. 45N. 7E. Bp. of Anselm, Archb. of Canterbury (1033-1109).

Arbroath (Aberbrothock), Forfar, Scot. 56N. 2W. Bell rock and lighthouse; Dr. Johnson at, 1773. (Sc. (Fairport) Scott, 'Antiquary;' see Southey, 'The Inchcape Rock.')

Arcis-sur-Aube, France. 48N. 4E. Victory of Allies over Napoleon, March, 1814.

Arcola, Italy. 45N. 11E. Famous victory of Napoleon over Austrians, 1796.

Arden, or Woodland, Warwick, En. 52N. 1W. Site of the forest of 'As You Like It.'

Arezzo, Italy. 45N. 11E. Bp. of Guido d'Arezzo, inventor of musical scale, of Petrarch, Leonardo Bruni, Vasari, etc. (See Browning, 'Ring and the Book.')

Argenteuil, France. 48N. 2E. Heloise, abbess of priory.

Arles, France. 43N. 4E. Roman amphitheatre, Constantine's palace, etc.

Armagh, Ulster, Ir. 54N. 6W. Graves of Brian Boru and his son, killed at Clontarf, 1014.

Arqua, Italy. 45N. 11E. Petrarch d. 1374.

Arques, France. 49N. 1E. Famous victory of Henri IV. over Leaguers, 1589.

Arran, island, Scot. 55N. 5W. 'King's Cave,' Robert Bruce's hiding-place.

Arras, France. 50N. 2E. Bp. of the poet Jean Bodel, 14th century; of Robespierre.

Arroyo Molinos, Spain. 39N. 6W. Victory of Lord Hill over the French, 1811.

Arundel, Sussex, En. 51N. 1W. Taken by Henry I.; by Waller, 1644; res. of the queen after Henry I.'s death.

Aschaffenburg, Bavaria. 49N. 9E. Prussian victory over Austrians, 1866.

Ashbourne, Derby, Eng. 53N. 1W. Cottage where Moore wrote part of 'Lalla Rookh.'

Ashby-de-la-Zouche, Leicester, En. 52N. 1W. Prison of Mary Stuart. (Sc. Scott, 'Ivanhoe.')

Ashdown (Aescdun), Berks, En. 51N. 1W. Defeat of Danes by West Saxons under Ethelred and Alfred, 871.

Ashe, Devon, En. Bp. of Marlborough (1650-1722).

Ashiestiel, Selkirk, Scot. 55N. 2W. Res. of Sir W. Scott, 1804-12, and where he wrote part of 'Waverley,' and his chief poems.

Ashingdon (Assandun), Essex, En. 51N. 0E. Defeat of the English under Edmund Ironsides by Canute, 1016.

Asolo, Italy. 45N. 11E. Res. of Caterina Cornaro, Queen of Cyprus, after her abdication (1489); beloved by Browning, who was there the autumn before his death. (See Browning, 'Asolando.')

Aspern, Austria. 48N. 16E. Two days' battle between Napoleon and Austrians, 1809.

Aspromonte, Italy. 38N. 15E. Garibaldi wounded, and 'Red Shirts' obliged to surrender, Aug. 29, 1862.

Athelney, Isle of, Somerset, En. 51N. 2E. King Alfred's entrenchment against the Danes, 879; his 'Jewel' found near.

Atherton Moor, Lancashire, En. 53N. 2W. Victory of the Royalists over Fairfax, Jan. 30, 1643.

Athlone, Roscommon and Westmeath, Ir. 53N. 7W. Taken by English under William III.

Auburn, or Lissoy, Westmeath, Ir. 53N. 7W. Goldsmith's 'Deserted Village.'

Auchinleck, Ayr, Scot. 55N. 4W. Visited by Dr. Johnson and Boswell, 1773.

Auchmithie, near Arbroath, Forfar, Scot. 56N. 2W. (Sc. (Musselcrag) Scott, 'Antiquary.')

Auerstedt, Prussian Saxony. 51N. 11E. Victory of French over Prussians, and death of Duke of Brunswick, Oct. 14, 1806.

Augsburg (Augusta Vindelicorum), Bavaria. 48N. 10E. Diet, 1530 ('Confessions'), 1548 (Interim); Peace of (Catholics and Reformers), 1555; bp. of Holbein.

Auldearn, Nairn, Scot. 57N. 3W. Victory of Montrose over the Covenanters, 1645.

Auray, France. 47N. 3W. Battle between rival claimants to Brittany, John de Montford and Charles of Blois; Du Guesclin taken prisoner and Charles de Blois slain, 1364.

Aussig, Bohemia. 50N. 14E. Sigismund defeated by Ziska (Hussite W.). (See Count Lützen, 'Life of John Hus.')

Austerlitz, Moravia. 49N. 16E. 'Battle of the Three Emperors,' Dec. 2, 1805.

Avignon, France. 43N. 4E. Res. of Popes, 1309-78; res. of Petrarch, and where he first saw Laura.

Avoca, Ovoca, Wicklow, Ir. 52N. 6W. Vale of the meeting of the waters, sung by Moore.

Awe, Loch, Argyle, Scot. 56N. 5W. Fierce encounter between R. Bruce and Lord of Lorn, 1308.

Aylesford, Kent, En. 51N. 0E. Defeat of Vortigern by Hengist and Horsa, 456; of Danes by Alfred, 893; and by Edmund Ironsides, 1016.

Ayr, Scot. 55N. 4W. Burning of 'Barns of Ayr' by Wallace, 1297.

Azores, or Western Islands. 37N. 25W. Discovered and colonised by Portuguese, 1431-60.

Bach y Graig, Flint., Wa. 53N. 3W. Property of Mrs. Thrale; Johnson at, 1774. (See 'Journey into N. Wales.')

Badajoz, Spain. 38N. 6W. Taken by the French under Soult, 1811; by Wellington, 1812.

Badbury, Dorset, En. 50N. 1W. Mons

Badonicus (?), sc. defeat of Saxons by British chief Ambrosius, cir. 516. (See Gildas, ' Chronicle.')

Badenoch, Inverness, Scot. 56N. 4W. Son of Robert II. known as 'Wolf of B.'; hiding-ground of Macpherson, Jacobite, left in charge of hidden treasure. (See Stevenson, 'Catriona'; Lang, 'Pickle the Spy.')

Badminton, Gloucester, En. 51N. 2W. Grave of Lord Raglan, who died in the Crimea, 1855.

Baiæ (Baiæ), Italy. 40N. 14E. Favourite resort of Roman emperors.

Baireuth, or Bayreuth, Bavaria. 49N. 11E. Theatre erected for performance of Wagner's operas, 1872-6; grave of Wagner (1813-83); J. P. Richter d here in 1825.

Bakchiserai, the 'Garden Palace,' Russia. 44N. 33E Capital of the ancient khans of the Crimea.

Balaclava, Crimea. 44N. 33E. Battle between Russians under Mentschikoff and British under Lord Raglan, Oct. 25, 1854. (See Tennyson, 'Charge of the Light Brigade.')

Baldock, Herts, En. 51N. 0W. Monuments of Templars.

Baldoon, Galloway, Scot. Castle of Dunbar family, one of whom married Lucy of Lammermoor (See Scott)

Bale (Basel), Switzerland. 47N. 7E. Res. of Erasmus, d. 1536, great council, 1431-49; treaty, 1795 (Prussia and Spain withdrew from coalition against France).

Ballater, Aberdeen, Scot. 57N. 3W. Byron at farm near when a boy.

Ballitore, Kildare, Ir. 53N. 6W. Edmund Burke at school here.

Ballyclerahan, Tipperary, Ir. 52N. 7W. Castle taken by Cromwell

Ballymore, Westmeath, Ir. 53N. 7W. Taken from Loyalists by De Ginkell, 1691.

Ballymote, Sligo, Ir. 54N. 8W. Taken by Ireton and Coote, 1652; famous MS. known as 'Book of B.'

Ballynahinch, Down, Ir. 54N 5W. Defeat of rebels by Nugent, 1798.

Balmaclellan, Kirkcudbright, Scot. 55N. 4W. Stone to memory of 'Old Mortality.'

Balquhidder, Perth, Scot. 56N. 4W. Here Rob Roy died and was buried. (See Scott)

Balsall, see Temple-Balsall.

Bamberg, Bavaria. 49N. 10E. Tombs of Emperor Henry II. and his wife.

Bamborough, Northumberland, En. 55N. 1W. Capital of Ida, King of Northumbria.

Banbury, Oxford, En 52N. 1W. Defeat of Edward IV. by Warwick, 1469, held by Royalists after Edgehill.

Banff, Scot. 57N. 2W. Remains of Templars; Dr Johnson at, 1773

Bangor, Carnarvon, Wa. 53N. 4W. Graves of the Welsh princes, Gryffydd ap Cynan, Owen Gwynedd, and Cadwaladr, Dr. Johnson at, 1774.

Bangor, Flint, Wa. 53N. 4W. Massacre of over 1000 monks by Edelfrith of Northumbria, 593.

Bannockburn, Stirling, Scot. 56N. 3W. Battle, June 24, 1314

Bapaume, France. 50N. 2E. Battle (Franco-Prussian W.), 1871.

Bar, Russia. 49N. 27E. Confederation of Polish patriots, 1768.

Barbizon, Forest of Fontainebleau, France. 48N. 2E. School of painters, including Millet, Rousseau, Corot, etc.

Barcelona, Spain 41N. 2E. Surrendered to English, 1705 (W. of Spanish Succession).

Bard, Italy. 45N. 7E Fort taken by French after 8 days' siege, 1800.

Barden, York, En. 54N. 2W. Ruins of tower built by Clifford, the 'Shepherd Lord.' (See Wordsworth, 'Feast of Brougham Castle.')

Bardney, Lincoln, En. 53N. 0W. Supposed grave of King Ethelred

Bardsey, York, En. 53N. 1W. Bp of Congreve, dramatist (1670-1729).

Barfleur, France. 49N. 1W. Port of departure for England of William the Conqueror, 1066; near went down the 'White Ship' with Henry I.'s son. (See Rossetti's Ballad.)

Barholm, Kirkcudbright, Scot. 54N. 4W. Sc. (Ellangowan) Scott, 'Guy Mannering '

Bari, Italy 41N. 16E. Taken by Robert Guiscard, 1071.

Barnard Castle, Durham, En. 54N. 1W. Ruins of Barnard Baliol's castle. (See Scott, 'Rokeby ')

Barnes, Surrey, En. 51N. 0W. Res. of Sir Francis Walsingham House of Jacob Tonson, the bookseller, where Kit-cat Club met. Cowley, Fielding, ' Monk' Lewis, and Handel, residents.

Barnet, Herts, En. 51N 0W. Defeat of Lancastrians and death of Earl of Warwick, April 14, 1471. (See Lytton, 'Last of the Barons.')

Barnsdale, Yorks, En. 53N. 1W. Ass. Robin Hood.

Barnstaple, Devon, En 51N. 4W. Bp. of John Gay, A. of the ' Beggar's Opera ' (1685-1732).

Barosa, Spain. 36N. 6W. Defeat of French by Graham, 1811 (Peninsular W.).

Barra Island, Inverness, Scot. 56N. 7W. Victory of Robert Bruce, 1308.

Basing, Hants, En. 51N. 1W. Saxon defeat by Danes, 871, taken by Cromwell after 2 years' siege, 1645

Bass Rock, Scot. 56N. 2W. Prison of Covenanters Held against William III for 3 years. (Sc Stevenson's 'Catriona.')

Bassano, Italy. 45N. 11E. Victory of Napoleon over Austrians, 1796.

Bath (Aquæ Solis), Somerset, En. 51N 2W. Coronation of King Edgar, 973, lost and retaken by Royalists in Civil W.; Monmouth refused entry, 1685. Celebrated in works of earlier novelists.

Battle, Sussex, En. 50N. 0E. The Senlac of the Battle of Hastings, Oct 14, 1066

Bauge, France. 47N. 0W Defeat of English, 1421 (Hundred Years' W.).

Bautzen, Saxony. 51N. 14E. Napoleon's

victory over Prussians and Russians, 1813.

Bayeux, France. 49N. 0W. Tapestry, attributed to Queen Matilda, wife of William the Conqueror.

Bayonne, France 43N. 1W. Besieged by Spanish and English, 1814.

Beachy Head, Sussex, En. 50N. 0E. Defeat of English and Dutch fleet by French, 1690.

Beaconsfield, Bucks, En. 51N. 0W. Home and burial place of Waller the poet, and of Edmund Burke; Dr. Johnson, Mrs. Thrale, Crabbe, etc., entertained by Burke

Bearn, France. 43N. 0W. Ass. Marguerite d'Angoulême and Jeanne d'Albret, mother of Henri IV.

Beaugency, France. 47N. 1E. Retaken from English by Joan of Arc, 1429; defeat of French, 1870.

Beaulieu, Bewley, Hants, En. 50N. 1W. Refuge of Margaret of Anjou after battle of Barnet.

Beaumont, Ardennes, France. 49N. 4E. Defeat of the French, 1870.

Beaumaris, Anglesey, Wa. 53N. 4W. Castle described by Johnson ('Journey into N. Wales,' 1774).

Beaurevoir, France. 49N. 3E. Joan of Arc imprisoned.

Beauvais, France. 49N. 2E. Defended by women under Jeanne Hachette against Charles the Bold, 1472.

Bec, France. 49N. 0E Monastery made famous in 11th century by teaching of Lanfranc and Anselm.

Beckenham, Kent, En. 51N. 0W. Bp. of Grote, the historian (1794-1871).

Beddgelert, Carnarvon, Wa. 53N. 4W. Grave of dog Gelert, sc. part of Southey's 'Madoc.'

Bedfont, East, Middlesex, En. 51N. 0W. Famous yew trees, the 'Peacocks,' commemorated by Hood.

Bedford, En. 52N. 0W. Prison of John Bunyan, where he wrote many of his works.

Bedwin, Bedwyn, Great, Wilts, En. 51N. 1W. Battle between West Saxons and Mercians, 675; Wolf Hall, Jane Seymour's home near.

Belfort, France. 47N. 6E. Won by Germans after 3 months' siege, 1871.

Belgrade (White Town), Servia. 44N. 20E. Held against Turks by Hunyadi, 1456; taken by Prince Eugène, 1718, by Czerni George, 1806, re-taken by Turks, 1813-66; King Milan abdicated, 1889; murder of King Alexander and Queen Draga, 1903.

Bell Rock, or Inchcape, see Arbroath.

Belvoir, Rutland, En. 52N. 0W Crabbe chaplain to the Duke of Rutland, 1782-85.

Bemerton, Wilts, En. 51N. 1W. George Herbert rector, 1630-33.

Benbecula Island, Hebrides. 57N. 7W. Charles Edward at, after Culloden.

Bender, Bessarabia. 46N. 29E. Res. for years of Charles XII. of Sweden. (See Life by Voltaire.)

Benevento (Maleventum), Italy. 41N. 14E. Victory of Charles of Anjou and death of Manfred, 1266.

Bentworth, Hants, En. 51N. 1W. Sold by Withers the poet to raise a force during Civil W.

Bere-Regis, Dorset, En. 50N. 2W. Res. of Queen Elfrida, and of King John.

Beresina River, Russia. 52N. 29E. Disastrous passage of Napoleon on retreat from Moscow, Nov. 28, 1812.

Bergen, Norway 60N. 5E. Ancient res. of Norwegian kings.

Bergen, Holland. 51N. 4E. Russians defeated by Brune, 1799.

Bergholt, Suffolk, En. 51N. 1E. Bp. of Constable, the painter.

Berkeley, Gloucester, En. 51N. 2W. Edward II. murdered, 1327; taken by Parliamentarians, 1645; bp. and grave of Dr. Jenner, discoverer of vaccination.

Berkhampstead, Great, Herts, En. 51N. 0W. Bp. of the poet Cowper.

Berlin, Prussia. 52N. 13E. Congress (termination Russo-Turkish W.), 1878; Conference (Greco-Turkish Frontier), 1880; International Conference, 1885.

Berne, Switzerland. 46N 7E. Capitulated to French, 1798; Treaty with France, 1862; International (Postal Union), 1874; Convention (copyright), 1887.

Berwick-upon-Tweed, En. 55N 2W Frequently besieged during wars between Scots and English, cannon first used in England during siege of, 1406; taken by Cromwell, 1648.

Besancon, France. 47N 6E. Bp. of Victor Hugo (1802-85)

Bethune, France 50N. 2E. Taken by Gaston d'Orléans, 1645 (Thirty Years' W.); by Imperialists, 1707 (W. of Spanish Succession).

Bettws-y-Coed, Carnarvon, Wa. 53N. 3W. Tomb of Llewelyn's nephew; David Cox, painter, a yearly visitor to the 'Royal Oak.'

Beverley (Lake of Beavers), Yorks, En. 53N. 0W. Famous 'Percy' shrine, 14th century.

Beziers (Julia Beterra), France. 43N. 3E. Taken from Arabs by Charles Martel, 736; massacre by Simon de Montford, 1209 (Albigensian W.)

Biberach, Germany. 48N. 9E. Victory of Moreau over Austrians near, 1796.

Bicester, Oxon, En. 51N. 1W. Royalists defeated, 1643

Bickleigh, Devon, En. 50N. 4W. Bp. of Bamfylde Moore Carew, King of the Gypsies (1693-1758).

Bidford, Warwick, En. 52N. 1W. Falcon Inn, where Shakespeare is said to have caroused.

Bideford, Devon, En 51N. 4W. Fort taken by Royalists, 1643; here Kingsley wrote 'Westward Ho!', bp of Sir Richard Grenville, hero of the 'Revenge,' 1591. (See Tennyson's poem.)

Bienne (Biel), Switzerland. 47N. 7E. Town and lake. Rousseau on Ile St. Pierre, 1765

Bilbao, Spain. 43N. 2W. Taken by French, 1795 and 1808; besieged by Carlists, 1835 and 1874-75.

Bingen, Rhine. 49N. 7E. Mouse-tower of Bishop Hatto; statue of Germania. (See Southey's ballad.)

Birchington, Kent, En 51N. 1E. Tomb of Dante G Rossetti, who died here 1882.

Birmingham, Warwick, En. 52N. 1W. Sacked by Prince Rupert, 1643; Dr Priestley's house and library destroyed, 1791; Chartist riots, 1839; ass. names of Watt, Bright, Burne-Jones, etc.

Birnam, Perth, Scot. 56N. 3W. Wood, famous for its ass Shakespeare's 'Macbeth.'

Bishopsbourne, Kent, En. 51N. 1E. Richard Hooker rector, 1595-1600, the date of his death

Bishopwearmouth, Durham, En. 54N. 1W Bp of Sir Henry Havelock, b. 1795; died at Lucknow, 1857.

Bitche (Bitsch), France (Lorraine). 49N. 7E. Held against the Germans from Aug. 6, 1870, to March 21, 1871.

Bitonto, Italy. 41N. 16E. Defeat of Austrians by Spaniards, 1734 (W. of Polish Succession).

Blackbourton, Oxon, En. 53N. 2W. Bp. of Maria Edgeworth, 1767.

Blackheath, Kent, En. 51N. 0W. Gathering of rebels under Wat Tyler, 1381; under Jack Cade, 1450; under Lord Audley, 1497

Blair Atholl, Perth, Scot. 56N. 3W. 'Fiery Cross' sent out from, by Montrose, 1644; besieged by Lord George Murray, 1746; grave of Graham of Claverhouse, killed 1689.

Blakesware, Herts, En. 51N. 0W. (See Lamb's Blakesmoor, 'Essays of Elia ')

Blanquefort, France. 44N 0W. Defeat of the English, 1450 (Hundred Years' W.)

Blenheim, Bavaria, see Hochstädt.

Blenheim, Oxon, En. 51N. 1W. Presented by the nation to Marlborough after the battle. Dr. Johnson and Boswell at, 1776. (See Scott, 'Woodstock ')

Blickling, Norfolk, En. 51N. 1E. Former property of the Boleyn family, and perhaps bp of Anne Boleyn; famous library.

Blois, France. 47N. 1E. Joan of Arc at, 1429; Froissart at; bp. of Louis XII. and King Stephen, res. of Francis I and successors; assassination of Henri de Guise and Cardinal, 1588, capitulated to Germans, 1870 (See hist. novels (Valois kings), Balzac, Dumas, etc.)

Bloore Heath, Staffs, En. 52N. 2W. Defeat of Lancastrians (W. of the Roses)

Bobrouisk, Russia. 53N. 29E. Besieged by the French, 1812.

Bodmin, Cornwall, En. 50N. 4W. Taken by Fairfax (Civil W)

Bodvel, Carnarvon, Wa. 52N. 4W. Dr. Johnson at, 1774; bp. of Mrs Thrale.

Bois-le-Duc, France 51N. 5E. Moreau forced to retire by the Allies, 1794.

Bolingbroke, Lincoln, En. 53N. 0E. Bp. of Henry IV.

Bologna, Italy. 44N. 11E. Former noted school of law, Charles V. crowned, 1530, home of many famous painters.

Bolsover, Derby, En. 53N. 1W. Castle besieged, 1644.

Bolton, Lancs., En. 53N. 2W. Stormed during the Civil W.

Bolton Abbey, Yorks, En. 54N. 1W. Mary Queen of Scots here for a while a prisoner (See Wordsworth, 'White Doe of Rylstone,' 'The Force of Prayer,' and Rogers, ' Boy of Egremond.')

Bomarsund, Gulf of Bothnia. 60N. 20E. Bombarded by English and French, 1854.

Bonhill, Dumbarton, Scot. 55N. 4W. Smollett born at Dalquhurn Grange near (1721-71.)

Bonn, Rhenish Prussia. 50N. 7E. Bp. of Beethoven; graves of Schumann and Niebuhr

Boom, Belgium. 51N. 4E. Stevenson at. (See ' Inland Voyage.')

Bordeaux, France. 44N. 0W. English possession, 1152-1451; res. of Black Prince and bp. of Richard II.; Montaigne a student here, and later made counsellor.

Borghetto, Italy. 45N. 10E. Defeat of Austrians by French, 1796

Bormio, Italy. 46N. 10E. Defeat of Austrians by French, 1799.

Borny, Alsace-Lorraine. 48N. 7E. Battle, 1870 (Franco-German W.).

Borodino, Russia. 55N. 35E. Battle (known also as ' Moskowa '), Napoleon and Russians, Sept. 7, 1812 (See Tolstoy, ' War and Peace.')

Boroughbridge, Yorks., En. 54N. 1W. Rebels routed by Edward II., 1322.

Borrodale, Inverness, Scot 56N. 5W. Landing-place of Prince Charles Edward, 1745.

Borrowdale, Cumberland, En. 54N. 3W. Famous yew trees, commemorated by Wordsworth.

Borrowdale Valley, Cumberland, En. Bowder Stone, mentioned by Wordsworth.

Borthwick, Edin., Scot. 55N. 3W. Escape of Mary Stuart and Bothwell from, 1567.

Borysthenes, river of Sarmatia (Dnieper). Victory of Poles, 1512 (Russo-Polish W.).

Boscobel, Salop, En. 52N. 2W. 'Royal Oak' of Charles II.

Boscombe, Wilts, En 50N. 2W. Here Hooker as rector wrote part of his 'Ecclesiastical Polity,' 1591-95.

Bosham, Sussex, En. 50N. 0W. Harold's port of sail for Normandy.

Bosna-Serai, Bosnia. 43N. 18E. Taken by the Austrians, 1878

Bosworth, or Market Bosworth, Leicester, En. 52N. 1W. Defeat and death of Richard III., Aug. 21, 1485.

Bothwell, Lanark, Scot 55N. 4W Defeat of Covenanters by Monmouth, 1679.

Boughton-Malherbe, Kent, En. Bp. of Sir Henry Wotton. (See Life by Izaak Walton)

Boulogne, France. 50N. 1E. Taken by Henry VIII., 1544; Napoleon's camp pre-

paratory to invading England, 1803; Louis Napoleon imprisoned after insurrectionary attempt, 1840; bp. of Godfrey de Bouillon and Sainte-Beuve, the poet Campbell, and Le Sage, A. of 'Gil Blas,' died here; Treaty, Dauphin (Charles V.) and Edward III.

Bourg - en - Bresse, France. 46N. 5E. Church of Brou. (See M. Arnold's poem.)

Bourges, France. 47N. 2E. Bp. of Louis XI.

Bourn, Lincoln, En. 52N. 0W. Site of battle of Brunanburh, when the Danes were defeated by Athelstan, 937 or 938, commemorated in Anglo-Saxon poem, camp of Hereward the Wake. (See Kingsley's novel.)

Bournemouth, Hants En 50N. 1W. Graves of Mary Wollstonecraft, Mary Shelley, and Godwin.

Bouvines, France. 50N 4E. Victory of Philip Augustus over Otho IV., 1214; encounters between French and Austrians, 1794.

Bovey Tracey, Devon, En. 50N. 3W. Wentworth defeated by Cromwell, 1646.

Bowes (Roman Lavatræ), Yorks, En. 54N. 2W. Former school said to have been original of 'Dotheboy's Hall.'

Bowhill, Roxburghs., Scot. 55N. 2W. House of the Buccleughs, where Scott was a frequent visitor.

Bowscale, Cumberland, En. 54N 3W Tarn of the 'undying fish.' (See Wordsworth, 'Feast of Brougham Castle.')

Boxtel, Holland. 51N. 5E Victory of French over English and Dutch, 1794.

Boyne River, Ir. 53N. 6W. Defeat of James II by William III., July 1, 1690.

Bracewell, Yorks, En. 53N. 2W. Here Henry VI. took shelter after battle of Hexham, 1464.

Braddock, Cornwall, En. 50N. 4W. Defeat of Parliamentarians, 1643.

Bradenham, Bucks, En. 51N. 0W. Res. of Isaac d'Israeli, and bp. of his famous son.

Bradford-on-Avon, Wilts, En. 51N 3W. Church, 38 ft long, 7th-8th century. Saxon victory over British, 652.

Bradgate, Leicester, En. 52N. 1W. Bp. of Lady Jane Grey.

Bradninch, Devon, En. 50N. 3W. Charles I. at, 1644; Fairfax at, 1645.

Bramham Moor, Yorks, En. 53N 1W. Defeat of Northumberland and rebels by Henry IV., 1408.

Brandeis, Bohemia. 50N 14E. Defeat of Austrians by Swedes, 1639.

Branksome, Branxholm. 55N. 2W. Former castle owned by the 'bold Buccleugh' (15th century), ancestor of Sir Walter Scott. (See old ballad, 'Kinmount Willie'; Scott, 'Lay of the Last Minstrel.')

Brantwood, Lancs., En. 54N 3W. Res. of Ruskin.

Bray, Berks, En. 51N. 0W. Simon Aleyn, famous vicar, 1540 88.

Brechin, Forfar, Scot. 56N. 2W. Siege under Edward I., 1305; defeat of the rebel Douglases, 1452; plundered by Montrose, 1647.

Brecon, Brecknock, Wa. 51N. 3W. Mrs. Siddons born at the Shoulder of Mutton (1755-1831).

Breda, Holland. 51N. 4E. Taken by Spaniards, 1581; by Maurice of Orange, 1590; by Spinola, 1625; regained by Dutch, and taken later by French, peace of, 1667. (See Motley, 'Dutch Republic')

Bregenz, Austria 47N. 9E. Defeat of Swiss Leaguers by Austrians, 1408.

Breitenfeld, Saxony. 51N. 12E. Victory of Gustavus Adolphus over Tilly, 1631; of Swedes over Archduke Leopold and Piccolomini, 1643 (Thirty Years' W.), battle of Leipzig (q v.).

Brenneville, France. 49N. 1E. Victory of Henry I. over Louis VI., 1119.

Brentford, Middlesex, En. 51N. 0W. Defeat of Danes by Edmund Ironsides, 1016; of Parliamentarians by Prince Rupert, 1642.

Brescia, Italy. 45N. 10E. Assault and capture by Austrians under Haynau, 1849.

Breslau, Silesia. 51N. 17E Taken and retaken by Austrians and Prussians, 1757, and later by the French.

Brest, France. 48N. 4W. Victory of English under Lord Howard, 1512; repulse of English, 1694; victory of Lord Howe, 1794.

Bretigny, France. 48N. 1E. Peace between Edward III. and France, 1360.

Bridgewater, Somerset, En. 51N. 3W. Bp. of Admiral Blake.

Bridgnorth, Salop, En. 52N. 2W. Siege by Henry II. and Edward II., destroyed by Parliamentarians, bp. of Bishop Percy; Baxter minister in 1640.

Briel, The Brill 51N 4E. Taken from Spaniards by Netherlanders, 1572; bp. of Tromp and W de Witt.

Brienne - le - Chateau, France. 48N 4E. Napoleon military student at; his defence of town against Allies, and their final occupation of, 1814

Brihuega, Spain. 40N. 2W. Defeat of Stanhope by the French, 1710 (W. of Spanish Succession).

Bristol, Gloucesters., En. 51N. 2W. Bp. of John Cabot, and port whence he and his son Sebastian sailed on their voyages, of Southey, Chatterton, Sir Thomas Lawrence, ass. Wordsworth and Coleridge.

Brixham, Devon, En. 50N. 3W. Landing of William of Orange, Nov. 4, 1688.

Broadstairs, Kent, En. 51N. 1E. Favourite summer resort of Dickens. (See 'Bleak House.')

Brocken, Saxony. 51N. 10E. Sc. witches' meeting on Walpurgis night. (See Goethe, 'Faust.')

Brod, Bohemia. 45N. 18E. Emperor Sigismund defeated by Ziska, 1422.

Bromley, Kent, En. 51N. 0E. Grave of Dr. Johnson's wife.

Bruges, Belgium (Hanse town). 51N. 3E. Res. of the painters J. van Eyck and Memling, and of Colard Mansion, under

whom Caxton learned to print; occupied by French, 1745 and 1794.

Brunnen, Switzerland 47N. 8E. League of the Forest Cantons, 1315.

Brussels, Belgium. 50N. 4E. Execution of Counts Egmont and Horn, 1568; suffered greatly under Alva, and during wars of France with Spain and with Austria. (See Motley; Goethe, 'Egmont.')

Bucharest, Roumania 44N 26E. Sieges by Russians and Austrians, 1767-89, treaty, Russia and the Porte, 1812.

Buckhurst, Sussex, En 50N. ow Bp. of Lord Sackville, poet, joint author of the tragedy of 'Gorboduc' (1536-1608).

Buda-Pesth, Hungary 47N. 19E. Mongol invasion, 1241, taken by Soliman the Magnificent, 1529; re-conquest by Charles of Lorraine, and burning of Pesth, 1686.

Builth, Radnor, Wa. 52N. 3w. Llewelyn, Prince of Wales, killed near, 1282.

Burgh-by-Sands, Cumberland, En. 54N. 3w. Death of Edward I., 1307.

Burglen, Switzerland. 47N. 9E. Bp. of William Tell.

Burgos, Spain 42N. 3w. Taken by Wellington, 1813; bp. of the Cid, whose bones are here preserved.

Burntisland, Fife, Scot. 56N. 3w. Ass. Mary Stuart and the poet Chastelard. (See Swinburne's tragedy 'Chastelard.')

Bury St. Edmunds, Suffolk, En. 52N 0E. Coronation of Edmund (856) and of Henry II, oath taken by barons to force ratification of Magna Charta, 1214; insurrection under Jack Straw, 1381, tomb of Mary Tudor, widow of Louis XII.; the poet Lydgate, a monk of the abbey, res of Defoe (See Carlyle, 'Past and Present;' Dickens, 'Pickwick.')

Busento River, Calabria, Italy. 39N. 16E Alaric buried in bed of.

Buxton, Derby, En. 53N. 1w. Old Hall Hotel, built for Mary Queen of Scots.

Cadiz, Spain. 36N. 6w. Spanish fleet destroyed by Drake, 1587; pillaged by English, 1596; blockade by French, 1810-12.

Cadsant, islet near Flushing Defeat of French by Manny, 1337, beginning of Hundred Years' W.

Caen, France. 49N. 0w. William the Conqueror and Queen Matilda buried at, taken by the English, 1346 and 1417, Charlotte Corday brought up at; bp. of Malherbe (1555-1628). (See Sainte-Beuve, 'Causeries du Lundi,' vol. viii)

Caerlaverock, Dumfries, Scot. 55N. 3w. Wallace at, 1297; besieged by Edward I, 1300; grave of 'Old Mortality.'

Caerleon, Monmouthshire, Wa 51N. 2w. Ass Arthur and his 'Round Table.'

Cahors, France 44N. 1E. Bp. of poet Clément Marot (1495-1544).

Calais, France 50N. 1E Siege by Edward III., 1346-47; retaken by French, 1558.

Calatafimi, Sicily 37N. 12E. Neapolitans defeated by Garibaldi, 1860.

Caldiero, Italy. Napoleon defeated by Austrians, 1796; heights captured by Masséna, 1800

Calne, Wilts, En. 51N. 2w. Meeting of Witan, 978, when the floor fell, and Dunstan alone escaped.

Calvi, Corsica. 42N. 8E. Captured by English (fleet under Nelson), 1794; retaken, 1795.

Cambrai, France 50N. 3E. League (Austria, France, Spain, and Pope against Venice), 1508; 'Paix des Dames' (Charles V. and Francis I.), 1529.

Camelford, Cornwall, En. 50N. 4w Traditional sc. King Arthur's birth, and of his last fatal fight with Modred.

Camenz, Lusatia. 51N. 14E. Bp. of Lessing, poet and critic (1729-81).

Campaldino, Italy. 40N. 11E. Fight between Guelfs and Ghibellines, in which Dante took part, 1289.

Camperdown, Holland. 52N. 4E. Defeat of Dutch fleet by Admiral Duncan, 1797.

Candia, Crete. 35N. 25E. Twenty years' siege by Turks, 1645-69.

Canossa, Italy. 44N. 10E. Submission of Emperor Henry IV. to Gregory VII., 1077.

Canterbury, Kent, En 51N. 1w Murder of Becket, 1170; 'Canterbury Pilgrims' at Chequers Inn, tombs of Black Prince and Henry IV.; head of Sir T. More in S. Dunstan's; bp. of Marlowe, the dramatist, 1564-93). (See Stanley, 'Memorials of C')

Cape Finisterre, Spain 42N 9w. Defeat of French fleet by Admiral Anson, 1747, partial victory by Sir R Calder, 1805

Cape Passaro, Sicily 36N 15E Defeat of Spanish fleet by Sir G Byng (Battle of Messina), 1718.

Cappel, Switzerland 47N. 8E. Defeat of Reformers and death of Zwingli, 1531.

Caprera Island, Italy. 41N. 9E. Garibaldi's home (1854-82), and grave.

Capri Island, Italy. 40N. 14E Abode of Emperor Tiberius during last 11 years of life.

Caprona, Italy. 43N. 10E Dante at siege of, 1290

Capua, Italy. 41N. 14E. Taken by Garibaldi, 1860.

Caravaggio, Italy. 45N. 9E. Bp. of painters of that name.

Carberry, Midlothian, Scot. 55N. 3w. Surrender of Mary Stuart to confederates, 1567

Carbisdale, Ross, Scot. 57N. 5w. Final defeat of Montrose, 1650.

Carcassonne, France 43N. 2E. Sc. Albigensian persecution, 1210, besieged by Black Prince, 1356.

Cardiff, Glamorgans, Wa 51N. 3w. Prison for 28 years of Robert, Duke of Normandy; taken by Cromwell, 1648.

Cardross, Dumbartons., Scot. 55N. 4w. Death of Robert Bruce, 1329 (See Froissart.)

Carisbrooke, Isle of Wight. 50N. 1w. Charles I imprisoned, 1647-8.

Carlisle, Cumberland, En. 54N. 2w Mary Stuart imprisoned, 1568; taken by Parlia-

mentarians, 1614, 1648, by Jacobites, 1745; rescue of 'Kinmont Willie,' 1596. (See Branksome)

Carnarvon, capital of county. Wa. 53N. 4W. Edward II. born at, 1284

Carpi, Italy. 44N. 10E. Defeat of French by Prince Eugène, 1701.

Carrickfergus, Antrim, Ir. 54N.5W. Landing place of William III. before the battle of Boyne, 1690; taken by French, 1760, encounter between the 'Drake' and ship of the pirate Paul Jones, 1778.

Cartagena, Spain. 37N. 0W. Held by the 'Intransigeants' for five months, 1873-4.

Cashel, Tipperary, Ir. 52N. 7W. Ancient seat of Kings of Munster; Henry II. received homage of King of Thomond, 1172; burning of cathedral by Earl of Kildare, 1495.

Cassano, Italy. 45N. 9E. Victory of Prince Eugène over French (W. of Spanish Succession), 1705; of Suvarov, 1799.

Castalla, Spain. 38N 26W. Victory of Sir J. Murray and Allies over French, 1813 (Peninsular W.).

Castelfidardo, Italy. 43N. 13E. Rout of Papal troops by General Cialdini, 1860 (Unification of Italy).

Castelfranco, Italy. 45N. 12E. Austrians defeated by French, 1805; bp. of Giorgione.

Castelnaudary, France 43N. 1E. Rased by S Louis, 1229; burnt by Prince of Wales, 1355; Montmorenci defeated by Schomberg, 1632.

Castiglione, Italy. 45N. 10E. Battle (W. of Spanish Succession), 1706; victory of Napoleon, 1796.

Castillon, France. 44N. 0W. Last battle of Hundred Years' W.; Talbot defeated by Dunois and killed, 1453.

Castle Rising, Norfolk, En. 52N. 0E. Res of Edward II.'s queen, Isabella.

Castleton, Derby, En. 53N. 1W. Castle of 'Peveril of the Peak.'

Catanzaro, Italy. 38N. 16E. Robert Guiscard's castle.

Cateau - Cambresis, France. 50N. 3E. Treaty, France and Spain, 1559

Cauterets, France. 42N 0W. Court of Margaret of Navarre, sister of Francis I., A. of the 'Heptameron' (1492-1549)

Cephalonia, Greece, 38N. 20E. Death of Robert Guiscard, 1085

Ceresole, Italy. 44N. 7E. Victory of French over Charles V.'s troops, 1544.

Cerignola, Italy. 41N. 15E. Defeat of French by Gonsalvo de Cordova, 1503

Certaldo, Italy. 43N. 11E. Here Boccaccio passed his last years and died

Cesena, Italy. 44N. 12E. Austrians defeated by Murat, 1815.

Cevennes, France. 44N. 3E. Country of the Camisards. (See R. L. Stevenson, 'Travels with a Donkey.')

Chalfont St. Giles, Buckinghams., En. 51N. 0W Milton's cottage.

Chalgrove, Oxon., En. 51N. 1W. Victory of Prince Rupert; death of Hampden, 1643.

Chalons-sur-Marne, France. 48N 4E. At-

tila defeated by Aetius, 451; Crusade preached by S Bernard, 1147

Chaluz, France. 45N. 0E. Richard I. mortally wounded during siege, 1199.

Champ-Aubert, France. Allies defeated by Napoleon, 1814.

Charenton-le-Pont, France. 48N. 2E. Frequent sc. action during wars with England and religious wars; defended against Allies, 1814.

Chartres, France. 48N. 1E. Taken by Dunois, 1432; coronation of Henry IV, 1594. Contains first Cathedral in France dedicated to the Virgin Mary.

Chateaudun, France. 48N. 1E. Dunois buried in castle chapel.

Chateauneuf-di-Randon, France. Du Guesclin died during siege of, 1380.

Chateau-Thierry, France. 49N. 3E. Allies defeated by Napoleon, 1814; bp. of La Fontaine, chief of fabulists (1621-95).

Chatham, Kent, En. 51N. 0E. Ships burned by De Ruyter, 1667; ass. with Charles Dickens.

Chatillon-sur-Seine, France. 47N. 4E. Congress of Allies, 1814

Chelles, France. Murder of Chilperic I. by Frédegonde, 584.

Cherbourg, Normandy. 49N. 1W. English possession, 1418-50, taken again by English, 1758.

Cheriton, Kent, En. Defeat of Royalists by Waller, 1644.

Chertsey, Surrey, En. 51N. 0W. Last home of the poet Cowley, d 1667.

Chester, Cheshire, En. 53N. 2W. Royalists besieged, 1643-46

Chiari, Italy. 45N. 9E. Villeroi defeated by Prince Eugène, 1707 (W. of Spanish Succession).

Chichester, Sussex En. 50N. 0W. Bp. of Collins, poet (1721-59)

Chigwell, Essex, En 50N. 0E. The 'Maypole Inn' of 'Barnaby Rudge.'

Chillon, Switzerland 46N. 6E. Bonivard, 'prisoner of C.' commemorated by Byron, imprisoned, 1530-36.

Chinon, France. 47N. 0E. Death of Henry II., 1189; Joan of Arc received by Charles VII., 1428; bp. of Rabelais (1483-1553).

Chioggia, Chiozza, Italy. 45N 12E. W. of C. (Venetians and Genoese), 14th century.

Chislehurst, Kent, En. 51N. 0E. Bp of Sir Nicholas Bacon

Chiswick, Middlesex, En. 51N. 0W. Home of William Morris; grave of Hogarth (1697-1764).

Chize, France. 46N. 0W. Defeat of English by Du Guesclin, 1372.

Christianople, Sweden 56N. 16E. Taken from Danes by Gustavus Adolphus, 1611.

Churchill, Oxon, En 51N. 1W. Bp. of Warren Hastings (1732-1818).

Cintra, Portugal. 38N. 8W. Convention (England and France), 1808.

Cirencester, Gloucesters, En. 51N. 1W. Stormed by Prince Rupert, 1642 and 1643.

Ciudad Rodrigo, Spain. 40N. 6W. Taken by Wellington, 1812.

Civitella, Italy. 42N. 13E. Victory of Robert Guiscard and his Normans, 1033.

Clarendon, Wilts, En. Constitutions of C., signed by barons and clergy, 1164.

Clarens, Switzerland. 46N. 6E. Rendered famous by Rousseau.

Cleobury Mortimer, Salop, En 52N 2W. Probable bp. of Langland, the poet, author of 'Piers the Plowman,' 14th century.

Clermont-Ferrand, France. 45N. 3E. Council and first crusade preached by Urban II, 1095; frequent resort of French kings, 13th and 14th centuries, bp. of Pascal (1623-62).

Clevedon, Somersets., En. 51N. 2W. Coleridge at Myrtle Cottage, 1795, Thackeray's 'Castlewood' ('Esmond'), grave of the Arthur Hallam of 'In Memoriam.'

Clonmacnoise, King's County, Ir. 53N. 7W. Annals of Tigernach, the abbot (d. 1088), and other famous works compiled at; burial place of Irish kings and nobles.

Clonmel, Tipperary, Ir. 52N. 7W. Bp. of Sterne (1713 68).

Clontarf, Dublin, Ir. 53N. 6W. Defeat of Danes by Brian Boru and his son, and death of both the latter, Good Friday, 1014

Cnossus, Crete. 35N. 25E. Palace of Minos and famous labyrinth (in course of excavation).

Coburg, Germany 50N. 12E. Luther at, 1530; besieged by Wallenstein, 1632.

Cockermouth, Cumberland, En. 54N. 3W. Mary Stuart imprisoned, 1568; bp. of Wordsworth (1770-1850)

Cockthorpe, Norfolk, En. 52N. 1E. Admiral Sir Cloudesley Shovel baptised at (1650 1707).

Cognac, France. 45N. 0W. Bp. of Francis I

Coimbra, Portugal. 40N. 8W. Ancient capital.

Colchester, Essex, En. 51N. 0E. The 'Royal Town' of 'Cymbeline,' taken by Parliamentarians, 1648

Colinton, The Lothians, Scot. 55N 3W. R L Stevenson at, as a child. (See 'A Lowden Sabbath Morn.')

Coll Island, Scot. 56N. 6W. Dr. Johnson and Boswell storm-bound on, 1773. (See 'Journey to Western Islands.')

Cologne, Germany. 50N 6E. Famous Cathedral. Supposed bones of the 'Three Kings' preserved.

Colombey, France. 48N. 6E. Battle (Franco-German W), 1870.

Colombo, Ceylon 6N. 79E. Captured by English, 1796; bp. of Lord Napier of Magdala (1810-90)

Combe-Florey, Somersets., En. 51N. 3W. Sidney Smith rector, 1829-45.

Comines, France and Belgium. 50N. 2E. Bp of the historian Philippe de C (1445-1509).

Compiegne, France. 49N. 2E. Joan of Arc made prisoner, 1430; Stevenson at. (See 'An Inland Voyage.')

Compostella, (Santiago), Spain. 42N. 9W Famous shrine of San Iago.

Conflans, France. 49N. 5E. Treaty of, closing the W. of 'Bien Public,' signed by Louis XI., 1465.

Conisborough, Yorks, En. 53N 1W. Athelstan's fort. (See Scott, 'Ivanhoe.')

Coniston, Lancashire, En. 54N. 3W. Ruskin's home for many years till his death in 1900.

Connor, Antrim, Ir. 54N. 6W. Defeat of English by Edward Bruce, 1315.

Constance, Switzerland. 47N. 9E. Great Church Council, 1414-18.

Constantinople, Turkey. 41N. 29E. Capital of the Eastern empire from 395, taken by Crusaders, 1203 and 1204; Baldwin proclaimed Latin emperor, 1204; retaken by Greek emperor, 1261, taken by Turks, 1453. (See Finlay, 'Byzantine Empire')

Copenhagen, Denmark 55N. 12E. Naval victory of Parker and Nelson, 1801; bombardment by English, 1807; bp. of Thorwaldsen, sculptor (1770 1844).

Coppet, Switzerland. 46N. 6E. Res. of Mme de Staël; graves of her and her father.

Cordova, Spain. 38N. 5W. Taken from the Moors, 1236, bp. of Seneca, Lucan, Averroes, and Juan de Mena (Spanish poet). (See Irving, 'Conquest of Granada.')

Corfe, Dorset, En. 50N. 2W. Edward the Martyr murdered 978; defended by Lady Bankes, 1643; taken by Parliamentarians, 1646.

Corinth, Greece 38N. 22E. Besieged by Turks, 1715 (See Byron's 'Siege of Corinth.')

Cork, capital of county, Ir. 51N. 8W. Taken by Cromwell, 1649; by Marlborough, 1690

Corsica, island, Mediterranean. 42N 9E. Paoli's insurrection, and French conquest of, 1768.

Corte Nuova, Italy. 45N 9E. Victory of Frederick II. of Germany over Lombard League, 1237.

Corunna, Spain. 43N 8W. John of Gaunt at, 1386; port of sail of the Armada, 1588, battle and death of Sir John Moore, 1809. (See poem by C. Wolfe)

Cosenza, Italy. 39N. 16E. Taken by Robert Guiscard, 1060.

Coulmiers, France. 47N. 1E. Defeat of Bavarian army, 1870

Courtrai, Belgium. 50N. 3E. 'Battle of the Spurs,' 1302.

Coutras, France. 45N. 0W. Victory of Henri IV. over Catholics, 1587.

Coventry, Warwicks., En. 52N 1W. Lady Godiva, 11th century, commemorated by Tennyson; res. of George Eliot, 1841-2. (See Shakespeare, 'Rich. II.' i. 3.)

Cowes, Isle of Wight 50N. 1W. Queen Victoria d. 1901; bp of Dr. Arnold (1795-1842).

Cowslip Green, Somersets., En. 51N. 3W. Hannah More's home.

Cracow, Austria. 50N. 19E. Old Polish capital, graves of Sobieski, Poniatowski, and Kosciusko.

Craigenputtock, Dumfriess., Scot. 55N. 3W. Carlyle's home, 1828-34.

Craonne, France. 49N. 3E. Victory of Napoleon over Blucher, 1814.

Crayford, Kent, En. 51N. 0E. Defeat of Britons under Vortigern by Hengist, 456.

Crecy, France. 50N. 2E. Battle, Aug. 26, 1346.

Crefeld, Germany. 51N. 6E. Defeat of French (Seven Years' W.).

Cremona, Italy. 45N. 10E. Sc. struggles between Guelphs and Ghibellines in the middle ages; taken by Imperialists and Marshal de Villeroi made prisoner, 1702; by French, 1796, 1800; home of the great violin makers, Amati, Guarneri, Stradivarius.

Crimea, Russia. 45N. 34E. War, 1854-55.

Cropredy Bridge, Oxon., En. 52N. 1W. Victory of Royalists, 1644.

Crosthwaite, Cumberland, En. 54N. 3W. Grave of Southey the poet, d. 1843.

Crowndale, Devon, En. 50N. 3W. Bp. of Sir Francis Drake (1540 (?)-96).

Culloden, Inverness, Scot. 57N. 4W. Battle, April 16, 1746.

Cumnor, Berks, En. 51N. 1W. Sc. Amy Robsart's murder. (See Scott, 'Kenilworth,' and Mickle's poem.)

Custozza, Italy. 45N. 11E. Italians defeated by Austrians, 1848, 1866.

Dalquhurn, Dumbarton, Scot. 55N. 4W. Bp. of Smollett, 1721-71.

Dalry (Dal Righ, King's field), Perth, Scot. 56N. 3W. Defeat of Robert Bruce by Macdougal of Lorn (famous 'brooch of Lorn' torn from Bruce's plaid), 1306.

Dalton-in-Furness, Lancashire, En. 54N. 3W. Bp. of Romney, the painter (1734-1802).

Dangan, Meath, Ir. 53N. 6W. Early home of the Duke of Wellington.

Danzig, Prussia (Hanse town). 54N. 18E. Held by Poles against Gustavus Adolphus, 1627-9 (Thirty Years' W.); surrendered to French, 1807; besieged and taken by Allies, 1813.

Dardanelles, The, Turkey. 40N. 26E. Crossed by Xerxes and Alexander; ass. with tale of Hero and Leander; Byron swam across, 1810.

Dartford, Kent, En. 51N. 1E. First paper mill in England established, 1588.

Dartington, Devon, En. 50N. 4E. Bp. of Froude the historian (1818-94).

Dartmouth, Devon, En. 50N. 3W. Port of embarkation of Crusaders, 1190; taken by Prince Maurice, 1643; by Fairfax, 1646; bp. of Sir Humphrey Gilbert, navigator of the 16th century.

Daventry, Northamptons., En. 52N. 1W. Charles I. at, before Naseby, 1645.

Daylesford, Worcesters., En. 52N. 2W. Later res. and grave of Warren Hastings.

Deal, Kent, En. 51N. 1E. Colonel Hutchinson was imprisoned and died in Sandown Castle near. (See 'Memoirs' by his wife.)

Deddington, Oxon, En. 52N. 1W. Piers Gaveston captured, 1312.

Delft, Holland. 52N. 4E. Assassination of William the Silent, 1584; bp. and grave of Grotius, jurist (1583-1645).

Denain, France. 50N. 3E. Defeat of Allies by Villars, 1712 (W. of Spanish Succession).

Dennewitz, Prussia. 52N. 13E. Defeat of French under Ney by Allies, 1813.

Derby, cap. of county, En. 53N. 1W. Johnson married at S. Werburgh, 1735; monument to 'Bess of Hardwick' at All Saints.

Dereham, East, Norfolk, En. 52N. 1E. Last res. and burial place of the poet Cowper; bp. of Borrow, A. of 'The Bible in Spain,' etc. (1803-81). (See Borrow, 'Lavengro.')

Derg, Lough, Donegal, Ir. 54N. 8W. Ass. with legend of S. Patrick's Purgatory, the subject of a play by Calderon.

Dessau, Germany. 52N. 12E. Defeat of Protestants by Wallenstein, 1626 (Thirty Years' W.).

Dettingen, Bavaria. 50N. 9E. Defeat of the Duc de Noailles by George II., 1743.

Deutschbrod, Bohemia. 49N. 15E. Victory of Ziska over Sigismund, 1422 (Hussite W.).

Deventer, Netherlands. 52N. 6E. Erasmus and à Kempis students at.

Devizes, Wilts. En. 51N. 1W. Stormed by Cromwell, 1645; Sir T. Laurence's father landlord of the 'Bear Inn.'

Dieppe, France. 49N. 1E. Bombarded by English and Dutch, 1694.

Dieuze, Alsace-Lorraine. 48N. 6E. Bp. of Edmond About, French A. (1828-85).

Dijon, France. 47N. 5E. Burgundian king defeated by Clovis, 500; taken by Germans, 1870; Prussians held in check by Garibaldi, 1871; bp. of Dukes of Burgundy, and of Bossuet (1627-1704).

Dinan, France. 48N. 2W. Du Guesclin, Constable of France, born near, and his heart preserved at (cir. 1320-80).

Dirham (Deorham), Gloucester, En. 51N. 2W. Defeat of Welsh by Ceawlin, King of Wessex, 577.

Dirleton, Haddington, Scot. 56N. 2W. (See Stevenson, 'The Pavilion on the Links.')

Dniester, river, Russia. 46N. 29E. Defeat of Turks by Prince Gallitzin, 1769.

Dodbrooke, Devon, En. 50N. 3W. Bp. of Dr. John Wolcot (Peter Pindar), poet and satirist (1738-1819).

Dogger Bank, North Sea. 54N. 2E. Severe engagement, English and Dutch fleets, 1781; 'D. B. incident,' 1904.

Dollar, Clackmannan, Scot. 56N. 3W. John Knox at, 1536; burned by Montrose, 1645.

Dolni-Dubnik, Plevna. 43N. 24E. Redoubt taken by General Gourko, 1877 (Russo-Turkish W.).

Domokos, Thessaly. 39N. 22E. Engagement, Greco-Turkish W., 1879.

Domremy, France. 48N. 5E. Bp. of Joan of Arc (1412-31).

Donauworth, Germany. 48N. 10E. Victory of Marlborough over Marshal Tallard, 1704 (W. of Spanish Succession).

Donegal, Ulster, Ir. 54N. 8W. Famous 'Annals of the Four Masters' compiled at.

Donnybrook, Dublin, Ir. 53N. 6W. Celebrated old fair licensed by King John, 1204, abolished 1855.

Doonbeg, Clare, Ir. 52N. 9W. Vessel of the Armada wrecked off, and part of crew killed by natives.

Dorchester, Dorset, En. 50N. 2W. Cromwell at, 1645; Judge Jeffreys' 'Bloody Assize,' 1685.

Dord, Dordrecht, Holland. 51N. 4E. Independence of the United Provinces proclaimed, 1572; famous Protestant Synod, 1618-19; bp. of the De Witt, of Cuyp, and Ary Scheffer.

Dorking, Surrey, En. 51N. 1W. Lord Beaconsfield's 'Coningsby' (1844) written at 'Deepdene' near.

Douai, France. 50N. 3E. Surrendered to Prince Eugène, 1710 (W. of Spanish Succession).

Douglas, Lanark, Scot. 55N. 3W. Queen Mary and Darnley at, 1565. Sc. Scott's 'Castle Dangerous.'

Doune, Perth, Scot. 56N. 4W. Imprisonment and escape of Home, A. of 'Douglas,' after Falkirk, 1746; Charles Edward at, 1745-6; 'Waverley' brought a prisoner to.

Douro, river, Spain and Portugal. 41N. 8W. Victory of Wellington over Soult, 1809.

Dove, river, En. 52N. 1W. Cotton's little fishing house on, where he and Walton lived together.

Dover, Kent, En. 51N. 1E. Blake defeated by Van Tromp, 1652.

Down, Kent, En. 51N. 0E. Res. of Charles Darwin from 1842 to his death.

Downpatrick, County Down, Ir. 54N. 5W. Graves of S. Patrick and S. Columba.

Downs, The, En. 51N. 1E. Indecisive action between English and Dutch fleet, 1666.

Dresden, Saxony. 51N. 13E. Repulse of Allies by Napoleon, and death of Moreau, 1813.

Dreux, France. 48N. 1E. Taken and retaken by Henry II. and Philippe Auguste; Huguenots defeated and Condé made prisoner, 1562.

Drogheda, Louth, Ir. 53N. 6W. Siege by Irish rebels, 1641; stormed and garrison massacred by Cromwell, 1649; surrendered to William III., 1690.

Dromore, Down, Ir. 54N. 6W. Graves of the two famous bishops, Jeremy Taylor and Percy.

Drumclog, Lanarks., Scot. 55N. 4W. Defeat of Claverhouse by Covenanters, 1679.

Drummelzier, Peebles, Scot. 55N. 3W. Traditional grave of Merlin.

Drummond, Perths., Scot. 56N. 3W. Prince Charlie's room preserved in castle.

Dryburgh, Berwicks., Scot. 55N. 2W. Grave of Sir Walter Scott, his wife, and Lockhart.

Dubienka, Russia. 51N. 23E. Battle Russians and Kosciusko, 1792.

Dublin, Ir. 53N. 6W. Henry II. and court at, 1172; slaughter of English, 'Black Monday,' 1209; siege and surrender to Parliamentarians, 1646, 1647; bp. of Steele, R. B. Sheridan, Burke, and Swift.

Duddon, river, En. 54N. 3W. (See Wordsworth's Sonnet.)

Dumbarton, county of D., Scot. 55N. 4W. Wallace a prisoner, 1305; Mary Stuart carried off from to France, 1548; famous capture of Jordanhill by Craufurd, 1571; Smollett at grammar school.

Dumfries, county of D., Scot. 55N. 3W. Comyn stabbed by Bruce, 1306; res. of Burns, who here lies buried.

Dunbar, Haddington, Scot. 56N. 2W. Defeat of Scots by Edward I., and surrender of Baliol, 1296; Edward II. at after Bannockburn; defended against English by 'Black Agnes,' 1339; Mary Stuart carried off to by Bothwell, 1567; defeat of Leslie by Cromwell' ('Race of Dunbar'), 1650.

Dunboy, Bantry Bay, Ir. 51N. 9W. Brave defence and surrender to royal troops, 1601. (See Froude, 'The Two Chiefs of D.')

Dundalk, Louth, Ir. 54N. 6W. Defeat and death of Edward Bruce, 1318; taken by Cromwell, 1649; by Schomberg, 1689.

Dundee, Forfars., Scot. 56N. 2W. William Wallace here at school; Edward I. at, 1296, 1303; Bruce acknowledged king, 1309; taken and retaken during Scottish wars; sack by Montrose, 1645; sack and massacre by Monk, 1651.

Dundonald, Ayrshire, Scot. 55N. 4W. Death of Robert II., 1390.

Dundrennan, Kirkcudbrights., Scot. 54N. 3W. Traditional abode of Michael Scott the wizard; here Mary Stuart spent her last night in Scotland, 1568.

Dunfermline, Fife, Scot. 56N. 3W. Res. and burial place of Scottish kings; grave of Robert Bruce; bp. of Charles I.

Dungannon, Tyrone, Ir. 54N. 6W. Seat of the rebel O'Neills.

Dunkeld, Perths., Scot. 56N. 3W. Monument to the 'Wolf of Badenoch,' son of Robert II.; brave defence by Cameronians, 1689; 'Birnam wood' in neighbourhood.

Dunkirk, Dunkerque, France. 51N. 2E. Burned by English, 1388; held in turn by French and Spanish, 16th and 17th centuries; taken by Cromwell, 1658; sold by Charles II.

Dunmow, Essex, En. 51N. 0E. Prize of flitch of bacon to married couples instituted 1244.

Dunsinane, Perths., Scot. 56N. 3W. Defeat of Macbeth by Malcolm Canmore, Duncan's son, 1054.

Dunstable, Bedfords., En. 51N. 0W. First miracle play performed, 1110; court held by Cranmer for divorce of Catherine of Aragon.

Dunstaffnage, Argyles., Scot. 56N. 5W. Former resting-place of the 'stone of destiny.'

Dupplin, Perths., Scot. 56N. 3W. Victory

of Edward Baliol over forces of David, King of Scotland, 1332.

Duppel, Prussia. 54N. 9E. Victory of Danes over Germanic Confederation, 1848; taken by the Prussians, 1864.

Durazzo, Turkey. 41N. 19E. Taken by Robert Guiscard after a three months' siege, 1081.

Durham, county of D., En. 54N. 1W. Tombs of Bede and S. Cuthbert.

Durrenstein, Austria. 48N. 15E. Richard I. imprisoned by Leopold of Austria; Russians beaten back by French, 1805.

Dusseldorf, Germany. 51N. 6E. Bp. of Heinrich Heine (1797-1856).

Dwina, the western river, Russia. 64N. 40E. Defeat of Saxons by Charles XII., 1701 (Swedo-Polish W.).

Ebersberg, Austria. 48N. 14E. Austrians driven from (Wagram Campaign), 1809.

Ecclefechan, Dumfriess., Scot. 55N. 3W. Bp. and grave of Carlyle (1795-1881).

Eckmuhl, Bavaria. 49N. 12E. Victory of Napoleon over Austrians, 1809 (Wagram Campaign).

Eddystone, rocks, Cornwall, En. 50N. 4W. Lighthouse, Sir J. N. Douglas, 1882.

Edenhall, Cumberland, En. 54N. 3W. Goblet known as the 'Luck' still preserved.

Edgehill, border of Warwicks. and Oxfords., En. 52N. 1W. First battle of Civil W., Oct. 23, 1642.

Edgeworth, Lancashire, En. 53N. 2W. Battle (W. of the Roses), 1469.

Edgeworthstown, Longford, Ir. 53N. 7W. Home of Edgeworth family since 1583.

Edial, Staffords., En. 52N. 2W. Johnson opened school at, 1736.

Edinburgh, Scot. 55N. 3W. Reception of Margaret Tudor (see Dunbar, 'The Thistle and the Rose'); castle destroyed by Elizabeth's forces, 1573; Cromwell at siege of, 1650; castle held for James VII., 1689. (See Scott, 'Bonnie Dundee,' and 'The Heart of Midlothian.')

Edmonton, Middlesex, En. 51N. 0W. Graves of Charles Lamb and his sister. (See Cowper's 'John Gilpin.')

Ednam, Roxburghs., Scot. 55N. 2W. Bp. of Thomson the poet, A. of the 'Seasons,' etc. (1700-48).

Eger, Bohemia. 50N. 12E. Wallenstein murdered, 1634.

Egremont, Cumberland, En. 54N. 3W. See Wordsworth for legend of Horn.

Ehrenbreitstein, Germany. 50N. 7E. Captured by French, 1799.

Eigg, Egg, island, Scot. 56N. 6W. Slaughter of monks from Iona, 617; 200 Macdonalds smoked to death by Macleods, end 16th century; Scott at during his cruise in 1814.

Einsiedeln, Switzerland. 47N. 8E. Noted yearly pilgrimage to; Zwingli, reformer, preacher at, 1516-18; taken by French, 1798; bp. of Paracelsus, commemorated by Browning.

Eisenach, Germany. 50N. 10E. (See Wart-

burg.) Luther at as student; bp. of J. Seb. Bach (1685-1750).

Eisleben, Germany. 51N. 11E. Bp. of Luther (1483-1546).

Elba, island, Mediterranean. 42N. 10E. Napoleon on from May, 1814, to February, 1815.

Elchingen, Bavaria. 48N. 10E. Austrians driven out by Ney, 1805.

Elderslie, Renfrews., Scot. 55N. 4W. Traditional bp. of Wallace, and ancient patrimony of the Stuarts.

Elena, Bulgaria. 43N. 25E. Russian victory (Russo-Turkish W.), 1877.

Ellandune, Wilts, En. 51N. 2W. Egbert's victory over Mercians, 823 (5?).

Ellisland, Dumfriess., Scot. 55N. 3W. Home of Burns, 1788-90.

Elsinore, Denmark. 56N. 12E. Sc. 'Hamlet.'

Ely, Cambridge, En. 52N. 0E. Hereward's camp of refuge; surrendered to the Conqueror, 1071; res. of Cromwell, 1636-40.

Enfield, Middlesex, En. 51N. 0W. A royal res. of Edward VI.

Engen, Baden. 47N. 8E. Defeat of Austrians by Moreau, 1800.

Enger, Westphalia. 51N. 8E. Res. and burial place of Witikind, leader of the Saxons against Charlemagne, killed 807.

Enniscorthy, Wexford, Ir. 52N. 6W. Taken by Cromwell, 1649; destroyed by rebels encamped on Vinegar Hill, 1798.

Enniskillen, Fermanagh, Ir. 54N. 7W. Bravely defended against James II.'s forces, 1689.

Ensisheim, Alsace-Lorraine. 47N. 7E. Sc. warfare during Thirty Years' W.

Enzersdorf, Austria. 48N. 16E. Taken by French on first day of battle of Wagram, 1809.

Epernay, France. 49N. 3E. Taken from Leaguers by Henri IV., 1592.

Epinay, France. 48N. 2E. Ancient res. of Frankish kings.

Erbach, Hesse. 50N. 9E. Austrians driven back by French, 1800; tomb of Eginhard, Charlemagne's son-in-law.

Ercildoune, Berwicks., Scot. 55N. 2W. Traditional home of Thomas the Rhymer.

Erfurt, Saxony. 50N. 11E. Luther a student at; celebrated meeting of the monarchs of Europe, 1808.

Ermenonville, France. 49N. 2E. Here Rousseau died, 1778.

Ermin Street, Roman road running from London to York.

Espinosa-de-los-Monteros, Spain. 42N. 3W. Defeat of Spaniards by French, 1808.

Essling, Austria. 48N. 16E. Victory of Napoleon over Austrians, 1809 (Battle of Aspern).

Estella, Spain. 42N. 2W. Battle of 3 days, and death of General Concha, 1874 (Carlist W.).

Etampes, France. 48N. 2E. Clotaire defeated by Thierry, 604; destroyed by Rollo, 911; taken by Henri IV., 1590 (Religious W.).

Etaples, France. 50N. 1E. Treaty, Henry VII. and Charles VIII., 1492.

Ettlingen, Germany. 48N. 8E. Defeat of Austrians by French, 1796.

Ettrick, Selkirks., Scot. 55N. 3W. Bp. and grave of Hogg the 'Shepherd' (1770-1835).

Eupatoria, Crimea 45N. 33E. Anglo-French army at, 1855-56.

Evesham, Worcestershire, En 52N. 1W Defeat and death of Simon de Montfort, 1265.

Evora, Portugal. 38N. 7W. In possession of Moors, 715-1166.

Evreux, France. 49N. 1E. Taken and re-taken by English and French during Hundred Years' W.; occupied by Prussians, 1870.

Exeter, Devons., En. 50N. 3W. Sc. sieges by Danes, William the Conqueror, etc.; taken by Fairfax, 1646; bp. of the 'judicious' Hooker (1554-1600).

Exmoor, Devons., En. 51N. 3W. (See Blackmore, 'Lorna Doone.')

Eylau, Prussia. 54N. 20E. Two days' battle and victory of Napoleon, 1807.

Faenza, Italy. 44N. 11E. Bp. of Torricelli (1608-47), inventor of the barometer.

Falaise, France. 48N. 0W. Taken in turn by Henry V. and Charles VII., 1418, 1450, bp. of William the Conqueror.

Falkirk, Stirlingshire, Scot. 56N. 3W. Defeat of Wallace by Edward I., 1298; of George II 's force by Charles Edward, 1746.

Falkland, Fife, Scot. 56N. 3W. Young Duke of Rothesay starved to death, 1402, death of James V., 1542. (See Scott, 'Fair Maid of Perth.')

Famagusta, Cyprus. 35N. 33E. Guy de Lusignan crowned King of Jerusalem, 1191; besieged by Turks, Oct. 1570-Aug. 1571.

Fanjeaux, France. 43N. 2E. Burnt by Black Prince, 1355.

Fano, Italy. 43N. 13E. Taken and re-taken by Totila and Belisarius, 545.

Farnham, Surrey, En. 51N. 0W. Defeat of Danes by Alfred, 895; Moor Park, ass. with Swift, is in the neighbourhood.

Feldkirch, Austria. 47N. 9E. French victory, 1800.

Fenestrelle, Italy. 45N. 7E. Prison of Xavier de Maistre, and where he wrote 'Voyage autour de ma chambre.'

Fere, La, France. 49N. 3E. Sacked by Allies, 1814, taken by Germans, 1870.

Fere-Champenoise, La, France. 48N. 4E. Victory of Allies over Napoleon, 1814

Ferney, France. 46N. 6E. Home of Voltaire for last 20 years of his life.

Ferrara, Italy. 44N. 11E. Repulse of Murat by the Austrians, 1815 (Hundred Days' W.); bp. of Savonarola (1452-98).

Ferrieres, France. 48N. 2E. Consecration of Pepin le Bref, first Carlovingian king, and father of Charlemagne, 751.

Ferrol, Spain. 43N. 8W. French defeated by English fleet, 1805; taken later by French, 1809 and 1823.

Ferrybridge, Yorks., En. 53N. 1W. Defeat of Yorkists, 1461.

Ferte-Milon, France. 49N. 3E. Bp. of Racine (1639-99).

Fiesole, Italy. 43N. 11E. Home of Fra Angelico.

Finisterre, Cape, Spain. 42N. 9W. French fleet defeated by Anson, 1747; by Admirals Calder and Strachan, 1805.

Fismes, France. 49N. 3E. Summons to arms sent out to the nation from by Napoleon, 1814.

Flavigny, France. 47N. 4E. Taken by the English, 1359.

Fleche, La, France 47N. 0W. Descartes student at; Hume's first philosophical work written here (1737).

Fleurus, Belgium. 50N. 4E. Battle, 1622 (Thirty Years' W.), French victory over Augsburg league, 1690, of French over Austrians, 1794, defeat of Blücher by Napoleon (Battle of Ligny), 1815.

Flint, Wa. 53N. 3W Surrender of Richard II. to Bolingbroke, 1399.

Flodden, Northumberland, En. 55N. 2W. Defeat of Scots, and death of James IV. and his nobility, Sept. 9, 1513.

Florence, Italy 43N. 11E. Proclaimed a republic, 1250; Dante exiled, 1302, plague described by Boccaccio, 1348; Savonarola executed, 1498. Under the Medici it became the great centre of literature and art. The Florentine school of painters included Cimabue, Giotto, the Lippis, Del Sarto, etc.; bp. of Dante, Machiavelli, the sculptors Ghiberti and Donatello, etc., and of Florence Nightingale. (See George Eliot, 'Romola.')

Flores, westernmost of the Azores Islands. 39N. 31W. 'At Flores in the Azores, Sir Richard Grenville lay. (See Tennyson, 'The Revenge.')

Flushing, Holland. 51N. 3E. First town to rise against the Spaniards, 1572; bombarded by English, 1809.

Foggia, Italy. 41N. 15E. Manfred defeated by Charles d'Anjou, 1266.

Fontainebleau, France. 48N. 2E. Royal res. of early French kings; revocation of Edict of Nantes signed by Louis XIV., 1685, abdication of Napoleon, 1814.

Fontarabia, Spain. 43N. 1W. Sc. sieges by Francis I. and Conde; taken by Marshal Berwick, 1719; ass. with the hero Roland. (See Roncesvalles)

Fontenay (Fontanetum), France. 46N. 0W. Celebrated victory of Charles the Bald and Louis the German over Lothair, 841.

Fontenoy, Belgium. 50N. 3E. Defeat of Allies by Marshal Saxe, 1745 (W. of Austrian Succession).

Fontevrault, France. 47N. 0W. Tombs of Richard I., Henry II., and Plantagenet Queens excavated Aug. 1910, in Abbey.

Forli, Italy. 44N. 12E. Taken by French, 1797; joined the cause of liberty, 1860.

Formigny, France. 49N. 0W. Defeat of English, 1450 (Hundred Years' W).

Fornovo, Italy. 44N. 10E. Victory of Charles VIII. over Milanese, 1495.

Forres, Elgins., Scot. 57N. 3W. Victory of Malcolm II. over Danes, 1008 or 1010. (Sc. 'Macbeth.')

Fossalta, river, Emilia, Italy. 44N. 10E. Victory of Guelphs over Ghibellines and capture of Enzio, King of Sardinia, 1249.

Fossano, Italy. 44N. 7E. Taken by Charles V., 1536; by French, 1796.

Fotheringay, Northamptonshire, En. 52N. 0W. Mary Queen of Scots beheaded, 1587; bp. of Richard III.

Fougeres, France. 48N. 1W. Vendean victory over republicans, 1793.

Fraga, Spain. 41N. 0E. Alfonso I. of Aragon defeated by Moors, 1134.

Framlingham, Suffolk, En. 52N. 1E. Tomb of Earl of Surrey, poet, beheaded,1547.

Frankenhausen, Germany. 51N. 11E. Munzer, leader, taken and beheaded (Peasants' W.), 1525.

Frankfort-on-the-Main, Germany. 50N. 8E. Ancient capital of Eastern France; Barbarossa and later emperors elected at; Treaty of Peace (Franco-German W.), 1871; bp. of Goethe.

Frankfort-on-the-Oder, Germany. 52N. 14E. Occupied in turn by Wallenstein and Swedes (Thirty Years' W.); suffered during Seven Years' W.; French in possession, 1806, 1812-13.

Fraustadt, Prussia. 51N. 16E. Saxons defeated by Charles XII. of Sweden, 1706.

Fredericia, Jutland. 55N. 9E. Bombarded by Germans, 1849.

Frederikshald, Norway. 59N. 11E. Charles XII. of Sweden killed during siege of, 1718. (See Voltaire, 'Charles XII.')

Freiberg, Saxony. 50N. 13E. Defeat of Imperial forces by Prussians, 1762 (last of the Seven Years' W.).

Freiburg in Breisgau, Germany. 47N. 7E. Defeat of Imperialists by Condé and Turenne after 3 days' battle, 1644 (Thirty Years' W.).

Frejus, France. 43N. 6E. Landing of Napoleon from Egypt, 1799; his port of embarkation for Elba, 1814; bp. of Agricola.

Freshwater, Isle of Wight. 50N. 1W. Res. of Tennyson.

Freteval, France. 47N. 1E. Richard I.'s victory over Philippe Auguste, 1194.

Friedberg, Bavaria. 48N. 11E. Austrians defeated by Moreau, 1796.

Friedberg, Silesia. 52N. 15E. Austrians defeated by Frederick the Great, 1745.

Friedland, E. Prussia. 54N. 21E. Victory of Napoleon over Russians and Prussians, 1807.

Fuentes de Onoro, Spain. 40N. 6W. Masséna defeated by Wellington, 1811 (Peninsular W.).

Furnes, Belgium. 51N. 2E. Victory over Flemish (English Allies) by Comte d'Artois, 1297.

Furth, Bavaria. 49N. 12E. Battle between Wallenstein and Gustavus Adolphus, 1632.

Gadebusch, Germany. 53N. 11E. Victory of Danes, 1712 (Dano-Swedish W.).

Gadshill, Kent, En. 50N. 0E. Last home of Charles Dickens; ass. Falstaff.

Gaeta, Italy. 41N. 13E. Besieged in turn by French and Austrians, 1799-1821; capitulated to Piedmontese, 1861 (Unification of Italy).

Gainsborough, Lincolns., En. 53N. 0W. Marriage of Alfred the Great to chief's daughter, 868; King Sweyn assassinated, 1013; taken by Cromwell, 1643. The 'St. Oggs' of Geo. Eliot's novels.

Galatz, Roumania. 45N. 28E. Russian victory over Turks, 1789.

Galway, Connaught, Ir. 53N. 9W. Besieged and taken by Parliamentarians under Ludlow, 1652; surrendered after battle of Aghrim, 1691.

Garigliano, river, Italy. 41N. 14E. French defeated by Spaniards under G. de Cordova, Chevalier Bayard being among the French, 1503; defeat of Neapolitans by Italian patriots, 1850.

Gask, Perths., Scot. 56N. 3W. Home of the Scottish poetess, Lady Nairne, of the house of Jacobite Oliphants, A. of the 'Land o' the Leal,' etc.

Gastein, Austria. 47N. 13E. Convention, Austria and Prussia, for division of Schleswig-Holstein, 1865.

Gate Fulford, Yorks, En. 53N. 1W. English defeated by Harold Hardraga, 1066.

Gateshead, Durham, En. 54N. 1W. House in which Defoe wrote 'Robinson Crusoe.'

Gayhurst, Bucks, En. 52N. 0W. Bp. of Sir Kenelm Digby, one of the Gunpowder plotters.

Gembloux, Belgium. 50N. 4E. Defeat of Netherlanders by Don John of Austria, 1578.

Geneva, Lake, Switzerland. 46N. 6E. Ass. Voltaire, Mme de Staël, Rousseau, Byron, Gibbon.

Geneva, town, Switzerland. 46N. 6E. Res. of Calvin, 1541 to his death, 1564; bp. of Rousseau, Necker, Bonnet, and De Saussure.

Genoa, Italy. 44N. 8E. Austrians driven from, 1746; English naval victory over French, 1795; blockade, and capitulation of Masséna, 1800; chief old families: Doria, Spinola, Fieschi, Grimaldi; Columbus was a son of the territory.

Gerberoy, France. 49N. 2E. Robert, son of William the Conqueror, besieged and imprisoned by his father, 1080; taken by Henry II., 1160; Earl of Arundel defeated and killed by the 'Ecorcheurs,' 1435; taken and retaken later by English and French.

Gerona, Spain. 42N. 2E. Besieged during Peninsular W., 1809.

Ghent, Belgium. 51N. 3E. Revolts under the Arteveldes, 1336, 1379-83; against Charles V., 1538; pacification (United Provinces against Spain), 1576; treaty (England and United States), 1815; bp. of Jacob van Artevelde and of 'time-honoured Lancaster.' (See old ballad of 'Mary Ambree.')

Gibraltar, Spain. 36N. 5W. Finally taken from the Moors, 1462; in English possession since 1704; held by General Eliott against French and Spanish, 1779-83.

E

Gidding, Little, Hampshire, En. 52N. 0W. Community founded by Nicholas Ferrar, 1625. (See Shorthouse, ' John Inglesant.')

Gillingham, Dorset, En. 51N. 2W. Defeat of Danes by Edmund Ironsides, 1016.

Gisors, France. 40N. 1E. Victory of Richard I. over French, 1198.

Gitschin, Bohemia 50N. 15E. Defeat of Austrians by Prussians, 1866 (Seven Weeks' W.).

Gladsmuir, Haddingtons., Scot. 55N. 2W. Battle of Prestonpans, 1745.

Glamys, Forfars, Scot. 56N. 3W. Malcolm II., Duncan's grandfather, reported, wrongly, to have been murdered here; Scott passed a night in Macbeth's castle.

Glarus, Switzerland. 47N. 9E. Zwingli, reformer, pastor at, 1506-16.

Glastenbury, Somerset, En. 51N. 2W. Ass. legend of Joseph of Arimathea and the Grail.

Glenalmond, Perthshire, Scot. 56N. 3W. Grave of Ossian, commemorated by Wordsworth

Glencoe, Argylls., Scot. 56N. 4W. Massacre of Macdonalds, Feb. 13, 1692.

Glenfinnan, Inverness, Scot. 56N. 5W. Stuart standard raised, 1745.

Glenfruin, Dumbarton, Scot. 56N. 4W. Massacre by Macgregors, and consequent suppression of their surname. (Sc. ' Rob Roy.')

Glenlivet, Banffs., Scot. 57N. 3W. Defeat of Argyle by rebel earls under James VI., 1594.

Glenmoriston, Inverness, Scot. 57N. 4W. Prince Charles in hiding after Culloden.

Glenroy, Inverness, Scot. 56N. 4W. Celebrated ' parallel roads ' marking the shores of ancient lakes.

Glenshiel, Ross, Scot. 57N. 5W. Highlanders and Spanish Allies defeated by Hanoverians, 1719.

Glen Trool, Galloway, Scot. 55N. 4W. Sc. Bruce's wanderings and adventures.

Gloucester, cap. of county, En. 51N. 2W. Bishop Hooper martyred, 1555; shrine of Osric, King of Northumbria, and tomb of Edward II.

Godstow, Oxon, En. 51N. 1W. Res. and burial place of ' Fair Rosamond.'

Gorey, Jersey. 40N. 2W. William Prynne, A. of ' Histriomastix,' imprisoned, 1637-40.

Gorlitz, Germany. 51N. 15E. Home of the mystic, Jacob Boehme (1575-1624).

Goslar, Germany 51N. 10E. Sc. warfare during Thirty Years' W.

Gottingen, Germany. 51N. 9E. Occupied by the French, 1803-7, Coleridge, Longfellow, Motley, etc., students at; the brothers Grimm expelled for liberal views, 1837.

Gracedieu, Leicester, En. 52N. 1W. Bp. of Beaumont the dramatist (1584-1616).

Granada, Spain. 37N. 3W Last Moorish stronghold, capitulated 1491; tombs of Ferdinand and Isabella, and of Gonsalvo di Cordova, the ' great captain ' (1443-1515). (See Irving, ' Conquest of Granada.')

Grandson, Switzerland. 46N. 6E. Victory of the Swiss over Charles the Bold, 1476.

Grantham, Lincoln, En 52N. 0W. King John and court at, 1213, Buckingham's death-warrant signed by Richard III., 1483; Cromwell's first victory over Royalists, 1643; Sir Isaac Newton student at, 1655-6.

Grasmere, Westmoreland, En. 54N. 3W. Grave of Wordsworth

Gravelines, France. 51N. 2E. Defeat of French by Allies under Egmont, 1558; Armada dispersed, 1588.

Gravelotte, Alsace-Lorraine. 49N 6E. Defeat of Bazaine, 1870 (Franco-German W.).

Gravesend, Kent, En. 51N. 0E. The great navigators of the 16th century here assembled their fleets before starting on their perilous voyages.

Greenhithe, Kent, En. 51N. 0W. Sir J. Franklin's port of sail, 1845.

Greenock, Renfrews, Scot. 55N. 4W. Grave of Burns' ' Highland Mary '; raided by Rob Roy, 1715; bp. of James Watt and Kidd the pirate. (See Poe, ' The Gold Bug.')

Greenwich, Kent, En 51N. 0. Here Queen Elizabeth was born, 1533, and Edward VI. died, 1553.

Grochow, Poland. 52N 23E. Russians defeated by Poles under Radziwill, 1831.

Gubbio, Italy 43N. 12E. Discovery of ' Eugubine Tablets,' inscribed with rules of ancient brotherhood, 1444

Guildford, Surrey, En. 51N. 0W. Res. of early kings; Alfred the Atheling and his partisans massacred by Godwin's orders, 1036; taken by Louis the Dauphin, 1216.

Guinegatte, France. 50N. 2E. Battle of the Spurs, 1513.

Guines, France. 50N. 1E. Field of the Cloth of Gold held near.

Guise, France. 49N. 3E. Defended by its women against the Spaniards, 1650, bp. of Camille Desmoulins, guillotined 1794.

Gunzburg, Bavaria. 48N. 10E. Ney's victory over Austrians, 1805.

Haarlem, Holland. 52N. 4E. Siege and massacre by Duke of Alva, 1572, 1573, bp. of Laurens Coster, printer, Wouverman, Van der Helst, painters. (See Motley, op. cit)

Habbie's Howe, Midlothian, Scot. 55N. 3W. Sc. Allan Ramsay's ' Gentle Shepherd.'

Haddington, cap. of county, Scot. 55N. 2W. English besieged by Scots, 1549; Edward Irving head of mathematical school, 1810-12; ass. Wishart, reformer and martyr; bp of Knox and Jane Welsh Carlyle.

Hadleigh, Suffolk, En. 52N. 0E Supposed tomb of Danish king Guthrum, d. 889.

Hague, The, Holland. 52N. 4E. The brothers De Witt killed, 1672; Treaty of Triple Alliance, 1668; coalition against France, 1673, against Louis XIV., 1701; Peace conference, 1899; bp. of Rembrandt and Potter. (See Dumas, ' The Black Tulip.')

Hamburg, Austria. 48N. 16E. The Carnutum of the ' Nibelungenlied.'

Halidon Hill, Northumberland, En. 55N. 2W. English victory over Scots, 1333.

Halifax, Yorks, En. 53N. 1W. Sterne educated at.

Ham, France. 49N. 3E. State prison, in which Joan of Arc, Condé, Louis Napoleon, etc., were imprisoned.

Hameln (Hamelin), Hanover. 52N. 9E. Town freed from rats by the famous 'Pied Piper,' 1284. (See Browning's poem.)

Hampden, Great, Bucks, En. 51N. 0W. Bp. of John Hampden, and where he lies buried (1594-1643).

Hampstead, Middlesex, En. 51N. 0W. Meeting place of Kit Cat Club, ass. many of the chief names in literature.

Hampton, Middlesex, En. 51N. 0W. Bp of Edward VI.; escape of Charles I. from, Nov 1647, conference of bishops and Presbyterians, 1604.

Hanau, Germany. 50N. 8E. Austrians and Allies defeated by Napoleon, 1813; bp. of the brothers Grimm (Jakob, 1785-1863; Wilhelm, 1786-1859).

Hanover, Germany 52N 9E. Palace of Herrenhausen (fine works of art); bp of the brothers Schlegel and Sir F. W. Herschel (1738-1822).

Harby, Hardeby, Notts, En. 52N. 1W. Here Eleanor of Castile, queen of Edward I., died, 1290.

Harlaw, Aberdeens, Scot 57N. 2W See 'Ballad' in Scott's 'Antiquary.'

Harlech, Merionethshire, Wa. 52N 4W Successful siege by Yorkists, 1468, commemorated by the 'March of the Men of H.'

Harrogate, Yorkshire, En. 54N. 1W. (See Smollett, 'Humphry Clinker.')

Harrow, Middlesex, En. 51N. 0W. School among its famous scholars were Byron, Rodney, Sir R. Peel, Lord Palmerston, etc.

Harz Mountains, Germany. 51N. 10E. Brocken (q.v.) the highest summit.

Haslemere, Surrey, En. 51N. 0W. Aldworth, home and death place of Tennyson near

Hastings, Sussex, En. 50N. 0E. Battle, Oct. 14, 1066

Hatfield, Herts., En. 51N 0W. Elizabeth here when called to the throne; her first Privy Council held at, 1558.

Hatfield, Yorks, En. 53N. 1W Battle between Edwin, King of Northumbria, Cadwallo, and Penda of Mercia, 633.

Havre, France. 49N. 0E. Taken and retaken by English and French, 1562; bombarded by English, 1694, etc ; bp. of Bernardin de St Pierre, A. of 'Paul et Virginie,' Casimir Delavigne, and Georges and Mlle de Scudéry.

Hawarden, Flintshire, Wa. 53N 3W. Res. of W. E. Gladstone.

Hawick, Roxburghs., Scot. 55N. 2W. Ruined tower of Harden near, home of 'Auld Wat,' who married the 'Flower of Yarrow,' from whom Scott was descended.

Hawkshead, Lancashire, En. 54N. 3W. Wordsworth at Grammar School.

Haworth, Yorks, En. 53N 1W. Home of the Brontës.

Hawthornden, Midlothian, Scot. 55N. 3W. Bp. and home of Drummond the poet (1585-1649), visited by Ben Jonson, 1618-19 (see Drummond's 'Notes'); Dr. Johnson and Boswell at, 1773.

Hayes Barton, Devon, En. 50N. 3W. Bp. of Sir Walter Raleigh (1552 (?)-1618).

Heddington (Ethandune), En. 51N. 2W Alfred's victory over Danes, 878.

Hedgeley, Northumberland, En. 55N. 1W. Defeat of Lancastrians and death of Sir Ralph Percy, 1464.

Heidelberg, Germany. 49N. 8E. Former res. of electors palatine.

Heilbronn, Wurtemberg. 49N. 9E. Prison of Goetz v. Berlichingen, subject of Goethe's drama.

Heilsberg, Prussia. 54N. 20E. Indecisive battle between Soult and Russians, 1807.

Heligoland, North Sea. 54N. 7E. English possession, 1807-1890

Hellevoetsluys, Holland. 51N. 4E. Port of departure of William III., 1688.

Helsingborg, Sweden. 56N. 12E. Danish invaders driven back by Steinbock, 1710.

Hengsdown, Hengston, Cornwall, En. 50N. 4W. Danes defeated by Egbert, 835.

Herculaneum, Italy. 40N. 14E Destroyed by eruption of Vesuvius, A.D. 79.

Hereford, cap. of county, En. 52N. 2W. Old 'Mappa Mundi' in cathedral; sc. warfare during Wars of Roses and Civil Wars; bp. of Garrick, the actor.

Hericourt, France. 47N. 6E. Defeat of Burgundians by Swiss, 1474; three days' battle (Franco-Prussian W.) 1871.

Heristal, Herstal, Belgium. 50N. 5E. Bp. of King Pepin and frequent res. of Charlemagne.

Hernani, Spain. 43N. 1W. Battles, 1836, 1837 (Carlist W.).

Herrara, Spain. 42N. 4W. Victory of Don Carlos, 1837.

Herrnhut, Saxony. 51N. 14E. Chief seat of the Moravian Brethren.

Hexham, Northumberland, En. 54N 2W. Defeat of Lancastrians, 1464.

Highgate, Middlesex, En. 51N. 0W. Last home and burial place of Coleridge, graves of 'George Eliot,' Faraday, etc.

Hildesheim, Hanover. 52N. 9E. Town of extreme antiquarian interest.

Hochkirch, Saxony. 51N. 14E. Defeat of Frederick the Great by Austrians, 1758 (Seven Years' W); French defeated, 1813.

Hochstadt, Bavaria. 48N. 10E. Imperialists defeated by Villars, 1703, battle of Blenheim, 1704; Austrians defeated by Moreau, 1800.

Hoechst, Germany. 50N. 8E. Victory of Tilly (Thirty Years' W.).

Hof, Germany. 50N. 11E. J. P. Richter a student at when young, Austrians defeated by Prussians, 1759, Prussians by Murat, 1807.

Hohenfriedberg, Prussia. 51N. 16E. Vic-

tory of Frederick the Great (W. of Austrian Succession), 1745.

Hohenlinden, Germany. 48N. 11E. Defeat of Austrians by Moreau, 1800. (See poem by Campbell.)

Holy Island (Lindisfarne), Northumberland, En 55N. 1W. Famous old priory of Columban monks

Homildon Hill, Northumberland, En. 55N. 2W. Victory of English under Hotspur over Scots, 1402.

Honiton, Devon, En. 50N. 3W. Lacemaking introduced by Flemish refugees, 16th century.

Horsham, Sussex, En. 51N. 0W. Shelley born at Field Place near.

Hucknall Torkard, Notts , En. 53N. 1W. Grave of Lord Byron.

Huesca, Spain. 42N. 0W. Carlist victory, 1837.

Hughenden, Bucks, En. 51N. 0W. Res. for 30 years of D'Israeli, Earl of Beaconsfield (1804-81), and where he is buried.

Hull, Yorks, En. 53N. 0W. Defended by Fairfax against Royalists, 1643; bp. of William Wilberforce, philanthropist (1759-1833)

Huntingdon, cap. of county, En. 52N. 0W. Bp. of Oliver Cromwell, 1599, res of the poet Cowper, 1765-7.

Hursley, Hampshire, En. 51N 1W. Graves of Keble (vicar, 1835-66) and of Richard Cromwell.

Hurst Castle, Hampshire, En. 50N. 1W. Charles I. here Dec. 1-17 before his execution.

Huy, Belgium. 50N. 5E. Last home of Peter the Hermit.

Hyeres, France. 43N. 6E. Bp. of Massillon, French divine (1663-1742).

Iceland, Arctic Ocean. 65N. 18W First colony f. by Norwegian nobles, 874.

Icknield Street   Old Roman Road running west from Norfolk.

If, island, Mediterranean 43N. 5E. State prison; Mirabeau confined at, 1774. (See Dumas, 'Monte Christo')

Ilchester, Somersets., En. 51N. 2W. Bp. of Roger Bacon (1214-94 ?).

Imola, Italy. 44N. 11E. French victory, 1797.

Inchmahome, islet, Perths., Scot. 56N. 3W. Mary Queen of Scots at after Pinkie; her child-garden and bower still seen.

Ingelheim, Germany. 49N. 7E. Ancient res. of Charlemagne, and according to tradition his birthplace.

Ingelmunster, Belgium. 50N. 3E. Defeat of English and Hanoverians by French, 1794

Ingolstadt, Germany. 48N. 11E. Death of Tilly, who was mortally wounded during the sack, 1632.

Inkerman, Crimea. 44N. 33E. Battle, Nov. 5, 1854.

Innsbruck, Austria. 47N. 11E. Monument and statue to the patriot Andreas Hofer (1767-1810).

Inverlochy, Inverness, Scot. 56N. 5W.

Defeat of Campbells and Covenanters by Montrose, 1645.

Inverness, cap. of county, Scot. 57N. 4W. Castle of Malcolm Canmore and Macbeth; fort erected by Cromwell, since destroyed.

Iona (Icolmkill), Hebrides. 6N 6W. Convent of S. Columba, 6th century, ancient centre of learning; sepulchre of Kings of Scotland, Ireland, and Norway.

Ipswich, Suffolk, En. 52N. 1E The 'White Horse' (sc. 'Eatanswill' of 'Pickwick'), bp. of Cardinal Wolsey

Ischia, island, Bay of Naples. 40N. 13E. Destroyed by earthquake, 1883

Islay, island, Hebrides. 55N. 6W. Old chief seat of the Lords of the Isles.

Islip, Oxford, En. 51N. 1W. Bp. of Edward the Confessor

Ivica, Island, Mediterranean. 39N. 1E Taken from the Moors by the Spaniards, 1294.

Ivry, France. 48N. 1E. Victory of Henri IV. over Leaguers, 1590. (See Macaulay's poem)

Jaca, Spain. 42N. 0W. Former capital of Aragon; French in possession of, 1808-14.

Jaen, Spain 37N 3W. Moors defeated at, 1157; taken by Ferdinand III. of Castile, 1246.

Jargeau, France. 47N. 2E. Taken by Joan of Arc, 1429

Jarnac, France. 45N 0W. Defeat of the Huguenots under Condé, 1569.

Jarrow, Durham, En. 54N 1W. Monastic home of the Venerable Bede.

Jedburgh, Roxburghs., Scot. 55N. 2W Illness and supposed death of Mary Queen of Scots at, 1566, ass. Charles Edward, Scott, Wordsworth, etc.

Jemappes, Belgium. 50N. 3E. Defeat of Austrians by Dumouriez, 1792.

Jena, Germany. 50N. 11E. Napoleon's victory, Oct. 14, 1806.

Jersey, island, Channel. 49N. 2W. French fleet defeated by Sir William Winter, 1550.

Kaiserberg, Alsace - Lorraine. 48N. 7E. Bp. of the reformer Zell (1477-1548).

Kaiserlautern, Bavaria. 49N. 7E. French defeated, 1793, 1794; Austrians driven out by Moreau, 1795.

Kalisch, Poland. 51N. 18E. Swedes defeated by Russians, 1706.

Kappel, see Cappel.

Kara-sou-Bazar, Crimea. 45N. 34E. Here Mme. Krüdener, one of the remarkable figures of the 18th-19th century, ended her days.

Kars, Armenia. 40N. 43E Held for six months by the Turks, who finally capitulated, 1855 (Crimean W.), stormed by the Russians, 1877 (Russo-Turkish W).

Katrine, Loch, Scot. 56N. 4W. Immortalised by Scott in the 'Lady of the Lake.'

Katzbach River, Silesia. 51N.15E. French defeated by Blücher, 1813.

Kazanlik, Eastern Roumelia. 42N 24E. Sc.

of several actions between Turks and Russians, 1877-78.

Kazan, Russia. 55N. 49E. Taken from the Tartars by Ivan IV., 1552; Cossack rising, 1774.

Kehl, Baden, Germany. 48N. 7E. Taken in turn by French and Austrians during the 18th century; former celebrated printing-press at.

Kelloe, Durham, En. 54N. 1W. Mrs. Browning born in this parish, at Coxhoe Hall (1806-61).

Kelmscott, Oxon, En. 51N. 1W. Here William Morris set up his famous printing-press, and here he was buried, 1896.

Kells, Meath, Ir. 53N. 6W. Famous illuminated gospels, known as 'Book of Kells, a monument of early Christian art, now at Trinity, Dublin.

Kelso, Roxburghs., Scot. 55N. 2W. Abbey destroyed by Earl of Hertford, 1545; ass. the rising of 1715.

Kempen, Rhenish Prussia. 51N. 17E. Defeat of Allies near, 1760; bp. of Thomas à Kempis.

Kenilworth, Warwicks., En. 52N. 1W. Given to Leicester by Elizabeth; destroyed by Cromwell. (See Scott's novel.)

Kertch, Crimea. 45N. 36E. Taken and burnt by Anglo-French army, 1855.

Kesh, Russo-Turkistan. 34N. 66E. Bp. of Tamerlane, the famous Mongol conqueror (1336-1405).

Kesseldorf, Saxony. 51N. 15E. Saxons defeated by Prussians, 1745.

Kexholm, Finland. 60N. 28E. Possession in turns of Swedes and Russians; taken by Peter the Great, 1710.

Khotin (Choczim), Austria. 48N. 27E. Defeat of Turks by John Sobieski, 1673; by Russians, 1739.

Kieff, Russia. 50N. 30E. An ancient and sacred spot, visited yearly by some thousands of pilgrims.

Kilblain, Perths., Scot. 56N. 3W. Battle between Edward III. and Scots, 1335.

Kildare, Leinster, Ir. 53N. 6W. Ancient town; suffered under Elizabeth and during wars of 17th century.

Kilkenny, Leinster, Ir. 52N. 7W. Old Irish parliaments held at; 'Statute of K.' passed, 1367; capitulated to Cromwell, 1650; Swift and Congreve educated at.

Killala, Mayo, Ir. 54N. 9W. Landing of French under General Humbert, who were shortly after driven out by the royal troops, 1778.

Killaloe, Clare, Ir. 52N. 8W. Site of 'Kincora,' Brian Boru's palace, commemorated by Moore.

Killiecrankie, Perth, Scot. 56N. 3W. Defeat of royal troops by the Highlanders under Claverhouse, and death of latter, 1689.

Kilmarnock, Ayrshire, Scot. 55N. 4W. Ass. Burns.

Kilmeadan, Waterford, Ir. 52N. 7W. Castle taken by Cromwell.

Kilmuir, Skye, Scot. 57N 6W. Grave of Flora Macdonald.

Kilmun, Holy Loch, Argylls., Scot. 56N. 4W. Burial place of the Argyll family.

Kilpatrick, Dumbartons., Scot. 55N. 4W. Supposed bp. of St. Patrick.

Kilravock, Nairns., Scot. 57N. 3W. Prince Charles at, on the eve of Culloden, followed the next day by the Duke of Cumberland, 1746; Burns at, 1787.

Kilronan, Roscommons., Ir. 53N. 8W. Burial place of Carolan, 'last of the bards' (1670-1738).

Kilrush, Clare, Ir. 52N. 9W. Vessel of the Armada wrecked off.

Kilsyth, Stirlings., Scot. 55N. 4W. Covenanters defeated by Montrose, 1645.

Kilwinning, Ayrs., Scot. 55N. 4W. 'Popinjay' shooting (see 'Old Mortality'); Dr. Johnson and Boswell at, 1773.

Kimbolton, Huntingdons., En. 52N. 0W. Last res. of Queen Catherine of Aragon.

King's Cliffe, Northants., En. 52N. 0W. Bp. of William Law, A. of the 'Serious Call' (1686-1761), and where Mrs. Hutcheson and Miss Gibbon joined him in 1744.

King's Langley, Herts., En. 51N. 0W. Piers Gaveston buried at, 1315; first burial place of Richard II.

King's Lynn, Lynn Regis, Norfolk, En. 52N. 0E. Besieged by Parliamentarians, 1643; bp. of Frances Burney, Madame D'Arblay, novelist (1752-1840).

King's Norton, Worcesters., En. 52N. 1W. Hawkesley House, now disappeared, taken by Charles I., 1645.

Kingston-upon-Thames, Surrey, En. 51N. 0W. Saxon kings crowned at; headquarters of Fairfax, 1647.

Kingswinford, Staffs., En. 52N. 2W. Holbeach House, where gunpowder plotters were seized, and Percy and Catesby killed.

Kington, Herefords., En. 52N. 3W. The 'Red Book of Hergest,' famous monument of Welsh literature, now at Oxford, was named from the old mansion here.

Kinlochlochy, Inverness, Scot. 57N. 4W. 'Battle of the Shirts,' in which the Clan Ranald were dressed when they defeated the Frasers, 1544.

Kinloss, Moray Frith, Scot. 57N. 3W. Defeat of Scots by Danes under Sweyn, 1009.

Kinneff, Kincs., Scot. 56N. 2W. The Scottish regalia hidden under church floor during siege of Dunnottar Castle, whence they were secretly carried by the minister's wife.

Kinsale, Cork, Ir. 51N. 8W. Landing of James II., 1689; taken by Marlborough, 1690.

Kirby Wiske, Yorks., En. 54N. 1W. Bp. of Roger Ascham (1515-68), A. of the 'Schoolmaster,' and tutor to the royal children.

Kirkbean, Kirkcudbrights., Scot. 54N. 3W. Bp. of Paul Jones the 'freebooter' (1747-92). (See Fennimore Cooper, 'The Pilot' and 'The Pathfinder'; and Dumas, 'Captain Paul.')

Kirkcaldy, Fife, Scotland. 56N. 3W. Edward Irving and Carlyle teachers at,

1816-18; bp. of Adam Smith, A. of the 'Wealth of Nations' (1723-90).

Kirkconnel, Dumfriess., Scot. 55N. 4W. Graves of Helen of K. and her lover. (See old ballad.)

Kirklees, Yorks., En. 53N. 1W. Traditional death place of Robin Hood.

Kirkliston, Linliths., Scot. 55N. 3W. Burial place of 'Lady Ashton.' (See 'Bride of Lammermoor.')

Kirkoswald, Ayrs., Scot. 55N. 4W. Graves of 'Tam o' Shanter' and 'Soutar Johnnie,' and some of Burns' ancestors.

Kirkpatrick - Irongray, Kirkcudbrights., Scot. 55N. 3W. Grave of Jeanie Deans. (See Scott, 'Heart of Midlothian.')

Kirkwall, Orkney, Scot. 58N. 2W. Ruins of palace where King Haco died, 1263. (See Scott, 'The Pirate.')

Kirriemuir, Forfars., Scot. 56N. 3W. Bp. of the novelist Barrie (b. 1860), and commemorated in his 'Thrums.'

Kissingen, Bavaria. 50N. 10E. Defeat of Bavarians by Prussians, 1866 (Seven Weeks' W.)

Kitterland, off Isle of Man. 54N. 4W. (See Wilkie Collins's 'Armadale')

Klostercamp, Westphalia, Prussia. 51N. 8E. Hanoverians defeated by De Castries, 1760.

Knaresborough, Yorks., En. 54N. 1W. Richard II. imprisoned at; captured by Fairfax, 1644; sc. Eugene Aram's crime. (See Hood's poem.)

Knighton, Radnors., Wa. 52N. 3W. Neighbouring camp the traditional last stronghold of Caractacus.

Knoyle, East, Wilts., En. 51N. 2W. Bp. of Sir Christopher Wren (1632-1723).

Knutsford, Cheshire, En. 53N. 2W. Sc Mrs. Gaskell's 'Cranford.'

Koeniggratz, Bohemia. 50N. 15E. Austrians defeated by Prussians, 1866 (Battle of Sadowa); burial place of Ziska, the reformer.

Koenigsberg, Prussia. 54N. 20E. Here Kant was born and died (1724-1804).

Kolin, Bohemia. 50N. 15E. Defeat of Frederick the Great, 1757 (Seven Years' W.).

Kolomna, Russia. 55N. 38E. Ancient fortress and prison

Komorn, Hungary. 47N. 18E. Sacked in turn by Turks and Imperialists; relieved from Austrian besiegers, 1849 (Hungarian rising).

Kossovo, 'Field of Blackbirds,' Turkey. 43N. 20E. Battle, 1389, whereby the Turkish domination over Servia was secured, defeat of Hungarians under Hunyady by the Turks, 1448.

Koulikovo Plain, Russia. 52N. 36E. Tartars finally driven from the north of Europe by Dmitri Ivanovitch, 1380.

Kronborg, Denmark. 56N. 12E. Hamlet's castle, the old hero of romance, Ogier the Dane, is said to be asleep in the vaults.

Kulm, Bohemia. 53N. 18E. Defeat of French by Prussians and Russians, 1813.

Kunersdorf, Prussia. 52N. 15E. Defeat of

Frederick the Great by Allies, 1759 (Seven Years' W.).

Kussnacht, Switzerland. 47N. 8E. Ass. William Tell.

Kyffhauser, The, Thuringia. 50N. 11E. Frederic Barbarossa said to be still sleeping beneath, some day to return to life as Germany's helper.

La Hogue (Hougue), English Channel. 49N. 1W. French fleet under Tourville defeated by English and Dutch under Admirals Russell and Allemande, 1692.

La Rochelle, France. 46N. 1W. Huguenot stronghold, held against the Catholics by Lanoue, 1573, surrendered to Richelieu after 14 months' siege, 1627-28.

La Rothiere, France. 48N. 4E. Fierce battle between Napoleon and Allies, which left the former in possession of the field, 1814

La Vendee, France. 46N. 1W. Bravely withstood the Revolutionists. (See Hugo, 'Thirty-three'; Dumas, 'Companions of Jehu' and 'She-wolves of Machecoul.')

Laa, Austria. 48N. 16E. Austrians defeated by French, 1809. (See also Marchfeld.)

Lagos, Portugal. 37N. 8W French fleet defeated by Admiral Boscawen, 1759.

Laleham, Middlesex, En. 51N. 0W. Bp. and grave of Matthew Arnold.

Lanark, chief town of county, Scot. 55N. 3W. Near is the seat of the Lockharts, owners of the 'Lee-penny,' made famous by Scott's 'Talisman.'

Landau, Bavaria. 48N. 12E. Sc. various sieges; taken from the French, 1815

Landeshut, Silesia. 50N. 16E. Frederick II. defeated by Laudon, 1760.

Landrecies, France. 50N. 3E. Taken and retaken by Austrians and French, 1794.

Landshut, Bavaria. 48N. 12E. Taken several times by the French, 1796-1809.

Langensalza, Saxony. 51N. 10E. Defeat of Prussians by Hanoverians under their king, George, who was later forced to surrender to superior numbers, 1866 (Seven Weeks' W.).

Langport, Somersets., En. 51N. 2W. Royalists routed by Fairfax, 1645.

Langres, France 47N. 5E. Occupied by the Allies, 1814; bp. of Diderot, the encyclopedist (1713-84).

Langside, Glasgow, Lanarks., Scot. 55N. 4W. Defeat of Mary Queen of Scots' forces by Murray, 1568. (See Scott, 'The Abbot.')

Lannoy, France. 50N. 3E. Flemish Protestants under Cornaille cut to pieces by the Spaniards, 1567.

Lansdown, Somerset, En. 51N. 2W. Waller forced to retreat from his entrenchments by Cornish Royalists, 1643.

Laon, France 49N. 3E. Defeat of French by Allies under Blucher, 1814; taken by the Germans, 1870. Fine Cathedral.

Largo, Fife, Scot. 56N. 2W. Bp. of Alexander Selkirk, whose story suggested Defoe's 'Robinson Crusoe.'

Largs, Ayrs., Scot. 55N. 4W. Defeat of King Haco and his Norsemen by the Scots, 1263.

Las Navas de Tolosa, Spain. 37N. 3W. Celebrated victory of the Kings of Castile, Leon, Aragon, Navarre, and Portugal over the Moors, 1212.

Lasswade, Lothians, Scot. 55N. 3W. Grave of Drummond of Hawthornden; res. of Scott, 1798-1804; of De Quincey, 1840-59.

Lathom, Lancs, En. 53N. 2W. Lathom House gallantly defended for 3 months by the Countess of Derby, 1644; destroyed by Parliamentarians, 1645.

Lauder, Berwicks., Scot. 55N. 2W. Impromptu hanging of the Scotch king's favourites by Earl of Angus ('Bell the Cat'), 1483.

Launceston, Cornwall, En. 50N. 4W. Fox, the Quaker, imprisoned at, 1656.

Laupen, Switzerland. 46N. 7E. Burgundians routed by the Swiss under Rudolf v. Erlachs, 1339.

Lausanne, Switzerland. 46N. 6E. Here Gibbon wrote the chief part of his 'Decline and Fall'; bp. of H. Benjamin Constant (de Rebecque), A. and politician (1767-1830); grave of John Kemble, the actor.

Lauterbourg, Alsace-Lorraine. 48N. 8E. Taken in turns by Austrians, 1744, and by Prussians and French, 1793.

Laval, France. 48N. 0W. Republicans defeated by Larochejaquelin and the Vendéans, 1793; bp. of Ambroise Paré, the great French surgeon and court physician (1517-90).

Lavaur, France. 43N. 1E. Albigensian stronghold, sacked by Simon de Montfort, 1211.

Lawfeldt, or Laeffelt, Belgium. 50N. 5E. Defeat of English and Allies by Marshal Saxe, 1747 (W. of Austrian Succession).

Leadhills, Lanarks., Scot. 55N 3W. Bp. of Allan Ramsay, poet of the 'Gentle Shepherd' (1686-1758).

Lebrixa, or Lebrija, Spain. 36N. 6W. Bp. of the great Spanish navigator, J. Diaz de Solis, killed beside the Rio de la Plata, which he discovered.

Lech River, Bavaria. 48N. 10E. Tilly mortally wounded while holding the passage of, against Gustavus Adolphus, 1632.

Lechfeld Plain, Bavaria. 48N. 10E. Huns defeated by Charlemagne, 794.

Ledbury, Herefordshire, En. 52N. 2W. Hope End, Mrs. Browning's early home near.

Leeds, Yorks, En. 53N. 1W. Taken and retaken by Royalists and Fairfax, 1642, 1643.

Leghorn, Italy. 43N. 10E. Grave of Smollett.

Legnago, Italy. 45N. 11E. One of the Quadilateral; defeat of Barbarossa by Milanese, 1176; taken by French, 1796.

Leicester, cap. of county, En. 52N. 1W. Here Cardinal Wolsey died, 1530; site of 'Blue Boar,' where Richard III. slept two

nights before his death; his body was buried in Grey Friars.

Leipzig, Saxony. 51N. 12E. Famous yearly book fair; defeat of Tilly by Gustavus Adolphus, 1631 (Thirty Years' W.); second victory of Swedes, 1642; 'Battle of the Nations,' and defeat of Napoleon, Oct. 16-18, 1813; bp. of Wagner (1813-83).

Leith, Firth of Forth, Scot. 55N. 3W. Besieged for 9 months by the Lords of the Congregation, 1559-60; taken and plundered by Jacobites, 1715; bp. of J. Home, A. of 'Douglas' (1722-1808).

Le Mans, France, see Mans, Le.

Lens, France. 50N. 2E. Condé's victory over Archduke Leopold of Austria, 1648 (Thirty Years' W.).

Lentagio, Tagina, Italy. 43N. 13E. Totila the Ostrogoth defeated and mortally wounded by Narses, 552.

Lepanto, Greece. 38N. 21E. Defeat of Turkish fleet by Don John of Austria, 1571. (See Motley, 'Dutch Republic.')

Lerida, Spain. 41N. 0E. Taken by the French under Suchet, 1810.

Lerins Islands, Mediterranean. 43N. 7E. Ste. Marguerite, the prison of the 'Man with the Iron Mask,' and of Marshal Bazaine, who escaped, 1874.

Leuthen, Prussia (Silesia). 51N. 16E. Defeat of Austrians by Frederick the Great, 1757 (Seven Years' W.).

Leven, Loch, Kinross, Scot. 56N. 5W. Mary Queen of Scots imprisoned on Castle Island, 1567-68. (See Scott, 'The Abbot.')

Lewes, Sussex, En. 50N. 0E. Defeat of Henry III. by Simon de Montfort, 1264 (Barons' W.).

Leyden, Holland. 52N. 4E. Heroically held against the Spaniards, 1573-74 (see Motley, op. cit.); famous printing-house of the Elzevirs, 16th-17th centuries; Sir Thomas Browne, Evelyn, and Goldsmith among the celebrities who studied here.

Lichfield, Staffords., En. 52N. 1W. Bp. of Dr. Johnson, and where he, Garrick, and Addison were educated.

Liddesdale, Roxburghs., Scot. 55N. 2W. Hermitage Castle, where Sir Alex. Ramsay was starved to death, 1342; and thither Queen Mary rode over from Jedburgh to visit Bothwell, 1566. (See Scott, 'Guy Mannering.')

Liege, Belgium. 50N. 5E. Taken by Marlborough, 1702; by the French, 1792, 1794; ass. the 'Boar of Ardennes (see Scott, 'Quentin Durward'); bp. of Colin Maillard, Flemish soldier of 10th century, who fought on when blinded (hence perhaps French name for 'hide and seek').

Liegnitz, Silesia. 51N. 16E. Austrians defeated by Frederick the Great, 1760 (Seven Years' W.), and French by Blucher, 1813.

Lierre, Belgium. 51N. 4E. Taken by Allies under Marlborough, 1706.

Ligny, Belgium. 50N. 4E. Defeat of Blucher by Napoleon, June 16, 1815.

Lille, France. 50N. 3E. Surrendered to

Prince Eugène, 1708 (W. of Spanish Succession); French possession since 1713.

Limerick, Ir. 52N. 8W. Besieged by Ireton, 1651; death of latter here from plague, 1652; terrible siege and final surrender to William III., 1691.

Limoges, France. 45N. 1E. Sacked and burnt by Black Prince, 1370.

Lincoln, cap. of county, En. 53N. 0W. Stephen, after gallant fighting, taken prisoner by Empress Matilda's forces, 1141; 'Lincoln Fair,' fought in the streets between French and English, 1217; siege by Parliamentarians, 1644.

Linlithgow, cap. of county, Scot. 55N. 3W. James IV. received his mysterious Flodden warning in St. Michael's; murder of the regent Moray, 1570; bp. of James V. and Mary Stuart. (See Scott, 'Marmion.')

Lisbon, Portugal. 38N. 9W. Great earthquake, 1755; Armada sailed from, 1588; tombs of Camoens, poet of the 'Lusiads,' who died and was born (?) here; and of Vasco da Gama, who sailed from this port in 1497.

Lisburn, Antrim, Ir. 54N. 6W. Monument to John Nicholson, the hero of Delhi, who here spent part of his childhood.

Lisieux, France. 49N. 0E. Marriage of the future Henry II. with Eleanor of Guienne, 1152.

Lismore, Cork, Ir. 52N. 7W. Bp. of the philosopher Robert Boyle (1627-91).

Lissa, Silesia (see Leuthen).

Lissa Island, Adriatic. 43N. 16E. In English possession, 1810-15; Italian fleet defeated by Austrians, 1866 (Seven Weeks' W.).

Liverpool, Lancashire, En. 53N. 2W. Bp. of Mrs. Hemans and Gladstone; the writers Hall Caine, W. Watson, Le Gallienne, and J. A. Noble have been known as the 'Liverpool School.'

Llangollen, Denbighs., Wa. 52N. 3W. Res. of Lady Eleanor Butler (d. 1829) and Miss Sarah Ponsonby (d. 1831), the 'Ladies of L.,' who for 50 years lived in complete seclusion, and were visited by the chief celebrities of the day.

Llanthony, Monmouths., Wa. 51N. 3W. Abbey bought by Walter Savage Landor, where for a while he lived.

Llerena, Spain. 38N. 6W. French cavalry routed by English, 1812.

Loches, France. 47N. 0E. Old royal palace and prison; here were the 'cages' invented under Louis XI. by La Balue, who was the first to make trial of one; among other prisoners were Comines, the historian, and Ludovico Sforza, who died in confinement; tomb of Agnes Sorel; bp. of Alfred de Vigny, poet and prose writer (1797-1863). (See Scott, 'Quentin Durward.')

Lochmaben, Scot. 55N. 3W. Robert Bruce born here, or at Turnberry.

Lodi, Italy. 45N. 9E. Passage of the Adda forced by Napoleon, 1796.

Loftcha, Lovetz, Bulgaria. 43N. 24E. Turks driven from by Russians, 1877 (Russo-Turkish W.).

Loigny-Pouprey, 45N. 1E. Army of the Loire defeated by the Germans, 1870 (Franco-German W.).

Londonderry, cap. of county, Ir. 55N. 7W. Famous siege by James II.'s forces of 105 days, April to August, 1689, when the brave garrison was relieved.

Longworth, Berks, En. 51N. 1W. Bp. of Blackmore, A. of 'Lorna Doone,' etc. (1825-1900).

Longwy, France. 47N. 5E. Taken by Prussians, 1792, 1815, and 1871.

Lons-le-Saunier, France. 46N. 5E. Bp. of Rouget de Lisle, A. of the 'Marseillaise.'

Loudoun, Ayrs., Scot. 55N. 4W. English defeated by Bruce, 1306.

Loughborough, Leicesters., En. 52N. 1W. Great bell of St. Paul's cast at, 1881.

Louth, Lincs., En. 53N. 0E. Tennyson and Sir J. Franklin at grammar school.

Louvain, Belgium. 50N. 4E. Revolt in 1382, and subsequent emigration of many inhabitants to England; taken by the French, 1792 and 1794.

Louviers, France. 49N. 1E. Taken by English, 1418 and 1431.

Lovisa, Gulf of Finland. 60N. 26E. Bombarded by English, 1855.

Lowestoft, Suffolk, En. 52N. 1E. Defeat of Dutch off coast, 1665.

Lowositz, Bohemia. 50N. 13E. Defeat of Austrians by Frederick the Great, leading to surrender of Pirna, 1756 (Seven Years' W.).

Lubeck, Germany. 53N. 10E. Former capital of Hanseatic League; taken by the French, 1806; bp. of painters Kneller and Van Ostade.

Lucerne, Switzerland. 47N. 8E. Lion of L. hewn out of the rock in commemoration of the Swiss guards who perished at the Tuileries in defence of Louis XVI., Aug. 10, 1792; ass. of lake with William Tell.

Ludlow, Salop, En. 52N. 2W. Death at, of Prince Arthur, Henry VII.'s son, 1502; Milton's 'Comus' performed at, 1634.

Lugo, Spain. 43N. 7W. Taken by the French, 1809.

Lund, Sweden. 55N. 13E. Battle (Dano-Swedish W.), 1675.

Lundy Island, Bristol Channel. 51N. 4W. Old stronghold of smugglers and pirates. (See Kingsley's 'Westward Ho!')

Luneville, France. 48N. 6E. Treaty of Peace (Austria and French Republic), 1801.

Lutter, Germany. 52N. 10E. Christian IV. of Denmark defeated by Tilly (Thirty Years' W.).

Lutterworth, Leicesters., En. 52N. 1W. Wyclif rector, 1374 to his death, 1384; he was buried here, but his ashes were afterwards scattered.

Lutzen, Saxony. 51N. 12E. Defeat of Wallenstein by Gustavus Adolphus, and death of latter, 1632 (Thirty Years' W.); defeat of Allies by Napoleon, 1813.

Luzarches, France. 48N. 1E. Ancient royal res. of Merovingian kings.

Lyme Regis, Dorsets., En. 50N. 2W. Besieged by Prince Maurice, April-June, 1644;

landing of Duke of Monmouth, 1685; bp. of Sir G. Somers, coloniser of the Bermudas (1554-1611).

Lyndhurst, Hants., En. 50N. 1W. Stirrup used by Rufus the day he was killed preserved in Queen's House.

Lyons, France. 45N. 4E. Martyrdom of Christians (Pothinus and Blandina), 2nd century; massacre of Huguenots, 1572; destroyed and inhabitants slain by the Convention, 1792; centre of republicanism.

Macon, France. 46N. 4E. Engagement between French and Allies, 1814; bp. of Lamartine, poet (1790-1869).

Madrid, Spain. 40N. 3W. Finally taken from the Moors, 1083; made capital of Spain by Philip II., 1560; taken by the Allies under Wellington, 1812; bp. of Calderon, dramatic poet (1600-81).

Maestricht, Holland. 51N. 5E. Famous subterranean quarries; sacked by the Duke of Alva, 1576; taken by Kleber, 1794; Dutch possession since 1839. (See Motley, op. cit.)

Magdeburg, Saxony. 52N. 11E. Tombs of Otho the Great and his English wife Editha; 6 months' siege by Wallenstein, 1629; sack and massacre lasting 3 days by Tilly, 1631 (Thirty Years' W.); occupied by the French, 1806.

Magenta, Italy. 45N. 8E. Austrians defeated by French and Sardinians, 1859.

Magus Muir, Fife, Scot. 56N. 2W. Archbishop Sharpe murdered, 1679.

Maidenhead, Berks, En. 51N. 0W. Skirmish between forces of Richard II. and Henry IV., 1400; meeting between Charles I. and his children at 'The Greyhound,' 1647.

Maiden Way, old Roman road, running north through Westmoreland, Cumberland, and Northumberland.

Maidstone, Kent. 51N. 0E. Stormed by Fairfax, 1648; bp. of William Hazlitt (1778-1830).

Mainz, Germany. 50N. 8E. Taken by French, 1792; capitulated to Prussians, 1793; since, in turn, French and German possession; bp. of Gutenberg, printer, b. 1400.

Majorca, Balearic Islands. 39N. 3E. Captured from Spaniards by Sir John Leake, 1706; taken by French, 1715.

Malaga, Spain. 36N. 4W. Taken by Ferdinand and Isabella, 1487.

Malakoff, Sebastopol, Crimea. 44N. 33E. Fort stormed by the French, 1855.

Maldon, Essex, En. 51N. 0E. Defeat of East Saxons by Danes, and death of Byrthnoth, 991, commemorated in a contemporary ballad, 'one of the pearls of Old English poetry.'

Malmesbury, Wilts, En. 51N. 2W. Aldhelm, first abbott, 7th century; William of M., historian, cir. 1095-1143; grave of King Athelstan; bp. of Hobbes, A. of 'Leviathan' (1588-1679).

Malplaquet, France. 50N. 3E. French de-

feated by Marlborough and Prince Eugène, 1709.

Malta, Mediterranean. 35N. 14E. Given to the knights of S. John by Charles V., 1530; taken by French, 1798; British possession since 1814.

Man, Isle of, Irish Sea. 54N. 4W. Former property of Earls of Derby and Dukes of Athol, bought by crown, 1829.

Mancha, La, Spain. 37N. 3W. Country of Don Quixote.

Manchester, Lancs., En. 53N. 2W. Bp. of De Quincey (1785-1859).

Mannheim, Germany. 49N. 8E. Sacked in turns by Bavarians and French, 1622-1689; taken again by French, 1795.

Manor, Peebles, Scot. 55N. 3W. Cottage and grave of Scott's 'Black Dwarf'; traditional site of 'Macbeth's Castle.'

Manorbier, Pembrokes., Wa. 51N. 4W. Bp. of Giraldus Cambrensis, historian, etc. (1146 (?)-1220 (?)).

Manresa, Spain. 41N. 1E. Taken and burnt by French, 1811.

Mans, Le, France. 48N. 0E. Vendéans defeated, 1793; French defeated, 1871 (Franco-German W.); bp. of Henry II.

Mantes, France. 48N. 1E. Burnt by William the Conqueror, who here met with the injury from which he died, 1087.

Mantua, Italy. 45N. 10E. Ruled by the Gonzaga family, 1328-1708; taken by Napoleon after long siege, 1797; by Austrians, 1814; restored to Italy, 1866; crusade against Turks preached at Congress of, 1459; coalition against France, Congress, 1791.

Marburg, Prussia. 46N. 15E. Conference of reformers, 1529; William Tyndale, translator of the Bible, a student at.

Marchfeld, Austria. 48N. 16E. Defeat of Ottocar, King of Bohemia, by Rudolf of Hapsburg, 1278; the house of Hapsburg has since been that of Austria.

Marengo, Italy. 44N. 8E. Austrians defeated by Napoleon, 1800.

Marienthal, Mergentheim. 49N. 9E. Turenne defeated, 1645 (Thirty Years' W.).

Marignano, Melegnano, Italy. 45N. 9E. Swiss defeated by Francis I. (Battle of the Giants), 1515; Austrians defeated, 1859.

Market-Drayton, Salop, En. 52N. 2W. Yorkist victory at Bloreheath near, 1459.

Market-Harborough, Leicesters., En. 52N. 0W. Headquarters of Charles I. on the eve of Naseby, 1643. (See novel by Whyte Melville.)

Marlow, Great, Bucks, En. 51N. 0W. Shelley resident at, 1817.

Marsaglia, Italy. 44N. 7E. Defeat of English and Allies by Marshal de Catinat, 1693 (W. of Louis XIV.).

Marsala, Sicily. 37N. 12E. Landing of Garibaldi and his 'Thousand,' 1860.

Marseilles, France. 43N. 5E. Suffered under the Reign of Terror; sc. sanguinary riot on the return of the Bourbons, 1813; bp. of Thiers, historian and politician, 1797-1877.

Marston Moor, York, En. 53N. 1W. De-

feat of Royalists under Prince Rupert, 1644.

Mauchline, Ayrs., Scot. 55N. 4W. Burns married to Jean Armour, 1788; Mossgiel Farm, the poet's res. for a while, is near; sc. 'Jolly Beggars' and 'Holy Fair.'

Mayfield, Staffords., En. 53N. 1W. House where Thomas More wrote most of his 'Lalla Rookh.'

Mayfield, Sussex, En. 51N. 0E. Palace of Sir Thomas Gresham, visited by Elizabeth.

Meaux, France. 48N. 2E. Treaty, terminating Albigensian W., 1229; extermination of the Jacquerie by English and French, 1358; massacre of Huguenots, 1572; Bossuet made bishop, 1681.

Medina de Rio Seco, Spain. 41N. 5W. Spaniards defeated by French (Peninsular W.), 1808.

Meissen, Saxony. 51N. 13E. Famous porcelain factory, f. 1710, the first in Europe; Gellert and Lessing students at.

Melos, island, Greek Archipelago. 36N. 24E. Famous statue of Venus (Louvre) found on, 1820. (See Smith, Classical Dict.)

Melrose, Roxburghs., Scot. 55N. 2W. Burial place of the heart of Bruce, of the Douglases, among them the hero of Otterburn, of Michael Scott, the wizard, etc. (See 'Lay of the Last Minstrel.')

Melun, France. 48N. 2E. Royal res. of early Capétiens; taken by Du Guesclin, 1358; by English, 1420; revolt of inhabitants instigated by Joan of Arc, and capitulation of English, 1430.

Memmingen, Bavaria. 47N. 10E. Austrians defeated by Moreau, 1800.

Mentana, Italy. 42N. 12E. Garibaldians defeated, 1867.

Merton, Surrey, En. 51N. 0W. Cynewulf, King of the W. Saxons, attacked in his house and slain, 785; Ethelred, King of the W. Saxons, defeated by Danes and mortally wounded, 871; statutes of, 1235; Becket, and Walter de Merton, f. of Merton Coll., Oxford, were educated in old priory.

Messina, Sicily. 38N. 15E. Sicilian Vespers, 1282; bombarded by Neapolitans, 1848; surrendered to Italian troops, 1861; lately destroyed by earthquake.

Methven, Perths., Scot. 56N. 3W. Robert Bruce defeated, 1306.

Metz, Lorraine. 49N. 6E. French possession, 1552-1870; capitulation of Marshal Bazaine, 1870 (Franco-German War).

Meudon, France. 48N. 2E. Rabelais curé at, 1545.

Meulan, France. 49N. 1E. Taken by English, 1346; by Du Guesclin, 1363.

Mezieres, France. 49N. 4E. Held by Bayard against Charles V.'s army, 1521; held against Allies, 1815; capitulated, 1870-71 (Franco-German War.

Middelburg, Zealand. 51N. 3E. Taken from the Spaniards by Dutch, 1574; by the French, 1795; by English, 1809; the microscope invented at by Jansen. (See Motley, op. cit.)

Milan, Italy. 45N. 9E. Edict in favour of Christians issued by Constantine, 313; head of the Lombard League from 1167; old reigning families: Della Torre, Visconti, Sforza; occupied by the French, 1796; capital of Austro-Italian dominions, 1815-59 (battle of Magenta).

Milazzo, Sicily. 38N. 13E. Neapolitans defeated by Garibaldi, 1860.

Milford, Wales. 51N. 5W. Landing of Richmond, the future Henry VII., before Bosworth, 1485.

Millesimo, Italy. 44N. 8E. Austrians defeated by Napoleon, 1796.

Milston, Wilts., En. 51N. 1W. Bp. of Addison (1672-1719).

Mincio, river, Italy. 45N. 10E. Passage forced by Brune, 1800; Austrians defeated by Beauharnais, 1814.

Minden, Prussia. 52N. 8E. French defeated, 1759 (Seven Years' War).

Minorca, Balearic Islands. 39N. 4E. In hands of English and French in turns from 1708; Spanish possession since 1782.

Missolonghi, Greece. 38N. 21E. Besieged by Turks, 1821-2, and 1825-6, when it was taken by storm; here Byron died, 1824.

Modena, Italy. 44N. 10E. Reigning family, the Este, 13th to 19th century.

Mohacz, Hungary. 45N. 18E. Turkish possession, 1526-1687.

Mohileff, Mogileff, Russia. 53N. 30E. Russians defeated by French, 1812.

Mohrungen, Prussia. 53N. 19E. Russians defeated by Bernadotte, 1807.

Mollwitz, Prussia. 51N. 17E. Austrians defeated by Frederick the Great, 1741 (W. of Austrian Succession).

Monastier, France. 44N. 3E. (See Stevenson, 'Travels with a Donkey.')

Moncontour, France. 46N. 0W. Huguenot defeat, 1569.

Mondovi, Italy. 44N. 7E. Sardinians defeated by Napoleon, 1796.

Monmouth, Wa. 51N. 2W. The chronicle of Geoffrey of M. (? 1100-54) was the chief source of Arthurian legend; bp. of Henry V.

Montargis, France. 48N. 2E. Old tapestries representing tale of dog (hence known as dog of M.) who slew his master's murderer in the lists (see Chanson de Geste of 'Macaire.'); court of Renée de France, daughter of Louis XII.

Montauban, France. 44N. 1E. Held by the Huguenots for three months, 1621; taken by Richelieu, 1629; suffered from the 'dragonnades' under Louis XIV.

Montbeliard, France. 47N. 6E. Bp. of Cuvier, the naturalist, 1769-1832.

Monte Aperto, Italy. 44N. 11E. Defeat of Florentine Guelphs by Ghibellines, 1260.

Montebello Casteggio, Italy. 44N. 9E. Defeat of Austrians by French, 1800 and 1859.

Montenotte, Italy. 44N. 8E. Austrians defeated by Napoleon, 1796.

Montereau, France. 48N. 2E. Duke of Burgundy assassinated, 1419; Allies defeated by Napoleon, 1814.

Montgomery, Wa. 52N. 3W. Bp. of George Herbert (1593-1633).

Montilla, Spain. 37N. 4W. Bp. of Gonzalvo di Cordova, the Great Captain, 1443-1515.

Montmedy, France. 49N. 5E. Taken by Germans, 1815; and 1870 (Franco-German War).

Montmirail, France. 49N. 4E. Allies defeated by Napoleon, 1814.

Montpellier, France. 43N. 3E. Petrarch a student at; Rabelais doctor of medicine at, 1531; bp. of Comte, f. of Positivism (1798-1857).

Montrose, Forfars., Scot. 56N. 2W. Port of departure of the Old Pretender after the failure of 1715; held in turn by Jacobites and Hanoverians, 1745, 1746; Dr. Johnson at, 1773; ass. with Wishart, reformer and martyr; bp. of the 'great' marquis.

Mont St. Michel, France. 48N. 1W. Besieged in vain by Henry V.; Order of St. Michel f. by Louis XI., 1469.

Monza, Italy. 45N. 9E. Ancient Lombard capital; the Iron Crown preserved at.

Morat, Switzerland. 46N. 7E. Famous Swiss victory over Charles the Bold of Burgundy, 1476, one of 'true glory's stainless victories.' (See 'Childe Harold,' Cant. III. lxiv.)

Morazzone, Italy. 45N. 9E. Garibaldi, after long resistance to superior numbers, retreated to Arona, 1848.

Morella, Spain. 40N. 0W. Taken by Carlist general Cabrera, 1838; retaken by Espartero, 1840 (Carlist War).

Morgarten, Switzerland. 47N. 8E. Defeat of Austrians by small force of Swiss, 1315; Austrians defeated by French, 1799.

Morlaix, France. 48N. 3W. Bp. of General Moreau, and of Emile Souvestre, A. of 'Philosophe sous les Toits,' etc. (1806-54).

Mortara, Italy. 45N. 8E. Piedmontese driven from by Austrians, 1849 (Italian Rising).

Mortimer's Cross, Hereford, En. 52N. 2W. Lancastrians defeated, 1461.

Mortlake, Surrey, En. 51N. 0W. Bp. of famous Dr. Dee, the alchemist (1579-1651), and grave of Partridge, the almanac-maker, satirised by Swift (1644-1715).

Moscow, Russia. 55N. 37E. Former capital; czars crowned at; entry of Napoleon and burning of city, 1812.

Moskirch, 47N. 9E. Austrians defeated by Moreau, 1800.

Mossgiel, Ayrs., Scot. 55N. 4W. Res. of Burns, 1784-86.

Moulins, France. 46N. 3E. Assembly convened by Catherine de' Médicis, and famous ordinance passed for the reform of the administration of justice, etc., 1566. (See Sterne's 'Sentimental Journey.')

Moy, Loch, Inverness, Scot. 57N. 4W. Prince Charles at, saved by ruse of Lady Macintosh, 1746.

Muhlberg, Saxony. 51N. 13E. Protestants defeated by Charles V., 1547.

Mull, Argylls., Scot. 56N. 6W. Dr. Johnson on, 1773.

Munden, Hanover. 51N. 9E. Taken by Tilly, 1626; occupied by French, 1756 and 1805.

Munich, Bavaria. 48N. 11E. Taken by Swedes, 1632; thrice by Austrians, 1704-43; by French, 1800.

Munster, Westphalia. 51N. 7E. Suffered during Thirty and Seven Years' W.; Treaty of Westphalia (close of Thirty Years' W.) signed at, 1648.

Najera, Spain. 42N. 2W. Du Guesclin defeated by Black Prince, 1367 (also known as Battle of Navarete).

Nairn, cap. of county, Scot. 57N. 3W. Duke of Cumberland at on eve of Culloden, 1746; bp. of Grant, the African explorer, who also died here (1827-92).

Namur, Belgium. 50N. 4E. French possession, 1701-12; bombarded by Allies, 1704.

Nancy, Germany (Lorraine). 48N. 6E. Heroic defence by Swiss against Charles the Bold, Duke of Burgundy, killed besieging, 1477; res. and tomb of Stanislas, King of Poland, afterwards Duke of Lorraine. (See Scott, 'Anne of Geierstein.')

Nangis, France. 45N. 2E. Russians defeated by French, 1814.

Nantes, France. 47N. 1W. Celebrated edict signed by Henri IV., 1598; sc. Carrier's 'Noyades' and other atrocities; Cathelineau, Vendéan leader, killed during attack on, 1793; bp. of Fouché, of revolutionary celebrity; of Jules Verne (1828-1905).

Nantwich, Cheshire. 53N. 2W. Besieged by Royalists, 1644; Royalists defeated by Lambert, 1659.

Naples, Italy. 40N. 14E. Part of former kingdom of the Two Sicilies, successively under Norman, Hohenstaufen, Angevine, Arragonese, and Bourbon rule; Joseph Buonaparte king, 1806; Murat king, 1808; Bourbons finally overthrown by Garibaldi, 1860; an insurrection against Spanish rule was headed by Masaniello, 1647.

Narbonne, France. 43N. 3E. Order for arrest of Cinq-Mars signed by Louis XIII., 1642. (See A. de Vigny, 'Cinq-Mars.')

Narva, Russia. 59N. 28E. Russians defeated by Charles XII. of Sweden, 1700; taken by Peter the Great, 1704. (See Voltaire, op. cit.)

Naseby, Northamptons., En. 52N. 0W. Royalists defeated, 1645.

Navarete, see Najera.

Navarino, Greece. 36N. 21E. Turko-Egyptian fleet destroyed by English and Allies, 1827.

Neanderthal, Prussia. 51N. 7E. Skeleton of prehistoric man found, 1857.

Neerwinden, Belgium. 50N. 5E. English under William III. defeated by French, 1693; French defeated by Allies, 1793.

Neisse, Silesia. 50N. 17E. Taken by Frederick the Great, 1741; by Jérome Bonaparte, 1807.

Neuss, Rhenish prov. 51N. 6E. Russians defeated by French, 1813.

Neuwied, Rhenish prov. 50N. 7E. Victory of French over Austrians, 1796, 1797.

Neville's Cross, Durham, En. 54N. 1W.

David Bruce defeated and made prisoner, 1346.

Nevin, Carnarvons., Wa. 52N. 4W. Festival and pageant held by Edward I. in honour of final subjugation of Wales, 1284.

Newark-upon-Trent, Notts., En 53N. 0W. Death of King John at, 1216; thrice besieged during Civil War

Newbury, Berks, En. 51N. 1W. Royalists forced to retreat and Falkland killed, 1643, indecisive action, 1644.

Newcastle - upon - Tyne, Northumberland, En. 54N. 1W. Edward I. received homage of Baliol, 1292; taken by Scottish army, 1640 and 1644, Charles I. prisoner at, 1646-7.

New Forest, Hants, En. 50N. 1W. William Rufus killed in, 1100.

Newhaven, Edinburgh, Scot. 55N. 3W. (See C. Reade, 'Christie Johnstone')

Newport, Isle of Wight. 50N. 1W. Carisbrooke Castle near; negotiations between Charles and Parliamentarians, 1648.

Newstead, Notts., En. 53N. 1W. Sometime res. of Lord Byron. (See his two poems)

Newton-by-Usk, Brecon, Wa. 52N. 3W. Bp of Henry Vaughan, the poet (1622-95).

Nice, Italy 43N. 7E. French possession, 1792-1814; finally ceded to France by Sardinia, 1860, bp. of Garibaldi (1807-1882).

Niemen, river, Russia. 55N. 21E. Celebrated interview between Napoleon and Emperor Alexander on island of, resulting in peace of Tilsit, 1807, passage of French army, 1812.

Nieuport, Belgium. 51N. 2E. Victory of Dutch over Spaniards, 1600; three times taken by French, 1745-94.

Nimeguen, Holland. 51N. 5E. Peace congress (France, Holland, Spain, Austria), 1678-9.

Nimes, France. 43N. 4E. Celebrated amphitheatre and other Roman remains; sc. fierce religious conflicts, 1791 and 1815, bp. of Guizot, statesman and historian (1787-1874), and of Alphonse Daudet, novelist (1840-97).

Niort, France. 46N. 0W. Bp. of Madame de Maintenon.

Nogent-le-Retrou, France. 48N 0E. Remains of palace, and tomb of Henri IV.'s great minister, Sully (1560-1641); German victory (Franco-Prussian War).

Nohant, France. 46N. 1E. Home of George Sand (1804-76).

Nola, Italy. 40N. 14E. Bp. of Giordano Bruno, philosopher (1548, burnt 1600).

Norham, Northumberland, En. 55N. 2W. Sc. old Border warfare, King John and Edward I. at; besieged by James IV., 1497, taken by him 1513. (See Scott's 'Marmion.')

Northallerton, Yorks., En. 54N. 1W. Near was fought the battle of the Standard, when David I. of Scotland was defeated, 1138.

Northampton, cap. of county, En. 52N. 0W. Barons swore homage to Empress Matilda, 1131, Treaty of, establishing independence of Scotland, 1328; Henry VI. defeated by

Warwick and made prisoner, 1460; held by Parliamentarians during Civil W.; Holmby House near, Charles I.'s prison, 1647.

Norwich, Norfolk, En. 52N. 1E. Res. and grave of Sir T. Browne, A. of 'Religio Medici' (1605-82); Nelson educated at grammar school; bp. of Greene, the dramatist, and Harriet Martineau; early home of Elizabeth Fry. (See Borrow, 'Lavengro.')

Nottingham, cap. of county, En. 52N. 1W. Roger Mortimer seized and carried to his death, 1330; here Charles I. raised his standard, 1642; castle held for Parliamentarians by Colonel Hutchinson. (See Life, by his wife)

Novara, Italy. 45N. 8E. Piedmontese defeated, 1849 (Italian Rising).

Novi, Italy 44N. 8E. French defeated by Russians and Austrians under Suvarov, and Joubert killed, 1799.

Noyon, France. 49N. 2E. Charlemagne crowned, 768, Hughes Capet elected king, 987; bp. of Calvin (1509-64)

Nuneaton, Warwicks., En 52N. 1W. 'George Eliot' here at school.

Nuremberg, Bavaria. 49N. 11E. Watches (Nüremberg eggs), globes, air guns, etc., invented, splendid specimens of work by sculptors Krafft, Stoss, and Vischer; Treaty (Catholics and Protestants), 1532; fierce fighting between Wallenstein and Gustavus Adolphus, 1532; bp. of Albert Dürer and Hans Sachs, one of the 'Meistersingers.'

Ocana, Spain. 39N. 3W. Defeat of Spaniards by French under Soult (Peninsular War), 1809.

Odcombe, Somerset, En. 50N. 2W. Bp. of Thomas Coryat, A. of the 'Crudities' (1577(?)-1617).

Odense, Fünen. 55N. 10E. Bp. of Hans Andersen (1805-75).

Odessa, Russia. 46N. 30E. Bombarded by Anglo-French fleet, 1854.

Offley, Herts, En. 51N. 0W. Reported grave of King Offa, d. 796.

Olmutz, Moravia. 49N. 17E. Sacked during Thirty Years' W.; besieged by Frederick the Great (Seven Years' W.); Lafayette state prisoner at, 1792-97.

Olney, Bucks, En. 52N. 0W. Res. of the poet Cowper, 1767-86, and where he wrote 'John Gilpin.'

Oltenitza, Roumania. 44N. 26E. Russians defeated by Turks (Crimean W.), 1853.

Oporto, Portugal. 41N. 8W. Sc frequent insurrections; taken from the French by Wellington, 1809; rose against usurper Miguel, 1828, headquarters of Dom Pedro, 1832-3.

Oppenheim, Rhenish prov. 49N. 8E Suffered during Thirty Years' W; taken by French, 1792 and 1794.

Orange, France 44N. 4E. Triumphal arch and other fine Roman remains.

Orleans, France. 47N. 1E. Attacked by Attila, 450, and taken by Clovis, 486; besieged by English and delivered by Joan of Arc, 1428-9; taken by Mademoiselle de

Montpensier (Fronde W.), 1652, occupied by Germans, 1870.

Orthez, France. 43N. 0W. Froissart at, 1388; Soult defeated by Wellington near, 1814.

Ostend, Belgium. 51N. 2E. Besieged by Spaniards, July, 1601-September, 1604; surrendered to Allies, 1706; taken by French, 1745, 1792, and 1793; bombarded by English, 1798.

Ostrolenka, Russia. 53N. 21E. Russians defeated by Oudinot, 1807, by insurgent Poles, 1831; by Turks, 1853 (Crimean W.).

Ostrovno, Russia. 48N. 27E. Russian corps defeated by Ney and Prince Eugène, 1812.

Oswestry (Oswald's Tree), Salop, En. 52N. 3W. St. Oswald, King of Northumberland, slain in battle against Penda of Mercia, 642, taken and burnt by King John, and later by Llewellyn, taken by Parliamentarians, 1644

Otranto, Italy. 40N. 18E. Taken and inhabitants massacred by the Turks, 1480 (See Horace Walpole, 'Castle of O.')

Otterburn, Northumberland, En. 55N. 2W. Famous battle commemorated in old ballad; Hotspur made prisoner and Douglas slain.

Ottery St. Mary, Devons., En. 50N. 3W. Res. awhile of Sir W. Raleigh; bp. of Coleridge (1772-1834) (The Clavering St. Mary of Thackeray's 'Pendennis.')

Oudenarde, Belgium. 50N. 3E. Taken by Marlborough, 1706; French defeated by, 1708.

Oviedo, Spain. 43N. 5W. Taken by Ney, 1809; taken and retaken later during Peninsular W.

Oxford, En. 51N. 1W. First colls. f., Balliol, Merton, and University, latter half of 13th century, Edmund Ironside d., or killed here, according to some historians, 1016; Empress Maude besieged, 1142; 'Provisions of Oxford' drawn up by 'Mad Parliament,' 1258, Ridley and Latimer martyred, 1555, Cranmer, 1556; surrendered to Parliamentarians, 1646, bp. of Richard I. and John.

Paderborn, Westphalia. 51N. 8E. Charlemagne held several diets here; his headquarters during the war with the Saxons.

Padua, Italy 45N. 11E. Destroyed in turns by Alaric and Attila; restored by Charlemagne; the Carrara were rulers after 1318, taken by Venice, 1405, Austrian possession, 1797-1805, 1814-1866, when incorporated in kingdom of Italy; bp. of the painter Mantegna

Palermo, Sicily. 38N. 13E. Sicilian Vespers, 1282; revolt against Bourbon rule, 1820, 1848; freed by Garibaldi and his 'Thousand,' 1860.

Palestrina, Italy. 41N. 12E. Neapolitans routed by Garibaldi, 1849.

Palestro, Italy. 45N. 9E. Defeat of Austrians by Piedmontese and French, 1859 (Unification of Italy).

Pallas, Longford, Ir. 52N. 8W. Bp. of Oliver Goldsmith (1728-74).

Palos, Spain 37N. 6W. Old port where Columbus embarked for his great voyage.

Pampeluna, Spain. 42N. 1W. Ancient capital of Navarre; taken by Charlemagne, 778, taken and retaken later by French and Spaniards; Loyola, founder of the Jesuits, wounded during defence of, 1521; sc. conflicts during Civil W. (1831-42).

Parga, Turkey. 39N. 20E. Brought under Turkish control by Ali Pacha, 1819, when the inhabitants all migrated.

Paris, France. 48N. 2E. Bastille taken, 1789; occupied by Allies, 1814; entry of Louis XVIII., 1815; revolution and Louis Philippe king, 1830-48; coup d'état, 1851; invested by German army, Sept., 1870-Jan. 1871; insurrection and government of Commune, 1871. (See Lytton, 'The Parisians;' Daudet, 'Robert Helmont;' Zola, 'The Downfall,' Erckmann-Chatrian, 'The Plébiscite).

Parma, duchy and town of, Italy. 44N. 10E. Town besieged by Frederick II., 1245 and 1248, subsequently under rule in turn of the Correggio, Este, Visconti, the Pope, and Farnese.

Passau, Bavaria. 49N. 13E. Suffered during wars of 1808 and 1809.

Patay, France. 48N. 2E. English defeated by Joan of Arc and Richemont, and Talbot made prisoner, 1429; series of engagements between French and Germans, 1870.

Pau, France. 43N. 0W. Former capital of Béarn; bp. of Jeanne d'Albret and her son, Henri IV., and of Bernadotte (Charles XIV. of Sweden).

Pavia, Italy. 45N. 9E. Ancient capital of the Lombards from 584-775, when delivered into Charlemagne's hands; the Languschi and Beccaria were rival lords, 13th and 14th centuries, the latter exterminated by the Duke of Milan, 1418, Francis I. defeated under its walls and taken prisoner, 1525; taken by the French, 1796, bp. of Lanfranc, cir. 1005-1089.

Peel, Isle of Man 54N. 4W. (See Scott, 'Peveril of the Peak.')

Pembroke, cap. of county, Wa 51N. 4W. Taken by Cromwell, 1648; bp. of Henry VII.

Peniscola, Spain. 40N. 0E. In possession of French, 1811-14.

Penshurst, Kent, En. 51N. 0E. Bp. of Sir Philip and Algernon Sidney.

Penzance, Cornwall, En. 50N. 5W. Burned by small force of Spaniards, 1595; sacked by Fairfax, 1646; bp. of Sir Humphrey Davy (1778-1829).

Perigord, France. 45N. 0E. Bp. of Montaigne, essayist (1533-92).

Perigueux, France 45N. 0E. Suffered during Hundred Years' W. and the Fronde.

Peronne, France. 49N. 2E. Charles the Simple a prisoner here for 6 years before his death; Louis XI. held prisoner by Duc de Bourgogne, and forced to sign treaty, 1468; retaken by, 1477; treaty signed by nobles of Picardy, the beginning of the Ligue, 1576; taken by Germans, 1871.

Perpignan, Pyrenees. 42N. 2E. Old capital of Roussillon; taken by French after long siege, 1475, became in turns Spanish and French possession, 1493, 1642.

Perth, cap. of county, Scot. 56N. 3W. Famous sermon on 'Idolatry' by Knox, 1559; James I. of Scotland assassinated, 1437; Gowrie conspiracy, 1600; Chevalier proclaimed James VIII., 1715, 1745. (See Scott, 'Fair Maid of Perth.')

Perugia, Italy. 43N. 12E. Seven years' siege by Goths, 6th century; later in possession of Lombards; taken from Pope by Condottiere Forte-Braccio, 1416; possession of disputed by the Oddi and Baglioni, 15th-16th centuries; papal possession till 1860. (See Matarazzo's 'Chronicles.')

Pesaro, Italy. 43N. 12E. Destroyed by Totila, 6th century; bp. of Rossini, the composer.

Peschiera, Italy. 45N. 10E. One of the Quadrilateral, taken in turns by French and Allies, 1796-1801; by Sardinians and Austrians, 1848.

Peterborough, Northampton, En. 52N. 0W. Ass. Hereward the Wake; Queen Catherine of Aragon buried in cathedral, 1536; grave of Mary Queen of Scots, 1587-1612; portrait of 'Old Scarlett' who buried both; Cromwell at, 1643

Petherton, North, Somerset, En 50N 4W. Chaucer appointed forester, 1390-1.

Peterwardein, Austria-Hungary. 45N. 19E. Soldiers assembled by Peter the Hermit for first crusade; great victory of Prince Eugène over Turks, 1716, siege by Austrians and capitulation of Hungarians, 1848, 1849.

Pevensey, Sussex, En 50N. 0E. Landing-place of William the Conqueror.

Pezenas, France. 43N. 3W. Taken by Simon de Montfort, 1211; here Molière wrote his 'Précieuses Ridicules '

Phalsbourg, Lorraine. 48N. 7E. Defended against Allies, 1814, 1815; taken by Germans, 1870. (See Erckmann-Chatrian, 'Le Blocus.')

Philiphaugh, Selkirk, Scot. 55N. 2W. Montrose defeated by Leslie, 1645.

Philippsbourg, Germany. 49N. 8E. Sc frequent sieges, 1633-1734, Marshal de Berwick killed, 1734; taken by French, 1799.

Piacenza, Italy. 45N 9E. First crusade preached at Council, 1095; the Scotti in power from 1254; passed to Visconti, 1332-1447; sacked by Sforza, 1447; possession in turns of the Pope and Farnese from 1511; defeat of Franco-Spanish forces by Austro-Sardinian, 1746; occupied by French, 1799, 1800.

Picquigny, France 49N. 2E. William Long-sword assassinated, 942; treaty between Edward IV. and Louis XI, 1457.

Pidavro (Epidaure), Greece. 37N. 22E. National congress to proclaim independence of Greece, 1822.

Pilsen, Bohemia. 49N. 13E. Taken by Ziska (Hussite W.), by Mansfeld (Thirty Years' W.); headquarters of Wallenstein, 1633-4.

Pinerolo, Pignerol, Italy. 44N. 7E. Prison of Man with the Iron Mask, 1666-86.

Pinkie, Midlothian, Scot. 55N. 2W. Scots defeated by Protector Somerset (known also as Battle of Musselburgh), 1547; last battle fought between English and Scots.

Pirna, Saxony. 50N. 13E. Defeat of Austrians by Prussians, 1745; of Saxons, 1756; encounters between French and Allies, 1813.

Pisa, Italy. 43N. 10E. Supporter of the Ghibelline cause; under successive masters from 1361; famous church council, 1409; bp. of Galileo (1564-1642).

Pistoia, Italy 43N. 10E. Passed 1406 into power of Florence; Murat defeated by Austrians, 1815; bp. of Cino, poet and jurisconsult, 13th-14th centuries.

Pitgaveny, Elgin, Scot. 57N. 3W. King Duncan murdered at, 1040.

Plescow, Pskov, Russia. 57N. 28E. Besieged by Gustavus Adolphus, 1615 (Russo-Swedish W).

Plevna, Bulgaria. 43N 24E Osman Pasha surrendered to Russians after siege of 143 days, 1877 (Russo-Turkish W.).

Plymouth, Devons., En. 50N. 4W Sailing port of Drake, 1572, Sir Humphrey Gilbert, 1583, Sir J. Hawkins, 1595, the two last never returned; here the admirals assembled to await the Armada, 1588; 'Pilgrim Fathers' left in 1620; in hands of Parliamentarians during Civil W., bp. of Sir J. Hawkins.

Plympton, Devons., En. 50N. 4W. Prince Maurice at, 1643; taken by Essex, 1644; bp. of Sir Joshua Reynolds (1723-92).

Poitiers, France. 46N. 0E. Alaric II. defeated and killed by Clovis at Vouillé near, 507; Saracen power crushed by Charles Martel near, 732; King John defeated by Black Prince, 1356.

Pola, Austria-Hungary. 44N. 13E. Naval victory of Genoese over Venetians, 1379; headquarters of the Austrian Fleet.

Poligny, France. 46N. 5E. A res. of the Counts and Dukes of Burgundy; sc. several sieges from time of Louis XI., 1479 to 1674.

Polotsk, Russia 55N. 28E. Sc. two engagements between French and Russians during Moscow campaign, 1812.

Pompeii, Italy. 40N. 14E. Destroyed by eruption of Vesuvius, A.D. 79.

Pontefract, Yorkshire, En. 53N. 1W. Richard II. murdered, 1400; captured after successive sieges by Lambert, 1649.

Ponthieu, France. 50N. 1E. Harold wrecked off the coast of, and delivered up to William, 1064.

Pontoise, France. 49N. 2E. Here Louis IX made his vow to undertake a crusade; taken in turns by English and French during Hundred Years' W.

Pont Valain, France. 47N. 0E. English defeated by Du Guesclin, 1370.

Portisham, Dorsets, En. 50N. 2W. Bp. of Nelson's Hardy, vice-admiral (1769-1839).

Portland Dorset, En. 50N. 2W. Three

days' naval fight between Blake, Deane, and Monk, and the Dutch under Van Tromp, De Ruyter, and Evetzen; the latter were defeated, 1653.

Portsmouth, Hants, En. 50N. 1W. Duke of Buckingham assassinated by Felton, 1628; Charles II. married to Catherine of Braganza, 1661; bp. of Sir W. Besant (1836-1901), and of George Meredith; Dickens born at Portsea.

Possagno, Italy. 45N. 12E. Bp. of Canova, sculptor (1757-1822).

Potsdam, Prussia. 52N. 13E. Tombs of the Hohenzollerns; Sans Souci, res. of Frederick the Great; bp. of Wilhelm von Humboldt, philologist, friend of Schiller and Goethe (1767-1835).

Prague, Bohemia. 50N. 14E. Taken by Ziska and Hussites, 1419; 'Defenestration which began the Thirty Years' W.,' 1618; Elector Frederick defeated, 1620; Austrians defeated by Koenigsmarck, 1648; celebrated siege sustained by French, and famous retreat (W. of Austrian Succession), 1742; Austrians defeated by Frederick the Great (Seven Years' W.), 1757; Congress, 1813; insurrection, 1848; peace between Austria and Prussia, 1866.

Prenzlow, Prussia. 53N. 13E. Taken by Murat, 1806.

Presburg, Hungary. 48N. 17E. Later kings of Hungary crowned at; taken by Gabor Bethlen, who was proclaimed king the following year (1620); by Austrians, 1621; bombarded by Davoût, 1809; Treaty between Napoleon and Emperor after Austerlitz, 1805.

Prescott, Lancashire, En. 53N. 2W. Bp. of John P. Kemble the actor (1757-1823).

Preston, Lancashire, En. 53N. 2W. Royalists defeated, 1648; spinning-frame set up by Arkwright, a native, 1768.

Prestonpans, Haddingtons., Scot. 55N. 2W. English defeated by Prince Charles Edward, 1745.

Primolano, Italy. 45N. 11E. Austrians defeated by Napoleon, 1796.

Princes Risborough, Bucks., En. 51N. 0W. Site of palace of Black Prince.

Puente de la Reyna, Spain. 42N. 1W. Republicans defeated by Carlists, 1872.

Pultowa, Poltava, Russia. 49N. 34E. Charles XII. defeated by Peter the Great, 1709. (See Voltaire's Life of Charles XII.)

Pultusk, Poland. 52N. 21E. Saxons defeated by Charles XII., 1703; Russians by French, 1806.

Putney, Surrey, En. 51N. 0W. Bp. of Thomas Cromwell, Earl of Essex (1485 (?)-1540).

Quatre Bras, Belgium. 50N. 4E. Ney defeated by Wellington, June 16, 1815.

Quedlinburg, Prussia. 51N. 11E. Bp. of Klopstock, A. of the 'Messiah' (1724-1803).

Queenborough, Isle of Sheppey, En. 51N. 0E. Named after Queen Philippa.

Quesnoy, France. 50N. 3E. Taken and retaken by French and Imperialists, 1654,

1712; taken by Austrians, 1792, by French, 1794.

Quiberon, France. 47N. 3W. French fleet defeated by Hawke, 1759 (Seven Years' W.).

Quimper, France. 48N. 4W. Several times besieged by the English.

Quistello, Italy. 45N. 11E. Victory over French by Prince Eugène, 1734 (W. of Polish Succession).

Raab, Austria-Hungary. 47N. 17E. Defeat of Austrians by French under Eugène Beauharnais, 1809.

Radcot Bridge, England. 51N. 1W. Defeat of Richard II.'s forces by those of Henry IV., 1387.

Raeberry Castle, Galloway, Scot. 54N. 4E. The 'Ellangowan New Place' of 'Guy Mannering.'

Ragatz, Switzerland. 47N. 9E. Victory of Swiss confederates over Austrians, 1446 (Armagnac W.).

Raglan Castle, Monmouths., En. 51N. 2W. Charles I. at, after Naseby, 1645; surrendered to Fairfax, 1646.

Ragusa, Austria-Hungary. 42N. 18E. Formerly a small republic; occupied by the French, 1806; assigned to Austria by Congress of Vienna, 1815.

Rambervilliers, France. 48N. 6E. Held against the Germans, 1870.

Ramillies, Belgium. 50N. 4E. French defeated by Marlborough, 1706.

Ramsbottom, Lancashire, En. 53N. 2W. Home of Dickens' 'Cheeryble Brothers.'

Rapperschwyl, Switzerland. 47N. 8E. A republic from 1458-1798.

Rashult, Sweden. 56N. 14E. Bp. of Linnæus, Swedish naturalist (1707-78).

Rastadt, Baden. 48N. 8E. Austrians driven from heights by Moreau, 1796; Congress, 1797-9 (France and Germany), and assassination of French commissaries.

Rathenow, Prussia. 52N. 12E. Swedes defeated by Elector Frederick William, 1675.

Rathmines, suburb of Dublin, Ir. 53N. 6W. Royalists defeated, 1649.

Ratisbon (Regensburg), Bavaria. 49N. 12E. Several times besieged, 1631-41; taken by Napoleon after five days' fighting, 1809; Imperial diets held at, 1656-1806; Interim signed, 1541; armistice (France and Austria), 1684; bp. of F. M. Grimm, A. of the 'Correspondence' (1723-1807).

Ratzeburg, Germany. 53N. 10E. Coleridge at as student.

Ravenna, Italy. 44N. 12E. Made capital of Western Empire by Honorius, 404; res. of Odoacer, and of Theodoric, King of the Ostrogoths; later papal possession; victory over the Holy League and death of Gaston de Foix, 1512; Byron at, 1819-21; tombs of Theodoric and of Dante, who died here.

Ré, Rhé, island, France. 46N. 1W. Surrendered by English to Charles VII., 1457; fruitless siege under Duke of Buckingham, July-October, 1627.

Reading, Berks, En. 51N. 0W. Defeat of Ethelred and Alfred by Danes, 871; sur-

rendered to Parliamentarians, 1643; skirmish between troops of James II. and Prince of Orange, 1688; bp of Archbishop Laud (1573-1645).

Rebec, Italy. 45N. 10E. French defeated by Austrians, death of Bayard, 1524.

Reggio, Italy (Calabria). 38N 15E. Taken in turns by Alaric, Totila, Saracens, and Normans, 5th-11th centuries; sacked by Barbarossa, 1544; by Turks, 1588; destroyed by earthquake, 1783.

Reggio, Italy (Modena). 44N. 10E. Taken by Guiscard, 1060; by French and Imperialists, 1702, 1706; bp. of Ariosto (1474-1533).

Reigate, Surrey, En. 51N. 0W. Grave of Lord Howard of Effingham, Lord High Admiral at the time of the Armada (1510 (?)-73).

Reims, France. 49N. 4E. Famous cathedral town, sacked by Vandals and Attila, 5th century; Clovis baptised at, 496; French kings from Philippe Auguste consecrated at, besieged by Edward III., 1359; English possession, 1421-29, when taken by Joan of Arc; occupied by the Russians, 1814.

Rennes, France (Brittany). 48N. 1W Besieged by English, 1356; Parliament held by Henri II., 1553.

Rethel, France 49N 4E. Taken and retaken by Condé and Turenne during the wars of the Fronde, 1650-55.

Rheinberg, Rhenish Prussia. 51N. 6E. French victory over Hanoverians, 1760.

Rheinfelden, Switzerland. 47N. 7E. Two battles (Thirty Years' W.), in which first Austrians and then French were victors, 1638; Austrians defeated, 1678

Rhodes, island, Mediterranean. 36N. 28E. Knights of St. John established in 1310, vainly besieged by Turks, 1479; secured to Turks by Soliman II., 1522, famous 'Laocoon' found on in 1506.

Rhuddlan, Flints., Wa. 53N. 3W. Caradoc defeated by Offa, 795; statutes of issued by Edward I., 1284; taken by Parliamentarians, 1646

Richmond, Surrey, En. 51N. 0W. Tournament held by Henry VII., 1492; Queen Elizabeth died, 1603; Ass. Swift and 'Stella'; grave of Thomson, poet of the 'Seasons'

Rickmansworth, Herts, En. 51N. 0W. William Penn, f. of Pennsylvania, a resident, 1672-77.

Rieti, Italy 42N. 12E. Defeat of Neapolitans by Austrians, and reinstatement of King Ferdinand, 1821.

Riga, Russia. 57N. 24E. Held by small body of Poles, and finally taken by Gustavus Adolphus (Thirty Years' W.), 1621; held by Russia since 1710.

Rimini, Italy 44N. 12E. The Malatesta in power from 13th to 16th century, when they were driven out by Cæsar Borgia, 1528, Francesca di R. has been immortalised by Dante. (See also dramas by D'Annunzio and Stephen Phillips; Byron's 'Parisina' w²s a Malatesta.)

Rimnik, Roumania. 45N. 27E. Grand Vizier and his Turks routed by Austrians and Russians, 1789.

Rivoli, Italy (Venetia). 45N. 7E. Austrians defeated by Napoleon, 1797.

Robroyston, Ayr, Scot. 55N 4W Wallace captured, 1305.

Rochefort-sur-mer, France. 45N. 0W. Napoleon surrendered to Captain Maitland, of the 'Bellerophon,' 1815.

Rochelle, La, France. 46N. 1W. Huguenot stronghold, valiantly defended against Catholic forces, 1572 and 1573; taken by Richelieu after 13 months' siege, 1628.

Rochester, Kent, En. 51N. 0E. Commemorated in several of Dickens' works, his home, 'Gadshill,' is near.

Rochford, Essex, En. 51N. 0E. One of the places at which Anne Boleyn is said to have been born (see Blickling).

Rocourt, Belgium. 50N. 5E. Imperialists defeated by Maurice de Saxe (W. of Austrian Succession), 1746.

Rocroi, France. 49N. 4E. Victory of Condé over Spaniards, 1643 and 1653 (Thirty Years' W.).

Rodemack, Alsace - Lorraine. 49N. 6E. Bravely held against the Prussians in 1792 and 1815.

Rohrau, Austria. 48N. 16E. Bp of Haydn, the composer (1732-1809).

Rokeby, Yorks, En. 54N. 1W. Commemorated in Scott's poem.

Rolica, Portugal 39N 9W. French driven from by Wellington (Peninsular W.), 1808.

Romano, Italy (Piedmont). 45N. 7E. Austrians defeated by Napoleon, 1800.

Rome, Italy. 41N. 12E. Seat of empire removed from to Byzantium by Constantine, 330; division of empire into East and West, 364; overrun by barbarians, 5th century; Charlemagne crowned emperor at, 800; suffered several sieges during long struggle between popes and emperors, ending with death of Frederick II., 1250, republic proclaimed by Rienzi, 1347; by Berthier, 1798; made part of French empire, 1808, restored to pope, 1814; French in occupation, 1849-70, revolt of papal states, 1860, capital of the united kingdom of Italy since 1870

Roncesvalles, Spain. 42N. 1W. Charlemagne's rearguard attacked, and Roland and other peers slain, 778, subject of old Chanson de Geste; held by the English against Soult (Peninsular W.), 1813.

Rosbecque, Belgium. 50N. 3E. Defeat of Flemings by Charles VI., and death of Philip van Artevelde, 1382.

Roscoff, France. 48N. 3W. Landing of Mary Queen of Scots, 1548.

Roseneath, Ayr, Scot. 56N. 4W Seat of Duke of Argyle. (See Scott, 'Heart of Midlothian')

Roskild, Denmark. 55N. 12E. Ancient capital.

Rosny-sur-Seine, France. 49N. 1E. Bp of Sully, companion and minister of Henri IV. (1560 1641).

Ross, Hereford, En. 51N. 2W. House and grave of John Kyrle, 'Man of R.' (d. 1724), immortalised by Pope.

Rossbach, Prussia. 51N 11E. Victory of Frederick the Great over French and Austrians (Seven Years' W.), 1757.

Rosslyn, Midlothian, Scot. 55N. 3W. English defeated by Scots, 1303, ass. visits of Wordsworth, Burns, and Dr. Johnson. (See Scott, 'Lay of the Last Minstrel')

Rostock, Mecklenburg-Schwerin. 54N. 12E. Defeat of Swedes by Danes, 1677; tomb of Grotius (1583-1646); bp. of Blücher, our ally at Waterloo.

Rothesay, Bute, Scot. 55N. 5W. Res. of early Stuart kings.

Rothiere, La, France. Fierce fight between Allies and Napoleon, leaving the latter victor, 1814.

Rotterdam, Holland. 51N 4E. Suffered during wars of the Revolution; bp. of Erasmus (1465-1536.) (See Motley, op cit.)

Rouen, France. 49N. 1E. Possession of Dukes of Normandy from 9th to 13th century, taken by Philippe Auguste, 1204; by Henry V., 1419, trial and death of Joan of Arc, 1431, suffered during religious warfare in 16th century; bp. of Corneille, the father of French tragedy (1606-84) Famous Cathedral at.

Roulers, Belgium. 50N. 3E. Austrians defeated by French, 1794.

Roundway Down, Wilts, En. 51N. 1W. Waller defeated by Royalists, 1643.

Rouvray, France 48N. 1E. 'Battle of the Herrings' in which Sir John Fastolf distinguished himself, 1429.

Roveredo, Tyrol 45N. 11E. Austrians defeated by Napoleon, 1796.

Rowton, Salop, En 52N. 2W. Bp. of Richard Baxter (1615-91).

Rowton Heath, Cheshire, En. 53N. 2W. Royalists defeated, 1645.

Roxburgh, Scot 55N. 2W. Taken from English by James II of Scotland, who was killed by explosion of a gun, 1460.

Rullion Green, Pentlands, Scot. 55N. 3W. Covenanters defeated by Royalists, 1666.

Rumersheim, Alsace - Lorraine. 47N. 7E. Imperialists defeated by French (W of Spanish Succession), 1709.

Runnimede, Surrey, En 51N. 0W. Magna Charta signed by King John, 1215.

Rustchuk, Bulgaria. 43N. 25E Former Turkish fort, fought for by Russians and Turks, 1809-11 and 1854; taken by Russians, 1877

Rutherglen, Lanark, Scot 55N 4W. Several times besieged in the days of the Bruces; destroyed by Regent Moray, 1568; now a thriving suburb of Glasgow.

Ruthwell, Dumfries, Scot. 55N. 3W. Famous cross, inscribed with verses from Anglo-Saxon poem.

Ruth, Grütli, Switzerland. 46N. 8E. Meadow where the men of the cantons took the oath to drive out the Austrians, 1307.

Rye, Sussex, En. 50N. 0E. Bp. of Fletcher, the dramatist (1579-1625). (See Thackeray's 'Denis Duval.')

Ryswick, Holland. 52N. 4E. Treaty of Peace (France, England, Spain, Germany, and Netherlands), 1697.

Saalfeld-an-der-Saale, Saxe-Meiningen, Germany. 50N. 11E. Prussians defeated by the French, 1806

Saarbruck, Prussia. 49N. 6E. First engagement of Franco-German W, 1870

Saardam (Zaandam), Holland. 52N 4E. Here Peter the Great apprenticed himself as a carpenter to learn shipbuilding, 1697.

Saarlouis, Prussia 49N. 6E Bp of Marshal Ney, who rejoined Napoleon in 1815, fought at Waterloo, and was shot that same year.

Sables-d'Olonne, France. 46N. 1W. Destroyed by English-Dutch fleet, 1696.

Sabugal, Portugal. 40N. 7W. French driven back by Wellington, 1811 (Peninsular W.)

Sacile, Italy. 45N. 12E. Eugène Beauharnais defeated by Austrians, 1809.

Sadowa, Bohemia 50N. 15E. Austrians defeated by Prussians, 1866 (known also as battle of Koniggratz).

Sagres, Portugal. 37N 8W. Burnt by Drake, 1597.

Sagunto (Murviedro), Spain. 39N. 16W. Siege by Soult and final surrender to, 1811 (Peninsular W.).

St. Albans, Herts, En. 51N 0W. Ancient cathedral town. Tombs of Sir Francis Bacon and Duke Humphrey of Gloucester, at Sopwell Nunnery near Juliana Berners wrote her famous book of the chase, known as 'The Boke of S. Albans,' written in the early 15th century; the Yorkists won a victory here in 1455; the Lancastrians, 1461.

Saint-Amant-Mont-Rond, France 47N. 2E. Taken in turns by English and by Charles VI.

St Andrews, Fife, Scot 56N. 2W. Wishart martyred and Cardinal Beaton murdered, 1546.

St. Aubin-du-Cormier, France. 48N 1W Victory of La Tremoille over the Bretons, 1488

Saint-Cast, France. 48N. 3W. English defeated, 1758

St. Cloud, France. 48N. 2E. Henri III. assassinated, 1589; a favourite res. of Napoleon, capitulation of Paris signed, 1815, castle destroyed, 1870 (Franco-Prussian W.).

St. Cyr, France. 48N. 2E. Here Mme de Maintenon died and was buried

St. Davids, Pembrokes., Wa. 51N 5W. Former resort of pilgrims, among them the Conqueror and later kings; tomb of Edmund Tudor, father of Henry VII.

St. Denis, France. 48N. 2E. For twelve centuries the necropolis of the French kings (tombs of Dagobert, Louis XII., Francis I, Henri II' and Catherine de' Medici, etc, also of famous generals, Du Guesclin, Turenne, etc.), Suger, the great statesman (cir. 1081-1151), was brought up here, victory of Catholics over Protestants, and death

F

of Montmency, 1567; bombarded by Germans, 1871.

Saint-Dizier, France. 48N. 4E. Allies defeated near by Napoleon, 1814.

St. Gall, Switzerland. 47N. 9E A chief source for the history of Charlemagne was the work of a monk of this abbey.

St. Germain-en-Laye, France. 48N. 2E. Former res of French kings and where Louis XIV. and several of his predecessors were born; res. of James II of England for the last two years of his life, and where he lies buried

Saint-Gilles-sur-Vie, France 46N. 1W Victory of Louis XIII. over Protestants, 1622, defeat of Vendéans, 1815.

Saint-Gothard, Hungary. 46N. 16E. Turks driven out of Hungary by Austrians under Montecuculli and French under Coligny, 1664.

St. Helena, Atlantic. 15S. 5W. English possession since 1673; Napoleon a prisoner on from 1815 to his death.

St. Ives, Huntingdons, En. 52N. 0W. Res. of Cromwell, 1631-36.

Saint-Jacques, Basle, Switzerland. 47N. 7E Celebrated for the stand made by a small body of Swiss, who were all slain, against a large French force, 1444.

Saint-Jean-de-Losne, France. 47N 4E. Held by a small garrison against besieging Germans and Spaniards, 1636.

Saint-Jean-de-Luz, Pyrenees. 43N. 1W. Louis XIV. married at.

Saint-Just, Estramadura, Spain 50N. 5W. To this monastery Charles V. retired after his abdication, and here two years later died, 1558.

Saint-Leu-Taverny, France. 48N 2E. Tombs of Napoleon's father, and of his brother Louis, King of Holland, and of Marshal Ney.

St. Lô, France. 49N. 1W. Taken in turns by French and English, 1203-1449; bp. of Octave Feuillet, novelist and dramatist.

St. Macaire, France 44N 0W. Taken by Henry III. of England, 1253; sc. several later sieges

St. Malo, France. 48N. 2W. Bp. of the early navigator Jacques Cartier, of Chateaubriand, who is also buried here (1768-1848), and of Lamennais (1782-1854)

St. Michel, France, see Mont St. Michel.

Saint-Omer, France. 50N 2E. Sc. many sieges by French kings and Imperialists from the 11th century; saved from Marlborough and Prince Eugène by the efforts of a woman, Jacqueline Robin, 1711; bp. of Suger, the great French statesman of the early 12th century.

St. Petersburg, Russia. 59N. 30E. F. by Peter the Great, 1703

Saint-Pierre-Port, Guernsey. 49N. 2W. Hugo's home during his exile, 1856-70.

Saint-Point, France 46N 4E. Castle and tomb of the poet Lamartine (1790-1869).

St. Quentin, France. 49N. 3E. French defeated by English and Spanish forces, 1557, French defeated by Germans, 1871. (See Dumas, 'The Two Dianas.')

Saint-Remy, France. 45N. 5E. Bp. of the famous astrologer, Nostradamus (1503-66).

Saint-Valery-sur-Somme, France 50N. 1E. Whence William the Conqueror set sail for England, 1066.

St. Vincent, Cape, Portugal. 37N. 9W. Rooke defeated by French off, 1693; success of Rodney over Spaniards, 1780, defeat of Spaniards by Jervis, 1797; victory of Sir Charles Napier over Don Miguel, 1833.

Sainte-Sévère, France 46N. 1E. Taken from the English by Du Guesclin, 1372.

Salamanca, Spain 40N. 5W. Taken by French, 1812; victory of Wellington over Marmont, 1812 (Peninsular W); contains one of the oldest monasteries in Europe.

Salcombe, S Devon, En. 50N. 3W. Grave of Froude, the historian.

Salerno, town and province, Italy. 40N. 14E. Defeat of Saracens by Norman knights, 1016; taken by Robert Guiscard, 1075; town destroyed by Emperor Henry IV., 1193.

Salisbury, Wilts, En. 51N. 1W. Famous circular group of stones known as Stonehenge. The 'Barset' of Trollope.

Salonica, Turkey 40N. 22E. Taken from Venetians by Turks, 1430.

Saluzzo, Italy 44N. 7E. Bp. of Silvio Pellico, dramatist and prose writer (1788-1854).

Salzbach, Baden. 48N. 7E. Marshal Turenne killed, 1675.

Salzburg, Austria. 47N. 13E. Emigration of persecuted Protestants, 1732. (See Goethe, 'Hermann u. Dorothea')

Sandridge, near Dartmouth, En. 50N. 3W. Bp of John Davis, navigator of the 16th century.

Sandwich, Kent, En. 51N 1E Defeat of Danes by Athelstan, 851; landing-place of Sweyn and Canute, more than once burnt by the French in 15th century.

Sandy Knowe, Roxburgh, Scot. 55N. 2W. Sir Walter Scott some years at when a child.

Sanquhar, Dumfriess, Scot. 55N. 3W. Taken by Scots and English garrison slaughtered, 1297; hither Mary Queen of Scots rode in hot haste after disaster of Langside, and hence escaped to England, Declaration of Covenanters, 1680 (see Aird's Moss); bp. of the 'Admirable' Crichton (cir. 1560-82).

San Sebastian, Spain. 43N. 1W. Taken by the French, 1808; stormed by Wellington, 1813; Carlists forced to raise siege, 1836 (Carlist W).

Santander, Spain. 43N. 3W. Sacked by Soult, 1808.

Santiago de Compostella, Spain. 42N. 8W. Famous resort of pilgrims in the Middle Ages

Saorge, Maritime Alps. 44N. 6E. Taken by Masséna, 1794.

Saragossa, Spain. 41N. 0W. Taken from the Moors after a 5 years' siege, 1118; besieged by French, June to August, 1808, December to February, 1808-9, when the

'Maid of Saragossa' distinguished herself. (See Byron, 'Childe Harold,' Canto I)

Sardinia, Mediterranean 40N. 9E Transferred from Spain to Austria by Treaty of Utrecht, 1714, since then in possession in turns of Dukes of Savoy and the French.

Sarzeau, Brittany, France 47N. 2W. Bp. of Le Sage, A of 'Gil Blas' (1668-1747)

Sasun (Sassoon), Armenia. 39N. 42E. Sc. atrocities committed by Kurds and Turks, 1893-4

Sauchie (Sauchieburn), Stirling, Scot 56N. 3W. James III of Scotland defeated and slain, 1488.

Saulieu, France. 47N 4E. Burnt by the English, 1359

Saumur, France 47N. 0W. Centre of Calvinism until revocation of Edict of Nantes, 1685, taken by Vendéans, 1793, insurrection under General Berton, 1822

Sauve, France 43N. 3E. Sided with Calvinists, 1620; taken, and soon lost again, by Camisards, 1702, Florian, French versifier of fables, was born near (1755-94).

Savenay, France. 47N 1W. Vendéans defeated by republicans, 1795.

Savernake, Wilts, En 51N 1W. Wolf Hall, bp of Jane Seymour.

Savona, Italy. 44N. 8E. Bombarded by English, 1746; taken by French, 1809, and the Pope held prisoner by Napoleon till 1812.

Scandiano, Italy. 44N. 10E Bp. of the poet Bojardo, A. of 'Orlando Innamorato' (1430-94).

Scarborough, Yorks, En 54N 0W. Bp. of Sir F. Leighton (1830-96); grave of Anne Brontë, d 1849.

Schellenberg, Austria. 47N. 13E. Austrians defeated by Marlborough, 1704.

Scheveningen, Holland. 52N. 4E. Dutch fleet defeated and Tromp killed by English under Monk, 1653.

Schlettstadt, Alsace-Lorraine 48N 7E Taken by Germans, 1870; bp. of Bucer, the Reformer (1491-1551).

Schlusselburg, Russia 60N. 32E. Fort, where Ivan VI. was for 23 years imprisoned and then murdered.

Schmalkalden, Prussia. 50N. 10E. Protestant League concluded, 1537.

Schoenbrunn, Austria 48N. 16E. Peace signed between Napoleon and Austria, 1809, death of his son, the Duke de Reichstadt, 1832. (See 'L'Aiglon' by Rostand)

Schweidnitz, Prussia. 50N. 16E. Held against Frederick the Great during long siege, 1761-2, taken by French, 1807.

Schweinfurt, Bavaria 50N 10E. Bp. of the poet Rückert (1789-1866).

Scilly Islands, Cornwall, En. 49N. 6W. Taken by Athelstan, 938; leased by Elizabeth to Sir F. Godolphin, Sir Cloudesley Shovel, Admiral, drowned off, with loss of his ship, 1707.

Scone, Perth, Scot 56N. 3W. Coronation place of Scottish kings, 'stone' carried off by Edward I, 12 .

Scutari, Turkey   41 2E   Military

hospital during Crimean W. ass. with Florence Nightingale.

Sebastopol, Crimea, Russia. 44N. 33E Eleven months' siege during Crimean W, 1854-55. (See Tolstoi, 'Sevastopol ')

Sedan, France. 49N. 4E. Capitulated to the Germans, 1815; defeat and surrender of Napoleon III., 1870; bp. of Marshal Turenne (1611-75).

Sedgemoor, Somerset, En. 51N. 2W Monmouth defeated by royal forces, 1685.

Segovia, Spain. 40N. 4W. Sacked by the French, 1808

Selborne, Hants, En 51N. 0W. House where Gilbert White, A. of 'Natural History of S' was born and died (1720-93)

Selby, Yorks, En 53N. 1W. Bp. of Henry I , taken by Fairfax, 1644.

Seminara, Italy Gonzalvo de Cordova defeated by D'Aubigné, 1495; himself victor, 1503; Neapolitans defeated by French, 1807.

Semlin, Hungary. 44N. 20E. Remains of castle of John Hunyadi, where he died.

Sempach, Switzerland 47N 8E. Memorable victory of the Swiss over Austrians, 1386

Senlac, see Hastings.

Sens, France. 48N 3E. Besieged for a fortnight by the Allies, 1814.

Seville, Spain. 37N 5W Taken from the Moors by Ferdinand III. of Castile, 1248; treaty between England and Spain signed, 1729; French in possession, 1810-12; bp. of the Spanish painters Murillo and Velasquez

Sezannes, France. 48N. 3E. Besieged by the English, 1423, by the Huguenots, 1566, sacked by the Allies, 1814.

Shaftesbury, Dorset, En. 51N 2W. Death of Canute at, 1035; burial place of Edward the Martyr, murdered at Corfe Castle, 978

Shanklin, Isle of Wight. 50N. 1W. Keats at, 1817, here he began his 'Endymion.'

Sheerness, Kent, En. 51N 0E. Taken by De Ruyter, 1667.

Sheffield, Yorks, En. 53N. 1W. Castle taken by Parliamentarians, 1644.

Sherbourne, Dorset, En. 50N 2W Castle built by Raleigh and taken by Fairfax, 1645, graves of Asser, bishop of S., King Alfred's biographer, and of two of the king's brothers.

Sheriffmuir, Perth, Scot. 56N. 3W. Indecisive action between Jacobites and Hanoverians, 1715

Sherwood Forest, Notts, En 53N 1W Ass. Robin Hood, the hero of many old ballads

Shetland Islands, Scot. 60N. 1W. (See Scott, 'Pirate ')

Shipka Pass, Balkans. 42N. 25E. Held by the Russians against severe odds, 1877 (Russo-Turkish W.).

Shrewsbury, Salop, En. 52N 2W. Battle in which Hotspur was killed, 1403.

Sicily, Italy. 37N. 14E. Part of the kingdom of the Two Sicilies under the Normans, and again at intervals under succeeding dynasties governed in turns by the house of Anjou, Hohenstaufen, Aragon, Savoy,

Hapsburg, and Bourbon; finally incorporated with Italy, 1861.

Siena, Italy 43N. 11E. Powerful republic in the Middle Ages, the Piccolomini were among its noble families; in possession of Charles V., 1540-53, retaken by him, 1554; centre of a famous school of painting

Silistria, Bulgaria. 44N. 27E. Besieged unavailingly by Russians (Crimean W); occupied by the Russians, 1878.

Simancas, Spain. 41N. 4W. Repository of national archives since 1563; indecisive battle between Christians and Moors, 939

Simplon, Switzerland. 46N. 8E. Military route over, constructed by Napoleon, 1800-7

Sinsheim, Baden. 49N. 8E. Imperialists defeated by Turenne, 1674, the Austrians by Ney, 1799.

Skien, Norway. 59N. 9E. Bp. of Ibsen, 1828.

Skipton, Yorks, En. 53N 2W. Traditional bp of ' Fair Rosamond.'

Skye, Hebrides, Scot. 57N. 6W Ass Flora Macdonald and Prince Charlie; Dr Johnson at Dungevan Castle, 1773, Scott at, 1814. (See Scott, ' Lord of the Isles.')

Slains (Slenach), Aberdeen, Scot. 57N. 1W. Comyn defeated by Bruce, 1307.

Sleswick-Holstein, Prussia. 54N. 9E. Taken from the Danes by Austria and Prussia, 1864, cause of war between these powers, 1866.

Sligo, Connaught, Ir. 54N. 8W. Taken by Sir F. Hamilton, 1641; by Sir C. Coote, 1645.

Slough, Bucks, En 51N 0W Home of Sir F. William Herschel (1786-1822), and afterwards of his son.

Sluys, Holland. 51N. 3E. Defeat of French by naval forces of Edward III., 1340, taken by the French, 1747 and 1794.

Smailholm, Roxburgh, Scot. 55N. 2W. Scott passed some years of childhood at Sandy Knowe farm, near. Sc. Avenel Castle, Scott, ' Monastery.'

Smerwick, Kerry, Ir. 52N. 10W. Fort taken by Lord Grey and butchery of Spanish and Italian defenders, 1580 (See Kingsley, ' Westward Ho! ')

Smolensk, Russia. 54N. 32E. Russians defeated by Napoleon, 1812.

Sofia, Bulgaria. 42N. 23E. Present capital of principality.

Soissons, France. 49N 3E. Victory of Clovis over Roman general Syagrius, 486 (ass. the episode of the ' Vase de Soissons '); of Charles Martel over Chilpéric, 719, and Charles the Simple over Robert, who was killed, 922, Charles himself defeated, 923; sc frequent sieges during Hundred Years', religious, and Napoleonic W.; taken by Germans, 1870.

Soldau, Prussia. 53N 20E. Prussians and Russians defeated by Ney, 1806.

Solferino, Italy. 45N. 10E. Austrians under Francis Joseph defeated by French and Piedmontese under Napoleon III, 1859.

Solway Moss, Cumberland. En. 55N. 2W. Scots defeated by English, 1542.

Somersby, Lincoln, En. 53N. 0E. Bp. of Tennyson.

Somerton, Somerset, En. 51N. 2W. Res. of Saxon kings; pillaged by Danes, 877; French King John imprisoned at.

Sommershausen, Bavaria. 49N. 9E. Imperialists defeated by Turenne and Wrangel, 1648.

Soncino, Italy. 45N. 10E. Milanese defeated by Robert Sforza, 1440; taken, but soon lost, by Prince Eugène, 1720

Sondershausen, Germany. 51N 10E. English and Allies defeated by French, 1758.

Sonnethal, Germany. 52N 10E. Traditional defeat of Charlemagne's forces by Witikind, the Saxon chief, 782.

Sorrento, Italy. 40N. 14E. Bp. of Tasso (1544-95).

Souli, Albania 40N 20E Brave defence against attacks by Ali Pasha, and final emigration of inhabitants, 1804. (See picture by Ary Scheffer.)

Sound, The. 55N. 12E. Forced by Nelson, 1801.

Southampton, Hants, En. 50N. 1W. Ass. Sir Bevis, hero of old romance; bp of Dr. Isaac Watts, Dibdin (song writer), and Millais.

Southwell, Notts, En. 53N. 0W. Charles I. surrendered to Scots Commissioners, 1646.

Southwold, Suffolk, En. 52N. 1E. Indecisive naval battle between English and Dutch, 1672.

Spandau, Prussia. 52N. 13E. Taken by the French, 1806.

Spanish Point, Ireland. 52N. 9W. Burial place of many of the crews of the wrecked Armada.

Spezzia, Italy. 44N. 9E. Shelley at, during last months of life.

Spicheren, Lorraine. 49N. 6E. French defeated by Germans, 1870.

Spielberg, Moravia. 49N. 16E. Silvio Pellico (1788-1854) imprisoned. (See his ' Le Mie Prigioni.')

Spilsby, Lincoln, En. 53N 0E. Bp. of Sir John Franklin, Arctic explorer (1786-1847).

Spires, Rhenish Bavaria. 49N. 8E. Famous diet of 1529, when the Reformers gained their name of Protestant; destroyed by French, 1689, and occupied by them several times during the 18th century.

Squillace, Italy. 38N. 16E. Bp. of Cassiodorus, historian and general writer, and minister of Theodoric, King of the Ostrogoths, who died about 575, after a life of nearly a hundred years.

Staffa, Hebrides, Scot. 56N. 6W. Fingal's cave

Stafford, cap. of county, En. 52N. 2W. Bp of Isaac Walton (1593-1683).

Stamford Bridge, Yorks, En 53N. 0W. Death of Tostig and Harold Hardrada, defeated by Harold, 1066, first encounter in the W. of the Roses, 1453.

Stanhope, Durham, En. 54N. 2W. Bishop Butler, A. of the ' Analogy,' rector, 1725-40.

Steinkirk, Belgium. 50N. 4E. William III. defeated by French, 1692.

Stendal, Saxony. 52N. 11E. Bp of Winckelmann, the archæologist (1717-68).

Stevershausen (Sievershausen), Prussia. 53N. 10E. Maurice, Elector of Saxony, mortally wounded, 1553.

Stirling, Scot. 56N. 3W. Contains famous castle; victory of Wallace, 1297; besieged and taken by Edward I, 1304; Douglas stabbed by James II, 1452; the infant Mary Stuart (1543) and James VI. crowned at; Regent Lennox killed, 1571; taken by Monk, 1651, vainly besieged by Jacobites, 1746.

Stockholm, Sweden. 59N. 18E. Besieged by Margaret of Denmark, 1389; massacre of nobles by Christian II. of Denmark, 1520; treaty between Sweden and England, 1719; bp. of Swedenborg (1688-1772).

Stoke Poges, Bucks, En. 51N. 0W. Grave of Gray in the churchyard immortalised by him in his 'Elegy.'

Stone, Staffs, En. 52N 2W. Bp. of Peter de Wint, painter (1784-1849).

Stowmarket, Suffolk, En. 52N. 1E Milton's tutor, Dr. Young, vicar of, and here visited by his pupil.

Stralsund, Prussia. 54N. 13E. Vainly besieged by Wallenstein, 1628; fierce bombardment and capitulation to Elector of Brandenburg, 1715; heroically defended by Schill against Prussia and Allies, 1809, finally ceded to Prussia, 1815.

Strasburg, Alsace-Lorraine. 48N. 7E Memorable siege, August 10 to September 27, 1870 (Franco-Prussian W).

Stratford-on-Avon, Warwick, En. 52N. 1W. Bp. of Shakespeare, and where he and Anne Hathaway and his daughters were buried.

Streatham, Surrey, En. 51N. 0W. Ass. Johnson and Mrs. Thrale.

Stromness, Orkney, Scot. 58N. 3W. Bp of Gow, Scott's 'Pirate.'

Stuhlweissenburg, Hungary. 47N. 18E For 500 years the res. and necropolis of kings of Hungary, and where they were anciently crowned.

Stuttgart, Würtemberg. 48N 9E. Suffered much during Thirty Years W. and under Louis XIV; bp. of Hegel, the philosopher (1770-1831).

Sudbury, Suffolk, En. 52N. 0E. Bp. of Gainsborough (1727-88).

Sudeley, Gloucester, En. 51N. 2W. Tomb of Catherine Parr, who lived here as wife of Admiral Seymour.

Sveaborg, Helsingfors, Finland. 60N. 24E. Bombarded by Allied fleets, 1855 (Crimean W.).

Swanage, Dorset, En. 50N. 1W. Danes defeated by Alfred, 877.

Swanston, The Lothians, Scot 55N. 3W. R. L Stevenson at when a child (see his 'St. Ives.').

Swilly, Lough, Donegal, Ir. 55N. 7W. French fleet destroyed, 1798.

Swineshead, Lincoln, En. 52N. 0W. Here King John indulged in the feast of peaches and beer which finally caused his death.

Taganrog, Russia. 47N. 38E Bombarded by French and English fleets, 1855 (Crimean W.).

Tagliacozzo, Italy. 42N. 13E. Victory of Charles of Anjou over Conradin, rightful heir to Naples, the latter taken and beheaded, 1268.

Tain, Ross, Scot. 57N 4W. Bruce's queen captured and delivered to the English, 1306.

Talavera, Spain. 39N. 4W. French defeated by Wellington, 1809 (Peninsular W)

Talley (Tal-y-Llychau), Carmarthens., Wa. 51N. 3W. Traditional grave of the famous bard, David ap Gwilym, 14th century.

Tantallon, Haddings, Scot. 56N. 2W. Old stronghold of the Douglases; taken by Oliver Cromwell, 1639. (See Scott's 'Marmion.')

Tara, Meath, Ir. 53N. 6W. Palace and burial place of ancient kings of Ireland, commemorated by Moore in his well-known ballad.

Tarascon, France. 43N. 4E. Made famous by Daudet's works. (See 'Tartarin de Tarascon,' etc.).

Tarbes, France. 43N. 0E. English in possession, 1360-1406; bp. of Théophile Gautier, poet and novelist (1811-72)

Tarento, Italy. 46N. 13E. Taken by Gonzalvo de Cordova, 1502.

Tarifa, Spain. 36N. 5W. Held against the French by English under Gough, and Spaniards, 1811-12.

Tarragona, Spain. 41N. 1E. Occupied by English, 1705 (W. of Spanish Succession); taken by General Suchet, 1811 (Peninsular War).

Tarvis, Austria-Hungary. 46N. 13E. Austrians defeated by Masséna, 1797.

Taunton, Somerset, En 51N. 3W. Seized by Perkin Warbeck, 1497; held by Admiral Blake, 1644-45; standard presented to Monmouth, 1685, 'Bloody Assize' held by Jeffreys, 1685; bp. of Samuel Daniel, poet (1562-1619), and of Kinglake, A. of 'Eothen' (1809-91).

Tchernaya River, Crimea. 46N. 33E. Gortschakoff defeated by French and Allies under Marmora, 1855 (Crimean W.).

Teignmouth, Devon. 50N. 3W. Burned by the French, 1338 and 1690.

Temesvar, Hungary. 45N. 21E. Hungarians defeated by Austrians under Haynau, after long bombardment, 1849 (Hungarian Rising).

Temple Newsam, Yorks., En. 53N. 1W. Bp. of Darnley, Mary Stuart's husband, 1545. (Sc. Templestowe, Scott's 'Ivanhoe.')

Terni, Italy. 42N. 12E. Falls of Velino near. (See Byron, 'Childe Harold,' Canto IV. lxix-lxxii)

Tettenhall, Staffs., En. 52N. 2W. Danes defeated by Edward the Elder, 910.

Tewkesbury, Gloucester, En. 51N. 2W. Famous Yorkist victory and murder of Prince Edward of Lancaster, 1471; grave of the Duke of Clarence, murdered in the Tower.

Texel Island, Zuider Zee. 53N. 4E. Tromp (who was killed) and De Ruyter defeated by Monk and Blake, 1653; Dutch fleet, blocked by ice, taken by French cavalry, 1795; blockaded by Duncan, 1797; Dutch fleet surrendered to Mitchell, 1799

Thames River, En. 51N. 1W. (See Spenser, 'Prothalamion', Denham, 'Cooper's Hill,' etc).

Thaxted, Essex, En. 51N. 0E. Bp. of Samuel Purchas, A. of 'Purchas; his Pilgrimage,' a record of early voyages (1575 (?) 1626).

Thetford, Norfolk and Suffolk, En 52N. 0E. Danes defeated by Anglians, 870.

Thionville, Lorraine 49N 6E. Taken by Condé, 1643; later sieges by Austrians and Prussians, 1792, 1814, by the Germans, 1870.

Thorn, Prussia. 53N. 18E. Sc. of many sieges; taken by Charles XII. from the Poles, 1703, bp. of Copernicus, the celebrated astronomer (1473-1543)

Thornton, Yorks, En. 53N. 1W. Bp. of Charlotte Brontë (1816-55).

Thrieve, Galloway, Scot. 54N. 3W. 'Mons Meg' forged for the reduction of this castle.

Tiflis, Caucasia 41N. 44E. Taken by Genghis Khan, 12th century, by Tamerlane, 1386, later by Turks, Persians, and Russians, treaty, 1814 (Russia and Persia)

Tilbury, Essex, En. 51N. 0E. Review of troops by Elizabeth, 1588.

Tilsit, Prussia 55N 21E. Treaty signed between Napoleon and Alexander, 1807.

Tinchebrai, France. 48N. 0W. Robert of Normandy defeated by Henry I., who took possession of Normandy, 1106

Tintagel, Cornwall, En. 50N. 4W. Ruins of King Arthur's castle

Tintern, Monmouth, En. 51N. 2W. Ruins of abbey, immortalised by Wordsworth

Tippermuir, Perth, Scot. 56N. 3W. Covenanters defeated by Montrose, 1644.

Tirlemont, Belgium. 50N. 4E. Austrians defeated by French, 1793, 1794.

Tiverton, Devon, En. 50N 3W. Blackmore and his 'John Ridd' at school here. (See 'Lorna Doone ')

Toboso, El, Spain. 39N. 2W. Home of Don Quixote's Dulcinea.

Tolentino, Italy. 43N. 13E. Treaty (Napoleon and Pope), 1797; Murat defeated by Austrians, 1815.

Torbay, Devon, En. 50N. 3W. William III. landed, 1688.

Torgau, Prussia. 51N. 13E. Austrians defeated by Frederick the Great, 1760 (Seven Years' W.).

Torrington, Great, Devon, En. 50N. 4W. Victory of Fairfax, 1646.

Toulon, France. 43N. 5E. Attacked by Sir Cloudsley Shovel, 1707 (W. of Spanish Succession); defeat of British fleet, 1744 (W. of Austrian Succession); taken from English, 1793—siege memorable as the beginning of Napoleon's military reputation.

Toulouse France. 43N 1E. Simon de Montfort killed besieging, 1217-18 (Albigensian W), French defeated by Wellington, 1814

Tournay, Belgium. 50N. 3E. Bravely defended by Princess d'Epinoy against Parma, 1581 (Dutch W. of Independence); surrendered to the English under Marlborough, 1709 (W. of Spanish Succession), retaken later by French.

Tours, France. 47N 0E. Famous victory near, of Charles Martel over Saracens, one of the decisive battles of the world, 732; bp. of Honoré de Balzac (1799-1850) (See Creasy.)

Towton, Yorks, En 53N. 1W. Yorkist victory, 1461.

Trafalgar, Spain. 36N. 6W. Combined fleets of France and Spain defeated by Nelson, 1805.

Trebbia, Italy. 44N. 9E. French defeated by Suvarov, 1799.

Treguier, France 48N. 3W. Bp. of J. Ernest Renan (1823-92).

Treves (Trier), Prussia. 49N. 6E. Sc. frequent sieges by barbarians, and in 17th and 18th centuries by the French, who held it from 1794-1815, when it was given to Prussia.

Trim, Meath, Ir. 53N. 6W Wellington here at school when young, Henry of Lancaster imprisoned by Richard II ; Sir G. Coote, military commander in Ireland, killed, 1642, taken by Cromwell, 1649.

Trondhjem, Norway. 63N. 10E. Norwegian kings crowned at.

Tubingen, Würtemberg 48N. 9E. Suffered severely during Thirty Years' W.; the leader of the ' Tübingen School ' was Baur, the theologian (1792-1860); bp of Uhland, the poet (1787-1862)

Tudela, Spain. 42N. 1W. Spaniards defeated by French under Lannes, 1808 (Peninsular W.).

Turbigo, Italy. 45N 8E Austrians repulsed by Napoleon III., 1859 (Franco-Austrian W.).

Turin, Italy. 45N. 7E. Besieged by French, 1640, in 1706 (W. of Spanish Sucession), and during later wars; in possession in turns of French and House of Savoy, 1800-60, it then became the capital of Italy till 1865.

Turnau, Bohemia 50N. 15E. Austrians defeated by Prussians, 1866

Turnberry, Ayrs., Scot 55N. 4W. Robert Bruce born here or at Lochmaben.

Turnhout, Belgium. 51N. 4E. Spaniards defeated by Maurice of Nassau, 1597 (Dutch W. of Independence) (See Motley, op. cit.).

Tutbury, Staffords, En. 52N. 1W. Mary Queen of Scots here for a while a prisoner, 1569; surrendered to Parliamentarians, 1646

Twickenham, Middlesex, En. 51N. 0W. Res. of Horace Walpole (Strawberry Hill), and of Pope (also buried here) from 1719 to his death, 1744, ass. many other celebrities.

Ulm, Würtemberg 8N. 9E. Mack for d to capitulate by Napoleon, 1805

Upsala, Sweden. 59N. 17E. Tombs of Gustavus Adolplius and the naturalist Linnæus; famous 'Silver Codex' of Gothic translation of Scripture by Bhp. Ulfilas, 4th century.

Urbino, Italy. 43N. 12E. Bp of Raphael.

Ushant, island, France. 48N. 5W. Howe's naval victory, 1794

Utrecht, Netherlands. 52N. 5E. Declaration of Independence of the United Provinces, known as Union of U., 1579 (see Motley); Treaty (W. of Spanish Succession), 1713.

Valenciennes, France. 50N. 3E. Taken by Allies after long siege, 1793, retaken by French, 1794, bp. of Froissart, 14th century.

Valetta, Malta. 35N. 14E. Capitulated to Napoleon after five days' attack, 1798; taken by English after nearly 2 years' siege, 1800.

Valladolid, Spain. 41N. 4W. Sacked by the French, 1808, Napoleon's headquarters, 1809.

Vallombrosa, Italy. 43N. 11E. Milton here in 1639; 'Thick as autumnal leaves that strow the brooks in Vallombrosa.' (See 'Paradise Lost,' i. 302-3.)

Valmy, France. 49N. 4E. Prussians defeated by Dumouriez, 1792.

Varennes, France 49N. 5E. Louis XVI. and his family captured on their flight, 1791. (Sc. Carlyle, 'French Revolution')

Varna, Bulgaria. 43N. 27E. Taken from Turks after long siege by Russians under Mentschikoff, 1828.

Vaucluse, France. 44N. 5E. Res. for a while of Petrarch, who has immortalised its 'Fountain.'

Vendome, France. 47N. 1E. German victory near, 1870 (Franco-Prussian W.)

Venice, Italy. 45N. 12E. First doge, 697; chief maritime power of the Adriatic, in rivalry with Genoa, 13th and 14th centuries; chief commercial power of Europe until discovery of other routes to India at close of 15th century; Austrian possession, 1798-1805, and from 1814 till incorporated in kingdom of Italy, 1866, although bravely struggling for independence in 1849. (See Ruskin, 'Stones of Venice.')

Verdun, France. 49N. 5E. Taken by Germans after long siege, 1870.

Verona, Italy. 45N. 11E. Home of the Capulets and Montagues (see 'Romeo and Juliet'), the Scala family in power, 13th-14th centuries; in turns, Venetian and Austrian possession, 1405-1805, Italian, 1805-15; Austrian, 1815-66, Congress of the Holy Alliance, of which Chateaubriand left an account, 1822.

Versailles, France 48N. 2E Peace of (England and United States) 1783; meeting of states-general, 1789, capitulation of Paris signed, 1871.

Vezelay, France. 47N. 3E. Here the first crusade was preached by St Bernard, 1145, and Richard I. and Philippe Auguste took the cross, 1187.

Vienna, Austria. 48N. 16E. Taken by Mathias Corvin, King of Hungary, 1485; twice besieged by Turks, 1529 and 1683, when relieved by Sobieski; occupied by Napoleon, 1805-9; famous Congress of Allied Powers, 1814-15.

Vigo, Spain. 42N 8W. Victory of Drake, 1585, 1589; of Sir George Rooke (capture of Spanish galleons), 1702, of Lord Cobham, 1719.

Villafranca, Italy. 45N. 10E. Peace of (France and Austria), 1859.

Villers-Cotterets, France. 49N. 3E. Bp. of Alexandre Dumas (1803-70).

Vimiero, Portugal. 39N. 9W. Junot defeated by Wellington, 1808.

Vinegar Hill, Wexford, Ir. 52N. 6W. Irish rebels defeated by Lake, 1798.

Vionville, Lorraine. 48N. 6E. French defeated by Prussians, 1870.

Volturno, Italy. 41N. 14E. Victory of Garibaldi over Neapolitans, 1860.

Wagram, Austria. 48N. 16E. Austrians defeated by Napoleon, 1809.

Wakefield, Yorks, En. 53N. 1W. Defeat of Yorkists, and death of Richard, Duke of York, 1460.

Walcheren, island, Holland. 51N. 3E. Disastrous expedition against, by English, 1809.

Walmer, Kent, En. 51N. 1E. Death of the Duke of Wellington, Lord Warden of the Cinque-ports, 1852.

Walsingham, Norfolk, En. 52N. 0E. Ancient resort of pilgrims, among whom was Erasmus, who left an account of his visit

Waltham, Essex, En. 51N. 0. Traditional grave of Harold and his two brothers, slain at Hastings, cross to Queen Eleanor.

Walthamstow, Essex, En. 51N. 0E. Bp. of William Morris (1834-96).

Wantage, Berks, En. 51N. 1W. Bp of King Alfred.

Ware, Herts, En. 51N. 0W. 'Town of fame.' (See 'John Gilpin.')

Warsaw, Poland 52N 21E. Taken by Charles XII. (See Voltaire, op cit), 1703, by Suvarov, 1794; taken from Prussians by Murat, 1806, ceded to Russia. 1815, revolt of Poland in 1830, 1848, 1863.

Wartburg. 50N. 10E. Celebrated contest of the 'Minnesinger' 1207 at the Court of the Landgrave of Thuringia. Here Luther wrote his translation of the Bible, 1522.

Warwick, cap. of county, En. 52N. 1W. Unsuccessfully besieged by Royalists, 1642.

Waterford, cap. of county, Ir. 52N. 7W. Early Danish settlement, taken by Strongbow, 1170; capitulated to Ireton, 1650. (Sc. Kingsley, 'Hereward the Wake.')

Waterloo, Belgium. 50N. 4E. Battle of, June 18, 1815.

Watling Street, old Roman road running North and West from Dover.

Wavre, Belgium. 50N. 4E. Prussians held Grouchy in check, 1815 (Battle of Waterloo).

Wedmore, Somerset. 51N. 2W. Peace

of, between Alfred and Danes, after battle of Edington, 878.

Weimar, Germany. 50N. 11E. Res. of Goethe, of Schiller, Herder, Wieland, etc., bp. of Kotzebue (1761-1819).

Wellow, East, Hants. 50N. 1W. Early home and grave of Florence Nightingale, d 1910.

Welwyn, Herts, En. 51N. 0W. Young, as vicar (1730-65), wrote his 'Night Thoughts' here, and is buried in the church.

Wemyss, Fife, Scot. 56N. 3W. Here Mary and Darnley first met.

Wexford, cap. of county, Ir. 52N. 6W. Res in 12th century of Strongbow, stormed by Cromwell, 1649; massacre of inhabitants by rebels, 1798.

Whitby, Yorks, En. 54N. 0W Caedmon, A -Saxon poet, 7th century, lay brother under the Abbess Hilda (see Scott, 'Marmion '), here had the vision that inspired his poetic genius

Whitchurch, Middlesex, En. 51N. 1W. Handel for 3 years chapel master at 'Canons'; his organ preserved in church; grave of the 'Harmonious Blacksmith' in churchyard.

Wigan, Lancashire, En. 53N. 2W. Defeat of Royalists, 1651.

Wimbledon, Surrey, En. 51N. 0W. Here Linnæus is said to have knelt in ecstacy at his first sight of the gorse in bloom.

Winchester, Hants, En. 51N. 1W. Here King Alfred was educated, held his court, and was buried, Emperor Charles V. entertained by Henry VIII.; taken in turn by Waller, the Royalists, and Cromwell, 1645; graves of Jane Austen, Izaak Walton, also traditional tomb of Rufus; bp. of Henry III.

Windsor, Berks, En. 51N 0W Famous Herne's Oak ' (see ' Merry Wives of Windsor '), fell 1863.

Woodstock, Oxon., En. 51N. 1W. Elizabeth's verses, 'writ with charcoal on a shutter' while a prisoner here (1555), are preserved in the Percy ballads, ass. 'Fair Rosamond.' (See Scott, 'Woodstock.')

Woolton, Kent, En 51N. 0E. Tappington Court near. (See ' Ingoldsby Legends.')

Worcester, cap. of county, En. 52N. 2W. Charles II. defeated by Cromwell, 1651.

Workington, Cumberland, En. 54N. 3W. Here Mary Queen of Scots arrived in a fish-ing-boat when escaping from Scotland after Langside, 1568.

Worms, Germany. 49N. 8E. Ass. Siegfried and Kriemhild (see Nibelungenlied); Concordat (question of Investiture), 1122; famous Diet, where Luther appeared, 1521.

Worth, Alsace. 48N. 7E. French defeated by Germans, 1870 (Franco-Prussian W.).

Wurzburg, Bavaria. 49N. 9E. Grave of Walther v. der Vogelweide, one of the early minnesingers.

Wylam, Northumberland, En. 54N. 1W. Bp. of George Stephenson, the engineer (1781-1848).

Xeres, Spain. 36N 6W. Roderic, the last of the Goths, defeated by the Moors under Tarik, 711; retaken from Moors, 1255.

Yarrow, river, Scot 55N 3W. See poems by Hamilton (' Braes of Yarrow '), Wordsworth, and old ballads

Yetholm, Cheviots, Scot. 55N. 2W. Colony of gipsies, under the royal family of Faa.

York, cap. of county, En. 53N. 1W. Marriage of Edward III. with Philippa, 1328; Richard III. crowned, 1483; surrendered to Parliamentarians, 1644, bp. of Flaxman, sculptor (1755-1826).

Youghal, Ir. 51N. 7W. Sir W. Raleigh's house, known as Myrtle Grove, where he entertained Spenser, and where the first potato was planted in Ireland.

Yvetot, France. 49N. 0E. Former possessors known as ' Kings.'

Zamora, Spain. 41N. 5W. Moors defeated by Alfonso the Great, 901; finally taken from them by the Cid, 1093, ruins of latter's palace.

Zierickzee, Holland 51N. 3E. Siege of, 1575 (W. of Dutch Independence).

Zorndorf, Prussia. 52N 14E. Russians defeated by Frederick the Great (Seven Years' W.), 1758.

Zurich, Switzerland. 47N. 8E. Centre of reform under Zwingli; Austrians defeated by Swiss, 1443; Allies by Masséna, 1799.

Zutphen, Holland 52N 6E. Sir Philip Sidney killed, 1586. (See Spenser's elegy, ' Astrophel.')

Zwolle, Holland. 52N. 6E. A Kempis lived and died in the monastery of Agnetenberg near.

INDEX

Those places marked with an asterisk (*) appear also in the Gazetteer

	PAGE
Aachen, Germany. 51N. 6E.	77
Aalborg, Denmark. 57N. 10E.	89
*Aalesund, Norway. 62N. 6E.	89
Aar, R., Switzerland. 47N. 8E.	86
Aarberg, Switzerland. 47N. 7E.	86
Aarhuus, Denmark. 56N. 10E.	89
Abbazia, Austria. 45N. 14E.	78
Abbeville, France. 50N. 2E.	73
Abbeyfeale, Ireland. 52N. 9w.	68
Abbeyleix, Ireland. 53N. 7w.	69
Abbotsford, Scotland. 56N. 3w.	65
Aberaeron, Wales. 52N. 4w.	56
Aberavon, Wales. 52N. 4w.	56
Aberchirder, Scotland. 58N. 3w.	63
Aberdare, Wales. 52N. 3w.	56
*Aberdeen, Scotland. 57N. 2w.	63
*Aberdour, Scotland. 56N. 3w.	65
*Aberdour, Scotland. 58N. 2w.	63
Aberdovey, Wales. 53N 4w.	56
Aberfeldy, Scotland. 57N. 4w.	63
Aberffraw, Wales. 53N. 4w.	54
*Aberfoyle, Scotland. 56N. 4w.	65
*Abergavenny, England. 52N. 3w.	56
*Abergele, Wales. 53N. 4w.	54
Abersoch, Wales. 53N. 5w.	54
Aberthaw, Wales. 51N. 3w.	56
*Aberystwith, Wales. 52N. 4w.	56
*Abingdon, England. 52N. 1w.	57
Abington, Scotland. 55N. 4w.	65
Abo, Russia. 60N. 22E.	90
Aboyne, Scotland. 57N. 3w.	63
*Abrantes, Portugal. 40N. 8w.	84
Abruzzi, Italy. 42N. 14E.	83
Accrington, England. 54N. 2w.	54
Acerenza, Italy. 41N. 16E.	81
Achill Hd., Ireland. 54N. 10w.	66
Achill Is., Ireland. 54N. 10w.	66
Achill Sd., Ireland. 54N. 10w.	66
Achnasheen, Scotland. 58N. 5w.	62
Achtyrka, Russia. 51N. 35E.	91
Acireale, Sicily. 38N. 15E.	81
Aclare, Ireland. 54N. 9w.	66
Acquapendente, Italy. 43N. 12E	83
*Acqui, Italy. 45N. 9E.	82
Ada, Hungary. 46N. 20E.	79
Adaja, R., Spain. 41N. 5w.	84
Adamello, Mt., Italy. 46N. 11E.	82
Adare, Ireland. 53N. 9w.	68
Adda, R., Italy. 45N. 10E.	82
Adda, R, Italy. 46N. 9E.	82
Adelsberg, Austria. 46N. 14E.	78
Adelsheim, Germany. 49N. 9E.	77
Ademuz, Spain. 40N. 1w.	85
Adenau, Germany. 50N. 7E.	77
Aderno, Sicily. 38N. 15E.	81
Adige, R., Italy. 45N. 12E.	83
Adjud, Roumania. 46N. 27E.	94

	PAGE
Adler Gebirge, Austria. 50N. 16E.	78
Adour, R., France. 44N. 1w.	72
Adra, Spain. 37N. 3w.	85
Adria, Italy. 45N. 12E.	83
Adrianople (Edirne), Turkey. 42N. 27E.	94
Adula Group, Switzerland. 46N. 9E.	87
Ægades, Is., Sicily. 38N. 12E.	81
Ægina, Greece. 38N. 23E.	95
Ærschot, Belgium. 51N. 5E.	71
Agathopoli, Turkey. 42N. 28E.	94
Agde, France. 43N. 3E.	73
*Agen, France. 44N. 1E.	72
Aggerminde, Denmark. 57N 8E.	89
*Agincourt, France. 51N. 2E.	73
Aghsh, Ireland. 52N. 8w.	69
Agno, Switzerland. 46N. 9E.	87
Agnone, Italy. 42N. 14E.	83
Agogna, R., Italy. 45N. 9E.	82
Agout, R., France. 44N. 2E.	73
Agram, Hungary. 46N. 16E.	94
Agri, R., Italy. 40N. 17E.	81
Agrinion, Greece. 39N. 21E.	95
Agropoli, Italy. 40N. 15E.	81
Aguilas, Spain. 37N. 1w.	85
Ahascragh, Ireland. 53N. 8w.	66
Ahaus, Germany. 52N. 7E.	76
Ahoghill, Ireland. 55N. 6w.	67
Ahrweiler, Germany. 51N. 7E.	77
Aig, d'A., Switzerland. 46N. 7E.	86
Aigle, Switzerland. 46N. 7E.	86
*Ailsa Craig, Scotland. 55N. 5w.	64
Ain, France. 46N. 5E.	73
Ain, R., France. 46N. 5E.	73
Aird, Pt. of, Scotland. 58N. 6w.	62
Airdrie, Scotland. 56N. 4w.	65
Aire, R., England. 54N. 1w.	55
*Airolo, Switzerland. 46N. 9E.	87
Aisch, R., Germany. 50N. 11E.	77
Aisne, France. 50N. 3E.	73
Aisne, R., France. 50N. 3E.	73
Aix, France. 44N. 5E.	73
*Aix-la-Chapelle, Germany. 51N. 6E.	77
Aix-les-Bains, France. 46N. 6E.	73
Ajaccio, Corsica. 42N. 9E.	80
*Ajaccio, Gulf of, Corsica. 42N. 9E.	80
Akhaltsikh, Russia. 42N. 43E.	91
Akherman, Russia. 46N. 30E.	91
Alagna, Italy. 46N. 8E.	82
Alagon, R, Spain. 40N. 7w.	84
Alais, France. 44N. 4E.	73
Aland Is., Russia. 60N. 20E.	90
Alands Haf, Sweden. 60N. 19E.	89
Alapaiysk, Russia. 58N. 62E.	90
Alassio, Italy. 44N. 8E.	82

	PAGE
Alatri, Italy. 42N. 13E.	83
Alava, Spain. 43N. 3w.	85
Alba, Italy. 45N. 8E.	82
Albacete, Spain. 39N. 2w.	85
Albani, Mt., Italy. 42N. 13E.	83
Albania, Turkey. 40N. 20E.	95
Albano, Italy. 42N. 13E.	83
Albaracin, Spain. 40N. 1w.	85
Albegna, R., Italy. 43N. 11E.	83
Albenga, Italy. 44N. 8E.	82
Alberche, R., Spain. 40N. 5w.	84
Alberique, Spain. 39N 1w	85
Albertville, France. 46N. 6E.	73
Albis, Switzerland. 47N. 9E.	87
Alboran Is., Spain. 36N. 3w.	85
Albula P., Switzerland. 47N. 10E.	87
Albula R., Switzerland. 47N. 9E.	87
Albuquerque, Spain. 39N. 7w.	84
Alby, France. 44N. 2E.	73
*Alcala de Henares, Spain. 41N. 3w.	84
*Alcala de Real, Spain. 37N. 4w.	84
Alcamo, Sicily. 38N. 13E.	81
Alcaniz, Spain. 41N 0w.	85
*Alcantara, Spain. 40N. 7w.	84
Alcaraz, Spain. 39N. 2w.	85
Alcazar, Spain. 39N. 3w	84
Alcester, England 52N. 2w.	56
Alcira, Spain. 39N. 0w.	85
Alcoy, Spain. 39N. 0w.	85
Alcudia, Majorca. 40N 3E.	85
*Aldeburgh, England. 52N. 2E.	57
Alderney, Channel Is. 49N. 2w.	56
Aldershot, England. 51N. 1w.	57
Ale Water, Scotland. 56N. 3w.	65
Alefleyevka, Russia. 51N. 39E.	91
Alemtejo, Portugal. 39N. 8w.	84
*Alencon, France. 48N. 0E.	72
*Alessandria, Italy. 45N. 9E.	82
Alessio, Turkey 42N. 19E.	94
Aletsch Glacier, Switzerland. 46N. 8E	86
Aletschhorn, Switzerland. 46N. 8E.	86
Alexandrapol, Russia. 41N. 44E.	91
Alexandrovo, Russia. 53N. 19E.	75
Alexandrovski, Russia. 69N. 32E.	90
Alexinatz, Servia 44N. 22E.	94
Alfaro, Spain. 42N 2w.	85
Alford, England. 53N. 0E.	55
*Alford, Scotland. 57N. 3w.	63
*Alfreton, England. 53N. 1w.	55
Algarve, Portugal. 37N. 8w	84
*Algeciras, Spain. 36N. 5w.	84
Alghero, Sardinia. 41N. 8E.	81
Alhama, Spain. 38N. 1w.	85
Aliaga, Spain. 41N. 1w.	85
*Alicante, Spain. 38N. 0w.	85
*Alkmaar, Holland. 53N. 5E.	70
Alice, Pta dell', Italy. 39N. 17E	81
Alicudi Is., Italy. 39N. 14E.	81
Allalin, Switzerland. 46N. 8E.	86
Allan R., Scotland. 56N. 4w.	65
Alle, Germany. 54N. 20E	75
Allen, Lough. Ireland. 54N 8w.	67
Allendale, England. 55N. 2w	54
Allenstein, Germany. 54N. 20E.	75
Aller, R., Germany. 53N. 9E.	76
Allier, France. 46N. 3E.	73
Alliers, R , France. 47N. 3E.	73
Allingsas, Sweden. 58N 13E.	89
*Alloa, Scotland. 56N. 4w.	65
Allua, Lough, Ireland. 52N. 9w.	68
Almaden, Spain 39N. 5w	84
Almansa, Spain. 39N. 1w.	85
Almaraz, Spain. 40N. 6w.	84
Almazan, Spain. 41N. 3w.	85
Almeida, Portugal. 41N. 7w.	84
Almelo, Holland. 52N. 7E.	70
Almendralejo, Spain. 39N. 6w.	84
*Almeria, Spain. 37N. 2w.	85
Almodovar, Spain. 39N. 4w.	84
Almond R., Scotland. 56N. 4w	65
Almorchon, Spain. 39N. 5w.	84
Almunecar, Spain. 37N. 4w.	84
Aln, R., England. 55N. 2w.	55
Alness, Scotland. 58N. 4w.	63
Alness, R., Scotland. 58N. 4w.	63
Alnmouth, England. 55N. 2w.	55
*Alnwick, England. 55N. 2w.	54
Alora, Spain 37N. 5w.	84
*Alost, Belgium. 51N. 4E	71
Alpes, Maritimes, France. 44N. 7E.	73
Alresford, England. 51N. 1w.	57
*Alsace, Germany. 48N. 7E.	77
Alsasua, Spain. 43N. 2w.	85
Alsen Is., Germany. 55N. 10E.	74
Alseuz, Germany. 50N. 8E.	77
Alsfeld, Germany. 51N. 9E.	77
Alsh, Loch, Scotland. 57N. 6w.	62
Alstahong, Norway. 66N. 13E.	88
Alston, England. 55N. 2w.	54
Altamura, Italy. 41N. 16E.	81
*Altdorf, Switzerland. 47N. 9E.	87
Altels, Switzerland. 46N. 8E.	86
Alten Fd, Norway. 70N. 23E.	88
Altenburg, Germany. 51N. 12E.	76
Alten Elf, Norway. 70N. 23E.	88
Altengaard, Norway. 70N. 23E.	88
Alte Vand, Norway. 69N. 20E.	88
Altkirch, Germany. 48N. 7E.	77
Altmühl, R., Germany. 49N. 12E.	77
Alton, England. 51N. 1w.	57
Altona, Germany. 54N 10E.	76
Altrincham, England. 53N. 2w.	54
Altsohl, Hungary. 49N 19E.	79
Altstälten, Switzerland. 47N. 10E.	87
Altvater, Austria. 50N. 17E.	78
Aluta R., Roumania. 44N. 25E.	94
Alva, Scotland. 56N 4w.	65
Alyth, Scotland. 57N. 3w.	63
Alz, R., Germany. 48N. 13E.	77
Alzey, Germany. 50N. 8E.	77
Amaxiki, Greece. 39N. 21E	95
Ambelakia, Greece. 40N. 22E.	95
Amberg, Germany. 49N. 12E.	77
Amble, England. 55N. 2w.	55
*Ambleside, England. 54N. 3w.	54
Ambleve R., Belgium. 50N. 6E.	71
*Amboise, France. 47N. 1E.	72
Ameland, Holland. 53N. 6E.	70
Amer, Spain. 42N. 3E.	85
Amersfoort, Holland. 52N. 5E.	70
Amesbury, England. 51N. 2w.	56

PAGE

Amiata, Mt., Italy. 43N. 11E. 83
*Amiens, France. 50N. 2E. 73
Amminster, England. 51N. 3W. 56
Amlwch, Wales. 53N. 4W. 54
Ammer See, Germany. 48N. 11E. 77
Amorbach, Germany. 50N 9E. 77
Amorgos, Greece. 37N. 26E. 95
Amper, R., Germany. 48N. 12E. 77
*Ampthill, England. 52N. 1W. 57
Amstel, R., Holland 52N. 5E 70
*Amsterdam, Holland. 52N. 5E. 70
Amstetten, Austria. 48N. 15E. 78
Anagni, Italy. 42N. 13E. 83
Anaphi, Greece. 36N 26E. 95
*Ancona, Italy. 44N. 14E. 83
And Fd., Norway. 69N. 16E 88
Andail, Loch, Scotland. 56N. 6W. 61
Andalusia, Spain. 37N. 5W. 84
Andelfingen, Switzerland. 48N. 9E. 87
*Andermatt, Switzerland. 47N. 9E. 87
Andorra, Spain. 43N 2E. 85
Andover, England. 51N. 1W. 57
Andrea Is., S., Austria. 43N.16E. 78
Andria, Italy. 41N. 16E. 81
Andros, Greece. 38N. 25E. 95
Andujar, Spain. 38N. 4W. 84
Angerburg, Germany. 54N. 22E. 75
Angerman Elf, Sweden. 63N. 18E. 88
Angermunde, Germany. 53N. 14E. 76
*Angers, France. 84N. 1W. 72
*Anglesey, Wales. 53N. 4W. 54
*Angoulême, France. 46N. 0E. 72
Angus, Braes of, Scotland. 57N. 3W. 63
Anhalt, Germany. 52N. 12E. 76
Anholt, Denmark. 57N. 12E. 89
Anina, Hungary. 45N. 22E 79
Anklam, Germany. 54N. 14E. 76
Annaberg, Germany. 51N. 13E. 77
Annalee R., Ireland. 54N. 7W. 67
*Annan, Scotland. 55N. 3W. 65
Annan, R., Scotland. 55N. 3W. 65
Annecy, France. 46N. 6E 73
*Annonay, France. 45N. 5E 73
Ansbach, Germany. 49N. 10E. 77
Annunciata, T. d., Italy. 41N. 15E. 81
Anstruther, Scotland. 56N 3W. 65
Antepucra, Spain. 37N. 5W. 84
Antibes, France. 44N. 7E. 73
Antivari, Montenegro. 42N. 19E. 94
Antrim, Ireland. 55N. 6W. 67
*Antwerp, Belgium. 51N 4E. 71
Anzin, France. 50N. 3E. 73
*Aosta, Italy. 46N. 7E. 82
Apatin, Hungary. 46N. 19E. 79
Apeldoorn, Holland. 52N. 6E. 70
Apennines, Italy. 11N. 15E. 81
Apoldo, Germany. 51N. 11E. 76
Appenzele, Switzerland. 47N. 9E 87
Appin, Scotland. 57N. 5W. 62
Appleby, England. 55N. 3W. 54
Applecross, Scotland. 57N. 6W. 62
Aquila, Italy. 42N. 13E. 83

PAGE

Aracena, Spain. 38N. 7W. 84
Arad, Hungary. 46N. 21E. 79
Aragon, Spain. 41N. 1W. 85
Aragon, R., Spain. 42N. 2W. 85
Aran Is., Ireland. 53N. 10W. 68
Aranda, Spain. 42N. 4W. 84
Aranjuez, Spain. 40N. 4W. 84
Aranmore Is., Ireland. 55N. 9W. 66
Aranyos, Hungary. 46N. 24E 79
Ararat Mt., Russia. 40N. 44E. 91
Aras R., Russia. 40N. 48E. 91
Arboga, Sweden. 59N. 16E. 89
Arbon, Switzerland. 48N. 9E. 87
*Arbroath, Scotland. 57N. 3W. 63
Arcachon, Basin d', France. 45N. 1W. 72
Archangel, Russia. 64N. 41E. 90
Archipelago, Greek, Greece. 37N. 25E. 95
Arcidossa, Italy. 43N. 12E. 83
*Arcis-sur-Aube, France. 49N. 4E. 73
*Arcole, Italy. 45N. 11E. 83
Arcos, Spain. 37N. 6W. 84
Ardagh, Ireland 54N. 8W. 67
Ardara, Ireland. 55N. 8W. 66
Ardèche, France. 45N. 4E. 73
Ardèche, R., France. 44N. 5E. 73
Ardee, Ireland. 54N. 7W. 67
Ardennes, Belgium. 50N. 5E. 71
Ardennes, France. 50N. 5E. 73
Ardfert, Ireland. 52N 10W. 68
Ardglas, Ireland. 54N 6W. 67
Ardila R., Portugal. 38N. 7W. 84
Ardle Water. 57N. 3W. 63
Ardlui, Scotland. 56N 5W 64
Ardmore, Ireland. 52N. 8W. 69
Ardnamurchan Pt., Scotland 57N. 6W. 62
Ardrahan, Ireland. 53N. 9W. 68
Ardrishaig, Scotland. 56N. 5W. 64
Ardrossan, Scotland. 56N. 5W. 64
Arendal, Norway. 59N. 9E. 89
Arevalo, Spain. 41N. 5W. 84
*Arezzo, Italy. 43N. 12E. 83
Arganda, Spain. 40N. 3W. 84
Argens, R., France. 43N. 7E. 73
Argenta, Italy. 45N. 12E. 83
Argentaro, Mt., Italy. 42N. 11E. 83
Argos, Greece. 38N. 23E. 95
Argostoli, Greece. 38N. 21E. 95
Argyll, Scotland. 56N. 5W 64
Argyrakastro, Turkey. 40N. 20E. 95
Ariano, Italy. 41N. 15E. 81
Ariano, Italy. 45N. 12E. 83
Ariège, France. 43N 1E 72
Ariège, R., France. 44N. 1E. 72
Arigna, Ireland. 54N. 8W. 66
Arisaig Pt., Scotland. 57N. 6W. 62
Arjish, R., Roumania. 44N. 27E. 94
Arkadia, Greece. 37N. 22E. 95
Arkaig, Loch, Scotland. 57N. 5W. 62
Arklow, Ireland. 53N. 6W. 69
Arlanza, R., Spain. 42N 4W. 84
Arlanzon, R., Spain. 42N. 4W. 84
Arlberg, Austria. 47N 10E. 78
Arles, France. 41N. 5E. 73

	PAGE
Arlon, Belgium. 50N. 6E.	71
Armadale, Scotland. 56N. 4W.	65
*Armagh, Ireland. 54N. 7W.	67
Armentieres, France. 51N. 3E.	73
Armoy, Ireland. 55N. 6W.	67
Arnhem, Holland. 52N. 6E.	70
Arno, R., Italy. 44N. 10E.	82
Arno R., Italy. 43N. 12E.	83
Arnsberg, Germany. 51N. 8E.	76
Arnswalde, Germany. 53N. 15E.	75
Arolsen, Germany. 52N. 9E.	76
Arona, Italy. 46N. 9E.	82
Arpino, Italy. 42N. 14E.	83
Arquata, Italy. 45N. 9E.	82
*Arran, Scotland. 56N. 5W.	64
*Arras, France. 50N. 3E.	73
Arree, Mts. d', France. 48N. 4W.	72
Arrone, R., Italy. 42N. 12E.	83
Arrow, Lough, Ireland. 54N. 8W.	66
Arsamas, Russia. 55N. 44E.	91
Arsie, Italy. 46N. 12E.	83
Arta, Greece. 39N. 21E.	95
Arta Gulf, Greece. 39N. 21E.	95
Arth, Switzerland. 47N. 9E.	87
Arun, R., England. 51N. 1W.	57
*Arundel, England. 51N. 1W	57
Arva, R., Hungary. 49N. 20E.	79
Arvagh, Ireland. 54N. 8W	67
*Aschaffenburg, Germany. 50N 9E.	77
Aschersleben, Germany. 52N. 11E	76
Asciano, Italy. 43N. 12E.	83
Ascoli, Italy. 43N. 14E.	83
Ascona, Switzerland. 46N. 9E.	87
Ascot, England. 51N. 1W.	57
Asele, Sweden. 64N. 17E.	88
*Ashborne, England. 53N. 2W.	51
Ashbourne, Ireland. 54N. 6W.	67
Ashburton, England. 51N. 4W.	56
*Ashby-de-la-Zouche, England. 53N. 1W.	57
Ashford, England. 51N. 1E.	57
Ashford, Ireland. 54N. 9W.	66
Ashton, England. 53N. 2W.	54
Asiago, Italy. 46N. 12E.	83
Asinalunga, Italy. 43N 12E.	83
Asinara, Gulf of, Sardinia. 41N. 8E.	81
Asinara Is., Sardinia. 41N. 8E.	81
Askeaton, Ireland. 53N. 9W.	68
Aso, R., Italy. 43N. 14E.	83
Asola, Italy. 45N. 10E.	82
*Asolo, Italy. 46N. 12E.	83
Aspang, Austria. 48N. 16E.	78
Aspro Potamo, Greece. 39N. 21E.	95
Assen, Holland. 53N. 7E.	70
Assisi, Italy. 43N. 13E.	83
Assynt, Loch, Scotland. 58N. 5W.	62
Asti, R, Italy. 45N. 9E	82
Astorga, Spain. 43N. 6W.	84
Astrakhan, Russia. 46N. 48E.	91
Asturias, Spain. 43N. 6W.	84
Atalanti, Greece. 39N. 23E.	95
Atessa, Italy. 42N. 14E.	83
Ath, Belgium. 51N. 4E.	71
Athboy, Ireland. 54N. 7W.	67
Athenry, Ireland. 53N. 9W.	66
Athens, Greece. 38N. 24E.	95
Atherstone, England. 53N. 2W.	57

	PAGE
*Athlone, Ireland. 53N. 8W.	66
Atholl, Scotland. 57N. 4W.	63
Athos Mt., Turkey. 40N. 24E.	95
Athy, Ireland. 53N. 7W.	69
Atri, Italy. 43N. 14E.	83
Atter S., Austria. 48N. 14E.	78
Attleborough, England. 53N. 1E.	57
Aube, France. 48N. 4E.	73
Aube, R., France. 48N. 4E.	73
Aubert, Switzerland. 47N. 7E.	86
Aubonne, Switzerland. 46N. 6E.	40
*Auburn, Ireland. 54N. 8W.	67
Aubusson, France. 46N. 2E.	73
Auch, France. 44N. 1E.	72
*Auchinleck, Scotland. 55N. 4W.	65
Auchterarder, Scotland. 56N. 4W.	65
Auchtermuchty, Scotland. 56N. 3W.	65
Aude, France. 43N. 3E.	73
Aude, R., France. 43N. 3E.	73
Augher, Ireland. 54N. 7W.	67
Aughnacloy, Ireland. 54N. 7W.	67
Aughrim, Ireland. 53N 8W.	66
Aughrim, Ireland. 53N. 6W.	69
*Augsburg, Germany. 48N. 11E.	77
Augusta, Sicily. 37N. 15E.	81
*Auldearn, Scotland. 58N. 4W.	63
Aurdal, Norway 61N. 10E.	89
Aurich, Germany. 54N. 8E.	76
Aurillac, France. 45N. 2E.	73
Auronzo, Italy. 46N. 12E.	80
*Aussig, Austria. 51N. 14E.	78
*Austerlitz, Austria. 49N. 17E.	78
Austria, Lower, Austria. 48N. 16E.	78
Austria, Upper, Austria. 48N. 14E.	78
Autun, France. 47N. 4E.	73
Auvergne Mts., France. 45N. 3E.	73
Auxerre, France. 48N. 4E.	73
Auxonne, France. 47N. 5E.	73
Aveiro, Portugal. 41N. 9W.	84
Avellino, Italy. 41N 15E.	81
Avenches, Switzerland. 47N. 7E.	86
Aversa, Italy. 41N. 14E.	81
Aveyron, France. 44N. 3E.	73
Avezzano, Italy. 42N. 13E.	83
Aviano, Italy. 46N. 13E.	83
Aviemore, Scotland. 57N. 4W.	63
*Avignon, France. 44N. 5E.	73
Avila, Spain. 41N. 5W.	84
Aviles, Spain. 44N. 6W.	84
Avlana, Turkey. 40N. 20E.	95
Avoca, R., Ireland. 53N. 6W.	69
*Avoca, Vale of, Ireland. 53N. 6W.	69
Avoch, Scotland. 58N. 4W.	63
Avola, Sicily. 37N. 15E.	81
Avon, R., England. 52N. 2W.	56
Avon, R., England. 52N. 1W.	57
Avon, R., England. 51N. 2W.	56
Avon, R., England. 51N. 3W.	56
Avon R., Scotland. 56N. 4W.	65
Avon R., Scotland. 57N. 3W.	63
Avonmouth, England. 52N. 3W.	56
Avranches, France. 49N. 1W.	72
Avricourt, Germany. 49N. 7E.	77
*Awe, Loch, Scotland. 56N. 5W.	64
Axbridge, England. 51N. 3W.	56

PAGE

Axe, R., England. 51N. 3W. 56
Axe Edge, England. 53N. 2W. 54
Axminster, England. 51N. 3W. 56
Axmouth, England. 51N. 3W. 56
Aylesbury, England. 52N. 1W. 57
Aylsham, England. 53N. 1E. 55
Aylort, Loch, Scotland. 57N. 6W. 62
Aynho, England. 52N. 1W. 57
*Ayr, Scotland. 55N. 5W. 64
Ayr R., Scotland. 55N. 5W. 64
Ayre Pt., Isle of Man. 54N. 4W. 54
Azov, Russia. 47N. 39E. 91
Azov, Sea of, Russia. 46N. 37E. 91

Babadagh, Roumania. 45N. 29E. 94
Babia Gura, Austria. 50N. 20E. 79
Bacchiglione R., Italy. 45N. 12E. 83
Bacs, Austria-Hungary. 45N. 19E. 79
Bacup, England. 54N. 2W. 54
Baeza, Spain. 38N. 4W. 84
Bad Nauheim, Germany. 50N. 9E. 77
*Badajoz, Spain. 39N. 7W. 84
Baden, Austria. 48N. 16E. 78
Baden, Switzerland 47N. 8E. 86
Baden, Germany 49N. 8E. 77
Badenweiler, Germany. 48N. 8E. 77
Badstadt, Austria. 48N. 13E. 78
Baena, Spain. 38N. 4W. 84
Bagenalstown, Ireland. 53N. 7W. 69
Bagheria, Sicily 38N. 14E. 81
Bailen, Spain. 38N. 4W. 84
Baillieborough, Ireland. 54N. 7W. 67
*Baireuth, Germany. 50N 11E. 77
Baise, R., France. 44N. 0E. 72
Baja, Hungary. 46N 19E. 79
Bakewell, England. 53N. 2W. 55
Bakhmut, Russia. 49N. 38E. 91
Bakony, Hungary. 47N. 18E. 78
Baku, Russia. 40N. 50E. 91
Bala, Wales. 53N. 4W. 54
Bala Lake, Wales. 53N. 4W. 74
Balaguer, Spain. 42N. 1E. 85
Balassa Gyarmat, Hungary. 48N. 20E 79
Balbriggan, Ireland. 54N. 6W. 67
Bald L., Switzerland 47N. 8E. 86
Balearic Is., Spain 39N. 3E. 85
Balfron, Scotland. 56N 4W 65
Balkan Mts., Bulgaria. 43N. 25E. 94
Balla, Ireland. 54N. 9W. 66
Ballachulish, Scotland. 57N. 5W. 62
Ballaghadereen, Ireland. 54N. 9W. 66
Ballantrae, Scotland. 55N. 5W. 64
*Ballater, Scotland. 57N. 3W. 63
Ballaton L., Hungary. 47N. 18E. 78
Ballickmoyler, Ireland. 53N. 7W. 69
Ballina, Ireland. 54N. 9W. 66
Ballina, Ireland. 53N. 8W. 68
Ballinafad, Ireland. 54N. 8W. 66
Ballinakill, Ireland. 53N. 7W. 69
Ballinamore, Ireland. 54N 8W. 67
Ballinasloe, Ireland. 53N. 8W. 66
Ballincollig, Ireland. 52N. 9W. 68
Ballinderry R., Ireland. 55N. 7W. 67
Ballindine, Ireland. 54N. 9W. 66
Ballingarry, Ireland. 52N. 9W. 68
Ballinrobe, Ireland. 54N. 9W. 66

PAGE

Ballinskelligs B., Ireland. 52N. 10W. 68
Ballintober, Ireland. 54N. 8W. 66
Ballintogher, Ireland. 54N. 8W. 66
Ballintra, Ireland. 55N. 8W. 66
Ballitore, Ireland. 53N. 7W. 69
Ballivor, Ireland. 54N. 7W. 67
Balloch, Scotland. 56N. 5W. 64
Ballon, Ireland. 53N. 7W. 69
Ballsadare, Ireland. 54N. 9W. 66
Ballybay, Ireland. 54N. 7W. 67
Ballybofey, Ireland. 55N. 8W. 67
Ballybrittas, Ireland. 53N. 7W. 69
Ballybunion, Ireland. 53N. 10W. 68
Ballycastle, Ireland. 54N. 9W. 66
Ballycastle, Ireland. 55N. 6W. 67
Ballyclare, Ireland. 55N. 6W. 67
Ballyconnell, Ireland. 54N. 8W. 67
Ballycottin B., Ireland. 52N 8W. 69
Ballydehob, Ireland. 52N. 9W. 68
Ballyduff, Ireland. 52N. 8W. 69
Ballygar, Ireland. 54N. 8W. 66
Ballygawley, Ireland. 54N. 7W. 67
Ballygeary, Ireland. 52N. 6W. 69
Ballyhahill, Ireland. 53N. 9W. 68
Ballyhaise, Ireland. 54N. 7W. 67
Ballyhaunis, Ireland. 54N. 9W. 66
Ballyheige B., Ireland. 52N. 10W. 68
Ballyhoura Hills, Ireland. 52N. 9W. 68
Ballyjamesduff, Ireland. 54N. 7W. 67
Ballylanders, Ireland. 52N. 8W. 68
Ballylongford, Ireland. 53N. 9W. 68
Ballymahon, Ireland. 54N. 8W. 67
Ballymena, Ireland. 55N. 6W. 67
Ballymoe, Ireland. 54N. 8W. 66
Ballymoney, Ireland. 55N. 7W. 67
Ballymore, Ireland. 53N. 8W. 67
*Ballymore Eustace, Ireland. 53N. 7W. 69
*Ballymote, Ireland. 54N. 9W. 66
Ballymurphy, Ireland. 53N. 7W. 69
*Ballynahinch, Ireland. 54N. 6W. 67
Ballynakill Harbour, Ireland. 54N. 10W. 66
Ballyneen, Ireland. 52N. 9W. 68
Ballyness B., Ireland. 55N. 8W. 66
Ballyragget, Ireland. 53N. 7W. 69
Ballyrosey, Ireland. 54N. 6W. 67
Ballyshannon, Ireland. 55N. 8W. 66
Ballyteige B., Ireland. 52N. 7W. 69
Ballyvaghan, Ireland. 53N. 9W. 68
Ballywalter, Ireland. 55N. 5W. 67
Balmacarra, Scotland. 57N. 6W 62
Balmoral Castle, Scotland. 57N. 3W. 63
*Balquhidder, Scotland. 56N. 4W. 64
Bals Fd., Norway. 69N. 19E. 88
Balta, Russia. 48N. 30E. 91
Baltchik, Bulgaria. 43N. 28E. 94
Baltimore, Ireland. 51N. 9W. 68
Baltinglass, Ireland. 53N. 7W. 69
*Bamberg, Germany. 50N. 11E. 77
*Bamborough Castle, England. 56N. 2W. 55
Bampton, England. 51N 3W. 56
Banagher, Ireland. 53N. 8W. 69
Banavie, Scotland. 57N 5W. 62

PAGE

Banbridge, Ireland. 54N. 6w 67
Banbury, England. 52N. 1w. 57
Banchory, Scotland. 57N. 2w. 63
Bandon, Ireland. 52N. 9w. 68
Bandon, R., Ireland. 52N 9w. 68
*Banff, Scotland. 58N. 3w. 63
Banffi Hunyad, Hungary. 47N.23E.79
Bangor, Ireland. 54N. 10w. 66
Bangor, Ireland. 55N. 6w. 67
*Bangor, Wales. 53N. 4w. 54
Banialuka, Bosnia. 45N. 18E. 94
Bann, R., Ireland. 53N. 7w. 69
Bann, R., Ireland. 55N. 7w. 67
*Bannockburn, Scotland. 56N 4w. 65
Banreve, Hungary. 48N. 22E. 79
Banteer, Ireland. 52N. 9w. 68
Bantiger, Switzerland. 47N. 8E. 86
Bantry, Ireland. 52N. 9w. 68
Bantry B., Ireland. 52N. 10w. 68
Banya, Hungary. 48N. 24E. 79
*Bar, Russia. 49N. 28E. 91
Barbastro, Spain. 42N. 0E. 85
*Barcelona, Spain. 41N. 2E. 85
Barcs, Hungary. 46N. 17E. 78
Bardi, Italy. 45N. 10E. 82
Bardsey Is., Wales. 53N. 5w. 54
*Bari, Italy. 41N. 17E. 81
Barken, Germany. 52N. 7E. 76
Barking, England. 52N. 0E. 57
Barkum Is., Germany. 54N. 7E. 76
Bar-le-Duc, France. 49N 5E. 73
Barletta, Italy. 41N. 16E. 81
Barmen, Germany. 51N. 7E. 76
Barmouth, Wales. 53N. 4w. 54
*Barnard Castle, England. 55N. 2w. 54
Barnsley, England. 54N. 1w. 55
*Barnstaple, England. 51N. 4w. 56
Barnstaple B., England. 51N. 4w. 56
Barquero, Spain. 44N. 8w. 84
Barr, Germany. 48N. 7E. 77
Barr, Scotland. 55N. 5w. 64
Barreiro, Portugal. 39N. 9w. 84
Barrels Rock, Ireland. 52N. 6w. 69
Barrhead, Scotland. 56N. 4w. 65
Barrhill, Scotland. 55N. 5w. 64
Barrow, R., Ireland. 52N. 7w. 69
Barrow-in-Furness, England. 54N. 3w. 54
Barry, Wales. 51N. 3w. 56
Bar-sur-Aube, France. 48N. 5E. 73
Bar-sur-Seine, France. 48N. 4E. 73
Barton, England. 54N. 0w. 55
Bartsh R., Germany. 52N. 16E. 75
Barvas, Scotland. 58N. 7w. 62
Basel, Switzerland. 48N. 8E. 86
Basi, Russia. 46N. 47E. 91
Basenta R., Italy. 40N. 17E. 81
Basingstoke, England. 51N. 1w. 57
Basque Provinces, Spain. 43N. 3w. 85
*Bass Rock, Scotland. 56N. 3w. 65
*Bassano, Italy. 46N. 12E. 83
Basses-Alpes, France. 44N. 6E. 73
Basses-Pyrenees, France. 43N. 1w. 72
Bastia, Corsica 43N. 9E. 80
Bastogne, Belgium. 50N. 6E. 71
Bataszek, Hungary. 46N. 19E. 79

PAGE

*Bath, England. 51N 2w. 56
Bathgate, Scotland. 56N. 4w. 65
Batley, England. 54N. 2w 55
Batoum, Russia. 42N. 42E. 91
*Battle, England. 51N. 0E. 57
Battock, Mt., Scotland. 57N. 3w. 63
Batya, Hungary. 48N. 22E. 79
*Bautzen, Germany. 51N. 14E. 76
Bavaria, Germany. 49N. 12E. 77
Bavaria, Lower, Germany. 49N. 13E. 77
Bavaria, Upper, Germany. 48N. 12E. 77
Bawtry, England. 53N 1w. 55
*Bayonne, France. 44N. 2w. 72
Bayrischer Wald, Germany. 49N. 13E. 77
Baza, Spain. 38N. 3w. 85
Bazardjik, Burgaria. 44N. 28E. 94
Bazarudi, Turkey. 40N. 24E. 95
Bazias, Hungary. 45N. 22E. 94
*Beachy Head, England. 51N. 0E. 57
*Beaconsfield, England. 52N. 1w. 57
Beal, England. 56N. 2w. 54
Beaminster, England. 51N. 3w. 56
Beattock, Scotland. 55N. 3w. 65
Beaucaire, France. 44N. 5E. 73
Beaugen, France. 48N. 1E. 72
Beauly, Scotland. 57N. 5w. 62
Beauly Firth, Scotland. 57N. 4w. 63
Beauly, R., Scotland. 57N. 5w. 62
*Beaumaris, Wales. 53N. 4w. 54
Beaumaris B., Wales. 53N. 4w. 54
*Beaumont, Belgium. 50N. 4E. 71
Beaune, France. 47N. 5E. 73
*Beauvais, France. 50N. 2E. 73
Beccles, England. 52N. 2E. 57
Becerrea, Spain. 43N. 7w. 84
Becskerek, Hungary. 45N. 20E. 79
Bedale, England. 54N 2w 55
Bedarieux, France. 44N. 3E. 73
*Bedford, England. 52N. 0w 57
Bedford R., England. 51N. 0E. 57
Bedlington, England. 55N. 2w. 55
Beer Berg, Germany. 51N. 11E. 77
Beg, Lough, Ireland. 55N. 6w. 67
Bega, Hungary. 45N. 20E. 79
Beilaia R., Russia 53N 57E. 91
Beira, Portugal. 40N. 8w. 84
Beira alta, Portugal. 41N. 8w. 84
Beira baixa, Portugal. 40N. 7w. 84
Beith, Scotland. 56N. 5w. 64
Beja, Portugal. 38N. 8w. 84
Bejar, Spain. 40N. 6w. 84
Bekes, Hungary. 47N. 21E 79
Belbino, Austria. 46N. 12E. 78
Belbo R., Italy. 45N. 9E. 82
Belchite, Spain. 41N. 1w. 85
Belcoo, Ireland. 54N. 8w. 67
Belem, Portugal. 39N. 9w. 84
Belfast, Ireland. 55N. 6w. 67
Belfast Lough, Ireland. 55N. 6w. 67
Belford, England. 56N. 2w. 54
*Belfort, France. 48N. 7E. 73
Belgard, Germany. 54N. 16E. 75
*Belgrade, Servia. 45N. 21E. 94
*Bell Rock Lighthouse, Scotland. 56N. 2w. 65

PAGE

Bellahy, Ireland   54N. 9W.   66
Bellananagh, Ireland.   54N. 7W.   67
Bellavary, Ireland.   54N. 9W.   66
Bellavista, C. di, Sardinia.   40N.
    10E.   81
Belle Isle, France.   47N. 3W.   72
Belleek, Ireland.   55N. 8W.   66
Bellew, Mt., Ireland.   53N. 8W.   66
Belley, France.   44N. 6E.   73
Bellingham, England.   55N. 2W.   54
Bellinzona, Switzerland.   46N. 9E.   87
Belluno, Italy.   46N. 12E.   83
Belmez, Spain.   38N. 5W.   84
Belmullet, Ireland.   54N. 10W.   66
Belper, England.   53N. 1W.   55
Beltra Lough, Ireland.   54N. 9W.   66
Belturbet, Ireland.   54N. 7W.   67
Belvedere, Italy.   40N. 16E.   81
Belzig, Germany.   52N. 12E.   76
Ben Alligin, Scotland.   58N. 6W.   62
Ben Attow, Scotland.   57N. 5W   62
Ben Avon, Scotland.   57N. 3W.   63
Ben Cleuch, Scotland.   56N. 4W.   65
Ben Cruachan, Scotland.   56N. 5W.   64
Ben Dearg, Scotland.   58N. 5W.   62
Ben Hee, Scotland.   58N. 5W.   62
Ben Hope, Scotland.   58N. 5W.   62
Ben Ime, Scotland.   56N. 5W.   64
Ben Klibreck, Scotland.   58N. 4W.   63
Ben Lawers, Scotland.   57N. 4W.   63
Ben Ledi, Scotland.   56N. 4W.   65
Ben Lomond, Scotland.   56N. 5W.   64
Ben Lui, Scotland.   56N. 5W.   64
Ben Macdhui, Scotland   57N. 4W.   63
Ben More, Scotland.   56N. 4W.   65
Ben More, Scotland.   58N. 5W.   62
Ben Nevis, Scotland.   57N. 5W.   62
Ben Resipol, Scotland.   57N 6W.   62
Ben Scrial, Scotland.   57N. 6W.   62
Ben Venue, Scotland.   56N. 4W.   64
Ben Voirlich, Scotland.   56N. 4W.   65
Ben Vorlich, Scotland.   56N. 5W.   64
Ben Wyvis, Scotland.   58N. 5W.   62
Benavente, Spain.   42N. 6W.   84
*Benbecula Sd , Scotland.   57N. 7W.   62
Bencroy, Ireland.   54N. 8W.   67
Bendery, Russia.   47N. 29E.   91
*Benevento, Italy.   41N. 15E.   81
Bengore Hd., Ireland.   55N. 6W.   67
Benicarlo, Spain.   40N. 0E.   85
Benkovaz, Dalmatia.   44N. 16E.   78
Benmore Hd., Ireland.   55N 6W.   67
Bennettsbridge, Ireland.   53N. 7W.   69
Bentheim, Germany   52N. 7E.   76
Benwee Hd., Ireland.   54N. 10W.   66
Ben-y-Gloe, Scotland.   57N 4W.   63
Beragh, Ireland.   55N. 7W.   67
Berat, Turkey.   41N. 20E.   95
Berbir, Bosnia.   45N. 17E.   94
Berdiansk, Russia.   47N. 38E.   91
Berditchev, Russia.   50N. 29E.   91
Bere Haven, Ireland.   52N. 10W.   68
Bere Is., Ireland.   52N. 10W.   68
*Bere Regis, England.   51N. 2W.   56
*Beresina R., Russia.   53N. 30E.   91
Berettya, Hungary.   47N. 21E.   79
Berezna, Hungary.   49N. 22E.   79
Berg, Germany.   50N. 9E.   77

PAGE

Berga, Spain.   42N. 2E.   85
Bergamo, Italy.   46N. 10E.   82
Bergen, Germany.   54N. 13E.   76
*Bergen, Norway.   60N. 5E.   89
*Bergen op Zoom, Holland.   51N.
    4E.   71
Bergerac, France.   45N. 0E.   72
Bergsjö, Sweden.   62N. 17E.   89
Berici, Monti, Italy.   45N. 11E.   83
*Berkeley, England.   52N. 2W.   56
Berkshire, England.   51N. 1W.   57
Berlad, Roumania.   46N. 28E.   94
*Berlin, Germany.   53N. 14E.   76
Bermeo, Spain.   43N. 3W.   85
Bernburg, Germany.   52N. 12E.   76
Berne, Germany.   53N. 8E.   76
*Berne, Switzerland.   47N. 7E.   86
Berneray Is., Scotland   58N. 7W. 62
Bernese Alps, Switzerland.   46N.
    8E.   86
Bernina P., Switzerland.   46N. 10E   87
Bernina P., Switzerland.   47N. 9E.   87
Bernkastel, Germany.   50N. 7E.   77
Berridale, Scotland.   58N. 3W.   63
Bertraghboy B., Ireland.   53N.
    10W.   66
Bervie, Scotland.   57N. 2W.   63
Berwick, Scotland.   56N. 2W.   65
*Berwick-upon-Tweed,   England.
    56N. 2W.   54
Berwyn Mt., Wales.   53N. 3W.   54
Berzava, Hungary.   45N. 21E.   79
*Besançon, France.   47N. 6E.   73
Beskiden, Austria.   50N. 19E.   79
Bessarabia, Russia.   47N. 29E.   91
*Bettws-y-coed, Wales.   53N. 4W. 54
Bettyhill, Scotland.   59N. 4W.   63
Beuthen, Germany.   50N. 19E.   75
Bevagna, Italy.   43N. 13E.   83
Beverland, North, Holland.   52N.
    4E.   70
Beverland, South, Holland.   51N.
    4E.   71
Beverley, England.   54N 0W.   55
Beverwyk, Holland.   52N. 5E.   70
Bewdley, England.   52N. 2W.   56
Bex, Switzerland.   46N. 7E.   86
Bexhill-on-Sea, England   51N. 0E. 57
*Beziers, France.   43N. 3E.   73
Biarritz, France.   44N. 2W.   72
Biasca, Switzerland.   46N. 9E.   87
*Biberach, Germany.   48N. 10E.   77
*Bicester, England.   52N. 1W.   57
Bidassoa, R., Spain.   43N. 2W.   85
Bidean-nan-Bian, Scotland.   57N.
    5W.   62
*Bideford, England.   51N. 4W.   56
Bielaia R., Russia.   55N. 55E.   90
Bielefeld, Germany.   52N. 8E.   76
Bielgorod, Russia.   51N. 37E.   91
Biella, Italy.   46N. 8E.   82
Bielo Sero L., Russia.   60N. 38E. 90
Bielopolie, Russia.   51N. 35E.   91
*Bienne, Switzerland.   47N. 7E.   47
Bienne, L. of, Switzerland.   47N.
    7E.   86
Biggar, Scotland.   56N. 4W.   65
Biggleswade, England.   52N. 0W. 57

PAGE

Bigorre, France. 43N. 0E. 72
Bihacs, Bosnia. 45N 16E. 91
Bihar Gura, Hungary. 47N. 23E. 79
Bila Mts., Hungary. 46N. 17E. 78
*Bilbao, Spain. 43N. 3w. 85
Bill of Portland, England. 51N.
 2w. 56
Bills of Achill, Ireland. 54N 10w. 66
Bilston, England. 53N. 2w. 56
Bimel, Switzerland. 47N. 6E. 86
*Bingen, Germany. 50N. 8E. 77
Bingham, England. 53N. 1w. 55
Bingley, England. 54N. 2w. 54
Birkenfeld, Germany. 50N. 7E. 77
Birkenhead, England. 53N. 3w. 54
*Birmingham, England. 52N. 2w. 56
Birr, Ireland. 53N. 8w. 69
Birs R., Switzerland 47N. 8E 86
Biscay, Bay of, France. 46N. 3w. 72
Bisceglie, Italy. 41N. 17E. 81
Bischoffsoell, Switzerland. 47N.
 9E. 87
Bishop Auckland, England. 55N.
 2w. 55
Bishop Stortford, England 52N.
 0E. 57
Bishops Castle, England. 52N.
 3w. 56
Bishops Waltham, England. 51N.
 1w. 57
Bistritz, Hungary. 47N. 24E. 79
Bitburg, Germany. 50N. 6E. 77
Bitna R., Russia. 57N. 24E. 90
Bitolfa, Turkey. 41N. 21E 95
*Bitonto, Italy. 41N. 17E. 81
*Bitsch, Germany. 49N. 7E. 77
Bitterfeld, Germany. 52N. 12E. 76
Björneborg, Russia. 61N. 21E. 90
Bjuken Fos, Norway. 60N. 8E. 89
Black Hd., Ireland. 53N 9w. 68
Black Isle, Scotland. 58N. 4w. 63
Black Koros, Hungary. 47N. 21E. 79
Black Rock, Ireland. 53N 6w. 67
Black Sea, Russia. 43N 35E. 91
Blackadder, R., Scotland. 56N.
 2w. 65
Blackburn, England. 54N. 3w. 54
Blacklarg, Scotland. 55N. 4w. 65
Blackpool, England. 54N. 3w. 54
Blacksod B., Ireland. 54N. 10w. 66
Blackwater Bank, Ireland. 53N.
 6w. 69
Blackwater, R., England. 52N.
 1E. 57
Blackwater, R., Ireland. 52N. 8w. 69
Blackwater R., Ireland. 54N. 7w. 67
Blackwater R., Ireland. 55N 7w. 67
*Blair Atholl, Scotland. 57N. 4w. 63
Blairgowrie, Scotland. 57N. 3w. 63
Blakeney Harbour, England.
 53N. 1E. 55
Blanc, Mont, France. 46N. 7E. 73
Blandford, England. 51N. 2w. 56
Blanes, Spain. 42N. 3E. 85
Blankenberghe, Belgium. 51N. 3E. 71
Blankenburg, Germany 52N. 11E. 76
Blantyre, Scotland 56N. 4w. 65
Blarney, Ireland. 52N. 9w. 68

PAGE

Blavands Huk., Denmark. 56N.
 8E. 89
Blaven, Scotland. 57N. 6w. 62
Blaye, France. 45N. 1w. 72
Blessington, Ireland. 53N. 7w. 69
Bletchley, England. 52N. 1w. 57
Blisworth, England. 52N. 1w. 57
*Blois, France. 48N 1E. 72
Blokzyl, Holland. 53N. 6E. 70
Bloody Foreland, Ireland. 55N.
 8w. 66
Blore, England. 53N. 2w. 54
Bludenz, Austria. 47N. 10E. 78
Bluestack, Ireland. 55N. 8w. 66
Blumlis Alps, Switzerland. 46N.
 8E. 86
Blyth, R., England. 55N. 2w. 55
Boat of Garten, Scotland. 57N.
 4w. 63
Bobadilla, Spain. 37N. 5w. 84
Bobbio, Italy. 45N. 9E. 82
Bober R., Germany. 52N. 15E. 75
*Bobruisk, Russia. 53N. 29E. 91
Bocairente, Spain. 39N. 1w. 85
Bochum, Germany. 52N. 7E. 76
Boddam, Scotland. 57N. 2w. 63
Bode R., Germany. 52N. 11E. 76
Boderg Lough, Ireland. 54N. 8w. 66
*Bodmin, England. 50N. 5w. 56
Bodö, Norway. 67N. 14E. 88
Bognor, England. 51N. 1w. 57
Bogragh Mts., Ireland. 52N 9w 68
Bohemia, Austria. 50N 14E. 78
Boherboy, Ireland. 52N. 9w. 68
Bohmer Wald, Austria. 49N. 13E. 78
Boisdale, Loch, Scotland. 57N.
 7w. 62
*Bois-le-Duc, Holland. 52N. 5E. 70
Bolkhov, Russia. 54N. 36E. 91
Bolnas, Sweden. 61N. 16E. 89
*Bologna, Italy. 44N. 11E. 83
Bolsena, L. di, Italy. 43N. 12E. 83
*Bolton, England. 54N 2w. 54
Bolus Hd., Ireland. 52N 10w. 68
Bomst, Germany. 52N. 16E. 75
Bonar Bridge, Scotland. 58N. 4w. 63
Bonawe, Scotland. 56N. 5w. 64
Bo'ness, Scotland. 56N. 4w. 65
Bonfol, Switzerland. 47N. 7E. 86
Bonifacio, Corsica. 41N. 9E. 80
Bonifacio, Strait of, Italy. 41N.
 9E. 81
*Bonn, Germany. 51N. 7E. 77
Bonneville, France. 46N 6E. 73
Bonorva, Sardinia 40N. 9E. 81
Bonyhad, Hungary. 46N. 18E. 79
*Boom, Belgium. 51N. 4E. 71
Bootle, England. 53N. 3w. 54
Bootle, England. 54N. 3w. 54
Boras, Sweden. 58N. 13E. 89
*Bordeaux, France. 45N. 1w 72
Bordenone, Italy. 46N. 13E. 83
Borgataro, Italy. 44N. 10E. 82
Borgholm, Sweden. 57N. 17E. 89
Borgomanero, Italy. 46N. 9E. 83
Borgonure, Italy. 45N. 10E. 82
Borgo San Donino, Italy. 45N.
 10E. 82

PAGE

Borgo San Sepolcro, Italy. 44N. 12E.   83
Borisoghebsk, Russia. 51N. 42E. 91
Borisov, Russia. 54N. 29E. 91
Borja, Spain. 42N. 2w. 85
Bormida R., Italy. 45N. 9E. 82
Bornholm, Denmark 55N. 15E. 89
Boros Sebes, Hungary. 46N. 22E. 79
Boroughbridge, England. 54N. 1w. 55
Borris, Ireland. 53N. 7w. 69
Borrisokane, Ireland. 53N. 8w. 69
Borrisoleigh, Ireland. 53N. 8w. 69
Borsawa, Hungary. 48N. 22E. 79
Boryslaw, Austria. 49N. 24E. 79
Bosa, Sardinia. 40N 9E. 81
Bosna R., Bosnia. 45N. 18E. 94
Bosnia, Austria-Hungary. 44N. 18E.   79
Bosphorus, Turkey. 43N. 29E. 94
Boston, England. 53N. 0w. 55
Bothnia, Gulf of, Sweden 65N. 24E.   88
Boti, Russia. 42N. 42E. 91
Botoshany, Roumania. 48N. 27E. 94
Bouches-du-Rhone, France. 44N. 5E.   73
Boudry, Switzerland. 47N. 7E. 86
Bouillon, Belgium. 50N. 5E. 71
*Boulogne, France. 51N. 2E. 73
Bourbonne, France. 48N. 6E. 73
*Bourg, France. 46N. 5E. 73
*Bourges, France. 47N. 2E. 73
*Bourn, England. 53N. 1w. 55
*Bournemouth, England. 51N. 2w. 56
Bourtange, Holland. 53N. 7E. 70
Bourton, England. 52N. 2w. 56
Bouveret, Switzerland. 46N. 7E. 86
*Boves, Italy. 44N. 8E. 82
Bow, England. 51N. 4w. 56
Bowes, England. 55N. 2w. 54
Bowfell, England. 54N. 2w. 54
Bowmore, Scotland. 56N. 6w. 64
Boyle, Ireland. 54N 8w. 66
Boyle R., Ireland. 54N. 8w. 66
*Boyne R., Ireland. 54N. 6w. 67
Bozen, Austria. 47N. 11E. 78
Bra, Italy. 45N. 8E. 82
Brabant, Belgium. 51N. 5E. 71
Bracadale, Scotland. 57N. 6w. 62
Bracciano, L. di, Italy. 42N. 12E. 83
Brackley, England. 52N. 1w.   57
Brad, Hungary. 46N. 23E. 79
Bradano R , Italy. 40N. 17E. 81
*Bradford, England. 51N. 2w. 56
Bradford, England. 54N. 2w. 54
Braeriasch, Scotland. 57N. 4w. 63
Braga, Portugal. 42N. 8w. 84
Braganca, Portugal. 42N 7w. 84
Bragar, Scotland. 58N. 7w. 62
Brahilov, Roumania. 45N. 28E. 94
Braich-y-Pwll, Wales. 53N. 5w. 54
Braine-le-Comte, Belgium. 51N. 4E.   71
Braintree, England. 52N. 1E. 57
Brampton, England. 55N. 3w. 54
Bran, R., Scotland. 57N. 4w. 65
Brandenburg, Germany. 52N. 14E. 76

PAGE

Brandenburg, Germany. 52N 12E.76
Brandon, England. 52N. 1E. 57
Brandon B., Ireland. 52N. 10w. 68
Brandon Hd., Ireland. 52N. 10w. 68
Brandon Hill, Ireland. 52N. 10w. 68
Braunau, Austria. 48N. 13E 78
Braunsberg, Germany. 54N. 21E. 75
Braviken B., Sweden. 59N. 17E. 89
Bray, Ireland. 53N. 6w. 67
Bray Hd., Ireland. 52N. 10w. 68
Brazza Is., Dalmatia. 43N. 16E. 94
Breadalbane, Scotland. 56N. 4w. 65
*Brechin, Scotland. 57N. 3w. 63
Brecknock Beacon, Wales. 52N. 3w.   56
*Brecon, Wales. 52N. 3w. 56
*Breda, Holland. 52N. 5E. 70
Brede, R., England. 51N. 1E. 57
Bredevoort, Holland. 52N. 7E. 70
*Bregenz, Austria. 47N. 10E. 78
Breisach, A., Germany. 48N. 8E. 77
Breisach, N., Germany. 48N. 8E. 77
Brelostok, Russia. 53N. 23E. 91
Bremangerland, Norway. 62N. 5E. 89
Bremen, Germany. 53N. 9E. 76
Bremerhaven, Germany. 54N. 9E. 76
Bremgarten, Switzerland. 47N. 8E. 87
Breno, Italy. 46N. 10E. 82
*Brentford, England. 51N. 0w 57
Brentwood, England. 52N. 0E. 57
*Brescia, Italy. 46N. 10E. 82
*Breslau, Germany. 51N. 17E. 75
Bressay Is , Scotland. 60N. 1w. 63
*Brest, France. 48N. 5w. 72
Brest Litovsk, Russia. 52N. 23E. 91
Breukelen, Holland. 52N. 5E. 70
Brezezany, Austria. 50N. 25E. 79
Briancon, France. 45N. 6E. 73
Briansk, Russia. 53N. 35E. 91
Bridge of Allan, Scotland 56N. 4w.   65
Bridgend, Scotland. 56N. 6w. 64
Bridgend, Wales. 52N. 4w. 56
*Bridgewater, England. 51N. 3w. 56
Bridgewater Bay, England. 51N. 3w.   56
*Bridgnorth, England. 53N. 2w. 56
Bridlington, England. 54N. 0w. 55
Bridlington Quay, England. 54N. 0w.   55
Bridport, England. 51N. 3w. 56
Brieg, Germany. 51N. 17E. 75
Brieg, Switzerland. 46N. 8E. 86
*Brielle, Holland. 52N. 4E. 70
Brienz, Switzerland. 47N. 8E. 86
Brienz, Lake of, Switzerland. 47N. 8E.   86
Brierley Hill, England. 52N. 2w. 56
Bries, Hungary. 49N. 20E. 79
Brightlingsea, England. 52N. 1E. 57
Brighton, England. 51N. 0w. 57
Brig of Earn, Scotland. 56N. 3w. 65
Brims Ness, Scotland. 59N. 4w. 63
Brindisi, Italy. 41N. 18E. 81
Brissago, Switzerland. 46N. 9E. 87
*Bristol, England. 51N. 3w 56
Bristol Channel, England. 51N. 4w.   56

	PAGE
Brittle, Loch, Scotland. 57N. 6W.	62
Brives, France. 45N. 1E.	72
Brixen, Austria. 47N. 12E.	78
*Brixham, England. 50N. 3W.	56
Briljita, Bulgaria. 44N. 22E.	94
Broad Bay, Scotland. 58N. 6W.	62
Broadford, Scotland. 57N. 6W.	62
Broad Haven, Ireland. 54N. 10W.	66
*Brocken, Germany. 52N. 11E.	76
*Brod, Bosnia. 45N. 18E.	94
Brodick, Scotland. 56N. 5W.	64
Brody, Austria. 50N. 25E.	79
Bromberg, Germany. 53N. 18E.	75
Bromsgrove, England. 52N. 2W.	56
Bromyard, England. 52N. 3W.	56
Brookeborough, Ireland. 54N. 7W.	67
Broom, Loch, Scotland. 58N. 5W.	62
Broos, Austria-Hungary. 46N. 23E.	79
Brora, Scotland. 58N. 4W.	63
Brora, R., Scotland. 58N. 4W.	63
Broseley, England. 53N. 3W.	56
Brosna, R., Ireland. 53N. 7W.	67
Brosna, R., Ireland. 53N. 8W.	69
Brough, England. 55N. 2W.	54
Broughton, England. 54N. 3W.	54
Broughton, Scotland. 56N. 3W	65
Broughty Ferry, Scotland. 56N. 3W.	65
Brown Willy, England. 51N. 5W	56
Broye R., Switzerland 47N. 7E.	86
Bruchsal, Germany. 49N. 9E.	77
Bruck, Austria. 47N. 15E.	78
Bruff, Ireland 52N. 9W.	68
*Bruges, Belgium. 51N. 3E.	71
Brugg, Switzerland. 47N. 8E.	86
Brünig, Switzerland. 47N. 8E.	86
Brunn, Austria. 49N. 16E.	78
Brunsbüttel, Germany. 54N 9E.	76
Brunswick, Germany. 52N. 10E.	76
Brunswick, Germany. 52N. 11E.	76
Bruree, Ireland. 52N. 9W.	68
*Brussels, Belgium. 51N. 4E.	71
Bruster Ort, Germany. 55N. 20E.	75
Bruton, England. 51N. 2W.	56
Brux, Bohemia. 51N. 14E.	78
Buccari, Croatia. 45N. 14E.	78
Buchan Ness, Scotland. 57N. 2W.	63
Buchholz, Germany. 53N. 10E.	76
Buchnia, Austria. 50N. 20E.	79
Bückeburg, Germany. 52N. 9E.	76
Buckenham, England. 52N. 1E.	57
Buckhaven, Scotland. 56N. 3W.	65
Buckingham, England. 52N. 1W.	57
Buckie, Scotland. 58N. 3W.	63
Bucklyvie, Scotland. 56N. 4W.	65
Buczacz, Austria. 49N. 25E.	79
*Budapest, Hungary. 47N 19E.	94
Buddon Ness, Scotland. 56N. 3W.	65
Bude, England. 51N 5W.	56
Bude Bay, England. 51N. 5W.	56
Budrio, Italy. 45N. 12E.	83
Budua, Dalmatia. 42N. 19E.	79
Budweis, Austria. 49N. 14E.	78
Buffalvria, Italy. 40N. 16E.	81
Bug R., Russia. 47N. 32E.	91
Bug R., Russia. 53N. 21E	91
Bugulma, Russia. 55N. 53E.	91
Bugurastan, Russia. 54N. 52E.	91
*Builth, Wales. 52N. 3W.	56
*Bukharest, Roumania. 44N. 26E.	94
Bukke Fd., Norway. 59N. 6E.	89
Bukowina, Austria. 48N. 26E.	79
Bülach, Switzerland. 48N. 9E.	87
Bull Rock Lighthouse, Ireland. 52N. 10W.	68
Bulle, Switzerland. 47N. 7E.	86
Bumasco, Switzerland. 46N. 9E.	87
Buncrana, Ireland. 55N. 7W.	67
Bundoran, Ireland. 54N. 8W.	66
Bungay, England. 52N. 1E.	57
Bunzlau, Germany. 52N. 15E.	75
Burano, Italy. 45N. 12E.	83
Bure, R., England. 53N. 2E.	55
Buren, Switzerland. 47N. 7E.	86
Burg, Germany. 52N. 12E.	76
Burg, Germany. 54N. 11E.	76
Burgdorf, Switzerland. 47N. 8E.	86
Burgh, England. 53N 0E.	55
Burghas, Bulgaria. 42N. 28E.	94
Burghead, Scotland. 58N. 3W.	63
*Bürglen, Switzerland 47N. 9E.	87
*Burgos, Spain. 42N. 4W.	84
Burnham, England. 52N. 1E.	57
Burnham, England. 51N. 3W.	56
Burnham Thorpe, England. 53N. 1E.	55
Burnley, England. 54N. 2W.	54
*Burntisland, Scotland. 56N. 3W.	65
Burra Is., Scotland. 60N. 1W.	63
Burray Is., Scotland. 59N. 3W.	63
Burriana, Spain. 40N. 0W.	85
Burrow Head, Scotland. 55N. 4W.	65
Burry Inlet, Wales. 52N. 4W.	56
Burslem, England. 53N. 2W.	54
Burton Port, Ireland. 55N. 8W.	66
Burton-upon-Trent, England. 53N. 2W.	55
Bury, England. 54N. 2w.	54
*Bury St. Edmunds, England. 52N. 1E.	57
Busa Cape, Crete. 36N. 24E.	95
Busby, Scotland. 56N. 4W.	65
Busen, Roumania. 45N. 27E.	94
Busen R., Roumania. 45N. 28E.	94
Bush, R., Ireland. 55N. 7W.	67
Bushmills, Ireland. 55N. 7W.	67
Busto Arizio, Italy. 46N. 9E.	82
Busuluk, Russia. 53N. 52E.	91
Busum, Germany. 54N. 9E.	76
Bute, Scotland. 56N. 5W.	64
Bute Sd., Scotland. 56N. 5W.	64
Butt of Lewis, Scotland. 59N. 6W.	62
Buttevant, Ireland. 52N. 9W.	68
Butzow, Germany. 54N. 12E.	76
*Buxton, England. 53N. 2W.	54
Bystrica, Austria-Hungary. 49N. 25E.	79
Byth, England. 55N. 1W.	55
Cabeza, Spain. 39N. 5W.	84
Cabezon, Spain. 43N. 4W.	84
Cabra, Spain. 37N. 4W.	84
Cabrera, Balearic Isles. 39N. 3E.	85
Cabriel, R., Spain. 39N. 1W.	85
Caceres, Spain. 39N. 6W.	84
Cader Idris, Wales. 53N. 4W.	56

PAGE

*Cadiz, Spain. 36N. 6W. 84
*Caen, France. 49N. 0W. 72
Caergwrle, Wales. 53N. 3W. 54
*Caerleon, England. 52N. 3W. 56
Caerphilly, Wales. 52N. 3W. 56
Caghari, Sardinia. 39N. 9E. 81
Caghari, Gulf of, Sardinia. 39N. 9E. 81
Caha Mts., Ireland. 52N. 10W. 68
Caher, Ireland. 52N. 8W. 69
Caherconlish, Ireland. 53N. 8W. 68
Cahirciveen, Ireland. 52N. 10W 68
Cahore Pt , Ireland. 53N. 6W. 69
*Cahors, France. 44N. 1E. 72
Cairn Table, Scotland. 55N. 4W. 65
Cairnbawn, Loch, Scotland. 58N. 5W. 62
Cairngorm, Scotland. 57N. 4W. 63
Cairnsmuir, Scotland. 55N. 4W. 65
Cairnsmuir of Fleet, Scotland. 55N. 4W. 65
Cairntoul, Scotland. 57N. 4W. 63
Caister, England. 53N. 2E. 57
Caistor, England. 53N. 0W. 55
Caithness, Scotland. 58N. 3W. 63
Calabrian Mts., Italy. 39N. 16E. 81
*Calais, France. 51N. 2E. 73
Calanca, V., Switzerland. 46N. 9E. 87
Calatayud, Spain. 41N. 2W. 85
Calder, R., Scotland. 56N. 3W. 65
Calder, Mid, Scotland. 56N. 3W. 65
Calder, West, Scotland. 56N. 3W. 65
Caldew, R., England. 55N. 3W. 54
Caldy Is., Wales. 52N. 5W. 66
Caledon, Ireland. 51N. 7W. 67
Caledonian Canal, Scotland 57N. 5W. 62
Calf of Man, Isle of Man. 54N 5W 54
Callan, Ireland 53N. 7W. 69
Callander, Scotland 56N. 4W. 65
Callington, England 51N. 4W. 56
Calmar, Sweden. 57N. 16E. 89
*Calne, England. 51N. 2W. 56
Caltagirone, Sicily. 37N. 15E. 81
Caltanisetta, Sicily. 37N. 14E. 81
Caluso, Italy. 45N. 8E. 82
Calvados, France. 49N. 0W. 72
*Calvi, Corsica. 43N. 9E. 80
Calzada, Spain. 39N. 4W 84
Cam, R., England. 52N. 0E 57
Camacchio, Italy. 45N. 12E 83
Camborne, England. 50N. 5W. 56
*Cambray, France. 50N. 3E. 73
Cambrian Mts., Wales. 52N. 4W. 56
Cambridge, England. 52N. 0E. 57
Camel, R., England. 51N. 5W. 56
*Camelford, England. 51N. 5W. 56
Camerino, Italy. 43N. 13E. 83
Camisano, Italy. 46N. 12E. 83
Camlin, R., Ireland. 54N 8W. 67
Cammin, Germany. 53N. 15E. 76
Camolin, Ireland. 53N. 6W. 69
Campania, Italy. 41N. 15E. 81
Campbeltown, Scotland. 55N. 6W 64
Campli, Italy. 43N. 14E. 83
Campo Maior, Portugal. 39N 7W. 84
Campobasso, Italy. 42N. 15F. 80
Campofarmio, Italy. 46N. 13E. 83

PAGE

Campsie, Scotland. 56N. 4W. 65
Campsie Fells, Scotland. 56N. 4W. 65
Can, Germany. 54N. 9E. 76
Cancale, France. 49N. 2W. 72
*Candia, Crete. 35N. 25E. 95
Canea, Crete. 35N. 24E. 95
Cangas de Tineo, Spain. 43N. 7W. 84
Canicatti, Sicily. 37N. 14E. 81
Canisbay, Scotland. 59N. 3W. 63
Canna Is., Scotland. 57N. 7W. 62
Cannes, France. 44N. 7E. 73
Cannstadt, Germany. 49N. 9E. 77
Canonbie, Scotland. 55N. 3W. 65
*Canossa, Italy. 45N. 10E. 82
Canpile, Ireland. 52N. 7W. 69
Cantabrian Chain, Spain. 43N. 4W. 84
Cantal, France. 45N. 3E. 73
Cantal, Mt., France. 45N. 3E. 73
*Canterbury, England. 51N. 1E. 57
Cantyre, Scotland. 56N. 6W. 64
Capannori, Italy. 44N. 11E. 82
Capolago, Switzerland. 46N. 9E. 87
Cappamore, Ireland. 53N. 8W. 68
Cappoquin, Ireland. 52N. 8W. 69
Capraja Is., Italy. 43N. 10E. 80
*Caprera Is., Sardinia. 41N. 10E. 81
*Capri Is., Italy. 41N. 14E 81
Caprino, Italy. 46N. 11E. 83
*Capua, Italy. 41N. 14E. 81
Carballino, Spain. 42N. 8W. 84
Carballo, Spain. 43N. 9W. 84
Carbonara, C., Sardinia. 39N. 10E. 81
Carboneras, Spain. 37N. 2W. 84
Carbost, Scotland. 57N. 6W. 62
Carbury, Ireland. 53N. 7W. 17
*Carcassonne, France. 43N. 2E. 73
*Cardiff, Wales. 51N. 3W. 56
Cardigan, Wales. 52N. 5W. 56
Cardigan Bay, Wales. 53N. 4W. 56
Carese, Italy. 42N. 13E. 83
Cargill, Scotland. 57N. 3W. 65
Carignano, Italy. 45N. 8E. 82
Carinthia, Austria. 47N. 14E. 78
Carlingford, Ireland. 54N. 6W. 67
Carlingford Lough, Ireland. 54N. 6W. 67
*Carlisle, England. 55N. 3W. 54
Carlow, Ireland. 53N. 7W. 69
Carlshafen, Germany. 52N. 10E. 76
Carlshamn, Sweden. 56N. 16E 89
Carlsruhe, Germany. 49N 8E. 77
Carlstad, Sweden. 59N. 13E. 89
Carluke, Scotland. 56N. 4W. 65
Carmagnola, Italy. 45N. 8E. 82
Carmarthen, Wales. 52N. 4W. 56
Carmarthen B., Wales. 52N. 4W. 56
Carmylie, Scotland. 57N. 3W. 63
Carna, Ireland. 53N. 10W. 66
*Carnarvon, Wales. 53N. 4W. 54
Carnarvon B , Wales. 53N. 4W. 54
Carndonagh, Ireland. 55N. 7W. 67
Carney, Ireland. 54N. 9W 66
Carnforth, England. 54N. 3W. 54
Carnic Alps, Austria. 47N. 13E. 78
Carniola, Austria. 46N. 14E. 78
Carnlough, Ireland. 55N 6W. 67
Carnoustie, Scotland. 57N. 3W. 65
Carnsore Pt., Ireland. 52N. 6W. 69

PAGE

Carnwath, Scotland. 56N. 4W.   65
Carpathians, Hungary. 49N. 23E.79
Carpentras, France. 44N. 5E.   73
*Carpi, Italy. 45N. 11E.   83
Carrantual, Ireland. 52N 10W. 68
Carrara, Italy. 44N. 10E.   82
Carrick, Ireland 55N. 9W.   66
Carrickbeg, Ireland. 52N. 7W. 69
*Carrickfergus, Ireland. 55N. 6W. 67
Carrickmacross, Ireland. 54N.7W. 67
Carrickmore, Ireland. 55N. 7W. 67
Carrick-on-Shannon, Ireland. 54N.
    8W.   66
Carrick-on-Suir, Ireland. 52N. 7W. 69
Carrigallen, Ireland. 54N 8W. 67
Carrigans, Ireland. 55N. 7W.   67
Carril, Spain. 43N. 9W.   84
Carrion R., Spain. 42N. 5W.   84
Carron, Scotland. 56N. 4W.   65
Carron, Loch, Scotland. 57N. 6W. 62
Carron, R., Scotland. 57N. 5W. 62
Carrowmore Lough, Ireland. 54N.
    10W.   66
Carse of Gowrie, Scotland. 56N.
    3W.   65
Carsphairn, Scotland. 55N. 4W. 65
Carstairs, Scotland. 56N. 4W. 65
*Cartagena, Spain. 38N. 1W.   85
Carter Fell, England. 55N. 2W. 54
Carvoeiro, C, Portugal. 39N. 10W. 84
Carwen, Wales. 53N 3W   54
Casale, Italy. 45N. 8E.   82
Caserta, Italy. 41N. 14E.   81
*Cashel, Ireland. 53N. 8W.   69
Cashen, R., Ireland. 53N. 10W. 68
Casoli, Italy. 42N. 14E.   83
Caspe, Spain. 41N. 0W.   85
Caspian Sea, Russia. 42N. 50E. 91
Cassalmaggiore, Italy. 45N. 10E. 82
Cassandra Gulf, Turkey 40N 24E 95
Cassel, Germany. 51N. 10E.   77
Cassino, Italy. 42N 14E.   80
Castel Bolognese, Italy 44N. 12E. 83
Castel di Sangro, Italy 42N 14E. 83
Castel Sardo, Sardinia 41N. 9E. 81
Castel San Pietro, Italy. 44N.12E. 83
*Castelfranco, Italy. 46N. 12E. 83
Castellamare, G. of, Sicily. 38N.
    13E.   81
Castellammare, Italy. 41N. 14E. 81
Castello Branco, Portugal. 40N.
    7W.   84
Castellon de la Plana, Spain. 40N.
    0W.   85
*Castelnaudary, France. 43N. 2E. 73
Castelnuovo, Dalmatia. 42N. 18E. 79
Castelvetere, Italy. 38N. 16E. 81
Castelvetrano, Sicily. 38N. 13E. 81
*Castiglione, Italy. 45N. 10E.   82
Castle Dawson, Ireland. 55N. 7W.67
Castle Donnington, England. 53N.
    1W.   55
Castle Douglas,Scotland. 55N.4W. 65
Castle Eden, England. 55N. 1W. 55
*Castle Rising, England. 53N. 0E. 55
Castlebar, Ireland. 51N. 9W.   66
Castlebellingham, Ireland. 54N.
    6W.   67

PAGE

Castleblaney, Ireland. 54N. 7W. 67
Castlebridge, Ireland. 52N. 6W. 69
Castlecomer, Ireland. 53N. 7W. 69
Castleconnell, Ireland. 53N. 8W. 68
Castlederg, Ireland. 55N. 8W   67
Castledermot, Ireland. 53N 7W. 69
Castlefinn, Ireland 55N 8W.   67
Castlegrove, Ireland. 52N. 10W. 68
Castleisland, Ireland. 52N. 9W. 68
Castlemaine, Ireland. 52N. 10W. 68
Castlemartyr, Ireland. 52N. 8W. 69
Castlepollard, Ireland. 54N 7W. 67
Castlerea, Ireland. 54N. 8W.   66
*Castleton, England. 53N. 2W. 54
Castletown, Isle of Man. 54N. 5W. 54
Castletown, Scotland. 59N 3W 63
Castletown of Braemar, Scotland.
    57N. 3W.   63
Castle-wellan, Ireland. 54N. 6W. 67
Castres, France. 44N. 2E.   73
Castro Urdiales, Spain. 43N. 3W. 84
Castrovillari, Italy. 40N. 16E. 81
Catalonia, Spain. 42N. 2E.   85
Catania, Sicily. 38N. 15E.   81
Catania, G. of, Sicily. 37N. 15E. 81
*Catanzara, Italy. 39N. 17E.   81
Caterham, England. 51N. 0W. 57
Cattaro, Montenegro. 42N. 19E. 94
Caucasia, Russia. 43N. 45E.   91
Caucasus, Russia. 43N. 44E.   91
Cavan, Ireland. 54N. 7W.   67
Caveller Maggiore, Italy. 45N. 8E. 82
Cawdor, Scotland. 58N. 4W.   63
Cawsand Beacon, England. 51N.
    4W.   56
Cawston, England. 53N. 1E.   55
Cazalla, Spain. 38N 6W.   84
Cecina, Italy. 43N. 11E.   82
Cecina, R., Italy 43N 11E.   82
Cedeira, Spain. 44N. 8W.   84
Cefalu, Sicily. 38N. 14E.   81
Ceglie, Italy. 41N. 18E.   81
Celano, Italy. 42N. 14E.   83
Celbridge, Ireland. 53N. 7W.   67
Cellar Hd., Scotland. 58N. 6W. 62
Celle, Germany 53N. 10E.   76
Cenis Tunnel, Mt., France. 45N.
    7E.   82
Cento, Italy. 45N 11E.   83
*Cephalonia, Greece. 38N 21E 95
Ceres, Scotland. 56N. 3W.   65
*Cerignola, Italy. 41N. 16E.   81
Cerigo, Greece. 36N. 23E.   95
Cerigotto, Crete. 36N. 23E.   95
Cervera, Spain. 42N. 1E.   85
Cervia, Italy. 44N. 12E.   83
Cesano, R., Italy. 44N. 13E.   83
*Cesena, Italy. 44N. 12E.   83
Cetinge, Montenegro. 42N. 19E. 94
Cette, France. 43N. 4E.   73
Ceva, Italy 44N. 8E.   82
*Cevennes, France. 44N. 5E.   73
Cevio, Switzerland. 46N. 9E.   87
Chalcis, Greece. 38N. 24E.   95
*Chalons-sur-Marne, France. 49N.
    4E.   73
Chalone-sur-Saone, France. 47N.
    5E.   73

PAGE

Cham, Germany. 49N. 12E. 77
Chambery, France. 46N. 6E. 73
Chambord, France. 48N. 2E. 73
Chamouni, France. 46N. 7E. 73
Champagne, France. 49N. 5E. 73
Champéry, Switzerland. 46N. 7E. 86
Channel Is., England. 49N. 2w. 56
Chantada, Spain. 43N. 8w. 84
Chapel-en-le-Frith, England. 53N.
2w. 54
Chara, Greece. 39N. 23E. 95
Chard, England. 51N. 3w. 56
Charente, France. 46N. 0E. 72
Charente, R., France. 46N. 1w. 72
Charente Inférieure, France. 46N.
1w 72
Charing, England. 51N. 1E. 57
Charleroi, Belgium. 50N. 4E. 71
Charlestown, Ireland. 54N. 9w. 66
Charlestown, Scotland 56N. 4w. 65
Charleville, Ireland. 52N. 9w. 68
Charlottenburg, Germany. 52N.
13E. 76
Chartres, France. 48N. 1E. 72
Chasseral, Switzerland. 47N. 7E. 86
Château d'Oex, Switzerland. 46N.
7E. 86
Chateaubriant, France. 48N. 1w. 72
Chateauroux, France. 47N. 2E. 73
Chateau-Salins, Germany. 49N.
6E. 77
Chateau-Thierry, France. 49N. 3E. 73
Chatelet, Belgium. 50N 5E. 71
Châtellerault, France. 47N. 0E. 72
Chatel St. Denis, Switzerland. 47N.
7E. 86
Chatham, England. 51N. 1E. 57
Chatillon, France. 48N. 5E. 73
Chatillon, Italy. 46N. 8E. 82
Chaumont, France. 48N. 5E. 73
Chaumont, Switzerland. 47N. 7E. 86
Chaves, Portugal. 42N. 8w. 84
Cheadle, England. 53N. 2w. 54
Cheddar, England. 51N. 3w. 56
Chelmer, R., England. 52N. 1E. 57
Chelmsford, England. 52N. 0E. 57
Cheltenham, England. 52N. 2w. 56
Chelva, Spain. 40N. 1w. 85
Chemnitz, Germany. 51N. 13E. 77
Chepstow, England. 52N. 3w. 56
Cher, France. 47N. 2E. 73
Cher, R., France. 47N. 0E. 72
Cherasco, Italy. 45N. 8E. 82
Cherbourg, France. 50N. 2w. 72
Cherso, Austria. 45N. 14E. 78
Chertsey, England. 51N. 1w. 57
Cherwell R., England. 52N. 1w. 57
Chesham, England. 52N. 1w. 57
Cheshire, England. 53N. 3w 51
Chesil Bank, England 51N. 3w. 56
Chesilton, England. 51N. 2w. 56
Chester, England. 53N. 3w. 54
Chesterfield, England. 53N 1w. 55
Chester-le-Street, England. 55N.
2w. 55
Cheviot, England. 55N. 2w. 54
Chiara, Italy. 46N. 10:. 82
Chiavari, Italy. 44N. 9E. 82

Chiavenna, Italy. 46N. 9E. 80
Chichester, England. 51N. 1w. 57
Chiem See, Germany. 48N. 12E. 77
Chienti R., Italy. 43N. 14E. 83
Chieri, Italy. 45N. 8E. 82
Chieti, Italy. 42N. 14E. 83
Chilivani, Sardinia. 41N. 9E. 81
Chillon, Switzerland. 46N. 7E. 86
Chiltern Hills, England. 52N. 1w. 57
Chimay, Belgium. 50N. 4E. 71
Chinchilla, Spain. 39N. 2w. 85
Chinon, France. 47N 0E. 72
Chiny, Belgium. 50N. 5E. 71
Chioggia, Italy. 45N. 12E. 83
Chipiona, Spain. 37N. 6w. 84
Chippenham, England. 51N. 2w. 56
Chipping Barnet, England. 52N.
0w. 57
Chipping Campden, England. 52N.
2w. 56
Chipping Norton, England. 52N.
2w. 57
Chipping Ongar, England. 52N.
0E. 57
Chiusa, Italy. 44N. 8E. 82
Chiusi, Italy. 43N. 12E. 83
Chivasso, Italy. 45N. 8E. 82
Chollet, France. 47N. 1w. 72
Cholmogory, Russia. 64N. 42E. 90
Chorley, England. 54N. 3w. 54
Christchurch, England. 51N. 2w. 56
Christiania, Norway. 60N. 11E. 89
Christiania Fd., Norway. 59N.
11E. 89
Christiansand, Norway. 59N. 8E. 89
Christiansand, Norway. 58N. 8E. 89
Christianstad, Sweden. 56N. 14E. 89
Christiansund, Norway. 63N. 8E. 88
Christineham, Sweden. 59N. 14E. 89
Chulmleigh, England. 51N. 4w. 56
Church Stretton, England. 53N.
3w. 56
Chyrow, Austria. 50N. 23E. 79
Cieza, Spain. 38N 1w. 85
Cilli, Austria. 46N. 15E. 78
Cimone, M., Italy. 44N 11E. 83
Cinca, R., Spain. 41N. 0E. 85
Cintra, Portugal. 39N. 10w. 84
Circello, C., Italy. 41N. 13E. 81
Cirencester, England. 52N. 2w. 56
Cirie, Italy. 45N. 8E. 82
Citta di Castella, Italy. 43N. 12E. 83
Cittadella, Italy. 46N. 12E. 83
Ciudad Real, Spain. 39N. 4w. 84
Ciudad Rodrigo, Spain. 41N. 6w. 84
Ciudadela, Minorca. 40N. 4E. 85
Cividale, Italy. 46N. 13E. 83
Civita Castellana, Italy. 42N. 12E. 83
Civita della Pieve, Italy. 43N. 12E. 83
Civita San Angelo, Italy. 43N.
14E. 83
Civita Vecchia, Italy. 42N 12E. 83
Clackmannan, Scotland. 56N. 4w. 65
Clacton, England. 52N. 1E. 57
Clain, R., France. 47N. 0E. 72
Clamecy, France. 47N. 3E. 73
Clane, Ireland. 53N. 7w. 67
Clara, Ireland. 53N. 8w. 67

PAGE

Clare, Ireland. 53N. 9W. 68
Clare Is., Ireland. 54N. 10W. 66
Clare, R., Ireland. 54N. 9W. 66
Claregalway, Ireland. 53N 9W. 66
Claregalway R., Ireland. 53N. 9W. 66
Claremorris, Ireland. 54N 9W. 66
Clashmore, Ireland. 52N. 8W. 69
Claudy, Ireland. 55N. 7W. 67
Clausthal, Germany. 52N. 10E. 76
Clay, Loch, Scotland 58N. 7W. 62
Clear, Cape, Ireland. 51N. 10W. 68
Clear Is., Ireland. 51N. 9W. 68
Cleator Moor, England. 55N. 4W. 54
Cleethorpes, England. 54N. 0W 55
*Cleobury Mortimer, England. 52N. 2W. 56
Clerf, Luxemburg. 50N. 6E 71
Clerf, R., Luxemburg 50N. 6E. 71
*Clermont, France. 46N. 3E. 73
*Clevedon, England. 51N 3W. 56
Cleveland, England. 54N. 1W. 55
Cleves, Germany. 52N. 6E 76
Clew B., Ireland. 54N 10W. 66
Clifden, Ireland. 53N. 10W. 66
Cliffony, Ireland. 54N 8W. 66
Cliffs of Moher, Ireland. 53N 9W. 68
Clitheroe, England. 54N. 2W. 54
Clogh R., Ireland. 55N. 6W. 67
Cloghan, Ireland. 53N. 8W. 69
Clogheen, Ireland. 52N 8W. 69
Clogher, Ireland. 54N 7W. 67
Clogher Hd., Ireland. 54N 6W. 67
Clonakilty, Ireland. 52N. 9W. 68
Clonakilty B., Ireland. 52N. 9W. 68
Clonaslee, Ireland. 53N. 8W. 69
Clonegall, Ireland 53N 7W. 69
Clones, Ireland. 51N. 7W. 67
*Clonmel, Ireland. 52N. 8W. 69
*Clontarf, Ireland. 53N. 8W. 67
Cloone, Ireland 54N. 8W. 67
Closeburn, Scotland. 55N. 4W. 65
Clova, Scotland. 57N 3W. 63
Clovelly, England 51N 4W. 56
Cloyne, Ireland. 52N. 8W. 69
Clun, England. 52N. 3W. 56
Clunie, Loch, Scotland. 57N. 5W. 62
Clusone, Italy. 46N. 10E. 82
Clyde, Firth of, Scotland. 56N. 5W. 61
Clyde, R., Scotland. 56N. 5W. 65
Clydebank, Scotland. 56N. 4W. 65
Clyne, Scotland. 58N 4W. 63
Coachford, Ireland. 52N. 9W. 68
Coatbridge, Scotland. 56N. 4W 65
Cobbler, The, Scotland. 56N. 5W. 64
Coblenz, Germany. 50N 8E. 77
*Coburg, Germany. 50N. 11E. 77
Cockburnspath, Scotland. 56N. 2W. 65
*Cockermouth, England. 55N. 3W. 54
Codroipo, Italy. 46N. 13E. 83
Coervorden, Holland. 53N. 7E. 70
Coggeshall, England 52N. 1E 57
*Cognac, France. 46N. 0W. 72
*Coimbra, Portugal. 40N. 8W. 84
Coire (Chur), Switzerland. 47N. 10E. 87
Col de Balme, Switzerland. 46N. 7E. 86

PAGE

Col de Ferret, Switzerland. 46N. 7E. 86
Col di Cadibona, Italy. 44N. 8E. 82
Col di Tenda, Italy. 44N. 8E. 82
Col du Jaman, Switzerland. 46N. 7E. 86
Colberg, Germany. 54N. 15E. 76
*Colchester, England. 52N. 1E. 57
Coldingham, Scotland. 56N 2W 65
Coldstream, Scotland. 56N. 2W. 65
Coleraine, Ireland. 55N. 7W. 67
*Coll, Scotland. 57N 7W. 64
Coll, Passage of, Scotland. 57N. 6W. 62
Collieston, Scotland. 57N 2W. 63
Collioure, France. 43N. 3E. 73
Collon, Ireland. 54N 6W. 67
Collooney, Ireland. 54N. 8W. 66
Colmar, Germany. 48N. 7E. 77
Coln R., England. 52N. 2W 56
Colne, England 54N. 2W 54
Colne, R., England. 51N. 1W 57
*Cologne, Germany. 51N. 6E 76
Colon Mt., Switzerland. 46N. 7E. 86
Colonna C., Italy. 39N. 17E. 81
Colonsay, Scotland. 56N. 6W. 64
Colonsay, Passage of, Scotland. 56N. 6W. 64
Colorno, Italy. 45N. 10E. 82
Columbretes, Spain 40N. 1E. 85
Colwyn, Wales. 53N. 4W. 54
Comask, Scotland. 57N. 6W. 62
Comber, Ireland. 55N. 6W. 67
Combin Mt., Switzerland. 46N. 7E. 86
Comeragh Mts, Ireland. 52N. 8W. 69
Comero, Mt., Italy. 44N. 12E. 83
Comino, C., Sardinia. 41N. 10E. 81
Como, Italy. 46N. 9E. 82
Como, L. di, Italy. 46N. 9E. 82
*Compiègne, France. 50N. 3E. 73
Comrie, Scotland. 56N. 4W 65
Condom, France. 44N. 0E. 72
Cone, France. 47N. 3E. 73
Conegliano, Italy 46N 12E. 83
Cong, Ireland. 54N. 9W. 66
Congleton, England. 53N. 2W. 54
*Coniston L., England. 54N. 3W. 54
Conn, Lough, Ireland. 54N 9W. 66
Connaught, Ireland. 54N. 9W. 66
Connemara, Ireland. 54N. 10W. 66
Constadt, Germany. 51N. 18E. 75
*Constance, Switzerland. 48N 9E. 87
Constance, L. of, Switzerland. 48N. 9E. 87
*Constantinople, Turkey. 41N. 28E. 95
Constantza, Roumania. 44N. 29E 94
Conthey, Switzerland. 46N 7E. 86
Contrexéville, France. 48N. 6E. 73
Conway, Wales. 53N. 4W. 54
Conway R., Wales. 53N. 4W. 54
Cookstown, Ireland 55N. 7W. 67
Coolaney, Ireland. 54N. 9W. 66
Coolgreany, Ireland. 53N 6W. 69
Cootehill, Ireland 54N 7W. 67
Copeland Is., Ireland. 55N. 6W. 67
*Copenhagen, Denmark. 56N. 12E. 89
Copinshay Is., Scotland. 59N. 3W. 63

PAGE

Coppenburg, Germany. 53N. 7E. 76
*Coppet, Switzerland. 46N 6E. 86
Coquet Is., England. 55N. 1w. 55
Coquet, R., England. 55N. 2w. 55
Carabid, Roumania. 44N. 24E. 94
Corato, Italy. 41N. 16E. 81
Corbeil, France. 49N. 2E. 73
Corbières, Switzerland. 47N. 7E. 86
Corby, England. 53N. 1w. 55
*Cordova, Spain. 38N. 5w. 84
Corfu Is , Greece. 40N. 20E. 95
Coria, Spain. 40N 6w. 84
*Corinth, Greece. 38N. 23E. 95
Corinth Gulf, Greece. 38N. 23E. 95
*Cork, Ireland. 52N 8w. 68
Cork Harbour, Ireland. 52N 8w. 68
Corleone, Sicily. 38N. 13E. 81
Cormons, Italy. 46N. 13E. 83
Corneto, Italy. 42N. 12E. 83
Cornia, R., Italy. 43N. 11E. 82
Corno, Mt , Italy. 42N. 13E. 83
Cornwall, England. 50N. 5w. 56
Correze, France. 45N. 2E. 73
Corrib, Lough, Ireland. 53N 9w. 66
Corrofin, Ireland 53N. 9w. 68
Corsewell Pt., Scotland. 55N. 5w. 64
*Corsica, France. 42N. 9E. 80
Corso, C., Corsica 43N 9E 80
Corsoer, Denmark. 55N. 11E. 89
Corte, Corsica. 42N. 9E. 80
Cortona, Italy. 43N. 12E. 83
*Corunna, Spain. 43N. 8w. 84
Coryvreckan, G. of, Scotland. 56N. 6w. 64
*Cosenza, Italy. 39N. 16E. 81
Cöslin, Germany. 54N. 16E. 75
Cossonay, Switzerland 47N. 7E. 86
Cote d'Or, France. 48N. 5E. 73
Cotes du Nord, France. 48N. 3w. 72
Cotrone, Italy. 39N. 17E. 81
Cotswold Hills, England. 52N. 2w. 56
Cottian Alps, Italy. 45N. 7E. 82
Coupar Angus, Scotland. 57N. 3w. 63
Courland, Russia. 57N. 23E. 90
Courmayeur, Italy 46N. 7E 82
Courtelary, Switzerland. 47N. 7E. 86
Courtmacsherry, Ireland. 52N. 9w. 68
Courtmacsherry B., Ireland. 52N. 9w. 68
*Courtrai, Belgium. 51N. 3E. 71
Coutances, France. 49N. 1w. 72
Couvin, Belgium. 50N 4E. 71
*Coventry, England. 52N. 2w. 57
Covilha, Portugal. 40N. 7w. 84
Cowbridge, Wales. 51N. 3w. 56
*Cowes, England. 51N. 1w. 57
*Cracow, Austria. 50N. 20E. 79
Craiguenamanagh, Ireland. 53N. 7w. 69
Craignish, Loch, Scotland. 56N. 6w. 64
Crail, Scotland. 56N. 3w. 65
Cranborne, England. 51N. 2w. 56
Cranbrook, England 51N. 1E. 57
Crarae, Scotland. 56N. 5w. 64
Crathie, Scotland. 57N. 3w. 63
Crati, R., Italy. 40N. 17E. 81

Craughwell, Ireland. 53N. 9w. 68
Crediton, England. 51N. 4w. 56
Cree, R., Scotland. 55N. 4w 64
Creetown, Scotland. 55N. 4w. 65
*Crefeld, Germany. 51N. 6E. 76
Crema, Italy. 45N. 10E. 82
*Cremona, Italy. 45N. 10E. 82
Creran, Loch, Scotland. 57N. 5w. 64
*Cressy, France. 50N 2E. 73
Crete Is., Mediterranean. 35N. 25E. 95
Creuse, France. 46N. 2E. 73
Creuse, C., Spain. 42N. 3E. 85
Creuse, R., France. 47N. 1E. 72
Creux, C., Spain. 42N. 3E. 73
Crewe, England. 53N. 2w. 54
Crewkerne, England 51N. 3w. 56
Crianlarich, Scotland. 56N 5w. 64
Criccieth, Wales. 53N. 4w. 54
Crickhowel, Wales. 52N. 3w. 56
Cricklade, England. 52N. 2w. 56
Crieff, Scotland. 56N. 4w. 65
Criffell, Scotland. 55N. 4w. 65
*Crimea, Russia. 45N. 34E. 91
Croagh Patrick, Ireland. 54N. 10w. 66
Croatia, Hungary. 45N 16E. 78
Croix, Is., France. 48N 3w. 72
Cromarty, Scotland. 58N. 4w. 63
Cromarty Firth, Scotland. 58N. 4w. 63
Cromer, England. 53N. 1E. 55
Crookhaven, Ireland. 51N. 10w. 68
Croom, Ireland. 53N. 9w. 68
*Cropredy Bridge, England. 52N. 1w. 57
Cross Fell, England. 55N. 2w. 54
Crossgar, Ireland. 54N. 6w. 67
Crosshaven, Ireland. 52N. 8w. 68
Crossmaglen, Ireland. 51N. 7w. 67
Crossmolina, Ireland. 54N. 9w. 66
Crow Head, Ireland. 52N. 10w. 68
Crowborough, England 51N. 0E. 57
Crowle, England. 54N. 1w. 55
Croydon, England. 51N. 0w. 57
Cruden B., Scotland. 57N. 2w. 63
Crumlin, Ireland. 55N 6w. 67
Crummock Water, England. 55N. 3w. 54
Crusheen, Ireland. 53N 9w. 68
Csaba, Hungary. 47N. 21E. 79
Csap, Hungary. 49N. 22E. 79
Csukas, Mt., Hungary. 46N. 26E. 79
Cuckfield, England. 51N. 0w. 57
Cudrefin, Switzerland. 47N. 7E. 86
Cuenca, Spain. 40N. 2w. 85
Cuevas, Spain. 37N. 2w. 85
Culcagh, Ireland. 54N. 8w. 67
Cuillin Hills, Scotland. 57N. 6w. 62
Cuillin Sd., Scotland. 57N. 6w. 62
Culenborg, Holland. 52N. 5E. 70
Cullen, Scotland. 58N. 3w. 63
Cullera, Spain. 39N. 0w. 85
*Culloden, Scotland. 57N. 4w 62
Cullompton, England. 51N. 3w. 56
Cully, Switzerland. 46N. 7E. 86
Culross, Scotland. 56N. 4w. 65
Culter, Scotland. 57N. 2w. 63
Cumberland, England. 55N 3w. 54

	PAGE
Cumbrian Mts., England. 55N. 3w.	54
Cumnock, Scotland. 55N. 4w.	65
Cuneo, Italy. 44N. 8E.	82
Cupar, Scotland. 56N. 3w.	65
Currane, Lough, Ireland. 52N. 10w.	68
Curraun Peninsula, Ireland. 54N. 10w.	66
Curry, Ireland. 54N. 9w.	66
Curzola Is., Austria. 43N. 17E.	94
Cushendall, Ireland. 55N. 6w.	67
Cushendun, Ireland. 55N. 6w.	67
*Custozza, Italy. 45N 11E.	83
Cüstrin, Germany. 52N. 15E.	75
Cuxhaven, Germany. 54N. 9E.	76
Cyclades, Greece. 37N. 25E.	95
Czegled, Hungary. 47N. 20E.	79
Czengrad, Hungary. 47N. 20E.	79
Czerna Gora, Mt., Austria. 48N. 25E.	79
Czernowitz, Austria. 48N. 26E.	79
Czibles, Hungary. 48N. 24E.	79
Daghestan, Russia. 42N 47E.	91
Dago, Russia. 59N. 22E.	90
Dahme, Germany. 52N. 13E.	76
Dailleul, France. 51N 3E.	73
Dakau, Roumania. 47N. 26E.	94
Dal Elf, Sweden. 60N. 17E.	89
Dal Elf, Sweden. 61N. 14E.	89
Dalbeattie, Scotland. 55N. 4w.	65
Dale-carlia, Sweden. 61N. 16E.	89
Dalen, Norway. 60N. 8E.	89
Dalkeith, Scotland. 56N. 3w.	65
Dalkey, Ireland. 53N. 6w.	67
Dalmally, Scotland. 56N. 5w.	64
Dalmellington, Scotland. 55N. 4w.	65
Dalry, Scotland. 56N 5w.	64
*Dalry, Scotland. 55N. 4w.	65
*Dalton, England. 54N. 3w.	54
Dalwhinnie, Scotland. 57N. 4w.	63
Damme, Belgium. 51N. 3E.	71
Dan, Lough, Ireland. 53N. 6w.	69
Dannemora, Sweden. 60N 18E.	89
Dannenberg, Germany. 53N. 11E.	76
Danube, Roumania. 45N. 29E.	94
Danun, Germany. 53N. 14E.	76
*Danzig, Germany. 54N. 19E.	75
Danzig, G. of, Germany. 55N. 19E.	75
*Dardanelles, The, Turkey. 40N 26E.	95
Dargle R., Ireland. 53N. 6w.	69
Darlington, England. 55N. 1w.	55
Darmstadt, Germany. 50N. 9E.	77
Daroca, Spain. 41N. 1w.	85
Dart, R., England. 50N. 4w.	56
Dartmoor Forest, England. 51N. 4w.	56
*Dartmouth, England 50N. 4w.	56
Darwen, Lower, England. 54N. 3w.	54
Daunt Rock Light Vessel, Ireland. 52N. 8w.	68
*Daventry, England. 52N. 1w.	57
Daviot, Scotland. 57N. 4w.	63
Davos Platz, Switzerland. 47N. 10E.	87

	PAGE
Dawlish, England. 51N. 3w.	56
Dawros Hd., Ireland. 55N. 9w.	66
Dax, France. 44N. 1w.	72
De Honde, Holland 51N. 4E.	71
De Krammer, Holland. 52N. 4E.	70
De Maas, Holland. 52N. 4E.	70
*Deal, England. 51N. 1E.	57
Deben, R., England. 52N. 1E.	57
Debenham, England. 52N. 1E.	57
Debreczin, Hungary 47N. 22E.	94
Dedeh Agatch, Turkey. 41N. 26E.	95
Dee, R., England. 53N. 3w.	54
Dee R., Ireland. 54N. 6w.	67
Dee, R., Scotland. 55N. 4w.	65
Dee, R., Scotland. 57N. 2w.	63
Deel, R., Ireland. 53N. 9w.	68
Deer Ness, Scotland 59N. 3w.	63
Dées, Hungary. 47N. 24E.	79
Deggendorf, Germany. 49N. 13E.	77
Dejuchin, Russia. 60N. 57E.	90
Delden, Holland. 52N. 7E.	70
Delémont, Switzerland 47N. 7E.	86
*Delft, Holland. 52N. 4E.	70
Delfzy, Holland. 53N 7E.	70
Delgany, Ireland. 53N. 6w.	69
Dellen L , Sweden. 62N 17E	89
†Delphi Mt , Greece. 39N. 24E.	95
Delvino, Turkey. 40N. 20E	95
Demmin, Germany. 54N. 13E.	76
Demonte, Italy. 44N. 7E	82
Demotika, Bulgaria. 42N. 26E.	91
Den Burg, Holland. 53N. 5E.	70
Denbigh, Wales. 53N. 3w.	54
Dender R , Belgium 51N. 4E.	71
Deneshkin Kamen, Russia. 61N. 60E.	90
Denholm, Scotland. 55N. 3w.	65
Denia, Spain. 39N. 0E.	85
Denny, Scotland. 56N. 4w.	65
Dent Blanche, Switzerland. 46N. 8E.	86
Dent du Midi, Switzerland. 46N. 7E.	86
Deptford, England. 51N. 0w.	57
Derbend, Russia. 42N. 48E.	91
*Derby, England. 53N. 1w.	55
Derevaragh, L , Ireland. 54N. 7w.	67
*Derg, L., Ireland. 55N. 8w.	66
Derg, R , Ireland. 55N. 8w.	67
Derrygonnelly, Ireland. 54N. 8w.	67
Derrynasaggart Mts., Ireland. 52N. 9w.	68
Derryveagh Mts., Ireland. 55N. 8w.	66
Dervock, Ireland. 55N. 6w.	67
Derwent R., England. 54N 0w.	55
Derwent, R., England. 53N 1w.	55
Derwent, R., England. 55N. 2w.	55
Derwent R., England. 55N. 4w.	54
Derwent Water, England. 55N. 3w.	54
Desna R., Russia. 52N. 32E.	91
Despoco-Dagh, Bulgaria. 42N.25E.	91
*Dessau, Germany. 52N. 12E.	76
Detmold, Germany. 52N. 9E.	76
Detra, Hungary. 49N. 20E.	79
*Deutsch Brod, Austria. 50N. 16E.	78
Deux Sevres, France. 47N. 0w.	72

PAGE

Deva, Hungary. 46N. 23E. 79
Deva, Spain. 43N. 2w. 85
*Deventer, Holland. 52N. 6E. 70
Deveron R., Scotland. 58N. 2w. 63
Devil's Bridge, Wales. 52N. 4w. 56
*Devizes, England. 51N. 2w. 56
Devon, England. 51N. 4w. 56
Devon R., Scotland. 56N. 4w. 65
Devonport, England. 50N. 4w. 56
Dewsbury, England. 54N. 2w. 55
Dhomoko, Greece. 39N. 22E. 95
Dhu Heartach, Scotland. 56N.
7w. 64
Dia Is., Crete. 35N. 25E. 95
Diakovar, Slavonia. 45N. 19E. 79
Diekirch, Luxemburg. 50N. 6E. 71
Diemel R., Germany. 52N. 9E. 76
Diepholz, Germany. 53N. 9E. 76
*Dieppe, France. 50N. 1E. 72
Diest, Belgium. 51N. 5E. 71
Dieu, Is., France. 47N. 2w. 72
Dievenow, Germany. 51N. 15E. 76
Dieze R., Holland. 52N. 5E. 70
Digne, France. 44N. 6E. 73
*Dijon, France. 47N. 5E. 73
Dimitrov, Russia. 57N. 38E. 90
*Dinan, France. 48N. 2w. 72
Dinant, Belgium. 50N. 5E. 71
Dinaric Alps, Austria. 44N. 16E 94
Dinas Mowddy, Wales. 53N. 4w. 54
Dingle, Ireland. 52N. 10w. 68
Dingle B., Ireland. 52N. 10w. 68
Dingwall, Scotland. 58N. 5w. 62
Dinkelsbühl, Bavaria. 49N. 10E. 77
*Dirleton, Scotland. 56N. 3w. 65
Dirschau, Germany. 54N. 18E. 75
Disentis, Switzerland. 47N. 9E. 87
Diss, England. 52N. 1E 57
Divra, Turkey. 42N. 20E. 94
Divre Mt., Ireland. 55N. 6w. 67
Dixmude, Belgium. 51N 3E. 71
Dnieper R., Russia. 47N. 32E. 91
*Dniester R., Russia. 47N. 30E. 91
Doagh, Ireland. 55N. 6w. 67
Döbeln, Germany. 51N. 13E. 76
Doberan, Germany. 54N. 12E. 76
Dobrudja, Roumania. 44N. 28E. 94
Dobshau, Hungary. 49N. 21E. 79
Dodder, R., Ireland 53N. 6w. 67
Dodman Pt., England. 50N. 5w. 56
Doesborgh, Holland. 52N. 6E 70
Doldenhorn, Switzerland. 46N. 8E. 86
Dole, France. 47N. 5E. 73
Dolgelly, Wales. 53N. 4w. 54
*Dollar, Scotland. 56N. 4w. 65
Dollart, The, Germany. 53N. 7E. 76
Dom, Switzerland. 46N. 8E. 86
Domen, Norway. 71N. 31E. 88
Domo d'Ossolo, Italy. 46N. 8E. 82
*Domremy, France. 48N. 6E. 73
Don R., England. 54N. 1w. 55
Don R., Russia. 47N. 39E. 91
Don, R., Scotland. 57N. 2w. 63
Don Benito, Spain. 39N. 6w. 84
Don Cossacks, Russia. 49N. 42E. 91
Donaghadee, Ireland. 55N. 6w. 67
Donauworth, Germany. 49N. 11E. 77
Doncaster, England. 54N. 1w. 55

PAGE

Donegal, Ireland. 55N. 8w. 66
Donegal B., Ireland. 55N. 8w. 66
Doneraile, Ireland. 52N. 9w. 68
Donington, England. 53N. 0w. 55
Donnaeso, Norway. 66N. 13E. 88
Donnaz, Italy. 46N. 8E. 82
Donoughmore, Ireland. 52N. 9w. 68
Doogort, Ireland. 54N. 10w. 66
Doo Lough, Ireland. 54N. 10w. 66
*Doonbeg, Ireland. 53N. 10w. 68
Doon, Loch, Scotland. 55N. 4w. 65
Doon, R., Scotland. 55N. 5w. 64
Dora Baltea R., Italy. 45N 9E. 82
Dora Repairo R., Italy. 45N. 7E. 82
*Dorchester, England. 51N. 2w. 56
Dordogne, France. 45N. 1E. 72
Dordogne, R., France. 45N. 0w. 72
Dordogne, R., France. 45N. 2E. 73
Dordrecht, Holland. 52N. 5E. 70
Dore, Mt., France. 46N. 3E. 73
Doriah, Turkey. 41N. 23E. 95
*Dorking, England. 51N. 0w. 57
Dormitor, Montenegro. 43N. 19E. 94
Dornaas, Norway. 62N. 9E. 89
Dornbirn, Austria. 47N. 10E. 78
Dornoch, Scotland. 58N. 4w. 63
Dornoch Firth, Scotland. 58N. 4w.63
Dorohoi, Roumania. 48N. 27E. 94
Dorpat Yuryev, Russia. 58N. 28E. 90
Dorset, England. 51N. 2w. 56
Dortmund, Germany. 52N. 8E. 76
Douarnenez B., France. 48N. 5w. 72
*Douay, France. 50N. 3E. 73
Doubs, France. 47N 6E. 73
Doubs, R., France. 47N 5E. 73
*Douglas, Scotland. 56N. 4w. 65
Douglas, Isle of Man. 54N. 5w. 54
Douglas W., Scotland. 56N. 4w. 65
*Doune, Scotland. 56N. 4w. 65
Dour, Belgium. 50N. 4E. 71
Douro, Portugal. 41N. 8w. 84
*Douro, R., Portugal. 41N. 9w. 84
*Dove, R., England. 53N. 2w. 55
*Dover, England. 51N. 1E. 57
Dover, Strait of, England. 51N.
1E. 57
Dovey, R., Wales. 53N. 4w. 56
Dovre Fjeld, Norway. 62N. 9E. 89
Dowlais, Wales. 52N. 3w. 56
Down, Ireland. 54N. 6w. 67
Downham Market, England. 53N.
0E. 57
*Downpatrick, Ireland. 54N. 6w. 67
Downpatrick Hd., Ireland. 54N.
9w. 66
*Downs, The, England. 51N. 1E. 57
Dragten, Holland. 53N. 6E. 70
Draguignan, France. 44N. 6E. 73
Drama, Turkey. 41N. 24E. 95
Drammen, Norway. 60N. 10E. 89
Drammen R , Norway. 60N. 10E. 89
Drau R., Austria. 46N. 17E. 94
Dranse R., Switzerland. 46N. 7E 86
Draperstown, Ireland. 55N. 7w. 67
Drave R., Hungary. 46N. 17E. 94
Drenthe, Holland. 53N. 7E. 70
*Dresden, Germany. 51N. 14E. 76
*Dreux, France. 49N. 1E. 72

H

PAGE

Drewenz, Germany. 53N. 19E.　75
Drimoleague, Ireland. 52N. 9w.　68
Drin, R., Turkey. 42N. 20E.　94
Drina R., Bosnia. 45N. 19E.　94
*Drogheda, Ireland. 54N. 6w.　67
Drohobycz, Austria. 49N. 24E.　79
Droitwich, England. 52N. 2w.　56
Dromara, Ireland. 54N. 6w.　67
Dromcolliher, Ireland. 52N. 9w.　68
Drome, France. 45N. 5E.　73
Drome, R., France. 45N. 0w.　72
Drome, R., France. 45N. 5E.　73
*Dromore, Ireland. 54N. 6w.　67
Dromore, Ireland. 55N. 7w.　67
Dromore, Ireland. 54N. 9w.　66
Dronfield, England. 53N. 1w.　55
Drontheim, Norway. 63N. 11E.　88
Drontheim Fd., Norway. 63N.10E.　88
Drumahaire, Ireland. 54N. 8w.　66
Drumburg, Germany. 54N. 16E.　75
Drumcliff, Ireland. 54N. 8w.　66
Druminn, Ireland. 55N. 8w.　66
Drumkeeran, Ireland 54N. 8w　66
Drumlish, Ireland. 54N. 8w.　67
Drumlithie, Scotland. 57N. 2w　63
*Drummelzier, Scotland. 56N. 3w.　65
Drummer, Germany. 53N. 8E.　76
Drumquin, Ireland. 55N. 8w.　67
Drumshanbo, Ireland. 54N. 8w.　67
*Dryburgh Abbey, Scotland. 56N.
　3w.　65
Drymen, Scotland. 56N. 4w.　64
*Dublin, Ireland. 53N. 6w.　67
Dublin B., Ireland. 53N. 6w.　67
Dubooka, Russia. 49N. 45E.　91
*Duddon, R., England. 54N. 3w.　54
Dudley, England. 53N. 2w.　56
Dufftown, Scotland. 57N. 3w.　63
Duich, Loch, Scotland. 57N. 5w.　62
Duisburg, Germany. 52N. 6E　76
Dukinfield, England. 53N. 2w.　54
Dulcigno, Montenegro. 42N. 19E　94
Duleek, Ireland. 54N. 6w.　67
Dulnan, R., Scotland. 57N. 4w.　63
Dulverton, England. 51N. 4w.　56
*Dumbarton, Scotland. 56N. 5w.　64
*Dumfries, Scotland. 55N. 3w.　65
Dunaburg, Russia. 56N. 27E.　90
Dunajec R., Austria. 50N. 21E.　79
Dunany Pt., Ireland. 54N. 6w.　67
*Dunbar, Scotland. 56N. 3w　65
Dunbeath, Scotland. 58N. 3w.　63
Dunblane, Scotland. 56N. 4w.　65
Dunboyne, Ireland. 53N. 6w.　67
Duncansbay Hd., Scotland. 59N.
　3w.　63
Duncormick, Ireland. 52N. 7w.　69
*Dundalk, Ireland. 54N. 6w.　67
Dundalk B., Ireland. 54N. 6w.　67
*Dundee, Scotland. 56N. 3w.　65
Dundrum, Ireland. 54N. 6w.　67
Dundrum B., Ireland. 54N. 6w.　67
*Dunfermline, Scotland. 56N. 3w.　65
*Dungannon, Ireland. 55N. 7w　67
Dungarvan, Ireland. 52N. 8w.　69
Dungarvan Harbour, Ireland.
　52N. 8w.　69
Dungeness, England. 51N. 1E.　57

PAGE

Dungiven, Ireland. 55N. 7w.　67
Dunglow, Ireland. 55N. 8w.　66
*Dunkeld, Scotland. 57N. 4w.　63
Dunkerry Beacon, England. 51N.
　4w.　56
*Dunkirk, France. 56N. 2E.　73
Dunleer, Ireland. 54N. 6w.　67
Dunlavin, Ireland. 53N. 7w.　69
Dunlop, Scotland. 56N. 5w.　64
Dunloy, Ireland. 67N. 6w.　67
Dunmanus B., Ireland. 52N. 10w.　68
Dunmanway, Ireland. 52N. 9w.　68
Dunmore, Ireland. 52N. 7w.　69
Dunmore, Ireland. 54N. 9w.　66
Dunmore Hd., Ireland. 52N. 10w.　68
*Dunmow, England. 52N. 0E.　57
Dunnet, Scotland. 59N. 3w.　63
Dunnet B., Scotland. 59N. 3w　63
Dunnet Hd., Scotland. 59N. 3w.　63
Dunning, Scotland. 56N. 4w.　65
Dunnottar Castle, Scotland. 57N
　2w.　63
Dunoon, Scotland. 56N 5w.　64
Dunranagh, Ireland. 55N. 8w.　66
Dunrobin Castle, Scotland. 58N.
　4w.　63
Duns, Scotland. 56N. 2w.　65
Dunscore, Scotland. 55N. 4w.　65
Dunshaughlin, Ireland. 53N. 7w.　67
*Dunstable, England. 52N. 1w.　57
Dunstanborough Castle, England.
　56N. 2w.　55
Dunster, England. 51N. 3w　56
Dunvegan Loch, Scotland. 58N.
　7w.　62
Durance, R., France. 44N 5E.　73
Duratch, Turkey. 41N. 19E.　95
*Durazzo, Turkey. 41N. 19E.　95
Durbuy, Belgium. 50N. 5E.　71
Duren, Germany. 51N. 6E.　77
Durham, England. 55N. 2w.　55
Durness, Scotland. 59N. 5w.　62
Durrow, Ireland. 53N. 7w.　69
Dursey Is., Ireland. 52N 10w.　68
Dursley, England. 52N. 2w　56
*Dusseldorf, Germany. 52N. 6E.　76
*Dvina R., Russia. 64N. 41E.　90
Dyce, Scotland. 57N. 2w.　63
Dyle, R., Belgium. 51N 5E.　71
Dysart, Scotland. 56N. 3w.　65

Eagle Is., Ireland. 54w. 10w.　66
Earlston, Scotland. 56N. 3w.　65
Earn, L., Scotland. 56N. 4w.　65
Earn R., Scotland. 56N. 4w.　65
Eask, Lough, Ireland. 55N. 8w.　66
Easky, Ireland. 54N. 9w.　66
East Beskiden, Austria. 49N. 22E.　79
East Dereham, England. 53N. 1E　57
East Flanders, Belgium. 51N. 4E　71
East Friesian Is., Germany. 54N.
　7E.　76
East Kilbride, Scotland. 56N 4w.　65
East Linton, Scotland. 56N 3w.　65
East Retford, England. 53N. 1w.　55
East Riding, Yorkshire. 54N. 1w.　55
Eastbourne, England. 51N. 0E.　57
Eastleigh, England. 51N. 1w.　57

PAGE

Easter Schelde, Holland. 52N. 4E. 70
Eastern Roumelia, Bulgaria. 42N.
  26E. 94
Eaux Vives, Switzerland. 46N. 6E.46
Eberswalde, Germany. 53N. 14E. 76
Ebingen, Germany. 48N. 9E. 77
Ebnat, Switzerland. 47N. 9E. 87
Ebro, R., Spain. 41N. 1E. 85
Ecclefechan, Scotland. 55N. 3W. 65
Eccleshall, England. 53N. 2W. 54
Echallens, Switzerland. 47N. 7E. 86
Ecija, Spain. 38N. 5W. 84
Ecloo, Belgium. 51N. 4E. 71
Edam, Holland. 53N. 5E. 70
Eday Is., Scotland. 59N. 3W. 63
Edderton, Scotland. 58N. 4W. 63
Eddrachilles B., Scotland. 58N. 4W.62
*Eddystone Lighthouse, England.
  50N. 4W. 56
Eden, R., England. 55N. 3W. 54
Eden, R., Scotland. 56N. 3W. 65
Edenburg, Germany. 51N. 13E. 76
Edenderry, Ireland. 53N. 7W. 67
Eder R., Germany. 51N. 9E. 76
Ederny, Ireland. 55N. 8W. 67
*Edge Hill, England. 52N. 1W. 57
*Edgeworthstown, Ireland. 54N.8W.67
*Edinburgh, Scotland. 56N. 3W. 65
Edinkillie, Scotland. 57N. 4W. 63
Edirne, Turkey. 42N. 27E. 94
Edzell, Scotland. 57N. 3W. 63
Effretikon, Switzerland. 47N. 9E. 87
*Eger, Hungary. 50N. 12E. 78
Eger, R., Austria. 50N. 13E. 78
Eglisau, Switzerland. 48N. 9E. 87
*Egremont, England. 54N. 4W. 54
Egripos, Greece. 38N. 24E. 95
Eibenschitz, Austria 49N. 16E. 78
Eichstadt, Germany. 49N. 11E. 77
Eider R., Germany. 54N. 9E. 76
Eidsvold, Norway 60N. 11E. 89
Eifel, Germany. 50N. 7E. 77
Eiger, Switzerland. 47N. 8E 86
*Eigg Is., Scotland. 57N. 6W. 62
Eil Loch, Scotland. 57N. 5W. 62
Embeck, Germany. 52N. 10E 76
Eindhove, Holland. 51N. 5E. 71
Einfisch Th., Switzerland. 46N.
  8E. 86
*Einsiedeln, Switzerland. 47N. 9E. 87
*Eisenach, Germany. 51N. 10E. 76
Eisenerz, Austria 48N. 15E. 78
Eishort, L., Scotland. 57N. 6W. 62
*Eisleben, Germany. 52N. 11E. 76
Ejea, Spain. 42N. 1W. 85
Ekaterinburg, Russia. 57N. 61E. 90
Ekaterinodar, Russia. 51N. 39E. 91
Ekaterinoslav, Russia. 48N. 35E. 91
Ekersund, Norway. 58N. 6E. 89
Elanchove, Spain. 43N. 3W. 85
*Elba Is., Italy. 43N. 10E. 82
Elbassan, Turkey. 41N. 20E. 95
Elbe R., Germany. 54N. 9E. 76
Elberfeld, Germany. 51N. 7E. 76
Elbeuf, France. 49N. 1E. 72
Elbing, Germany. 54N. 19E. 75
Elbrus, Russia. 43N. 43E. 91
Elburg, Holland. 52N. 6E. 70

PAGE

Elche, Spain. 38N. 1W. 85
Elde R., Germany. 53N. 12E. 76
Elets, Russia. 53N. 33E. 91
Elfros, Sweden. 62N. 15E. 89
Elgin, Scotland. 58N. 3W. 63
Elie, Scotland. 56N. 3W. 65
Elizabetgrad, Russia. 48N. 32E. 91
Elizabethpol, Russia. 41N. 46E. 91
Elland, England. 54N. 2W. 54
Ellesmere, England. 53N. 3W. 54
Ellon, Scotland. 57N. 2W. 63
Ellwangen, Germany. 49N. 10E 77
Elmsharn, Germany. 54N. 11E. 76
Elphin, Ireland. 54N. 8W. 66
Elsfleth, Germany. 53N. 8E. 76
*Elsinore, Denmark. 56N. 12E. 89
Elster R., Germany. 51N. 12E. 76
Elvas, Portugal. 39N. 7W. 84
*Ely, England. 52N. 0E. 57
Emden, Germany. 53N. 8E. 76
Emilia, Italy. 45N. 11E. 83
Emlagh Pt., Ireland. 54N. 10W. 66
Emmenthal, Switzerland. 47N. 8E.86
Empoli, Italy. 44N. 11E. 83
Ems, Germany. 50N. 8E. 77
Ems R., Germany. 53N. 7E. 76
Emyvale, Ireland. 54N. 7W. 67
Enara L., Russia 69N. 29E. 90
Enard B., Scotland. 58N. 5W. 62
*Enfield, England. 52N. 0E 57
Engadin, Switzerland. 47N. 11E. 78
Engelberg, Switzerland. 47N. 8E. 87
Enghien, Belgium. 51N. 4E. 71
English Channel, England. 50N.
  2W. 56
Enkhuizen, Holland. 53N. 5E. 70
Enköping, Sweden. 60N. 17E 89
Ennell Lough, Ireland. 53N. 7W. 67
Ennis, Ireland. 53N. 9W. 68
*Enniscorthy, Ireland. 53N. 7W. 69
*Enniskillen, Ireland. 54N. 8W. 67
Ennistimon, Ireland. 53N. 9W. 68
Enns, Austria. 48N. 14E. 78
Enos, Turkey. 41N. 26E. 95
Enschede, Holland. 62N. 7E. 70
Entlebuch, Switzerland. 47N. 8E. 86
Entre Douro e Mino, Portugal.
  42N. 8W. 84
Entrecamiento, Portugal. 39N.
  8W. 84
Enz R., Germany. 49N. 9E. 77
Enza R., Italy. 45N. 10E. 82
Eperies, Hungary. 49N. 21E. 79
*Epernay, France. 49N. 4E. 73
Epinal, France. 48N. 7E. 73
Epirus, Turkey. 39N. 20E. 95
Epsom, England. 51N. 0W. 57
Erba, Italy. 46N. 9E. 82
Erding, Germany. 48N. 12E. 77
*Erfurt, Germany. 51N. 11E. 76
Ergene R., Turkey. 42N. 27E. 94
Eriboll Loch, Scotland. 59N. 5W. 62
Ericht Loch, Scotland. 57N. 4W.63
Ericht Water, Scotland. 57N. 3W. 63
Erisa Loch, Scotland. 57N. 6W. 62
Erisort Loch, Scotland. 58N. 6W. 62
Erivan, Russia. 40N. 44E. 91
Erlach, Switzerland. 47N. 7E. 86

PAGE

Erlangen, Germany. 50N. 11E. 77
Erlau, Hungary. 48N. 20E. 79
Erne L., Ireland. 55N. 8w. 67
Erne, R., Ireland. 54N. 7w. 67
Erne R., Ireland. 55N. 8w. 66
Erne, Upper Lough, Ireland. 54N.
  8w. 67
Erriff R., Ireland. 54N. 10w. 66
Errigal, Ireland. 55N. 8w. 66
Erris Hd., Ireland. 54N. 10w. 66
Errol, Scotland. 56N. 3w. 65
Erz Gebirge, Germany. 51N. 13E.77
Esbjerg, Denmark. 56N. 8E. 89
Escalona, Spain. 40N. 4w. 84
Escatron, Spain. 41N. 0w. 85
Escaut R., Belgium. 51N. 4E. 71
Esch, Luxemburg. 50N 6E. 71
Eschwege, Germany. 51N. 10E. 76
Escorial, Spain. 41N. 4w. 84
Esino R., Italy. 44N. 13E 83
Esk R., England. 54N 1w. 55
Esk R., England. 54N. 3w. 54
Esk, R., Scotland. 55N. 3w. 65
Esk R., North, Scotland. 57N. 2w. 63
Esk R., South, Scotland. 57N. 3w. 63
Eski-djuma, Bulgaria. 43N. 27E.94
Eski-Saghra, Bulgaria. 43N. 26E.94
Eskilstuna, Sweden. 59N. 17E. 89
Esla R., Spain. 42N. 6w. 84
Espichel C., Portugal. 38N. 9w. 84
Essek, Slavonia. 45N. 19E. 79
Essen, Germany. 52N. 7E. 76
Esslingen, Germany. 49N. 9E. 77
Estaca de Vares, Pt., Spain. 44N.
  8w. 84
*Estella, Spain. 43N. 2w. 85
Estepona, Spain. 36N. 5w. 84
Esthonia, Russia. 59N. 25E. 90
Estrada, Spain. 43N. 8w. 84
Estremadura, Portugal. 39N. 9w.84
Estremadura, Spain. 39N. 6w. 84
Estremoz, Portugal. 39N. 7w. 84
*Etampes, France. 49N. 2E. 73
Etive L., Scotland. 56N. 5w. 64
Etna Mt., Sicily. 38N. 15E. 81
Eton, England. 52N. 1w 57
Etruscan Apennines, Italy. 44N.
  11E. 83
Etsch R., Austria. 46N. 11E. 78
*Ettrick Pen., Scotland. 55N. 3w. 65
Ettrick Water, Scotland. 55N. 3w. 65
Euboea, Greece. 38N. 24E. 95
Euganei, Colli, Italy. 45N. 12E. 83
Eure, France. 49N. 1E. 72
Eure R., France. 49N. 1E. 72
Eure-et-Loir, France. 48N. 1E. 72
Europa Pt., Spain. 36N. 5w. 84
Eutin, Germany. 54N. 11E. 76
Evanton, Scotland. 58N. 4w. 63
Evenlode R., England. 52N. 2w. 57
*Evesham, England. 52N. 2w. 56
*Evora, Portugal. 39N. 8w. 84
*Evreux, France. 49N. 1E. 72
Ewe L., Scotland. 58N. 6w. 62
Exe R., England. 51N. 3w. 56
Exeter, England. 51N. 4w. 56
*Exmoor Forest, England. 51N. 4w. 56
Exmouth, England. 51N. 3w. 56

PAGE

Eye, England. 52N. 1E. 57
Eye Pen., Scotland. 58N. 6w. 62
Eyemouth, Scotland 56N. 2w. 65
Eynort L., Scotland. 57N. 7w. 62
Eyrecourt, Ireland. 53N. 8w. 69

Faa Fd., Norway. 62N. 5E. 89
Fabriano, Italy. 43N. 13E. 83
Faedis, Italy. 46N. 13E. 83
Fœmund L., Norway. 62N. 12E. 89
*Faenza, Italy. 44N 12E. 83
Fahlun, Sweden. 61N. 16E. 89
Faido, Switzerland. 46N. 9E. 87
Fair Hd., Ireland. 55N. 6w. 67
Fair Is., Scotland. 60N. 2w. 63
Fairford, England. 52N. 2w. 56
Fairlie, Scotland. 56N. 5w. 64
Fakenham, England. 53N. 1E. 55
*Falaise, France. 49N. 0w. 72
Falconara, Italy. 44N. 13E. 83
Falkenberg, Germany. 52N. 13E. 76
Falkingham, England. 53N. 0w. 55
*Falkirk, Scotland. 56N. 4w. 65
*Falkland, Scotland. 56N. 3w. 65
Fall of Foyers, Scotland. 57N. 4w 63
Falls of Clyde, Scotland. 56N. 4w. 65
Falmouth, England. 50N. 5w. 56
Falmouth B., England. 50N. 5w. 56
Falster, Denmark. 55N 12E. 89
Falterona Mt., Italy. 44N. 12E. 83
Famund Lake, Norway. 62N. 12E. 89
Fanad Hd., Ireland. 55N. 8w. 67
Fane R., Ireland. 54N. 6w. 67
Fannich Loch, Scotland. 58N. 5w. 62
*Fano, Italy. 44N. 13E. 83
Fano Is., Turkey. 40N. 19E. 95
Faringdon, England. 52N. 2w. 57
Farland, Ireland. 55N 7w. 67
Farnborough, England. 51N. 1w. 57
*Farnham, England. 51N. 1w. 57
Farne Is., England. 56N. 2w. 55
Faro, Portugal. 37N. 8w. 84
Farr Pt., Scotland. 59N. 4w. 63
Farsund, Norway. 58N. 7E. 89
Fastnet Lighthouse, Ireland. 51N.
  10w. 68
Faulhorn, Switzerland. 47N. 8E. 86
Faversham, England. 51N. 1E. 57
Favignana, Sicily. 38N. 12E. 81
Feale R., Ireland. 52N. 10w. 68
Fécamp, France. 50N. 0E. 72
Feeagh Lough, Ireland. 54N. 10w. 66
Fehmern, Germany. 54N. 11E. 76
Fehrbellin, Germany. 53N. 13E. 76
Felanitx, Majorca. 39N. 3E. 85
Feld Berg, Germany. 48N. 8E. 77
*Feldkirch, Austria. 47N. 10E. 78
Felegyhaza, Hungary. 47N. 20E. 79
Fels, Luxemburg. 50N. 6E. 71
Fels Berg, Germany. 50N. 9E. 77
Felixstowe, England. 52N. 1E. 57
Feltre, Italy. 46N. 12E. 83
Fenit, Ireland. 52N. 10w. 68
Fenny Compton,England. 52N.1w. 57
Fens Fd , Norway. 61N. 5E. 89
Ferbane, Ireland. 53N. 8w. 67
Ferentino, Italy. 42N. 13E. 83
Fergus R., Ireland. 53N. 9w. 68

	PAGE
Ferintosh, Scotland. 58N. 4W.	63
Fermanagh, Ireland. 51N. 8W.	67
Ferno, Italy. 43N. 14E.	83
Fermont, Switzerland. 47N. 10E.	87
Fermoselle, Spain. 41N. 6W.	84
Fermoy, Ireland. 52N. 8W.	68
*Ferney, Switzerland. 46N. 6E.	86
Ferns, Ireland. 53N. 6W.	69
*Ferrara, Italy. 45N. 12E.	83
*Ferrol, Spain. 44N. 8W.	84
Festiniog, Wales. 53N. 4W.	54
Fethard, Ireland. 52N. 7W.	69
Fethard, Ireland. 52N. 8W.	69
Fetlar Is., Scotland. 60N. 1W.	63
Fetter-cairn, Scotland. 57N. 3W.	63
Feuerstein, Switzerland. 47N. 8E.	86
Fiarenzuola, Italy. 45N. 10E.	82
Fichtel Gebirge, Germany. 50N. 12E.	77
Fidra Lighthouse, Scotland. 56N. 3W.	65
Fife, Scotland. 56N. 3W.	65
Fife Ness, Scotland. 56N. 3W.	65
Figeac, France. 45N. 2E.	73
Figueras, Spain. 42N. 3E.	85
Figueira, Portugal. 40N. 9W.	84
Filey, England. 54N. 0W.	55
Filias, Roumania. 45N. 24E.	94
Fihcuri Is., Italy 39N. 15E.	81
Finale, Italy. 45N. 11E.	83
Finale Borgo, Italy. 44N. 8E.	82
Findhorn, Scotland. 58N. 4W.	63
Findhorn R., Scotland. 58N. 4W.	63
Findon, Scotland. 57N. 2W.	63
Finistère, France. 48N. 4W.	72
*Finisterre, C., Spain. 43N. 9W.	84
Finland, Russia. 64N. 25E.	90
Finland G. of, Russia. 60N. 25E.	90
Finn R., Ireland. 55N. 8W.	66
Finow Canal, Germany. 53N. 14E.	76
Finst, Switzerland. 47N. 8E.	86
Fintona, Ireland. 55N. 7W.	67
Firth of Forth, Scotland. 56N. 3W.	65
Firth of Tay, Scotland. 56N. 3W.	65
Fishguard, Wales. 52N. 5W.	56
Fiume, Austria. 45N. 14E.	78
Fiumicino, Italy. 42N. 12E.	83
Five Mile Town, Ireland. 54N.7W.	67
Fladdachuan Is.,Scotland. 58N.6W.	62
Flamatt, Switzerland. 47N. 7E.	86
Flamborough Hd., England. 54N. 0W.	55
Fleet Loch, Scotland. 58N. 4W.	63
Flekkcfjord, Norway. 58N. 6E.	89
Flensburg, Germany. 55N. 9E.	74
Flesk R., Ireland. 52N. 10W.	68
Fletschhorn, Switzerland. 46N. 8E.	86
*Flint, Wales. 53N. 3W.	54
*Flodden, England. 56N. 2W.	54
*Florence, Italy 44N. 11E.	83
Flotta Is., Scotland. 59N. 3W.	63
Fluchth, Switzerland. 47N. 10E.	87
Fluela Pass, Switzerland. 47N. 10E.	87
Fluelen, Switzerland. 47N. 9E.	87
Flühen, Switzerland. 47N. 7E.	86
Flumendosa, Sardinia. 39N. 10E.	81
*Flushing, Holland. 51N. 4E.	71
Fochabers, Scotland. 58N. 3W.	63
Fogaras, Hungary. 46N. 25E.	79
*Foggia, Italy. 41N. 16E.	80
Foinaven, Scotland. 58N. 5W.	62
Foix, France. 43N. 1E.	72
Fokshany, Roumania. 46N. 27E.	94
Folden Fd., Norway. 65N. 11E.	88
Földvar D., Hungary. 47N 19E.	79
Folge Pond, Norway. 60N. 7E.	89
Foligno, Italy. 43N. 13E.	83
Folkestone, England. 51N. 1E.	57
Follonica, Italy. 43N. 11E.	83
Folticheni, Roumania. 48N. 26E.	94
*Fontainebleau, France. 48N. 3E.	73
Fontana, Italy. 46N. 13E.	83
*Fontenay-le-Comte, France. 47N. 1W.	72
Fonzaso, Italy. 47N. 12E.	83
Forbach, Germany. 49N. 7E.	77
Forchheim, Germany. 50N. 11E.	77
Förde Fd., Norway. 62N. 5E.	89
Fordingbridge, England. 51N. 2W.	56
Fordon, Germany. 53N. 19E.	75
Foreland, The, England. 51N. 4W.	56
Forest of Harris, Scotland. 58N. 7W.	62
Forfar, Scotland. 57N. 3W.	63
*Forli, Italy. 44N. 12E.	83
Forlimpopoli, Italy. 44N. 12E.	83
Formby, England. 54N. 3W.	54
Formby Hd., England. 54N. 3W.	54
Formentera Balearic Is., 39N. 1E.	85
Formica Is., Italy. 42N. 10E.	82
*Fornovo, Italy. 45N. 10E.	82
*Forres, Scotland. 58N. 4W.	63
Forst, Germany. 52N. 14E.	76
Fort Augustus, Scotland. 57N. 5W.	62
Fort Bard, Italy. 46N. 8E.	82
Fort George, Scotland. 58N. 4W.	63
Fort William, Scotland. 57N. 5W.	62
Forth R., Scotland. 56N. 4W.	65
Fortrose, Scotland. 58N. 4W.	63
*Fossano, Italy. 45N. 8E.	82
Fossombrane, Italy. 44N. 13E.	83
Fotcha, Turkey. 44N. 19E.	94
*Fougères, France. 48N. 1W.	72
Foula Is., Scotland. 60N. 2W.	63
Foulness, England. 53N. 1E.	55
Foulness Is., England. 52N. 1E.	57
Fowey, England. 50N. 5W.	56
Foxford, Ireland. 54N. 9W.	66
Foyle Lough, Ireland. 55N. 7W.	67
Foyle R., Ireland. 55N. 7W.	67
Foynes, Ireland. 53N. 9W.	68
*Framlington, England. 52N. 1E.	57
Francavilla, Italy. 41N. 18E.	81
Franken Wald, Bavaria, 50N. 12E.	77
Frankenberg, Germany. 51N. 9E.	76
Frankford, Ireland. 53N. 8W.	69
*Frankfort, Germany. 50N. 9E.	77
*Frankfurt, Germany. 52N. 14E.	76
Frascati, Italy. 42N. 13E.	83
Fraserburgh, Scotland. 58N. 2W.	63
Fratesti, Roumania. 44N. 26E.	94
Frauenfeld, Switzerland. 48N 9E.	87
*Fredericia, Denmark. 56N. 10E.	89

	PAGE
*Frederickshald, Norway. 59N. 11E.	89
Frederiksham, Denmark. 58N. 11E.	89
Frederickstad, Norway. 59N. 11E	89
Fregenal, Spain. 38N. 7W.	84
*Freiberg, Germany. 51N 13E.	77
*Freiburg, Germany. 48N. 8E.	77
Freienwald, Germany. 53N. 14E.	76
Frenchpark, Ireland 54N. 8W.	66
Freshford, Ireland. 53N. 7W.	69
Freswick B., Scotland 59N. 3W.	63
Freudenstadt, Germany. 48N. 8E.	77
Freystadt, Austria. 49N. 14E.	78
Freyung, Germany. 49N. 14E.	77
Fribourg, Switzerland. 47N. 7E.	86
Frick, Switzerland. 47N. 8E.	86
*Friedland, Germany. 54N. 14E.	76
Friedrich, Germany. 52N. 14E.	76
Friedrichsart, Germany. 54N. 10E.	76
Friedrichshafen, Germany. 48N. 9E.	77
Friesian Is., Holland. 53N. 6E.	70
Friesing, Germany. 48N. 12E.	77
Friesland, Holland. 53N. 6E.	70
Frische Haff, Germany 54N. 21E.	75
Fritzlar, Germany. 51N. 9E.	76
Frome, England 51N. 2W.	56
Frome R., England. 51N. 2W.	56
Frosinone, Italy. 42N. 13E.	83
Froyen, Norway. 64N. 9E.	88
Frutigen, Switzerland. 47N. 8E.	86
Fucecchio, Italy. 44N. 11E	83
Fuenterrabia, Spain. 43N. 2W.	85
Fulda, Germany. 50N. 10E	77
Fulda R., Germany. 51N. 10E.	76
Funen, Denmark. 55N. 10E	89
Funfkirchen, Hungary. 46N. 18E	79
Furka Pass, Switzerland. 47N. 9E.	87
*Furness, England 51N 3W.	54
Furstenberg, Germany. 53N. 13E	76
Furstenwalde, Germany 52N. 14E.	76
Furth, Germany. 49N. 11E.	77
*Furth, Germany. 49N. 13E	77
Fussen, Germany. 47N. 11E	77
Fyne, Loch, Scotland 56N. 5W.	64
Fyvie, Scotland. 57N. 2W.	63
*Gaeta, Italy. 41N. 14E.	81
Gaeta, G. of, Italy. 41N. 14E	81
*Gainsborough, England. 53N. 1W.	55
Gairloch, Scotland. 58N 6W	62
Gais, Switzerland 47N 9E	87
Galashiels, Scotland. 56N. 3W.	65
*Galatz, Roumania. 46N. 28E.	94
Galdhoppigen, Norway. 62N. 8E.	89
Galens, Switzerland. 47N. 9E.	87
Galicia, Austria-Hungary. 50N. 22E.	79
Galicia, Spain. 43N. 8W.	84
Galisteo, Spain. 40N 6W.	84
Gallarate, Italy. 46N. 9E.	82
Galley Hd., Lighthouse, Ireland. 52N. 9W.	68
Gallipol, Italy. 40N. 18E.	81
Gallipoli, Turkey 40N. 26E.	95
Gallo Cape, Greece. 37N. 22E.	95
Gallon Hd , Scotland. 58N. 7W.	62
Galston, Scotland. 56N. 4W.	65
Galty Mts., Ireland. 53N. 8W.	68
Galtymore, Ireland. 52N 8W.	69
*Galway, Ireland. 53N. 9W.	66
Galway B., Ireland. 53N. 9W.	66
Gand, Belgium. 51N. 4E.	71
Gandia, Spain. 39N. 0W.	85
Gap, France. 45N. 6E	73
Gara Lough, Ireland. 54N 8W.	66
Gard, France. 44N. 1E.	73
Garda, L. di, Italy. 46N. 11E.	82
Garde, France. 44N. 4E.	73
Gardelegen, Germany. 53N. 11E.	76
Garelochhead, Scotland. 56N. 5W.	64
Gargano, Mt., Italy. 42N. 16E.	80
Gargnano, Italy. 46N. 11E.	82
Garliestown, Scotland. 55N. 4W.	65
Garmouth, Scotland. 58N. 3W.	63
Garonne, R., France. 45N. 1W.	72
Garron, Pt., Ireland. 55N. 6W.	67
Garry Loch, Scotland. 57N 5W.	62
Garstang, England. 51N. 3W.	54
Garvagh, Ireland. 55N. 7W.	67
Garz, Germany. 53N. 14E.	76
*Gastein, Austria. 47N. 13E.	78
Gasturi, Greece. 38N. 21E.	95
Gata, C. de, Spain. 37N. 2W.	85
Gatchouse of Fleet, Scotland. 55N. 4W.	65
Gateig, Switzerland. 46N. 7E.	86
*Gateshead, England. 55N. 2W.	55
Gatzko, Bosnia. 43N. 18E.	94
Gandos, Crete. 35N. 24E.	95
Gausta, Norway. 60N. 9E.	89
Gave de Pau, France. 44N. 1W.	72
Gay, Turkey. 39N. 20E.	95
Gebweiler, Germany. 48N. 7E.	77
Geertrui, Holland. 52N. 5E.	70
Gefle, Sweden. 61N. 17E.	89
Geifswald, Germany. 54N. 13E.	76
Gelderland, Holland. 52N. 6E.	70
Gellivara, Sweden. 67N 21E	88
Gelsenkirchen, Germany. 52N. 7E	76
Gelstemunde, Germany. 54N. 9E.	76
*Gembloux, Belgium. 51N. 5E.	71
Gemmi, Switzerland. 46N. 8E	86
Gemunden, Germany 50N 10E	77
Genappe, Belgium. 51N. 4E.	71
Genemuiden, Holland. 53N. 6E.	70
*Geneva, Switzerland. 46N. 6E.	86
*Geneva, L. of, Switzerland. 46N. 7E.	86
Genil, R., Spain. 38N. 5W	84
Gennargentu, Mt., Sardinia. 40N. 9E.	81
Gennep, Holland. 52N. 6E.	70
*Genoa, Italy. 44N. 9E	82
Gulf of Genoa, Italy. 44N. 9E.	82
Genthin, Germany. 52N. 12E.	76
Genzano, Italy. 42N. 13E.	83
Gera, Germany. 51N. 12E.	77
Gerace, Italy. 38N. 16E.	81
Gerlsdorfer Sp., Hungary. 49N. 21E.	79
Germain, France. 49N. 2E.	73
Germersheim, Germany. 49N. 8E.	77

PAGE

Germünd, Germany. 51N. 6E. 77
*Gerona, Spain. 42N. 3E. 85
Gers, France. 44N. 0E. 72
Gersan, Switzerland. 47N. 9E. 87
Gheel, Belgium. 51N. 5E. 71
Giannutri, Italy. 42N. 11E. 83
Giant's Causeway, Ireland. 55N.
7w. 67
*Gibraltar, Spain. 36N. 5w. 84
Gibraltar, Strait of, Spain. 36N.
6w. 84
Giessen, Germany. 50N 9E 77
Gifford, Scotland. 56N 3w. 65
Gifharn, Germany. 53N. 10E. 76
Gigha Is, Scotland. 56N. 6w. 64
Giglio Is., Italy. 42N. 11E. 83
Giguela, R., Spain. 39N. 4w. 84
Gijon, Spain. 44N. 6w. 84
Gilford, Ireland. 54N. 6w. 67
Gill, Lough, Ireland. 54N. 8w. 66
Gimildjina, Turkey. 41N. 25E. 95
Ginzo, Spain. 42N. 8w. 84
Giornico, Switzerland. 46N. 9E. 87
Girdle Ness, Scotland. 57N. 2w. 63
Girgenti, Sicily. 37N. 14E. 81
Gironde, France. 45N. 1w. 72
Gironde, R., France. 45N. 1w. 72
Girvan, Scotland. 55N. 5w. 64
Girvan Water, Scotland. 55N. 5w. 64
Giuhanova, Italy. 43N. 14E. 83
Giupuzcoa, Spain. 43N. 2w. 85
Giura, Greece. 39N. 24E. 95
Gladbach, Germany. 51N. 6E. 76
*Glamis, Scotland. 57N. 3w. 63
Glamorgan, Wales. 52N 4w. 56
Glanford Brigg, England. 54N.
0w. 55
Glärnisch, Switzerland. 47N. 9E. 87
*Glarus, Switzerland. 47N. 9E. 87
Glasgow, Scotland. 56N. 4w. 65
Glaslough, Ireland. 54N 7w. 67
Glasnevin, Ireland. 53N. 6w. 67
Glass Loch, Scotland. 58N. 5w. 62
*Glastonbury, England. 51N. 3w. 56
Glatz, Germany. 50N. 16E. 75
Glauchau, Germany. 51N. 12E. 77
Gleiwitz, Germany. 50N. 18E. 75
Glen, Ireland. 55N. 8w. 67
Glen Avon, Scotland. 57N. 3w. 63
Glen Binig, Scotland. 58N. 5w. 62
Glen Cannich, Scotland. 57N. 5w. 62
Glen Clova, Scotland. 57N. 3w. 63
*Glen Coe, Scotland. 57N. 5 w. 62
Glen Dochart, Scotland. 56N.
4w. 64
Glen Etive, Scotland. 56N. 5w. 64
Glen Garry, Scotland. 57N. 5w. 62
Glen Garry, Scotland. 57N. 4w. 63
Glen Isla, Scotland. 57N. 3w. 63
*Glen Livet, Scotland. 57N. 3w. 63
Glen Lochy, Scotland. 56N. 4w. 64
Glen Lyon, Scotland. 57N. 4w. 63
Glen More, Scotland. 58N. 5w. 62
Glen More nan Albin, Scotland
57N. 5w. 62
*Glen Moriston, Scotland. 57N.
5w. 62
Glen Orchy, Scotland. 56N. 5w. 62

PAGE

Glen Orrin, Scotland. 57N. 5w. 62
Glen Prosen, Scotland. 57N. 3w. 63
Glen Rannoch, Scotland. 57N.
4w. 63
*Glen Roy, Scotland. 57N. 5w. 62
Glen Shee, Scotland. 57N. 3w. 63
Glen Spean, Scotland. 57N. 5w. 62
Glen Strath Farrar, Scotland.
57N. 5w. 62
Glen Tilt, Scotland. 57N. 4w. 63
Glen Urquhart, Scotland. 57N.
5w. 62
Glenamaddy, Ireland. 54N. 9w. 66
Glenariff, Ireland. 55N. 6w. 67
Glenarm, Ireland. 55N. 6w. 67
Glenbeigh, Ireland. 52N. 10w. 68
Glendowan Mts, Ireland. 55N. 8w. 66
Glenelly, R., Ireland. 55N. 7w. 67
Glengad Hd., Ireland. 55N. 7w. 67
Glengarriff, Ireland 52N. 10w. 68
Glenluce, Scotland. 55N. 5w. 64
Glenties, Ireland. 55N. 8w. 66
Glin, Ireland. 53N. 9w. 68
Glogan, Germany. 52N. 16E. 75
Glommen R., Norway. 62N. 11E. 89
Glossa, Turkey. 40N. 19E. 95
Glossop, England. 53N. 2w. 54
*Gloucester, England. 52N. 2w. 56
Glubokoye, Russia. 55N. 28E. 90
Gluckstadt, Germany. 54N. 9E. 76
Glukhov, Russia. 52N. 34E. 91
Glynn, Ireland. 53N. 7w. 69
Gmund, Germany. 49N. 10E. 77
Gmund, Austria. 49N. 15E. 78
Gmunden, Austria. 48N. 14E. 78
Gnesen, Germany. 52N. 18E. 75
Gnoien, Germany. 54N. 13E. 76
Goat Fell, Scotland. 56N. 5w. 64
Godalming, England. 51N. 1w. 57
Godollo, Hungary. 48N. 20E. 79
Goerdereede, Holland. 52N. 4E. 70
Goeree, Holland. 52N. 4E. 70
Goes, Holland. 52N. 4E. 70
Gog Magog Hills, England. 52N.
0E. 57
Goil Loch, Scotland. 56N. 5w. 64
Goito, Italy. 45N. 11E. 82
Goktcha L., Russia. 40N. 45E. 91
Gol, Norway. 61N. 9E. 89
Golan Hd., Ireland. 53N. 10w. 66
Goldau, Switzerland. 47N. 9E. 87
Golspie, Scotland. 58N. 4w. 63
Gomel, Russia. 53N. 31E. 91
Gonzago, Italy. 45N. 11E. 83
Goodwin Sands, England. 51N. 2E. 57
Goole, England. 54N. 1w. 55
Goor, Holland. 52N 7E. 70
Goplo See, Germany. 52N. 18E. 75
Göppingen, Germany. 49N. 10E. 77
Goresbridge, Ireland. 53N. 7w. 69
*Gorey, Ireland. 53N. 6w. 68
Gorgona Is., Italy 43N. 10E. 82
Gorincham, Holland. 52N. 5E. 70
Göritz, Austria. 46N. 14E. 78
Goritza, Turkey. 40N. 21E. 95
*Gorlitz, Germany. 51N. 15E. 75
Gormanton, [Ireland]. 51N. 6w. 67
Gort, Ireland. 68

PAGE

Gorumna Is., Ireland. 53N. 10w. 66
Göschenen, Switzerland. 47N. 9E. 87
*Goslar, Germany. 52N. 10E. 76
Gospich, Hungary. 45N. 15E. 78
Gosport, England. 51N. 1w. 57
Gossau, Switzerland. 47N. 9E. 87
Gotha, Germany. 51N. 11E. 77
Gotha R., Sweden. 58N. 12E. 89
Gothenborg, Sweden. 58N. 12E. 89
Gothland, Sweden. 57N. 14E. 89
Gothland Is., Sweden. 57N. 19E. 89
*Göttingen, Germany. 52N. 10E. 76
Gottschee, Austria. 46N. 15E. 78
Gottska Sandö, Sweden. 58N. 19E. 89
Gouda, Holland. 52N. 5E. 70
Goudhurst, England. 51N. 0E. 57
Gourdon, France. 45N. 1E. 72
Gourock, Scotland. 56N. 5w. 64
Govan, Scotland. 56N. 4w. 65
Gower, Wales. 52N. 4w. 56
Gower, Port, Scotland. 58N. 4w. 63
Gowna, Lough, Ireland. 54N. 8w. 67
Gozzano, Italy. 46N. 8E. 82
Grabow, Germany. 54N. 14E. 76
Gracia, Spain. 41N. 2E. 85
Gradiska, Hungary. 45N. 17E. 94
Graian Alps, Italy. 45N. 7E. 82
Graigue, Ireland. 53N. 7w. 69
Grammont, Belgium. 51N. 4E. 71
Grampian Mts., Scotland. 57N. 4w. 63
Gran, Hungary. 48N. 19E. 79
Gran, R., Hungary. 48N. 19E. 79
Gran Sasso d'Italia, Italy. 42N.
    14E. 83
*Granada, Spain. 37N. 4w. 84
Granard, Ireland. 54N. 7w. 67
Grand Canal, Ireland. 53N. 7w. 67
*Grandson, Switzerland. 47N. 7E. 86
Grange, England. 54N. 3w. 54
Grangemouth, Scotland. 56N. 4w. 65
Granitola C., Sicily. 38N. 13E. 81
Gransele, Sweden. 65N. 18E. 88
*Grantham, England. 53N. 1w. 55
Granton, Scotland. 56N. 3w. 65
Grantown, Scotland. 57N. 4w. 63
Granville, France. 49N. 1w. 72
Grasse, France. 44N. 7E. 73
Grassington, England. 54N. 2w. 54
Graudenz, Germany. 53N. 19E. 75
Grave, Holland. 52N. 6E. 70
Gravedona, Italy. 46N. 9E. 82
*Gravesend, England. 51N. 0E. 57
Gray, France. 48N. 6E 73
Graz, Austria. 47N. 17E. 78
Gt. Belt, Denmark. 55N. 11E. 89
Gt. Bernera Is., Scotland. 58N.
    7w. 62
Gt. Blasket Is , Ireland. 52N. 11w. 68
Gt. Cumbrae, Scotland. 51N. 5w. 64
Gt. Driffield, England. 54N. 0w. 55
Gt. Glockner, Austria. 47N. 13E. 78
Gt. Grimsby, England. 54N. 0w. 55
Gt. Malvern, England. 53N. 2w. 56
Gt. Marlow, England. 53N. 1w. 57
Gt. Orme's Hd., Wales. 53N. 4w. 54
Gt. Pelvoux, France. 45N. 6E. 73
Gt. St. Bernard, Switzerland. 46N.
    7E. 86

PAGE

Gt. Sebütt I., Hungary, 48N. 18E. 78
Gt. Usen, Russia. 50N. 49E. 91
Gt. Whernside, England. 54N. 2w. 54
Gt. Yarmouth, England. 53N. 2E. 57
Greco, T. d., Italy, 41N. 14E. 81
Greding, Germany. 49N. 11E. 77
Greencastle, Ireland. 54N. 6w. 67
Greencastle, Ireland. 55N. 7w. 67
Greenlaw, Scotland. 56N. 2w. 65
*Greenock, Scotland. 56N. 5w. 64
Greenore, Ireland. 54N. 6w. 67
Greenore Pt., Ireland. 52N. 6w. 69
Greenstone Pt., Scotland. 58N.6w. 62
*Greenwich, England. 51N. 0E. 57
Greifenberg, Germany. 54N. 15E. 75
Greifenhagen, Germany. 53N. 14E. 76
Greifensee, Switzerland. 47N. 9E 87
Greina P., Switzerland. 47N. 9E. 87
Greiz, Germany. 51N. 12E. 77
Grenoble, France. 45N. 6E. 73
Gressoney, Italy. 46N. 8E. 82
Gretna Green, Scotland. 55N. 3w. 65
Greve, Italy. 44N. 11E. 83
Grevena, Turkey. 40N. 21E. 95
Grey Abbey, Ireland. 55N. 6w. 67
Griess Pass, Switzerland. 46N. 8E. 86
Grimsay Is., Scotland. 57N. 7w. 62
Grimma, Germany. 51N. 12E. 76
Grimsel, Switzerland. 47N. 8E. 87
Grinstead, England. 51N. 0w. 57
Grisons, Switzerland. 47N. 10E. 87
Grodek, Austria. 50N 24E. 79
Grodno, Russia-in-E., 51N. 24E. 91
Groenlo, Holland. 52N. 7E. 70
Groningen, Holland. 53N. 7E. 70
Gross Beeren, Germany. 52N. 13E. 76
Grossenhain, Germany. 51N. 14E. 76
Grosses Haf, Germany. 54N. 14E. 76
Grossetto, Italy. 43N. 11E. 83
Grosswardein, Hungary. 47N.
    22E. 94
Grunberg, Germany. 52N. 16E. 75
Gruinard B., Scotland. 58N 5w. 62
Gruningen, Switzerland. 47N. 9E. 87
Gruyères, Switzerland. 47N. 7E. 86
Guadalajara, Spain. 41N. 3w. 84
Guadalaviar, R., Spain. 40N. 0w. 85
Guadalimar, R., Spain. 38N. 4w. 85
Guadalope, R., Spain. 4N. 0E. 85
Guadalquivia, R., Spain. 37N. 6w.84
Guadiana, R., Portugal. 37N. 7w. 84
Guadiana menor, Spain. 38N. 3w. 84
Guadix, Spain. 37N. 3w. 84
Guarda, Portugal. 41N. 7w. 84
Guastalla, Italy. 54N. 11E. 82
*Gubbio, Italy. 43N. 13E. 83
Guben, Germany. 52N. 14E. 76
Gudvangen, Norway. 61N. 7E. 89
Gueret, France. 46N. 2E. 73
Guernsey, Channel Is., 49N. 3w. 56
*Guildford, England. 51N. 0w. 57
Guingamp, France. 49N. 3w. 72
Guisborough, England. 55N. 1w.55
Gullane, Scotland. 56N. 3w. 65
Gumbrinnen, Germany. 55N. 22E. 75
Guns, Hungary 47N. 16E. 78
Gunzenhausen, Germany. 49N.
    11E. 77

PAGE

Guorgne, Italy. 45N. 8E. 82
Gurgevo, Roumania. 44N. 25E. 94
Gurkfeld, Austria-Hungary. 46N.
16E. 78
Güstrow, Germany. 54N. 12E. 76
Guthrie, Scotland. 57N. 3w. 63
Gweebarra B., Ireland. 55N. 8w. 66
Gweebarra, R., Ireland. 55N. 8w. 66
Gweedore, Ireland. 55N. 8w. 66
Gweedore B., Ireland. 55N. 8w. 66
Gyergyo Sz. Miklos, Hungary.
47N. 26E. 79
Gyongyös, Hungary. 48N. 20E. 79
Gyula, Hungary. 47N. 21E. 79

Haag, Switzerland. 47N. 9E. 87
Haard, The, Germany. 52N. 7E. 76
*Haarlem, Holland. 52N. 5E. 70
Haarlem Meer, Holland. 52N. 5E. 70
Haase, R., Germany. 53N. 7E. 76
Hacketstown, Ireland. 53N. 7w. 69
*Haddington, Scotland. 56N. 3w. 65
Hadersleben, Germany. 55N. 9E. 74
Hadhaz, Hungary. 48N. 22E. 79
*Hadleigh, England. 52N. 1E. 57
Hagatz, Switzerland. 47N. 9E. 87
Hagen, Germany. 51N. 8E. 76
Hagenau, Germany. 49N. 8E. 77
Hagenow, Germany. 54N. 11E. 76
Hags Hd., Ireland. 53N 9w. 68
Hague, Cape de la, France. 50N. 2w. 72
*Hague, The, Holland. 52N. 4E. 70
Hailsham, England. 51N. 0E. 57
Hainault, Belgium. 50N. 4E. 71
Hal, Belgium. 51N. 4E. 71
Halas, Hungary. 46N. 20E. 79
Halberstadt, Germany. 52N. 11E. 76
Halesworth, England. 52N. 1E. 57
*Halifax, England. 54N. 2w 54
Halkirk, Scotland. 59N. 3w. 63
Hall, Germany. 49N. 10E. 77
Halle, Germany. 52N. 12E. 76
Hallwyl, Switzerland. 47N. 8E. 86
Hallwyl L., Switzerland. 47N. 8E. 86
Halmstad, Sweden. 57N. 13E. 89
Halstead, England. 52N. 1E. 57
Haltwhistle, England. 55N. 2w. 54
Hamar, Norway. 61N. 11E. 89
Hamburg, Germany. 54N. 10E. 76
*Hameln, Germany. 52N. 10E. 76
Hamilton, Scotland. 56N. 4w. 65
Hamm, Germany. 52N. 8E. 76
Hammar, Sweden. 59N. 15E 89
Hammerfest, Norway. 71N 24E. 88
Hampshire, England. 51N. 1w. 57
*Hanau, Germany. 50N. 9E. 77
Handa Is., Scotland. 58N. 5w. 62
Handeck, Switzerland. 47N. 8E. 87
Hangesund, Norway. 59N. 5E. 89
Hango Hd., Russia. 60N. 23E. 90
Hanley, England. 53N. 3w. 54
Hanover, Germany. 53N. 9E. 76
*Hanover, Germany. 52N. 10E. 76
Hansstock, Switzerland. 47N. 9E. 87
Haparanda, Sweden. 66N. 24E. 88
Harburg, Germany. 54N. 10E 76
Hardanger Fjeld, Norway. 61N.
8E. 89

PAGE

Hardanger Fd., Norway. 60N.
7E. 89
Hardenberg, Holland. 53N. 7E. 70
Harderwyk, Holland. 52N. 6E. 70
Hardt Geb, Germany. 49N. 8E. 77
Haringvliet, Holland. 52N. 4E. 70
*Harlech, Wales. 53N. 4w. 54
Harlingen, Holland. 53N. 5E. 70
Harmanly, Bulgaria. 42N. 26E. 94
Haro, Spain. 43N. 3w. 85
Harris Is., Scotland. 58N. 7w. 62
Harris, Sound of, Scotland. 58N.
7w. 62
*Harrogate, England. 54N. 2w. 55
Hart Fell, Scotland. 55N. 4w. 65
Hartland Pt., England. 51N. 5w. 56
Hartlepool, England. 55N. 1w. 55
Hartley, England. 55N. 1w. 55
Harwich, England. 52N. 1E. 57
*Harz Mts., Germany. 52N. 11E. 76
*Haslemere, England. 51N. 1w. 57
Hasli, Th., Switzerland. 47N. 8E. 86
Hasselt, Belgium. 51N. 5E. 71
Hasselt, Holland. 53N. 6E. 70
Hastings, England. 51N. 1E. 57
*Hatfield, England. 52N. 0w. 57
Hatherleigh, England. 51N. 4w. 56
Hatvan, Hungary. 48N. 20E. 79
Hauchstein, Switzerland. 47N. 8E. 86
Haute Garonne, France. 44N. 1E. 72
Haute Loire, France. 45N. 4E. 73
Haute Marne, France. 48N. 5E. 73
Haute Saone, France. 48N. 6E. 73
Haute Savoie, France. 46N. 6E. 73
Haute, Vienne, France. 46N. 1E. 72
Hautes Alpes, France. 45N. 6E. 73
Hautes Pyrenees, France. 43N. 0E. 72
Havant, England. 51N. 1w. 57
Havel R., Germany. 52N. 12E. 76
Haverfordwest, Wales. 52N. 5w. 56
Haverhill, England. 52N 0E. 57
*Havre, France. 50N. 0E. 72
*Hawarden, Wales. 53N. 3w. 54
Hawes, England. 54N. 2w. 54
*Hawick, Scotland. 55N 3w. 65
Hawkhurst, England. 51N. 0E. 57
*Haworth, England. 54N. 2w. 54
Hay, Wales. 52N. 3w. 56
Hay Sound, Scotland. 59N. 3w. 63
Hayle, England. 50N. 5w. 56
Headford, Ireland 53N. 9w. 66
Hebrides, Scotland. 56N. 7w. 62
Hebrides, Gulf of the, Scotland.
57N. 7w. 62
Hechingen, Germany. 48N. 9E. 77
*Hedgeley Moor, England. 55N. 2w. 54
Hedmora, Sweden. 60N. 16E. 89
Heerenberg, Holland. 52N 6E. 70
Heerenveen, Holland. 53N. 6E. 70
Heide, Germany. 54N. 9E. 76
*Heidelberg, Germany. 49N. 9E. 77
Heiden, Switzerland. 47N. 10E. 87
*Heilbronn, Germany. 49N. 9E. 77
Heiligendamm, Germany. 54N.
12E. 76
Heiligenstadt, Germany. 51N. 10E. 76
Helder, Holland. 53N. 5E. 70
Helensburgh, Scotland. 56N. 5w. 64

PAGE

Helford, England. 50N. 5w. 56
Helge R., Sweden. 56N 14E. 89
Helicon, Greece. 38N. 23E. 95
*Hellevoet Sluis, Holland. 52N. 4E. 70
Helmond, Holland. 51N. 6E. 71
Helmsdale, Scotland. 58N. 4w 63
Helmsdale, R., Scotland. 58N. 4w. 63
Helmsley, England. 54N. 1w. 55
Helmstedt, Germany. 52N. 11E. 76
*Helsingborg, Sweden. 56N. 14E. 89
Helsingfors, Russia. 60N. 25E. 90
Helston, England. 50N. 5w 56
Helvellyn, England. 55N. 3w. 54
Hemso, Sweden. 57N. 19E. 89
Henares, R., Spain. 40N. 4w. 84
Hengelo, Holland. 52N. 7E. 70
Henley, England. 52N 1w. 57
Herault, France. 44N. 3E. 73
Herault, R., France. 43N. 3E. 73
*Hereford, England. 52N. 3w. 56
Hérens, V. d'. Switzerland. 45N. 7E. 86
Herford, Germany. 52N. 8E. 76
Hergiswyl, Switzerland. 47N. 8E. 86
Herisau, Switzerland. 47N. 9E 87
Herm, Channel Is., 49N 2w. 56
Hermanstadt, Hungary. 46N. 24E. 94
Hermupolis, Greece. 37N. 25E. 95
Hernad, Hungary. 48N. 21E. 79
Herne Bay, England. 51N. 1E. 57
Hernösand, Sweden. 63N. 18E. 89
Hersfeld, Germany. 51N. 10E. 77
Hertford, England. 52N. 0w. 57
Hertogenbosch, S', Holland. 52N. 5E. 70
Hervas, Spain. 40N. 6w. 84
Herve, Belgium. 51N. 6E. 71
Herzogenbuchsee, Switzerland. 47N. 8E. 86
Herzegovina, Bosnia. 43N. 18E. 94
Hessen, Germany. 50N 9E. 77
Hessen, Germany. 51N 9E. 77
*Hexham, England. 55N. 2w. 54
Heysham, England. 54N. 3w. 54
Heyst, Belgium 51N 3E. 71
Heytesbury, England. 51N. 2w. 56
Heywood, England. 51N. 2w. 54
Hierapetra, Crete. 35N 26E. 95
High Is., Ireland 54N. 10w. 66
High Tauern, Austria. 47N. 12E. 78
High Wycombe, England. 52N. 1w. 57
Hildburghausen, Germany. 50N. 11E. 77
*Hildesheim, Germany. 52N. 10E. 76
Hill of Fare, Scotland. 57N. 2w 63
Hillsborough, Ireland. 54N. 6w. 67
Hillswick Is , Scotland. 60N. 1w. 63
Hilltown, Ireland. 54N. 6w. 67
Hilton, Scotland. 58N. 4w. 63
Hinckley, England. 53N. 1w. 57
Hindó, Norway. 69N. 16E. 88
Hindon, England. 51N. 2w. 56
Hinojosa de l'Iniquc, Spain. 39N. 5w. 8'
Hinter R. 'n Th. Switzerland. 47N 1 E. 87

PAGE

Hirschberg, Germany. 51N. 16E. 75
Hirsova, Roumania 45N. 28E. 94
Hitchin, England. 52N. 0w. 57
Hitteren, Norway. 64N. 9E. 88
Hjelmar L., Sweden. 59N. 16E. 89
Hochwang, Switzerland. 47N. 10E. 87
Hod Mezo Vasarhely, Hungary. 46N. 20E. 79
Hoe Pt., Scotland. 57N. 7w. 62
Hoek van Holland, Holland. 52N. 4E. 70
*Hof, Germany. 50N. 12E. 77
*Hohenlinden, Germany 48N. 12E. 77
Hohenstaufen, Germany. 49N. 10E. 77
Hohenzollern, Germany. 48N. 9E 77
Holbeach, England. 53N. 0E 55
Holl, England. 53N. 1E. 55
Holland, England. 53N. 0w. 55
Holm L., Sweden. 62N. 15E. 89
Holmfirth, England. 54N. 2w. 54
Holsworthy, England. 51N. 4w. 56
Holt, Wales. 53N 3w. 54
Holtenau, Germany. 54N. 10E. 76
*Holy Is., England. 56N. 2w. 54
Holy Is., Scotland. 56N. 5w. 64
Holy Is., Wales. 53N. 5w. 54
Holycross, Ireland. 53N. 8w. 69
Holyhead, Wales. 53N. 5w. 54
Holywell, Wales. 53N 3w. 54
Holywood, Ireland. 55N 6w. 67
Holzminden, Germany. 52N. 9E. 76
Homburg, Germany. 50N. 9E. 77
Homonna, Hungary. 49N. 22E. 79
Honfleur, France 49N. 0E 72
*Honiton, England. 51N. 3w. 56
Hoogeveen, Holland. 53N. 6E. 70
Hook Hd., Ireland. 52N. 7w. 69
Hoorn, Holland. 53N. 5E. 70
Hope, Loch., Scotland 58N. 5w. 62
Hopeman, Scotland 58N. 3w. 63
Hoppegarten, Germany. 52N. 14E. 76
Horgen, Switzerland. 47N. 9E. 87
Horn Afvan, Sweden 66N. 18E. 88
Horn Hd., Ireland. 55N. 8w. 66
Horncastle, England. 53N. 0w. 55
Hörnli, Switzerland. 47N. 9E. 87
Hornsea, England. 54N. 0w. 55
Horsens, Denmark. 56N. 10E. 89
*Horsham, England. 51N. 0w. 57
Hospital, Ireland 52N. 8w. 68
Houffalize, Belgium. 50N. 6E. 71
Hourn, Loch, Scotland. 57N. 6w. 62
Howden, England. 54N. 1w. 55
Howth, Ireland. 53N. 6w. 67
Howth Hd. Lighthouse, Ireland. 53N. 6w. 67
Höxter, Germany. 52N. 9E. 76
Hoy Is., Scotland. 59N. 3w. 63
Hoya, Germany. 53N. 9E. 76
Huddersfield, England. 54N. 2w. 54
Hudiksvall, Sweden. 62N. 17E. 89
Huelva, Spain. 37N. 7w. 84
*Huesca, Spain. 42N. 0w. 85
*Hull, England. 54N. 0w. 55
Hulst, Holland. 51N. 4E. 71
Humber, R., England. 54N. 1w. 55
Hungerford, England. 51N. 1w. 57

	PAGE
Hungry Hill, Ireland. 52N. 10w.	68
Hunmanby, England. 54N. 0w.	55
Hunsruck, Germany. 50N. 7E.	77
Hunstanton, England. 53N. 1E.	55
Hunte R., Germany. 53N. 8E.	76
*Huntingdon, England. 52N. 0E.	57
Huntingford, England. 52N 0w.	57
Huntly, Scotland. 57N. 3w.	63
Hushi, Roumania. 47N. 28E.	94
Husiatyn, Austria. 49N. 26E.	79
Huszt, Hungary. 48N. 23E.	79
Hutwyl, Switzerland. 47N. 8E.	86
Hyde, England. 53N. 2w.	54
Hydra, Greece. 37N. 23E.	95
*Hyères, France. 43N. 6E	73
Hysker Is., Scotland. 57N. 7w.	62
Hythe, England. 51N. 1E.	57
Ibar R., Servia. 43N. 20E.	94
Ibraila, Roumania. 45N. 28E.	94
Iburg, Germany. 52N. 8E.	76
Ichtiman, Bulgaria. 42N. 24E.	94
Ida Mount, Crete. 35N. 25E	95
Idle, R , England. 53N. 1w	55
Iglau, Austria. 48N. 16E.	78
Iglesias, Sardinia. 39N. 8E.	81
Igualada, Spain 42N. 2E.	85
Ihna R., Germany. 53N. 14E.	76
Ilanz, Switzerland. 47N. 9E	87
*Ilchester, England. 51N. 3w.	56
Ilfracombe, England. 51N. 4w.	56
Ilkeston, England. 53N. 1w.	55
Ilkley, England. 54N. 2w.	54
Ill R., Germany. 49N. 8E.	77
Ille, R., France. 48N. 2w.	72
Ille et Vilaine, France. 48N. 2w.	72
Iller, R., Germany. 48N. 10E	77
Illowo, Germany. 53N. 21E.	75
Ilmen L., Russia. 58N. 31E.	90
Ilsley, England. 52N. 1w.	57
Immenstadt, Germany. 47N. 10E.	77
*Imola, Italy. 44N. 12E.	83
Inca, Majorca. 40N. 3w.	85
Inchard, Loch, Scotland. 58N. 5w.	62
Inchigeelagh, Ireland. 52N. 9w.	68
Inchkeith Lighthouse, Scotland. 56N. 3w.	65
Incoronata, Austria. 44N. 15E.	78
Indre, France. 47N. 1E.	72
Indre, R., France. 47N 0E.	72
Indre-et-Loire, France 47N 1E.	72
Indre Sulen, Norway. 61N. 5E.	89
Inellan, Scotland. 56N 5w.	64
Infiesto, Spain 43N. 5w.	84
Ingleborough, England 54N. 2w.	54
Ingleton, England. 54N. 2w.	54
*Ingolstadt, Germany. 49N. 11E.	77
Inishbofin, Ireland. 54N. 10w.	66
Inishbofin, Ireland. 55N. 8w.	66
Inisheer, Ireland. 53N. 10w.	68
Inisherone, Ireland. 54N. 9w.	66
Inishkea, N. and S., Ireland. 54N. 10w.	66
Inishmaan, Ireland. 53N. 10w.	68
Inishmore, Ireland. 53N. 10w.	68
Inishmurray Is., Ireland. 54N. 8w.	66
Inishowen Hd., Ireland. 55N. 7w.	67
Inishshark, Ireland. 54N. 10w.	66
Inishtrahull Is., Ireland. 55N. 7w.	67
Inishturk, Ireland. 54N. 10w.	66
Inistioge, Ireland. 53N. 7w.	69
Inn, R., Austria. 49N. 14E.	78
Inner Sd., Scotland. 57N. 6w.	62
Innerleithen, Scotland. 56N. 3w.	65
Innishannon, Ireland. 52N. 9w.	68
*Innsbruck, Austria. 47N. 11E.	78
Inny, R., Ireland. 52N. 10w.	68
Inny, R., Ireland. 54N 7w.	67
Inowraclaw, Germany. 53N. 18E.	75
Insch, Scotland. 57N. 3w.	63
Insterburg, Germany. 55N. 22E.	75
Interlaken, Switzerland. 47N. 8E.	86
Intra, Italy. 46N. 9E.	82
Inver, Loch, Scotland. 58N. 5w.	62
Inveran, Ireland. 53N. 9w.	66
Inverary, Scotland. 56N. 5w.	64
Inveravon, Scotland. 57N. 3w.	63
Invergordon, Scotland. 58N. 4w.	63
Inverkeithny, Scotland. 57N 3w.	63
*Inverness, Scotland. 57N. 4w.	63
Inverness Firth, Scotland 58N. 4w.	63
Invershin, Scotland. 58N. 4w	63
Inverury, Scotland. 57N. 2w.	63
*Iona, Scotland. 56N. 6w.	64
Iona Sd , Scotland. 56N. 6w	64
Ionian Is., Greece. 38N. 21E.	95
Ionian Sea, Italy. 38N. 17E.	81
Ipek, Turkey. 43N. 20E.	94
Ipoly, Hungary. 48N 19E.	79
Ipsala, Turkey. 41N. 26E.	95
*Ipswich, England. 52N 1E.	57
Irbit, Russia. 57N. 64E.	90
Irelands Eye, Ireland. 53N. 6w.	67
Irgis R., Russia-in-E., 52N. 48E.	91
Iron Gate, Roumania. 45N. 22E.	94
Irthing, R., England. 55N. 3w.	54
Irun, France. 44N. 2w.	72
Irvine, Scotland. 56N. 5w.	64
Irvine, R., Scotland. 56N. 5w.	64
Irvinestown, Ireland. 55N. 8w.	67
Isar, R., Germany. 49N 13E.	77
*Ischia, Italy. 41N. 14E.	81
Ischl, Austria. 48N 14E.	78
Ise Fd., Norway. 62N. 6E.	89
Iseghem, Belgium. 51N. 3E.	71
Iseo, Italy 46N. 10E.	82
Iseo, L. d', Italy. 46N. 10E.	82
Isère, France. 45N. 6E.	73
Isère, R., France. 45N. 5E.	73
Iserlohn, Germany. 51N. 8E.	76
Ishevsk, Russia. 57N 53E	90
Ishma R., Russia. 65N 54E.	90
Isili, Sardinia. 40N. 9E	81
Isker R., Bulgaria. 44N 24E.	94
Isla, R., Scotland. 57N 3w.	63
Island Magee, Ireland. 55N. 6w.	67
*Islay, Scotland. 56N. 6w.	64
Islay, Sound of, Scotland 56N. 6w.	64
Isle, R , France. 45N 0w.	72
Isle d'Hyères, France. 43N. 6E.	73
Isleworth, England. 51N. 0E.	57
Isle of Man, England. 54N. 5w.	54

PAGE

Isle of May Lighthouse, Scotland.
  56N. 3W.   65
Isle of Purbeck, England.   51N.
  2W.   56
Isle of Wight, England 51N. 1W. 57
Ismail, Russia. 45N. 29E.   94
Ismilan, Bulgaria. 42N. 25E.   94
Isny, Germany. 48N. 10E.   77
Isset, R., Russia. 56N. 62E.   60
Issoire, France. 45N. 3E.   73
Issoudun, France. 47N. 2E.   73
Isthmia, Greece. 38N. 23E.   95
Istib, Turkey. 42N. 23E.   94
Istria, Austria. 45N. 14E.   78
Isuela R., Spain. 42N. 0E.   85
Itchen, R., England. 51N. 1W.   57
Ithaka Is., Greece. 39N. 21E.   95
Itzehoe, Germany. 54N. 9E.   76
*Iviça, Balearic Isles. 39N. 1E.   85
Ivrea, Italy. 45N. 8E.   82
Ixworth, England. 52N. 1E.   57

Jabalon, Spain. 39N. 3W.   84
*Jaca, Spain. 43N. 1W.   85
Jacova, Turkey. 42N. 19E.   94
Jade B., Germany. 53N. 8E.   76
*Jaen, Spain. 38N. 4W.   84
Jagodina, Servia 44N. 22E.   94
Jagst, R., Germany. 49N. 10E.   77
Jalomitza R., Roumania. 45N.28E.94
Jalon, R., Spain. 42N. 1W.   85
Jamestown, Ireland. 54N. 8W.   66
Janina, Turkey. 40N. 21E.   95
Jankovac, Hungary. 46N. 19E.   79
Jar Connaught, Ireland. 53N.
  9W.   66
Jarama, R., Spain. 40N. 4W.   84
Jaroslau, Austria. 50N. 23E.   79
*Jarrow, England. 55N. 1W.   55
Jaslo, Austria. 50N. 21E.   79
Jassy, Roumania. 47N. 28E.   94
Jasz-Bereny, Hungary. 48N. 20E.   79
Jativa, Spain. 39N. 0W.   85
Jauer, Germany. 51N. 16E.   75
Javea, Spain. 39N 0E.   85
Jeantown, Scotland. 57N. 5W.   62
*Jedburgh, Scotland. 55N 3W.   65
*Jemappes, Belgium. 50N. 4E.   71
Jemelle, Belgium. 50N. 5E.   71
*Jena, Germany. 51N. 12E.   77
Jerez, Spain. 37N. 6W.   84
*Jersey, Channel Is. 49N. 2W.   56
Jesi, Italy. 44N. 13E.   83
Jever, Germany. 54N. 8E.   76
Jiloca, R., Spain. 41N. 2W.   85
Joacimsthal, Austria. 50N. 13E.   78
Joensuu, Russia. 63N. 30E.   90
John o' Groat's House, Scotland.
  59N. 3W.   63
Johnnisburg, Germany. 54N.
  22E.   75
Johnshaven, Scotland. 57N 2W 63
Johnstone, Scotland. 56N. 5W.   64
Johnstown, Ireland. 53N. 7W.   67
Joigny, France. 48N. 3E.   73
Joux, L. of, Switzerland. 47N.6E. 86
Joyces Country, Ireland. 54N.
  10W.   66

PAGE

Judenburg, Austria. 47N. 14E.   78
Julian Alps, Austria. 46N. 14E.   78
Julier, P., Switzerland. 46N. 10E. 87
Jumilla, Spain. 39N. 1W.   85
Jung Bunzlau, Austria. 51N. 15E.   78
Jura, France. 47N. 6E.   73
Jura, Scotland. 56N. 6W.   64
Jura Mts., France. 47N. 7E.   73
Jura, Sound of, Scotland. 56N.
  6W.   64
Jüterbog, Germany. 52N. 13E.   76
*Kaiserslautern, Germany. 49N. 8E. 77
Kaiserstuhl, Switzerland.   48N.
  8E.   86
Kaiser Wilhelm, Germany.   54N.
  9E.   76
Kakonya, Hungary. 46N. 17E.   78
Kalafat, Roumania. 44N. 24E.   94
Kalamata, Greece. 37N. 22E.   95
Kalamata Gulf, Greece. 37N. 22E. 95
Kalatch, Russia. 50N. 41E.   91
Kaliakra Cape, Bulgaria.   45N.
  29E.   94
*Kalisz, Germany. 52N. 18E.   75
Kalisz, Russia. 53N. 18E.   91
Kalix Elf, Sweden. 66N. 23E.   88
Kalkanden, Turkey. 42N. 21E.   94
Kall L., Sweden. 64N. 13E.   88
Kalmazui R., Roumania.   45N.
  28E.   94
Kalocsa, Hungary. 47N. 19E.   79
Kalofer, Bulgaria. 42N 25E.   94
Kalvarde, Germany. 53N. 11E.   76
Kama R , Russia. 60N. 56E.   90
Kamenetz Podolsk, Russia.   49N.
  27E.   91
Kampen, Holland. 53N. 0E.   70
Kampalung, Roumania.   45N.
  25E.   94
Kamsko Votimskoi, Russia.   57N.
  53E.   90
Kamtchyk R., Bulgaria. 43N. 28E. 94
Kamyshin, Russia. 50N. 46E.   91
Kandelaksha, Russia.   67N. 33E. 90
Kanin Pen., Russia. 68N. 45E.   90
Kanizsa, Gr., Hungary. 47N. 17E. 78
Kanturk, Ireland. 52N. 9W.   68
Kaposvar, Hungary. 46N. 18E.   78
Kara Sea, Russia. 70N. 61E.   90
Karakal, Roumania. 44N. 24E.   94
Karasu, Turkey. 41N. 25E.   95
Karatchev, Russia-in-E. 53N. 35E. 91
Karatova, Turkey. 42N. 23E.   94
Karawauken, Austria. 46N. 14E.   78
Karditza, Greece 39N. 22E.   95
Karfried, Austria. 46N. 14E   78
Kargopol, Russia.   62N. 39E.   90
Karlsbad, Austria. 50N. 13E.   78
Karlsburg, Hungary. 46N. 24E.   79
Karlstadt, Croatia. 45N. 16E.   78
Karnabad, Bulgaria. 43N. 28E.   94
Karpathos, Crete. 36N. 27E.   95
*Kars, Russia. 41N. 43E.   91
Karytana, Greece. 38N. 22E.   95
Kashau, Hungary. 49N. 21E.   79
Kasimov, Russia. 55N. 42E.   91
Kasos, Crete. 35N. 27E.   95

PAGE

Kastoria, Turkey. 40N. 21E. 95
Katharine Har., Russia. 69N. 34E. 90
Katrine, Loch, Scotland. 56N. 4w. 64
Katwijk, Holland. 52N. 4E. 70
Katzenbuckel, Germany. 49N. 9E. 77
Kavaia, Turkey. 41N. 20E. 95
Kavala, Turkey. 41N. 24E. 95
Kazan, Russia. 56N. 49E. 90
Kazanlik, Bulgaria. 43N. 26E. 94
Kazbek, Russia. 43N. 45E. 91
Keady, Ireland. 54N. 7w. 67
Kealkill, Ireland. 52N. 9w. 68
Kecskemet, Hungary. 47N. 20E. 79
Keeper, Mt , Ireland. 53N. 8w. 68
Kehl, Germany. 49N. 8E. 77
Keighley, England. 54N. 2w. 54
Keil Berg, Germany. 51N. 13E. 77
Keiss, Scotland. 59N. 3w. 63
Keith, Scotland. 58N. 3w. 63
Kells, Ireland. 55N. 6w. 67
Kells, Ireland. 53N. 7w. 69
Kelso, Scotland. 56N. 2w. 65
Kelvedon, England. 52N. 1E. 57
Kem, Russia. 65N. 35E. 90
Kempen, Germany. 51N. 18E 75
Kempten, Germany. 48N. 10E. 77
Ken Water, Scotland. 55N. 4w. 65
Kendal, England. 54N. 3w. 54
Kenfig, Wales. 52N. 4w. 56
Kenilworth, England. 52N. 2w. 57
Kenmare, Ireland. 52N. 10w. 68
Kenmare R., Ireland. 52N. 10w. 68
Kenmore, Scotland. 57N. 4w. 63
Kennedy, Mt., Ireland. 53N. 6w. 69
Kennet, R., England. 51N. 1w. 57
Kenoru, Hungary. 48N. 18E. 79
Kent, England. 51N. 1E. 57
Keos, Greece. 38N. 24E. 95
Kephesia, Greece. 38N. 24E. 95
Kerrera Is., Scotland. 56N. 6w. 64
Kerry, Ireland. 52N. 10w. 68
Kerry Hd., Ireland. 52N. 10w. 68
Kertch, Russia. 45N. 36E 91
Kertch, G. of, Russia. 45N. 37E. 91
Kesh, Ireland. 55N. 8w. 67
Kessock, Scotland. 58N. 4w. 63
Kesteven, England. 53N. 0w. 55
Keswick, England. 55N. 3w. 54
Kettering, England. 52N. 1w. 57
Key, Lough, Ireland. 54N. 8w. 66
Kharkov, Russia. 50N. 36E. 91
Khaskoi, Bulgaria. 42N. 25E. 94
Khelmos, Mt., Greece. 38N. 22E.95
Kherson, Russia. 47N. 33E. 91
Khoper R., Russia. 50N. 42E. 91
Khotin, Russia. 49N. 27E. 91
Kidderminster, England. 52N. 2w. 56
Kidwelly, Wales. 52N. 4w. 56
Kiel, Germany. 54N. 10E. 76
Kiel B., Germany. 54N. 10E. 76
Kiev, Russia. 51N. 31E. 91
Kikashu, Roumania. 47N. 26E. 94
Kikiuda, Hungary. 46N. 20E. 79
Kilashandra, Ireland. 54N. 8w. 67
Kilbeggan, Ireland. 53N. 7w. 67
Kilbirnie, Scotland. 56N. 5w 64
Kilbrennan, Sd., Scotland. 56N.
5w. 64

Kilbrittain, Ireland. 52N. 9w. 68
Kilcar, Ireland. 55N. 9w. 66
Kilcock, Ireland. 53N. 7w. 67
Kilconnell, Ireland. 53N. 8w. 66
Kilcoole, Ireland. 53N. 6w. 69
Kilcullen, Ireland. 53N. 7w. 69
*Kildare, Ireland. 53N. 7w. 68
Kildrummy, Scotland. 57N. 3w. 63
Kilfenora, Ireland. 53N. 9w. 68
Kilfinnane, Ireland. 52N. 8w. 68
Kilgarvan, Ireland. 52N. 9w. 68
Kilia, Roumania. 46N. 29E. 94
Kilia Mouth, Roumania. 46N.
30E. 94
Kilkee, Ireland. 53N. 10w. 68
Kilkee B., Ireland 53N. 10w. 68
Kilkeel, Ireland. 54N. 6w. 67
Kilkelly, Ireland. 54N. 9w. 66
*Kilkenny, Ireland. 53N. 7w. 69
Kilkieran B., Ireland. 53N. 10w. 66
Kill, Ireland. 52N. 7w. 69
Killadysert, Ireland. 53N. 9w. 68
*Killala, Ireland. 54N. 10w. 66
Killala, B., Ireland. 54N. 9w. 66
*Killaloe, Ireland. 53N. 8w. 68
Killard, Pt., Ireland. 53N. 10w. 68
Killarney, Ireland. 52N. 10w. 68
Killary Harb., Ireland. 54N. 10w. 66
Killenaule, Ireland. 53N. 8w. 69
*Killiecrankie Pass, Scotland. 57N.
4w. 63
Killimor, Ireland. 53N. 8w. 68
Killin, Scotland. 56N. 4w. 65
Killintringan Hd., Scotland. 55N.
5w. 64
Killisport, Loch, Scotland. 56N.
6w. 64
Killorglin, Ireland. 53N. 10w. 68
Killough, Ireland. 54N. 6w. 67
Killurin, Ireland. 52N. 7w. 69
Killybegs, Ireland. 55N. 8w. 66
Killygordon, Ireland. 55N. 8w. 67
Killylea, Ireland. 54N. 7w. 67
Killyleagh, Ireland. 54N. 6w. 67
Kilmacthomas, Ireland. 52N. 7w. 69
Kilmaine, Ireland. 54N. 9w. 66
Kilmainham, Ireland. 54N. 7w. 67
Kilmalcolm, Scotland. 56N. 5w. 64
Kilmallock, Ireland. 52N. 9w. 68
*Kilmarnock, Scotland. 56N. 4w. 65
Kilmessan, Ireland. 54N. 7w. 67
Kilmichael Pt., Ireland. 53N. 6w. 69
Kilmore, Ireland. 52N. 7w. 69
Kilmory, Scotland. 55N. 5w. 64
*Kilmuir, Scotland. 57N. 7w. 62
Kilnaleck, Ireland. 54N. 7w. 67
Kilninver, Scotland. 56N. 6w. 64
Kilrea, Ireland. 55N. 7w. 67
Kilrenny, Scotland. 56N. 3w. 65
*Kilrush, Ireland. 53N. 9w. 68
*Kilsyth, Scotland. 56N. 4w. 65
Kiltamugh, Ireland. 54N. 9w. 66
Kiltyclogher, Ireland. 54N. 8w. 66
*Kilwinning, Scotland. 56N. 5w. 64
Kimpolung, Austria. 48N. 26E. 79
Kinaird Hd., Scotland. 58N. 2w.63
Kincardine, Scotland. 57N. 2w. 63
Kincardine, Scotland. 56N. 4w. 65

PAGE

Kineschma, Russia. 57N. 42E. 90
Kings Co., Ireland. 53N. 7w. 67
*King's Lynn, England. 53N. 0E 57
Kinghorn, Scotland. 56N. 3w. 65
Kingsbarns, Scotland. 56N. 3w. 65
Kingsbridge, England. 50N. 4w. 56
Kingsclere, England. 51N. 1w. 57
Kingscourt, Ireland. 54N. 7w. 67
*Kingston, England. 51N. 0w. 57
Kingston-upon-Hull, England.
  54N. 0w. 55
Kingstown, Ireland. 53N. 6w. 67
Kingswear, England. 50N. 4w. 56
*Kington, England 52N. 3w. 56
Kingussie, Scotland. 57N. 4w. 63
Kinlough, Ireland. 54N. 8w. 66
Kinross, Scotland. 56N. 3w. 65
*Kinsale, Ireland. 52N. 9w. 68
Kinsale Harb., Ireland. 52N. 9w. 68
Kintore, Scotland. 57N. 2w. 63
Kinvarra, Ireland. 53N. 9w. 68
Kinzig, R., Germany. 50N. 9E. 77
Kiölen Mts., Norway. 65N. 14E. 88
Kipen, Germany. 55N. 9E. 74
Kippure, Ireland 53N. 6w. 69
Kirghiz Horde, Russia. 48N. 49E. 91
Kirkby Lonsdale, England. 54N.
  3w. 54
Kirkby Stephen, England. 54N.
  2w. 54
*Kirkcaldy, Scotland. 56N. 3w. 65
Kircubbin, Ireland. 54N. 6w. 67
Kirkcudbright, Scotland. 55N. 4w. 65
Kirkcudbright B., Scotland. 55N.
  4w. 65
Kirkgunzeon, Scotland. 55N. 4w 65
Kirkintilloch, Scotland. 56N. 4w. 65
Kirk-Kilissia, Turkey. 42N 27E.94
Kirkmaiden, Scotland. 55N. 5w. 66
Kirkmichael, Scotland. 57N. 3w. 63
Kirkoswald, England. 55N. 3w. 54
*Kirkoswald, Scotland. 55N. 5w. 64
*Kirkwall, Scotland. 59N. 3w. 63
Kirn, Scotland. 56N. 5w 64
*Kirriemuir, Scotland. 57N. 3w. 63
Kirton-in-Lindsey, England. 53N.
  1w. 55
Kisilskaya, Russia-in-E. 54N. 59E.91
Kishinev, Russia. 47N. 29E. 91
Kishorn, Loch, Scotland. 57N. 6w.62
Kishenev, Russia. 47N. 28E. 94
*Kissingen, Germany. 50N. 10E. 77
Kirsovo Mount, Greece. 40N. 23E.95
Kitsbuhel, Austria. 47N. 12E. 78
Kitzingen, Germany. 50N. 10E. 77
Klagenfurt, Austria. 47N. 14E. 78
Klar Elf, Sweden. 60N. 13E. 89
Klattau, Austria. 49N. 13E. 78
Klausenberg, Hungary. 47N. 24E. 94
Kleines Haf, Germany 54N. 14E. 76
Kheshe, Turkey. 42N. 20E. 94
Klinlehamn, Sweden 57N. 19E. 89
Kloster, Switzerland. 47N. 10E. 87
Kliutch, Bosnia 45N. 17E. 94
*Knaresborough, England. 54N. 1w.55
*Knighton, Wales. 52N. 3w. 56
Knin, Dalmatia. 44N. 16E. 94
Knockmahon, Ireland. 52N. 7w. 69

PAGE

Knockmealdown Mts., Ireland.
  55N. 8w. 69
*Knutsford, England. 53N. 2w. 54
Kochem, Germany. 50N. 7E 77
Kocher, R., Germany. 49N. 9E. 77
Koekel, Hungary. 46N 24E 79
Kola Penin., Russia. 67N. 37E 90
Kolguev, Russia 69N. 49E. 90
*Kolin, Austria. 50N. 15E. 78
Kolomea, Austria. 49N. 25E. 79
*Kolomna, Russia. 55N. 39E. 91
Kom Mt, Turkey. 43N 20E. 94
Kongsberg, Norway. 60N. 10w. 89
Kongsvinger, Norway. 60N. 12E. 89
Konietza, Bosnia. 44N. 18E. 94
*Königgratz, Austria. 50N. 16E 78
Königs See, Germany. 47N. 13E. 77
Konitz, Germany. 53N. 17E. 75
Konitza, Turkey. 40N. 21E. 95
Königsberg, Germany. 53N. 15E. 75
*Königsberg, Germany. 55N. 20E. 75
Konigshutte, Germany. 50N. 19E.75
Konigstein, Germany. 51N. 14E. 76
Kontehakov, Russia. 60N. 59E. 90
Koping, Sweden. 60N. 16E. 89
Koprili, Turkey. 42N. 21E. 94
Kornneuburg, Austria. 48N. 16E. 78
Koroni, Greece. 37N. 22E. 95
Korsehen, Germany. 54N 21E. 75
Kosel, Germany. 51N. 18E 75
Kosiajnica, Croatia 45N. 16E. 78
Koslov, Russia. 53N. 40E. 91
Kostendil, Bulgaria. 42N. 25E 94
Kostroma, Russia. 58N. 41E. 90
Kothen, Germany. 52N. 12E. 76
Kotlas, Russia. 61N. 47E. 90
Kottbus, Germany. 52N. 14E. 76
Kovno, Russia. 55N. 24E. 90
Kowel, Russia. 52N. 24E. 91
Krajova, Roumania. 44N. 24E. 94
Kramburg, Austria. 46N. 14E. 78
Krapina, Croatia. 46N. 16E 78
Kraqushevatz, Servia. 44N. 20E. 94
Krasne, Austria. 50N. 24E. 79
Krasnoborsk, Russia. 62N. 46E. 90
Krasno Ufimsk, Russia. 57N. 58E. 90
Kremenets, Russia. 50N. 26E. 91
Krementchug, Russia. 49N. 34E.91
Kremnitz, Austria-Hungary. 49N.
  19E. 79
Krems, Austria. 49N. 16E. 78
Kreutz, Germany. 53N. 16E. 75
Kreuz, Austria-Hungary. 46N. 16E.78
Kreuznach, Germany. 50N. 8E. 77
Krichava, Turkey. 41N. 21E. 94
Krio C., Crete. 35N. 24E. 95
Kronstadt, Hungary. 46N 25E. 94
Kronstadt, Russia. 60N. 30E. 90
Krumau, Austria. 49N. 14E. 78
Krushevatz, Servia. 43N 21E. 94
Kryoneri, Greece. 38N. 22E. 95
Kuba, Russia. 41N. 49E. 91
Kuban Distr., Russia. 45N. 40E. 91
Kuban R., Russia. 45N. 38E. 91
Kubinskoie L., Russia 60N. 40E. 90
Kufstein, Austria. 48N. 12E. 78
Ku stein, Germany. 47N. 12E. 77
Kuinre, Holland. 53N. 6E. 70

PAGE

Kuleti, Turkey. 42N. 26E. 94
Kulmbach, Germany. 50N. 12E. 77
Kulpa, Croatia. 45N. 16E. 78
Kungur, Russia. 57N. 57E. 90
Kunzelsau, Germany. 49N. 10E. 77
Kuopio, Russia. 63N. 27E. 90
Kura R, Russia. 40N. 49E. 91
Kurdszag, Hungary. 47N. 21E. 79
Kurfursten, Switzerland. 47N. 9E. 87
Kurische Nerung, Germany. 55N. 21E. 75
Kurisches Haff, Germany. 55N. 21E. 75
Kursk, Russia. 52N. 36E. 91
Kusnetsk, Russia. 53N. 47E. 91
Kussnacht, Switzerland. 47N. 8E. 87
Kustendji, Roumania. 44N. 29E. 94
Kustenland, Austria. 46N. 14E. 78
Kustrin, Germany. 52N. 14E. 76
Kutais, Russia. 42N. 43E. 91
Kuttenberg, Austria. 50N. 15E. 78
Kuty, Austria. 48N 25E. 79
Kvalynsk, Russia. 53N. 48E. 91
Kvenangen Fd, Norway. 70N. 21E. 88
Kyle Akin, Scotland. 57N. 6w. 62
Kyle More, Scotland 57N. 6w. 62
Kyle of Durness, Scotland. 59N. 5w. 62
Kyle of Lochalsh, Scotland. 57N. 6w. 62
Kyle of Tongue, Scotland. 59N. 4w. 63
Kyles of Bute, Scotland. 56N. 5w. 64
Kyritz, Germany. 53N. 12E. 76
Kyrtashan, Roumania. 44N. 25E. 94
Kyrthausen, Germany. 51N. 10E. 76

La Belle Alliance, Belgium. 51N 4E. 71
La Chaux de Fonds, Switzerland. 47N. 7E. 86
La Dôle, Switzerland. 46N. 6E. 86
La Flèche, France. 48N. 0w. 72
La Mancha, Spain. 39N. 3w. 85
La Palma, Spain. 37N. 7w. 84
La Roche, Belgium. 50N. 6E. 71
La Roche sur Yonne, France. 47N. 1w. 72
La Rochelle, France. 46N. 1w. 72
La Roda, Spain. 39N. 2w. 85
La Sagra, Spain. 38N. 3w. 85
La Teste de Buch, France. 45N. 1w. 72
La Union, Spain. 38N. 1w. 85
Laaland, Denmark. 55N. 12E. 89
Laasphe, Germany. 51N. 8E. 76
Labiana, Spain. 43N. 6w. 84
Labiau, Germany. 55N. 21E. 75
Lachen, Switzerland. 47N. 9E. 87
Ladoga L., Russia. 61N. 31E. 90
Laerdals, Norway. 61N. 7E. 89
Lacsö, Denmark. 57N. 11E. 89
Lagan, R., Ireland. 55N 6w. 67
Laganai, Russia. 56N. 60E. 90
Lagonegro, Italy. 40N. 16E. 81
Lagos, Portugal. 37N. 9w. 84

PAGE

Lagosta Is., Dalmatia. 43N. 17E. 78
Lahu, Germany. 50N. 8E. 77
Laibach, Austria. 46N. 14E. 78
Laigle, France. 49N. 1E. 72
Lainio, Sweden. 68N. 23E. 88
Lainza, Russia. 53N. 22E. 91
Lairg, Scotland. 58N. 4w. 63
Lakocz, Hungary. 46N. 26E. 79
Lambay Is., Ireland. 53N. 6w. 67
Lambourn, England. 52N. 2w. 57
Lambs Hd., Ireland. 52N. 10w. 68
Lamia, Greece. 39N. 23E. 95
Lamlash, Scotland. 56N. 5w. 64
Lamego, Portugal. 41N. 8w. 84
Lammermuir Hills, Scotland. 56N 3w. 65
Lampeter, Wales. 52N. 4w. 56
*Lanark, Scotland. 56N. 4w. 65
Lancashire, England. 54N. 3w. 54
Lancaster, England. 54N. 3w. 54
Lanciano, Italy. 42N. 14E. 83
*Landau, Germany. 49N. 13E. 77
Landau, Germany. 49N. 8E. 77
Landeron, Switzerland. 47N. 7E. 86
Landes, France. 44N. 1w. 72
Landquart, Switzerland. 47N. 10E. 87
Lands End, England. 50N. 6w. 56
Landsberg, Germany. 53N. 15E. 75
Landsberg, Germany. 48N. 11E. 77
*Landshut, Germany. 49N. 12E. 77
Landskrona, Sweden. 56N. 13E. 89
Lanesborough, Ireland. 54N. 8w. 66
Langeland, Denmark. 55N. 11E. 89
Langenthal, Switzerland. 47N. 8E. 86
Lang Field, Norway. 62N. 8E. 89
Langholm, Scotland. 55N. 3w. 65
Langnau, Switzerland. 47N. 8E. 86
*Langres, France. 48N. 5E. 73
*Laon, France. 50N. 3E. 73
Lanzo, Italy. 45N. 7E. 82
Lapland, Russia. 68N. 29E. 90
Laraisel, Sardinia. 40N. 10E. 81
Larbert, Scotland. 56N. 4w. 65
Laredo, Spain. 43N. 3w. 84
*Largo, Scotland. 56N. 3w. 65
Largo B., Scotland. 56N. 3w. 65
Larino, Italy. 42N. 15E. 80
Larissa, Greece. 40N. 22E. 95
Lark, R., England. 52N. 0E. 57
Larne, Ireland. 55N. 6w. 67
Larne, Lough, Ireland. 55N. 6w. 67
*Largs, Scotland. 56N. 5w. 64
Latheron, Scotland. 58N. 3w. 63
Latisana, Italy. 46N 13E 83
*Lauder, Scotland. 56N. 3w. 65
Lauenbg, Germany. 55N. 18E. 75
Lauenburg, Germany. 53N. 11E. 76
Laufen, Switzerland. 47N. 7E. 86
Laufen, Switzerland. 48N. 9E. 87
Laufenburg, Switzerland 48N. 8E. 86
Laukas, Russia. 63N. 26E. 90
*Launceston, England. 51N. 4w. 56
Laune, R., Ireland. 52N. 10w. 68
*Laupen, Switzerland. 46N. 7E. 86
Laurion, Greece. 38N. 24E. 95
Laurvig, Norway. 59N. 10E. 89
*Lausanne, Switzerland. 47N. 7E. 86

	PAGE
Lauterbrunnen, Switzerland. 47N. 8E.	86
Lauwer Zee, Holland. 53N. 6E.	70
*Laval, France. 48N. 1w.	72
Lavenham, England. 52N. 1E.	57
Lavena, Italy. 46N. 9E.	82
Law, Scotland. 56N. 3w.	65
Lawrence-kirk, Scotland. 57N. 2w.	63
Laxe Fd., Norway. 71N. 27E.	88
Laxey, Is. of Man. 54N. 4w.	54
Laxford, R., Scotland. 58N. 5w.	62
Lea, R., England. 52N. 0E.	57
Leach, R., England. 52N. 2w.	56
*Leadhills, Scotland. 55N. 4w.	65
Leamington, England. 52N. 2w.	57
Leba, Germany. 55N. 18E.	75
*Lebrija, Spain. 37N. 6w.	84
Lecce, Italy. 40N. 18E.	81
Lecco, Italy. 46N. 9E.	82
*Lech R., Germany. 49N. 11E.	77
Lechlade, England. 52N. 2w.	56
Le Creuzot, France. 47N. 4E.	73
Lectoure, France. 44N. 1E.	72
Leda, Crete. 35N. 25E.	95
*Ledbury, England. 52N. 2w.	56
Lee, R., Ireland. 52N. 9w.	68
*Leeds, England. 54N. 2w.	55
Leek, England. 53N. 2w.	54
Leer, Germany. 53N. 8E.	76
Leeuwarden, Holland. 53N. 6E.	70
*Leghorn, Italy. 44N. 10E.	82
*Legnago, Italy. 45N. 11E.	83
Lehrte, Germany. 52N. 10E	76
Leibnitz, Austria. 47N. 16E.	78
*Leicester, England. 53N. 1w.	57
Leigh, England. 53N. 3w.	54
Leighlinbridge, Ireland. 53N. 7w.	69
Leighton Buzzard, England. 52N. 1w.	57
Leine R., Germany. 53N. 10E.	76
Leinster, Ireland. 53N. 7w.	69
Leinster, Mt., Ireland. 53N. 7w.	69
*Leipzig, Germany. 51N. 13E.	76
Leiria, Portugal. 40N. 9w.	84
*Leith, Scotland. 56N. 3w.	65
Leitmeritz, Austria. 51N. 14E.	78
Leitrim, Ireland. 54N. 8w.	66
Leixlip, Ireland. 53N. 6w.	67
Lek, R., Holland. 52N. 5E.	70
Le Locle, Switzerland. 47N. 7E.	86
*Le Mans, France. 48N. 0w.	72
Le Puy, France. 45N. 4E.	73
Le Treport, France. 50N. 1E.	72
Lemberg, Austria. 50N 24E.	79
Lemmer, Holland. 53N. 6E.	70
Lena, Spain 43N. 6w.	84
Lenadoon Pt., Ireland. 54N. 9w.	66
Lenk, Switzerland. 46N. 7E.	86
Lenne R., Germany. 51N. 8E.	76
Lennoxtown, Scotland 56N. 4w.	65
Lensie Jun , Scotland. 56N. 4w.	65
Lentini, Sicily. 37N. 15E.	81
Lenzburg, Switzerland, 47N. 8E.	86
Leoben, Austria. 47N. 15E.	78
Leobschütz, Germany. 50N. 18E	75
Leominster, England. 52N. 3w.	56
Leon, Spain. 43N. 6w.	84
Leone Mt., Switzerland. 46N. 8E.	86

	PAGE
Leonidi, Greece. 37N. 23E.	95
*Lepanto, Greece. 38N. 22E.	95
Le Pont, Switzerland. 47N. 6E.	86
Lerici, Italy. 44N. 10E.	82
*Lerida, Spain. 42N. 1E.	85
*Lerins, France. 44N. 7E.	73
Lerwick, Scotland. 60N. 1w.	63
Lesina Is., Dalmatia. 43N. 17E.	94
Leskovatz, Servia. 43N. 22E.	94
Leslie, Scotland. 56N 3w.	65
Lesmahago, Scotland. 56N. 4w.	65
Le Sentier, Switzerland. 47N. 6E.	86
Lesse R., Belgium. 50N. 5E.	71
Lessines, Belgium. 51N. 4E.	71
Letterfrack, Ireland. 54N. 10w.	66
Letterston, Wales. 52N. 5w.	56
Letterkenny, Ireland. 55N. 8w.	67
Leti Is , Roumania. 45N. 30E	94
Leuchars, Scotland. 56N. 3w.	65
Leuk, Switzerland. 46N. 8E.	86
Leuker Rad., Switzerland. 46N. 8E.	86
Leuze, Belgium. 51N. 4E.	71
Leva, Hungary. 48N. 19E.	79
Levanger, Norway. 64N. 12E.	88
Levanto, Italy. 44N. 10E.	82
Levanzo Is., Sicily. 38N. 12E.	81
*Leven, Scotland. 56N 3w.	65
Leven, L., Scotland. 56N. 3w.	65
Leventina R., Switzerland 46N. 9E.	87
*Lewes, England. 51N. 0E.	57
Lewis Is., Scotland. 58N 7w.	62
Leyburn, England. 54N. 2w.	54
*Leyden, Holland. 52N. 5E.	70
Leytha, R., Hungary. 48N. 18E.	78
Libau, Russia. 57N. 21E.	90
Libourne, France. 45N. 0w.	72
Licata, Sicily. 37N. 14E.	81
*Lichfield, England. 53N. 2w.	56
Lichtenfels, Germany 50N. 11E.	77
Lichtensteig, Switzerland. 47N. 9E.	87
Licosia, Pta. della, Italy. 40N. 15E.	81
Liddel Water, Scotland. 55N. 3w.	65
Lidköping, Sweden. 59N. 13E.	89
*Liege, Belgium. 51N. 6E.	71
Liegnitz, Germany. 51N. 16E.	75
Lienz, Austria. 47N. 13E.	78
*Lierre, Belgium. 51N. 5E.	71
Liestal, Switzerland. 48N. 8E.	86
Liesh, Turkey. 42N. 20E.	94
Lietzen, Austria. 48N. 14E.	78
Liffey, R., Ireland. 53N. 6w.	67
Lifford, Ireland. 55N. 8w.	67
Liguria, Italy. 44N. 9E.	82
Ligurian Apennines, Italy. 44N. 9E.	82
Ligurian Sea, Italy. 44N. 9E.	82
Lileh-Bergas, Turkey. 42N. 27E.	94
*Lille, France. 51N. 3E.	73
Lillehammer, Norway. 62N. 10E.	89
Lim R., Turkey. 43N. 20E.	94
Limavady, Ireland. 55N. 7w.	67
Limburg, Belgium. 51N. 5E.	71
Limburg, Germany. 50N. 8E.	77
Limburg, Holland. 51N 6E.	71
Limia, R., Portugal. 42N. 9w.	84
*Limerick, Ireland. 53N. 9w.	68
Limmat R., Switzerland. 47N. 8E.	87

PAGE

*Limoges, France. 46N. 1E. 72
Limoux, France. 43N. 2E. 73
Linares, Spain. 38N. 4W. 84
Linaro, C., Italy. 42N. 12E. 83
Linas Hd., Wales. 53N. 4W. 64
*Lincoln, England. 53N. 1W. 55
Lindau, Germany. 48N. 10E. 77
Linden, Germany. 52N. 10E. 76
Lindsey, England. 53N. 0W. 55
Line, R., England. 55N. 3W. 54
Lingen, Germany. 53N. 7E. 76
Linkoping, Sweden. 58N. 16E. 89
*Linlithgow, Scotland. 56N. 4W. 65
Linth R., Switzerland. 47N. 9E. 87
Linththal, Switzerland. 47N. 9E. 87
Linz, Austria. 48N. 14E. 78
Lions, G. of., France. 43N. 4E. 73
Lipari I., Italy. 39N. 15E. 81
Lipari Is., Italy. 39N. 15E. 81
Lipetsk, Russia. 53N. 40E. 91
Lippe, Germany. 52N. 9E 76
Lippe R., Germany. 52N. 6E. 76
Liptau Geb., Hungary. 49N. 20E. 79
Liria, Spain. 40N. 1W. 85
*Lisbon, Portugal. 39N. 9W. 84
*Lisburn, Ireland. 55N. 6W 67
Liscannor, Ireland. 53N. 9W. 68
Liscannor B., Ireland. 53N 9W. 68
Lisdoonvarna, Ireland. 53N. 9W. 68
Liskeard, England. 50N. 5W. 56
Lismore, Ireland. 52N. 8W. 69
*Lismore, Scotland. 56N. 6W. 64
Lisnaskea, Ireland. 54N. 7W. 67
*Lissa, Dalmatia 43N. 16E. 78
Lissa, Germany. 52N 17E. 75
Lister Fd., Norway. 58N. 6E. 89
Listowel, Ireland. 52N. 9W. 68
Lithinos, Crete. 35N. 25E. 95
Littay, Austria. 46N 15E. 78
Little Belt, Denmark. 55N. 10E. 89
Little Cumbrae, Scotland. 56N. 5W. 64
Lit. Karpathians, Hungary. 49N. 18E. 78
Little Killary B., Ireland. 54N. 10W. 66
Little Loch Broom, Scotland. 58N. 5W. 62
Little Minch, Scotland. 58N. 7W. 62
Little Ouse R., England. 53N. 0E. 57
Little St. Bernard, Italy. 46N.7E. 82
Little Usen, Russia. 50N 48E. 91
Littlehampton, England. 51N. 0W. 57
Littleport, England. 52N. 0E. 57
Littlestone, England. 51N. 1E. 57
Livadia, Greece. 38N. 23E. 95
Livadia, Russia. 44N. 34E. 91
*Liverpool, England. 53N. 3W. 54
Livna, Bosnia. 44N. 17E. 94
Livny, Russia. 53N. 33E. 91
Livonia, Russia. 58N. 25E. 90
Livorno, Italy. 44N. 10E. 82
Lizard Hd., England. 50N. 5W. 56
Lizieux, France. 49N. 0E. 72
Ljungan R., Sweden. 62N. 16E. 89
Ljusne, Sweden. 62N. 16E. 89
Llanberis, Wales. 53N. 4W. 54
Llandaff, Wales. 52N. 3W. 56

PAGE

Llandilofawr, Wales. 52N. 4W. 56
Llandovery, Wales. 52N. 4W. 56
Llandudno, Wales. 53N. 4W. 54
Llanelly, Wales. 52N. 4W. 56
Llanfair, Wales. 53N. 3W. 56
Llanfyllin, Wales. 53N. 3W. 54
Llangadock, Wales. 52N. 4W. 56
*Llangollen, Wales. 53N. 3W. 54
Llangynog, Wales. 53N. 3W. 54
Llanidloes, Wales. 52N. 4W. 56
Llanrwst, Wales. 53N. 4W. 54
Llantrisaint, Wales. 52N. 3W. 56
*Llerena, Spain. 38N. 6W. 84
Loanhead, Scotland. 56N. 3W. 65
Lobau, Germany. 53N. 20E. 75
Lotschen Th., Switzerland. 46N. 8E. 86
Locarno, Switzerland. 46N 9E. 87
Loch-an-Dorbh, Scotland. 57N. 4W. 63
Loch Laxford, Scotland. 58N. 5W. 62
Lochearnhead, Scotland. 56N. 4W. 65
Lochee, Scotland. 56N. 3W 65
Lochem, Holland. 52N. 6E. 70
Lochgelly, Scotland. 56N. 3W. 65
Lochgilphead, Scotland. 56N. 5W 64
Loch Langabhat, Scotland. 58N. 7W. 62
Loch Leven, Scotland. 57N. 5W. 62
Loch Linnhe, Scotland. 57N. 5W. 62
*Lochnaben, Scotland. 55N. 3W. 65
Lochnagar, Scotland. 57N. 3W. 63
Loch na Keal, Scotland. 56N. 6W. 64
Loch Lochy, Scotland. 57N. 5W. 62
Loch Lomond, Scotland. 56N. 5W. 64
Loch Long, Scotland. 56N. 5W. 64
Loch Loyal, Scotland. 58N. 4W. 63
Loch Lubnaig, Scotland. 56N. 4W. 65
Loch Luichart, Scotland. 58N. 5W. 62
Loch Lydoch, Scotland. 57N. 5W. 62
Loch Monar, Scotland. 57N. 5W. 62
Lochwinnoch, Scotland. 56N. 5W. 64
Lochy, R., Scotland. 57N. 5W. 62
Lodève, France. 44N. 3E. 73
*Lodi, Italy. 45N. 9E. 82
Lodz, Russia. 53N. 20E. 91
Lofoden Is., Norway. 69N. 15E. 88
Logierait, Scotland. 57N. 4W. 63
Logrono, Spain. 43N. 2W. 85
Loire (prov.), France. 46N. 4E. 73
Loire, R., France. 47N. 2W. 72
Loire Inférieure, France. 47N. 2W. 72
Loiret, France. 48N. 2E. 73
Loiret, R., France. 48N. 2E. 73
Loire et Cher, France. 48N. 1E. 72
Loja, Spain. 37N. 4W. 84
Lockerbie, Scotland. 55N. 3W. 65
Lokeren, Belgium. 51N 4E. 71
Lombardy, Italy. 46N. 10E. 82
Lomello, Italy. 45N. 9E. 82
Lomond Hills, Scotland. 56N. 3W. 65
Lom Palanka, Bulgaria. 44N. 23E. 94
Lomza, Russia. 54N. 22E. 91
London, England. 53N. 0W. 57
*Londonderry, Ireland. 55N. 7W. 67
Longa Is., Scotland. 58N. 6W. 62
Longfad, Ireland. 54N. 8W. 67
Longnor, England. 53N. 2W. 54

I

PAGE

Longridge, England. 53N. 3w. 54
Long Stratton, England. 53N. 1E. 57
Longton, England. 53N. 2w. 54
Longtown, England. 55N. 3w. 54
*Lons de Saulnier, France. 47N. 6E. 73
Loop Hd., Ireland. 53N. 10w. 68
Lorraine, Germany. 49N. 6E. 77
Lorca, Spain. 38N. 2w. 85
Loreto, Italy. 43N. 14E 83
Lorient, France. 48N. 3w. 72
Lorne, Scotland. 56N. 4w. 64
Lorne, Firth of, Scotland. 56N. 6w. 64
Lörrach, Germany. 48N 8E. 77
Los Santos, Spain. 39N. 6w. 84
Lossie. R., Scotland. 58N. 3w. 63
Lossiemouth, Scotland. 58N.3w. 63
Lostwithiel, England. 50N. 5w. 56
Lot, France. 44N. 2E. 73
Lot, R., France. 44N. 0E. 72
Lot et Garonne, France. 44N. 0E. 72
Lötzen, Germany. 54N. 22E. 75
Louisburgh, Ireland. 54N. 10w. 66
Loughar, Wales. 52N. 4w. 56
*Loughborough, England. 53N. 1w. 57
Lough Derg, Ireland 53N. 8w. 68
Lough Graney, Ireland. 53N. 9w. 68
Lough Leane, Ireland. 52N 10w. 68
Loughrea, Ireland. 53N. 9w. 68
Loughros More B., Ireland. 55N. 9w. 66
Loule, Portugal. 37N. 8w. 84
Louriçal, Portugal. 40N. 9w. 84
*Louth, England. 53N. 0w. 55
Louth, Ireland. 54N. 7w. 67
Louther Hills, Scotland. 55N. 4w. 65
*Louvain, Belgium. 51N. 5E. 71
*Louviers, France. 49N. 1E. 72
Lovat R., Russia. 58N. 31E. 90
Lovatz, Bulgaria. 43N. 24E. 94
Looe, England. 50N. 5w. 56
Lovere, Italy. 46N. 10E. 82
Lower Engadine, Switzerland. 47N. 10E. 87
Lower Franconia, Germany. 50N. 10E. 77
*Lowestoft Ness, England. 53N. 2E. 57
Lowtherstown, Ireland. 55N. 8w. 67
Lozère, France. 44N. 3E. 73
Loznitza, Servia. 45N. 19E. 94
Lucan, Ireland. 53N. 6w. 67
Lübbecke, Germany. 52N. 8E. 76
*Lubeck, Germany. 54N 11E. 76
Lubeck B., Germany. 54N. 11E. 76
Lubben, Germany. 52N. 14E. 76
Lublin, Russia. 51N. 22E 91
Lubtinitz, Germany. 51N. 19E. 75
Lucca, Italy. 44N. 10E. 82
Luce B., Scotland. 55N. 5w. 64
Lucena, Spain. 37N. 4w. 84
Lucera, Italy. 41N. 15E. 80
*Lucerne, Switzerland. 47N. 8E. 86
Lucerne, L. of, Switzerland. 47N. 8E. 87
Luchon, France. 43N. 0E. 72
Luchow, Germany. 53N. 11E. 76
Luckau, Germany. 52N 13E. 76
Luckenwald. Germany. 52N. 13E. 76
Lucifer Shoal, Ireland. 53N. 6w. 69

Ludgershall, England. 51N. 2w. 57
*Ludlow, England. 52N. 3w. 56
Ludwigsburg, Germany. 49N. 9E. 77
Ludwigshafen, Germany. 49N. 8E. 77
Ludwigslust, Germany. 53N. 11E. 76
Luga, Russia. 59N 30E. 90
Lugano, Italy. 46N. 9E 82
Lugano, Switzerland. 46N. 9E. 87
Lugano, L. of, Switzerland. 46N. 9E. 87
Lugansk, Russia. 49N. 39E. 91
Lugg, R., England. 52N. 3w. 56
Luguarmilla, Ireland. 53N. 6w. 69
Lugo, Italy. 44N. 12E. 83
*Lugo, Spain. 43N. 8w. 84
Lugos, Hungary. 46N. 22E. 79
Luina, Italy. 46N. 9E. 82
Luing Is., Scotland. 56N. 6w. 64
Lukmanier P., Switzerland. 47N. 9E. 87
Lulea R., Sweden. 66N. 22E. 88
Lum Fd., Denmark. 57N. 9E. 89
Lunan, Scotland. 57N. 3w. 63
*Lund, Sweden. 56N. 13E. 89
Lunderburg, Austria. 49N. 17E. 78
*Lundy Is., England. 51N. 5w. 56
Lune, R., England. 54N. 3w. 54
Luneburg, Germany. 53N. 10E. 76
Luneburg Heath, Germany. 53N. 10E. 76
*Luneville, France. 47N. 6E. 73
Lunga, Dalmatia. 44N. 15E. 78
Lurgan, Ireland. 55N. 6w. 67
Lusk, Ireland. 54N. 6w. 67
Luss, Scotland. 56N. 5w. 64
*Lutterworth, England. 52N. 1w. 57
Lutjenberg, Germany. 54N. 10E. 76
Luton, England. 52N 0w. 57
Lutry, Switzerland. 46N. 7E. 86
Lutsk, Russia. 51N. 26E. 91
Luxemburg, Belgium. 50N. 5E. 71
Luxemburg, Grand Duchy of, Belgium. 50N. 6E. 71
Luz, France. 43N. 0w. 72
Lybster, Scotland. 58N. 3w. 63
Lyck, Germany. 54N. 22E. 75
Lyme B., England. 51N. 3w. 56
*Lyme Regis, England. 51N. 3w 56
Lymington, England. 51N. 2w. 57
Lyne Water, Scotland. 56N. 3w. 65
Lyngen Fd., Norway. 70N. 20E. 88
Lynton, England. 51N 4w. 56
Lyon, R., Scotland. 57N. 4w. 63
*Lyons, France. 46N. 5E. 73
Lys, R., Belgium. 51N. 4E. 71
Lyss, Switzerland. 47N. 7E. 86
Lytham, England. 54N. 3w. 54

Maas, R., Holland. 52N. 5E. 70
Maaseyk, Belgium. 51N 6E. 71
Maastrich, Holland. 51N. 6E. 71
Mablethorpe, England. 53N. 0E. 55
Macclesfield, England. 53N. 2w. 54
Macduff, Scotland. 58N. 2w. 63
Macedonia, Turkey. 41N 22E. 95
Macerata, Italy. 43N. 13E. 83
Macgillicuddys Rocks, Ireland. 52N. 10w. 68

PAGE

Machrihanish, Scotland. 55N. 6w. 64
Machynlleth, Wales. 53N. 4w. 56
Macnean, Upper Lough, Ireland.
　54N. 8w. 66
Macomer, Sardinia. 40N. 9E. 81
*Macon, France. 46N. 5E. 73
Macroom, Ireland. 52N. 9w. 68
Madaras, Hungary. 47N. 21E. 79
Maddaloni, Italy. 41N. 14E. 81
Maddy, Loch, Scotland. 58N. 7w. 62
Madras Mts., Crete. 35N. 24E. 95
*Madrid, Spain. 40N. 4w. 84
Maelstrom, Norway. 68N. 13E. 88
Magdalena, Sardinia. 41N 9E. 81
*Magdeburg, Germany. 52N. 12E. 76
*Magenta, Italy. 45N. 9E 82
Mageroe, Norway. 71N. 25E. 88
Maggia, Switzerland. 46N. 9E. 87
Maggia R., Switzerland. 46N. 9E. 87
Maggiore, L., Italy. 46N. 9E. 82
Maghera, Ireland. 55N. 7w. 67
Magherafelt, Ireland. 55N. 7w. 67
Magilligan Pt, Ireland. 55N. 7w. 67
Maglai, Bosnia. 45N. 18E. 94
Magliano, Italy. 42N. 12E. 83
Magra B., Italy. 44N. 10E. 82
Mague, R., Ireland. 53N. 9w. 68
Maguires Bridge, Ireland. 54N. 7w. 67
Magurelli, Roumania. 44N. 25E. 94
Mahon, Minorca. 40N. 4E. 85
*Maidenhead, England. 52N. 1w. 57
Maidens Is., Ireland 55N. 6w. 67
*Maidstone, England. 51N. 1E. 57
Main, R., Germany. 50N. 9E. 77
Main, R., Ireland. 55N. 6w. 67
Maine et Loire, France. 48N. 1w. 72
Maine, R., Ireland. 52N. 10w 68
Mainland Is., Scotland. 59N. 3w. 63
Maira R., Italy. 45N. 8E. 82
*Majorca, Balearic Isles. 39N. 3E. 85
Mako, Hungary. 46N. 20E. 79
Mal Bal, Ireland. 53N. 9w. 68
Maladetta, Spain. 43N. 1E. 85
*Malaga, Spain. 37N. 4w. 84
Malahide, Ireland. 53N. 6w. 67
Malar L., Sweden. 59N. 17E. 89
Malchin, Germany. 54N. 12E. 76
*Maldon, England. 52N. 1E. 57
Malgara, Turkey. 41N. 27E. 95
Malia C., Greece. 36N. 23E. 95
Malin, Ireland. 55N. 7w. 67
Malin Hd., Ireland. 65N. 7w. 67
Malinmore Hd , Ireland. 55N. 9w. 66
Mallaig, Scotland. 57N. 6w. 62
Mallow, Ireland. 52N. 9w. 68
Malmberg, Sweden. 67N. 21E. 88
*Malmesbury, England. 52N. 2w. 56
Malmö, Sweden. 56N. 13E 89
Malmysh, Russia. 57N. 51E. 90
Maloja, Switzerland. 46N. 10E. 87
Malpas, England. 53N. 3w. 54
Malton, England. 54N. 1w. 55
Malvaglia, Switzerland. 46N. 9E. 87
Malvern Hills, England. 52N. 2w. 56
Mam Soul, Scotland. 57N. 5w. 62
Mamturk Mts., Ireland 54N. 10w. 66
Manacles, England. 50N. 5w. 56
Manacor, Majorca. 40N. 3E. 85

PAGE

*Manchester, England. 53N. 2w. 54
Manchester Ship Canal, England.
　53N. 3w. 54
Mandal, Norway. 58N. 7E. 89
Manfredonia, Italy. 42N. 16E. 80
Manfredonia, G. of, Italy. 42N.
　16E. 80
Mangalia, Roumania. 44N. 29E. 94
Mangerton, Upper Lough, Ireland.
　52N. 9w. 68
*Mannheim, Germany. 49N. 9E. 77
Mannin B., Ireland. 53N. 10w. 66
Manningtree, England. 52N 1E. 57
Manor Hamilton, Ireland. 54N. 8w. 66
Manresa, Spain. 42N. 2E. 85
Mansfield, England. 53N. 1w. 55
Mansilla, Spain. 43N. 5w. 84
*Mantua, Italy. 45N. 11E. 83
Manulla, Ireland. 54N. 9w. 66
Manytch, Russia. 46N. 44E. 91
Manzanares, Spain. 39N. 3w. 84
Manzanares, R., Spain. 40N. 4w. 84
Mar Menor, Spain. 38N. 1w. 85
Marargui, C., Sardinia. 40N. 8E. 81
Marathon, Greece. 38N. 24E. 95
Marathonisi G., Greece. 37N. 23E. 95
Marbella, Spain. 37N. 5w. 84
*Marburg, Austria. 47N. 16E. 78
*Marburg, Germany. 51N. 9E. 77
March, R., Austria. 48N. 17E. 78
Marche, Belgium. 50N. 5E. 71
Marchena, Spain. 37N. 5w. 84
Marches, Italy. 43N. 13E. 83
Marecchia, R., Italy. 44N. 12E. 83
Maree, Loch, Scotland. 58N. 5w. 62
Maremma, Italy. 44N. 10E. 82
*Marengo, Italy. 45N. 9E. 82
Margate, England. 51N. 1E. 57
Margitta, Hungary. 46N. 26E 79
Maria Theresiopel, Hungary. 46N.
　20E. 94
Marienbad, Austria. 50N. 12E 78
Marienbourg, Belgium. 50N. 5E. 71
Marienwurder, Germany. 54N. 19E. 75
Mariestad, Sweden. 59N. 14E. 89
Marino, Italy. 42N. 13E 83
Maritime Alps, Italy. 44N. 7E. 82
Maritimo Is., Sicily. 38N. 12E. 81
Maritza R., Bulgaria. 42N. 26E. 94
Mariupol, Russia. 47N. 38E. 91
Marken, Holland. 52N. 5E. 70
Market Bosworth, England. 53N.
　1w. 57
Market Deeping, England. 53N.
　0w. 55
*Market Drayton, England. 53N.
　2w. 54
*Market Harborough, England.
　52N. 1w. 57
Market Rasen, England. 53N. 0w. 55
Market Weighton, England. 51N.
　1w. 55
Markethill, Ireland. 54N. 7w. 67
Markinch, Scotland. 56N. 3w. 65
Markirch, Germany. 48N. 7E. 77
Marlborough, England. 51N. 2w. 56
Marmora, Sea of, Turkey. . N. 28E. 95
Marne, France. 49N. 4E. 73

PAGE

Marne, R., France. 49N. 2E. 73
Maros R., Hungary. 46N. 21E. 94
Maros Vasarhely, Hungary. 46N.
25E. 94
Maros Vasarhely, Hungary. 47N.
25E. 79
Marsal, Germany. 49N. 7E. 77
*Marsala, Sicily. 38N. 12E. 81
*Marseilles, France. 43N. 5E. 73
Martelange, Belgium. 50N. 6E 71
Martenburg, Germany. 54N. 19E.75
Martigny, Switzerland. 46N. 7E. 86
Martos, Spain. 38N 4W. 84
Maryborough, Ireland. 53N. 7W. 69
Marykirk, Scotland. 57N. 3W. 63
Maryport, England. 55N. 4W. 54
Mask, Lough, Ireland 54N. 9W. 66
Masham, England. 54N. 2W. 55
Massa, Italy. 43N. 11E. 83
Massa, Italy. 44N. 10E. 82
Matapan C., Greece. 36N. 22E. 95
Mataro, Spain. 42N. 2E. 85
Mate Szalka, Hungary. 48N. 22E. 79
Matera, Italy. 41N 17E. 81
Matlock, England 53N. 2W. 55
Matterhorn, Switzerland. 46N 8E. 86
Mauch, Scotland. 56N. 4W. 64
Mauche, France 49N 1W. 72
*Mauchline, Scotland. 56N. 4W. 65
Mawddach, R., Wales. 53N. 4W 56
Maxwelltown, Scotland. 55N. 4W. 65
Maybole, Scotland. 55N. 5W. 64
Maydan, Austria. 50N. 22E. 79
Mayen, Germany. 50N. 7E. 77
Mayence, Germany. 50N. 8E 77
Mayenne, France. 48N. 1W. 72
Mayenne, R., France. 47N. 1W. 72
Maynooth, Ireland. 53N. 7W. 67
Mazamet, France. 44N. 2E. 73
Mazarron, Spain. 38N. 1W. 85
Mazzara, Sicily. 38N. 13E. 81
Mealfourvounnie, Scotland. 57N.
5W. 62
Meath, Ireland. 54N. 7W. 67
*Meaux, France. 49N. 3E. 73
Mecklenburg, Germany. 54N.
12E. 76
Medemblik, Holland. 53N. 5E. 70
Mediasch, Hungary. 46N. 24E. 79
Medina, Spain. 42N. 5W. 84
Medina del Campo, Spain. 41N. 5W.84
Medina Sidonia, Spain. 36N. 6W. 84
Medjidie, Roumania. 44N. 29E. 94
Medoc, France. 45N. 1W. 72
Meerane, Germany. 51N. 12E. 77
Megara, Greece. 38N. 24E. 95
Megri, Turkey. 41N. 26E. 95
Mehadia, Hungary. 45N. 22E. 79
Meigle, Scotland. 57N. 3W. 63
Meilen, Switzerland. 47N. 9E. 87
Meiningen, Germany. 51N. 10E. 77
Meiningen, Switzerland. 47N. 8E. 86
*Meissen, Germany. 51N. 14E. 76
Melada I., Dalmatia. 44N. 15E 78
Melbourne, England. 53N. 1W. 55
Melcombe Regis, England. 51N.
2W. 56
Meleda Is., Dalmatia. 43N. 18E. 94

PAGE

Melegnano, Italy. 45N. 9E. 82
Melfi, Italy. 41N. 16E. 81
Melfort, Loch, Scotland. 56N. 6W. 64
Melness, Scotland. 59N. 4W. 62
Melnik, Austria. 50N. 14E. 78
Melnik, Turkey. 12N. 23E. 94
*Melrose, Scotland. 56N. 3W. 65
Meltham, England. 54N. 2W. 54
Melton Mowbray, England 53N.
1W. 55
*Melun, France. 49N. 3E. 73
Melvich, Scotland. 59N. 4W. 63
Melvin, Lough, Ireland. 54N. 8W. 66
Memel, Germany. 56N. 21E. 75
Memel R., Germany. 55N. 21E. 75
*Memmingen, Germany 48N. 10E.77
Menaggio, Italy. 46N. 9E. 82
Menai Strait, Wales. 53N. 4W 54
Mende, France. 44N 3E. 73
Mendip Hills, England. 51N 3W. 56
Mendrisio, Switzerland. 46N. 9E. 87
Menin, Belgium. 51N. 3E. 71
Mentone, France. 44N. 7E. 73
Meppel, Holland. 53N. 6E. 70
Meppen, Germany. 53N. 7E. 76
Merida, Spain. 39N 6W. 84
Merioneth, Wales. 53N. 4W. 54
Meron, Austria 47N. 11E. 78
Merrick, Scotland. 55N. 4W. 64
Mersch, Luxemburg. 50N. 6E. 71
Merseburg, Germany. 52N. 12E. 76
Mersey, R., England. 53N. 3W. 54
Merthyr Tydfil, Wales. 52N. 3W. 56
Merzig, Germany. 49N. 7E. 77
Meseritz, Germany. 53N. 16E. 75
Mesocco, Switzerland. 46N. 9E. 87
Mesocco R , Switzerland. 46N. 9E. 87
*Messina, Sicily. 38N. 16E. 81
*Messina Strait of, Italy. 38N. 16E. 81
Messini, Greece. 37N. 22E. 95
Mesta R., Turkey 41N 24E 95
Mestre, Italy. 46N. 12E. 83
Metaponto, Italy. 40N. 17E. 81
Metauro, R., Italy. 44N. 13E. 83
Methil, Scotland. 56N 3W. 65
Methlick, Scotland. 57N. 2W. 63
*Methven, Scotland. 56N. 4W. 65
Metkovitz, Bosnia. 43N. 18E. 94
Metsova, Turkey. 40N. 21E. 95
*Metz, Germany. 49N. 6E. 77
Meurthe, R., France. 49N. 6E. 73
Meurthe et Moselle, France. 49N.
6E. 73
Meuse, France. 49N. 5E. 73
Mew Lighthouse, Ireland. 55N.
6W. 67
Mexborough, England. 53N. 1W. 55
Mezen, Russia. 66N. 44E. 90
Mezen, G. of, Russia. 67N. 44E. 90
Mezen, R., Russia. 66N. 44E. 90
*Mezières, France. 50N. 1E. 73
Mezo Havas, Hungary 47N 26E. 79
Mezotur, Hungary. 47N. 21E. 79
Mhor, Loch, Scotland. 57N. 4W. 63
Miava, Hungary. 49N. 18E. 78
Mid Calder, Scotland. 56N. 3W. 65
Midd, R., England. 54N. 1W. 55
*Middelburg, Holland. 51N. 4E. 70

	PAGE
Middle Franconia, Germany. 49N. 10E.	77
Middlesborough, England. 55N. 1w.	55
Middlesex, England. 52N. 0w.	57
Middleton, England. 54N. 2w.	54
Middleton, Ireland. 52N. 8w.	68
Middlewich, England. 53N. 2w.	54
Midhurst, England. 51N. 1w.	57
Midia, Turkey. 42N. 28E.	94
Mies, R., Austria. 50N. 14E.	78
Milan, Italy. 45N. 9E.	82
Milanovatz, Servia. 44N. 22E.	94
Milazzo, Sicily. 38N. 15E.	81
Mildenhall, England. 52N. 1E.	57
Milford, England. 54N. 1w.	55
Milford, Ireland. 55N. 8w.	67
Milford, Wales. 52N. 5w.	56
Milford Haven, Wales. 52N. 5w.	56
Milk Haven, Ireland. 54N. 8w.	66
Milkovatz, Bulgaria. 44N. 23E.	94
Milleau, France. 44N. 3E.	73
Millstreet, Ireland. 52N. 9w.	68
Milltown Malbay, Ireland. 53N. 9w.	68
Milnathom, Scotland. 56N. 3w.	65
Milne, Loch, Scotland. 58N. 5w.	62
Milngavie, Scotland. 56N. 4w.	65
Milos, Greece. 37N. 24E.	95
Minas, Spain. 38N. 7w.	84
Minch, The, Scotland. 58N. 6w.	62
Mincio, R., Italy. 45N. 11E.	83
Minden, Germany. 52N 8E	76
Mine Hd., Lighthouse, Ireland. 52N. 8w.	69
Minehead, England. 51N. 3w.	56
Minho, R., Spain. 43N. 9w.	84
Minorca, Balearic Isles. 40N. 4E.	85
Minsk, Russia. 54N. 29E.	91
Miosen, L., Norway. 61N. 11E.	89
Mirabella, Crete. 35N. 26E.	95
Miranda, Spain. 43N. 3w.	85
Mirandella, Portugal. 42N. 7w.	84
Mirandola, Italy. 45N. 11E.	83
Mirecourt, France. 48N. 6E.	73
Miskolcz, Hungary. 48N. 21E.	79
Missolongi, Greece. 38N. 22E.	95
Mistretta, Sicily. 38N. 14E.	81
Mitan, Russia. 57N 23E.	90
Mitcheldean, England. 52N. 2w.	56
Mitchelstown, Ireland. 52N 8w.	68
Mitrovitz, Hungary. 45N. 20E.	79
Mitrovitza, Turkey. 43N 21E.	94
Mittel Geb., Austria. 51N. 14E.	78
Mizen Hd , Ireland. 51N. 10w.	68
Mizen Hd., Ireland. 53N. 6w.	69
Moate, Ireland. 53N. 8w.	67
Modena, Italy. 45N. 11E.	83
Modica, Sicily. 37N 15E.	81
Moen, Denmark. 55N. 12E.	89
Moerdyke, Holland. 52N. 5E.	70
Moffat, Scotland. 55N. 3w.	65
Mohacs, Hungary. 46N. 19E.	79
Mohilev, Russia. 54N. 30E.	91
Mohill, Ireland. 54N. 8w.	67
Moidart, Loch, Scotland. 57N. 6w.	62
Moissac, France. 44N. 1E.	72
Mojacar, Spain. 37N. 2w.	85
Mokshan, Russia. 53N. 45E.	91
Mola, Italy. 41N. 17E.	81
Mold, Wales. 53N. 3w.	54
Moldau, R., Austria. 50N. 14E.	78
Moldavia, Roumania. 47N. 27E.	94
Molde, Norway. 63N. 7E.	88·
Molde Fjord, Norway. 63N. 7E.	88
Mole R., England. 51N. 0w.	57
Molfetta, Italy. 41N 17E.	81
Molina, Spain. 41N. 2w.	85
Molise, Italy. 42N. 14E.	83
Monadhliath Mts. Scotland. 57N. 4w.	63
Monaghan, Ireland. 54N. 7w.	67
Monalto, Italy. 43N. 14E.	83
Monastir, Bulgaria. 43N. 26E.	94
Monastir, Turkey. 41N. 21E.	95
Monasterevin, Ireland. 53N. 7w.	69
Mönch, Switzerland. 47N. 8E.	86
Mondego, C., Portugal. 40N. 9w.	84
Mondego, R., Portugal. 40N. 9w.	84
*Mondovi, Italy. 44N. 8E.	82
Moneglia, Italy. 44N. 9E.	82
Moneygall, Ireland. 53N. 8w.	69
Moneymore, Ireland. 55N. 7w.	67
Monferrat, Italy. 45N 8E.	82
Moniave, Scotland. 55N. 4w.	65
Monikie, Scotland. 57N. 3w.	63
Monivea, Ireland. 53N. 9w.	66
*Monmouth, England. 52N. 3w.	56
Monnow, R., England. 52N. 3w.	56
Monopoli, Italy. 41N. 17E.	81
Mons, Belgium. 50N. 4E.	71
Monselice, Italy. 45N. 12E.	83
Mt. Adamello, Austria. 46N. 11E.	78
Mt. Cenis, France 45N. 7E.	73
Mont de Marsan, France. 44N. 0w.	72
Mt. Maladena, France. 43N 1E.	72
Mt. Marmolade, Austria. 46N. 12E.	78
Mont Terrible, Switzerland. 47N. 7E.	86
Montalcino, Italy. 43N. 11E.	83
Montalto, Italy. 42N. 12E.	83
*Montargis, France. 48N. 3E.	73
*Montauban, France. 44N. 1E.	72
Montbrison, France. 46N. 4E.	73
Monte Carlo, France. 44N 7E.	73
Monte Cristo Is., Italy. 42N. 10E.	82
Monte Rosa, Switzerland. 46N. 8E.	86
Monte Santo G., Turkey. 40N. 24E.	95
Montechiaro, Italy. 45N. 10E.	82
Montefiascone, Italy. 43N. 12E.	83
Montelcone, Italy. 39N. 16E.	81
Montelimart, France. 45N. 5E.	73
Montepulciano, Italy. 43N. 12E.	83
Monterrubio, Spain. 42N. 3w.	84
Montes de Toledo, Spain. 40N 5w.	84
Montevarchi, Italy. 44N. 12E.	83
*Montgomery, Wales. 53N. 3w.	56
Monthey, Switzerland. 46N. 7E.	86
Monti, Sardinia. 41N. 9E.	81
*Montilla, Spain. 38N. 5w.	84
Montluçon, France. 46N. 3E.	73
Montoro, Spain. 38N. 4w.	84
Montraz, Switzerland. 47N. 7E.	86
*Montpellier, France. 44N. 4E.	73

PAGE

Montreux, Switzerland. 46N. 7E. 86
*Montrose, Scotland. 57N. 2w. 63
Monymusk, Scotland. 57N. 2w. 63
*Monza, Italy. 46N. 9E. 82
Monzon, Spain. 42N. 0E. 85
Moor of Rannoch, Scotland. 57N.
  5w. 62
Moorfoot Hills, Scotland. 56N. 3w. 65
Moosberg, Germany. 49N. 12E. 77
Mora, Spain. 40N. 1w. 85
Morar, Loch, Scotland. 57N. 6w. 62
Morar, R., Scotland. 57N. 6w. 62
*Morat, Switzerland. 47N. 7E. 86
Morat, L. of, Switzerland. 47N. 7E. 86
Morava R., Servia. 45N. 21E. 94
Moravia, Austria. 49N. 17E. 78
Moravian Plateau, Austria. 49N.
  16E. 78
Moray Firth, Scotland. 58N. 4w. 63
Morbegno, Italy. 46N. 9E. 82
Morbihan, France. 48N. 3w. 72
Morbihan B., France. 48N. 3w. 72
Morcone, Italy. 41N. 15E. 81
Morea, Greece. 38N. 22E. 95
Morecambe B., England. 54N. 3w. 54
*Morella, Spain. 41N. 0w. 85
Moreton Hampstead, England.
  51N. 4w. 56
*Morgarten, Switzerland. 47N. 9E. 87
Morges, Switzerland. 47N. 6E. 86
Morgex, Italy. 46N. 7E. 82
Moritza R., Turkey. 41N. 26E. 95
*Morlaix, France. 49N. 4w. 72
Moron, Spain. 37N. 5w. 84
Morpeth, England. 55N. 2w. 54
*Mortara, Italy. 45N. 9E. 82
*Mortimer's Cross, England. 52N.
  3w. 56
Morven, Scotland. 57N. 6w. 62
Morven, Scotland. 58N. 4w. 63
*Moscow, Russia. 55N. 38E. 91
Mosdok, Russia. 44N. 45E. 91
Moselle, R., France. 49N. 6E. 73
Moselle, R., Germany. 50N. 7E. 77
Moss, Norway. 59N. 11E. 89
Mosso Santa Maria, Italy. 46N.
  8E. 82
Mostar, Bosnia. 43N. 18E. 94
Mosyr, Russia. 52N. 29E. 91
Motala, Sweden. 59N. 16E. 89
Motherwell, Scotland. 56N. 4w. 65
Motilla, Spain. 40N. 2w. 85
Motril, Spain. 37N. 4w. 84
Moudan, Switzerland. 47N. 7E. 86
*Moulins, France. 46N. 3E. 73
Mountains of Castile, Spain. 41N.
  4w. 84
Mountmellick, Ireland. 53N. 7w. 69
Mountrath, Ireland. 53N. 7w. 69
Mountshannon, Ireland. 53N. 8w. 68
Mounts B., England. 50N. 5w. 56
Mourne Mts., Ireland. 54N. 6w. 67
Mourne, R., Ireland. 55N. 7w. 67
Mouths of the Rhone, France.
  44N. 4E. 73
Moutier, Switzerland. 47N. 7E. 86
Moutier, V. de, Switzerland. 47N.
  7E. 86

PAGE

Moutiers, France. 45N. 6E. 73
Moville, Ireland. 55N. 7w. 67
Moy, Ireland. 54N. 7w. 67
Moy, R., Ireland. 54N. 9w. 66
Moynalty, Ireland. 54N. 7w. 67
Moyola R., Ireland. 55N. 7w. 67
Moyvally, Ireland. 53N. 7w. 67
Much Wenlock, England. 53N.
  3w. 56
Muck Is., Scotland. 57N. 6w. 62
Muckish, Ireland. 55N. 8w. 66
Muckno Lough, Ireland. 54N. 7w. 67
Muff, Ireland. 55N. 7w. 67
Muhlbach, Hungary. 46N. 24E. 79
Muhldorf, Germany. 48N. 12E. 77
Muhlhausen, Germany. 51N. 10E. 76
Muirkirk, Scotland. 56N. 4w. 65
Muldberg, Germany. 52N. 13E. 76
Mulde, Germany. 51N. 13E. 76
Mulde R., Germany. 52N. 12E. 76
Mülhausen, Germany. 48N. 7E. 77
Mulheim, Germany. 51N. 7E. 76
*Mull, Scotland. 56N. 6w. 61
Mull, Sound of, Scotland. 57N.
  6w. 62
Mull of Cantyre, Scotland. 55N.
  6w. 64
Mull of Galloway, Scotland. 55N.
  5w. 64
Mull of Oa, Scotland. 56N. 6w. 64
Mullaghmore, Ireland. 54N. 8w. 66
Mullcear, R., Ireland. 53N. 9w. 68
Mullinavat, Ireland. 52N. 7w. 69
Mullingar, Ireland. 54N. 7w. 67
Mulrea Mt., Ireland. 54N. 10w. 66
Mulroy B., Ireland. 55N. 8w. 67
Mumbles, Wales. 52N. 4w. 56
Mundesley, England. 53N. 1E. 55
*Munich, Germany. 48N. 12E. 77
Munkacs, Hungary. 49N. 23E. 79
Münster, Germany. 48N. 7E. 77
*Munster, Germany. 52N. 7E. 76
Munster, Ireland. 52N. 9w. 68
Munster, Switzerland. 47N. 8E. 86
Muonio, Sweden. 68N. 23E. 88
Mur, R., Hungary. 46N. 17E. 78
Muradly, Turkey. 41N. 27E. 95
Muravera, Sardinia. 39N. 10E. 81
Murcia, Spain. 38N. 1w. 85
Murias, Spain. 43N. 6w. 84
Muritz See, Germany. 53N. 12E. 76
Murom, Russia. 56N. 42E. 90
Muros, Spain. 43N. 9w. 84
Murren, Switzerland. 47N. 8E. 86
Murviedro, Spain. 40N. 0w. 85
Musselburgh, Scotland. 56N.
  30w. 65
Mustafa, Bulgaria. 42N. 26E. 94
Mustanly, Turkey. 42N. 26E. 94
Muthill, Scotland. 56N. 4w. 65
Mutton Is., Ireland. 53N. 10w. 68
Mykonos, Greece. 37N. 26E. 95
Mylus, Greece. 37N. 23E. 95
Mynydd Epynt, Wales. 52N. 4w. 56
Mythen, Switzerland. 47N. 9E. 87

Naarden, Holland. 52N. 5E. 70
Naas, Ireland. 53N. 7w. 67

PAGE

Nab, Germany. 50N. 12E. 77
Näfels, Switzerland. 47N. 9E. 87
Nagy-Kanissa, Hungary. 46N. 18E. 94
Nagy-Karoly, Hungary. 48N. 22E. 79
Nagy-Köros, Hungary. 47N. 20E. 79
Nailsworth, England. 52N. 2w. 56
*Nairn, Scotland. 58N. 4w. 63
Nakitchevan, Russia. 47N. 40E. 91
Nakshoy, Denmark. 55N. 12w. 89
Namsen, Norway. 65N. 12E. 88
Namsos, Norway. 64N. 12E. 88
*Namur, Belgium. 50N. 5E. 71
Nanas, Hungary. 48N. 21E. 79
*Nancy, France. 49N. 6E. 73
Nanny, R., Ireland. 54N. 6w. 67
*Nantes, France. 47N. 2w. 72
Nantua, France. 46N. 6E. 73
*Nantwich, England. 53N. 3w. 54
Nao, C. de la, Spain. 39N. 0E. 85
Napf, Switzerland. 47N. 8E. 86
*Naples, Italy. 41N. 14E. 81
Naples, B. of, Italy. 41N. 14E. 81
Narberth, Wales. 52N. 5w. 56
*Narbonne, France. 43N. 3E. 73
Nardo, Italy. 40N. 18E. 81
Narni, Italy. 43N. 13E. 83
Naro, Sicily. 37N. 14E. 81
*Narva, Russia. 59N. 28E. 90
Narvik, Norway. 68N. 17E. 88
Nassau, Germany. 50N. 8E. 77
*Naseby, England. 52N. 1w. 57
Nash Pt., Wales. 51N. 4w. 56
Nasice, Slavonia. 45N. 18E. 78
Nässjo, Sweden. 58N. 15E. 89
Nauen, Germany. 53N. 13E. 76
Nauplia, Greece. 38N. 23E. 95
Nauplia G., Greece. 37N. 23E. 95
Nava, Spain. 41N. 5w. 84
Navan, Ireland. 54N. 7w. 67
Navarra, Spain. 43N. 2w. 85
Navea, Spain. 44N. 7w. 84
Naver, Loch, Scotland. 58N. 4w. 63
Naxos, Greece. 37N. 26E. 95
Naze, The, England. 52N. 1E. 57
Naze, The, Norway. 58N. 7E. 89
Neagh, Lough, Ireland. 55N. 6w. 67
Neath, Wales. 52N. 4w. 56
Neath, R., Wales. 52N. 4w. 56
Needles, The, England. 51N. 2w. 57
Negoi, Hungary. 46N. 25E. 79
Negor Mt., Roumania. 46N. 25E. 94
Negropont, Greece. 38N. 24E. 95
Neidenburg, Germany. 53N. 21E. 75
Neilston, Scotland. 56N. 4w. 65
Neiss R., Germany. 52N. 15E. 76
*Neisse, Germany. 51N. 17E. 75
Neisse R., Germany. 51N. 17E. 75
Nekar, R., Germany. 49N. 9E. 77
Nelson, England. 54N. 2w. 54
Nen, R., England. 53N. 0E. 55
Nenagh, Ireland. 53N. 8w. 68
Nephin Mt., Ireland. 54N. 9w. 66
Nephin Beg Mt.,Ireland. 54N. 10w. 66
Nera R., Italy. 42N. 12E. 83
Neretva R., Bosnia. 43N. 18E. 94
Nerone Mt., Italy. 44N. 12E. 83
Ness, Loch, Scotland. 57N. 4w. 63
Ness, R., Scotland. 57N. 4w. 63

Nesthorn, Switzerland. 46N. 8E. 86
Neston, England. 53N. 3w. 54
Nettuno, Italy. 41N. 13E. 81
Netze R. Germany. 53N. 17E. 75
Neu Brandenburg, Germany. 54N. 13E. 76
Neuburg, Germany. 49N. 11E. 77
Neuchâtel, Switzerland. 47N. 7E. 86
Neufchâteau, Belgium. 50N. 6E. 71
Neufchâtel, France. 50N. 1E. 72
Neuhaus, Austria. 49N. 15E. 78
Neuhäusel, Hungary. 48N. 18E. 79
Neumünster, Germany. 54N. 10E. 76
Neunkirch, Switzerland. 48N. 9E. 87
Neu Ruppin, Germany. 53N. 12E. 76
Neusatz, Hungary. 45N. 20E. 94
Neusiedler, Hungary. 48N. 17E. 78
Neusohl, Hungary. 49N. 19E. 79
Neustadt, Germany. 50N. 18E. 75
Neustadt, Germany. 54N. 11E. 76
Neustadt, Germany. 48N. 8E. 77
Neustadt, Germany. 50N. 11E. 77
Neustadt, Austria. 48N. 16E. 78
Neu Stettin, Germany. 54N. 16E. 75
Neu Strelitz, Germany. 53N. 13E. 76
Neuss, Germany. 51N. 7E. 76
Neutra, R., Hungary. 49N. 18E. 78
Neutraer Geb, Hungary. 49N. 18E. 78
Neu Ulm, Germany. 48N. 10E. 77
Neuveville Switzerland. 47N. 7E. 86
Neva R., Russia. 60N. 31E. 90
Nevers, France. 47N. 3E. 73
*Nevin, Wales. 53N. 5w. 54
Nevis, Loch, Scotland. 57N. 6w. 62
Nevrekon, Turkey. 42N. 24E. 94
New R., England. 52N. 0w. 57
New Abbey, Scotland. 55N. 4w. 65
*Newark, England. 53N. 1w. 55
Newbiggin, England. 55N. 2w. 55
New Birmingham, Ireland. 53N. 8w. 69
Newbliss, Ireland. 54N. 7w. 67
New Bolingbroke, England. 53N. 0w. 55
Newbridge, Ireland. 53N. 7w. 69
New Brighton, England. 53N. 3w. 54
Newburgh, Scotland. 56N. 3w. 65
*Newbury, England. 51N. 1w. 57
New Byth, Scotland. 58N. 2w. 63
New Castile, Spain. 40N. 3w. 85
Newcastle, Ireland. 54N. 6w. 67
Newcastle, Ireland. 52N. 9w. 68
Newcastle Emlyn, Wales. 52N. 4w. 56
Newcastleton, Scotland. 55N. 3w. 65
Newcastle-under-Lyme, England. 53N. 2w. 54
*Newcastle - upon - Tyne, England. 55N. 2w. 55
New Cumnock, Scotland. 55N. 4w. 65
New Deer, Scotland. 58N. 2w. 63
Newent, England. 52N. 2w. 56
New Forest, England. 51N. 2w. 57
New Galloway, Scotland. 55N. 4w. 65
*Newhaven, England. 51N. 0E. 57
New Holland, England. 54N. 0w. 55
Newmarket, England. 52N. 0E. 57

PAGE

Newmarket, Ireland. 53N. 9w. 68
New Milford, Wales. 52N. 5w. 56
Newmilns, Scotland. 56N. 4w. 65
New Pitsligo, Scotland. 58N. 2w. 63
Newport, England. 53N. 2w. 54
Newport, England. 52N. 3w. 56
*Newport, England. 51N. 1w. 57
Newport, Ireland. 54N. 10w. 66
Newport B., Ireland. 54N. 10w. 66
Newport, Ireland. 53N. 8w. 68
Newport, Scotland. 56N. 4w. 65
Newport, Wales. 52N. 5w. 56
Newport Pagnell, England. 52N.
   1w. 57
New Quay, England. 50N. 5w. 56
New Radnor, Wales. 52N. 3w. 56
New Romney, England. 51N. 1E. 57
New Ross, Ireland. 52N. 7w. 69
Newry, Ireland. 54N. 6w. 67
New Shoreham, England. 51N. 0w.57
Newton, England. 53N. 3w. 54
Newton Abbot, England. 51N. 4w. 56
Newton Stewart, Scotland. 55N.
   5w 64
*Newtown, Wales. 53N. 3w. 56
Newtown, Ireland. 53N. 6w. 69
Newtownards, Ireland. 55N. 6w. 67
Newtown-barry, Ireland. 53N 7w. 69
Newtown Bellew, Ireland. 53N.
   9w. 66
Newtown Butler, Ireland. 54N.
   7w. 67
Newtown Hamilton, Ireland. 54N.
   7w. 67
Newtown Stewart, Ireland. 55N.
   7w. 67
Niamtzo, Roumania. 47N. 26E. 94
*Nice, France. 44N. 7E. 73
Nicopoli, Bulgaria. 44N. 25E. 94
Nicosia, Sicily. 38N 15E. 81
Nicostro, Italy. 39N. 17E. 81
Nicotera, Italy. 39N. 16E. 81
Nidau, Switzerland. 47N. 7E. 86
Nidder, R., Germany. 50N. 9E. 77
Nienburg, Germany. 53N. 9E. 76
Nienten R., Germany. 55N. 21E. 75
Niesen, Switzerland 47N. 8E. 86
Nieshin, Russia 51N. 32E. 91
*Nieuport, Belgium. 51N. 3E. 71
Nieuwediep, Holland. 53N. 5E. 70
Nieuwpoort, Holland. 52N. 5E. 70
Nievre, France. 47N. 3E. 73
Nigg, Scotland. 58N 4w. 63
Nijar, Spain. 37N. 2w. 85
Nijni Novgorod, Russia. 56N.
   44E. 90
Nijni Tagilsk, Russia. 59N. 58E. 90
Nikolaicvsk, Russia. 52N 49E. 91
Nikolaistadt (Vasa), Russia. 64N.
   22E. 90
Nikolaos, H., Greece. 36N. 23E. 95
Nikolayev, Russia. 47N. 32E. 91
Nikolsburg, Austria. 49N. 17E. 78
Niksics, Montenegro. 43N. 19E. 94
Nilly, Lough, Ireland. 54N. 8w. 67
Nimes, France. 44N. 4E. 73
*Niort, France. 46N. 0w. 72
Nios, Greece. 37N. 25E. 95

PAGE

Nish, Servia. 43N. 22E. 94
Nishegorod, Russia. 56N. 44E. 90
Nissa R., Sweden. 57N. 13E. 89
Nith R., Scotland. 55N. 4w. 65
Nivelles, Belgium. 51N. 4E. 71
Nizza, Italy. 45N. 8E. 82
Noale, Italy. 46N. 12E. 83
Nobber, Ireland. 54N. 7w. 67
Nocera, Italy. 43N. 13E. 83
Nogent-sur-Seine, France. 48N. 4E. 73
Noguera Pallaresa, R., Spain. 42N.
   1E. 85
Noguera Ribagorzana, R., Spain.
   42N. 0E. 85
Noirmoutier, Is., France. 47N. 2w. 72
Norcia, Italy. 43N. 13E. 83
Nord, France. 50N. 3E. 73
Norden, Germany. 54N. 7E. 76
Nordeney Is., Germany. 54N. 7E. 76
Nordenham, Germany. 54N. 8E. 76
Nordhausen, Germany. 52N. 11E. 76
Nordkyn, Norway. 71N. 28E. 88
Nordlingen, Germany. 49N. 10E.77
Nordrach, Germany. 48N. 8E. 77
Nore, England. 51N. 1E. 57
Nore, R., Ireland. 52N. 7w. 69
Norfolk, England. 53N. 1E. 57
*Norham, England. 56N. 2w. 54
Noric Alps, Austria. 47N. 14E. 78
Norris Mt., Ireland 54N. 6w. 67
Norrköping, Sweden. 59N. 16E. 89
Norrland, Sweden. 65N 18E. 88
*Northallerton, England. 54N. 1w. 55
*Northampton, England. 52N 1w. 57
North Berwick, Scotland. 56N. 3w.65
N. Beverland, Holland. 52N. 4E. 70
North Brabant, Holland. 52N. 5E. 70
North Cape, Norway. 71N. 26E. 88
North Channel, Ireland. 55N. 6w. 67
N. Dorogi, Russia. 53N. 28E. 91
North Downs, England. 51N. 1w. 57
Nortkeim, Germany. 53N. 10E. 76
N. Foreland, England. 51N 1E. 57
N Frisian Is., Germany. 55N. 8E. 74
North Kvalo, Norway. 70N. 19E.88
N. Queensferry, Scotland. 56N.
   3w. 65
North Riding, Yorkshire. 54N. 2w. 54
N. Ronaldshay Is., Scotland. 59N.
   2w. 63
N. Shields, England. 55N. 1w. 55
N. Somkut, Hungary. 48N. 23E. 79
North Sd., Ireland. 53N. 10w. 68
N. Tyne R., England. 55N. 2w. 54
N. Uist Is., Scotland. 58N. 7w. 62
Northumberland, England. 55N.
   2w. 54
N. Walsham, England. 53N. 1E. 55
Northwich, England. 53N. 3w. 54
*Norwich, England. 53N. 1E. 57
Noss Hd., Scotland. 58N. 3w. 63
Noto, Sicily. 37N. 15E. 81
*Nottingham, England. 53N. 1w. 55
Noya, Spain. 43N. 9w. 84
Noyon, France. 50N. 3E. 73
Novaia Zemlia, Russia. 71N. 55E. 90
*Novara, Italy. 45N. 9E. 82
Novgorod, Russia. 59N. 31E. 90

PAGE

*Novi, Italy. 15N. 9E. 82
Novi, Bosnia. 45N. 16E. 94
Novibazar, Turkey. 43N. 20E. 94
Novorossisk, Russia. 45N. 38E. 91
Novo Tcherkask, Russia. 47N. 40E. 91
Nufenen P., Switzerland. 46N. 9E. 87
Nugen, Mt., Ireland. 54N. 7W. 67
Nukha, Russia. 41N. 47E. 91
Nules, Spain. 40N. 0W. 85
*Nuneaton, England. 53N. 1W. 57
Nuoro, Sardinia. 40N. 9E. 81
Nüremburg, Germany. 51N. 12E. 76
*Nürnberg, Germany. 49N. 11E. 77
Nyeborg, Denmark. 55N. 11E. 89
Nykerk, Holland. 52N. 5E. 70
Nyiregyhaza, Hungary. 48N. 22E. 79
Nykjöbing, Denmark. 55N. 12E. 89
Nyköping, Sweden. 59N. 17E. 89
Nymegen, Holland. 52N. 6E. 70
Nyon, Switzerland. 46N. 6E. 86

Oakham, England. 53N. 1W. 57
Oban, Scotland. 56N. 5W. 64
*Ober Ammergau, Germany. 48N. 11E. 77
Oberhaltstein, Switzerland. 47N. 10E. 87
Oberhausen, Germany. 52N. 6E. 76
Oberwald, Switzerland. 47N. 8E. 87
Obra R., Germany. 52N. 16E. 75
Obrenovatz, Servia. 45N. 20E. 94
Ochil Hills, Scotland. 56N. 4W. 65
Ocker R., Germany. 53N. 10E. 76
Odde, Norway. 60N. 6E. 80
Odemira, Portugal. 38N. 9W. 84
*Odense, Denmark. 55N. 10E. 89
Odenwald, Germany. 49N. 9E. 77
Oder R., Germany. 53N. 15E. 75
Oderberg, Austria. 50N. 18E. 79
Oderburg, Germany. 50N. 18E. 75
Oderzo, Italy. 46N. 12E. 83
*Odessa, Russia. 46N. 31E. 91
Odiel, R., Spain. 37N. 7W. 84
Oebisfelde, Germany. 53N. 11E. 76
Oedenburg, Austria. 48N. 16E. 78
Oels, Germany. 51N. 18E. 75
Oesel, Russia. 58N. 22E. 90
Ofanto R., Italy. 41N. 16E. 81
Ofen P., Switzerland. 47N. 10E. 87
Ofenhorn, Switzerland. 46N. 8E. 86
Offenbach, Germany. 50N. 9E. 77
Offenburg, Germany. 48N. 8E. 77
Ofoten Fd., Norway. 68N. 17E. 88
Oglio R., Italy. 46N. 10E. 82
Ogulin, Croatia. 45N. 15E. 78
Oignon, R. l', France. 47N. 5E. 73
Oise, R., France. 49N. 2E. 73
Oka R., Russia. 55N. 40E. 91
Okehampton, England. 51N. 4W. 56
Okhrida, Turkey. 41N. 21E. 95
Okhrida L., Turkey. 41N. 21E. 95
Okna, Roumania. 46N. 26E. 94
Oland, Sweden. 57N. 17E. 89
Old Aberdeen, Scotland. 57N. 2W. 63
Oldbury, England. 53N. 2W. 56
Oldcastle, Ireland. 54N. 7W. 67
Old Deer, Scotland. 58N. 2W. 63

PAGE

Oldenburg, Germany. 53N. 8E. 76
Oldenburg, Germany. 54N. 11E. 76
Oldenhorn, Switzerland. 46N. 7E. 86
Oldenzaal, Holland. 52N. 7E. 70
Oldestoe, Germany. 54N. 10E. 76
Oldham, England. 54N. 2W. 54
Old Hd. of Kinsale, Ireland. 52N. 9W. 68
Old Man of Hoy, Scotland. 59N. 3W. 63
Old Meldrum, Scotland. 57N. 2W. 63
Oleggio, Italy. 46N. 9E. 82
Oléron, Is. d', France. 46N. 1W. 72
Oleszyce, Austria. 50N. 23E. 79
Olivenza, Spain. 39N. 7W. 84
Olivone, Switzerland. 47N. 9E. 87
Ollerton, England. 53N. 1W. 55
Olmeneta, Italy. 45N. 10E. 82
*Olmütz, Austria. 50N. 17E. 78
*Olney, England. 52N. 1W. 57
Olona R., Italy. 45N. 9E. 82
Olonetz, Russia. 61N. 33E. 90
Oloron, France. 43N. 1W. 72
Olot, Spain. 42N. 3E. 85
Olpe, Germany. 51N. 8E. 76
Olten, Switzerland. 47N. 8E. 86
Oltenitza, Roumania. 44N. 26E. 94
Olympia, Greece. 38N. 22E. 95
Olympus Mt., Turkey. 40N. 22E. 95
Omagh, Ireland. 55N. 7W. 67
Ombrone, R., Italy. 43N. 11E. 83
Ommen, Holland. 53N. 6E. 70
Onda, Spain. 40N. 0W. 85
Ondawa, Hungary. 49N. 22E. 79
Onega, Russia. 64N. 38E. 90
Onega, G. of, Russia. 64N. 36E. 90
Onega L., Russia. 62N. 35E. 90
Onega R., Russia. 64N. 38E. 90
Oneglia, Italy. 44N. 8E. 82
O'Neil, Scotland. 57N. 3W. 63
Onteniente, Spain. 39N. 1W. 85
Oosterhout, Holland. 52N. 5E. 70
Ootmarsum, Holland. 52N. 7E. 70
*Oporto, Portugal. 41N. 9W. 84
Oppeln, Germany. 51N. 18E. 75
*Orange, France. 44N. 5E. 73
Oranmore, Ireland. 53N. 9W. 66
Orba R., Italy. 45N. 9E. 82
Orbe, Switzerland. 47N. 7E. 86
Orbe R., Switzerland. 47N. 6E. 86
Orbetello, Italy. 42N. 11E. 83
Orbigo R., Spain. 42N. 6W. 84
Orchy, R., Scotland. 56N. 5W. 64
Ord of Caithness, Scotland. 58N. 4W. 63
Ore, R., Scotland. 56N. 3W. 65
Orebro, Sweden. 59N. 15E. 89
Orenburg, Russia. 52N. 55E. 91
Orel, Russia. 53N. 31E. 91
Orense, Spain. 42N. 8W. 84
Orfani, Turkey. 41N. 24E. 95
Orfordness, England. 52N. 2E. 57
Orhuela, Spain. 38N. 1W. 85
Oristano, Sardinia. 40N. 9E. 81
Oristano, G. of, Sardinia. 40N. 9E. 81
Orkhanie, Bulgaria. 43N. 24E. 94
Orkney Is., Scotland. 59N. 3W. 63
Orlando C., Sicily. 38N. 15E. 81

PAGE

*Orleans, France. 48N. 2E. 73
Ormonts, Switzerland. 46N. 7E. 86
Ormskirk, England. 54N 3W. 54
Orne, France. 49N. 0E. 72
Ornsköldsviksköping, Sweden. 63N. 19E. 88
Oropesa, Spain. 40N. 5W. 84
Orosei, Sardinia. 40N. 10E. 81
Orosei, G. of, Sardinia. 40N. 10E. 81
Oroszhaza, Hungary. 47N. 21E. 79
Orphir, Scotland. 59N. 3W. 63
Orsières, Switzerland. 46N. 7E. 86
Orskaia, Russia. 51N. 59E. 91
Orsova, Roumania. 45N. 22E. 94
Orta, Italy. 46N. 8E. 82
Orta, L., Italy. 46N. 8E. 82
Orte, Italy. 42N. 12E. 83
Ortegal, C., Spain. 44N. 8W. 84
Ortler, Austria. 47N. 10E. 78
Ortona, Italy. 42N. 14E. 83
Orvieto, Italy. 43N. 12E. 83
Orwell, R., England. 52N. 1E. 57
Osborne, England. 51N 1W. 57
Oschersleben, Germany. 52N. 11E. 76
Osimo, Italy. 43N. 13E. 83
Osma, Spain. 42N. 3W. 85
Osnabruck, Germany. 52N. 8E 76
Osso Mt., Greece. 40N. 23E. 95
Ostashkov, Russia. 57N · 33E. 90
Oste R., Germany. 54N 9W. 76
*Ostende, Belgium 51N 3E 71
Osterburg, Germany. 53N. 12E. 76
Ostersund, Sweden. 63N. 15E. 88
Ostia, Italy. 42N. 12E. 83
Ostiglia, Italy. 45N. 11E. 83
Ostrovskaya, Russia. 56N. 62E. 90
Ostrov, Russia. 58N. 28E. 90
Ostrova, Turkey. 41N. 21E. 95
Ostrovitza, Bosnia. 45N. 16E. 94
Ostrovskaya, Russia. 56N. 62E. 90
Ostrowo, Germany. 52N. 18E. 75
Osung, Spain. 37N. 5W. 84
Ostuni, Italy. 41N. 18E. 81
*Oswestry, England. 53N. 3W. 54
Otley, England. 54N. 2W. 55
*Otranto, Italy. 40N. 18E. 81
Otranto, Strait of, Turkey. 40N 19E. 95
Otta, Norway. 62N. 10E. 89
Ottensen, Germany. 54N. 10E. 76
Otter, R., England. 51N. 3W. 56
*Otterburn, England. 55N. 2W. 54
Ottochatz, Croatia. 45N. 15E. 78
Ottone, Italy. 45N. 9E. 82
Ottweiler, Germany. 49N. 7E. 77
Oudawa, Austria-Hungary. 49N 22E. 79
*Oudenharde, Belgium. 51N. 4E. 71
Oudewater, Holland. 52N. 5E. 70
Oughter, Lough, Ireland 54N. 7W. 67
Oughterard, Ireland. 53N. 9W. 66
Oulart, Ireland. 53N. 6W. 69
Oulx, Italy. 45N. 7E. 82
Oundle, England. 53N. 0W. 57
Our, R, Germany. 50N. 6E. 77
Our, R., Luxemburg 50N. 6E. 71
Ourique, Portugal. 38N. 8W. 84
Ourthe, R., Belgium. 51N. 6E. 71

PAGE

Ouse, R., England. 54N. 1W. 55
Ouse, R., England. 53N. 0E. 57
Ovada, Italy. 45N. 9E. 82
Ovar, Portugal. 41N. 9W. 84
Over Flakkee, Holland. 52N. 4E. 70
Overton, Wales. 53N. 3W. 54
Overton, England. 51N. 1W. 57
Overyssel, Holland. 52N. 7E. 70
*Oviedo, Spain. 43N. 6W 84
Ovrutch, Russia. 51N. 29E. 91
Owel, Lough, Ireland 54N. 7W 67
Owenkillew, R., Ireland. 55N. 7W. 67
Owenmore R, Ireland. 54N. 10W. 66
Ox Mts., Ireland. 54N. 9W. 66
*Oxford, England. 52N. 1W. 57
Oykel, R, Scotland. 58N. 4W. 62
Oystermouth, Wales. 52N. 4W. 56
Ozieri, Sardinia. 41N. 9E. 81

Paar, R., Germany. 49N. 11E. 77
Pabbay Is, Scotland. 58N. 7W. 62
Pacho, Hungary. 49N. 18E. 78
*Paderborn, Germany. 52N. 9W. 76
Padron, Spain. 43N. 9W. 84
Padstow, England 51N. 5W. 56
*Padua, Italy. 45N. 12E 83
Pae Khoi Mts., Russia. 69N. 63E. 90
Paestum, Italy. 40N. 15E. 81
Pageni, Italy. 41N. 15E. 81
Pago, Dalmatia. 45N. 15E. 78
Paignton, England. 50N. 4W. 56
Paimbœuf, France. 47N. 2W. 72
Paisley, Scotland. 56N. 4W. 64
Pakraoz, Slavonia. 45N. 17E. 78
Palafrugell, Spain. 42N. 3E. 85
Palamos, Spain. 42N. 3E. 85
Palatinate, Germany. 49N. 8E. 77
Palazzola, Italy. 46N. 10E. 82
Palencia, Spain. 42N. 4W. 84
*Palermo, Sicily. 38N. 13E. 81
*Palestrina, Italy. 42N. 13E. 83
Pali C., Turkey. 41N. 19E. 94
*Pallas Green, Ireland. 53N. 8W. 68
Pallaskenry, Ireland. 53N. 9W. 68
Palma, Majorca. 40N. 3E. 85
Palmanava, Italy. 46N. 13E. 83
Palmi, Italy. 38N. 16E. 81
Palo, Italy. 42N. 12E. 83
Palo, Italy. 41N. 17E. 81
Palos, C. de, Spain. 38N. 1W. 85
Pamiers, France. 43N. 2E. 73
Pampilliosa, Portugal. 41N. 9W. 84
Pamplona, Spain. 43N. 2W. 85
Panaria Is., Italy. 39N. 15E. 81
Panaro, R., Italy. 45N 11E. 83
Panayas, Portugal. 38N. 8W. 84
Pancsova, Hungary. 45N. 21E. 94
Pantellaria Is., Italy. 37N. 12E. 81
Paola, Italy. 39N. 16E. 81
Pap, The, Scotland. 57N. 5W. 62
Papa, Hungary. 47N. 17E. 78
Papa Stour Is., Scotland. 60N. 2W. 63
Papenburg, Germany. 53N. 7E. 76
Paps, The, Ireland. 52N. 9W. 68
Paps of Jura, Scotland. 56N. 6W. 64
Parchim, Germany. 54N. 12E. 76
Pardubitz, Austria. 50N. 16E. 78

PAGE

*Parga, Turkey. 39N. 20E.   95
*Paris, France. 49N. 2E.   73
Parkmore, Ireland. 55N. 6w.   67
*Parma, Italy. 45N. 10E.   82
Parma R., Italy. 45N. 10E.   82
Parnassus, Greece. 39N. 23E.   95
Paros, Greece. 37N. 25E.   95
Parret, R., England. 51N. 3w.   56
Parsonstown, Ireland. 53N. 8w.   69
Parta Rinteln, Germany. 52N.
   9E.   76
Partenkirchen, Germany. 47N. 11E. 77
Partinico, Sicily. 38N. 13E.   38
Partry Mts., Ireland. 54N. 9w.   66
Partumna, Ireland. 53N. 8w.   68
Parys, Mt., Wales. 53N. 4w.   54
Pas de Calais, France. 51N. 2w.   73
Pasewalk, Germany. 53N. 14E.   76
Pashkani, Roumania. 47N. 26E.   94
Paskallavik, Sweden. 57N. 17E.   89
Passage, Ireland. 52N. 7w.   69
Passage West, Ireland. 52N. 8w.   68
*Passau, Germany. 49N. 13E.   77
Passero C., Sicily. 37N. 15E.   81
Pateley Bridge, England. 54N.
   2w.   54
Patras G., Greece. 38N. 22E.   95
Patrington, England. 54N. 0w.   55
*Pau, France. 44N. 0w.   72
Pauillac, France. 45N. 1w.   72
Paullo, Italy. 44N. 11E.   83
Pausula, Italy. 43N. 14E.   83
*Pavia, Italy. 45N. 9E.   82
Pavoa de Varzim, Portugal. 41N.
   9w.   84
Paxo Is , Turkey. 39N. 20E.   95
Peak, The, England. 53N. 2w.   54
Peebles, Scotland. 56N. 3w.   65
*Peel, Is. of Man. 54N. 5w.   54
Peel Fell, England. 55N. 3w.   54
Peel Fell, Scotland. 55N. 3w.   65
Peel Marsh, Holland. 51N. 6E.   71
Peene R., Germany. 54N. 13E.   76
Peipus L., Russia. 59N. 28E.   90
Peissenburg, Germany. 48N. 11E.   77
Pelestrina, Italy. 45N. 12E.   83
Pembridge, England. 52N. 3w.   56
*Pembroke, Wales. 52N. 5w.   56
Peña Golosa, Spain. 40N. 0w.   85
Peñaranda, Spain. 41N. 5w.   84
Penarth, Wales. 51N. 3w.   56
Peñas, C. de, Spain. 44N. 6w.   84
Penicuik, Scotland. 56N. 3w.   65
Penistone, England. 54N. 2w.   55
Penkridge, England. 53N. 2w.   56
Penne, Italy. 42N. 14E.   83
Pennine Alps, Italy. 46N. 8E.   82
Pennine Chain, England. 54N.
   2w.   54
Penrith, England. 55N. 3w.   54
Penryn, England. 50N. 5w   56
Pentland Firth, Scotland. 59N.
   3w.   63
Pentland Hills, Scotland. 56N. 3w. 65
Pentland Skerries, Scotland. 59N.
   3w.   63
Penyghent, England. 54N. 2w.   54
Penza, Russia. 53N. 45E.   91

PAGE

*Penzance, England. 50N. 5w.   56
Penzberg, Germany. 48N. 11E.   77
Pera, Turkey. 41N. 29E.   95
Perdu, Mt., Spain. 43N. 0E.   85
Perdu, Mt., France. 43N. 0E.   72
Perekop, Russia. 46N. 34E.   91
Pergola, Italy. 44N. 13E.   83
*Perigueux, France. 45N. 1E.   72
Perim-dagh, Turkey. 41N. 24E.   94
Perleberg, Germany. 53N. 12E.   76
Perm, Russia. 58N. 57E.   90
Pernau, Russia. 58N. 25E.   90
*Perpignan, France. 43N. 3E.   73
Pershore, England. 52N. 2w.   56
*Perth, Scotland. 56N. 3w.   65
*Perugia, Italy. 43N. 12E.   83
Peruwetz, Belgium. 50N. 4E.   71
*Pesaro, Italy. 44N. 13E.   83
Pescara, Italy. 42N. 14E.   83
*Peschiera, Italy. 45N. 11E.   82
Pescina, Italy. 42N. 14E.   83
Petch, Turkey. 43N. 20E.   94
Petchora R., Russia. 68N. 54E.   90
Peterhead, Scotland. 58N. 2w.   63
Petersfield, England. 51N. 1w.   57
*Peterwardein, Hungary. 45N. 20E. 79
Petrina, Slavonia. 45N. 16E.   78
Petrocseny, Hungary. 45N. 24E.   94
Petrovsk, Russia. 43N. 48E.   91
Petrovsk, Russia. 53N. 45E.   91
Petroyskoie, Russia. 51N. 41E.   91
Pettau, Austria. 46N. 16E.   78
Petterill, England. 55N. 3w.   54
Pettigoe, Ireland. 55N. 8w.   67
Petworth, England. 51N. 1w.   57
*Pevensey, England. 51N. 0w.   57
Pewsey, England. 51N. 2w   56
Pfafers, Switzerland. 47N. 9E.   87
Pfalzburg, Germany. 49N. 7E.   77
Pfeife, Switzerland. 47N. 7E.   86
Pfirt, Germany. 48N. 7E.   77
Pforzheim, Germany. 49N. 8E.   77
Phersala, Greece. 39N. 22E.   95
Philiatea, Turkey. 40N. 21E.   95
Philiatra, Greece. 37N. 22E.   95
Philippeville, Belgium. 50N. 5E. 71
Philippopolis, Bulgaria. 42N. 25E. 94
Philipstad, Sweden. 60N. 14E.   89
Philipstown, Ireland. 53N. 7w.   67
Phonia Lake, Greece. 38N. 22E.   95
*Piacenza, Italy. 45N. 10E.   82
Pianella, Italy. 42N. 14E.   83
Pianoso Is., Italy. 43N. 10E.   82
Pias, Portugal. 38N. 7w.   84
Piatra, Roumania. 47N 26E.   94
Piave, R., Italy. 46N. 13E.   83
Piazza, Sicily 37N. 14E.   81
Pickering, England. 54N. 1w.   55
Piedmont, Italy. 45N. 8E.   82
Pieve di Cadore, Italy. 46N. 12E. 80
Pilatus Mt., Switzerland. 47N.
   8E.   86
Pillau, Germany. 55N. 19E.   75
Pillicoultry, Scotland. 56N. 4w.   65
Pilling, England. 54N. 3w.   54
Pillkillen, Germany. 55N. 22E.   75
Piltown, Ireland 52N. 7w.   69
*Pilsen, Austria. 50N. 13E.   78

	PAGE
Pindus Mts Greece. 39N. 21E.	95
*Pinerolo, Italy. 45N. 7E.	82
Pinsk, Russia. 52N. 27E.	91
Piombino, Italy. 43N. 10E.	83
Piosckov, Russia. 52N. 20E.	91
Piove, Italy. 45N. 12E.	83
Pirano, Austria. 46N. 14E.	78
Pirmaseus, Germany. 49N. 7E.	77
*Pirna, Germany. 51N. 14E.	76
Piræus, Greece. 38N. 24E.	95
Pirot, Servia. 43N 22E.	94
*Pisa, Italy. 44N. 10E.	82
Pisek, Austria. 49N 14E.	78
Piski, Hungary. 46N. 23E.	79
Pisogne, Italy. 46N. 10E.	82
*Pistoja, Italy. 44N. 11E.	83
Pisuerga, R., Spain 42N. 5w.	84
Pitea, Sweden. 65N. 21E.	88
Pitea E., Sweden. 66N. 21E.	88
Pitesti, Roumania. 45N. 25E.	94
Pitigliano, Italy. 43N. 12E.	83
Pitlochry, Scotland. 57N 4w.	63
Pittenweem, Scotland 56N. 3w.	65
Piz Aul, Switzerland. 47N. 9E.	87
Piz Languard, Switzerland. 46N. 10E.	87
Piz Linard, Switzerland. 47N. 10E.	87
Pizzighettone, Italy. 45N. 10E	82
Pizzo, Italy. 39N. 16E.	81
Pladda, Scotland. 55N. 5w.	64
Plaffeyen, Switzerland. 47N. 7E.	86
Planca, Pta della, Dalmatia. 43N. 16E.	78
Plasencia, Spain. 40N. 6w.	84
Plasencia, Spain. 40N. 6w.	84
Platamona, Turkey. 40N. 23E.	95
Platani R., Sicily. 37N. 13E.	81
Plau, Germany. 53N. 12E.	76
Plauen, Germany. 51N. 12E.	77
Pleschen, Germany. 52N. 18E.	75
Pleisse R., Germany. 51N. 12E.	76
Plessidi Mt., Greece. 39N. 23E.	95
*Plevna, Bulgaria. 44N. 24E.	94
Plinlimmon, Wales. 53N. 4w.	56
Plock, Russia. 53N. 20E.	91
Ploesti, Roumania 45N. 26E.	94
Plombières, France. 48N. 6F.	73
Plön, Germany. 54N. 10E	76
*Plymouth, England. 50N. 4w.	56
Plymouth Sd , England 50N. 4w.	56
Po, R., Italy. 45N 12E	83
Po della Mæstre, Italy. 45N. 12E	83
Po di Primaro, Italy. 45N. 12E.	83
Pocklington, England. 54N 1w.	55
Podhorce, Austria. 49N 26E.	79
Podolia, Russia. 49N. 28E.	91
Podolsk, Russia. 49N 27E.	91
Podwoloozyska, Austria. 50N. 26E.	79
Poggibonsi, Italy. 43N. 11E.	83
Poitiers, France 47N. 0E.	72
Pojana Ruska, Hungary. 46N 22E.	79
Poking, Germany. 48N. 13E.	77
*Pola, Austria. 45N. 14E.	78
Poland, Russia. 52N. 20E.	91
Policastro, Italy. 40N. 16E.	81
Policastro, G. of, Italy. 40N. 16E.	81
Polmone, Scotland. 56N. 4w.	65
Polna, Austria. 50N. 16E.	78
*Polotsk, Russia. 56N. 29E.	90
Poltava, Russia. 50N. 35E.	91
Polykandros, Greece. 36N. 25E.	95
Pomerania, Germany. 54N. 16E.	75
Pomeranian B., Germany. 54N. 14E.	76
Pomeroy, Ireland. 55N. 7w	67
Pomona Is., Scotland. 59N. 3w.	63
Pompeii, Italy. 41N. 15E.	81
Ponferrada, Spain. 43N. 7w.	84
Pons, Spain. 42N. 1E.	85
Pont-à-Mousson, France. 49N. 6E.	73
Pontassieve, Italy. 44N. 11E.	83
Ponte, Capo di, Italy. 46N 12E.	83
Pontebba, Italy. 46N 14E	80
Pontecorvo, Italy. 41N. 14E.	81
Pontedera, Italy. 44N. 11E.	82
*Pontefract, England. 54N. 1w	55
Pontevedra, Spain. 42N. 9w.	84
Pontevico, Italy. 45N. 10E	82
Pontine Is., Italy. 41N. 13E.	81
Pontine Marshes, Italy. 41N.13E.	81
Pontivy, France. 48N. 3w.	72
*Pontoise, France. 49N. 2E.	73
Pontremoli, Italy. 14N. 10E.	82
Pontresina, Switzerland. 47N. 10E.	87
Pontrilas, England. 52N. 3w	56
Pontypool, England. 52N. 3w.	56
Pontypridd, Wales. 52N. 3w.	56
Ponza, Italy. 41N 13E.	81
Poole, England. 51N. 2w	56
Poole B , England. 51N. 2w.	56
Poolewe, Scotland. 58N. 6w.	62
Pooltiel, Loch, Scotland. 57N. 7w.	62
Poperinghe, Belgium. 51N. 3w.	71
Poretta, Italy. 44N. 11E.	83
Porrentruy, Switzerland. 47N. 7E.	86
Porsanger Fjord, Norway. 71N. 26E.	88
Porsgrund, Norway. 59N. 10E.	89
Port Askaig, Scotland. 56N. 6w.	64
Port Carlisle, England 55N 3w.	64
Port Clarence, England. 55N 1w.	55
Port Ellen, Scotland. 56N. 6w.	64
Port Erin, Is. of Man. 54N. 5w.	54
Port Errol, Scotland. 57N. 2w.	63
Port Gordon, Scotland. 58N. 3w.	63
Port Madoc, Wales. 53N. 4w.	54
Port Glasgow, Scotland. 56N. 5w.	64
Port Patrick, Scotland. 55N. 5w.	64
Port Stewart, Ireland. 55N. 7w.	67
Port Talbot, Wales. 52N. 4w.	56
Port Vendres, France. 42N. 3E.	73
Port William, Scotland 55N. 5w.	64
Porth Nigel, Wales. 53N. 5w.	54
Porto d'Anzio, Italy. 41N. 13E.	81
Porto Empedocle, Sicily. 37N. 14E.	81
Porto Ferrajo, Elba Is., 43N. 10E.	82
Porto Longone, Elba Islands. 43N. 10E.	82
Porto Maurizio, Italy. 44N. 8E	82
Porto Palo, Sicily. 37N. 15E.	81
Porto San Stefano, Italy. 42N. 11E	83
Porto Torres, Sardinia. 41N. 8E.	81
Porto Vecchio, Corsica. 42N. 9E.	80
Portadown, Ireland. 54N. 6w	67

PAGE

Portaferry, Ireland. 54N. 6W. 67
Portalegre, Portugal. 39N. 7W. 84
Portarlington, Ireland. 53N. 7W. 69
Portglenone, Ireland. 55N. 6W. 67
Porthcawl, Wales. 51N. 4W. 56
Portishead, England. 51N. 3W. 56
*Portland Is., England. 51N. 2W. 56
Portlaw, Ireland. 52N. 7W 69
Portmagee, Ireland. 52N. 10W. 68
Portmahomack, Scotland. 58N. 4W. 63
Portmore, Lough, Ireland. 55N. 6W. 67
Portobello, Scotland. 56N. 3W. 65
Portogruano, Italy. 46N. 13E. 83
Portopus, Dalmatia. 43N. 18E. 78
Portoscuso, Sardinia. 39N. 8E. 81
Portovesme, Sardinia. 39N. 9E. 81
Portree, Scotland. 57N. 6W. 62
Portrush, Ireland. 55N. 7W. 67
*Portsmouth, England. 51N. 1W. 57
Portsoy, Scotland. 58N. 3W. 63
Portugalete, Spain. 43N. 3W. 85
Poschiavo, Switzerland. 46N. 10E. 87
Posen, Germany. 52N. 17E. 75
Potchinki, Russia. 55N. 45E. 91
Potgoritza, Montenegro. 43N. 20E. 94
Potenza, Italy. 41N. 16E. 81
Potenza R., Italy. 43N. 14E. 83
Potes Mts., Austria. 48N. 26E. 79
*Potsdam, Germany. 52N. 13E. 76
Poulton, England. 54N. 3W. 54
Poyntzpass, Ireland. 54N. 6W. 67
Pozoblanco, Spain 38N. 5W. 84
Praechia, Italy. 44N. 11E. 83
*Prague, Austria. 50N. 14E. 78
Prato, Italy. 44N. 11E. 83
Prattigau, Switzerland. 47N. 10E. 87
Prawle Pt , England. 50N. 4W. 56
Preceley Top, Wales. 52N. 5W. 56
Pregel R., Germany 55N. 21E. 75
*Prenzlau, Germany. 53N. 14E. 76
*Prescot, England. 53N. 3W. 54
*Pressburg, Hungary. 48N. 17E. 78
Presteigne, Wales. 52N. 3W. 56
*Preston, England. 51N. 3W. 54
*Prestonpans, Scotland. 56N. 3W. 65
Prestwick, Scotland. 55N. 5W. 64
Prevesa, Turkey. 39N. 21E. 95
Pribram, Austria. 50N. 14E. 78
Priego, Spain. 40N. 2W. 35
Priepolie, Turkey. 43N 20E. 94
Prilip, Turkey. 41N. 22E. 95
Priluki, Russia. 51N 33E. 91
Pripet R., Russia. 52N. 29E. 91
Prisrend, Turkey. 42N. 20E 94
Pristina, Turkey. 43N. 21E. 91
Pritzwalk, Germany. 53N. 12E. 76
Privas, France. 45N. 5E. 73
Prosna R., Germany. 52N. 18E. 75
Prosperous, Ireland. 53N. 7W. 67
Prossnitz, Austria. 49N 17E. 78
Prunelli, Corsica. 42N. 9E. 80
Prussia East, Germany. 54N. 21E. 75
Prussia West, Germany. 54N. 19E. 75
Pruth R., Roumania. 45N. 28E. 94
Przemysl, Austria. 50N. 23E. 79
Pskov, Russia. 58N. 28E. 90

Puebla de Tribes, Spain. 42N. 7W. 84
Pulborough, England. 51N. 0W. 57
Pulteneytown, Scotland. 58N. 3W. 63
Pura, Switzerland. 46N. 9E. 87
Purchena, Spain. 37N. 2W. 85
Purmerend, Holland. 52N. 5E. 70
Putbus, Germany. 54N. 13E. 76
Puy de Dome, France. 46N 3E. 73
Pwllheli, Wales. 53N. 4W. 54
Pyle, Wales 52N. 4W 56
Pylos, Greece. 37N. 22E. 95
Pyrenees, France. 43N. 1E. 72
Pyrenees Orientales, France. 43N. 2E. 73
Pyrgos, Greece. 38N. 21E. 95
Pyritz, Germany. 53N. 14E. 76

Quakenbruck, Germany. 53N. 8E. 76
Quantock Hills, England. 51N. 3W. 56
Quarnero, Austria. 45N. 14E. 78
*Quatre Bras, Belgium. 51N. 4E. 71
*Quedlinburg, Germany. 52N. 11E. 76
*Queenborough, England. 51N. 1E. 57
Queen's Co., Ireland. 53N. 7W 69
Queensberry, Hill, Scotland. 55N. 4W. 65
Queenstown, Ireland. 52N. 8W. 68
Quesada, Spain. 38N. 3W. 85
Quirang, Scotland. 58N. 6W. 62
Quimper, France. 48N. 4W. 72
Quintanar, Spain. 40N. 3W. 85
Quoich, Loch, Scotland. 57N. 5W. 62

*Raab, Hungary. 48N. 18E. 78
Raab R., Hungary. 48N. 18E. 78
Raasay Is., Scotland. 57N. 6W. 62
Raasay Sd., Scotland. 57N. 6W. 62
Racconigi, Italy. 45N. 8E. 82
Race of Alderney, Channel Islands. 49N. 2W. 56
Radautz, Austria. 48N. 26E. 79
Radnor, Wales. 52N. 3W. 56
Radom, Russia. 51N. 21E. 91
Radomir, Bulgaria. 42N. 23E. 94
Radstock, England. 51N. 2W. 56
*Ragusa, Dalmatia. 43N. 18E. 94
Ragusa, Sicily. 37N. 15E. 81
Raheen, Ireland. 54N. 10W. 66
Rahova, Bulgaria. 44N. 24E. 94
Ramelton, Ireland. 55N. 8W. 67
Ramsey, Isle of Man. 54N. 4W. 54
Ramsey, England. 52N. 0E. 57
Ramsey Is., Wales. 52N. 5W. 56
Ramsgate, England. 51N. 1E. 57
Randalstown, Ireland. 55N. 6W. 67
Randers, Denmark. 57N. 10E. 89
Ranea, Sweden. 66N. 22E 88
Ranen Fd., Norway. 66N. 14E. 88
Rannoch, Loch, Scotland. 57N. 4W. 63
Rapallo, Italy. 44N. 9E. 82
Raphoe, Ireland. 55N. 8W. 67
Rapid Koros, Hungary. 47N. 21E. 79
Rapolano, Italy. 43N. 12E 83
*Rapperswyl, Switzerland. 47N. 9E. 87
Raron, Switzerland. 46N. 8E. 86
Rasgrad, Bulgaria. 44N. 26E. 94

	PAGE
Rasharkin, Ireland. 55N. 6w.	67
*Rastatt, Germany. 49N. 8E.	77
Ratan, Sweden. 64N. 21E.	88
Rathcormack, Ireland. 52N. 8w.	68
Rathdowney, Ireland. 53N. 8w.	69
Rathdrum, Ireland. 53N. 6w	69
*Rathenow, Germany. 52N. 12E.	76
Rathfryland, Ireland. 54N. 6w.	67
Rathkeale, Ireland. 53N 9w.	68
Rathlin Is , Ireland. 55N. 6w.	67
Rathlin O'Birne Is., Ireland. 55N. 9w.	66
Rathmullan, Ireland. 55N. 8w.	67
Rathnew, Ireland. 53N. 6w.	69
Rathnolyon, Ireland. 53N. 7w.	67
Ratho, Scotland. 56N. 3w.	65
Rathowen, Ireland. 54N. 8w.	67
Ratibor, Germany. 50N. 18E.	75
*Ratisbon, Germany. 49N. 12E.	77
Rattray Hd., Scotland. 58N 2w	63
Ratzeburg, Germany. 54N. 10E.	76
Ravenglass, England. 54N. 3w.	54
Ravenna, Italy. 44N. 12E.	83
Ravensburg, Germany. 48N. 10E.	77
Rawaruska, Austria. 50N. 24E.	79
Rawicz, Germany. 52N. 17E.	75
Rayerne, Switzerland. 47N. 7E.	86
*Ré, Is. de, France. 46N. 1w.	72
*Reading, England. 51N. 1w.	57
Reay, Scotland. 59N. 4w.	63
Recknitz R., Germany. 54N. 12E.	76
Recoaro, Italy. 46N. 11E.	83
Red B., Ireland. 55N. 6w.	67
Redcar, England. 55N. 1w.	55
Redditch, England. 52N. 2w.	56
Rede, R., England. 55N. 2w.	54
Redosto, Turkey. 41N. 27E.	95
Redruth, England. 50N. 5w.	56
Ree, Lough, Ireland. 54N. 8w.	66
Reeth, England. 54N. 2w.	54
Regen, Germany. 49N. 13E.	77
Regen R., Germany. 49N. 12E.	77
Regensburg, Switzerland. 47N. 8E.	87
*Reggio, Italy. 45N. 11E.	82
*Reggio, Italy. 38N. 16E.	81
Regnitz, R., Germany. 50N. 11E.	77
Reichenberg, Austria. 51N. 15E.	78
Reichenhall, Germany. 48N 13E.	77
*Reigate, England. 51N. 0w.	57
Reinosa, Spain. 43N. 4w.	84
Remiremont, France. 48N. 6E.	73
Remscheid, Germany. 51N. 7E.	76
Renaix, Belgium. 51N. 4w.	71
Rendina G , Turkey. 41N. 24E.	95
Rendsburg, Germany. 54N. 10E.	76
Renfrew, Scotland. 56N. 4w.	64
Reni, Roumania. 46N. 28E.	94
*Rennes, France. 48N. 2w.	72
Reno, R., Italy. 45N. 12E.	83
Rens, Spain. 41N. 1E.	85
Reps, Hungary. 46N. 25E.	79
Requena, Spain. 40N. 1w.	85
Resiczabanya, Hungary. 45N. 22E.	79
Resort, Loch, Scotland. 58N. 7w.	62
Reston, Scotland. 56N. 2w.	65
Retrosav R., Russia. 61N. 34E.	90
Retz, Austria. 49N. 16E.	78
Reuss, Germany. 50N. 12E.	77
Reuss, R., Switzerland. 47N. 8E.	86
Reutlingen, Germany. 49N. 9E.	77
Revel, Russia. 59N. 24E.	90
Rhatian Alps, Austria. 47N. 11E.	78
Rhatikon, Switzerland. 47N. 10E.	87
Rhayader, Wales. 52N. 3w.	56
Rheido, R., Wales. 52N. 4w.	56
*Rheims, France. 49N. 4E.	73
Rheine, Germany. 52N. 8E	76
Rheineck, Switzerland. 47N. 10E.	87
*Rheinfelden, Switzerland 48N. 8E.	86
Rheingau, Germany. 50N. 8E.	77
Rhenen, Holland 52N 6E.	70
Rhenish Prussia, Germany. 50N. 7E.	77
Rheydt, Germany. 51N. 6E.	76
Rhone, R., France. 44N. 5E.	73
Rhone Geb., Germany. 50N. 10E.	77
Rhine, R Holland. 52N. 4E.	70
Rhine Falls, Switzerland 47N. 9E.	87
Rhu Stoir, Scotland. 58N 5w.	62
*Rhuddlan, Wales. 53N. 4w.	54
Rhyl, Wales. 53N. 4w.	54
Rhynie, Scotland. 57N. 3w.	63
Rhynns Pt., Scotland. 56N. 7w.	64
Rhys Vand, Norway. 66N. 14E.	88
Ria de Arosa, Spain. 42N. 9w.	84
Ria de Lisboa, Portugal 39N. 9w.	84
Ria de Muros a Noya, Spain. 43N. 9w.	84
Ria de Tinamayor, Spain. 44N. 4w.	84
Ria de Vigo, Spain. 42N. 9w.	84
Riano, Spain. 43N. 5w.	84
Riasan, Russia. 55N. 40E.	91
Ribble, R., England. 54N. 3w.	54
Ribe, Denmark. 55N. 9E.	89
Riccarton, Scotland. 55N 3w.	65
Rich Hill, Ireland. 54N. 7w.	67
*Richmond, England. 51N 0w.	57
Richmond, England. 54N. 2w.	54
Ried, Austria. 48N. 13E.	78
Riesa, Germany. 51N. 13E.	76
Riesen Gebirge, Austria. 51N. 16E.	78
*Rieti, Italy. 42N. 13E.	83
*Riga, Russia. 57N. 25E.	90
Riga, G. of, Russia. 58N. 23E.	90
Rigi, Switzerland. 47N. 9E.	87
Rilo-Dagh, Bulgaria. 42N. 23E.	94
*Rimini, Italy. 44N. 13E.	83
Rimnik Roumania 45N. 24E.	94
*Rimnik, Roumania. 45N. 27E.	94
Ringkjobing Fd., Denmark. 56N. 8E.	89
Ringville, Ireland. 52N. 8w.	69
Ringwood, England. 51N. 2w.	56
Rio Jacar, Spain. 39N. 0w.	85
Riom, France. 46N. 3E.	73
Rionero, Italy. 41N. 16E.	81
Ripatransone, Italy. 43N. 14E.	83
Ripley, England. 54N. 2w.	56
Ripon, England. 54N. 2w.	55
Risca, England. 52N. 3w.	56
Riva, Austria. 46N. 11E.	78
Rivadeo, Spain. 44N. 7w.	84
Rivadesella, Spain. 44N. 5w.	84
Rivarolo, Italy. 44N. 9E.	82
Rivarolo, Italy. 45N. 8E.	82

PAGE

Rive de Gier, France. 46N. 4E. 73
Riverstown, Ireland. 54N. 8W. 66
Riviera di Levante, Italy. 44N. 9E. 82
Riviera di Ponente, Italy. 44N. 8E. 82
*Rivoli, Italy. 45N. 8E. 82
Rivoli, Italy. 46N. 11E. 83
Rixhoft, Germany. 55N. 18E. 75
Rizzuto C., Italy. 39N. 17E. 81
Roag, Loch, Scotland. 58N. 7W. 62
Roanne, France. 46N. 4E. 73
Roaring Water B., Ireland. 52N. 10W. 68
Robe, R., Ireland. 54N. 9W. 66
Robertstown, Ireland 53N. 7W. 67
Robin Hood B., England. 54N. 1W. 55
Roca, C. de, Portugal. 39N. 10W. 84
Rochdale, England. 54N. 2W. 54
Rocher de Naye, Switzerland. 46N. 7E. 86
*Rochefort, France. 46N. 1W. 72
Rockabill Lighthouse, Ireland. 54N. 6W. 67
Rockcorry, Ireland. 54N. 7W. 67
Rockingham, England. 53N. 1W. 57
*Rocroy, France. 50N. 4E. 73
Roden R., England. 53N. 3W. 54
Rodez, France. 44N. 3E. 73
Roding, R., England. 52N. 0E. 57
Rodo, Norway. 67N. 13E. 88
Roer, Germany. 51N. 6E. 76
Roer, R., Holland. 51N. 6E. 71
Roermonde, Holland. 51N. 6E. 71
Roeskilde, Denmark. 56N. 12E 89
Rogart, Scotland. 58N. 4W. 63
Roldal, Norway. 60N. 7E. 89
Rolle, Switzerland. 46N. 6E. 86
Roman, Roumania. 47N. 27E. 94
Roman Apennines, Italy. 43N. 13E. 83
Romans, France. 45N. 5E. 73
Romanshorn, Switzerland. 48N. 9E. 87
*Rome, Italy. 42N. 12E. 83
Romford, England. 52N. 0E. 57
Romont, Switzerland. 47N. 7E. 86
Romorantin, France. 47N 2E. 73
Romsdal Is., Norway. 63N. 6E. 88
Romsdalen, Norway. 62N. 8E. 89
Romsey, England. 51N. 1W. 57
Rona Is., Scotland. 57N. 7W. 62
Roncade, Italy. 46N. 12E. 83
*Roncesvalles, Spain. 43N. 1W. 85
Ronda, Spain. 37N. 5W. 84
Rönne, Sweden. 55N. 15E. 89
Roodeschool, Holland. 53N. 7E. 70
Rooskey, Ireland. 54N. 8W. 66
Roquetas, Spain. 37N. 3W. 85
Roraas, Norway. 63N. 11E. 89
Roray Hd., Scotland 59N. 3W. 63
Rorschach, Switzerland. 47N. 10E. 87
Rosas, G. of, Spain. 42N. 3E. 85
Roscommon, Ireland. 54N. 8W. 66
Roscrea, Ireland. 53N. 8W. 69
Rösenberg, Germany. 51N. 19E. 75
Rosenheim, Germany. 48N. 12E. 77
Rosignano, Italy. 43N. 10E. 82

PAGE

*Roslin, Scotland. 56N. 3W. 65
*Ross, England. 52N. 3W. 56
Ross Carbery, Ireland. 52N. 9W. 68
Ross of Mull, Scotland. 56N. 6W. 64
Rossberg, Switzerland. 47N. 9E. 87
Rosscarbery B., Ireland. 52N. 9W. 68
Rossieny, Russia. 55N. 23E. 90
Rosslare Harb., Ireland. 52N. 6W. 69
*Rostock, Germany. 54N. 12E. 76
Rostov, Russia. 47N. 40E. 91
Rostov, Russia. 57N. 39E. 90
Rostrevor, Ireland. 54N. 6W. 67
Rotenburg, Germany. 51N. 10E. 76
Rotenburg, Germany. 53N. 10E. 76
Rothbury, England. 55N 2W. 54
Rothenburg, Germany. 49N. 10E. 77
Rother, R., England. 51N. 1E. 57
Rother, R., England. 53N. 1W. 55
Rotherham, England. 53N. 1W. 55
Rothes, Scotland. 57N. 3W. 63
*Rothesay, Scotland. 56N. 5W. 64
Rothhorn, Switzerland. 47N. 8E. 86
Rothiemay, Scotland. 58N. 3W. 63
Rothiemurchus, Scotland. 57N.4W 63
Rotondo, Mt., Corsica. 42N. 9E. 80
Rott, R., Germany. 49N. 13E. 77
*Rotterdam, Holland. 52N. 5E. 70
Roubaix, France. 51N. 3E. 73
*Rouen, France. 50N. 1E. 72
Roughty, R., Ireland. 52N. 10W. 68
*Roulers, Belgium. 51N. 3E. 71
Roumelia, Greece. 39N 22E. 95
Rousay Is., Scotland 59N. 3W. 63
Rova, R., Italy. 44N. 8E. 82
Roverbella, Italy. 45N 11E 83
*Rovereto, Austria. 46N. 11E. 78
Rovigno, Austria. 45N 14E 78
Rovigo, Italy. 45N. 12E. 83
Rowno, Russia. 51N. 26E. 91
*Roxburgh, Scotland. 55N 3W. 65
Roxen L., Sweden. 59N. 16E. 89
Royal Canal, Ireland. 53N. 7W. 67
Royan, France. 46N. 1W. 72
Royston, England. 52N. 0E 57
Rozendaal, Holland. 52N. 4E. 70
Rozwadow, Austria. 51N. 22E. 79
Rshev, Russia. 56N. 34E. 90
Ru Coygach, Scotland. 58N. 5W. 62
Ru Rea, Scotland. 58N. 6W. 62
Ru Renish, Scotland. 58N. 7W. 62
Ruabon, Wales. 53N. 3W. 54
Rudolstadt, Germany. 51N. 11E. 77
Rue, Switzerland. 47N 7E 86
Rugby, England. 52N. 1W. 57
Rugeley, England. 53N. 2W. 56
Rugen Is., Germany. 54N. 13E. 76
Rügen B., Germany. 54N. 14E. 76
Rügenwalde, Germany. 54N. 16E. 76
Ruhr R., Germany. 51N. 8E. 76
Rum Is., Scotland. 57N. 6W. 62
Runcorn, England. 53N. 3W. 54
Runn L., Sweden. 60N. 16E. 89
Rupel R., Belgium. 51N. 4E. 71
Rush, Ireland. 54N. 6W. 67
*Rustchuk, Bulgaria. 44N. 26E. 94
*Rutherglen, Scotland. 56N. 4W. 65
Ruthin, Wales. 53N 5W. 54
Rutland, England. 52N. 1W. 57

PAGE

Ryan, Loch, Scotland. 55N. 5w. 64
Rybinsk, Russia. 58N. 39E.   90
Ryde, England. 51N. 1w.   57
*Rye, England. 51N. 1E.   57
Rye, R., England. 54N 1w.   55
Ryssen, Holland. 52N. 7E.   70
Rzeszow, Austria. 50N. 22E.   79

Saale, R., Germany. 50N. 10E.   77
Saales, Germany. 48N. 7E.   77
Saane, R., Switzerland. 47N. 7E. 86
Saanen, Switzerland. 46N 7E.   86
Saar, R., Germany. 50N. 6E.   77
*Saarbruck, Germany. 49N. 7E.   77
Saarburg, Germany. 50N. 6E.   77
Saargemund, Germany. 49N. 7E   77
*Saarlouis, Germany. 49N. 7E.   77
Saas, Switzerland. 46N. 8E.   86
Saaz, Austria. 50N. 14E.   78
Sabadell, Spain. 42N. 2E.   85
Sabbioncello, Dalmatia. 43N.17E   78
Sabine Mts., Italy 42N. 13E.   83
*Sables d'Olonne, France. 47N. 2w. 72
Sablia, Russia. 65N. 59E.   90
Sabor, R., Portugal. 41N. 7E.   84
Saborsio, Hungary. 46N. 22E.   79
Sacco, R., Italy. 41N. 14E   81
*Sacile, Italy. 46N. 13E.   83
Sackingen, Germany. 47N. 8E.   77
Saddell, Scotland. 56N. 6w.   14
Saddle Hd., Ireland. 54N. 10w.   66
Saddleback, England. 55N. 3w.   54
Sado, R., Portugal 38N. 9w.   84
*Sadowa, Hungary. 50N. 16E.   78
Saffron Walden, England 52N. 0E   57
Sagan, Germany. 52N. 15E   75
Sahagun, Spain. 42N. 5w.   84
Saillon, Switzerland. 46N. 7E.   86
Saima L., Russia. 62N. 29E.   90
St. Abbs Hd., Scotland. 56N. 2w. 65
St. Affrique, France. 44N. 3E.   73
*St. Albans, England. 52N. 0w.   57
St. Albans Hd., England. 51N. 2w. 56
*St. Amand, France. 47N 2E.   73
*St. Andrews, Scotland. 56N. 3w. 65
St. Andrews B , Scotland. 56N. 3w.65
St. Anne's, England. 45N. 3w.   54
St. Austell, England. 50N. 5w.   56
St. Austell B., England. 50N. 5w. 56
St. Asaphs, Wales. 53N. 3w.   54
St. Bees Hd., England. 55N. 4w.   54
St. Bernardino, Mt., Switzerland.
  46N. 9E.   87
St. Boswells, Scotland. 56N 3w. 65
St. Brides Bay, Wales. 52N. 5w.   56
St. Brieux, France 49N. 3w.   72
St. Catherine's Pt., England. 51N.
  1w.   57
St. Combs, Scotland. 58N. 2w.   63
*St. Davids, Wales. 52N. 5w.   56
St. David's Hd., Wales. 52N. 5w. 56
*St. Denis, France. 49N. 3w.   73
St. Die, France. 48N 7E.   73
St. Etienne, France. 46N. 4E.   73
St. Fergus, Scotland. 58N. 2w.   63
St. Fillans, Scotland. 56N. 4w. 65
St. Flour, France. 45N. 3E.   73
*St. Gall, Switzerland. 47N. 9E. 87

PAGE

St. George Is , Roumania. 45N.
  30E.   94
St. George Mouth, Roumania. 45N.
  30E.   94
St. Gingolph, Switzerland. 46N.
  7E.   86
St. Girons, France. 43N 1E.   72
St. Goar, Germany. 50N. 8E.   77
*St. Gotthard, Switzerland. 47N.
  9E.   87
St. Gowans Hd., Wales. 52N. 5w.   56
St. Helens, England. 53N. 3w.   54
St. Helier, Jersey. 49N. 2w.   56
St Hubert, Belgium. 50N. 5E.   71
*St. Ives, England. 50N. 5w.   56
St Ives, England. 52N. 0E.   57
S. Jean, France. 45N. 6E   73
St. John's Pt. Lighthouse, Ireland.
  55N. 8w.   66
St. Leonards on Sea, England. 51N.
  1E.   57
*St. Lo, France. 49N. 1w.   72
St. Magnus B , Scotland. 60N. 1w 63
*St. Malo, France. 49N. 2w.   72
St Mary's Loch, Scotland. 55N.
  3w.   65
St. Matthieu Pt , France. 48N 5w. 72
St. Maurice, Switzerland. 46N. 7E 86
St. Michael, Russia. 64N. 27E. 90
St. Michaels Mt., England. 50N. 5w 56
St. Nazaire, France. 47N. 2w.   72
St. Neots, England. 52N. 0E   57
St. Nicolas, Belgium. 51N. 4E. 71
*St. Omer, France. 51N 2E.   73
*St. Petersburg, Russia. 60N.30E. 90
St. Polten, Austria. 48N. 16E   78
*St. Quentin, France. 50N. 3E.   73
St. Servan, France. 49N. 2w.   72
St. Sulpice, Switzerland. 47N. 7E. 86
St. Trond, Belgium. 51N 5E.   71
St. Tropez, France. 43N. 7E.   73
St. Ursane, Switzerland. 47N. 7E. 86
*St. Vincent, C., Portugal. 37N. 9w. 84
St. Vith, Germany. 50N. 6E.   77
St. Wendelo, Germany. 50N. 7E.   77
St Yrieux, France. 46N. 1E.   72
Saintes, France. 46N. 1w.   72
Saintfield, Ireland. 54N. 6w.   67
Saitchar, Servia. 44N. 22E.   94
Sajo, Hungary. 48N. 21E.   79
Sala, Sweden. 60N. 16E.   89
*Salamanca, Spain. 41N. 6w.   84
Salen, Scotland. 57N. 6w.   64
*Salerno, Italy. 41N. 15E.   81
Salerno, G. of, Italy. 41N. 15E. 81
Salford, England. 53N. 2w.   54
Saline, Italy. 43N. 11E.   83
Salina Is., Italy. 39N. 15E.   81
*Salisbury, England. 51N. 2w.   56
Salisbury Plain, England. 51N.
  2w.   56
Salins, France. 47N. 6E.   73
Sallins, Ireland. 53N. 7w.   67
Salo, Italy. 46N. 11E.   82
*Salonica, Turkey. 41N. 23E   95
Salonika G., Turkey. 40N. 23E. 95
Salso, R., Sicily. 37N. 14E.   81
Saltash, England. 50N. 4w.   56

PAGE

Saltau, Germany. 53N. 10E. 76
Saltburn, England. 55N. 1W. 55
Saltcoats, Scotland. 56N. 5W. 64
Saltfleet, England. 53N. 0E. 55
Saltmills, Ireland. 52N. 7W. 69
Saltee Is, Ireland. 52N. 7W. 69
Saltees Light Vessel, Ireland. 52N.
7W. 69
Salto, R, Italy. 42N. 13E. 83
*Saluzzo, Italy. 45N. 7E. 82
Salzach, R, Germany. 48N. 13E. 77
*Salzburg, Austria. 47N. 13E. 78
Salzkammergut, Austria. 48N.
14E. 78
Salzwedel, Germany. 53N. 11E. 76
Samaden, Switzerland. 47N 10E.87
Samakov, Bulgaria. 42N. 24E. 94
Samara, Russia 53N 50E 91
Samassi, R., Sardinia. 39N. 9E. 81
Sambor, Austria 50N 23E 79
Sambre, R., Belgium. 50N. 5E. 71
Samoiedes, Russia. 67N. 55E. 90
Samter, Germany. 53N. 16E. 75
San, Austria. 50N. 22E. 79
San Adrian, C. de, Spain. 43N. 9W. 84
San Antioco Is., Sardinia. 39N.
8E. 81
San Antonio, Portugal. 37N. 7W.84
San Benedetto, Italy. 43N. 14E. 83
San Carlos de la Rapita, Spain.
41N. 1E. 85
San Casciano, Italy. 44N. 11E. 83
San Feliu, Spain. 42N. 3E. 85
San Fernando, Spain. 36N. 6W. 84
San Gines de la Jara, Spain. 38N.
1W. 85
San Jorje, G. of, Spain. 4N. 1E. 85
San Juan, Spain. 42N. 2E. 86
San Marino, Italy. 44N. 12E. 83
San Moritz, Switzerland. 47N. 10E. 87
San Pier d'Arena, Italy. 44N 9E. 82
San Pietro Is., Sardinia. 39N.
8E. 81
San Remo, Italy. 44N. 8E. 82
San Roque, Spain. 36N. 5W. 84
San Salvatore, Switzerland. 46N.
9E. 87
*San Sebastian, Spain. 43N 2W. 85
San Vito C., Sicily. 38N. 13E. 81
Sanaig Pt., Scotland. 56N. 6W. 64
Sanda Is, Scotland. 55N. 6W. 64
Sanday Is., Scotland. 59N 2W. 63
Sandec, Austria. 50N. 21E. 79
Sandeid, Norway. 59N. 6E. 89
Sandomir, Russia. 51N. 22E. 91
Sandown, England. 51N. 1W. 57
Sandringham Hall, England. 53N.
1E. 55
*Sandwich, England. 51N. 1E. 57
Sandymount, Ireland 53N. 6W. 67
Sangro, R., Italy. 42N. 14E. 83
Sanguesa, Spain. 43N 1W. 85
Sanlucar, Spain. 37N. 6W. 84
Sanok, Austria. 50N. 22E. 79
*Sanquhar, Scotland. 55N. 4W. 65
Santa Eufemia, Italy. 39N. 16E. 81
Santa Eufemia, G. of, Italy. 39N.
16E. 81

PAGE

Santa Maria, C. de, Portugal. 37N.
8W. 84
Santa Maria di Leuca, C., Italy.
40N. 18E. 81
Santa Maura, Greece. 39N. 21E. 95
Sta. Teresa, Sardinia. 41N. 9E. 81
*Santander, Spain. 44N. 4W. 84
Santarem, Portugal. 39N. 9W. 84
Santhia, Italy. 45N. 8E. 82
*Santiago de Compostella, Spain.
43N. 9W. 81
Säntis, Switzerland. 47N. 9E. 87
Santoña, Spain. 44N. 4W. 84
Saone et Loire, France. 46N. 4E. 73
Saone, R., France. 46N 5E. 73
*Saragossa, Spain. 42N. 1W. 85
Saransk, Russia. 51N. 45E. 91
Saras, Hungary. 47N. 20E. 79
Saratov, Russia. 52N. 46E. 91
Sarclet, Scotland 58N. 3W. 63
*Sardinia, Italy. 40N. 9E. 81
Sargans, Switzerland. 47N. 9E. 87
Sark, Channel Is. 49N. 2W. 56
Sarlat, France. 45N. 1E. 72
Sarnen, Switzerland. 47N. 8E. 86
Sarnico, Italy. 46N 10E. 82
Saronna, Italy. 46N. 9E. 82
Saros, Turkey. 40N. 26E. 95
Sarthe, France. 48N. 0E. 72
Sarthe, R., France. 48N. 1W. 72
Sartona, Corsia. 42N. 9E. 80
Sarzana, Italy. 44N. 10E. 82
Saseno Is., Turkey. 40N. 19E. 95
Sassari, Sardinia. 41N. 8E. 81
Sas van Gent, Holland 51N. 4E. 71
Satoralja Ujheli, Hungary 49N.
22E. 79
Sauer, R., Luxemburg 50N. 6E. 71
Sauerland, Germany. 51N. 8E. 76
*Saumur, France. 47N. 0W. 72
Savigliano, Italy. 45N. 8E. 82
Savio R., Italy. 44N. 12E. 83
Save, R., Hungary. 46N. 16E. 94
Savoie, France. 45N. 6E. 73
Savona, Italy. 44N. 8E. 82
Sawel Mt., Ireland. 55N. 7W. 67
Saxilby, England. 53N. 1W. 55
Saxmundham, England. 52N. 2E.57
Saxony, Germany. 51N. 13E. 76
Saxony, Germany. 52N. 11E. 76
Sazawa, Austria. 50N. 14E. 78
Scafell, England. 54N. 3W. 54
Scaffery Is., Ireland. 53N. 10W. 68
Scalpa Is., Scotland. 57N. 6W. 62
Scalpa Is., Scotland. 58N. 7W. 62
Scapa, Scotland. 59N. 3W. 63
Scapa Flow, Scotland. 59N. 3W. 63
Scarba Is., Scotland. 56N. 6W. 64
*Scarborough, England. 54N. 0W.55
Scariff Is., Ireland. 52N. 10W. 68
Scarpa Is., Scotland. 58N. 7W. 62
Scarriff, Ireland. 53N. 9W. 68
Scar Water, Scotland. 55N. 5W. 65
Scavaig, Loch, Scotland. 57N. 6W. 62
Scesaplane, Switzerland. 47N. 10E. 87
Schagen, Holland. 53N. 5E. 70
Schaffhausen, Switzerland. 48N.
9E. 87

K

PAGE

Schässburg, Hungary. 46N. 25E. 79
Schavli, Russia. 56N. 23E. 90
Scheibbs, Austria. 48N. 15E. 78
Schelde R., Belgium. 51N. 4E. 71
Schemnitz, Hungary. 49N. 19E. 79
*Scheveningen, Holland. 52N. 4E. 70
Schiedam Holland. 52N. 4E. 70
Schiehallion, Scotland. 57N. 4w. 63
Schiermonnikoog, Holland. 53N. 6E. 70
Schinznacht, Switzerland. 47N. 8E. 86
Schio, Italy. 46N. 11E. 83
Schleiz, Germany 50N. 12E. 77
Schleswig, Germany. 55N. 10E. 74
Schleswig-Holstein, Germany. 54N. 10E. 76
*Schlettstadt, Germany. 48N. 8E. 77
Schlüchtern, Germany. 50N. 9E. 77
*Schmalkalden, Germany. 51N. 10E. 77
Schneeberg, Germany. 51N. 12E. 77
Schneidemuhl, Germany. 53N. 17E. 75
Schokland, Holland. 53N. 6E. 70
Schönebeck, Germany. 52N. 12E. 76
Schönhausen, Germany. 52N. 12E. 76
Schouwen, Holland. 52N. 4E. 70
Schreckhorn, Switzerland. 47N. 8E. 86
Schüttenhoffen, Austria. 49N. 14E. 78
Schwandorf, Germany. 49N. 12E.77
Schwarzawa, Austria. 48N. 17E. 78
Schwarzburg, Germany. 51N. 10E. 76
Schwarzburg, Germany. 51N. 11E. 76
Schwarz-Elster, Germany. 52N. 13E. 76
Schwarzenburg, Switzerland. 47N. 7E. 86
Schwarzenegg, Switzerland. 47N. 8E. 86
Schwarz Wald, Germany. 48N. 8E. 77
Schwedt, Germany. 53N. 14E. 76
*Schweidnitz, Germany. 51N. 17E. 75
*Schweinfurt, Germany. 50N. 10E. 77
Schwerin, Germany. 54N. 11E. 76
Schwys, Switzerland. 47N. 9E. 87
Schyl R., Roumania 44N. 24E. 94
Scalloway, Scotland. 60N. 1w. 63
Sciacca, Sicily. 37N. 13E. 81
Scilla, Italy. 38N. 16E. 81
*Scilly Is., England. 49N. 6w. 56
Sciur na Lapich, Scotland. 57N. 5w. 62
*Scone, Scotland. 56N. 3w. 65
Score, Loch, Scotland. 58N. 6w. 62
Scourie, Scotland. 58N. 5w. 62
Scour Ouran, Scotland. 57N. 5w. 62
Scramoge, R., Ireland. 54N. 8w. 66
Scregg, Ireland. 54N. 9w. 66
Scridan, Loch, Scotland. 56N. 6w. 64
Scuir of Eigg, Scotland. 57N. 6w. 62
*Scutari, Turkey. 41N. 29E. 95
Seaford, England. 51N. 0E. 57
Seaforth Loch, Scotland. 58N. 7w. 62

PAGE

Seaham Harb., England. 55N. 1w. 55
Sealg, Loch, Scotland. 58N. 6w. 62
Sebenico, Dalmatia. 44N 16E. 78
*Sedan, France. 50N. 5E. 73
Sedbergh, England. 54N. 3w. 54
Sedgefield, England. 55N. 1w. 55
See, Hungary. 48N. 17E. 78
Séez, France. 49N. 0E. 72
Segeberg, Germany. 54N. 10E. 76
Segorbe, Spain. 40N. 0w. 85
Segosero L., Russia 63N. 33E. 90
*Segovia, Spain. 41N. 4w. 84
Segre, R., Spain. 41N. 0E. 85
Segura, Spain. 41N. 1w. 85
Segura, R., Spain. 38N. 1w. 85
Seil Is., Scotland. 56N 6w. 64
Seine, France. 49N. 2E. 73
Seine et Marne, France. 49N. 3E. 73
Seine et Oise, France. 49N. 2E. 73
Seine, R., France. 50N. 1E. 72
Seine Inférieure, France. 50N. 1E. 72
*Selby, England. 54N. 1w. 55
Selkirk, Scotland. 56N. 3w. 65
Selsey, England. 51N. 1w. 57
Selsey Bill, England. 51N. 1w. 57
Sembrancher, Switzerland. 46N. 7E. 86
Semendria, Servia. 45N. 21E. 94
Semeni R., Turkey. 41N. 19E. 95
*Semlin, Servia. 45N. 20E. 94
Semoy, R., Belgium. 50N. 5E. 71
*Sempach, Switzerland. 47N. 8E. 86
Senjen Is., Norway. 69N. 18E. 88
Senlis, France. 49N. 3E. 73
Senne, R., Belgium. 51N. 4E. 71
*Sens, France. 48N. 3E. 73
Sense R., Switzerland. 47N. 7E. 86
Sentinas, Pt., Spain. 37N. 3w. 85
Seo de Urgel, Spain. 42N. 2E. 85
Sepey, Switzerland. 46N 7E. 86
Sepuveda, Spain. 41N. 4w. 84
Seraievo, Bosnia. 44N. 19E. 94
Seraing, Belgium. 51N. 6E. 71
Serchio R., Italy. 44N. 10E. 82
Serdobsk, Russia. 53N. 44E. 91
Sered, Austria. 49N. 26E. 79
Seres, Turkey. 41N. 24E. 95
Sereth, Austria. 48N. 26E. 79
Sereth R., Roumania. 45N. 27E 94
Sergiyevsku, Russia. 56N. 38E. 90
Serio R., Italy. 46N. 10E. 82
Seriphos, Greece. 37N. 24E. 95
Serpa, Portugal. 38N. 7w 84
Serpukhov, Russia. 55N. 38E. 91
Serra de Monchique, Portugal. 37N. 9w. 84
Serriana de Cuenca, Spain. 40N. 2w. 85
Serravezza, Italy. 44N. 10E. 82
Settle, England. 54N. 2w. 54
Setubal, Portugal. 39N. 9w. 84
Setubal, B. of, Portugal. 38N. 9w. 84
*Sevastopol, Russia. 45N. 34E. 91
Seven Churches, Ireland. 53N. 6w. 69
Seven Heads, Ireland. 52N. 9w. 68
Seven Oaks, England. 51N. 0E. 57
Severinu, Roumania. 44N. 22E. 94
Severn R., England. 52N. 2w. 56

	PAGE
Severn Bridge, England. 52N. 2w.	56
Severn Tunnel, England. 52N. 3w.	56
*Seville, Spain. 37N. 5w.	84
Sèvre Nantaise, R., France. 47N. 2w.	72
Sèvre Niortaise, R., France. 46N. 1w.	72
Shabatz, Servia. 45N. 20E.	94
*Shaftesbury, England. 51N. 2w.	56
Shamatz, Bosnia. 45N. 19E.	94
Shambria, Greece. 40N. 22E.	95
*Shanklin, England. 51N. 1w.	57
Shannon, R., Ireland. 53N. 8w.	68
Shannonbridge, Ireland. 53N. 8w.	66
Shannon Canal, Ireland 54N 8w.	67
Shap, England. 55N. 3w.	54
Shar-dagh, Turkey. 42N. 21E.	94
Shatista, Turkey. 40N. 22E.	95
Sheelin, Lough, Ireland. 54N. 7w.	67
Sheep Haven, Ireland. 55N. 8w.	66
Sheep Hd., Ireland. 52N. 10w.	68
Sheep, R., Ireland. 52N. 8w.	68
*Sheffield, England. 53N. 1w.	55
Shelford, England. 52N 0E	57
Shell, Loch, Scotland. 58N. 6w.	62
Shemaka, Russia. 41N. 49E.	91
Shenkursk, Russia. 62N. 43E.	90
Sheppey Is., England. 51N. 1E.	57
Sheptche, Bosnia. 44N. 18E.	94
Shepton Mallet, England. 51N. 3w.	56
*Sherborne, England. 51N. 3w.	56
Shercock, Ireland. 54N. 7w.	67
Sheringham, England. 53N. 1E.	55
*Shetland Is., Scotland. 60N. 1w.	63
Shiant Is., Scotland. 58N. 6w.	62
Shiel, Loch, Scotland. 57N. 6w.	62
Shieldag, Scotland. 58N. 6w.	62
Shifnal, England. 53N. 2w.	56
Shillelagh, Ireland. 53N. 7w.	69
Shin, Loch, Scotland. 58N. 5w.	62
Shinrone, Ireland. 53N. 8w.	69
*Shipka, Bulgaria. 43N. 25E.	94
Shipley, England. 54N. 2w.	54
Shipston-on-Stour, England. 52N. 2w.	57
Shipton, England. 52N. 2w.	57
Shisdra, Russia. 54N. 35E.	91
Shitomir, Russia 50N 29E.	91
Shklov, Russia. 54N. 32E.	91
Shoeburyness, England. 52N. 1E.	57
Shorncliffe, England. 51N. 1E.	57
Shotts, Scotland. 56N. 4w.	65
*Shrewsbury, England. 53N. 3w.	56
Shropshire, England. 53N. 3w.	56
Shrule, Ireland. 54N 9w	66
Shtiplie, Turkey. 42N. 23E	94
Shuma R., Turkey. 41N. 23E	95
Shumla, Bulgaria. 43N. 27E.	94
Shuna Is., Scotland. 56N. 6w.	64
Shupfhein, Switzerland. 47N. 8E.	86
Shusha, Russia. 40N. 47E.	91
*Sicily, Italy. 38N. 14E.	81
Sidelhorn, Switzerland. 46N. 8E.	87
Sidero C., Crete. 35N. 26E.	95
Sidlaw Hills, Scotland. 56N. 3w.	65
Sidmouth, England. 51N. 3w.	56
Sieben Geb, Germany. 51N. 7E.	77
Siedlce, Russia. 52N. 22E.	91
Sieg, R., Germany. 51N. 7E.	77
Siegen, Germany. 51N. 8E.	77
*Siena, Italy 43N. 11E.	83
Sierck, Germany. 49N. 6E.	77
Siero, Spain. 43N. 6w.	84
Sierra de Albarracin, Spain. 41N. 1w.	85
Sierra da Cabreira, Portugal. 42N. 8w.	84
Sierra de la Demanda, Spain. 42N. 3w.	85
Sierra de Espuna, Spain 38N. 2w	85
Sierra de Estrella, Portugal. 40N. 8w.	84
Sierra de Gata, Spain. 40N. 6w.	84
Sierra de Gredos, Spain. 40N. 5w.	84
Sierra do Guadalupe, Spain. 40N. 5w.	84
Sierra de Guadarrama, Spain. 41N 4w.	84
Sierra de la Guara, Spain. 42N. 0w.	85
Sierra del Moncayo, Spain. 42N. 2w.	85
Sierra Morena, Spain. 38N. 6w.	84
Sierra Morena, Spain. 39N. 4w.	84
Sierra Nevada, Spain. 37N 3w.	84
Sierra de Ossa, Portugal. 39N. 8w.	84
Sierra de la Pena, Spain. 42N. 1w.	85
Sierre, Switzerland. 46N. 8E.	86
Sieve, R., Italy. 44N. 11E.	83
Sigmaringen, Germany. 48N. 9E.	77
Sigmunsherberg, Austria. 49N.16E.	78
Siguenza, Spain. 41N. 3w.	85
Sihl, Switzerland. 47N. 9E.	87
Silesia, Germany. 51N. 17E.	75
*Silistria, Roumania. 44N. 28E.	94
Siljan L., Sweden. 61N. 15E.	89
Sillian, Austria. 47N. 12E.	78
Silloth, England. 55N. 3w.	54
Silvermines Mts., Ireland. 53N. 8w.	68
Simbirsk, Russia. 55N. 49E.	91
Simeto R., Sicily. 37N. 15E.	81
Simferop, Russia. 45N. 34E.	91
Simmen Thal, Switzerland. 47N. 7E.	86
Simnitza, Roumania. 44N. 25E.	94
Simpeln, Switzerland. 46N. 8E.	86
*Simplon, Switzerland. 46N. 8E.	86
Sinau, Roumania. 45N. 26E.	94
Sinclair B., Scotland. 59N. 3w.	63
Sines, C. de, Portugal. 38N. 9w.	84
Sinigaglia, Italy. 44N. 13E.	83
Sinn, R., Germany. 50N. 10E.	77
Sinno R., Italy. 40N. 17E.	81
Sion, Switzerland. 46N. 7E.	86
Siphnos, Greece. 37N. 25E.	95
Silesia, Austria. 50N. 18E.	78
Sillein, Hungary. 49N. 19E.	79
Silvretta, Switzerland. 47N. 10E.	87
Sissach, Switzerland. 47N. 8E.	86
Sissek, Slavonia. 45N. 16E.	78
Sisteron, France. 44N. 6E.	73
Sistova, Bulgaria. 44N. 26E.	94
Sitjes, Spain. 41N. 2E.	85
Six Mile Cross, Ireland. 55N. 7w.	67

PAGE

Sixmilebridge, Ireland. 53N. 9W. 68
Skagen, Denmark 58N. 11E. 89
Skagstolstind, Norway. 62N. 8E. 89
Skaw, The, Denmark. 58N. 11E. 89
Skegness, England. 53N. 0E. 55
Skeleftea, Sweden. 65N. 21E. 88
Skeleftea, E., Sweden. 65N 21E. 88
Skerkin Is., Ireland. 51N. 9W. 68
Skerries, Ireland. 54N. 6W. 67
Skerries, Wales. 53N. 5W 54
Skerryvore, Scotland. 56N. 7W. 64
Skibbereen, Ireland. 52N. 9W. 68
Skiddaw, England. 55N. 3W. 54
*Skien, Norway. 59N. 10E. 89
Skipness, Scotland. 56N. 5W. 64
Skiport, Loch, Scotland. 57N. 7W. 62
*Skipton, England. 54N. 2W. 54
Skive, Denmark. 57N. 9E. 89
Skogshorn, Norway. 61N 8E. 89
Skopelos, Greece. 39N. 24E. 95
Skopin, Russia 54N. 40E 91
Skopie, Turkey. 42N. 22E. 94
Skole, Austria. 49N. 24E 79
Skomer Is., Wales. 52N. 5W. 56
Skull, Ireland. 52N 10W. 68
Skutari, Turkey. 42N. 20E. 94
Skutari Lake, Montenegro. 42N. 19E. 94
Skyros, Greece. 39N. 24E. 95
Slamannan, Scotland. 56N. 4W. 65
Slane, Ireland. 54N. 7W. 67
Slaney, R., Ireland. 52N. 7W. 69
Slapin, Loch, Scotland. 57N. 6W. 62
Slatina, Roumania. 45N. 25E. 94
Slatitza, Bulgaria. 43N. 24E. 94
Slatoust, Russia. 55N. 59E. 90
Slaviansk, Russia. 49N. 38E. 91
Slavonia, Hungary. 45N. 18E. 94
Slea Hd., Ireland. 52N. 10W. 68
Sleaford, England. 53N. 0W. 55
Sleat Pt., Scotland. 57N. 6W. 62
Sleat, Sound of, Scotland. 57N. 6W. 62
Slieve Aughty Mts., Ireland. 53N. 9W. 68
Slieve Bloom Mts., Ireland. 53N. 8W. 69
Slieve Donard, Ireland. 54N. 6W. 67
Slieve Gamph, Ireland. 54N. 9W. 66
Slieve Gullion, Ireland. 54N. 6W. 67
Slieve League, Ireland. 55N. 9W. 66
Slieve Mish, Ireland. 52N. 10W. 68
Shevenaman, Ireland 52N. 8W. 69
Slieve Snaght, Ireland. 55N. 7W. 67
Slieve Tobey, Ireland. 55N. 9W. 66
*Sligo, Ireland. 54N. 8W. 66
Sligo B., Ireland. 54N. 9W. 66
Slinitza, Bulgaria. 43N. 23E. 94
Slivno, Bulgaria. 43N. 26E. 94
Slonim, Russia. 54N. 25E. 91
Sloten, Holland. 53N. 6E. 70
Sluin, Croatia. 45N. 16E. 78
Slyne Hd., Ireland. 53N. 10W. 66
*Smerwick Harb., Ireland. 52N. 10W. 68
Smethwick, England. 52N. 2W. 56
Smichow, Austria. 50N. 14E. 78
Smölen, Norway. 63N. 8E. 88

PAGE

*Smolensk, Russia. 55N. 32E. 91
Snaasen Vand, Norway. 64N 11E. 88
Snaefell, Is. of Man. 54N 4W. 54
Snaith, England. 54N. 1W. 55
Sneek, Holland. 53N. 6E. 70
Sneen, Ireland. 52N. 10W. 68
Snehattten, Mt., Norway. 62N. 10E. 89
Sniatyn, Austria. 49N. 25E. 79
Snizart, Loch, Scotland. 58N. 6W. 62
Snowdon, Wales. 53N 4W 54
Soay Is., Scotland. 57N. 6W. 62
Soclona, Greece. 38N. 22E. 95
Soderhamn, Sweden. 61N. 17E. 89
Soest, Germany. 52N. 8E. 76
*Sofia, Bulgaria. 43N. 23E. 94
Sogne Fd , Norway. 61N. 7E. 89
Soignies, Belgium. 51N. 4E. 71
*Soisson, France. 49N. 3E. 73
Sokal, Austria. 51N. 24E. 79
Sokal, Russia. 51N. 24E. 91
Soke of Peterborough, England. 53N. 0W. 57
Solent, England. 51N. 1W. 57
Soleure (Solothurn), Switzerland. 47N. 8E. 86
*Solferino, Italy. 45N 11E. 82
Solihull, England. 52N. 2W. 56
Solingen, Germany. 51N. 7E. 76
Solmona, Italy. 42N. 14E. 83
Solo, Russia 66N. 40E 90
Solombola, Russia. 65N. 41E. 90
Solothurn, Switzerland. 47N. 8E. 86
Somlyo Vasarhely, Hungary. 47N. 17E. 78
Somme, France. 50N. 2E. 73
Somme, R., France. 50N. 2E. 73
Sommen L., Sweden. 58N. 15E 89
Somerset, England. 51N. 3W. 56
*Sondershausen, Germany. 52N. 11E. 76
Sondrio, Italy. 46N. 10E. 82
Sonneberg, Germany. 50N. 11E. 77
Soperga, Italy. 45N. 8E. 82
Sora, Italy. 42N. 14E 83
Sorau, Germany. 52N. 15E. 75
Soresiano, Italy. 46N. 12E. 83
Sorgano, Sardinia. 40N. 9E. 81
Soria, Spain. 42N. 3W. 85
Sorö, Norway. 71N. 22E. 88
Sorraia, R., Portugal. 39N. 9W. 84
Sovana, Italy. 43N. 12E. 83
Sotteville, France. 50N. 1E. 72
Souccbaz, Switzerland. 47N. 7E. 86
*Sound, The, Denmark. 56N 13E. 89
*Southampton, England 51N 1W. 57
Southampton Water, England. 51N. 1W. 57
South Beverland, Holland. 51N. 4E. 71
South Downs, England. 51N 0W. 57
Southend, England. 52N. 1E. 57
South Foreland, England. 51N. 1E. 57
South Holland, Holland. 52N. 4E. 70
South Kvalo, Norway. 70N. 19E. 88
Southminster, England. 52N. 1E. 57
South Molton, England. 51N. 4W. 56
Southofen, Germany. 47N. 10E. 77
Southport, England. 54N. 3W. 54

	PAGE
South Queensferry, Scotland. 56N. 3w.	65
South Ronaldshay Is., Scotland. 59N. 3w.	63
Southsea, England. 51N. 1w.	57
South Shields, England. 55N. 1w.	55
South Sound, Ireland. 53N. 9w.	68
South Tyne R., England. 55N. 2w.	54
South Uist Is., Scotland. 57N. 7w.	62
South Walls, Scotland. 59N. 3w.	63
*Southwell, England. 53N. 1w.	55
*Southwold, England. 52N. 2E.	57
Spa, Belgium. 50N. 6E.	71
Spada, C., Crete. 36N. 24E.	95
Spalato, Dalmatia. 43N. 16E.	78
Spalding, England. 53N. 0w.	55
*Spandau, Germany. 52N. 13E.	76
Sparta, Greece. 37N. 22E.	95
Spartivento, C., Sardinia. 39N. 9E.	81
Spartivento C., Italy. 38N. 16E.	81
Spean, R., Scotland. 57N. 5w.	62
Sperrin Mts., Ireland. 55N. 7w.	67
Spessart, Germany. 50N. 9E.	77
Spey, Loch, Scotland. 57N. 5w.	62
Spey, R., Scotland. 58N. 3w.	63
*Spezia, Italy. 44N. 10E.	82
Spezia, G of, Italy. 44N. 10E.	82
Spezzia, Greece. 37N. 23E.	95
Sphakia, Crete. 35N. 24E.	95
Spiddle, Ireland. 53N. 9w.	66
Spiez, Switzerland. 47N. 8E.	86
Spilimbergo, Italy. 46N. 13E.	83
*Spilsby, England. 53N. 0E.	55
Spirding See, Germany. 54N. 21E.	75
*Spires, Germany. 49N. 8E.	77
Spithead, England. 51N 1w.	57
Spittal, Austria. 47N. 14E.	78
Spittal of Glenshee, Scotland 57N. 3w.	63
Spitza, Dalmatia. 42N. 19E	79
Splugen, Switzerland. 47N. 9E.	87
Splugen (Mt.), Switzerland. 46N. 9E.	87
Spoleto, Italy. 43N. 13E.	83
Sporades, N., Greece. 39N. 24E.	95
Spree, R., Germany. 52N. 14E.	76
Spree Wald, Germany. 52N. 14E.	76
Spremberg, Germany. 52N. 14E.	76
Spurn Hd., England. 54N. 0E.	55
*Squillace, Italy. 39N. 17E.	81
Squillace, G. of, Italy. 39N. 17E	81
Stade, Germany. 54N. 9E.	76
Stadt Prom , Norway. 62N. 5E.	89
*Staffa, Scotland. 56N. 6w.	64
Staffin, Loch, Scotland. 58N. 6w.	62
*Stafford, England. 53N. 2w.	54
Staines, England. 51N. 0E.	57
Stalbridge, England. 51N. 2w.	56
Stalden, Switzerland. 46N. 8E.	86
Stalybridge, England. 53N. 2w.	54
Stamboul, Turkey 41N. 28E	95
*Stamford, England. 53N. 1w.	57
Stanhope, England. 55N. 2w.	54
Stanislawow, Austria. 49N. 25E.	79
Stanley, Scotland. 56N. 3w.	65
Stans, Switzerland. 47N. 8E.	87
Staraia Russa, Russia. 58N. 31E.	90
Starcross, England. 51N. 3w.	56
Stargard, Germany. 53N. 15E.	75
Starodul, Russia. 53N. 33E.	91
Start B., England. 50N. 4w.	56
Start Pt., England. 50N. 4w.	56
Stassfurt, Germany. 52N. 12E.	76
Stavanger, Norway. 59N. 5E.	89
Stavelot, Belgium. 50N. 6E.	71
Stavoren, Holland. 53N. 5E.	70
Stavropol, Russia. 45N 42E.	91
Steckborn, Switzerland 48N. 9E.	87
Steenbergen, Holland. 52N. 4E.	70
Stein, Switzerland. 48N. 9E.	87
Steinach, Austria. 48N. 14E.	78
Steinamanger, Hungary. 47N. 17E.	78
Steinfurt, Germany. 52N. 7E.	76
Stelvio P., Austria. 46N. 10E.	78
*Stendal, Germany. 53N. 12E.	76
Sternberg, Austria. 50N. 17E.	78
Sterzing, Austria. 47N. 11E.	78
Stettin, Germany. 53N. 14E.	76
Stevan, Russia. 51N. 26E.	91
Stevenage, England. 52N. 0w.	57
Stewarton, Scotland. 56N. 4w.	65
Stewartstown, Ireland. 55N. 7w.	67
Steyer, Austria. 48N. 14E.	78
Stilton, England. 53N 0E.	57
Stinchar, R , Scotland. 55N. 5w.	64
*Stirling, Scotland. 56N. 4w.	65
Stirlitamak, Russia. 54N. 56E.	91
Stjernö, Norway. 70N. 22E.	88
Stockach, Germany. 48N. 9E.	77
*Stockholm, Sweden. 59N. 18E.	89
Stockhorn, Switzerland. 47N. 8E.	86
Stockport, England. 53N. 2w.	54
Stockton, England. 55N. 1w.	55
Stod, Norway. 65N. 12E.	88
Stoke, R., England. 53N. 0E.	57
Stokesley, England. 54N. 1w.	55
Stoke-upon-Trent, England. 53N. 2w.	54
Stolp, Germany. 54N. 17E.	75
Stolpmunde, Germany. 55N. 17E.	76
Stonehaven, Scotland. 57N. 2w.	63
Stonehenge, England. 51N. 2w.	56
Stonehouse, Scotland. 56N. 4w.	65
Stoneykirk, Scotland. 55N. 5w.	64
Stony Strafford, England. 52N. 1w.	57
Stor Afvan, Sweden. 66N. 18E.	88
Stora Lulea Jaur, Sweden. 68N. 20E.	88
Store Borge Fd., Norway. 65N. 14E.	88
Stören, Norway. 63N. 10E.	88
Store Vigel, Sweden. 62N. 13E.	89
Stornoway, Scotland. 58N. 6w.	62
Stornoway Harb., Scotland. 58N. 6w.	62
Storsa L., Sweden. 63N. 14E.	88
Stor Uman, Sweden. 65N. 17E.	88
Storr, The, Scotland. 58N. 6w.	62
Stour, R., England. 51N. 2w.	56
Stour, R., England. 52N. 1E.	57
Stour, R., England. 51N. 1E.	57
Stourbridge, England. 52N. 2w.	56
Stourport, England. 52N. 2w.	56
Stow, Scotland. 56N. 3E.	65
Stow Market, England. 52N. 1E.	57
Strabane, Ireland. 55N. 7w.	67

	PAGE
Strachur, Scotland. 56N. 5w.	64
Stradbally, Ireland. 52N. 7w	69
Stradbally, Ireland. 53N. 7w.	69
Stradella, Italy 45N. 9E.	82
Stradone, Ireland. 54N. 7w.	67
*Stralsund, Germany. 54N 13E.	76
Strande Fd., Norway. 60N 5E	89
Strangford, Ireland. 54N. 6w.	67
Strangford Lough, Ireland. 54N. 6w.	67
Stranorlar, Ireland 55N. 8w.	67
Stranraer, Scotland. 55N. 5w.	64
Strassburg, Germany. 53N 20E.	75
*Strassburg, Germany. 49N. 8E.	77
Stratford, Ireland. 53N. 7w	69
*Stratford-on-Avon, England. 52N. 2w.	57
Strath Affrick, Scotland. 57N. 5w.	62
Strathaven, Scotland. 56N. 4w.	65
Strathblane, Scotland. 56N. 4w.	65
Strathbungo, Scotland. 56N. 3w.	65
Strathdon, Scotland 57N. 3w.	63
Strathearn, Scotland. 56N. 4w.	65
Strath Brora, Scotland. 58N. 4w.	63
Strath Carron, Scotland. 58N. 4w.	62
Strath Conan, Scotland 58N. 5w.	62
Strath Dearn, Scotland. 57N 4w.	63
Strath Garve, Scotland. 58N. 5w.	62
Strath Halladale, Scotland 58N. 4w.	63
Strathmore, Scotland. 56N. 3w.	65
Strathmore, Scotland. 58N. 4w.	63
Strath Nairn, Scotland. 57N. 4w.	63
Strath Naver, Scotland. 58N. 4w.	63
Strathpeffer, Scotland. 58N. 5w.	62
Strathspey, Scotland. 57N. 4w	63
Strath Ulhe, Scotland. 58N. 4w	63
Strathy, Scotland. 59N. 4w.	63
Strathy Pt., Scotland. 59N. 4w.	63
Stratton, England. 51N. 5w.	56
Straubing, Germany. 49N. 13E.	74
Streamstown B., Ireland. 54N. 10w.	66
Streedagh Pt., Ireland. 54N. 9w.	66
Strelitz, To, Germany. 54N 11E.	76
Strichen, Scotland. 58N. 2w.	63
Striven, Loch, Scotland. 56N. 5w.	64
Strokestown, Ireland. 54N. 8w.	66
Strom, Sweden. 64N. 16E.	88
Stromboli, Is., Italy. 39N. 15E.	81
Strome Ferry, Scotland. 57N. 6w.	62
*Stromness, Scotland. 59N 3w.	63
Ströms Vatterdal, Sweden. 64N. 15E.	88
Stronsay Is., Scotland. 59N. 2w.	63
Stroud, England. 52N. 2w.	56
Strumble Hd., Wales. 52N. 5w.	56
Strumitza, Turkey. 42N. 23E.	94
Stry, Austria. 49N. 24E.	79
*Stuhlweissenburg, Hungary. 47N. 19E.	79
Stura, R., Italy. 45N. 8E.	82
Sturminster Newton, England. 51N. 2w.	56
*Stuttgart, Germany. 49N. 9E.	77
Stylis, Greece. 39N. 23E.	95
Styria, Austria. 47N. 15E.	78

	PAGE
Suances, Spain. 44N. 4w.	84
Subiaco, Italy. 42N. 13E.	83
Sucha, Austria. 50N. 20E.	79
Suck, R., Ireland. 53N. 8w.	66
Sudenc, Austria. 50N. 17E.	78
Suczawa, Austria. 48N. 26E.	79
Suda B., Crete. 35N. 24E.	95
*Sudbury, England. 52N. 1E.	57
Sudetic Chain, Germany. 50N. 17E.	75
Sueca, Spain. 39N. 0w.	85
Suffolk, England. 52N 1E.	57
Sugatag, Hungary. 48N. 24E.	79
Suhl, Germany. 51N. 11E.	77
Suhr, Switzerland. 47N. 8E.	86
Suhr, R., Switzerland. 47N. 8E.	86
Suir, R., Ireland. 52N. 7w.	69
Sukhona R., Russia 60N 45E.	90
Sulgen, Switzerland. 48N. 9E.	87
Sulina, Roumania. 45N. 30E	94
Sulitelma, Sweden. 67N. 17E.	88
Sulzbach, Germany. 50N. 12E.	77
Sumburgh Hd., Scotland. 60N. 1w.	63
Summer Isles, Scotland. 58N. 5w	62
Sunart, Loch, Scotland. 57N. 6w.	62
Sunderland, England. 55N 1w	55
Sundsvall, Sweden. 62N. 17E.	89
Sunion, Greece. 38N. 24E.	95
Surian, Hungary. 46N. 23E.	79
Surrey, England. 51N. 0w	57
Sursee, Switzerland. 47N. 8E.	86
Surzara, Roumania. 48N. 26E.	94
Susa, Italy. 45N. 7E.	82
Sussex, England. 51N. 0w.	57
Sutton, England. 53N. 0E.	55
Sutton Bridge, England 53N. 0E.	55
Suvalki, Russia. 54N. 23E.	91
Suzzaca, Italy. 45N. 11E.	83
Svardsjo, Sweden. 61N. 1CE.	89
Svendborg, Denmark. 55N. 11E.	89
Svenigorodka, Russia. 49N. 31E.	91
Svilainatz, Servia. 44N. 22E.	94
Svir R., Russia. 61N. 33E.	90
Swabia, Germany. 48N. 10w.	77
Swabian Jura, Germany. 49N. 10E.	77
Swaffham, England. 53N. 1E.	57
Swale, England. 51N. 1E.	57
Swale, R., England. 54N 1w.	55
*Swanage, England. 51N. 2w.	56
Swanlinbar, Ireland. 54N. 8w.	67
Swansea, Wales. 52N. 4w.	56
Swansea B., Wales. 52N. 4w.	56
Swartisen, Norway. 67N. 14E	88
Sweden (Province) Sweden. 60N. 15E.	89
Swilly R., Ireland. 55N 8w.	67
*Swilly, Lough, Ireland. 55N. 8w.	67
Swin, Loch, Scotland. 56N. 6w.	64
Swindon, England. 52N. 2w.	56
Swineford, Ireland. 54N. 9w.	66
Swinemünde, Germany. 54N. 14E.	76
Swing, Switzerland. 47N. 9E.	87
Swinton, Scotland. 56N 2w.	65
Swona Is., Scotland. 59N 3w.	63
Swords, Ireland. 53N. 6w.	67
Sybil Hd., Ireland. 52N. 10w.	68
Symington, Scotland. 56N. 4w.	65
Syracuse, Sicily. 37N. 15E.	81

PAGE

Syros, Greece. 37N. 25E. 95
Sysran, Russia. 53N. 49E. 91
Szagszard, Hungary. 46N. 18E. 79
Szamos, Hungary. 48N. 22E. 79
Szamos R., Hungary. 47N. 24E. 94
Szarvas, Hungary. 47N. 20E. 79
Szasz Regen, Hungary. 47N. 25E. 79
Szathmar Nemeti, Hungary.
48N. 23E. 79
Szdagy Somlyo, Hungary.47N.23E.79
Szegedin, Hungary. 46N. 20E. 94
Szentes, Hungary. 47N. 20E. 79
Szent Miklos, Hungary. 49N. 20E. 79
Sziget, Hungary. 48N. 24E. 79
Szolnok, Hungary. 47N. 20E. 79

Tabor, Austria. 49N. 15E. 78
Tadcaster, England. 54N. 1W. 55
Taff, R., Wales. 51N. 3W. 56
*Taganrog, Russia. 47N. 39E. 91
Taghmon, Ireland. 52N. 7W. 69
Tagliomento R., Italy. 46N. 13E. 83
Tagus, R., Portugal 39N. 9W. 84
*Tain, Scotland. 58N. 4W. 63
Tajo, R., Portugal. 39N. 9W. 84
Tajuna, R., 40N. 4W. 84
Takhyno L., Turkey. 41N. 24E. 95
Talamone, Italy. 43N. 11E. 83
*Talavera, Spain. 40N. 5W. 84
Talbert, Pt. de, France. 49N. 3W. 72
Talbot, Mount, Ireland. 54N. 8W. 66
Talgarth, Wales. 52N. 3W. 56
Talisker, Scotland. 57N. 6W. 62
Tallaght, Ireland. 53N. 6W. 67
Tallow, Ireland. 52N. 8W. 69
Tamar, R., England. 51N. 4W. 56
Tamaro, Switzerland. 46N. 9E. 87
Tambov, Russia. 53N. 42E. 91
Tamega, R., Portugal. 41N. 8W. 84
Tamina R., Switzerland. 47N. 9E. 87
Tamins, Switzerland. 47N. 9E. 87
Tammerfors, Russia. 62N. 24E. 90
Tamsweg, Austria. 47N. 14E. 78
Tamworth, England. 53N. 2W. 56
Tana Elf, Norway. 70N. 28E. 88
Tana Fd., Norway. 71N. 29E. 88
Tanaro R., Italy. 44N. 8E. 82
Tanderagee, Ireland. 54N. 6W. 67
*Tantallon Castle, Scotland. 56N.
3W. 65
*Tara, Ireland. 54N. 7W. 67
Tara R., Turkey. 43N. 20E. 94
Taransay Is., Scotland. 58N. 7W. 62
Taranto, Italy. 40N. 17E. 81
Taranto, G. of, Italy. 40N. 17E. 81
Tarare, France. 46N. 4E. 73
*Tarascon, France. 44N. 4E. 73
Tarasp, Switzerland. 47N. 10E. 87
Tarazona, Spain. 42N. 2W. 85
Tarbat Ness, Scotland. 58N. 4W. 63
Tarbeg, Scotland. 56N. 5W. 64
Tarbert, Ireland. 53N. 9W. 68
Tarbert, Scotland. 56N. 5W. 64
Tarbert, Scotland. 58N. 7W. 62
Tarbert, Loch, Scotland. 56N. 6W. 64
Tarbert, Loch E., Scotland. 56N.
5W. 64

PAGE

Tarbert, Loch E., Scotland. 58N.
7W. 62
Tarbert, Loch W., Scotland. 56N.
6W. 64
Tarbert, Loch W., Scotland. 58N.
7W. 62
*Tarbes, France. 43N. 0E. 72
*Tarifa, C., Spain. 36N. 6W. 84
Tarland, Scotland. 57N. 3W. 63
Tarn, France. 44N. 2W. 73
Tarn et Garonne, France. 44N. 1E. 72
Tarnopol, Austria. 50N. 26E. 79
Tarnow, Austria. 50N. 21E. 79
Taro, R., Italy. 45N. 10E. 82
Tarporley, England. 53N. 3W. 54
*Tarragona, Spain. 41N. 1E. 85
Tartaro, R., Italy. 45N. 12E. 83
Tartlau, Hungary. 46N. 26E. 79
Tarn, R., France. 44N. 1E. 73
Tatar-Bazarjik, Bulgaria. 42N.
25E. 94
Tatra Mts., Austria-Hungary. 49N.
20E. 79
Tattershall, England. 53M. 0W. 55
Tauber, R., Germany. 50N. 9E. 77
Tauern Chain, Austria. 47N. 14E. 78
*Taunton, England. 51N. 3W. 56
Taunus, Germany. 50N. 8E. 77
Taur, Ireland. 52N. 9W. 68
Taurida, Russia. 46N. 35E. 91
Taus, Austria. 50N. 13E. 78
Tavastehus, Russia. 61N. 24E. 90
Tavira, Portugal. 37N. 8W. 84
Tavistock, England. 51N. 4W. 56
Tavolara Is., Sardinia. 41N. 10E. 81
Taw, R., England. 51N. 4W. 56
Tawe, R., Wales. 52N. 4W. 56
Tay, Loch, Scotland. 56N. 4W. 65
Tay, R., Scotland. 56N. 3W. 65
Tay, R., Scotland. 57N. 4W. 63
Taygetos Mts., Greece. 37N. 22E. 95
Tayport, Scotland. 56N. 3W. 65
Tchachak, Servia. 44N. 21E. 94
Tchataldja, Turkey. 41N. 28E. 95
Tchelyabinsk, Russia. 55N. 62E. 90
Tcherdyn, Russia. 60N. 57E. 90
Tcherkazy, Russia. 50N. 32E. 91
Tchernavoda, Roumania. 44N.28E.94
Tchernigov, Russia. 52N. 31E. 91
Tcheskaia B., Russia. 67N. 47E. 90
Tchistopol, Russia. 55N. 51E. 90
Tchusovaia R., Russia. 58N. 58E. 90
Teano, Italy. 41N. 14E. 81
Tebay, England. 54N. 3W. 54
Teelin B., Ireland. 55N. 9W. 66
Tees B., England. 55N. 1W. 55
Tees R., England. 55N. 1W. 55
Tegern See, Germany. 48N. 12E. 77
Teifi, R., Wales. 52N. 5W. 56
Teign R., England. 51N. 4W. 56
*Teignmouth, England. 51N. 3W. 56
Teith, R., Scotland. 56N. 4W. 65
Tekutchin, Roumania. 46N. 28E. 94
Teme R., England. 52N. 2W. 56
Temes, Hungary. 45N. 21E. 79
*Temesvar, Austria. 46N. 21E. 94
Templo, Sardinia. 41N. 9W. 81
Templemore, Ireland. 53N. 8W. 69

PAGE

Templetouhy, Ireland. 53N. 8w. 69
Templin, Germany. 53N. 14E. 76
Tenbury, England. 52N. 3w. 56
Tenby, Wales 52N. 5w. 56
Tenda, Italy. 44N. 8E. 82
Tendre Mt., Switzerland. 47N. 6E. 86
Tenna, R., Italy. 43N. 14E. 83
Tenterden, England. 51N. 1E. 57
Teplitz, Austria. 51N. 14E. 78
Ter, R., Spain. 42N. 3E. 85
Ter Distr., Russia. 44N. 45E. 91
Teramo, Italy. 43N. 14E 83
Terek R., Russia. 44N. 47E. 91
Tergovist, Roumania. 45N. 26E. 94
Termini, Sicily. 38N. 14E. 81
Termoli, Italy. 42N. 15E. 80
Termonde, Belgium. 51N. 4E. 71
Termonfeckin, Ireland. 54N. 6w. 67
Tern R., England. 53N. 3w. 54
*Terni, Italy. 43N. 13E. 83
Terracina, Italy. 41N. 13E 81
Terranova, Sardinia. 41N. 10E. 81
Terranova, Sicily. 37N. 14E. 81
Terschelling, Holland. 53N. 5E. 70
Teruel, Spain. 40N. 1w. 85
Teschen, Austria. 50N. 19E. 79
Tetbury, England. 52N. 2w. 56
Teterow, Germany. 54N. 12E. 76
Teulada, C., Sardinia. 39N. 9E. 81
Teutoburger Wald, Germany. 52N. 8w. 76
Teverone, R., Italy. 42N. 12E. 83
Teviot, R., Scotland. 55N. 3w. 65
*Tewkesbury, England. 52N. 2w. 56
*Texel, Holland. 53N. 5E. 70
Thame, England. 52N. 1w. 57
*Thames, R., England. 51N. 0E. 57
Thanet Is., England. 51N. 1E. 57
Thann, Germany. 48N. 7E. 77
Tharsis, Spain. 38N. 7w. 84
Thasos, Turkey. 41N. 25E. 95
*Thaxted, England. 52N. 0E. 57
Thaya, Austria 49N 17E. 78
Theiss R., Hungary. 45N. 20E. 94
Theodosija, Russia. 45N. 35E. 91
Thera, Greece. 36N. 25E. 95
Theresientstadt, Austria. 51N. 14E. 78
Thermia, Greece. 37N. 24E. 95
Thermopyle, Greece. 39N. 22E. 95
Thessaly, Greece. 39N. 22E. 95
*Thetford, England. 52N. 1E. 57
Thielt, Belgium. 51N. 3E. 71
Thiers, France. 46N. 4E. 73
Thil, R., Belgium. 51N. 5E 71
Thirlmere, England. 55N. 3w. 54
Thirsk, England. 54N. 1w. 55
Thisted, Denmark. 57N. 9E. 89
Thiva, Greece. 38N. 23E. 95
Tholen, Holland. 52N. 4E. 70
Thomar, Portugal. 40N. 8w. 84
Thomastown, Ireland 53N. 7w 69
Thonon, France. 46N. 6E 73
*Thorn, Russia. 53N 19E 91
Thornhill, Scotland. 55N. 4w. 65
Thorpe, England. 54N. 1w. 55
Thosen Fd., Norway. 65N. 12E. 88
Thourout, Belgium. 51N. 3E. 71

PAGE

Thrapston, England. 52N. 1w. 57
Thuin, Belgium. 50N. 4E. 71
Thun, Switzerland. 47N 8E. 86
Thun, L. of, Switzerland. 47N. 8E. 86
Thur R., Switzerland. 48N. 9E. 87
Thuringer, Germany. 51N. 11E. 77
Thuringia, Germany. 51N. 11E. 77
Thurles, Ireland. 53N. 8w. 69
Thurso, Scotland 59N. 4w. 63
Thurso R., Scotland. 59N. 4w. 63
Thusis, Switzerland. 47N. 9E. 87
Tiarine P., Switzerland. 47N. 9E 87
Tiber, R., Italy. 42N. 12E. 83
Ticino, R., Italy. 45N. 9E. 82
Tidworth, England. 51N. 2w. 57
Tiefen Kasten, Switzerland. 47N. 10E. 87
Tiel, Holland. 52N. 5E. 70
*Tiflis, Russia. 42N. 45E 91
Tighnabruaich, Scotland. 56N. 5w. 64
Tilburg, Holland. 52N 5E. 70
*Tilbury, England. 51N. 0E. 57
*Tilsit, Germany. 55N. 22E. 75
Timan Ra., Russia. 65N. 52E 90
Timok, R., Servia. 44N. 22E. 94
Tinahely, Ireland. 53N. 6w. 69
Tinos, Greece. 37N. 25E. 95
*Tintagel Castle, England 51N. 5w. 56
*Tintern Abbey, England. 52N. 3w. 56
Tintern Abbey, Ireland. 52N. 7w.69
Tinto Hill, Scotland. 56N. 4w. 65
Tipperary, Ireland. 52N. 8w. 68
Tiranna, Turkey. 42N. 20E. 94
Tirano, Italy. 46N. 10E. 82
Tiraspol, Russia. 47N. 30E. 91
Tiree, Scotland. 57N. 7w. 64
Tirgoschyl, Roumania. 45N. 24E. 94
*Tirlemont, Belgium. 51N. 5E. 71
Tirnova, Bulgaria. 42N. 26E. 94
Tirnova, Bulgaria. 43N. 25E. 94
Tirschenreut, Germany. 50N. 12E. 77
Tirso, R., Sardinia. 40N. 8E. 81
*Tiverton, England. 51N. 3w. 56
Tivoli, Italy. 42N. 13E. 83
Tobercurry, Ireland. 54N. 9w. 66
Tobermore, Ireland. 55N. 7w. 67
Tobermory, Scotland. 57N. 6w. 62
Toberscanavan, Ireland. 54N. 8w. 66
Todi, Switzerland. 47N. 9E. 87
Todi, Italy 43N. 12E. 83
Todi Chain, Switzerland. 47N. 9E. 87
Todmorden, England. 54N. 2w. 54
Toe Hd., Ireland. 51N. 9w. 68
Toe Hd., Scotland. 58N. 7w. 62
Tokay, Hungary. 48N 22E. 79
Toledo, Spain. 40N. 4w. 84
*Tolentino, Italy. 43N. 13E. 83
Toll-pos Is, Russia. 64N. 59E. 90
Tolmezzo, Italy. 46N. 13E. 80
Tolosa, Spain. 43N. 2w. 85
Tolsta Hd., Scotland. 58N. 6w. 62
Tolua, Hungary. 47N. 19E. 47
Tolz, Germany. 48N. 11E. 77
Toming, Germany. 54N. 9E. 76
Tomintoul, Scotland. 57N. 3w. 63
Tomo Pass, Roumania. 46N. 25E. 94

PAGE

Tonbridge, England. 51N. 0E. 57
Tondern, Germany. 55N. 9E. 74
Tone, R., England. 51N. 3W. 56
Tongres, Belgium. 51N. 5E. 71
Tongue, Scotland. 58N. 4W. 63
Tonnerre, France. 48N. 4E. 73
Tonsberg, Norway. 59N. 10E. 89
Toome, Ireland. 55N. 6W. 67
Toomyvara, Ireland. 53N. 8W. 69
Topla, Hungary. 49N. 22E. 79
Topolias L., Greece. 38N. 23E. 95
*Tor B., England. 50N. 4W. 56
Torda, Hungary. 47N. 24E. 79
Tordesillas, Spain. 42N. 5W. 84
Tordino, R., Italy. 43N. 14E. 83
*Torgau, Germany. 52N. 13E. 76
Toriñana, C., Spain. 43N. 9W. 84
Tormes, R., Spain. 41N. 6W. 84
Torna, Hungary. 49N. 21E. 79
Torneå, Russia. 66N. 24E. 90
Torneå, Sweden. 66N. 24E. 88
Tornea, Sweden. 68N. 22E. 88
Tornea Elf, Sweden. 66N. 24E. 88
Tornea Traesk, Sweden. 68N. 21E. 88
Toro, Spain. 42N. 5W. 84
Torquay, England. 50N. 4W. 56
Torre Pellice, Italy. 45N. 7E. 82
Torrelavega, Spain. 43N. 4W. 84
Torrenieri, Italy. 43N. 12E. 83
Torres Novos, Portugal. 39N. 9W 84
Torres Vedras, Portugal. 39N. 9W. 84
Torrevieja, Spain. 38N. 1W. 85
Torridge, R., England. 51N. 4W. 56
Torridon, Loch, Scotland. 58N. 6W. 62
*Torrington, England. 51N. 4W. 56
Torrisdal, Norway. 58N. 8E. 89
Torshok, Russia. 57N. 36E. 90
Tortona, Italy. 45N. 9E. 82
Tortosa, Spain. 41N. 1E. 85
Tory Is., Ireland. 55N. 8W. 66
Toscanella, Italy. 42N. 12E. 83
Toscolano, Italy. 46N. 11E. 82
Toss R., Switzerland. 48N. 9E. 87
Totana, Spain. 38N. 1W. 85
Totma, Russia. 60N. 43E. 90
Totnes, England. 50N. 4W. 56
Toul, France. 49N. 6E. 73
*Toulon, France. 43N. 6E. 73
-*Toulouse, France. 44N. 1E. 72
*Tournai, Belgium. 51N. 3W. 71
*Tours, France. 47N. 1E. 72
Tovis, Hungary. 46N. 24E. 79
Towcester, England. 52N. 1W. 57
Towy, R., Wales 52N. 4W. 56
Towyn, Wales. 53N. 4W 56
*Trafalgar, C., Spain. 36N. 6W. 84
Tralee, Ireland. 52N. 10W. 68
Tralee B., Ireland. 52N. 10W. 68
Tramore, Ireland. 52N. 7W. 69
Tramore B., Ireland. 52N. 7W. 69
Tranent, Scotland. 56N. 3W. 65
Transylvania, Hungary. 46N. 24E. 94
Transylvanian Alps, Roumania. 45N. 24E. 94
Trant, Italy. 41N. 16F 81
Trapani, Sicily. 38N. 13E. 81
Traquair, Scotland. 56N. 3W. 65

PAGE

Trasimeno, L., Italy. 43N. 12E. 83
Traun S., Austria 48N. 14E. 78
Traunstein, Germany. 48N. 13E.77
Trautenau, Austria. 51N. 16E. 78
Trave R., Germany. 54N. 11E. 76
Travemunde, Germany. 54N. 10E. 76
Travnik, Bosnia. 44N. 18E. 94
Trawbreaga B., Ireland. 55N. 7W. 67
Trawenagh B., Ireland. 55N. 8W. 66
Traz oz Montes, Portugal. 42N. 7W. 84
*Trebbia R., Italy. 45N. 10E. 82
Trebinje, Bosnia. 43N. 18E. 94
Tredegar, England. 52N. 3W. 56
Tregaron, Wales. 52N. 4W. 56
Treig, Loch, Scotland. 57N. 5W. 62
Treja, Italy. 43N. 13E. 83
Tremadoc B., Wales. 53N. 4W. 54
Tremp, Spain. 42N. 1E. 85
Trent, Austria. 46N. 11E. 78
Trent, R., England. 54N. 1W 55
Treskavitza, Mt., Bosnia. 44N. 19E.94
*Treves, Germany. 50N. 7E. 77
Treviglio, Italy. 46N. 10E. 82
Treviso, Italy. 46N. 12E. 83
Trevoux, France. 46N. 5E. 73
Tricarico, Italy. 41N. 16E. 81
Trieste, Austria. 46N. 14E. 78
Trikhala, Greece. 40N. 22E. 95
Trillick, Ireland. 54N. 7W. 67
*Trim, Ireland. 54N. 7W. 67
Tring, England. 52N. 1W. 57
Trino, Italy. 45N. 8E. 82
Trionto, C. del, Italy. 40N. 17E. 81
Tripolitza, Greece. 37N. 23E. 95
Trocadero, Spain. 36N. 6W. 84
Trogen, Switzerland. 47N. 9E. 87
Troitsk, Russia. 54N. 63E 90
Trollhätta Falls, Sweden. 58N. 12E.89
Tromsö, Norway. 70N. 19E. 88
*Trondhjem, Norway. 63N. 10E. 88
Tronto R., Italy. 43N. 14E. 83
Troon, Scotland. 56N. 5W. 64
Troppau, Austria. 50N. 18E. 78
Trostan, Ireland. 55N. 6W. 67
Trossachs, Scotland. 56N. 4W. 65
Troup Hd., Scotland. 58N. 2W. 63
Trouville, France. 49N. 0E. 72
Trowbridge, England. 51N. 2W. 56
Troyes, France. 48N. 4E. 73
Trujillo, Spain. 40N. 6W. 84
Truro, England. 50N. 5W. 56
Tsaritsya, Russia. 49N. 44E. 91
Tuadh, Loch, Scotland. 57N. 6W. 64
Tuam, Ireland. 54N. 9W. 66
*Tubingen, Germany. 49N. 9E. 77
*Tudela, Spain. 42N. 2W. 85
Tukkum, Russia. 57N. 23E. 90
Tula, Russia. 54N. 38E. 91
Tulla, Ireland. 53N. 9W. 68
Tullamore, Ireland. 53N. 7W. 67
Tulle, France. 45N. 2E. 73
Tulloch, Scotland. 57N. 5W. 62
Tullow, Ireland. 53N. 7W. 69
Tultcha, Roumania. 45N. 29E. 94
Tummel, Loch, Scotland. 57N. 4W. 63
Tummel, R., Scotland. 57N. 4W. 63

PAGE

Tuna, Sweden. 60N. 16E. 89
Tunbridge Wells, England. 51N. 0E. 57
Tunja R., Bulgaria. 42N. 27E. 94
Tunstall, England. 53N. 2w 54
Turano R., Italy. 42N. 13E. 83
*Turin, Italy 45N. 8E. 82
Turn Ness, Scotland. 59N. 3w. 63
*Turnberry Pt, Scotland. 55N. 5w. 64
*Turnhout, Belgium. 51N. 5E. 71
Turnu, Roumania. 44N. 23E. 94
Turriff, Scotland. 58N. 2w. 63
Turtukai, Bulgaria. 44N. 27E. 94
Tuscany, Italy. 43N. 11E. 83
Tuskar Rock, Ireland. 52N. 6w 69
*Tutbury, England. 53N. 2w. 55
Tuttlingen, Germany. 48N. 9E. 77
Tuxford, England. 53N. 1w. 55
Tuy, Spain. 42N. 9w. 84
Tuzla, Bosnia. 44N. 19E. 94
Tver, Russia. 57N. 36E. 90
Tweed, R., England. 56N. 2w. 54
Tweedmouth, England. 56N. 2w. 65
Twelve Pins, Ireland. 54N. 10w. 66
Tyndrum, Scotland. 56N. 5w. 64
Tyne, R., England 55N 2w. 55
Tyne, R., Scotland. 56N 3w. 65
Tynemouth, England 55N. 1w. 55
Tyrhenian Sea, Italy. 40N. 12E. 81
Tyrnau, Hungary. 49N 18E. 78
Tyrnavo, Turkey. 40N. 22E. 95
Tyrol, Austria. 47N. 11E. 78
Tyrone, Ireland. 55N. 7w. 67
Tys Fd., Norway. 68N. 16E. 88

Ub, Servia. 44N. 20E. 94
Ubeda, Spain. 38N. 3w. 84
Uberlingen, Germany. 48N. 9E. 77
Uckermunde, Germany. 54N. 14E 76
Uckfield, England. 51N. 0E. 57
Ucunkopri, Turkey. 43N. 27E. 94
Uddevalla, Sweden. 58N. 12E. 89
Udine, Italy. 46N. 13E. 83
Udvarhely, Hungary. 46N. 25E. 79
Ufa, Russia. 55N. 56E 90
Ufa R., Russia. 56N. 57E. 90
Uffenheim, Germany. 50N. 10E. 77
Ugie, R., Scotland. 58N. 2w. 63
Uglitch, Russia. 58N. 38E. 90
Uig, Scotland. 58N. 6w. 62
Ulbster, Scotland. 58N. 3w. 63
Uleaborg, Russia. 65N. 26E. 90
Ullapool, Scotland. 58N. 5w. 62
Ullswater, England. 55N. 3w. 54
*Ulm, Germany. 48N. 10E. 77
Ulster, Ireland. 54N. 7w 67
Ulster Canal, Ireland. 54N. 7w. 67
Ulva, Scotland. 56N. 6w. 64
Ulverston, England. 54N. 3w. 54
Uman, Russia. 49N. 30E. 91
Umbria, Italy. 43N. 13E. 83
Umea, Sweden. 64N. 21E. 88
Umea E., Sweden. 14N. 20E. 88
Under Cliffe, England. 51N. 1w. 57
Ung Hradisch, Austria. 49N.17E. 78
Unghvar, Hungary. 49N. 22E. 79
Unna R., Bosnia. 45N. 16E. 94
Unst Is., Scotland. 61N. 1w. 63

PAGE

Unstrut R., Germany. 51N. 12E. 76
Unter See, Germany. 48N. 9E. 77
Unterseen, Switzerland. 47N. 8E. 86
Unterwalden, Switzerland. 47N. 8E 86
Upper Engadine, Switzerland. 47N. 10E. 87
Upper Franconia, Germany. 50N. 11E. 77
Upper Palatinate, Germany. 49N. 12E. 77
Uppingham, England. 53N. 1w. 57
*Upsala, Sweden. 60N. 18E. 89
Ural Mts., Russia. 60N. 60E. 90
Ural, R., Russia. 47N. 52E. 91
*Urbino, Italy. 44N. 13E. 83
Ure, R., England. 54N. 1w. 55
Uri, Switzerland. 47N 9E. 87
Uri, B. of, Switzerland. 47N. 9E. 87
Urk, Holland. 53N. 6E 70
Urlingford, Ireland. 53N. 8w. 69
Ury, R., Scotland. 57N. 2w. 63
Usedon, Germany. 54N. 14E. 76
*Ushant Is., France 48N. 5w. 72
Ushitze, Servia. 44N. 20E. 94
Usk, England. 52N 3w. 56
Usk, R., England. 52N 3w. 56
Uskub, Turkey. 42N. 22E. 94
Ussa, R., Russia. 69N. 64E. 90
Ust Sysolsk, Russia. 62N. 51E. 90
Ust Tsylma, Russia. 66N. 52E. 90
Ust Ussa, Russia. 66N. 57E. 90
Uster, Switzerland. 47N. 9E. 87
Ustica Is., Italy. 39N. 13E. 81
Utiel, Spain. 40N. 1w. 85
*Utrecht, Holland. 52N. 5E. 70
Utrera, Spain. 37N. 6w 84
Uttoxeter, England. 53N. 2w. 54
Utznach, Switzerland. 47N 9E. 87
Uxbridge, England. 52N. 0w. 57

Vaags Fd., Norway. 69N. 17E. 88
Vacha, Germany. 51N. 10E. 77
Vadsö, Norway. 70N. 30E 88
Vakuf, D., Bosnia. 44N 17E. 94
Valdai Hills, Russia. 58N 33E. 90
Valdepeñas, Spain. 39N 3w. 84
Valderaduey, R., Spain. 42N. 6w. 84
Valemi, Roumania. 45N. 26E. 94
Valence, France. 45N. 5E. 73
Valencia Harb., Ireland. 52N. 10w. 68
Valencia, Spain. 39N. 0w. 85
Valencia, Spain. 42N 5w. 84
Valencia de Alcantara, Spain. 39N. 7w. 84
Valencia Is., Ireland. 52N. 10w 68
*Valenciennes, France. 50N. 4E. 73
Valenza, Italy. 45N. 9E. 82
Valievo, Servia. 44N. 20E. 94
*Valladolid, Spain. 42N. 5w. 84
Vallengin, Switzerland. 47N. 7E 86
Valli di Comacchio, Italy. 45N. 12E. 83
*Vallombrosa, Italy. 44N. 12E. 83
Vellorbes, Switzerland. 47N. 6E. 86
Valls, Spain. 41N 1E. 85
Valverde, Spain. 37N. 7w. 84

PAGE

Vannes, France. 48N. 3w. 72
Var, France. 44N. 6E. 73
Var, R., France. 44N. 7E. 73
Vara, R., Italy. 44N. 10E. 82
Varag Njard, Norway. 70N. 29E. 88
Varanger Fd., Norway. 70N. 30E. 88
Varata R., Italy. 45N. 8E. 82
Vardar, Turkey. 41N. 22E. 95
Varel, Germany. 53N. 8E. 76
Varello, Italy. 46N. 8E. 82
Varese, Italy. 46N. 9E. 82
•Varna, Bulgaria 43N. 28E. 94
Vartry R., Ireland. 53N. 6w. 69
Vasilkov, Russia. 50N 30E. 91
Vaskon, Hungary. 47N. 22E. 79
Vaslui, Roumania. 47N 28E. 94
Vasto, Italy. 42N. 15E. 80
Vaternish Pt., Scotland. 58N. 7w. 62
Vathi, Greece. 38N. 21E. 95
Vaticano C., Italy. 39N. 16E. 81
•Vaucluse, France. 44N. 5E. 73
Vecht, R., Holland. 52N. 5E. 70
Vechta, Germany. 53N. 8E. 76
Vechte, R., Holland. 53N. 6E. 70
Vede R., Roumania. 44N. 26E 94
Vegen, Norway. 66N. 12E. 88
Vegesuck, Germany. 53N. 9E. 76
Veglia, Austria. 45N. 15E. 78
Veile, Denmark. 56N. 10E 89
Vejer de la Frontera, Spain. 36N. 6w. 84
Velez Malaga, Spain. 37N. 4w. 84
Velez Rubio, Spain. 38N 2w. 85
Veliki Ustyuk, Russia. 61N. 46E. 90
Vellebich G., Hungary. 45N. 15E. 78
Velletri, Italy. 42N. 13E. 83
Velsk, Russia. 61N. 42E. 90
Velzen, Germany. 53N. 10E. 76
Vendée, France. 47N. 1w. 72
•Vendôme, France. 48N 1E. 72
Vendrell, Spain. 41N. 1E. 85
Venetia, Italy. 46N 12E. 83
•Venice, Italy. 45N. 12E. 83
Venice, G. of, Italy. 45N. 13E. 83
Venidieh, Turkey. 41N. 25E 95
Venlo, Holland. 51N. 6E 71
Vennacher, Loch, Scotland. 56N 4w. 65
Venoge R., Switzerland 47N. 7E. 86
Ventimiglia, Italy. 44N. 8E. 82
Ventnor, England. 51N. 1w. 67
Ventoteni, Italy. 41N. 13E. 81
Vercelli, Italy. 45N. 9E. 82
Verden, Germany. 53N. 10E. 76
Verdon, R., France. 44N. 6E. 73
•Verdun, France. 49N. 5E. 73
Vergato, Italy. 44N. 11E. 83
Veria, Turkey. 40N. 22E. 95
Verin, Spain. 42N. 7w. 84
Verkotwine, Russia. 59N. 61E. 90
Verolanova, Italy. 45N. 10E. 82
•Verona, Italy. 45N. 11E. 83
•Versailles, France. 49N. 2E. 73
Versoix, Switzerland. 46N. 6E. 86
Verviers, Belgium. 51N 6E. 71
Vesdre, R., Belgium. 51N. 6E. 71
Vesoul, France. 48N. 6E. 73
Vesuvius Mt., Italy. 41N. 14E. 81

PAGE

Veszprim, Hungary. 47N. 18E. 78
Vetluga, Russia. 58N. 56E 90
Vetluga R., Russia. 57N. 56E. 90
Vetroz, Switzerland 46N. 7E. 86
Vevey, Switzerland. 46N. 7E. 86
Via Mala, Switzerland. 47N. 10E. 87
Viadana, Italy. 45N. 10E. 82
Vianden, Luxemburg. 50N. 6E. 71
Vianna, Portugal. 42N. 9w. 84
Viareggio, Italy. 44N. 10E. 82
Viasma, Russia. 56N. 34E. 90
Viatka, Russia. 59N. 50E. 90
Viatka R., Russia. 59N. 51E. 90
Viborg, Denmark. 57N. 9E. 89
Viborg, Russia. 61N. 29E. 90
Vicenza, Italy. 46N. 12E. 83
Vich, Spain. 42N. 2E. 85
Vichy, France. 46N. 3E. 73
•Vienna, Austria. 48N. 16E. 78
Vienne, France. 45N. 5E. 73
Vienne, France. 47N 0E. 72
Viersen, Germany. 51N. 6E 76
Vierzon, France. 47N. 2E. 73
Vieste, Italy. 42N. 16E. 80
Vigevano, Italy. 45N. 9E. 82
Viggiano, Italy. 40N. 16E. 81
•Vigo, Spain. 42N. 0w. 84
Vigten Is., Norway. 65N. 11E. 88
Vilaine, R., France. 48N. 2w. 72
Villa Nova, Portugal. 37N. 8w. 84
Villa Real, Portugal. 41N. 8w. 84
Villa Real, Spain. 40N. 0w. 85
Villach, Austria. 47N. 14E. 78
Villafranca, Italy. 45N. 7E. 82
•Villafranca, Italy. 45N. 11E 83
Villafranca, Spain. 41N. 2E. 85
Villafranca, Spain. 43N. 7w. 84
Villajoyosa, Spain. 39N. 0w. 85
Villalba, Spain. 43N. 8w. 84
Villanova y Geltra, Spain. 41N. 2E. 85
Villaricos, Spain. 37N. 2w. 85
Villaviciosa, Spain. 44N. 5w. 84
Villanueva de la Serena, Spain. 39N. 6w. 84
Villefranche, France. 44N. 2E 73
Villefranche, France. 46N. 5E. 73
Villena, Spain. 39N. 1w. 85
Villeneuve, Switzerland. 46N. 7E. 86
Villeneuve d'Agen, France. 44N. 1E. 72
Villingen, Germany. 48N. 8E. 77
Vilna, Russia. 55N. 25E. 90
Vilna, Russia. 55N. 26E. 91
Vils, R., Germany. 49N. 13E. 77
Vinalapo, R., Spain. 38N. 1w. 85
Vinaroz, Spain. 40N. 0E. 85
Vinkovcze, Slavonia. 45N. 19E. 79
Vinnitza, Russia. 49N. 29E. 91
Vir, Montenegro. 42N. 19E. 94
Vira, Switzerland. 46N. 9E. 87
Virginia, Ireland. 54N. 7w. 67
Virton, Belgium. 50N. 6E. 71
Visa, Turkey. 42N. 28E. 94
Viscaya, Spain. 43N 3w. 85
Vishegrad, Servia. 44N. 19E. 94
Vishni Volotchok, Russia. 58N. 35E. 90

	PAGE
Viso, Mt., Italy. 45N. 7E.	82
Visp, Switzerland. 46N. 8E	86
Vistritsa R., Turkey. 40N. 22E.	95
Vistula, Germany. 54N. 20E.	75
Vistula R., Russia. 53N. 19E.	91
Vitebsk, Russia. 55N. 30E.	91
Viterbo, Italy. 42N. 12E.	83
Vitoria, Spain. 43N. 3W.	85
Vitre, France. 48N. 1W.	72
Vittorio, Italy. 46N. 12E.	83
Vivero, Spain. 44N. 8W.	84
Vizen, Portugal. 41N. 8W.	84
Vlaardingen, Holland. 52N. 4E.	70
Vladikavkas, Russia. 43N. 44E.	91
Vladimir, Russia. 56N. 41E.	90
Vlieland, Holland. 53N. 5E.	70
Vodena, Turkey. 41N. 22E.	95
Vogels, Germany. 50N. 9E.	77
Voghera, Italy. 45N. 9E.	82
Vohenstrauss, Germany. 50N. 12E.	77
Voil, Loch, Scotland 56N. 4W.	65
Voldon, Norway. 62N. 7E.	89
Volga R., Russia. 46N. 48E.	91
Volhyna, Russia. 51N 27E.	91
Volkov R., Russia. 60N 32E	90
Vollenhove, Holland. 53N. 6E.	70
Volo, Greece. 39N. 23E.	95
Volo G., Greece. 39N. 23E.	95
Vologda (tn), Russia. 59N. 40E.	90
Vologda, Russia. 61N. 49E.	90
Volsk, Russia. 52N. 47E.	91
Volterra, Italy. 43N. 11E.	83
Voltri, Italy. 44N. 9E	82
*Volturno, R., Italy. 41N. 14E	81
Vomano R., Italy. 43N 14E	83
Vomtsa, Greece. 39N 21E.	95
Voorne, Holland. 52N. 4E.	70
Vorarlberg, Austria. 47N. 10E.	78
Vorder Rhein Thal, Switzerland. 47N. 9E.	87
Vorings Fos, Norway. 60N. 7E.	89
Vorjas, Austria. 46N. 21E.	79
Voronesh, Russia. 52N. 39E.	91
Vosges, France. 48N 6E.	73
Vosges Mts., France. 48N. 7E.	77
Vosse, Norway. 61N. 7E.	89
Vostitsa, Greece. 38N. 22E.	95
Vourne, Belgium. 51N 3E	71
Vovussa R., Turkey. 40N. 19E.	95
Vranja, Servia. 44N. 22E.	94
Vratza, Bulgaria. 43N. 24E.	94
Vulcano Is., Italy. 38N. 15E.	81
Vulkan Pass, Roumania. 45N. 23E.	94
Vuollerim, Sweden. 66N 21E.	88
Vyrnwy, L., Wales. 53N. 4W.	54
Vyrnwy R., Wales. 53N. 3W.	54
Vytchegda R., Russia. 62N. 50E.	90
Vytegra, Russia. 61N. 37E.	90
Waag, Hungary. 48N. 18E.	79
Waal, R., Holland. 52N. 5E.	70
Wadhurst, England. 51N. 0E.	57
Wadensweil, Switzerland. 47N. 9E.	87
Wadowice, Austria 50N 20E.	79
Wadsbridge, England. 51N 5W.	56
Wageningen, Holland. 52N. 6E	70
Waigatz Is., Russia. 70N. 60E.	90
Wainfleet, England. 53N. 0E.	55
Waitzen, Hungary. 48N. 19E.	79
*Wakefield, England. 54N. 1W.	55
Walchen S., Germany. 47N. 11E.	77
*Walcheren, Holland. 52N. 4E.	70
Wald, Germany. 51N 11E.	77
Wald, Switzerland. 47N. 8E.	87
Waldeck, Germany. 51N. 9E.	76
Waldenburg, Germany. 51N. 16E.	75
Waldenburg, Switzerland. 47N. 8E.	86
Waldkirch, Germany. 48N. 8E.	77
Waldsee, Germany. 48N. 10E.	77
Waldshut, Germany. 48N. 8E.	77
Walk, Russia. 58N. 26E	90
Wallachia, Roumania. 45N. 26E.	94
Wallenstadt, Switzerland. 47N. 9E.	87
Wallenstadt, L. of, Switzerland. 47N. 9E.	87
Wallingford, England. 52N. 1W.	57
*Walmer, England. 51N. 1E.	57
Walney Is., England 54N. 3W.	54
Walsall, England. 53N. 2W.	56
*Waltham Abbey, England. 52N. 0E.	57
Walton, England. 52N 1E.	57
Wangen, Switzerland. 47N. 8E.	86
Wangeroog Is., Germany. 54N. 8E.	76
Wanlockhead, Scotland. 55N. 4W.	65
Wansbeck, R., England. 55N. 2W.	54
*Wantage, England. 52N. 1W.	57
Wapper R., Germany. 51N. 7E.	76
Warasdin, Slavonia. 46N. 16E.	78
Warberg, Sweden. 57N. 12E.	89
Warburg, Germany. 52N. 9E.	76
*Ware, England. 52N. 0W.	57
Wareham, England. 51N. 2W.	56
Waren, Germany. 53N. 13E.	76
Wark, England. 55N 2W.	54
Warkworth, England. 55N. 2W.	55
Warminster, England. 51N. 2W.	56
Warnemünde, Germany. 54N 12E.	76
Warnow R., Germany. 54N. 12E	76
Warrenpoint, Ireland. 54N. 6W.	67
Warrington, England. 53N. 3W.	54
*Warsaw, Russia 52N. 21E.	91
Warstein, Germany. 52N. 8E.	76
Warta R., Germany. 51N. 19E.	75
*Wartburg, Germany. 51N. 10E.	77
Warthe R., Germany. 52N. 18E.	75
Warthe R., Germany. 53N. 15E.	75
*Warwick, England. 52N. 2W.	57
Wash, The, England. 53N. 0E.	55
Wasmes, Belgium. 50N. 4E	71
Wassen, Switzerland. 47N. 9E.	87
Wast Water, England. 54N. 3W.	54
Watchet, England. 51N. 3W.	56
*Waterford, Ireland. 52N. 7W	69
Waterford Haven, Ireland. 52N. 7W.	69
Watergate B., England. 50N. 5W.	56
Watergrasshill, Ireland. 52N. 8W.	68
*Waterloo, Belgium. 51N. 4E.	71
Waterville, Ireland. 52N. 10W.	68
Watford, England. 52N. 0W.	57

PAGE

Watlington, England. 52N. 1w. 57
Watten, Scotland. 58N. 3w. 63
Watten, Loch, Scotland. 58N. 3w. 63
Wattenwyl, Switzerland 47N. 8E. 86
Watton, England. 53N. 1E. 57
Watzman, Germany. 47N. 13E. 77
Waveney, R., England. 53N. 2E. 57
Waveren, Belgium. 51N. 5E. 71
Wear Hd., England. 55N. 2w. 54
Wear, R., England. 55N. 1w. 55
Wednesbury, England. 53N. 2w. 56
Weert, Holland. 51N. 6E. 71
Weesp, Holland. 52N. 5E. 70
Welden, Germany. 50N. 12E. 77
*Weimar, Germany. 51N. 12E. 76
Weinfelden, Switzerland. 48N. 9E. 87
Weirden, Holland. 52N. 7E. 70
Weissenburg, Germany. 49N. 8E. 77
Weissenfels, Germany. 51N. 12E 76
Weissensee, Germany. 51N. 11E. 76
Weisshorn, Switzerland. 46N. 8E. 86
Weisskirchen, Hungary. 45N. 21E. 79
Welland, R., England. 53N. 0w. 55
Wellingborough, England. 52N.1w. 57
Wellington, England. 51N. 3w 56
Wellington, England. 53N. 3w. 56
Wells, England. 51N. 3w. 56
Wells-next-the-Sea, England. 53N
1E. 55
Welshpool, Wales. 53N. 3w. 56
Wem, England. 53N. 3w. 54
*Wemyss B., Scotland. 56N. 5w. 64
Wener L., Sweden. 59N. 13E. 89
Wenersborg, Sweden. 58N. 12E. 89
Wensum, R., England. 53N. 1E. 55
Weobly, England. 52N 3w. 56
Werdenberg, Switzerland. 47N. 9E. 87
Werra R., Germany. 52N. 10E. 76
Werre R., Germany. 52N. 8E. 76
Werschetz, Hungary. 45N. 21E. 79
Wertach, R , Germany. 49N. 11E. 77
Wertheim, Germany. 50N. 9E. 77
Wesel R., Germany. 51N. 7E. 76
Wesen, Switzerland. 47N. 9E. 87
Weser R., Germany. 54N 8E 76
Wessenstein, Switzerland. 47N. 8E. 86
West Bromwich, England 53N.
2w. 56
West Calder, Scotland. 56N. 4w. 65
West Fjord, Norway. 68N. 15E. 88
West Flanders, Belgium. 51N 3E. 71
West Hartlepool, England. 55N.
1w. 55
West Kilbride, Scotland. 56N. 5w. 61
West Linton, Scotland. 56N. 3w. 65
West Meath, Ireland. 54N. 7w. 67
West Riding, Yorkshire. 54N. 2w. 55
Westbury, England. 51N. 2w. 56
Wester Dal, Sweden. 61N. 14E. 89
Wester Schelde, Holland. 51N. 4E. 71
Westerås, Sweden. 60N. 17E. 89
Westervik, Sweden. 58N. 17E. 89
Westerwald, Germany. 51N. 8E. 77
Westmoreland, England. 55N 3w. 54
Weston-super-Mare, England. 51N.
3w. 56
Westphalia, Germany. 52N. 8E. 76
Westport, Ireland. 54N. 10w. 66

PAGE

Westport B., Ireland. 54N. 10w. 66
Westray Is., Scotland. 59N. 3w. 63
Westward Ho, England. 51N. 4w. 56
Wetherby, England. 54N. 1w. 55
Wetter L., Sweden. 58N. 14E. 89
Wetter, R., Germany. 50N. 8E. 77
Wetteren, Belgium. 51N. 4E. 71
Wetherhorn, Switzerland. 47N. 8E. 86
Wetzlar, Germany. 51N. 9E. 77
*Wexford, Ireland. 52N. 6w. 69
Wexford Harb., Ireland. 53N. 6w. 69
Wexio, Sweden. 57N. 15E. 89
Wey R., England. 51N. 0w. 57
Weyer, Austria. 48N.15E. 78
Weymouth, England. 51N. 2w. 56
Whalsey Is., Scotland. 60N. 1w. 63
Wharfe, R., England. 54N. 1w. 55
Whernside, England. 54N. 2w. 54
*Whitby, England. 54N. 1w. 55
*Whitchurch, England. 51N. 1w. 57
Whitstable, England. 51N. 1E. 57
White Hd., Ireland. 55N. 6w. 67
White Körös, Hungary. 47N. 21E. 79
White Sea, Russia. 66N. 38E. 90
Whiteadder, R., Scotland. 56N.
2w. 65
Whitechurch, England. 53N. 3w. 54
Whitehaven, England. 55N. 4w. 54
Whiten Hd., Scotland. 59N. 5w. 62
Whithorn, Scotland. 55N. 4w. 65
Whittlesea, England. 53N. 0E. 57
Wiay Is., Scotland. 57N. 7w. 62
Wick, Scotland. 58N. 3w. 63
Wick B., Scotland. 58N. 3w. 63
Wicklow, Ireland. 53N. 6w. 69
Wicklow Hd., Ireland. 53N. 6w. 69
Wicklow Mts., Ireland. 53N. 6w. 69
Wickwar, England. 52N. 2w. 56
Widin, Bulgaria. 44N. 23E. 94
Wiedlisbach, Switzerland. 47N. 8E. 86
Wieliczka, Austria. 50N. 20E. 79
Wieringen, Holland. 53N. 5E. 70
Wiesbaden, Germany. 50N. 8E. 77
Wieselburg, Hungary. 48N. 17E. 78
Wig L., Russia 63N. 35E. 90
*Wigan, England. 54N 3w. 54
Wiggern, Switzerland. 47N. 8E. 86
Wigton, England. 55N. 3w 54
Wigtown, Scotland. 55N. 4w. 64
Wigtown B., Scotland. 55N. 4w 65
Wildbad, Germany. 49N. 8E. 77
Wildhelm Can, Germany. 52N.
14E. 76
Wilhelmshaven, Germany. 54N.
8E. 76
Wilhelmshohe, Germany. 51N. 9E. 76
Wildhorn, Switzerland. 46N. 8E. 86
Wilkinstown, Ireland. 54N. 7w. 67
Willenhall, England. 53N. 2w. 56
Willisau, Switzerland. 47N. 8E. 86
Wilsontown, Scotland. 56N. 4w. 65
Wilton, England. 51N. 2w. 56
Wiltshire, England. 51N. 2w. 56
Wily, R., England. 51N. 2w. 56
Wilz, Belgium. 50N. 6E. 71
Wimborne, England. 51N. 2w. 56
Wincanton, England. 51N. 2w. 56
Winchelsea, England. 51N. 1E. 57

PAGE

*Winchester, England. 51N. 1w.   57
Windau, Russia. 58N. 21E.   90
Windel E., Sweden. 64N. 20E.   88
Windermere L., England. 54N. 3w. 54
Windrush R., England. 52N. 1w.   57
*Windsor, England. 51N. 1w.   57
Winschoten, Holland. 53N 7E.   70
Winslow, England. 52N. 1w.   57
Winster, England. 53N. 2w.   55
Winterthur, Switzerland. 47N. 9E. 87
Wirksworth, England 53N 2w.   55
Wisbech, England. 53N. 0E.   57
Wisby, Sweden. 58N. 19E.   89
Wishaw, Scotland. 56N. 4w.   65
Wisloka, Austria. 50N. 21E.   79
Wismar, Germany. 54N. 12E.   76
Wiston, Wales. 52N. 5w.   56
Witham, R., England. 53N. 0E.   55
Withernsea, England. 51N. 0E.   55
Witney, England. 52N. 1w.   57
Witten, Germany. 51N. 7E.   76
Wittenberg, Germany. 52N. 13E 76
Wittenberge, Germany. 53N. 12E. 76
Wittengen, Germany. 53N. 10E. 76
Wittingau, Austria. 49N. 15E.   78
Wittlich, Germany. 50N. 7E.   77
Wittstock, Germany. 53N. 12E. 76
Woerden, Holland. 52N. 5E.   70
Wohlhusen, Switzerland. 47N. 8E. 86
Woking, England. 51N. 1w.   57
Wokingham, England. 51N. 1w.   57
Wolderas, Sweden. 61N. 13E.   89
Wolds, The, England. 54N. 0w   55
Wolfenbüttel, Germany. 52N. 11E. 76
Wolgast, Germany. 54N. 14E.   76
Wollin, Germany. 54N. 14E.   76
Wollin Is., Germany. 54N. 14E. 76
Wolsingham, England. 55N. 2w. 54
Wolverhampton, England. 53N. 2w.   56
Wongrowitz, Germany. 53N. 18E. 75
Woodbridge, England. 52N. 1E.   57
Woodford, Ireland. 53N. 8w.   68
Woodside, Scotland. 57N. 2w.   63
*Woodstock, England. 52N. 1w.   57
Wooler, England. 56N. 2w.   54
Woolwich, England. 51N. 0E.   57
Wootton Bassett, England. 52N. 2w.   56
Worbis, Germany. 52N. 10E.   76
*Worcester, England. 52N. 2w.   56
Wörgl, Austria. 47N. 12E.   78
*Workington, England. 55N. 4w.   54
Worksop, England. 53N. 1w.   55
Workum, Holland. 53N. 5E.   70
*Worms, Germany. 50N. 8E.   77
Worms Hd., Wales. 52N. 4w.   56
*Wörth, Germany. 49N. 8E.   77
Worthing, England. 51N. 0w.   57
Wragby, England. 53N. 0w.   55
Wrath, C., Scotland. 59N. 5w.   62
Wrekin, The, England. 53N. 3w. 56
Wreschen, Germany. 52N. 18E.   75
Wrexham, Wales. 53N. 3w.   54
Wronke, Germany. 53N. 18E.   75
Wumme R., Germany. 53N. 9E.   76
Würm S., Germany. 48N. 11E.   77
Wurtemberg, Germany. 49N. 9E. 77

PAGE

*Wurzburg, Germany. 50N 10E. 77
Wurzen, Germany. 52N. 13E.   76
Wye, R., England   52N. 3w.   56
Wyk, Holland. 52N. 5E.   70
Wyl, Switzerland. 47N. 9E.   87
Wylye, England. 51N. 2w.   56
Wymondham, England. 53N. 1E.   57

Xerokhori, Greece. 39N. 23E.   95

Yalping Nor, Russia. 61N. 59E.   90
Yamboli, Bulgaria. 42N. 27E.   94
Yare R., England. 53N. 2E.   57
Yarm, England. 54N. 1w.   55
Yarmouth, England. 51N. 1w.   57
Yaroslavl, Russia   57N 42E.   90
*Yarrow, Scotland. 56N. 3w.   65
Yarrow Water, Scotland. 56N. 3w. 65
Yatton, England. 51N. 3w.   56
Yecla, Spain. 39N. 1w.   85
Yefremov, Russia. 53N. 38E.   91
Yeisk, Russia   47N. 38E.   91
Yell Is., Scotland. 61N. 1w.   63
Yell Sd , Scotland 60N. 1w.   63
Yeni, Bulgaria. 42N. 26E.   94
Yenikale, Russia. 45N. 37E.   91
Yeovil, England. 51N. 3w.   56
Yes Tor, England. 51N. 4w.   56
*Yetholm, Scotland. 56N. 2w.   65
Ymes Fd., Norway. 62N. 8E.   89
Yonköping, Sweden. 58N. 14E.   89
Yonne, France. 48N. 4E.   73
Yonne, R., France. 48N. 3E.   73
*York, England.   51N. 1w.   55
Yorkshire Moors, England. 54N. 1w.   55
*Youghal, Ireland. 52N. 8w.   69
Youghal B. and Harb., Ireland. 52N. 8w.   69
Ypres, Belgium. 51N. 3E.   71
Yssel, R., Holland. 53N. 6E.   70
Ystad, Sweden. 17N. 14E.   89
Ystwith, R., Wales. 52N. 4w.   56
Ytham R., Scotland. 57N. 2w.   63
Yugovski, Russia   58N. 57E.   90
Yverdon, Switzerland. 47N. 7E.   86
Yzendyke, Holland. 51N. 4E.   71

Zaandam, Holland. 52N. 5E.   70
Zabern, Germany. 49N. 7E.   77
Zafra, Spain. 39N. 6w.   84
Zakynthos, Greece. 38N 21E.   95
Zala R., Hungary. 47N. 17E.   78
Zala Egerszeg, Hungary. 47N. 17E. 78
Zalamea, Spain. 38N 7w.   84
Zaleszczyk, Austria. 49N. 26E.   79
Zam, Austria. 46N. 22E.   79
*Zamora, Spain. 42N. 6w.   84
Zancara, R., Spain. 39N. 3w.   84
Zara, Dalmatia. 44N. 15E.   78
Zaribrod, Bulgaria. 43N. 22E.   94
Zealand, Denmark. 56N. 12E.   89
Zeebrugge, Belgium. 51N. 3E.   71
Zeeland, Holland. 51N. 4E.   70
Zeitz, Germany. 51N. 12E.   76
Zell, Germany. 48N. 8E.   77
Zell, Germany. 50N. 7E.   77
Zeng, Croatia. 45N. 15E.   78

PAGE

Zerbst, Germany. 52N. 12E. 76
Zermatt, Switzerland. 46N. 3E. 86
Zernetz, Switzerland. 47N. 10E. 87
Zevendar, Holland. 52N. 6E. 70
*Zierikzee, Holland. 52N. 4E. 70
Zihl, R., Switzerland. 47N. 7E. 86
Zittau, Germany 51N. 14E. 76
Zizers, Switzerland. 47N. 10E. 87
Zloczow, Austria. 50N. 25E. 79
Znaim, Austria. 49N. 16E. 78
Zofingen, Switzerland. 47N. 8E. 86
Zolkiew, Austria. 50N. 24E. 79
Zombor, Hungary. 46N. 19E. 91
Zoptau, Austria. 50N. 17E. 78
Zorn, R., Germany. 49N. 8E. 77
*Zorndorf, Germany. 53N. 14E. 76
Zug, Switzerland. 47N. 9E. 87

PAGE

Zug, L. of, Switzerland. 47N. 9E. 87
Zuider Zee, Holland 53N. 6E. 70
Zumarraga, Spain. 43N. 2w. 85
Zurgena, Spain. 37N. 2w. 85
*Zurich, Switzerland. 47N. 9E. 87
Zurich, L. of, Switzerland. 47N. 9E. 87
Zurl, Dalmatia. 44N. 15E. 78
Zursach, Switzerland. 48N. 8E. 86
*Zutfen, Holland. 52N. 6E 70
Zvornik, Bosnia. 44N. 19E. 91
Zwartsluis, Holland. 53N. 6E 70
Zweibrucken, Germany. 49N. 7E. 77
Zweysimmen, Switzerland. 47N. 7E. 86
Zwickau, Germany. 51N. 12E. 77
Zwittau, Austria. 50N. 16E. 78
*Zwolle, Holland. 53N. 6E. 70

THE TEMPLE PRESS LETCHWORTH ENGLAND